How to Use This

This book is about writing Windows code. It has been designed from the bottom up to teach you this subject in the most lucid, enjoyable, and thorough manner possible.

An extremely wide range of material has been packed between the covers of this book. This book starts out with the basics by presenting you a number of very easy-to-build Windows programs that are approximately ten lines in length. After you've had a chance to get a few of these short programs up and running, the book goes on to carefully introduce you to the proper method of constructing a classic Windows program. This second portion of the book was painstakingly designed and developed to show you the most flexible, up-to-date, and powerful methods for writing Windows code.

After you spread your wings and climb to a suitable vantage point, the text proceeds to introduce you to all the classic elements in Windows programming. Included in this middle, and largest, portion of the book are lively, in-depth discussions of many crucial topics, from dialogs and controls to callbacks and graphics.

After you've earned your wings, and know how to fly from one end of the realm of Windows programming to the other, the final portion of the book introduces you to such advanced topics as subclassing, dynamic link libraries, and multimedia.

Every page of this book was written with energy and the sure conviction that Windows programming can be not only challenging, but also exciting and fun. These pages present you not only with all the basic knowledge you need to write good Windows code, but they give you a chance to have some fun designing and playing graphics-based games, and writing multimedia programs that can play and record sounds, conversation, and music.

Special Features of This Book

This book contains some special features that will aid you in your quest to become a Windows programmer. Syntax boxes show you how to use specific features of the Windows API. Each box provides concrete examples and a full explanation of the best way to use each feature. To get a feel for the style of the syntax boxes, look at the following example. (Don't worry if the material doesn't make sense at this stage. You don't have to learn anything yet, I'm just showing off the nice features you're going to find in this book!)

SwapMouseButton

```
BOOL SwapMouseButton(BOOL)
```

BOOL bSwap: If TRUE then swap left and right mouse button messages.

SwapMouseButton returns TRUE if the mouse buttons are reversed; otherwise it returns FALSE.

This function swaps the functionality of the mouse buttons. You might want to give the user a chance to do this if they are left-handed, or if they have some other reason for wanting to change the way the mouse normally functions.

Example:

```
SwapMouseButton(TRUE);
```

Another feature of this book is the DO/DON'T boxes. These boxes can help you clear a straight path through complicated terrain:

DO	DON'T

DO take the time to experiment with the code you read in this book. The best possible teaching tool you can find is the challenge you face when you decide to bring one of your own programming ideas to fruition.

DON'T be afraid to take chances or to try something new. The best programmers are those who are always writing code that tests and explores the limits of the system. You need to test those bounds before you can write code that stays within safe limits.

Conventions Used in This Book

This book uses different typefaces to help you differentiate between code and regular English, and also to help you indentify important concepts. Windows code is typeset in a special monospace font. Placeholders—terms used to represent what you actually type in code—are typeset in an *italic monospace* font. New and important terms are typeset in *italic* for emphasis.

Onward, into the Breach

This book is designed to give you a very thorough knowledge of Windows programming. Ultimately, however, the responsibility for becoming a good Windows programmer rests on your shoulders. Specifically, if you want to become good at this challenging subject, you need to write lots of code. Nothing pays off like prolonged periods of serious hacking!

Teach
Yourself

Windows™
Programming

in 21 Days

Teach Yourself
Windows
Programming
in 21 Days

Charlie Calvert

SAMS
PUBLISHING

A Division of Prentice Hall Computer Publishing
201 West 103rd Street Indianapolis, Indiana 46290

This book is dedicated to my family, which includes all members of the Battle, Calvert, Kephart, and Masselink clans. In particular, I want to mention my father, Vice Admiral James Calvert, my brother, Dr. James Calvert, my wife, Marjorie Calvert, and especially, my wonderful sister, Margaret Norman.

Trademarks

Overview

Contents

Acknowledgments

As the author of this book, I owe an enormous debt of gratitude to the people who aided in its production. This section of the book gives me a chance to acknowledge those who helped bring some of the best portions of this book to completion.

At the top of the list is my wife Margie, who has supplied patience, love, and understanding in unimaginable and seemingly endless quantities. I have no idea what I ever did to deserve such a wonderful wife.

Another individual I owe a big note of thanks to is Sams' author and former Borland employee Paul Perry, who recommended me to the good folks at Sams Publishing, and who has also given me excellent technical advice on a number of occasions. Thank you, Paul!

Next on the list are Borland employees Bruneau Babet, Tommy Hui, and Lar Mader. I took almost all of my most complicated or delicate questions to these three fine programmers, and they all willingly gave freely of their time and expert advice. Much of what's best in this book from a technical viewpoint springs from their contributions.

Bruneau also served as technical editor for this book. There is no possible way I can ever thank him for all the excellent contributions he made in that context. Many of the most advanced and technically enlightened sections of this book owe their existence to his suggestions or advice, and there are innumerable sections that he saved from mediocrity or from the slough of egregious error. I want to stress, however, that any technical problems found in this book exist in spite of his efforts to steer me in the right direction, and not because of any oversights or erroneous suggestions on his part.

While I was writing this book, Lester Jackson, Rich Jones, Xavier Pacheco, Jason Sprenger, Robert Warren, and Dave Wilhelm were my immediate teammates or superiors where I work at the Borland Tech Support Department. These fine men not only answered umpteen-thousand of my questions, but they also put up with me when I wandered into work bleary eyed and grouchy after another long night of hacking or writing. In particular, I should probably single out Rich for all the help he has given me on a daily basis since I came to Borland; and Jason, who has come to my rescue many times with his expert knowledge of DOS and the 8086 architecture.

Other Borland employees who supplied me with technical advice or materials while writing this book include Tom Orsi, Jeff Peters, Peter Williams, Steve Barnette, Rich

Wesson, Bob Brahms, David Schneider, Gary Johnson, Kirsten Konopaski, Jim Alisago, Ed James-Bechkam, and Bill Dunlap. Thanks to you all.

Last, but by no means least, are the wonderful people at Sams Publishing who deserve a very large percentage of the credit for what's best in this book. In particular, I want to thank Keith Davenport, Stacy Hiquet, Mary Inderstrodt, and Dean Miller. I consider myself extremely lucky to work with these fine people and with all the other Sams employees who I have never met but whose talents help to redeem and clarify my work.

Hopefully you understand my drift here, but perhaps it won't hurt to spell it out one last time. Producing a book like this takes a tremendous amount of effort not only on my part, but on the part of highly talented artists, craftsmen, and engineers such as Keith, Mary, Dean, and Bruneau. Anyone who enjoys or learns from this book owes them a debt of gratitude.

About the Author

Charlie Calvert has a B.S. degree in Computer Science and a B.A. degree in Journalism from Evergreen State College in Olympia, Washington. He has worked as a journalist for *The Morton Journal* in Morton, Washington, and as an English teacher at an extension of Centralia College in Centralia, Washington. He also has worked as a programmer, doing contract work using Turbo Pascal and Borland C. He is currently employed as a Technical Support Engineer at Borland International. He lives with his wife, Marjorie, in Felton, California.

Charlie is the author of *Turbo Pascal Programming 101,* also available from Sams Publishing.

CIS: 76711,533

From the first chapter to the last, this book is written for people who like to program, and who have a strong desire to become a good programmer. This book is filled with many working examples, nearly all of which are meant to serve as starting points for top-notch hacks. Everyone who works this book through to the end will end up with a solid foundation in Windows programming. However, those who benefit the most will be readers who not only complete the basic course outlined in the book, but who use the included programs as starting points or inspirations for their own creations.

The goal of this book is to start you off with crystal clear explanations of the basics, and then to move on to increasingly exciting and challenging examples. By the end of the book, you'll be able to write dazzling multimedia Windows code, replete with stunning graphics and an interface that draws the user into even the most advanced and technically complex applications.

This book is meant to give you a hands-on introduction to Windows programming. You are going to be happiest with it if you come equipped with a good computer and a copy of a top C++ compiler such as Borland's or Microsoft's. This isn't an object-oriented programming book, but the code is meant to be compiled with the enhanced type checking that comes with a C++ compiler.

Each chapter in this book ends with a few hypothetical questions to which I supply the answers, as well as a quiz and a few exercises. By all means, don't neglect to read the hypothetical questions in the Q&A section! Windows is a vast subject, and many important points (which aren't worked into the narrative flow of a particular chapter) are raised in the Q&A section. Don't forget to read the questions and answers!

You'll also benefit from completing the quiz at the end of each chapter. Most of the time, the quizzes aren't particularly difficult to complete. Their purpose is not to trick you, but to let you review key points in the chapter. If you find that you draw a blank on two or three of the points covered in a particular quiz, you might want to reread some sections of the chapter. Answers to all the quiz questions appear at the back of the book in Appendix A.

Approach these exercises and questions, not as a test, but as an aid to use as you see fit. I'm totally uninterested in measuring your talents as a student. Instead, I want to give you everything you need to become a talented programmer. The fastest way to achieve that goal is to sit down at your computer and write code! This is not a tricky technique, nor some miracle course that will magically imbue you with remarkable programming talents. It's a practical, proven way to learn something truly worth achieving. The exercises at the end of each chapter are meant to inspire you to write real Windows code, and to do so with a spirit of excitement and commitment!

Where You're Going

The goal of Week 1 is to get you familiar with the formidable (but quite comprehensible) basics of Windows programming. If you are familiar with the DOS or UNIX command prompt, Windows programming can come as a bit of a shock. It's my contention that with a little effort, you can get over this initial hump and arrive safely at the place in which you feel you have a sure foothold in a new land.

The first three chapters are designed to ease you into the world of Windows code as comfortably as possible. The key issues are orientation and perspective. If I simply threw a full-scale Windows program at you right off the bat, I'm afraid that your heart would darken and your spirit flicker and possibly dim. This approach is not meant to coddle you, but to lead you to an understanding of the underlying themes that run like broad rivers through the vast Windows programming environment.

Days 4 and 5 familiarize you with the basic concepts behind an event-oriented, message-based operating system. They introduce a set of macros called WINDOWSX that greatly simplifies the task of Windows programming—simultaneously helping to delineate and illuminate the key principles that lie at the root of the task before you.

The final two chapters in Week 1 show off Windows resources, which add color and power to a program—with a minimum amount of effort on the programmer's part. These chapters are meant to reward you for your hard work in the early chapters. They should signal that your new knowledge gives you a remarkable opportunity to produce creative and powerful programs that your users will enjoy and respect.

When you are finished with Week 1, you'll be ready to move on to the greater and more exciting challenges in Week 2.

Getting Your Feet Wet

WEEK
1

1

D A Y

In this chapter, I provide a brief introduction to Windows programming, and then give two short example programs that are designed to get you up and running quickly.

After you have had a chance to get some hands-on experience, I discuss more general topics. Specifically, the last half of this chapter covers

☐ Graphical User Interfaces (GUIs)

☐ Recommended hardware

☐ Windows compilers

☐ Coding styles

☐ An overview of Windows

☐ An overview of upcoming chapters

General Overview

This book is about how you can use the C or C++ language to program Windows applications. My intention is to talk to you about this subject using words that are friendly, easy to understand, and technically correct.

It's my belief that if you have a solid foundation, you will be able to climb to almost any height; but if you try to build on sand, every edifice you construct will eventually crumble. Therefore, this book moves along at a slow, stately pace, always taking the time to outline all the major issues so you can see them clearly, even from a distance. To balance out this perhaps excessively conservative impulse, I've tried to keep the general mood of the text cheerful and high-spirited.

My task is considerably simplified by the Windows environment—which by its very nature is entertaining and exciting. In just a few lines of Windows code, you can implement tasks that DOS makes prohibitively complicated.

For instance, graphics, sound, and multitasking are three tasks that have challenged, frustrated, and often defeated a wide array of experienced DOS programmers. But these features are free for the asking when you're in the Windows environment. Graphics and sound capabilities have even evolved to the point that users can now show movies and write music on their PCs. Even more importantly, the new developments in Windows NT (*New Technology*) enable programmers to write multithreaded code that can use multiple processors at the same time. It also provides a simplified, 32-bit memory addressing scheme, as well as increased networking capabilities.

All these features are enormously intriguing. Windows programmers are standing with power at their fingertips—power that far outreaches even some of the wilder dreams of yesterday's science fiction writers. Ten years ago, it was hard to foresee that so much was going to happen so quickly, and that such technology was going to be available to almost everyone for relatively small sums of money.

Yet, I imagine you wouldn't have picked up this book if you weren't already convinced of the importance of Windows in today's and tomorrow's cultural and economic marketplace. As a result, you are probably eager to hear what this book covers, and about how you can get started writing real Windows code.

How to Use This Book

The basic goal of this book is to give you a solid introduction to the fundamentals of Windows programming. To accomplish these ends, I need two skills. The first is a solid knowledge of how Windows code is put together, and the second is a love of writing and teaching. When I sat down each evening to work on this book, I tried to be prepared. That is, I tried to have a thorough knowledge of the material to be covered, and a heartfelt willingness to share that information with you.

From your end, you need to come prepared with a desire to do some work, and with a decent knowledge of programming. The scope of this book is such that there is no room to give a general introduction to the C++ language, or to the fundamentals of using a computer. I assume, for instance, that you know how to use the Program Manager, File Manager, and how to work with the DOS directory structure.

I have, however, made every attempt to make this material as approachable as possible. If you have had some experience programming, you should do fine with the material in this book as long as you study it in the order it's presented. In particular, you should come to the party with some knowledge of structured programming, variables, types, and computer memory. You should also know how to run a compiler and an editor.

There is no need, however, for you to be an expert programmer. My goal in writing this book is to show you that you don't need to be a genius to become a first-rate Windows programmer. All you need is a lot of heart, and a willingness to experiment and have some fun. Whenever technical material is particularly challenging, and I feel you need to understand it, I take the time to explain it to you as clearly as possible.

I picture my ideal reader as someone who has modest knowledge of the basics of the C or C++ language. Starting from that point, I want to give you the tools you need to become an expert Windows programmer.

In order to accomplish this goal, I've tried to start out by making the first third of this book a kind of "Quickstart for Windows programming." That is, I try to give you the major tools you'll need to start producing standard Windows applications. In the second third of the book, I give you a more in-depth knowledge of how to use each of these fundamental Windows programming tools. In the last third of the book, I cover advanced material.

I hope this approach makes this a dynamic and intuitive book. In particular, I try not to introduce a topic, and then force the reader to study it in such depth that they put the book down in frustration—or find themselves skipping back and forth in search of the "good stuff." In contrast, I aim to give you the information you want when you want it. The details get covered, but only when you are ready to move past the basics.

Some programming books attempt to be comprehensive references, while others aim to present an organized method of study—with a beginning, middle, and end. My goal has been to find a middle ground between these two approaches, but when in doubt, I almost always forsook the reference model. Most compilers are equipped with good references. What's in short supply is plain talk about the core technical issues.

Before showing you your first program, I want to point out that this book has been designed and formatted so that you can make your way through its contents in just 21 days. However, it should come as no surprise to you to learn that it wasn't written in that short of a period. In fact, it took quite some time to put together. As a result, I won't mind at all if you spend longer than 21 days getting through it. In fact, you should feel free to take your time, if you have that luxury. To me, the key issue is not how fast you get through this book, but how much you can learn from it.

So, get ready for a spirited examination of the Windows programming environment. Be prepared to have some fun, to learn some new tricks, and to surprise yourself with how easily you can learn a new and exciting skill.

Your First C++ Windows Program

Whenever I start working with a new computer program, or a new language, I'm always anxious to get some hands-on experience as quickly as possible. Because you might feel exactly as I do, I've developed the following short C++ Windows program (Listing 1.1.) that you can get up and running in just a few minutes.

 Listing 1.1. **Your very first Windows program!**

```
1: // Program SHORT.CPP
2: #include <windows.h>
3: int PASCAL WinMain(HINSTANCE hInst,
4:                    HINSTANCE hPrevInstance,
5:                    LPSTR lpszCmdParam, int nCmdShow)
6: {
7:   WinExec("NOTEPAD.EXE", SW_SHOWNORMAL);
8:   return 1;
9: }
```

 Figure 1.1 shows the output from Listing 1.1.

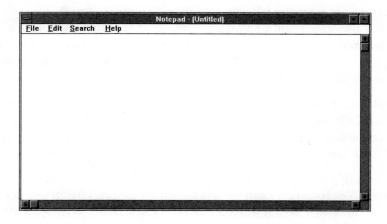

Figure 1.1. *The SHORT.EXE program launches NOTEPAD.EXE, which comes with every copy of Windows.*

 This is a totally legitimate C++ Windows program that follows the conventions and rules laid out for Windows programmers. The sole function of these simple lines of code is to launch NOTEPAD.EXE, which is the small text editor that comes with every copy of Windows.

9

Note: If you are not using either the Borland or the Microsoft compilers, you may not be able to compile the program in Listing 1.1 without the aid of module definition files and makefiles. If that's the case, you might want to just follow along through the ensuing discussion as best you can or use the code on the accompaning disk set. Then, in Chapter 2, "A Windows Frame of Mind," you get a chance to see an in-depth discussion of both module definition files and makefiles. After Chapter 2, all the programs in this book contain module definition files and makefiles. I'm omitting them now, so you can get started programming Windows with the simplest possible examples.

To run SHORT.CPP, all you need to do is launch your development environment, type in the code in Listing 1.1, and compile it. This process (see the following description) is really quite simple. So for now, just go ahead and follow the outlined plan —even if you don't really understand what the code means or why it works. The point of the SHORT.CPP isn't to teach you how Windows programs work, but to show you how simple they can be.

For instance, if you are using Borland C++, you can type in the code, save the file as SHORT.CPP, and start it by pressing Alt-R to bring down the run menu; then press R to run the program. That's all there is to it! Now, who said Windows programming in C++ has to be difficult?

If you are using the elegant new Microsoft Visual C++ package, the process involved in getting the program up and running is equally simple. First, type in the previous program and save it as SHORT.CPP. Next, press Ctrl-F5 to compile the program. When the compilation is finished, press Ctrl-F5 again to run the program. Voilá! What could be simpler?

The *WinExec* command

```
WinExec(progname, SW_ShowStatus);
```

The WinExec command takes two parameters. The first, *progname*, is the name of the program you want to launch, and the second, SW_ShowStatus is the way you want that program to be shown on the desktop. For instance, if you pass SW_SHOWMAXIMIZED, the Notepad program will first appear in a maximized state. Here are a few other possibilities:

SW_HIDE	Makes the window invisible.
SW_MINIMIZE	Minimizes the launched program.

SW_SHOWNORMAL	Starts and displays a program in its current size and position.
SW_SHOWMAXIMIZED	Starts a program in its maximized state.
SW_SHOWMINIMIZED	Starts a program in its minimized state.

Example:

```
WinExec("NOTEPAD.EXE", SW_SHOWNORMAL);
```

I like the preceding program, primarily because it shines a little light on the many yards of black newsprint that have been dedicated to discussions of just how complicated Windows and C++ can be when mixed together. Although there is some truth to all this talk, I think it has reached the kind of fever pitch in which rhetoric begins to overshadow reality. So, I want to get you started with a simple program that gives you a sense of mastery over the exciting features of the Windows environment.

Of course, the previous program doesn't do anything all that useful. If you want code that's not only easy to use, but also practical, you might like the following tidbit that launches a DOS batch file in a minimized Window. After it begins, you can let the batch file run in the background while you go on about another task (such as writing code or hammering away on a word processor). You'll know that the batch file is finished when the icon of your minimized program disappears from the desktop (see Figure 1.2).

Figure 1.2. *Working on a program while a batch file runs in the background. (Note the icon at the lower left of the screen.)*

Note: Before you run the following program, be sure that a batch file called UPDATE.BAT exists on your hard drive. The batch file you use can perform any one of a number of tasks, such as copying hundreds of files from the hard drive to a couple of floppies. There's no need, though, for you to create anything so elaborate. In fact, the following short batch file will do.

```
@echo off
rem -- Back up system files
c:
cd\
if exist c:\bak\config.sys goto copy
md bak
:copy
copy c:\config.sys bak
copy c:\autoexec.bat bak
copy c:\windows\win.ini bak
copy c:\windows\system.ini bak
exit
```

To create the batch file, just enter the preceding text into the Notepad program, and save it as "C:\DOS\UPDATE.BAT." The purpose of the batch file is simply to make sure that important system files are backed up.

Needless to say, on some systems you may have to make minor modifications to this batch file. But if you have installed Microsoft Windows on your C drive in a directory called Windows, you should be able to run the batch file as is.

Other than having the correct batch file, you'll also need to make sure that the DOSPRMPT.PIF file, placed by default in your Windows directory, has been modified so that it looks like the image in Figure 1.1. Before you worry about the PIF file, however, why don't you type in the code in Listing 1.2?

Note: PIF is an acronym that stands for *Program Information File*. A PIF is a file that contains information that Windows uses to run non-Windows applications. In particular, PIFs enable you to designate how much memory should be available for a particular task, how much of the processor's time should be allocated to it, and what configuration its window should have. These features are discussed in detail in the next few pages.

Listing 1.2 shows a more substantial Windows program.

Listing 1.2. A Windows program with a little more substance.

```
1: // SHORTBAT.CPP
2: #include <windows.h>
3: int CALLBACK WinMain(HINSTANCE hInst,
4:                      HINSTANCE hPrevInstance,
5:                      LPSTR lpszCmdParam, int nCmdShow)
6: {
7:
8:    WinExec("Dosprmpt.pif /C c:\\dos\\update.bat",
9:            SW_SHOWMINIMIZED);
10:   return TRUE;
11: }
```

The output for Listing 1.2 is displayed in Figure 1.3.

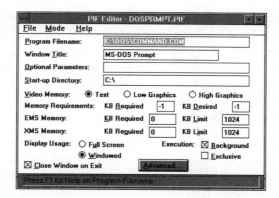

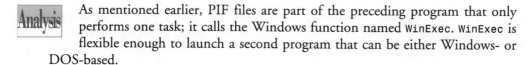

Figure 1.3. *The DOSPRMPT.PIF file as it should look before you run SHORTBAT.CPP. Notice the Background checkbox is selected.*

As mentioned earlier, PIF files are part of the preceding program that only performs one task; it calls the Windows function named WinExec. WinExec is flexible enough to launch a second program that can be either Windows- or DOS-based.

SHORTBAT.CPP specifies the name of the program to be launched, which in this case turns out to be nothing more than a PIF file that runs COMMAND.COM. The parameters passed to COMMAND.COM are /C, followed by the name and path of the batch file to be run. The /C syntax has nothing to do with Windows, but it is a convention required by the DOS command processor.

PIF files are part of the standard Windows environment. They are used to define the requirements for a DOS box that will be launched by Windows. DOS boxes are opened every time a DOS program is run in Windows.

The DOSPRMPT.PIF file comes with every copy of Windows and is used, by default, whenever you click the MSDOS icon in the Program Manager. If you are using a Program Manager substitute, such as the Norton Desktop for Windows, the same principles apply. Folks like myself, who use 4DOS, can substitute 4DOS.PIF for DOSPRMPT.PIF. When using 4DOS, the /C syntax should be omitted.

This book is not a tutorial on the Windows environment, but I should take the time to say that the most important part of a PIF file is the place where the programs memory requirements are specified. Placing a -1 in the KB Required or KB Desired box tells Windows to give the DOS program as much memory as is requested or as is available.

Okay. Hopefully, the two previous programs have started you in your Windows C++ programming career. With just a little imagination, I'm sure you can see how both programs can be modified to perform all sorts of useful tasks. (Note that there is no reason why you can't call WinExec many times inside one program!) If you come up with something truly useful, give your program a meaningful name and add its icon to one of your program groups. To me, nothing is more satisfying than creating programs of my own (that I can use on a regular basis).

The next two short sections in this book give you brief overviews of some of the more technical aspects of the previous two programs. Nothing you see in this chapter, however, is meant to give you anything more than a brief overview of topics you will hear about in more depth later on.

What Is WINDOWS.H?

This is not the place to get bogged down in a discussion of too many technical details. You might find it helpful, however, to know something about the broad structure of the two programs presented previously.

Both SHORT.CPP and SHORTBAT.CPP begin by including a header file called WINDOWS.H:

```
#include <windows.h>
```

Every Windows program includes this file, because it defines a very wide range of constants, structures, macros, and functions—all of which make up the backbone of all Windows programs. Both SHORT.CPP and SHORTBAT.CPP begin by including a file called WINDOWS.H. (See Figure 1.4.)

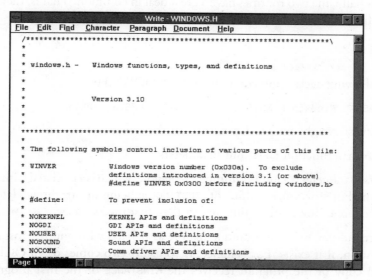

```
                              Write - WINDOWS.H
 File  Edit  Find  Character  Paragraph  Document  Help
 /***********************************************************************\
 *
 *
 * windows.h -    Windows functions, types, and definitions
 *
 *
 *
 *                Version 3.10
 *
 *
 *
 ***********************************************************************
 *
 * The following symbols control inclusion of various parts of this file:
 *
 * WINVER            Windows version number (0x030a).  To exclude
 *                   definitions introduced in version 3.1 (or above)
 *                   #define WINVER 0x0300 before #including <windows.h>
 *
 * #define:          To prevent inclusion of:
 *
 * NOKERNEL          KERNEL APIs and definitions
 * NOGDI             GDI APIs and definitions
 * NOUSER            USER APIs and definitions
 * NOSOUND           Sound APIs and definitions
 * NOCOMM            Comm driver APIs and definitions
 Page 1
```

Figure 1.4. *WINDOWS.H provides the structure upon which most Windows programs are built.*

All the programs in this book use WINDOWS.H. It's the key to the whole Windows programming experience. This book, and most other books that have been written on Windows programming, are really nothing more than commentaries on that essential document.

DO   DON'T

DO take the time to locate WINDOWS.H on your system. If you own Visual C++, the WINDOWS.H file was placed by default in the \msvc\include directory. If you own Borland C++, the file was placed by default in the \borlandc\include directory.

DON'T start reading the next chapter without first locating a copy of WINDOWS.H.

What Is *WinMain*?

Traditional C/C++ programs, from the DOS or UNIX environment, use the `main()` function as the program entry point. Windows programs, however, use `WinMain`. Functionally, the two routines have a great deal in common. That is, they both serve as the first function that gets called within a particular program.

The *WinMain* Function

The following declaration comes from WINDOWS.H:

```
int PASCAL WinMain(HINSTANCE, HINSTANCE, LPSTR, int);
```

This line shows the proper declaration for the program entry point.

The `WinMain` function takes four parameters:

The first parameter is a unique number, or handle, which is associated with the current program. For now, you can think of `HINSTANCE` as being an `int`; though later you'll see that there is a little more to this subject than first meets the eye.

The second parameter is a unique handle associated with another instance of this application, if it exists. For instance, if you start two copies of CLOCK.EXE, the second copy of the program receives the `HINSTANCE` of the first program in this parameter. If no previous instance of the program exists, this parameter is set to `NULL`.

The third parameter is a string containing any parameters passed to the program. The `LPSTR` type is Windows talk meaning a *long pointer to a string*. As you will see in the next chapter, it's really just a fancy name for `char * far` type.

The fourth parameter specifies whether the program should begin in a normal state, a maximized state, or a minimized state. A detailed example of how this is done is shown in Chapters 8 and 13.

`WinMain` returns an integer that Windows never actually examines. In other words, your application ends whenever `WinMain` ends; specific values returned are meant primarily to aid in debugging, or by making your code more readable. Therefore, it wouldn't really matter whether `WinMain` returns `TRUE` or `FALSE` at any particular point. I like to return `FALSE` when an error occurs, simply because it helps make the code readily comprehensible.

Example:
```
int CALLBACK WinMain(HINSTANCE hInst,
                     HINSTANCE hPrevInstance,
                     LPSTR lpszCmdParam, int nCmdShow)
```

Okay, that's enough for now. I'm sure you are interested in knowing more about the technical details that make up the SHORT.CPP and SHORTBAT.CPP programs, but I'd rather leave that kind of discussion for the next chapter. For now, you might want to just play around with your compiler and the Windows environment. Hands-on work is very important. Anyway, there will be plenty of time for technical discussions later in this book.

The rest of this chapter contains a few words about the kinds of compiler and hardware you'll need to write Windows code with the C++ language. I also mention a few stylistic issues, and from a theoretical standpoint, I give a general overview of the Windows environment. The chapter ends with a brief overview of the topics covered in the rest of this book.

The Sticky Matter of GUIs

Windows has a *Graphical User Interface* (GUI). This word is pronounced "gooey," as in a "gooey mass of cotton-candy flavored bubble gum."

As a participant in the rapidly changing high-tech world of computers, you no doubt have heard people say that Windows is slow. Well, the reason for its reputed slowness is not that it's a protected-mode application, and not that it multitasks, but because it is a GUI.

GUIs were created primarily to make life simpler for the users of applications. They were most definitely not created to make life simpler for programmers.

In particular, GUIs enable users to begin to think in terms of colors, icons, and graphics. The mere idea of multiple, resizable windows is not at all unique to a GUI. In fact, many DOS text-mode applications make excellent use of all these features. The bread and butter of a GUI are its graphical features (such as scrollbars that appear to exist in three dimensions and toolbars that are filled with intricate multicolored icons). These aren't merely bells and whistles designed to make Windows appear slick and sophisticated. GUIs were created to make applications more usable, more functional, and more approachable.

People who live near the heart of the computer world can forget how utterly baffling these machines can be to outsiders. The average person, even the average very bright person, needs all the help he or she can get when sitting down at a computer. This is not just a minor point, not just a nicety addressed to humor weak-kneed technophobes. Rather, the whole idea of making computers user-friendly has become a necessity— a hard-core art or science—which is being studied by the best minds in the world.

How Much Hardware Do You Need?

The GUI, which floats over Windows core like a big dome, is a crucially important feature that every programmer who reads this book is going to have to come to terms with sooner or later. Specifically, you need to understand that GUIs are here to stay, and that they take up massive amounts of system resources.

You cannot dodge this issue. The whole idea of computing has changed because of the presence of GUIs, and because of the current move to 32-bit operating systems. As a result, you need to think seriously about the kind of hardware you are using when you program Windows.

There was a time when a 286 with a couple megs of RAM was considered a hot machine. Those days are over. If you want to program Windows, you want the fastest possible machine you can lay your hands on.

Most of the time, this doesn't mean that you should run down to the store and attempt to upgrade you current computer. Trying to assemble a modern computer, out of bits and pieces of this and that, rarely works out right in the long run. If you can possibly afford it, you need a computer with some serious horsepower and with parts that work well together.

Let me just take a moment to underline this point. In my work, I have occasions to talk to people who are having trouble getting some very reliable programming tools up and running on their system. After the smoke clears, the discussions I have with these people usually focuses on one of two problems. The first, and more common, is that these people patched hardware together out of a hodgepodge of parts, some of which are four or five years old. The other problem represents the opposite extreme, namely, people who own some supposedly super-hot piece of hardware that exists on the bleeding edge of technology.

A reasonable machine on which to program Windows is a reliable 386 or 486 with at least four megs of memory, a VGA or SuperVGA monitor, and at least a one-hundred megabyte hard drive. A comfortable configuration, that treats you right, is a 486 DX with at least eight megs of memory and a two- or three-hundred megabyte hard drive. Anything less than a 386 33 MHz, with 4 megs of memory, would probably be too big of a strain on your sanity—though the patient could probably get along somehow on a 386SX. (I don't think I'd like to work too closely with someone using one!) Figure 1.5 uses the MSD.EXE program that comes with Windows to illustrate the features of a typical Windows development machine.

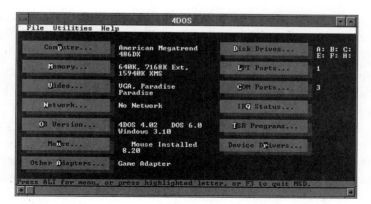

Figure 1.5. *The MSD.EXE program displays the features of a typical Windows development machine, circa summer, 1993.*

Notice that I don't mention my idea of an ideal machine. That's because every machine I've ever used in the last four or five years, has been a little slower than I wanted it to be. Back in the old days—when all I had was an XT—I was satisfied. But, ever since I got my hands on my first 286, I've had this inexplicable longing for a faster, more powerful machine! This appetite increased nearly tenfold when Windows came along. There's something about Windows that makes me dream about Pentiums, Septiums, and beyond....

At any rate, I'm quite serious about recommending that you get the most powerful machine you can afford. You would definitely not being going overboard if you decide to buy a 486 50 MHz machine with 8 to 16 megs of RAM. No one who really understands Windows programming would claim that such a machine is overkill.

The Compiler

Just as important as your hardware, is the compiler you choose. All the code in this book is guaranteed to run on either Microsoft Visual C++ or Borland C++. In most cases, the only differences in the code is in the makefiles, and even those differences are minor.

Either of these tools are more than adequate for the task. In fact, a number of other excellent compilers are on the market. I have not, however, had time to test this code on all those platforms. As a result, using this code on any other compiler could be problematic.

I want to stress again that I'm not promoting any one particular compiler. I simply want to write a good technical book that you'll find useful. I'm interested in programming—not PR.

I have, however, made every attempt to make the code in this book as up-to-date as possible. This means you'll be much better off if you own Borland C++ version 3.1 or Microsoft Visual C++ version 1. These are the compilers I used when writing this code. In particular, this book makes heavy use of both Windows 3.1 features and of a very important file called WINDOWSX.H. This file serves to extend and compliment WINDOWS.H, and to make your code nearly compatible with the new 32-bit operating environments. So before going further, you should check to be sure you have a copy of both Windows 3.1 and WINDOWSX.H.

It pains me to have to stress the need for powerful equipment and up-to-date compilers. Ordinarily, I'm not the type to be hip to all the latest trends. Windows, however, does exist very much on the cutting edge of existing computer technology, so you have to be prepared to make a considerable investment before you can sit down to play this particular game.

Coding Styles and Other Nitty-Gritty Issues

Most of the code for this book was written using Borland C++ for Windows. As I was creating the programs, I developed project files, and only later converted those project files into makefiles. I made the conversion, because I think makefiles provide a convenient format that lets me share code with you easily. If you want to have access to my project files, however, I have distributed the source code in this book on a wide a array of BBSs; and, there's a disk offer at the back of this book.

Note: This book's software is available on the CompuServe Information Service. When you GO SAMS, you enter the Prentice Hall Computer Publishing forum. Once there, enter the file library, and search in library 7 (Sams-ProgLang+DataB) for the keyword CALVERT.

All the code in this book is written to conform with C++ standards. This doesn't necessarily mean the code *won't* compile on a standard C compiler—only that the code takes full advantage of the strong type checking that is inherent in the C++ language.

At all stages of code development, I make heavy use of debuggers such as CodeView and Turbo Debugger for Windows (there are other powerful tools as well). I can't stress enough how vitally important debuggers can be to any successful coding project. Because this book is meant to appeal to you no matter which debugger you use, I don't concentrate on the techniques involved with using any particular debugging tool. Still, I believe it is of absolutely paramount importance that you learn to use the debugger that comes with your compiler—and that you lean on this friendly support as heavily as possible. The debugger is there to serve you. Learn to utilize its services, or you'll perish in a wasteland of lost messages, uninitialized pointers, and mind-boggling General Protection Faults!

What Is Windows?

I'm sitting here staring at the title of this section, realizing that I've managed to get myself in trouble again without having to exert myself in the least. All I've done is written out three fairly common English words that spell out a fairly simple question: "What is Windows?" Though it's an easy enough question to ask, I find myself wishing it were half as easy to answer. In fact, the mere phrasing of the question opens up a Pandora's box.

In the old days, programmers might have asked a presumably parallel question: "What is DOS?" In those simpler days, the answer was much easier: DOS is an operating system.

The same is not true of Windows. The 16-bit version of Windows 3.1, for instance, runs on top of DOS, and at least to some degree, depends upon and gives access to DOS services. So perhaps it's possible to at least "affirm" a negative by stating that Windows is not an operating system.

The only problem with that statement is that Windows NT *is* an operating system. Furthermore, many feel that DOS is *not* a true operating system, because it doesn't provide real preemptive multitasking or any form of protection against errors in ill-behaved programs. Windows NT provides all these things and much more. In fact, if you are interested in fancy features, I'm sure you know Windows for Workgroups already links large numbers of computers together in a nearly transparent manner. That is, you can be working on one machine, connect to a second machine, and access files or programs on that second machine as if they were on your own hard drive.

Hopefully by now, you can begin to understand why I introduced the metaphor of Pandora's box. In this section, I began by asking a simple question: What is Windows? After only a few moments of prying and poking, the question has led to a whole series of much more complicated questions. I need to answer these questions—making them fully evident (or at least comprehensible)—for anyone who hopes to be a real Windows programmer.

Make no mistake about this one issue: my goal, in this book, is to teach you to be a real Windows programmer. If you're looking for a miracle cure—for some incredible hitherto unknown shortcut to turn you into a dazzling professional overnight—you've come to the wrong place. My goal is to give you a friendly, high-spirited course in the real internals of the Windows programming environment.

This means that you have to proceed slowly and carefully, making sure not to brush aside important issues—just because they are a bit complicated or seemingly inconvenient.

Taking my own advice, I'm not going to try to rush ahead by offering a simplistic, and ultimately shallow, definition of Windows. Instead, I'm going to discuss the entire subject from several different angles over the next few pages. By the time you finish this chapter, the salient facts regarding Windows will be clear in your mind—and you'll have an intelligent and well-grounded understanding of Windows.

The API

In the last section, I wrestled with the paradoxical fact that Windows both is and isn't an operating system. This nasty Gordian knot† can yield rather quickly to the sword when you understand that Windows NT, the operating system, and Windows 3.1, the operating environment, remain linked together by a common API, or *Application Programming Interface*.

An API is a set of routines used to control either an entire computer, or a particular feature of a computer (such as a modem, video card, or a mouse). Suppose, for instance, you have a set of three routines designed to provide your program with a mouse interface. I'll call these routines `InitializeMouse`, `SetMousePosition`, and `GetMousePosition`.

These three routines could represent a simple API between your program and the mouse. They would let you start the mouse, set the mouse to a particular position, and get the current position of the mouse cursor. These simple capabilities are enough to form an *interface* between your *application* and a piece of hardware.

---

†The phrase *Gordian knot* is named after a knot tied by King Gordius of Phrygia. This knot was meant to only be untied by the future ruler, but Alexander the Great cut the knot with his sword. Today, a Gordian knot represents an intricate problem—especially one insoluble in its own terms.

The Windows API is nothing more than a similar set of routines that form an interface between your application and the entire computer. For instance, the Windows API gives you the ability to both set and get the current position of the mouse cursor. But it doesn't stop there. It also gives you functions for creating windows on the screen, for moving and resizing those windows, for controlling modems, files, directories, and memory—and much, much more. Windows is really only an API, but at the same time, it's an incredibly powerful API.

By now it should be clear that because Windows 3.1 and Windows NT have a common API, they are tied together. For instance, many Windows 3.1 programs make use of a function called `MoveWindow`. Naturally enough, this function can cause a Window to move from one location to another. Well, it should come as no surprise to learn that Windows NT also has a function called `MoveWindow`. It works exactly the same way the Windows 3.1 function works.

Of course, Windows 3.1 and Windows NT aren't exactly the same; they do have significant differences. Yet I am very much aware of the fact that many programmers want to program for both environments. As a result, in this book I use code that works in both environments—or that can be very easily ported from one environment to another. For instance, I frequently use a special header file called WINDOWSX.H that provides a common interface between 16-bit Windows 3.1 code and Win32 code (Win32 is 32-bit). As you learn to master WINDOWSX.H, you'll also learn how to write code that will run unchanged both in Windows 3.1 and in Windows NT.*

What's This Stuff About 32 Bits?

One of my goals in this book is to avoid using excessively technical language. I'm not interested in writing a book that has an erudite aura of arcane technical knowledge that leaves you feeling intimated, impressed, and not one whit the wiser.

Instead, I want to communicate things to you in the simplest possible terms. If you want to take that knowledge, and make something complicated out of it, then believe me: programming Windows in C++ is going to give you every opportunity imaginable for doing just that!

Rather than push you toward the brink of unfathomable complexity, I want to find the big themes that run through Windows programming like super-highways. I want you to have a very solid grounding in the basics, knowing that from there you can reach any region covered by the API, no matter how remote.

*If you want, you can purchase a copy of the code for this book that runs in a 32-bit environment. See the disk offer in back.

Therefore, it is important for you to come to terms right from the start with this business about the 8-bit, 16-bit, 32-bit operating systems, and also the 64K, 640K, and 4 gigabyte (a gigabyte is a billion bytes.) limits. Like it or not, these relatively technical subjects lie very much at the heart of Windows development. It's quite pos-sible that there wouldn't even be such a thing as Windows if it weren't for the 640K limit.

I'll start at the beginning by talking about bits. As you probably know, everything in a computer boils down to a bunch of on/off switches. These switches are represented by a series of zeros and ones called *binary* numbers.

For instance, the numbers zero and one each can be represented by a single binary digit. Here is the number zero in binary notation:

0

And here is the number one in binary notation:

1

Not very impressive looking, are they? When you see these tiny numbers standing all alone on the stage, it doesn't seem as if they can have the power to do much of anything. But hold on a moment.

Here is the number two in binary notation:

10

And here is the number three:

11

Here, for you personal delectation, is the number 255:

11111111

And finally, here is the number 65535 (also known as 64K):

1111111111111111

This last number has dominated computing on PCs for approximately the last five to seven years. The reason it's so important is because it's the largest number you can represent with 16 binary digits, that is, with a mere 16 *bits* of binary data.

 Note: The word *bit* comes from extracting letters from the phrase BInary digiT.

If you try to go one higher, that is to 65,536, you end with a binary number that looks like this:

```
10000000000000000
```

This number is represented with 17 bits of information. Unfortunately, the famous 80286 Intel processor can only handle 16 bits of information at any one time. That is what it is: a 16-bit processor that has dominated the computer industry *lo these many years....*

Of course, it's possible to work with numbers much larger than 65535 on a 286 computer. The problem is that you have to load up the coprocessor with several different bundles of information before you can count that high. That is fine when you are doing math, but it isn't fine when the computer is addressing memory. As a result, data structures on 8086 and 286 computers generally cannot be larger than 64K—at least not without performing some fancy behind-the-scenes manipulations. Anyone who has used arrays before is almost certainly painfully aware of this problem!

The 64K barrier is not the only limitation that DOS programmers have been wrestling with for some time now. The other problem involves the 640K limitation that represents the space inside which DOS and its family of programs can run.

At this late date, it's extremely easy to criticize the makers of DOS for limiting their operating system to such a relatively small memory space—and for not taking better advantage of the one meg of memory available to them. Yet sometimes, 20/20 hindsight is a bit too easy and too tempting. After all, DOS was the operating system that changed the face of the computing world and brought the wonders of the digital information age to nearly one-hundred million desktops. Given DOS's extraordinarily successful track record, it's really a bit much for all of us to suddenly stand up and say, "It was all a mistake."

The problem isn't so much that DOS was a mistake, but that programmers are now using computers to accomplish feats that the designers of the PC's memory architecture never imagined. On our desktops these days are 386s, 486s, Pentiums, and various RISC-based processors. A 286 computer can address 64K of memory at one time, but a 386 is a 32-bit computer that can address 4 gigabytes of memory at one time.

Here are 16 bits and 32 bits lined up one on top of the other:

```
16 bits: 1111111111111111
32 bits: 11111111111111111111111111111111
```

Here are the decimal numbers addressed by that many bits of information:

```
16 bits: 64,536
32 bits: 4,294,967,296
```

Four billion, two hundred ninety-four million, nine hundred and sixty-seven thousand, two hundred and ninety-six is a number that starts to slide off my scale of comprehension. All that I really know is that it's real, real big.

Certainly, it's large enough to utterly dwarf the old familiar limitations we find on 16-bit machines. What is 64K compared to 4 gigabytes? Nothing. It's irrelevant. It's simply ridiculous for owners of a 386 or better to sit around strapped in by the limitations imposed by DOS.

Once you begin to grasp these underlying facts, it becomes obvious that DOS, at least as we know it, is doomed. The computing world is moving inexorably towards 32-bit computing, and operating environments, such as Windows and 0S/2, will carry us across the great divide.

There you have it. That's one of the major underlying themes of this book. We're studying a way of programming that's ready to address the future. Windows straddles the gap between 16-bit and 32-bit computing, and therefore, it's a very likely route into the future. That's why somebody has hired me to write this book. That's why you're sitting there hopefully totally prepared to do the work necessary to master Windows programming.

The issue is simply that Windows, and its close cousin 0S/2, can lead the way into the future.

Even more remarkable is the fact that just as 16-bit computing has led to 32-bit computing, so will 32-bit computing inevitably lead to 64-bit computing, and even 128-bit computing. In other words, computing is going to go through a number of massive changes in the next five, ten, and twenty-five years. The computers we will work on ten years from now will make a 486 or a Pentium look like a child's toy. Without some understanding of these facts, you'll never really understand what Windows is about, or why it has taken on this particular shape.

Back Down from the Clouds

After this peek into the future, it's hard to come back down to reality. But right now, I want to concentrate on Windows 3.1, the main operating environment used to develop the programs in this book.

Win31 is not a 32-bit environment; it's a 16-bit environment that runs in *protected mode*. Before beginning to explore protected mode, I want to remind you that most of the programs in this book will compile unchanged for either 16-bit Win31, or 32-bit Windows NT. As a result, we sit uneasily on the edge of the future.

The past, however, in the form of 16-bit protected-mode programming, is still clinging to our shirt tails, holding us back. Two major features of 16-bit protected-mode programming set it apart from standard DOS programming.

In the DOS world, every address is made up of two 16-bit numbers, a segment and an offset, which are combined by the operating system to form a 20-bit number. In protected mode, however, the segment portion of an address is just an index into a table that holds 24-bit numbers. This index is called a *selector*.

Note: To convert two 16-bit numbers into a 20-bit number, use the following formula:

```
TwentyBitAddress = (Segment * 16) + Offset;
```

Multiplying by 16 is the same thing as shifting a number left four bits.

Right now, it's not necessary for you to get too bogged down in the details of how these addressing schemes work. Instead, concentrate on the fact that protected mode enables programmers to use a 24-bit number (whereas before, they could only use a 16-bit number). As a result, even "lowly" 16-bit protected-mode programs can address up to a total of 16 megabytes. In other words, protected mode makes it possible for your programs to utilize more than 16 times the amount of memory that a DOS application can address.

This doesn't mean that the old 64K limitation has disappeared. It's still a part of the 16-bit Windows 3.1 programming environment. Now, however, you can combine a selector and an offset to break the 640K limitation of real-mode DOS programs.

Note: Real-mode programs are so named, because their addressing scheme refers to actual, or "real" addresses in memory. Protected-mode programs, on the other hand, use selectors rather than "real" addresses.

In addition to enabling you to address a larger portion of memory, protected-mode programs also let you engage in a primitive form of multitasking. Selectors are the key to this process.

It's at the point when selectors come into play that you will finally begin to understand the meaning of protected mode. As I said earlier, selectors are only indexes into a table where real addresses are kept. As a result of this scheme, the operating system can monitor the use of every address so that it *protects* the user from careless or poorly written programs that try to write outside the program's memory space. In other words, protected-mode programs usually can't crash the system by writing to the wrong portions of memory. They are prohibited from doing so by the operating system itself, which monitors every address in the table where the selectors are kept.

At the same time, an efficient operating environment, such as Windows, can manipulate the memory addresses in this table so different programs can share close quarters without crowding one another out. This task is much too complicated for individual programmers to have to take on every time they sit down to write an application. Because protected-mode programs use selectors instead of real addresses, the actual nitty-gritty of multitasking is turned over to the operating system.

This is not the time or place to describe this process in any great detail. Instead, you just need to grasp two key concepts. The first is that 16-bit protected-mode applications can address, not 640K, but 16 megabytes of memory. Secondly, protected-mode programs can be multitasked, because the memory they address is kept in a special table that can be manipulated by the operating system.

So far, I have discussed the differences between 16-bit and 32-bit programs, and the difference between real-mode and protected-mode programs. But you don't actually need to know all these things to write Windows code.

I'm discussing these matters because I want you to understand what you are really doing when you write Windows code. If all I do is show you a set of rules to memorize, I can perhaps help you to become a fair Windows programmer of modest abilities. If, however, you learn the broad outlines of the underlying theory behind Windows, you'll be able to master any challenge. You will have not only knowledge, but also understanding.

A Look Ahead

The first third of this book is meant to be a general introduction to Windows programming. It acquaints you with the fundamentals without delving into too many details.

The second section includes an in-depth discussion of some important technical matters, as well as a full-length Windows program and game. By the time you finish the second third of this book, you should have a good feeling for how to write solid Windows programs that will appeal to a wide range of users.

The last third of this book covers advanced subjects, such as multimedia programming, OLE, and printing.

Summary

In this chapter, you read a brief introduction, and then ran two simple Windows programs. Once the preliminaries were out of the way, you had a chance to step back and take a look at Windows from a theoretical standpoint. You read a description of what Windows is, learned why it's important, and glimpsed its future.

You also read about the tools needed to best pursue your goal. In particular, you know that I believe Windows programming requires up-to-date programming tools and powerful computers.

Now that the ground work has been laid, the best thing you can do is to take some time to get set up. Load the compiler you want to work with and become familiar with its fundamentals. Take a look at the documentation you have available, and become familiar with it. Experiment with the editor you plan to use, and locate the compiler and debugger you'll depend on. Find the places in the manual that explain how to use these tools! To a good programmer, a debugger is nearly as essential as a compiler.

Take your time getting set up. I think programmers need to know how to putter. To me, programming isn't all just compulsive work, work, work, and more work. I need to enjoy playing with the tools I'm using when I'm on the job. If the whole thing doesn't seem at least a little bit like a large, very complicated, very elaborate game, I know something has gone wrong. As a rule, programmers work very, very hard. The thing that makes it possible is that some of that work is fun. So take the time to enjoy yourself, okay?

Q&A

1. Q: What is a program entry point?

   A: The program entry point is the place a program begins. When you click an icon and start a program, Windows loads that program into memory and then calls its WinMain function. This is the same process that goes on in DOS whenever a program is started. The big difference is that WinMain takes more parameters than does main().

2. Q: What is WINDOWS.H?

   A: WINDOWS.H is an include file that contains many of the most important constants, functions, structures, and macros used by Windows programs written in C++ or C. In some ways, it's the single most concise definition of the Windows programming environment available. As a commentary, however, it tends to be a bit too abbreviated, and so books such as this are written to explain WINDOWS.H in language that is easy to understand.

3. Q: Should I try to read WINDOWS.H from beginning to end?

   A: I guess I would consider reading WINDOWS.H in its entirety to be a fairly extreme act. On the other hand, a lot of the best Windows programmers tend to be a bit extreme by nature. Certainly no harm would come to you if you read the entire document. You might, however, want to start out by just dipping into it for a few minutes from time to time in order to get a feeling for the way it looks. Even if it seems a bit boring at first, I promise it will become more interesting as you learn more about the Windows environment.

4. Q: Will I be able to use my old 286 to program Windows?

   A: Yes. The Borland programming environment enables you to compile the code in this book on a 286. However, it's my strong opinion that such a machine is simply inadequate for the current task. If you're thinking about upgrading your computer, you might want to consider this an opportunity to treat yourself to something really special. If you are a professional, and the guys in hardware want to know what kind of machine you need, tell them you *require* a 486 66 MHz computer with 16 megs of RAM and a 500 megabyte hard drive. Tell 'em that's the minimum machine.

Workshop

The Workshop provides quiz questions to help you solidify your understanding of the material covered and exercises to provide you with experience in using what you've learned. Try to understand the quiz and exercise answers before continuing on to the next chapter. Answers are provided in Appendix A.

Quiz

1. What does the `WinExec` function do?

2. Name two differences between Windows and DOS.

3. What is a GUI?

4. Is Windows (that runs on top of DOS) a true operating system?

5. What is a PIF?

6. What is the name of the debugger that comes with your compiler?

7. Can two different Windows programs have the same `HINSTANCE`?

8. What is the name of the program entry point for a Windows program?

9. If only one copy of a program is running, what is the value of the second parameter passed to `WinMain`?

10. If two or more copies of a program are running, what is the value of the second parameter passed to `WinMain`?

Exercises

1. Write a program that "`WinExecs`" two other Windows programs.

2. Write a program that uses the third parameter of `WinMain` to specify, at runtime, which batch file you would like to run.

3. Write a batch file that runs a DOS batch file in a normal window, rather than in a minimized window.

Building Projects, Creating Windows

In this chapter, you get a chance to run several more short programs, and to see how to build Windows projects.

In particular, you will see how to

☐ Make sounds with your program, either through the multimedia extensions or through the standard MessageBeep function.

☐ Get better type checking by defining STRICT.

☐ Add a visual element to your program through the MessageBox function.

☐ Use module definition files.

☐ Use makefiles with Windows projects.

☐ Use project files in both Borland C++ and Visual C++.

☐ Pop up a traditional Window that can be resized, iconized, and maximized.

Sound

Windows programs engage the senses. Rather than simply showing line after line of written data, the goal of a Windows program is to present information conceptually through the use of pictures, graphs, and sounds.

In the last few chapters of this book you'll encounter a detailed look at the multimedia extensions to Windows. In those sections, you'll see how to add voices, music, and other audible features to your programs.

If, however, you have a Sound Blaster or another sound card, or if you have access to Microsoft's SPEAKER.DRV file, you can start using multimedia sound right away! All you need to do is run the short program called CHIMES.EXE. It enables you to use the SPEAKDER.DRV, or your sound card, to play WAV (wave) files. Wave files reproduce the sound of musical instruments, the human voice, and other realistic sounds. If you don't have access to any of these tools, don't worry; I have another simple program, called BEEPER.EXE, that you can use to tell your computer to start making short sounds (see Listing 2.2).

Note: The SPEAKER.DRV file is readily available. I got my copy by signing onto CompuServe, entering the Microsoft Library (GO MSL), and downloading the self-extracting file called SPEAK.EXE. This file also

is available when you download or purchase the software that comes with this book.

This book's software is available on the CompuServe Information Service. When you type GO SAMS, you enter the Prentice Hall Computer Publishing forum. Once there, enter the file library, and search in library 7 (Sams-ProgLang+DataB) for the keyword CALVERT.

Okay. Here are the two programs that show you how to start making sounds with your computer. The first version of this program (Listing 2.1) is the one you should use if you have SPEAKER.DRV or multimedia capabilities. The second version (Listing 2.2) runs on any system that has the built-in speaker that comes with nearly all PCs. If you can, run both programs, because you should know about the MessageBeep procedure.

Listing 2.1. CHIMES.CPP enables you to tap into the new multimedia capabilities provided by Microsoft.

```
 1: // Program CHIMES.CPP
 2: #define STRICT
 3: #include <windows.h>
 4: #include <mmsystem.h>
 5:
 6: int pascal WinMain(HINSTANCE hInst,
 7:                    HINSTANCE hPrevInstance,
 8:                    LPSTR lpszCmdParam, int nCmdShow)
 9: {
10:    sndPlaySound("Chimes.Wav", SND_ASYNC);
11:    return 0;
12: }
```

As shown in Listing 2.1, the Chimes program plays a file called CHIMES.WAV. This is a short musical file that, by default, the Windows SETUP program places in your Windows subdirectory. If you want to hear other sounds, songs, or voices, you can enter the name of a different WAV file.

This program calls a single function named sndPlaySound. sndPlaySound is part of the Multimedia extensions to Windows. The purpose of the function is to play a WAV file.

Notice the #define STRICT directive on line 2. Later in this chapter, you learn about STRICT programs. On line 4, I include the MMSYSTEM.H file. The letters "mm" in this file name stand for *multi*media. Since the advent of Windows 3.1, the MMSYSTEM.H header file is a standard part of the Windows programming environment. It's discussed in more depth later in the book, but for now you should probably open it inside an editor and take a brief look at it.

The sndPlaySound function is part of the Multimedia extensions to Windows. As a result, you must include MMSYSTEM.H in your program in order to use this function. (MMSystem stands for Multimedia system.)

sndPlaySound plays WAV files. These files usually have a .WAV extension and contain digital versions of analog sounds. As a result, they can hold nearly any kind of sound from voices to music.

The *sndPlaySound* Function

```
sndPlaySound(filename, SND_FORMAT);
```

The sndPlaySound function is a high-level multimedia command that gives you a simple way to play WAV files. The first parameter, *filename*, is the name of the WAV file you want to play. The Chimes program in Listing 2.1 plays CHIMES.WAV, which is placed on your system by default when you install Windows. Other files you might want to try include CHORD.WAV and DING.WAV.

The second parameter, SND_FORMAT, contains one of the following constants, which relay simple commands to Windows:

SND_SYNC	0x0000	Play synchronously (default)
SND_ASYNC	0x0001	Play asynchronously
SND_NODEFAULT	0x0002	Don't use default sound
SND_MEMORY	0x0004	First param is a memory file
SND_LOOP	0x0008	Loop sound until next sndPlaySound
SND_NOSTOP	0x0010	Don't stop any currently playing sound

Example:

```
sndPlaySound("Chord.Wav", SND_LOOP);
sndPlaySound("Ding.Wav", SND_SYNC);
```

Listing 2.2. The BEEPER.CPP program will make a sound on any PC system.

```
1: // Program BEEPER.CPP
2: #define STRICT
```

```
 3: #include <windows.h>
 4:
 5: int pascal WinMain(HINSTANCE hInst,
 6:                    HINSTANCE hPrevInstance,
 7:                    LPSTR lpszCmdParam, int nCmdShow)
 8: {
 9:   MessageBeep(-1);
10:   return 0;
11: }
```

The BEEPER.CPP file produces a short sound by using your system's built-in speaker.

This program uses the MessageBeep function to produce a beep or another sound, depending on how you set up your system. If you don't have multimedia sound available, you should always pass a -1 to the MessageBeep function.

The *MessageBeep* Function

```
MessageBeep(0);
```

The MessageBeep function is one of the simplest calls in the entire Windows API. It takes a single parameter, which is usually set to -1.

By default, the MessageBeep function makes a simple beep noise, very similar to what you hear so often in DOS programs. Systems that have multimedia capabilities, or systems equipped with SPEAKER.DRV, can associate other sounds with the MessageBeep function. To do this, simply pass one of the following constants to MessageBeep:

```
MB_ICONASTERISK
MB_ICONEXCLAMATION
MB_ICONHAND
MB_ICONQUESTION
MB_OK
```

You also can change the sounds associated with the preceding constants: just open the Control Panel and select the Sound icon. Match the Default sound from Column A with the WAV file of your choice from Column B (as shown in Figure 2.1). Now if you run the Beeper program, you'll hear an entirely new sound. (Remember, though, these later capabilities are only available on systems equipped with multimedia sound.

Example:

```
MessageBeep(MB_OK);
```

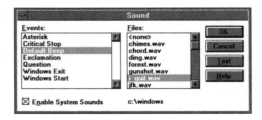

Figure 2.1. *Associating a particular sound with the* MessageBeep *function.*

Note: Built-in Windows API functions, such as sndPlaySound, WinExec, and MessageBeep are stored in DLLs. The acronym DLL stands for Dynamic Link Library. You'll see how to create your own DLLs later in this book. For now, all you need to know is that DLLs are libraries of routines that conceptually are somewhat similar to .LIB files. That is, they are libraries of code stored inside a single file. The big difference between LIB files and DLLs, however, is that LIB files are bound to your code at link time, whereas DLLs are linked in at runtime.

The major API calls, such as WinExec, sndPlaySound, and MessageBox, reside in DLLs and are linked dynamically at runtime. These DLLs have names such as GDI.EXE and USER.EXE. Also crucial are the "Kernal" DLLs, called KRNL386.EXE and KRNL286.EXE.

Don't worry if DLLs don't make complete sense to you yet. The topic comes up again in the last half of the book. For now, all you need to know is that they're much like LIB files.

Listings 2.1 and 2.2 contain only a few simple lines of code. In fact, their structure is identical to the programs you saw in the last chapter; except they're defined as STRICT. Take a moment to think about the important STRICT preprocessor directive.

Preprocessor Directives

```
#define CONSTANT value
```

Preprocessor directives are special messages written directly to the compiler. If you write:

```
#define MYNUMBER 35
```

this tells the compiler to swap in 35 whenever it sees the word MYNUMBER. The STRICT directive does something similar. It's a message telling the compiler to perform a certain action. The next few paragraphs of this book describe that action.

STRICT type checking gives special Windows-based integer types, such as HINSTANCE, a whole new power, thereby helping programmers avoid careless errors. This is not the time or place to discuss STRICT type checking in-depth. Indeed, you should know that the code in this book will run even if STRICT is not turned on. However, from here on out, all the programs in this book will be defined as STRICT by default. I strongly recommend that you follow this convention. The key point to remember is that STRICT code brings *strict type checking* to your program.

If STRICT isn't defined, HINSTANCE is declared as an unsigned int; if a program uses STRICT, however, HINSTANCE is declared as a pointer. This is done, because the compiler can perform careful type checking on pointers, whereas it quite naturally regards all integers as being the same type.

In this book, I often treat special Windows types, such as HINSTANCE, as simple variables (rather than pointers). This helps me present material in the clearest and simplest terms. In other words, even though I know that STRICT is turned on, I still speak of HINSTANCE as a simple integer value.

This brings us to a second important point: most of the time you should be able to ignore the presence of the STRICT directive altogether. It is meant to exist transparently and to raise its head only when it can help you correct an error.

When the STRICT option is used, the compiler can make distinctions between types to which it would normally be blind. For instance, the compiler usually doesn't distinguish the handle to a window from the handle to a picture (or bitmap, as pictures are often called in Windows). However, when you use the STRICT directive, the compiler can warn you (at compile time) of bugs that might normally take hours or days to track down.

Remember that the STRICT directive gives your program *strict type checking*. This helps you avoid careless errors that can delay projects for hours, days, or even weeks!

DEF Files and Visuals

So far, all the programs you've run have consisted of only one source file. Standard Windows programs, however, are usually made up of at least three sets of files. The first is the program's main module or modules, the second is a module definition file, and the third is a project or makefile.

The *module definition file* does more or less exactly what its name says it does; it defines the characteristics of the main module of a program. These characteristics include

☐ The file's name

☐ A short description of its purpose or primary characteristics

☐ The file's type

☐ The name of the stub program that will appear when the program is run from the DOS prompt

☐ It's stack and heap size

☐ A few statements, such as PRELOAD, DISCARDABLE, or MOVEABLE, that define the way the program handles memory

A *makefile*, of course, is used to orchestrate the act of bringing together the disparate source files of a project into a single executable. Most readers are probably familiar with makefiles, but I have provided a description of them in this chapter anyway. That way, you'll have a handy reference.

To give you a demonstration of how to use module definition files and makefiles, I have put together the following little program. It pops up a small window called a MessageBox. The message box contains a few words of wisdom, both inside it's main window, and inside its caption. Before you run this program, you need to learn how to compile using a Windows project or makefile. I'll explore that topic as soon as you type Listings 2.3 through 2.5.

Listing 2.3. The BOX1.CPP program displays words from an ancient Chinese text.

```
1: // Program LAOTZU.CPP
2: #define STRICT
3: #include <windows.h>
4:
5: #pragma argsused
6: int pascal WinMain(HINSTANCE hInst,
7:                    HINSTANCE hPrevInstance,
8:                    LPSTR lpszCmdParam, int nCmdShow)
9: {
10:   MessageBox(0,
11:              "He who knows does not speak",
12:              "He who speaks does not know",
13:              MB_OK | MB_ICONEXCLAMATION);
14:   return 0;
15: }
16:
17:
```

Listing 2.4. The BOX1 definition file.

```
 1:  ; LAOTZU.DEF
 2:
 3:  NAME            LAOTZU
 4:  DESCRIPTION     'LAOTZU Window'
 5:  EXETYPE         WINDOWS
 6:  STUB            'WINSTUB.EXE'
 7:  CODE            PRELOAD MOVEABLE DISCARDABLE
 8:  DATA            PRELOAD MOVEABLE MULTIPLE
 9:
10:  HEAPSIZE        4096
11:  STACKSIZE       5120
```

Listing 2.5. The Borland makefile.

```
 1:  # ------------
 2:  # Borland BOX1.MAK
 3:  # ------------
 4:
 5:  # macros
 6:  INCPATH = C:\BC\INCLUDE
 7:  LIBPATH = C:\BC\LIB
 8:  FLAGS = -W -m1 -v -w4 -I$(INCPATH) -L$(LIBPATH)
 9:
10:  # link
11:  BOX1.EXE: BOX1.OBJ BOX1.DEF
12:     bcc $(FLAGS) BOX1.OBJ
13:
14:  # compile
15:  BOX1.OBJ: BOX1.CPP
16:     bcc -c $(FLAGS) BOX1.CPP
```

Listing 2.6. The Microsoft makefile.

```
 1:  # ------------
 2:  # Microsoft BOX1.MAK
 3:  # ------------
 4:
 5:  # linking
 6:  BOX1.EXE: BOX1.OBJ BOX1.DEF
 7:     link Box1, /align:16, NUL, /nod llibcew libw, Box1
 8:
 9:  # compiling
10:  BOX1.OBJ: BOX1.CPP
11:     cl -c -AL -GA -Ow -W4 -Zp  BOX1.CPP
```

Figure 2.2 shows the output of the BOX.CPP program.

Figure 2.2. *The output from the BOX1.CPP program.*

 This program pops up the small window visible in Figure 2.2. Don't let this program give you the idea that windows are always this easy to create. In fact, its hard to create real windows that are maximizable, minimizable, and resizable. However, the `Messagebox` function serves as a nice interlude while building up to the real thing.

Before I talk about how to link and run the code in Listing 2.3, you might be interested in taking a quick look at the heart of the Box1 program. It includes only the `MessageBox` function, which is used over and over again in Windows code.

The *MessageBox* Function

```
int MessageBox(HWND, LPCSTR, LPCSTR, UINT);
```

The `MessageBox` function creates a window. It takes the following four parameters:

The first, an *HWND*, is a handle to the programs main window. In Listing 2.3, this is set to zero, because the Box1 program has no main window.

The second parameter, a long pointer to a constant string, is the text you want to appear in the main portion of the message box, as shown in Figure 2.2.

The third parameter, also a far pointer to a string, is the title of the message box.

The fourth parameter includes one or more of the following flags:

```
// Buttons
//----------------------------
#define MB_OK                 0x0000   Include okay button
#define MB_OKCANCEL           0x0001   Include cancel button
#define MB_ABORTRETRYIGNORE   0x0002   Abort, retry, ignore
#define MB_YESNOCANCEL        0x0003   Yes No Cancel buttons
#define MB_YESNO              0x0004   Yes No buttons
#define MB_RETRYCANCEL        0x0005   Retry, Cancel buttons

// Icons
#define MB_ICONHAND           0x0010   The stop icon
```

```
#define MB_ICONQUESTION      0x0020   The question mark icon
#define MB_ICONEXCLAMATION   0x0030   Exclamation mark icon
#define MB_ICONASTERISK      0x0040   Asterisk icon
#define MB_ICONINFORMATION   MB_ICONASTERISK
#define MB_ICONSTOP          MB_ICONHAND

// Scope and focus issues
#define MB_APPLMODAL         0x0000
#define MB_SYSTEMMODAL       0x1000
#define MB_TASKMODAL         0x2000
```

If you want to use more than one of these flags at a time, you should OR them together, as shown in the following example. To see how this works, try replacing the MB_ICONEXCLAMATION with MB_ICONINFORMATION.

The MessageBox function returns an integer that specifies the button the user selected when the MessageBox was on-screen. For instance, if the user presses an OK button, the function will return CMOK. If the user presses a CANCEL button, the function will return CMCANCEL. The following are the possible return values:

IDABORT	User selected the Abort button.
IDCANCEL	User selected the Cancel button.
IDIGNORE	User selected the Ignore button.
IDNO	User selected the No button.
IDOK	User selected the OK button.
IDRETRY	User selected the Retry button.
IDYES	User selected the Yes button.

Example:

```
MessageBox(0,
           "The astrolabe of the mysteries of God is love.",
           "Jalal-uddin Rumi said:",
           MB_OK | MB_ICONEXCLAMATION);
```

Overview of Compiling and Linking

The code for Listing 2.3 (the Box1 program) is quite a bit longer than the source for the previous programs in this book. Notice, however, that the BOX1.CPP file is very similar to the other programs you've seen. The added length comes entirely from the module definition file and the makefiles.

In the Chimes, Beeper, and Short programs, the compiler automatically generated internal module definition files that are very similar to the one accompanying the

BOX1 program. The compiler was capable of this, because module definition files for most simple Windows programs look almost identical.

> **Tip:** Once you've written and understood one module definition file, you can often copy it virtually unchanged from one program to the next! The same holds true for makefiles.

The point here is that you shouldn't feel overwhelmed by the presence of additional code. Most of the time, you can add makefiles and module definition files to your program with a simple copy and paste process, augmented by a quick search and replace procedure.

If you keep these thoughts in mind, you should find that the ensuing description of makefiles and module definition files are straightforward. So, without any further ado, you can start.

Project Files and Makefiles

There are two quite different ways to compile this program. The first is with a makefile; the second is with the relative simplicity of Borland's or Microsoft's convenient project files.

If you are using a project file, you need only add BOX1.CPP and BOX1.DEF to the project; then, compile and run. This is by far the simplest way to proceed. However, not everyone has the convenience of Borland's or Microsoft's programming environment, and many programmers prefer to use makefiles. As a result, the next few paragraphs are dedicated to an explanation of how to create and use a makefile.

You are probably familiar with makefiles. If you aren't, you should understand that makefiles are scripts run by a program called MAKE.EXE (Borland), or NMAKE.EXE (Microsoft). These scripts tell a compiler and linker how to build and link a program. The makefiles for the Box1 program can be run from the DOS prompt by typing one of the following commands:

```
make -fBox1          ( Borland )
```

or

```
nmake -fBox1.mak     ( Microsoft )
```

After typing and executing this command, you should have a working copy of BOX1.EXE on your hard disk. If this doesn't work, read the text (in the following section "The Microsoft Makefile") to learn how to set up the makefile for your particular system. If, however, typing the code did work, creating the executable isn't enough. If you are going to use makefiles, you also need to understand how to put one together.

Note: The next two sections are a rarity in this book; the first describes features of Microsoft's makefiles, whereas the second describes features of Borland's makefiles. In general, I try to avoid mentioning compiler-specific information. Makefiles are so important, however, that I decided to make an exception.

The Microsoft Makefile

If you are using Borland's compiler, you can skip this section and move on to the next.

The Microsoft makefile is read by a program called NMake, which performs the actual task of compiling and linking the program. The script, or makefile, which is passed to NMake, has three sections:

1. An optional title, which appears as a comment.

2. Two lines of code, which tell NMake how to link the program

3. Two lines of code, which tell NMake how to compile the program

The first part of the makefile begins with a pound (#) sign:

```
# Makefile for Box1
```

The pound (#) sign informs NMake that the remainder of the line is a comment.

The first line of fully processed code in the makefile explains the overall objective to NMake:

```
BOX1.EXE : BOX1.OBJ BOX1.DEF
```

This code states that the purpose of the makefile is to produce an executable called Box1, and that it will be made from (or more specifically, depend on) two source files called BOX1.OBJ and BOX1.DEF.

The next line of code shows the actual parameters passed to the linker:

```
link Box1, /align:16, NUL, /nod llibcew libw, Box1
```

If the parameters passed to link aren't already familiar, you should refer to your compiler's documentation for further details. However, I'll briefly explain that the "/align" option specifies that segments should be lined up on 16-byte boundaries. The NUL parameter tells the linker not to bother creating a map file. The /nod option specifies no default libraries. It's followed by the name of the small model Windows library, and the libw library that helps Windows link with the DLLs (where the API resides).

Before programs can be linked, the compiler must create the all-important object files. This is done by the last two lines in the project file:

```
BOX1.OBJ : BOX1.CPP
  cl -c -AL -GA -Ow -W4 -Zp  BOX1.CPP
```

As you can see, the first line informs NMake about the overall goal, which is to compile the source code file BOX1.CPP into BOX1.OBJ. The second line of code shows NMake the actual parameters to be passed to the Microsoft Command Line compiler, which is called cl.

- [ ] -c tells the compiler to compile without linking

- [ ] -AL tells the compiler to use the large memory model.

- [ ] The -GA switch tells Windows how to export certain Functions.

- [ ] The -Ow switch tells Windows to avoid some optimizations that don't work well in Windows.

- [ ] The -W4 switch instructs the compiler to give a complete list of warnings about potentially dangerous code.

- [ ] The -Zp switch tells the compiler to store structures and structure members on 1-byte boundaries.

Before leaving the subject of makefiles, I'll make one final change which enables you to reuse this makefile, with only minor changes, when compiling other programs:

```
# BOX1.MAK

APPNAME = Box1

# linking
$(APPNAME).exe : $(APPNAME).obj $(APPNAME).def
  link $(APPNAME), /align:16, NUL, /nod llibcew libw, $(APPNAME)
```

```
# compiling
$(APPNAME).obj : $(APPNAME).cpp
  cl -c -AL -GA -Ow -W4 -Zp $(APPNAME).cpp
```

This code uses a simple macro, which automatically substitutes the word `Box1` whenever it sees the word `APPNAME` in parentheses and proceeded by a dollar ($) sign.

You declare a macro by writing the macro name, followed by an equals (=) sign and the line of code you want to be represented by the macro. The end result is that you can alter multiple lines of code by changing one string. For instance, setting `APPNAME` equal to the string `AnyWind` affects every place mentioned in the makefile `APPNAME`. Therefore, changing only one line of code enables you to use this same makefile to compile a program called `AnyWind`.

> **Note:** At this point, people who have had a good deal of experience with makefiles might be itching for me to mention several further improvements that can be made to this script. For now, though, I will have to ask for patience. The style of this book is to begin with relatively clear and straightforward examples. After everyone has had a chance to grasp the basics, I move on to more advanced topics. That way, the reader can proceed easily by taking several passes over important subject matter.

Before wrapping up this discussion, I'll give you a second look at the three major sections of the Microsoft makefile:

☐ An optional title

☐ Instructions on how to link the program

☐ Instructions on how to compile the program

All in all, this makefile has just five lines of code. Though there are some fancy tricks you can perform with makefiles, most of what you see in this book is very straightforward. If some things don't make sense to you, the details will fall in place soon enough.

The Borland Makefile

If you are using the Microsoft compiler, you can skip this section and move on to the next.

There are four parts to the Borland makefile for Box1.

1. An optional title

2. A list of macros

3. An explanation about how to link the executable

4. An explanation about how to compile the object file

Each part starts with a comment to explain the purpose of the code. Comments in makefiles are proceeded by a pound (#) sign:

```
# Makefile for Box1
```

The three macros in the Borland makefile declare the path to the C++ include and library files, as well as the flags that are passed to the compiler:

```
INCPATH = C:\BC\INCLUDE
LIBPATH = C:\BC\LIB
FLAGS = -W -m1 -v -w+ -I$(INCPATH)
```

In other words, declare a macro by writing the macro name, followed by an equals (=) sign and the line of code you want to be represented by the macro. The end result is that you can reference a line of code by entering a dollar ($) sign, an open parenthesis (), and a macro name. For instance, the syntax following the -I directive inserts a macro into the fourth line of the makefile. Writing -I$(INCPATH) is exactly the same as writing -IC:\BC\INCLUDE.

The reason for including macros in a makefile is that it lets you alter multiple lines of code by changing one string. For instance, setting INCPATH equal to D:\BC\INCLUDE would affect every place in the makefile INCPATH (or FLAGS) is mentioned. Therefore, you can customize this makefile for your system by changing one line of code to fit your system's configuration.

Note: Four different flags are passed to this compiler. The first, -W, instructs the compiler to make a Windows application. The second, -m1, selects the large memory model. The third, -v, tells the compiler to include debugging information. The fourth, w+ tells the compiler to inform of any warnings regarding potential errors in the code.

The remaining lines in this file tell the command line compiler how to assemble the basic elements of the program. For instance, the following line tells Make that you

want to create a program called Box1 by using the two files, BOX1.OBJ and BOX1.DEF: `BOX1.EXE: BOX1.OBJ BOX1.DEF`

The next line of code tells Make what specific parameters to pass to the Borland command line compile, which is called BCC.EXE: `bcc $(FLAGS) BOX1.OBJ`

The final two lines of code in the makefile tell Make how to build the object file:

```
BOX1.OBJ: BOX1.CPP
 bcc -c $(FLAGS) BOX1.CPP
```

Notice that the FLAGS macro is expanded in two places, thereby automatically inserting into the command line the compiler directives and include directory (defined earlier in the makefile).

Before leaving this subject, it's worthwhile making one final change that enables you to reuse this makefile with only minor changes when compiling other programs:

```
# BOX1A.MAK -- alternate version

APPNAME = Box1
INCPATH = C:\BC\INCLUDE
LIBPATH=C:\BC\LIB
FLAGS = -W -m1 -v -w+ -I$(INCPATH)

$(APPNAME).exe: $(APPNAME).Obj $(APPNAME).def
  bcc $(FLAGS) $(APPNAME).obj

$(APPNAME).obj: $(APPNAME).cpp
  bcc -c $(FLAGS) $(APPNAME).cpp
```

Notice that this time, a new macro, called APPNAME, designates the name of the application. Sprinkling this macro throughout the makefile makes the script considerably more flexible. Now, only change one word of the makefile in order to use it with an entirely different application:

```
APPNAME = AnyWind
INCPATH = C:\BC\INCLUDE
LIBPATH=C:\BC\LIB
FLAGS = -W -m1 -v -w+ -I$(INCPATH)

$(APPNAME).exe: $(APPNAME).Obj $(APPNAME).def
  bcc $(FLAGS) $(APPNAME).obj

$(APPNAME).obj: $(APPNAME).cpp
  bcc -c $(FLAGS) $(APPNAME).cpp
```

This modified makefile builds an application called ANYWIND.EXE. The conversion occurred simply by changing Box1 to AnyWind.

Before wrapping up this discussion, here is a second look at the three major sections of the Borland makefile:

- [ ] An optional title
- [ ] Macro definitions
- [ ] Instructions on how to link the program
- [ ] Instructions on how to compile the program

This makefile is just a few lines of code. Although you can perform some fancy tricks with makefiles, most of what you see in this book is very straightforward. If things don't make sense to you, the details of how to create and use makefiles will surely fall into place.

Some High Falutin' Language

The next subject on the agenda is the module definition file, or DEF file (as it is commonly called).

Before delving into the details, it's perhaps worth pondering the sonorous title of this particular syntactical conglomeration: *The Module Definition File*, they call it. To hear this name, one might suppose that he or she has wandered into a lecture on Kant or Sartre. *The Critique of the Module Definition File*, perhaps, or maybe, *Being, Nothingness, and the Module Definition File*!

Before becoming too intimidated by the ominous ring of these words, you should know that one of the key aspects of Windows is an undocumented area of memory called by the somewhat farcical name—*BurgerMaster*. The BurgerMaster was named after a restaurant near Microsoft's headquarters.

My point is that the designers of Windows named one of its more esoteric and fascinating elements after a fast-food joint. Frankly, I think the name BurgerMaster reveals more about the true spirit of Windows than a stuffy name like the "module definition file." Like all truly interesting subjects, from Astronomy to Shakespeare, Windows isn't inherently somber or frightening. It's fun. If it weren't fun, it wouldn't be worth taking seriously.

At any rate, I'll return to the subject of DEF files. These little charmers usually perform several functions associated with the act of linking the final executable together.

One such task is to give the module a name:

```
NAME            Box1
```

A second is to designate the file as a Windows application:

```
EXETYPE        WINDOWS
```

The DESCRIPTION portion of the file is interesting, because this text is actually inserted into the programs header:

```
DESCRIPTION    'Box1 example'
```

The STUB, on the other hand, is just a little snippet of code that usually displays the well-known "This program requires Microsoft Windows" legend:

```
STUB           'WINSTUB.EXE'
```

If you want, you can write your own stub programs using a DOS compiler.

The last two lines of the DEF file designate the heap size and stack size:

```
HEAPSIZE       4096
STACKSIZE      5120
```

The stack for this application has been set at the recommended minimum. As a general rule, never try to build a Windows application with less than 5,120 bytes of stack space. This area, of course, is used to store information when the program calls local functions.

The HEAPSIZE designates an initial size for the program's local heap. If necessary, Windows can expand the local heap. Windows programs also can allocate memory from outside the local heap, if needed. In fact, DOS Windows programs have access to heap spaces that frequently climb above 16 megabytes in size. To find out how much heap is available on your machine, open the About box in the File Manager or Program Manager.

The remaining two lines from the DEF file describe how portions of the program are handled in memory :

```
CODE           PRELOAD MOVEABLE DISCARDABLE
DATA           PRELOAD MOVEABLE MULTIPLE
```

This is a somewhat more complicated subject, so I'll set aside a few paragraphs to go over it in-depth. Most of the subject matter revolves around the deep and murky ways Windows has of handling multitasking.

The PRELOAD MOVEABLE DISCARDABLE business, for instance, has the ring of some fairly heavy Kantian rhetoric. Indeed, these words should sound somewhat esoteric to DOS programmers who are not used to juggling more than one program in memory at a time.

The folks who created Windows surely had their hands full when writing the code that made multitasking in Windows possible. After all, they had to find ways to move a good deal of memory hither and yon, in a manner that would be totally transparent to ordinary programmers. Because they did such a good job, they left programmers with the task of understanding only a few relatively simple concepts.

Specifically, the code segment of this program is labeled MOVEABLE and DISCARDABLE. The MOVEABLE part means that Windows can move back and forth, in memory, the portions of this program that contain the actual code executed during runtime. Typically, Windows might do this in order to make room for another program recently brought to the forefront of the desktop. The DISCARDABLE part states that Windows can actual discard or remove the segment in question from memory, if necessary. If this happens, however, Windows will, of course, reload the code segment the moment it's needed.

Think of it this way: Windows can run several applications at the same time, but there is no guarantee that there will be a place to store the code for all these applications in memory. As a result, Windows shifts programs around in memory, or even temporarily discards portions of programs from memory.

So far so good. The rub comes from the fact that some pieces of code absolutely can't be moved. For instance, device drivers (which control printers or other pieces of hardware) must be loaded to a specific address and kept in place. To accomplish this feat, Windows enables you to designate the way certain segments in memory are treated.

The data segment, for instance, is designated as being MOVEABLE and MULTIPLE. This means that this memory block can be moved about at will, and that there also can be more than one copy of it in memory. (See Figure 2.3.) The need for multiple copies stems from the fact that there can be more than one copy of a program running at one time.

Some users, for instance, might want to have multiple copies of the Notepad program on the desktop at one time. They can easily switch back and forth between two documents, which is a very powerful and useful capability. To gain this capability, however, it's necessary that each copy of the program have its own data segment. If not, all the copies of Notepad would have to work with the same data.

The lesson here is that Windows flexibility comes at a price, and part of that price is using technical sounding words, such as MOVEABLE, DISCARDABLE, and MULTIPLE.

Figure 2.3. *When multiple copies of a single program are multitasked in Windows, each has its own data segment.*

By now, you should begin to understand why the data segment of most Windows programs must be declared as MULTIPLE. If it weren't, all the different copies of each program would be working on the same data. (See Figure 2.4). Notice, however, that the code segment for the Box1 program is not declared to be MULTIPLE. This means that each instance of the program shares the same code segment, even though it will have its own data segment.

DOS Windows programs traditionally work this way, because there is often a limited amount of RAM on a PC. When multiple instances of the program are on the desktop, only one copy of the code segment is needed. As a result, the smallest possible amount of space is used whenever a program is loaded into memory. This whole process is possible, because Windows doesn't enable you to write to the code segment of an application. If it did, you would have to declare code segments as multiple, because one instance of an application might have modified its code segment (whereas another might have left it untouched).

> **Note:** Other multitasking operating systems tend to give each instance of a program its own code segment. They can afford to do this, because they are running on hardware that's likely to have a plentiful supply of RAM.

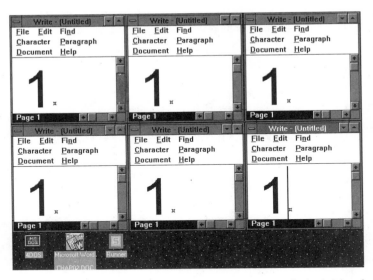

Figure 2.4. *Extreme example of what the Write program might look like if each copy on the desktop had the same data segment.*

Hopefully, you haven't found this lengthy discussion of the DEF file and related matters too confusing. It always frustrates me if I have to work with a black box that makes no sense. I want to understand a little something of what's actually going on, so I try to give you the same type of information.

If portions of this discussion have left you a little confused, don't worry. Everything's cool. In this book, you always can use the same basic DEF file over and over again, with only a few modifications. Specifically, all you usually need to do is change the name of the program and its description. The rest can be left untouched.

You really don't have to be too terribly clever to be a Windows programmer. What you must be is flexible and a little fast on your feet. If you can grasp new concepts, you are going to be okay. If you resist change, you'll have to be dragged kicking and screaming into this brave new world.

Creating Windows

So far, you've had a chance to look at several different Windows programs, but you haven't seen one real window! As it happens, there's a reason for this. And it's not that

I'm being stingy. I want to talk to you about creating windows, and in fact, almost all the remaining programs in this book contain at least one window (whereas many of them will contain multiple windows).

The problem, however, is that the actual act of creating a real window is far from trivial. In fact, I've spent a considerable amount of time clearing the boards, so to speak, so you can concentrate all your attention on one key subject: creating windows.

Let's not make any bones about this. What you are going to see in the next few paragraphs, and what you'll see throughout the entirety of the next chapter, is probably the most complicated single step you'll take in the beginning and intermediate stages of your Windows programming career. If you can master this one subject, everything else will fall into place.

At any rate, before you get too worried, you should know that, as with the previously shown DEF files and makefiles, the actual act of putting up a window is a three-step process that you can write once. Then, you can reuse it, almost completely unchanged, in many different programs.

Windows programmers don't sit down and say to themselves: "Okay, now I'm calling `CreateWindow`. What's the first parameter, and what should I set it to this time? Fine. Now, what's the second parameter...." Instead, all they do is perform a quick cut and paste operation, make a few minor changes, and forget the whole process.

The act of creating a window is a process with a bark that's a lot worse than its byte!

What you're about to see is the shortest program (50 lines) I could come up with that creates a real window—one that acts the way you would expect a window to act.

At this stage, you don't have to understand anything but the broadest outlines of how this program works. In fact, this program is stripped of a number of important syntactical elements that I feel are essential for the creation of robust, easily maintainable programs. I have even gone so far as to omit the DEF file and makefiles. I do this, because I want you to concentrate only on the broadest outlines of this program.

Don't worry about any of the details. Just get the program (shown in Listing 2.7) up and running so you can see that this code does all the things you would expect a real Windows program to do. That is, you can maximize it, minimize it, or resize it, just as you would any professional Windows application.

When you are done, come back to the text and read a brief discussion of the main sections of the program. After that, you can call it quits for the day. Tomorrow, you'll have a chance to go after a full-fledged Windows program in all the excruciating detail you could ever want. But that's tomorrow, and this is today.

Listing 2.7. The MakeWin program creates a traditional window with a caption, border, and system menu.

```cpp
 1: // Program MAKEWIN.CPP
 2: #define  STRICT
 3: #include <windows.h>
 4: #include <windowsx.h>
 5: #include <string.h>
 6:
 7: char Name[] = "MakeWin";
 8: LRESULT CALLBACK WndProc(HWND, UINT, WPARAM, LPARAM);
 9:
10: int pascal WinMain(HINSTANCE hInst,
11:                    HINSTANCE hPrevInstance,
12:                    LPSTR lpszCmdParam, int nCmdShow)
13: {
14:   HWND hwnd;
15:   MSG Msg;
16:   WNDCLASS W;
17:
18:   memset(&W, 0, sizeof(WNDCLASS));
19:   W.style = CS_HREDRAW ¦ CS_VREDRAW;
20:   W.lpfnWndProc = WndProc;
21:   W.hInstance = hInst;
22:   W.hbrBackground = GetStockBrush(WHITE_BRUSH);
23:   W.lpszClassName = Name;
24:   RegisterClass(&W);
25:
26:   hwnd = CreateWindow(Name, Name, WS_OVERLAPPEDWINDOW,
27:                       10, 10, 600, 400, NULL, NULL, hInst, NULL);
28:
29:   ShowWindow(hwnd,nCmdShow);
30:   UpdateWindow(hwnd);
31:
32:   while (GetMessage(&Msg, NULL, 0, 0))
33:   {
34:      TranslateMessage(&Msg);
35:      DispatchMessage(&Msg);
36:   }
37:
38:   return Msg.wParam;
39: }
40:
41: LRESULT CALLBACK _export WndProc(HWND hwnd, UINT Message,
42:                                  WPARAM wParam, LPARAM lParam)
43: {
44:   if (Message == WM_DESTROY)
45:   {
46:     PostQuitMessage(0);
47:     return 0;
48:   }
```

```
49:    return DefWindowProc(hwnd, Message, wParam, lParam);
50: }
```

This program creates a simple empty window with a title bar, minimize and maximize buttons, and a system menu (see Figure 2.5).

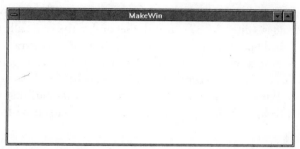

Figure 2.5. *The MakeWin program creates a window that can be minimized, maximized, resized, and normalized!*

The MakeWin program has two major parts:

1. The first part is the WinMain function.

2. The second part is the WndProc function.

The remainder of this chapter takes a brief look at each part.

The WinMain function can be divided into three sections:

☐ The first section (lines 18-24) is where the window is registered:

```
18:    memset(&W, 0, sizeof(WNDCLASS));
19:    W.style = CS_HREDRAW ¦ CS_VREDRAW;
20:    W.lpfnWndProc = WndProc;
21:    W.hInstance = hInst;
22:    W.hbrBackground = GetStockBrush(WHITE_BRUSH);
23:    W.lpszClassName = Name;
24:    RegisterClass(&W);
```

The Register procedure tells Windows about the characteristics of a window class. For now, there is no need to worry about why a window is registered or what this step means. You only need to note that this is the first thing that happens in a typical WinMain procedure. In later chapters, the complicated act of registering a Window will be isolated in its own procedure, as it should be according to the well-proven dictates of proper, structured design.

☐ The next step is to create the window (lines 26-30):

```
26:    hwnd = CreateWindow(Name, Name, WS_OVERLAPPEDWINDOW,
27:                        10, 10, 600, 400, NULL, NULL, hInst,
                          NULL);
28:
29:    ShowWindow(hwnd,nCmdShow);
30:    UpdateWindow(hwnd);
```

The act of creating a window involves two steps. The first is the call to CreateWindow (lines 26-27), and the second is the two calls to ShowWindow (line 29) and UpdateWindow (line 30). As with the registration procedure, the act of creating a window is usually handled in its own separate procedure. This is done to isolate complexity, and to create a well-structured, robust program. For now though, I've just run the whole business together so you can get a feeling for how it fits into what politicians used to call "the big picture."

☐ The third portion of the WinMain procedure is called the message loop (lines 32-36):

```
32:    while (GetMessage(&Msg, NULL, 0, 0))
33:    {
34:        TranslateMessage(&Msg);
35:        DispatchMessage(&Msg);
36:    }
```

When the user moves the mouse or strikes a key, messages are sent to the message loop. This is the *driver's seat* for a Windows program. This is command central, a loop that keeps repeating throughout much of the life of a program.

Don't worry if all of this doesn't make sense to you yet. Its not supposed to. The point of this last section of Day 2 is simply to give you an overview of a typical Windows program. Tomorrow, you get all the detail you could ever hope for, and then some.

Right now, you need only think about the broadest issues, such as the three steps in a WinMain procedure and the WndProc procedure, which responds to messages a program receives:

```
41: LRESULT CALLBACK _export WndProc(HWND hwnd, UINT Message,
42:                                  WPARAM wParam, LPARAM lParam)
43: {
44:    if (Message == WM_DESTROY)
45:    {
46:       PostQuitMessage(0);
47:       return 0;
48:    }
49:    return DefWindowProc(hwnd, Message, wParam, lParam);
50: }
```

The MakeWin program only responds explicitly to WM_DESTROY messages (line 44). All other messages get passed on to DefWindowProc (line 49). The DefWindowProc procedure, as you will see in the next chapter, does nothing more than handle the default behavior associated with a window. In other words, when you maximize a window, or minimize a window, the DefWindowProc procedure processes your message and knows what to do with it.

DefWindowProc doesn't, however, handle WM_DESTROY messages. That is your duty as a programmer. All you need to do, when the message comes down the pike, is call PostQuitMessage (line 46). When that's done, you can exit WndProc with a return value of 0 (line 47).

In the next chapter, you'll see how to handle standard Windows messages with macros, so you can move the message response functions outside of WndProc. The rationale is the same as for moving the Create and Register functions outside the WinMain procedure. That is, Windows programmers want to be able to create well-structured programs that are easy to maintain and debug. In this case, I have collapsed all these procedures back into the WinMain and WndProc functions, so you can see the overall structure of a typical Windows program.

For now, that's all you need to know about the MakeWin program. To summarize:

☐ There are two main parts in a program. The first is the WinMain procedure; the second is the WndProc procedure.

☐ The WinMain procedure has three parts. The first *registers* the Window, the second *creates* the window, and the third sends *messages* to the window through a loop.

☐ Any messages sent to a window pass through WndProc. This window procedure can explicitly handle the messages, or pass them on to DefWindowProc, which is the default message handler.

Summary

In this chapter, you learned how to make sounds with a Windows program, and how to pop up a MessageBox. You also learned how to deal with technical matters, such as using the STRICT directive and creating module definition files and makefiles. In the final portions of the chapter, you saw the broad outlines of the structure that lies behind most Windows programs.

After having completed these steps, you are ready to take an in-depth look at how to put together a full-fledged, totally functional program. All the gory details that go into that process will be discussed in-depth in the next chapter. For now, you can just sit back and rest on your laurels, and prepare for the things that lie ahead.

Q&A

1. **Q: How can I compile a Windows program?**

   A: There are two standard ways to compile a Windows program. The first is through the use of Microsoft's and Borland's powerful project files. Many programmers find this the ideal way to assemble a program from its disparate parts. Others prefer to use makefiles, which can be run from the DOS prompt. Some simple programs, which run on Microsoft's or Borland's compiler, don't absolutely need either a makefile or a project file. These simple programs turn out to be anomalies, however, because you'll usually need a makefile or project file in order to compile your project.

2. **Q: What is a module definition file?**

   A: A module definition file specifies certain major characteristics of a particular application. For instance, DEF files give an application a name, add a description to the executable's header, and specify how the program treats memory. Most of the time, you can simply copy a DEF file from one project to the next, with only modest changes. These fellows seem complicated at first, but after a few days, you'll find that they tend to fade into the background and require only minimal thought.

3. **Q: What memory model should I use?**

   A: Most of the programs in this book are designed to run in the large memory model. Your choice of memory model, is not so important in the earlier chapters of this book, but later on you will need to use the large memory model.

Workshop

The Workshop provides quiz questions to help you solidify your understanding of the material covered and exercises to provide you with experience in using what you've learned. Try to understand the quiz and exercise answers before continuing on to the next chapter. Answers are provided in Appendix A.

Quiz

1. What is the purpose of a Windows Stub file?

2. Name three things defined in a Module Definition File.

3. What are the two main procedures in the MakeWin program?

4. What are the three main parts of every WinMain function?

5. Every main window in an application must respond to one message. What is it?

Exercises

1. If you have multimedia, create a program that uses the lpszCmdParam argument to snag the name of a WAV file off the command line. Once it has the name, have the program play the associated WAV file.

2. Create a program that pops up a MessageBox that contains your name.

A Standard Windows Program

My goal in this chapter and the next is to analyze, in-depth, the underlying structure of a typical Windows program. Specifically, this chapter is where to turn for an overview of

- ☐ `WinMain`
- ☐ `RegisterClass`
- ☐ `CreateWindow`
- ☐ The Message Loop
- ☐ `WndProc`

Be aware, however, that `WndProc`s are covered again in the next chapter. These two chapters are the most important chapters in the book. They contain information you'll have to rely on again and again when doing serious Windows programming.

The First Functioning GUI

Windows has the reputation of being a very difficult environment to program. Whether or not this reputation is deserved is a matter of considerable debate.

Most programmers who try to master the art of coding in Windows come from the DOS environment. As a result, they are almost always startled, or even frightened, when they first see the brave new world of Windows code.

When reading this book, however, I hope you greet the new and the strange—not with a sense of fear and confusion—but with a sense of wonder and excitement. If Windows programming is sometimes difficult, it's only because it is ripe with possibilities. My hope is that you concentrate, not on the difficulties, but on the opportunities Windows provides for an alert and adventuresome programmer. Where others see complexity, I want you to see opportunity.

Without further ado, I'll show you a complete Windows program, designed to be both flexible and durable. For now, all you need do is type it in and get the program up and running (see Listing 3.1). When you are working with the program, remember that it consists of several modules, each of which must be tied into the whole through the use of a makefile or project file. This means that the Window1 program is made up of all of the files listed here, though, of course, some or all of the makefiles will be optional, depending on your circumstances.

It's time to get started, so here's the code (Listing 3.1).

Listing 3.1. Window1 is a multimodule program that illustrates all the major components of a standard Windows program.

Type

```
 1: // =============================================================
 2: // Program Name: Window1
 3: // Programmer: Charlie Calvert
 4: // Description: Example Windows program.
 5: // =============================================================
 6:
 7: #define STRICT
 8: #include <windows.h>
 9: #include <windowsx.h>
10: #pragma warning (disable: 4068)
11: #pragma warning (disable: 4100)
12:
13: static char szAppName[] = "Window1";
14: static HWND MainWindow;
15:
16: LRESULT CALLBACK _export WndProc(HWND hWindow, UINT Message,
17:                                 WPARAM wParam, LPARAM lParam);
18: BOOL Register(HINSTANCE hInst);
19: HWND Create(HINSTANCE hInst, int nCmdShow);
20:
21:
22: // =============================================================
23: // INITIALIZATION
24: // =============================================================
25:
26: ///////////////////////////////////////////////////////////////
27: // The WinMain function is the program entry point.
28: // Register the Window, create it, and enter the Message Loop.
29: // If either step fails, exit without creating the window.
30: ///////////////////////////////////////////////////////////////
31: #pragma argsused
32: int PASCAL WinMain(HINSTANCE hInst, HINSTANCE hPrevInstance,
33:                    LPSTR lpszCmdParam, int nCmdShow)
34: {
35:   MSG  Msg;
36:
37:   if (!hPrevInstance)
38:     if (!Register(hInst))
39:       return FALSE;
40:
41:   if (!(MainWindow = Create(hInst, nCmdShow)))
42:     return FALSE;
43:
44:   while (GetMessage(&Msg, NULL, 0, 0))
45:   {
46:     TranslateMessage(&Msg);
```

continues

Listing 3.1. continued

```
47:      DispatchMessage(&Msg);
48:    }
49:
50:    return Msg.wParam;
51: }
52:
53: /////////////////////////////////////////////////////////////
54: // Register the window
55: /////////////////////////////////////////////////////////////
56: BOOL Register(HINSTANCE hInst)
57: {
58:    WNDCLASS WndClass;
59:
60:    WndClass.style         = CS_HREDRAW | CS_VREDRAW;
61:    WndClass.lpfnWndProc   = WndProc;
62:    WndClass.cbClsExtra    = 0;
63:    WndClass.cbWndExtra    = 0;
64:    WndClass.hInstance     = hInst;
65:    WndClass.hIcon         = LoadIcon(NULL, IDI_APPLICATION);
66:    WndClass.hCursor       = LoadCursor(NULL, IDC_ARROW);
67:    WndClass.hbrBackground = GetStockBrush(WHITE_BRUSH);
68:    WndClass.lpszMenuName  = NULL;
69:    WndClass.lpszClassName = szAppName;
70:
71:    return RegisterClass (&WndClass);
72: }
73:
74: /////////////////////////////////////////////////////////////
75: // Create the window
76: /////////////////////////////////////////////////////////////
77: HWND Create(HINSTANCE hInstance, int nCmdShow)
78: {
79:    HWND hWindow = CreateWindow(szAppName, szAppName,
80:                   WS_OVERLAPPEDWINDOW,
81:                   CW_USEDEFAULT, CW_USEDEFAULT,
82:                   CW_USEDEFAULT, CW_USEDEFAULT,
83:                   NULL, NULL, hInstance, NULL);
84:
85:    if (hWindow == NULL)
86:      return hWindow;
87:
88:    ShowWindow(hWindow, nCmdShow);
89:    UpdateWindow(hWindow);
90:
91:    return hWindow;
92: }
93:
94: //===========================================================
95: // IMPLEMENTATION
96: //===========================================================
```

```
 97: #define Window1_DefProc      DefWindowProc
 98: void Window1_OnDestroy(HWND hwnd);
 99:
100: ////////////////////////////////////////////////////////////
101: // The window proc is where messages get processed
102: ////////////////////////////////////////////////////////////
103: LRESULT CALLBACK __export WndProc(HWND hWindow, UINT Message,
104:                                 WPARAM wParam, LPARAM lParam)
105: {
106:   switch(Message)
107:   {
108:     HANDLE_MSG(hWindow, WM_DESTROY, Window1_OnDestroy);
109:     default:
110:       return Window1_DefProc(hWindow, Message, wParam, lParam);
111:   }
112: }
113:
114: ////////////////////////////////////////////////////////////
115: // Handle WM_DESTROY message
116: ////////////////////////////////////////////////////////////
117: #pragma argsused
118: void Window1_OnDestroy(HWND hwnd)
119: {
120:   PostQuitMessage(0);
121: }
```

Listing 3.2 shows the Window1 definition file.

Type   **Listing 3.2. WINDOW1.DEF.**

```
 1: ;  WINDOW1.DEF
 2:
 3: NAME           Window1
 4: DESCRIPTION    'Window1 example'
 5: EXETYPE        WINDOWS
 6: STUB           'WINSTUB.EXE'
 7: CODE           PRELOAD MOVEABLE DISCARDABLE
 8: DATA           PRELOAD MOVEABLE MULTIPLE
 9:
10: HEAPSIZE       4096
11: STACKSIZE      5120
```

Listing 3.3 is the Window1 Borland makefile.

Listing 3.3. WINDOW.1MAK (Borland).

```
 1: # The MakeFile: WINDOW1.MAK
 2:
 3: # Macros
 4: INCPATH = C:\BC\INCLUDE
 5: LIBPATH = C:\BC\LIB
 6: FLAGS = -W -ml -v -w4 -I$(INCPATH) -L$(LIBPATH)
 7:
 8: # Link
 9: WINDOW1.EXE: WINDOW1.OBJ WINDOW1.DEF
10:    bcc $(FLAGS) WINDOW1.OBJ
11:
12: # Compile
13: WINDOW1.OBJ: WINDOW1.CPP
14:    bcc -c $(FLAGS) WINDOW1.CPP
```

Listing 3.4 is the Window1 Microsoft makefile.

 Listing 3.4. WINDOW1.MAK (Microsoft).

```
 1: # WINDOW1.MAK
 2:
 3: # linking
 4: WINDOW1.EXE : WINDOW1.OBJ WINDOW1.DEF
 5:    link /CO window1, /align:16, NUL, /nod llibcew libw, window1
 6:
 7: # compiling
 8: WINDOW1.OBJ : WINDOW1.CPP
 9:    cl -c -AL -GA -Ow -W4 -Zp -Zi WINDOW1.CPP
```

 The Windows1 program, which is produced by compiling all the preceding files, creates a simple example of the traditional window that is so familiar to all users of the Windows environment. An image of this window can be seen in Figure 3.1.

 If you haven't done so already, you should set this book aside long enough to see Window1 in action. To do so, you must first get the program up and running.

When compiling the program, remember that it consists of several different modules brought together to create a whole. Just as a gear shift, steering wheel, and transmission come together with other pieces of machinery to make up the sum total of a car, each module in a Windows program makes its own contribution toward creating a final executable file.

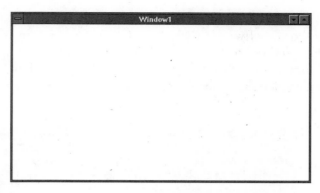

Figure 3.1. The output from running WINDOW1.CPP.

If you are working with project files inside of Borland C++ or Microsoft C++, the process of getting the program up and running should be fairly simple. If you aren't working with a project file, the first step is to run the makefile from the DOS prompt. Then, you can either start the program dynamically from a run menu, or add it as an icon to one of your program groups (and then start it from there).

Here is the command you should give if you want to use Borland C++ to compile Window1 from the DOS prompt:

```
make -f window1
```

Here is the command you should give if you want to use Microsoft Visual C++ to compile Window1 from the DOS prompt:

```
nmake -fwindow1.mak
```

Figure 3.2 shows a complete project as it appears when using Borland C++ version.

The Microsoft equivalent is visible in Figure 3.3.

Copies of the appropriate project and makefiles for Borland's and Microsoft's compiler are included with the disk or online file that is available for this book.

Note: It's crucial that you compile the programs in this book. If you are having trouble getting over this initial hurdle, you might consider purchasing or downloading the disk that accompanies this book. It comes with working code, guaranteed to compile and run correctly with either the Borland or Microsoft compilers.

This book's software is available on CompuServe Information Service. When you type GO SAMS, you enter the Prentice Hall Computer Publishing forum. Once there, enter the file library and search in library 7 (Sams-ProgLang+DataB) for the keyword CALVERT.

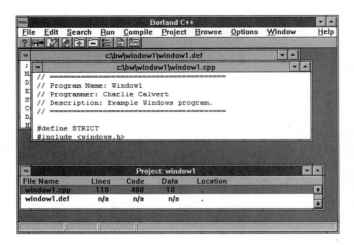

Figure 3.2. *The Borland IDE when creating the Window1 program.*

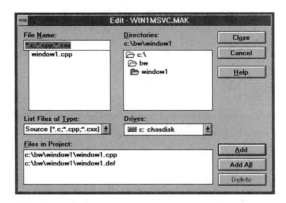

Figure 3.3. *The Microsoft project dialog when creating the Window1 program.*

When you have the program up and running, take the time to play with it for a few minutes. Even if you are already familiar with the Windows environment, you should experiment with the program by maximizing it, minimizing it, and changing its shape

by pulling on its borders. You need to understand what functionality is inherent in the lines of code you have typed in and compiled.

Of Apples, Oranges, Windows, and DOS

After you've spent a little time wrestling with the code from WINDOW1.CPP, you might find yourself feeling a little overwhelmed by its size. In fact, you might even feel yourself longing for the relative simplicity of the DOS world.

Certainly, a lot has been written about the relative merits of the DOS and Windows programming environments. Some folks even ask you to compare the rolling, thundering, seemingly opaque lines of a program (such as WINDOW1.CPP) with the sample code presented on the first few pages of a traditional DOS programming book:

```
#include <stdio.h>

main()
{
  printf("Hello, world");
}
```

I want to discourage you from wasting too much time with such thoughts. To my mind, its like comparing apples and oranges.

A peek beneath the surface reveals that there are really only a few parallels between the rococo-like richness of the Windows application (presented earlier) and the admirable simplicity of the DOS "Hello, world" program.

For instance, by changing only line 88 of the WINDOW1.CPP module, the program can be made to first appear in its minimized state (as a small icon at the bottom of the screen). That same line of code can be changed again to maximize the Window. Other very small changes can remove the caption, borders, and system menu—and minimize and maximize the icons from the window—so that it appears as presented in Figure 3.4. (In various parts of this book, you'll learn how to make all these changes.)

To make equally radical changes to the "Hello, world" program would require the addition of many lines of code, and days, if not weeks or months, of work. In the end, the code would have to be altered so radically that it wouldn't be recognizable as the same program.

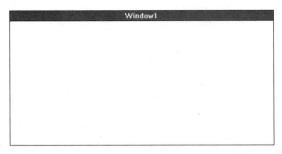

Figure 3.4. *Minor changes to the code in WINDOWS1.CPP can radically change the appearance of the Window it creates.*

Note: My point isn't that Windows is better than DOS, or that DOS is better than Windows. Rather, I believe that the two environments are radically different and they can't always be readily compared.

For instance, one can easily compare the relative merits of a Mercedes and a VW Beetle. It's more difficult, however, to compare a Mercedes to a motorcycle or sailboat. The statement "A Mercedes is roomier than a VW," is relatively valid. The same can't be said of the statement "A Mercedes is roomier than a motorcycle," or "A Mercedes is faster than a sailboat." I believe the same problem arises when people say "DOS is easier to program than Windows." Such statements aren't necessarily correct or incorrect, they're simply beside the point.

Ultimately, it may be unwise to try to see Windows and DOS as competing environments. Rather, I see them as complimenting one another. Of course, if you prefer Windows to DOS or DOS to Windows, that's fine with me. In fact, partisanship in this matter will probably lead to improvements in both environments, as each faction attempts to outdo the other. However, I hope they both survive so I can utilize the best features of each environment.

In the long run, the traditional "Hello, world" DOS program is probably not better or worse than a Windows program, only different. The computer world is very complex, and it's a mistake to always try to set one portion of it against another. The world isn't that simple. In this case, for instance, the one is an apple and the other an orange. As a result, the two can't be *fruitfully* compared!

Into the Code!

Well, it's time to start talking about the juicy stuff that forms the core of interest for all real programmers.

This is an extremely delicate part of the book. The things you'll learn about in the next few pages can appear a bit overwhelming, even to experienced Windows programmers. As a result, I want to be sure that you have some idea of what to expect.

☐ The next section presents a detailed overview of the WinMain procedure and the WndProc procedure—from a conceptual standpoint. My goal is to give you a bird's-eye view of an entire Windows program, without delving into too many specific lines of code. Once you have this image clear in your mind, you'll be prepared to see how the code is actually implemented. This section will appeal most to the theoretical, or abstract portions, of your intelligence.

☐ After the overview, the chapter swoops over the WinMain and WndProc code a second time. The purpose of this second pass is to take a careful look at the details of the WinMain, Create, and Register procedures. This section of the chapter features a line-by-line analysis of all three procedures, and will appeal to the practical side of your mind.

☐ The final section focuses on the details of the WndProc procedure. The WndProc procedure controls the program while it's running. In other words, the WinMain procedure launches the program, while the WndProc procedure helps run the program.

A Conceptual View of *WinMain* and *WndProc*

Following is the main function in the Window1 program.

```
32: int PASCAL WinMain(HINSTANCE hInst, HINSTANCE hPrevInstance,
33:                     LPSTR lpszCmdParam, int nCmdShow)
34: {
35:   MSG  Msg;
36:
37:   if (!hPrevInstance)
38:     if (!Register(hInst))
39:       return FALSE;
40:
41:   if (!(MainWindow = Create(hInst, nCmdShow)))
```

```
42:     return FALSE;
43:
44:   while (GetMessage(&Msg, NULL, 0, 0))
45:   {
46:       TranslateMessage(&Msg);
47:       DispatchMessage(&Msg);
48:   }
49:
50:   return Msg.wParam;
51: }
```

As stated earlier, function WinMain (lines 32-51) takes the place of function main() in a standard DOS program. Windows applications, written in C or C++, almost always begin with a call to WinMain.

WinMain is divided into three parts. The first is the call to Register (line 38), the second is the call to Create (line 41), and the third is the while loop that handles the program's messages (lines 44-47). Before I explain matters in detail, it might be helpful if you repeat these three steps as if they were a litany: Register, Create, enter the Message Loop. One more time: Register, Create, enter the Message Loop.

All right!

Take a moment to consider the following extended metaphor:

The Register function is roughly parallel to doing the paperwork when buying a car. You talk with the dealer about the particular "class" of car you want to buy. You tell him you want a Volvo station wagon with stick shift, or you want a Mercedes with power steering. That's the Register function.

The Create function, on the other hand, is similar to actually opening the door of a specific car, sitting down in the front seat, and turning the ignition. Now, it's officially yours. You've bought this particular vehicle—not just a particular class of vehicle, but a specific vehicle.

To complete this analogy, you can imagine that the message loop and WndProc are somewhat akin to the act of owning and maintaining a car. They are what you do after the cars is yours, and when you are taking care of it.

This analogy isn't without its flaws, but it serves as an image you can utilize during the upcoming discussion. It gives you something concrete to cling to when the conversation gets a bit abstract.

The act of *registering* a window is totally foreign to many DOS programmers. Nothing is parallel in the DOS world to the act of a program turning to the Windows environment and saying, in effect: "Ok, before my main window appears on the scene I want to register it with you so you know what class of window it is, and what it's up to."

To return to the parallel of buying a car, one can say that the `Register` procedure is akin to when you haggle over what type of car you want to buy. You are saying, "I want to buy this class of car. I want to buy a Toyota with four-wheel drive, or I want to buy a Chevy with air conditioning." You are not talking about a particular instance of a car, but about a general type of car and the actual features you want. Instead of establishing whether you want power steering or a fancy stereo, you establish what kind of icon you want, what kind of menu you want, what color window you want, and what name will be assigned to your window.

To summarize, the `Register` procedure enables you to register the class of window you want to use. The actual window you want to create is specified in the `CreateWindow` procedure.

> **Note:** The existence of the `Register` procedure implies that a window is a separate entity with an existence of its own. Furthermore, it has a caretaker (namely the program itself) that can talk with Windows proper (that is, with the operating environment).

After the window has been properly registered, the next step is to create it—to bring it into being. During this process, the shape, title and style of the window are established. Then, the window itself is brought into being, and the program takes over control of its existence.

This is roughly parallel to the act of actually buying a specific car. You sign the papers and become the owner of a particular vehicle. You can sit behind the wheel, and drive it off the lot. The program owns the window now, and is responsible for its future. You are no longer talking about a general class of car; you are now talking about a specific vehicle.

Notice that `WinMain` has a number of `if` clauses that must be navigated. If some of these clauses fail, the function will return `FALSE`, which means the window won't get created. In short, if the call to either `Register` or `Create` fails, the function `WinMain` is immediately aborted. It's as if your negotiations with the car dealer broke down, and you left without a purchase.

On the rare occasions when this happens, the application is summarily curtailed with little or no fanfare. These `if` clauses also ensure that if a previous instance of the application already exists, the window class won't be registered a second time. In other words, if you go into the dealer to buy a second car of the same type, you won't need to haggle over the type of car you are interested in or the features you want to include. You go straight to the `Create` function, which is where you *buy* a specific window.

Don't worry too much about the exact way these `if` clauses work. I discuss these lines of code in-depth later in this chapter.

The final step in `WinMain` is to enter the message loop. To continue the automotive analogy, one can think of the message loop and `WndProc` together as the driver's seat and controls of the newly purchased car. From here, the driver can see any new messages coming in, and can adjust the vehicle's course accordingly.

In order to fully understand the message loop and `WndProc`, you have to understand that Windows is, to some degree, object-oriented. That is, it has an existence of its own, just as a car is an object that has an existence of its own.

Each window can be treated as a separate object with an autonomous existence. As such, they aren't manipulated directly by the main program or by the operating system. Instead, the operating system can send messages to the window, and the window itself will "decide" what to do with those messages. Or perhaps it would be closer to the mark to say that the programmer teaches the window how to respond to the messages it gets.

It might help if I give a concrete example with which most readers should be familiar. At the end of the day, we usually decide to close Program Manager, or some Program Manager substitute, thereby shutting down Windows for the night. When this happens, messages are sent to all the windows on the desktop asking them if they are ready to close.

More specifically, the message is sent to the message loop that passes the message on to the `Wndproc`, or the message is sent directly to the `WndProc`. The `WndProc` decides what to do with the message.

Often, the `WndProc` replies: "Wait, I'm not ready! There's a file here that hasn't been saved." `WndProc` then pops up a window asking whether or not you want to save the file in question. If you do, `WndProc` saves the files and tells the operating system that it's ready to close. The entire process is summed up visually by Figure 3.5.

Figure 3.5. *A program turns to the user and asks a question.*

During much of this process, a window acts as an autonomous object with a life of its own. It knows enough to tell the Program Manager something needs to be done. Even more remarkably, it knows how to communicate with the user and request that any loose ends be tied up before anything else happens. This is quintessential object-oriented behavior.

DO   DON'T

DO remember to register a window class the first time it appears on the screen. When a window is registered, the operating environment is informed of several traits specific to that class. For instance, it learns about

- [ ] the name of the window class
- [ ] the icon of the window
- [ ] the cursor associated with the window
- [ ] the background color of the window
- [ ] the name of the menu associated with the window

DON'T forget to create a window whenever you call `WinMain`. While calling `CreateWindow`, you can define the window's title and dimensions, as well as perform other import initialization steps.

DON'T forget to set up the message loop properly. This is the driver's seat from which the window can view the rest of the world. A window without a message loop is like a car without any windows. The window won't know what's happening around it if it doesn't have a message loop. As a result, it will crash just as surely as a car will crash if a driver can't see!

So much for the overview of `WinMain` and `WndProc` in conceptual terms. Now it's time to change focus, to zoom in on the fine print. This is where you see the nitty-gritty that concerns most serious Windows programmers on a daily basis.

Calling *WinMain*

This section zooms in for a closer look at WinMain, which is the program entry point.

Start by taking another look at the header for the WinMain function:

```
32: int PASCAL WinMain(HINSTANCE hInst, HINSTANCE hPrevInstance,
33:                     LPSTR lpszCmdParam, int nCmdShow)
```

Even though you were given a brief overview of them in the first chapter, a great deal remains to be said about the four parameters passed to WinMain. Before focusing in too closely on the details, here's a quick review:

☐ The first parameter, hInst, is a unique number which identifies the program.

☐ The second parameter, hPrevInstance, is a unique number associated with any previous instance of this program. If there is no other instance on the desktop, hPrevInstance is set to NULL.

☐ The third parameter, lpszCmdParam, is a string containing any information passed from command line.

☐ The fourth parameter, nCmdShow, tells whether the program should appear minimized, maximized, or simply assume a default size and shape.

The first and second parameters passed to WinMain are declared to be of type HINSTANCE. The type HINSTANCE is really nothing but a handle, or unique number that Windows uses to identify a particular object on the desktop. In DOS, a similar situation occurs when the operating system assigns a handle to each open file.

The first parameter passed to an application identifies the *current instance* of an application. The second parameter identifies the *previous instance*, if it exists. Each of these instances can be thought of as nothing more than a unique number assigned to a particular object for means of identification.

The key issue is that Windows is a multitasking operating system that can support more than one copy of a program at a time. Therefore, the first order of business in any Windows program is to establish the "number" associated with the current instance of a program, and whether or not there is a previous instance of the program.

If no previous instance of the program exists, hPrevInstance is set to NULL. Therefore, it's possible to check whether or not a program has any siblings. This is done simply by typing

```
if(hPrevInstance)
  DoSomething();
```

Sometimes a programmer might decide that there should be only one copy of his or her program running at a time. As a result, a common use for this information is to preempt any attempt to create a second instance with something like the following code fragment:

```
if(hPrevInstance)
    return FALSE;
```

Of course, if you implement these two lines of code exactly as shown, your users would probably spend a lot of time clicking the icon for your application and wondering why nothing happens. In other words, it would probably be a good idea to pop up a MessageBox explaining the situation before returning NULL:

```
if(hPrevInstance)
{
  MessageBox(0, "Only 1 copy allowed", " Notice", MB_OK);
  return FALSE;
}
```

Earlier, I mentioned that Microsoft invented the HINSTANCE type to help you write easily readable, strongly type-checked code that helps you avoid careless errors. However, there is an important second reason for the creation of this type. This second reason has to do with creating code that will be portable between different architectures.

The issue here is that Microsoft wanted to be sure that the code for WinMain would compile even on an operating system that doesn't define an integer as it's defined on a 16-bit machine. As a result, Microsoft chose types that could be easily redefined in a new operating system. In other words, an int is the right type for an HINSTANCE in DOS Windows, but it might not be in Windows NT. As a result, the creators of Windows designed a system that would be flexible enough to enable you to use the same code on a number of different systems.

Before going on, I ought to talk some about the quaint notion of Hungarian notation. This particular conceit involves the habit of prefixing a letter to a variable name. This is done to help identify this variable's type. In other words, the "h," in hPrevInstance, is meant to indicate that hPrevInstance is of type HINSTANCE or of type HANDLE. Likewise, the "n" in nCmdShow designates that it's an integer.

This convention is a deep-rooted aspect of traditional Windows lore that also occasionally raises its head in the DOS world. Although Hungarian Notation can sometimes confuse newcomers, and though its value has been somewhat mitigated by the advent of the STRICT option, it can still be a useful tool in the hands of wary veterans.

3

Note: Certainly one nice feature of the notation convention is the way it got its name. The whole idea of Hungarian notation was created by an ace Microsoft programmer, Charles Simonyi, who was born in Hungary. The people who worked for him at Microsoft had always been taught to use this convention. To them it looked quite normal. However, observers of projects run by Simonyi have been known to comment on the strange appearance of the code produced in his shop. The traditional reply was to assume a deadpan expression and say that the code was strange-looking because it was written in Hungarian.

At any rate, I employ the convention because it is now, for better or for worse, an established part of the Windows coding tradition. I'll leave it up to you to decide whether or not you find it appealing.

The following often-quoted chart (see Table 3.1) should help you navigate through the Hungarian landscape:

Table 3.1. Windows typedefs, from WINDOWS.H.

Prefix	Type	Windows Type
b	int	BOOL
by	unsigned char	BYTE
c	char	
dw	unsigned long	DWORD
fn	function	
h	unsigned int (UINT)	HANDLE
i	int	
l	long	LONG
lp	long pointer	
n	int or short	
s	string	
sz	null-terminated string	
w	unsigned int	WORD

Notice the third column. It introduces you to various new types that are frequently used in Windows programs. They exist for the same reasons that the HINSTANCE type exists. Don't let their appearance in Windows code confuse you. Nothing about them

is tricky or difficult. In their simplest incarnation, they are just new names for the same old types that C programmers have been using for years. When STRICT is defined, however, they are often converted into pointers.

WINDOWS.H

Remember that the mother of all reference manuals is the WINDOWS.H file, which is referenced at the top of every Windows program. Inside WINDOWS.H, you'll find declarations and definitions for most of the functions and types native to the Windows environment. The following is a particularly important portion of WINDOWS.H that includes handy definitions:

```
/** Simple types & common helper macros **/

typedef int                 BOOL;
#define FALSE               0
#define TRUE                1

typedef unsigned char       BYTE;
typedef unsigned short      WORD;
typedef unsigned long       DWORD;

typedef unsigned int        UINT;

#ifdef STRICT
typedef signed long         LONG;
#else
#define LONG long
#endif

#define LOBYTE(w)           ((BYTE)(w))
#define HIBYTE(w)           ((BYTE)((UINT)(w) >> 8))

#define LOWORD(l)           ((WORD)(l))
#define HIWORD(l)           ((WORD)((DWORD)(l) >> 16))
```

A few choice moments spent pondering this code should help to clarify a number of interesting aspects of Windows programming. WINDOWS.H is the place where many mysteries are explained!

After studying the Hungarian notation chart, you might find that it's possible to make sense out of the third parameter to WinMain. The strange prefix before the identifier lpszCmdParam is meant to identify the parameter as a long pointer to a null-terminated string. In particular, this string happens to contain the command line passed to the program at startup.

The final parameter to WinMain helps designate whether or not the program is to begin in a maximized, minimized, or normal state. You encountered this same constant when using WinExec on Day 1, "Getting Your Feet Wet."

When nCmdShow is set to SW_SHOWMAXIMIZED, the program's main window appears in its maximized state. Conversely, when nCmdShow is set to SW_SHOWMINIMIZED, the window starts out minimized. The default is SW_SHOWNORMAL. To see what different results these values produce, you can take the time to experiment with them.

There is one last important part of the WinMain header that I've not yet discussed. This is the use of the word CALLBACK. In the old days, Windows programs used the words FAR PASCAL whereas programmers now use CALLBACK. The new word was chosen to provide compatibility with operating systems, such as Windows NT, which has no use for the keyword FAR. (*No use for the keyword FAR! What a wonderful, glorious, thought!*)

All procedures labeled CALLBACK are automatically declared with the *Pascal* calling convention. This means that when parameters are passed to this procedure, they are pushed onto the stack, starting with the parameter on the left, and ending with the parameter on the right. Traditional C programs take the opposite approach, but Windows uses the Pascal calling convention because it is faster.

A number of new conventions raised their heads in the last few paragraphs. But underneath all this syntactical sugar lie the same old types long familiar to C programmers. If you like, you can even think of the header for WinMain as "really" looking something like this:

```
int WinMain(int Instance, int PrevInstance,
            char far* CmdParam, int CmdShow)
```

If it helps you get a handle on this stuff, you can think of WinMain as being declared in this simple manner. The rest is just part of the carnival. Baffle your friends! Confound your enemies! Come join in—it's fun!

Registration

Here's the formidable Register function:

```
56: BOOL Register(HINSTANCE hInst)
57: {
58:    WNDCLASS WndClass;
59:
60:    WndClass.style        = CS_HREDRAW | CS_VREDRAW;
61:    WndClass.lpfnWndProc = WndProc;
62:    WndClass.cbClsExtra  = 0;
```

```
63:    WndClass.cbWndExtra      = 0;
64:    WndClass.hInstance       = hInst;
65:    WndClass.hIcon           = LoadIcon(NULL, IDI_APPLICATION);
66:    WndClass.hCursor         = LoadCursor(NULL, IDC_ARROW);
67:    WndClass.hbrBackground   = GetStockBrush(WHITE_BRUSH);
68:    WndClass.lpszMenuName    = NULL;
69:    WndClass.lpszClassName   = szAppName;
70:
71:    return RegisterClass (&WndClass);
72: }
```

This code introduces you to one of the great Windows traditions, namely, the existence of structures and declarations so numerous and complex, they are likely to send a distinct shiver down the spine of all but the most stout-hearted. Fortunately, these structures tend to lose their "byte" if you have either a good reference book handy or a good online help system.

Some day, you might want to memorize all the fields in the WNDCLASS structure. However, you don't need to do so immediately. Instead, you should probably dedicate your time to exploring the reference manuals or online help files in which these structures are listed.

For instance, both the SDK and Borland C++ come with information about the WNDCLASS structure. It looks like the image shown in Figure 3.6.

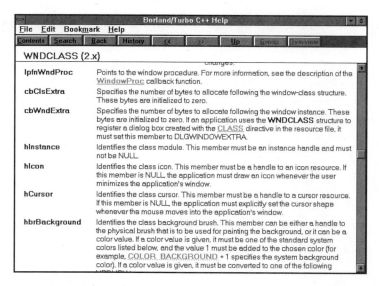

Figure 3.6. *An excerpt from the Borland C++ online help entry for the* WNDCLASS *structure.*

Alternatively, a few minutes spent perusing WINDOWS.H might help you find some additional information about the WNDCLASS structure:

```
typedef struct tagWNDCLASS
{
    UINT        style;
    WNDPROC     lpfnWndProc;
    int         cbClsExtra;
    int         cbWndExtra;
    HINSTANCE   hInstance;
    HICON       hIcon;
    HCURSOR     hCursor;
    HBRUSH      hbrBackground;
    LPCSTR      lpszMenuName;
    LPCSTR      lpszClassName;
} WNDCLASS;
```

The WNDCLASS structure lies at the heart of all Register procedures.

I've said that filling out the Register procedure is a bit like deciding what features you want to have on your new car. Now, you have a chance to see exactly what options are available whenever you register a new window:

☐ style field: What is the windows style? By changing the style field, you can radically alter the appearance of a window. This topic is discussed on Day 14, "Stylish Windows."

☐ wndProc field: Use this field to specify the name and address of the window procedure.

☐ cbClsExtra, cbWndExtra: Is there any extra data to be associated with the window class or instance? For now, you shouldn't worry too much about these two fields. They are discussed in-depth on Day 14.

☐ hInstance: Unique handle to an application

☐ hIcon: The window's icon, if any

☐ hCursor: The window's cursor, if any

☐ hbrBackground: The color of the window

☐ lpszMenuName: The menu for the window

☐ lpszClassname: The name of the window class

In WINDOW1.CPP, the style field is set to CS_HREDRAW and CS_VREDRAW (line 60). These two constants designate that the window is redrawn whenever the horizontal or vertical size of the window is changed. The presence of these two constants ensures that the contents of the window are always clearly visible to the user.

DO	**DON'T**

DO use the correct way to designate more than one Window style at a time by ORing them together with the ¦ symbol.

DON'T try to combine two window styles with an & or + operator.

The next step is to designate the window procedure. In some older code, `WndProc` is declared to return a `long`. If you define old code like that as `STRICT`, the resulting carefully monitored type-checking would force you to perform a typecast:

```
WndClass.lpfnWndProc    = (WNDPROC)WndProc;
```

But that extra bit of potentially confusing syntax can be avoided if `WndProc` is declared to return `LRESULT`:

```
WndClass.lpfnWndProc    = WndProc;
```

Of course, if you don't use `STRICT`, the latter syntax would probably compile on most standard C compilers (even if you did declare `WndProc` to return a `long`).

Of course, it goes without saying that typical Windows programs aren't going to get very far if you don't assign a window procedure to `lpfnWndProc`. So, no matter what path you take, all that really matters is that you somehow manage to assign a window procedure to `lpfnWndProc`. The actual technique you use is not nearly as important as the act itself!

The next two fields of the `WndClass` structure aren't important at this point. All `cbClsExtra` and `cbWndExtra` do is give you a chance to set aside some memory in which you can store information associated with your window. For now, there's no need to worry about such esoteric design issues.

The next step is to assign the `hInstance` field to the handle to your application. This is a simple, straightforward process:

```
WndClass.hInstance      = hInst;
```

The `hIcon`, `hCursor`, `hbrBackground` and `lpszMenuName` fields all describe common features of Windows. Later in the book, I describe how to tweak each of these features; for now, though, you might want to try a few simple experiments just to get a feel for what is going on. For instance, instead of assigning `IDI_APPLICATION` as your icon, try assigning `IDI_EXCLAMATION`, or `IDI_HAND`:

```
WndClass.hIcon      = LoadIcon(NULL, IDI_HAND);
```

After you run your application, minimize it and you'll see that it has a different icon.

You can do the same sort of trick with the cursor simply by substituting `IDC_WAIT`, `IDC_CROSS`, or `IDC_IBEAM` for `IDC_ARROW`:

```
WndClass.hCursor          = LoadCursor(NULL, IDC_CROSS);
```

If you use the `IDC_WAIT` icon as your main cursor, you'll see the familiar hourglass symbol, as shown in Figure 3.7. Even when I'm the guy who makes this change, it seems to confuse me. Normally, the hourglass symbol only appears when Windows is telling the user to wait. As a result, I tend to hesitate when I see it on-screen, even if I know that I put it there only on a whim.

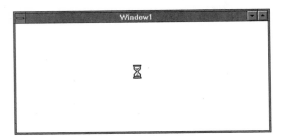

Figure 3.7. *A window using the famous hourglass cursor.*

Seemingly trivial experiences, such as this, help show how powerful icons and other symbols can be. The human brain interacts very intimately with symbols of all types. Learn to take advantage of their power! Or, if you want, you can simply play with icons and cursors in order to see what peculiar effects you can create. Now you are the programmer, and you can get Windows do to any crazy thing you want it to do. If you're at all like me, you'll probably relish the opportunity to create a little good-natured mischief!

If you want to change the background color of your application, just substitute `BLACK_BRUSH` or `GRAY_BRUSH` for the constant `WHITE_BRUSH`. Remember that all these constants are defined in WINDOWS.H and are listed in detail in any good reference book.

Right now isn't the time to begin working with the menu, but the `lpszClassName` field needs a few brief words of explanation. This field gives you a chance to name your window. This is a very important act, because it's under this name that your window is registered. The class name is a bit like the key to an automobile. Without it, you can't sit down in the driver's seat and turn on the engine. In other words, a window must be registered under a particular name before it can be created. Whenever you want to create a window, you'll be helpless if you don't have the key—that is, if you don't know the class name.

So at this point, further examination of the WNDCLASS structure isn't needed. The only thing left to do is to pass this information to Windows by calling RegisterClass and passing it the address of the WNDCLASS structure:

```
return RegisterClass (&WndClass);
```

There are two key points I hope you remember from this section:

☐ The Register procedure helps define the *class* of the window to appear on-screen. All windows are objects, and each object has a special set of traits. By filling out the WNDCLASS structure, a programmer tells Windows how he or she wants a particular object, or *class*, to be defined.

☐ You often don't have to think about the Register method at all. Just copy and paste it into your program, and call it without even thinking about its contents. The default settings (previously shown) do fine in many cases. The Register function isn't something you have to fuss with every time you code; it is a series of opportunities available to you.

Creating the Window

Now it's time to consider the Create routine. Remember, this is the portion of the program where you define a specific window. The Register procedure defines a general class of window, and the Create procedure defines a specific instance of a window class:

```
77: HWND Create(HINSTANCE hInstance, int nCmdShow)
78: {
79:   HWND hWindow = CreateWindow(szAppName, szAppName,
80:                   WS_OVERLAPPEDWINDOW,
81:                   CW_USEDEFAULT, CW_USEDEFAULT,
82:                   CW_USEDEFAULT, CW_USEDEFAULT,
83:                   NULL, NULL, hInstance, NULL);
84:
85:   if (hWindow == NULL)
86:     return hWindow;
87:
88:   ShowWindow(hWindow, nCmdShow);
89:   UpdateWindow(hWindow);
90:
91:   return hWindow;
92: }
```

The core of this function is the call to CreateWindow, which takes a total of 11 glorious parameters, none of which you should take too seriously now:

```
LPCSTR lpszClassName;       (address of registered class name )
LPCSTR lpszWindowName;      (address of window text )
DWORD dwStyle;              (window style )
int x;                      (horizontal position of window )
int y;                      (vertical position of window )
int nWidth;                 (window width )
int nHeight;                (window height )
HWND hwndParent;            (handle of parent window )
HMENU hmenu;                (handle of menu or child window )
HINSTANCE hinst;            (handle of application instance )
void FAR* lpvParam;         (address of window-creation data )
```

Clearly, this function is equipped with enough arguments to keep the wolves awake.

Some of these arguments can be changed in order to implement simple, relatively obvious changes in your program. For instance, if you call CreateWindow (with the following parameters), you'll get a window like the one depicted in Figure 3.8:

```
HWND hWindow = CreateWindow(szAppName,
                            "Tiny Window",
                            WS_OVERLAPPEDWINDOW,
                            1,
                            1,
                            100,
                            100,
                            NULL,
                            NULL,
                            hInstance,
                            NULL);
```

Figure 3.8. *Window1 after making some modifications to the parameters passed to* CreateWindow.

This example demonstrates how the second parameter passed to CreateWindow defines the window title, whereas the fourth through seventh parameters determine its initial shape. The constant, CW_USEDEFAULT, tells Windows to choose the coordinates for a program.

The first parameter passed to `CreateWindow` is the *class name*. Remember that every window on the desktop is a separate entity, with some degree of autonomy. As a result, windows should have names by which they can be identified. Traditionally, the name of a program's main window is also the name of the application itself—but this doesn't have to be the case.

The other parameters passed to `CreateWindow` are discussed at the beginning of Week 2, when the entire subject of registering and creating Windows is looked at in more detail. For now, use the previously listed defaults, unless there is some specific reason for doing otherwise.

> **Note:** Don't be confused by the seemingly cavalier way in which I put off discussing the other parameters passed to `CreateWindow`. Windows is not a difficult environment, but it *is* loaded with detail.
>
> I try to avoid bombarding you with too much material and cluttering the scene with a lot of information that isn't yet particularly relevant. Instead, I focus in on what is important at any particular stage.

Before moving on to a brief discussion of the `window` procedure and the `message` loop, take a glance at the two functions that make the window actually appear fully formed on the screen:

```
ShowWindow(hWindow, nCmdShow);
UpdateWindow(hWindow);
```

The `ShowWindow` function passes `nCmdShow` to Windows, thereby telling it to display the window in a particular state, such as minimized, maximized, or normal. The `UpDateWindow` call instructs Windows to send the `WM_PAINT` message to the window, which has just appeared on-screen. An in-depth explanation of how that process actually works will be included in the next chapter.

For now, you only need to know that both `ShowWindow` and `UpDateWindow` take `hWindow` as a parameter. In this case, `hWindow` is really a handle to the application's main window. The issue is that many windows can open on the desktop at any one time, but the current goal is only to show the particular one just created. Therefore, it's necessary to pass the handle to that window, so Windows knows which object needs to be shown.

What Goes Around Comes Around

The last few lines of the WinMain procedure look like this:

```
44:    while (GetMessage(&Msg, NULL, 0, 0))
45:    {
46:        TranslateMessage(&Msg);
47:        DispatchMessage(&Msg);
48:    }
```

You already know enough to understand the basic functionality associated with these few lines of code. The key point to remember is that throughout the life of an application, Windows is sending it messages that report on actions taken by the user, or by other portions of the environment.

These messages are placed in a queue, which the GetMessage function can dip into at will. As each message is retrieved, it's placed in a message structure that looks like this:

```
typedef struct tagMSG
{
  HWND    hwnd;
  UINT    message;
  WPARAM  wParam;
  LPARAM  lParam;
  DWORD   time;
  POINT   pt;
} MSG;
```

For now, you don't need to explore this structure in any depth, although you can rest assured that I'll return to it again (in the next chapter and elsewhere).

After the message is retrieved from the message queue, it's passed to TranslateMessage, where processing helps make a message more comprehensible. For instance, if a function key is pressed, the message is originally placed in the queue in a very abstract form. The TranslateMessage function performs the processing that makes this message much easier to understand.

The DispatchMessage function then proceeds to pass this message on to the specified window procedure, which, in this case, happens to be WndProc. After the message is dispatched, GetMessage is called to retrieve another message from the queue, if one is available.

It's important to understand that this loop, or one similar to it, is being executed over and over again throughout the entire life of an application. The process never stops. It lies very much at the heart of every Windows program. As such, it needs to be covered in-depth, so you'll find that the subject is broached repeatedly through this book.

The Window Procedure

The message loop revolves around and around in circles. This process is repeated in an endless loop throughout much of the life of a typical Windows program. First, it gets messages from the operating environment; then, it passes the messages to the `WndProc`:

```
#define Window1_DefProc    DefWindowProc
void Window1_OnDestroy(HWND hwnd);

// The window proc controls program flow
LRESULT CALLBACK __export WndProc(HWND hWindow,
                            UINT Message,
                            WPARAM wParam, LPARAM lParam)
{
  switch(Message)
  {
    HANDLE_MSG(hWindow, WM_DESTROY, Window1_OnDestroy);
    default: return Window1_DefProc(hWindow, Message,
                                    wParam, lParam);
  }
}

// The routine is called when the window is destroyed.
#pragma argsused
void Window1_OnDestroy(HWND hwnd)
{
  PostQuitMessage(0);
}
```

What this usually means is that messages go specifically to the window procedure where they can be handled individually. From there, they can be passed on to the default window procedure, `DefWindowProc`.

`DefWindowProc` knows how to handle nearly all the default behavior associated with a particular type of window. For instance, it knows how to handle mouse movements that minimize or maximize a window, as well as how to handle movements that expand or shrink a window.

Think about that last sentence for a moment. It states that one function handles all kinds of mouse movements and knows how to reshape a window. A great deal of functionality is packed into one simple call:

```
default:
  return Window1_DefProc(hWindow, Message, wParam, lParam);
```

If you look at this line of code from one perspective, it seems a bit long and convoluted. However, if you remember how much functionality it brings to a program, it no longer seems so complicated. It would take me hundreds, even thousands of lines of code to pack this much functionality into a standard DOS program. Windows lets me do it with a single line of code. Where some people might see complexity, I see a myriad of opportunities.

Note: This book usually encapsulates `DefWindowProc` inside a macro named after the program's main window: `Window1 DefProc`. Immediately preceding the call to this macro is the `HANDLE MSG` macro, which is defined in WINDOWSX.H. `HANDLE.MSG` parses the parameters associated with any one message and passes them on to a separate function, such as `Window1 OnDestroy`. Without the macros in WINDOWSX, most `WndPro` procedures would become mired in long, tangled case statements. The whole crucially important subject of WINDOWSX.H and message crackers is discussed in detail in the next chapter.

Note: It's important that you don't confuse WINDOWS.H and WINDOWSX.H. WINDOWS.H is a primary reference file. It's your primary bible, the sin qua non of Windows programming. WINDOWSX.H, however, is a relatively recent addition to Windows programming. It includes numerous refinements and time-saving improvements, but it is not absolutely essential to most programming endeavors. However, WINDOWSX.H can be an extremely important file that might save you hours, days, and even weeks of work.

As mentioned, WINDOWSX.H is explained in more depth in the next chapter (and in succeeding chapters). Be sure to read about it. Both WINDOWS.H and WINDOWSX.H are essential to the structure of this book. I discuss both files again and reference them in nearly every chapter of this book.

Before the default window procedure is called, `WndProc` has a chance to respond to most messages it receives. WINDOW.CPP is a minimal Windows programming example. As a result, it is only necessary to respond to the message that tells the main window it is about to be destroyed. The `HANDLE_MSG` macro parses the parameters passed to `WndProc` and sends only relevant ones to the `Window1_OnDestroy` message function handler:

```
void Window1_OnDestroy(HWND hwnd)
{
  PostQuitMessage(0);
}
```

Many different messages can bombard a window at one time. The WM_PAINT message, for instance, tells a window that it's time for it to repaint itself. Others, such as WM_MOUSEMOVE, tell a window that the mouse is moving over it at a certain coordinate. Other messages tell a window that it's being minimized, maximized, resized, pulverized—well, there's not really a WM_PULVERIZE message; but there might as well be, because so many other messages float in and out of WndProc throughout the life of a typical window.

I spend considerable time discussing WndProcs and the various ways they can be structured. For now, however, so you can get an overview of the whole process, I only want to introduce you to the main parts of this program.

Hopefully, you can visualize the main portions of a Windows program:

☐ First, the WinMain procedure contains Register, Create, and Message loop sections.

☐ Beneath WinMain is the WindProc, which has a chance to handle any messages being sent to a window.

These two functions represent the main structure and the main flow of the program. If you can grasp the rudiments of how this system works, you can get some feel for how the Windows environment is put together.

Summary

In this chapter, you took a detailed look at the very heart of Windows programming by examining a sample application. WINDOW1.CPP demonstrates many of the major features that are touched on again and again in this book.

Specifically, this chapter showed how a Windows program is initialized by calling the RegisterWindow and CreateWindow functions, and by showing the window to the user. In the process, you read about many of the major types unique to Windows, such as an HINSTANCE and WORD. I also discussed the Message Loop and the WndProc procedure, both of which handle the stream of messages constantly being sent to an application.

Q&A

1. Q: How can I find out about the special types used in a Windows application?

   A: There are several major sources of information. One is a book such as this. Other sources include reference books and online help systems. Perhaps the single most important reference is the WINDOWS.H file, which ships with your compiler and is included at the top of every Windows program. You can supplement the information found in WINDOWS.H by browsing through the important WINDOWSX.H file, which is covered in more detail in the next chapter.

2. Q: Windows is a *message-*, or *event-oriented* environment. What does this mean?

   A: In the DOS environment, a user usually interacts directly with a program. But in Windows, the user's actions are first trapped by the operating system, and then passed to an application in the form of messages or events. This system gives Windows applications a kind of autonomy and independence (entirely lacking from the traditional DOS environment).

Workshop

The Workshop provides quiz questions to help you solidify your understanding of the material covered and exercises to provide you with experience in using what you've learned. Try to understand the quiz and exercise answers before continuing on to the next chapter. Answers are provided in Appendix A.

Quiz

1. What is a `WNDCLASS`?

2. What is the purpose of the `register` function?

3. What is the purpose of the `Create` function?

4. What is the difference between `ShowWindow` and `UpDateWindow`?

5. What is the purpose of the `WndProc`?

6. What is the purpose of the `message loop`?

7. What is the purpose of the DefWindowProc?

8. What traditional C type is associated with a WORD?

9. What traditional C type is associated with a LONG?

10. What traditional C type is associated with a LPSTR?

Exercises

1. Create a program that appears in its maximized state.

2. Create a program that uses the hourglass cursor, which usually prompts the user to wait for a few moments.

3. Create a program that fails before even calling the Register function.

4. Create a program that has a light gray background.

5. Create a program that has your name visible in the title of its main window.

Messages, WINDOWSX, and Painting Text

Two major subjects are covered in this chapter:

1. The way Windows handles messages and how WINDOWSX.H can help simplify this process.

2. The most fundamental I/O issue, namely, how to display text.

Many of the traits that give Windows its special flavor owe their character to the fact Windows is an *event-oriented* (or message-based) system. If you don't understand messages, you won't understand Windows.

In this chapter, you get a chance to learn about event-oriented, message-based systems. You get an in-depth look at the window procedure, the messages sent to it, and the message crackers that help simplify Windows code. This is material that lies very much at the heart of Windows.

In particular, this chapter covers

- ☐ Messages
- ☐ WINDOWSX
- ☐ Message crackers
- ☐ Message handler functions
- ☐ Responses to WM_PAINT messages
- ☐ Device contexts
- ☐ Two ways to write text in a window

What Is a Message?

The last chapter presented a bird's-eye view of a standard Windows program. It gave you a flyby over all the major portions of a Windows program, including the WinMain, Register, Create, and WndProc functions, as well as the message loop. The next step is to narrow the focus so that you get a closer look at the window procedure and the messages that are sent to it.

By now you should have a feeling for the difference between a message (or event-driven program) and a standard procedural program. In the former case, the operating system (or operating environment) tells a program that an event has occurred. In the latter case, the program queries the system to find out what has happened:

- ☐ Windows message-based model: Once the program is launched, it simply waits for messages to be sent to it, and then responds accordingly. Windows

itself detects if a key has been pressed or if the mouse has been moved. When an event of this type occurs, Windows sends a predefined message to the program telling it what has happened. The program usually has the option of either ignoring the message or responding to the message.

☐ DOS Procedural Model: C++ code usually executes linearly; that is, it starts at the beginning of a program and advances through to the end by *stepping* through code one line at a time, or by branching or looping through various segments of code. The program discovers the user's commands by querying the system. That is, the program calls interrupt-based subroutines that are built into the operating system or the hardware. In return, these interrupts report whether a key has been pressed or the mouse has been moved.

When you have the concept of messages firmly in mind, it should come as no surprise to learn that messages are really just constants defined in WINDOWS.H. Here, for instance, are the WINDOWS.H declarations for messages that handle keyboard and mouse movements:

```
/* Keyboard messages */
#define WM_KEYDOWN          0x0100 // Key was pressed
#define WM_KEYUP            0x0101 // Key was released
#define WM_CHAR             0x0102 // Processed keystroke
#define WM_DEADCHAR         0x0103 // Composite key
#define WM_SYSKEYDOWN       0x0104 // Alt key was pressed
#define WM_SYSKEYUP         0x0105 // Alt key was released
#define WM_SYSCHAR          0x0106 // Processed system keystroke
#define WM_SYSDEADCHAR      0x0107 // Composite system keystroke

/* Mouse input messages */
#define WM_MOUSEMOVE        0x0200 // Mouse was moved
#define WM_LBUTTONDOWN      0x0201 // Left button pressed
#define WM_LBUTTONUP        0x0202 // Left button released
#define WM_LBUTTONDBLCLK    0x0203 // Double click of left button
#define WM_RBUTTONDOWN      0x0204 // Right button down
#define WM_RBUTTONUP        0x0205 // Right button up
#define WM_RBUTTONDBLCLK    0x0206 // Double click, right button
#define WM_MBUTTONDOWN      0x0207 // Middle button down
#define WM_MBUTTONUP        0x0208 // Middle button up
#define WM_MBUTTONDBLCLK    0x0209 // Double click, middle button
```

Don't try to memorize these messages. Just look them over and become familiar with the way they look and the kinds of services they provide.

Clearly, nothing is very mysterious about the messages themselves. They are simply constants with useful names that inform a program about the current state of the system. When an event occurs, these messages are bundled with other useful bits of information and sent to one or more appropriate window procedures. Exactly what should then be done with those messages is the topic of this chapter.

Note: A crucial point is that you don't have to understand how Windows knows that the mouse has been moved or a key has been pressed. All you need to know is that whenever a message with the number hexadecimal 200 comes down the pike, it's an indication that the mouse has been moved.

This kind of message-based system gives you a largedegree of platform independence. In other words, the Intel architecture usually uses `Int 33h` to track mouse movements. Another platform may use an entirely different system. But that won't matter to you, a Windows programmer. All you need do is respond to predefined messages.

Your Second Full-Scale Windows Program

The next few pages of this chapter focus on a three-part process that outlines exactly how messages are treated in a `WndProc`:

- Step one is to get a working example program up and running.

- Step two is to discuss WINDOWSX and message crackers. The discussion focuses primarily on two particular messages, `WM_DESTROY` and `WM_CREATE`.

- Step three takes a brief look at how WINDOWSX treats the default window procedure.

Note: Don't worry if you still are not totally clear on what WINDOWSX is all about. The WINDOWSX header file, and the macros it includes, represent a very broad topic that cannot be easily assim- ilated in just a few moments. Instead, you need to be prepared to allow for gradual increase in your knowledge of this complex and extremely important topic. For now you should feel content if you understand that the macros in WINDOWSX help to simplify Windows programming and help to ease the transition between 16-bit and 32-bit Windows code. The details will become clear in time as this book returns again and again to this intrigu- ing topic. As it happens, some of the most important aspects of WINDOWSX should be clear to you by the end of this chapter.

Most of the code in the program I am about to show you is similar to the code you saw in the last chapter. In fact, most Windows programs are based on a common template that changes little from program to program. As a result, you might want to copy the files used in making WINDOW1.EXE into a new subdirectory. Proceed to go through the files, changing the words Window1 to EasyText and renaming the files from WINDOW1.* to EASYTEXT.*. To perform this latter duty, enter the following command at the DOS prompt:

```
ren WINDOW1.* EASYTEXT.*
```

DO   DON'T

DO use pretested code as the basis of each program you write.

DON'T try to start each Windows program from scratch.

The steps previously outlined are very important. Almost every piece of Windows code you write will rest on the basic components created in the last chapter. In other words, that code is very much reusable. In fact, you might want to keep it in a separate subdirectory where you can access it whenever you need to start a new program. As you probably know, the idea of reusing packets of code is very important in most modern programming endeavors.

DO   DON'T

DO copy as many files as possible from one project to the next one.

DON'T try to copy old project files or makefiles from directory to directory without carefully reviewing them. Problems arise in such situations, because project files and some makefiles tend to keep track of the pathname of the files you add to a project. As a result, you should probably rebuild your project when you place it in a new subdirectory. Don't make the mistake of moving your files to a new subdirectory and accidentally modifying WINDOW1.CPP (or some other member of the original program), simply because it is still listed in your project file.

Okay, now that you have had a chance to see how to get started, see the code (in Listing 4.1) for EASYTEXT.CPP. Take the time to get this program up and running, so that you can understand the upcoming discussion.

Listing 4.1. The EASYTEXT.CPP main source file.

```
1: /////////////////////////////////////////
2: //   Program Name: EASYTEXT.CPP
3: //   Programmer: Charlie Calvert
4: //   Description: Demonstrate simple text I/O
5: //   Date: Feb 27, 1993
6: /////////////////////////////////////////
7:
8: #define STRICT
9: #include <windows.h>
10: #include <windowsx.h>
11: #include <string.h>
12: #pragma warning (disable: 4068)
13: #pragma warning (disable:4100)
14:
15: // -----------------------------------------
16: // Interface
17: // -----------------------------------------
18:
19: // variables
20: static char szAppName[] = "EasyText";
21:
22: // Class EasyText
23: #define EasyText_DefProc DefWindowProc
24: BOOL EasyText_OnCreate(HWND hwnd,
25:                         CREATESTRUCT FAR* lpCreateStruct);
26: void EasyText_OnDestroy(HWND hwnd);
27: void EasyText_OnPaint(HWND hwnd);
28:
29: // variables
30: char Directions[100];
31: static HWND MainWindow;
32: static HINSTANCE hInst;
33:
34: // functions
35: LRESULT CALLBACK _export WndProc(HWND hwnd, UINT Message,
36:                                   WPARAM wParam, LPARAM lParam);
37: BOOL Register(HINSTANCE hInst);
38: HWND Create(HINSTANCE hInst, int nCmdShow);
39:
40: // -----------------------------------------
41: // Initialization
42: // -----------------------------------------
43:
44: /////////////////////////////////////////
45: // Program entry point
46: /////////////////////////////////////////
47: #pragma argsused
```

```
48: int PASCAL WinMain(HINSTANCE hInst, HINSTANCE hPrevInstance,
49:                     LPSTR  lpszCmdParam, int nCmdShow)
50: {
51:   MSG  Msg;
52:
53:   if (!hPrevInstance)
54:     if (!Register(hInst))
55:       return FALSE;
56:
57:   if (!Create(hInst, nCmdShow))
58:     return FALSE;
59:
60:   while (GetMessage(&Msg, NULL, 0, 0))
61:   {
62:       TranslateMessage(&Msg);
63:       DispatchMessage(&Msg);
64:   }
65:
66:   return Msg.wParam;
67: }
68:
69: ////////////////////////////////////
70: // Register the window
71: ////////////////////////////////////
72: BOOL Register(HINSTANCE hInst)
73: {
74:   WNDCLASS WndClass;
75:
76:   WndClass.style          = CS_HREDRAW | CS_VREDRAW;
77:   WndClass.lpfnWndProc    = WndProc;
78:   WndClass.cbClsExtra     = 0;
79:   WndClass.cbWndExtra     = 0;
80:   WndClass.hInstance      = hInst;
81:   WndClass.hIcon          = LoadIcon(NULL, IDI_APPLICATION);
82:   WndClass.hCursor        = LoadCursor(NULL, IDC_ARROW);
83:   WndClass.hbrBackground  = GetStockBrush(WHITE_BRUSH);
84:   WndClass.lpszMenuName   = NULL;
85:   WndClass.lpszClassName  = szAppName;
86:
87:   return RegisterClass (&WndClass);
88: }
89:
90: ////////////////////////////////////
91: // Create the window
92: ////////////////////////////////////
93: HWND Create(HINSTANCE hInstance, int nCmdShow)
94: {
95:   HWND hwnd = CreateWindow(szAppName, szAppName,
96:                              WS_OVERLAPPEDWINDOW,
97:                              CW_USEDEFAULT, CW_USEDEFAULT,
98:                              CW_USEDEFAULT, CW_USEDEFAULT,
```

continues

Listing 4.1. continued

```
 99:                              NULL, NULL, hInstance, NULL);
100:
101:   if (hwnd == NULL)
102:      return hwnd;
103:1
104:   ShowWindow(hwnd, nCmdShow);
105:   UpdateWindow(hwnd);
106:
107:   return hwnd;
108: }
109:
110: // -----------------------------------
111: // WndProc and Implementation
112: // -----------------------------------
113:
114: ///////////////////////////////////////
115: // The Window Procedure
116: ///////////////////////////////////////
117: LRESULT CALLBACK _export WndProc(HWND hwnd, UINT Message,
118:                                  WPARAM wParam, LPARAM lParam)
119: {
120:   switch(Message)
121:   {
122:     HANDLE_MSG(hwnd, WM_CREATE, EasyText_OnCreate);
123:     HANDLE_MSG(hwnd, WM_DESTROY, EasyText_OnDestroy);
124:     HANDLE_MSG(hwnd, WM_PAINT, EasyText_OnPaint);
125:     default:
126:        return EasyText_DefProc(hwnd, Message, wParam, lParam);
127:   }
128: }
129:
130: ///////////////////////////////////////
131: // The destructor handles WM_DESTROY
132: ///////////////////////////////////////
133: #pragma argsused
134: BOOL EasyText_OnCreate(HWND hwnd, CREATESTRUCT FAR* lpCreateStruct)
135: {
136:   strcpy(Directions, "Try resizing this window.");
137:   return TRUE;
138: }
139:
140: ///////////////////////////////////////
141: // The destructor handles WM_DESTROY
142: ///////////////////////////////////////
143: #pragma argsused
144: void EasyText_OnDestroy(HWND hwnd)
145: {
146:   PostQuitMessage(0);
147: }
148:
```

```
149: /////////////////////////////////////
150: // Handle WM_PAINT messages
151: // Show how to use TextOut and DrawText.
152: /////////////////////////////////////
153: void EasyText_OnPaint(HWND hwnd)
154: {
155:   PAINTSTRUCT PaintStruct;
156:   RECT Rect;
157:
158:   HDC PaintDC = BeginPaint(hwnd, &PaintStruct);
159:
160:   TextOut(PaintDC, 10, 10, Directions, lstrlen(Directions));
161:
162:   GetClientRect(hwnd, &Rect);
163:
164:   DrawText(PaintDC, "The middle of the road", -1, &Rect,
165:            DT_SINGLELINE | DT_CENTER | DT_VCENTER);
166:
167:   EndPaint(hwnd, &PaintStruct);
168: }
```

Listing 4.2 is the EasyText definition file.

 Listing 4.2. **EASYTEXT.DEF.**

```
 1: ; EASYTEXT.DEF
 2:
 3: NAME            EasyText
 4: DESCRIPTION     'EasyText Window'
 5: EXETYPE         WINDOWS
 6: STUB            'WINSTUB.EXE'
 7: HEAPSIZE        4096
 8: STACKSIZE       5120
 9: CODE            PRELOAD MOVEABLE DISCARDABLE
10: DATA            PRELOAD MOVEABLE MULTIPLE
```

Listing 4.3 shows the Borland EasyText makefile.

Listing 4.3. **EASYTEXT.MAK.**

```
1: # EASYTEXT.MAK
2:
3: # macros
4: APPNAME = EasyText
```

continues

105

Listing 4.3. continued

```
 5: INCPATH = C:\BC\INCLUDE
 6: LIBPATH = C:\BC\LIB
 7: FLAGS = -H -ml -W -v -w4 -I$(INCPATH) -L$(LIBPATH)
 8:
 9: # link
10: $(APPNAME).exe: $(APPNAME).obj $(APPNAME).def
11:   bcc $(FLAGS) $(APPNAME).obj
12:
13: # compile
14: $(APPNAME).obj: $(APPNAME).cpp
15:   bcc -c $(FLAGS) $(APPNAME).cpp
```

Listing 4.4 shows the Microsoft EasyText makefile.

 Listing 4.4. EASYTEXT.MAK.

```
 1: # EASYTEXT.MAK
 2:
 3: APPNAME = EasyText
 4:
 5: # linking
 6: $(APPNAME).exe : $(APPNAME).obj $(APPNAME).def
 7:   link /CO $(APPNAME), /align:16, NUL, /nod llibcew libw, $(APPNAME)
 8:
 9: # compiling
10: $(APPNAME).obj : $(APPNAME).cpp
11:   cl -c -AL -GA -Ow -W4 -Zp -Zi $(APPNAME).cpp
```

 Figure 4.1 shows the output from Listing 4.1.

 This program pops up a standard window and prints two pieces of text on it. Notice that one piece of text always stays in the middle of the window, even when you resize it. The purpose of this program is to show you how to use message crackers and how to respond to WM_PAINT messages.

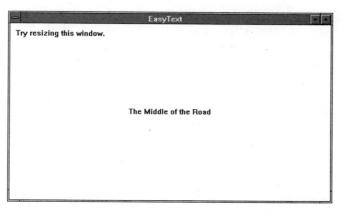

Figure 4.1. *EASYTEXT.EXE displays two pieces of text, one in the upper-left corner of the window, and one centered in the middle of the window.*

Note: You might notice that I add various pragmas to the code you see in this book. Pragmas contain compiler-specific information. For instance, I frequently include the following line of code:

```
#pragma argsused
```

This tells the Borland compiler to suppress any error messages about unused arguments passed to a particular function. Another pragma you will see me use a lot is this:

```
#pragma warning (disable: 4068)
```

This pragma tells the Microsoft compiler to ignore any pragmas that it doesn't understand. Normally, Microsoft's compiler informs the user through a warning when it encounters an unknown pragma. Because I'd prefer not to see those warnings, I turn them off with the preceding line of code.

The third pragma you might see from time to time in my code looks like this:

```
#pragma hdrstop
```

This pragma tells the Borland compiler to terminate the list of files used in precompiled headers. For instance, in the following example, WINDOWS.H and WINDOWSX.H are used in the precompiled header, but STRING.H and STDLIB.H are not:

```
#include <windows.h>
#include <windowsx.h>
#pragma hdrstop
#include <string.h>
#include <stdlib.h>
```

Overall, you should not be concerned about the pragmas included in this code. All the examples in this book will compile to the exact same binary code whether or not you include any of my pragmas. Their only purpose is to optimize or smooth the actual course of compilation. They have absolutely no effect on the final code that is generated.

Switch Statements, WINDOWSX, and Message Crackers

The most obvious new feature of this program is the presence of text in the client area of the window. Before taking a look at how that text is painted on-screen, it's important to first understand the mechanisms at play in the WndProc function:

```
117: LRESULT CALLBACK _export WndProc(HWND hwnd, UINT Message,
118:                                  WPARAM wParam, LPARAM lParam)
119: {
120:   switch(Message)
121:   {
122:     HANDLE_MSG(hwnd, WM_CREATE, EasyText_OnCreate);
123:     HANDLE_MSG(hwnd, WM_DESTROY, EasyText_OnDestroy);
124:     HANDLE_MSG(hwnd, WM_PAINT, EasyText_OnPaint);
125:     default:
126:       return EasyText_DefProc(hwnd, Message, wParam, lParam);
127:   }
128: }
```

Back in the bad old days before WINDOWSX.H, the window procedure could become an extremely formidable foe that Windows programmers had to wrestle to the

mat on nearly a daily basis. The source of the trouble was the notorious `switch` statement that, in even moderately complex programs, tended to stretch on in page after page of mind-boggling code.

Now that WINDOWSX.H is here, the `switch` statement (line 120) still exists, but it has been tamed by a series of message crackers that fairly effectively defang the serpent waiting within every window procedure. The message crackers do this by finding a simple way to move the body of your response to a message out of the `WndProc` and into functions that obey the basic rules of structured programming. Of course, using message crackers isn't an absolutely effortless process, but I believe you'll find them much easier to use than a lengthy `switch` statement.

Note: Because so much old code still exists, it's important for you to get a chance to see how to handle window procedures that consist solely of long `switch` statements. The solution comes in the form of dialog procedures, which are to dialogs what window procedures are to windows. For various reasons (not worth discussing right now), throughout most of this book you won't be seeing WINDOWSX.H used in dialog procedures. The big side benefit is that dialog procedures give you a chance to study the old style `switch` statements. Although none of these dialog procedures are present in this chapter, they make frequent appearances in later chapters.

When writing code, you need to set time aside to concentrate on the messages that are handled explicitly inside the `WndProc`. `EasyText` includes three such messages:

```
HANDLE_MSG(hwnd, WM_CREATE, EasyText_OnCreate);
HANDLE_MSG(hwnd, WM_DESTROY, EasyText_OnDestroy);
HANDLE_MSG(hwnd, WM_PAINT, EasyText_OnPaint);
```

As you can see, the messages are `WM_CREATE`, `WM_DESTROY`, and `WM_PAINT`. In the next few pages, you'll see how message crackers handle not only these messages, but all standard API messages.

When reading this discussion, remember that WINDOWSX helps shield you from complexity. Unfortunately, I have to delve right into the heart of that complexity in order to explain how message crackers work. But after you have a few basic ideas clear in your mind, you'll find that message crackers smooth the way for you over and over again.

Note: Message crackers help you use standard structured programming techniques throughout your WndProc. When I first learned structured programming, it seemed a bit complex. Over the years, however, it has saved me many, many frustrating days full of painful debugging. The same is true of message crackers—for many of the same reasons.

All right. It's time to gird your loins and focus your mind. The next few paragraphs contain a good deal of important information.

To begin, you need to know that WM_DESTROY messages are sent to a window whenever it's about to be closed. In the main window of an application, it's crucial that you remember to call PostQuitMessage in response to a WM_DESTROY message. If you don't do this, you'll immediately become involved in an inexplicable mass of bugs from which you'll never extract yourself until you finally figure out the nature of your error. In other words, if you forget to call PostQuitMessage, your application is toast!

Caution: As a rule, every program needs to call PostQuitMessage at some point. This function sends a WM_QUIT message to Windows, which is the signal to break out of the message loop back in WinMain. In other words, the message loop would continue indefinitely were it not for the call to PostQuitMessage. Therefore, this call is absolutely essential for proper application termination.

In EasyText, PostQuitMessage call is made in EasyText_OnDestroy function:

```
144: void EasyText_OnDestroy(HWND hwnd)
145: {
146:    PostQuitMessage(0);
147: }
```

If WINDOWSX were not being used, this whole process would have been handled in the WndProc, with the standard style for switch statements:

```
switch (Message)
{
  case WM_DESTROY:
    PostQuitMessage(0);
    break;
```

```
  case WM_PAINT:
    etc..
}
```

With WINDOWSX, however, programmers have the option of handling WM_DESTROY messages in a separate function. As I mentioned earlier, this entire process eliminates the endless switch statements that can be the bane of even the best thought-out Windows program.

You can see another big benefit of this style by turning to WINDOWSX.H itself. You can view the message cracker macros, which serve to "pick apart" the many parameters to WndProc and pass only the important ones to your message handler function. The issue is that every message sent to a window can be accompanied by additional information—that usually comes in the form of the hwnd, wParam, and lParam parameters.

Two problems occur as the result of sending messages in the hwnd, wParam, and lParam parameters:

1. Not all messages use all three of these parameters. As a result, programmers always have to look in their reference books to see which of these parameters are utilized by a particular message.

2. Different pieces of information often are packed into a particular parameter. For instance, a programmer might have to look in the first word of lParam to get a piece of information, and look in the first and second bytes of wParam to get different pieces of information. After engaging in this trying process, the programmer often needs to typecast the information before it's usable.

WINDOWSX eliminates this entire error-prone process through the mechanism of its message crackers. It's very important that you understand what message crackers do for you, and why they are so useful. So don't rush too quickly; take the time to absorb the information presented in the last few paragraphs.

You've learned that message crackers are really just a series of macros designed to "pick apart" the various parameters passed to WndProc. They usually consist of two parts. The first part handles the message itself; the second part can optionally pass the message on to DefWindowProc. For instance, here are the macros for WM_DESTROY messages as they are listed in WINDOWSX:

```
/* void Cls_OnDestroy(HWND hwnd); */
#define HANDLE_WM_DESTROY(hwnd, wParam, lParam, fn) \
    ((fn)(hwnd), 0L)
#define FORWARD_WM_DESTROY(hwnd, fn) \
    (void)(fn)((hwnd), WM_DESTROY, 0, 0L)
```

Declaring Functions to Deal with Messages

`Classname_OnMessagename`

The comment at the top of the previous excerpt from WINDOWSX, shows you how to declare a function that responds to WM_DESTROY messages. These functions are called message handler functions, or sometimes, message response functions. The convention for naming a message handler function is to start by writing the class name; follow that with an underscore, the word "on," and the name of the message.

Example:

In EasyText, this results in a function name that looks like this:

`EasyText_OnDestroy`

You can think of this syntax as saying, "Class EasyText executes this function on receipt of a WM_DESTROY message."

Probably the most important part of this excerpt from WINDOWSX is the definition of the HANDLE_WM_DESTROY macro. This code fragment picks apart the parameters passed to WndProc, singling out only hwnd as being important in this particular case:

`((fn)(hwnd), 0L)`

To reiterate, the purpose of this macro is to zero in on the important parameters passed to WndProc. In this particular case, neither the lParam nor the wParam arguments contain any useful information. As a result, the only important piece of associated infor-mation is the HWND parameter, which is duly passed on by the WM_DESTROY mes-sage cracker.

The second half of the message cracker is called FORWARD_WM_DESTROY. The FORWARD_WM_DESTROY macro is used only if you want to pass the message to another function, such as the default window procedure after you have handled it. To make this part of the process work correctly, encapsulate the default window procedure in a macro containing the class name, as previously explained.

The WM_DESTROY message cracker is a good place to start exploring message crackers, because it's so simple. However, it also might help to take a look at a somewhat more complicated macro. Fortunately, the WM_CREATE message cracker provides a good illustration of how WINDOWSX can be used to pick apart more complex macros.

 Note: The complement to the WM_DESTROY message is the WM_CREATE message. This latter message is sent to a main window procedure during the call to CreateWindow. In EasyText, the WM_CREATE message is responded to so a string can be initialized. Obviously, I could have declared the string as a constant (and thus avoided responding to WM_CREATE messages). However, I decided to handle things differently, so you can see how WM_CREATE messages work—and so you can see that they are put there explicitly to give you a place to perform initialization-oriented chores.

It might be helpful for you to know that whenever I explicitly handle either WM_CREATE or WM_DESTROY messages, I try to do it at the very beginning of a window procedure. That way, readers of my code can easily find the place where I handle the initialization (WM_CREATE) and the destruction (WM_DESTROY) of my window. Exactly why these two processes are so important becomes apparent in later examples. For now, you only need to remember that I like to handle these two chores first, and handle all other messages in alphabetical order.

Here is the WM_CREATE message cracker from WINDOWSX:

```
/* BOOL Cls_OnCreate(HWND hwnd,
                     CREATESTRUCT FAR* lpCreateStruct) */
#define HANDLE_WM_CREATE(hwnd, wParam, lParam, fn) \
    ((fn)((hwnd), (CREATESTRUCT FAR*)(lParam)) ? 0L : \
                                     (LRESULT)-1L)
#define FORWARD_WM_CREATE(hwnd, lpCreateStruct, fn) \
    (BOOL)(DWORD)(fn)((hwnd), WM_CREATE, 0, (LPARAM)(CREATESTRUCT
FAR*)(lpCreateStruct))
```

As you can see, HANDLE_WM_CREATE explicitly casts lParam as a pointer to a CREATSTRUCT and then ensures that this parameter, correctly typed, is passed on to the EasyText_OnCreate function:

```
BOOL EasyTxt_OnCreate(HWND hwnd,CREATESTRUCT FAR* lpCreateStruct)
```

At this point in the book, you don't need to ponder the many fields of a CREATSTRUCT, so I won't list them here. If you are interested, however, look them up in WINDOWS.H.

If it weren't for the message cracker, you would have to handle the typecasting yourself:

```
lpCreateStruct = (CREATESTRUCT FAR*)lParam;
```

This is undesirable, because it's an error-prone process that can prove especially tricky or confusing for people who are new to the Windows environment.

As you may notice, this macro returns either 0 or -1. If a program responds to a WM_CREATE message by returning 0, the program continues as usual. If it returns -1, however, the window will be summarily destroyed; that is, the CreateWindow function will return NULL.

These kinds of details can be confusing at times, so WINDOWSX clears the whole matter up in one clean stroke by declaring Cls_OnCreate a BOOL. As a result, all you need to do is return TRUE or FALSE, depending on whether or not you are able to initialize the areas in memory your program needed to access. If you return FALSE, the window is destroyed and your application ends.

The *HANDLE_MSG* Macro

Hopefully, the previous paragraphs have shown you exactly what kind of complexity message crackers are designed to eliminate. However, the icing on the cake comes in the form of one last macro, which serves to simplify your program even further. This is the HANDLE_MSG macro, declared in WINDOWSX.H like this:

```
#define HANDLE_MSG(hwnd, message, fn)     \
case (message): return HANDLE_##message((hwnd), (wParam), (lParam), (fn))
```

The purpose of this macro is to relieve you of the responsibility of having to pass on the value returned by your message handler function (the function you declared using the Cls_OnXXXX template). This is an important responsibility, because you must pass this value on even if your message handler function is declared void. In such cases, the macro always returns 0L. At any rate, if you use the HANDLE_MSG macro, you don't have to worry about this return value at all.

If you don't use HANDLE_MSG, you must be sure your macro returns a value. More explicitly, in the case of the WM_CREATE message, you would have to write the following code in your WndProc every time you use a message handler function:

```
switch(Message)
{
  case WM_CREATE:
      return HANDLE_WM_CREATE(hwnd, wParam, Cls_OnCreate);

  etc...
}
```

HANDLE_MSG relieves you of this responsibility by letting you write the following:

```
switch(Message)
{
  HANDLE_MSG(hwnd, WM_CREATE, Cls_OnCreate);
  etc...
}
```

When coding, it seems that nearly every programmer has a different set of priorities. In my case, I put a very high premium on techniques that help me write clear, easy-to-read code. As a result, the HANDLE_MSG macro appeals to me. It helps me write code that is as simple and straightforward as possible.

WINDOWSX and the Default Window Procedure

As you might recall from the last chapter, throughout the life of an application, the WndProc function is usually being bombarded by a vast array of messages. In many applications, most of these messages are being handled by the default window procedure. The purpose of this section is to show how WINDOWSX handles DefWindowProc.

In applications that make use of WINDOWSX, standard operating procedure is to wrap a macro around the standard Windows API function called DefWindowProc:

```
#define EasyText_DefProc DefWindowProc
```

The primary reason for doing this is to prevent you from making careless errors. To understand how this end is accomplished, you need to know that in some cases, a class of window might not pass its messages on to DefWindowProc; a window class might pass messages on to other functions, such as DefDlgProc or DefMDIChildProc. (For now, don't worry about when or why you might use these functions.)

The issue is that Windows programmers are always cutting and pasting their code from one program to another. As a result, it's easy to make a mistake, such as calling DefMDIChildProc when you mean to call DefWindowProc.

To prevent this, WINDOWSX programmers build the name of the class of the window right into the call to the DefWindowProc macro. This helps focus the programmer's mind on the primary issue—finding the correct default window procedure for this particular class.

Another big benefit of the entire WINDOWSX programming style is that it is very object-oriented. The call to the default window procedure, for instance, is explicitly marked as belonging to the EasyText window class:

```
return EasyText_DefProc(hwnd, Message, wParam, lParam);
```

This type of guide is invaluable when programmers are trying to write clean, readily comprehensible code. It fits in with an entire philosophy of modern programming practices— practices that have emerged at great cost and after much debate during the last 10 to 20 years.

DO	DON'T

DO declare a macro for handling the default window procedure in your window.

DON'T forget to name the macro after the class of your window; also, don't forget to check to be sure you are calling the correct default window procedure for your class.

Summing up Message Crackers

Before moving on to discuss the all-important WM_PAINT message, it might be worth indulging in a short recap of the last few sections.

Message crackers help simplify Windows programs and eliminate careless errors. They do this by three means:

☐ They break up the endless case statements typically found in WndProcs and help make your code conform to good structured programming practices.

☐ They help pick apart or parse the hwnd, lParam and wParam parameters by singling out the important ones and subjecting them to proper typecasting.

☐ They unify all the functions related to a window class under a single title, by virtue of the MyClass_OnXXX naming convention.

Hopefully, all this has sunk in; I don't cover it again in any detail. From here on out, message crackers are going to be taken for granted and treated as if they were the only sane way to handle messages in a window procedure. And indeed, that is the case.

It's possible to sum up most of the themes inherent in this discussion of WINDOWSX by showing you one tiny code fragment from EASYTEXT.CPP:

```
23: #define EasyText_DefProc DefWindowProc
24: BOOL EasyText_OnCreate(HWND hwnd,
25:                        CREATESTRUCT FAR* lpCreateStruct);
26: void EasyText_OnDestroy(HWND hwnd);
27: void EasyText_OnPaint(HWND hwnd);
```

These five lines give an overview of the entire functionality of the EasyText window class. When you see EASYTEXT.CPP for the first time, glance at these few lines. You should know immediately where to focus your attention. If there were three or four different classes in this module, you could look at each of the definitions for these classes, know immediately what they're about, and see how they differ from one another.

This kind of concision can help you organize and clean up your code quickly—whereas other programmers continue to flounder in the void! WINDOWSX helps bring structure and clarity to Windows code that has long been needed. Certainly it is possible to see ways it can be improved, and it does have its occasional disadvantages, but overall it will do much to aid you in the construction of readily comprehensible, error-free code.

> **Note:** If you want to learn more about message crackers, you can turn to some text files that come with your compiler. Microsoft users should look for a file called WINDOWSX.TXT, and Borland users should look for a file called WIN31.DOC.

4

Painting Text

Every message sent to a window procedure is important. Yet somehow, the WM_PAINT message ends up being singled out in my mind as *a* centrally important, perhaps even *the* centrally important message. Certainly, nobody could deny that WM_PAINT messages perform a vital function in the life of nearly all windows applications.

WM_PAINT messages are sent to a window every time it needs to redraw the contents of its client area. When programmers speak of the client area of a window, they are usually referring to the area inside a window's borders and title bar (see Figure 4.2). The client area is the space that programmers usually draw on, whereas Windows tends to take care of the rest of the application.

If there is a part of the client area that you do not specifically take control of, Windows fills it in with the designated background color. That is, it will do so if you don't prevent it from getting the required messages from the default window procedure. Specifically, trouble can occur if you don't pass a message on to DefWndProc that needs additional processing by the system. This is a subject to which I return in the next chapter.

Figure 4.2. *The client area is the portion of a window beneath the title bar and inside the frame or border.*

The main point of the last paragraph was that WM_PAINT messages get sent to a window whenever it needs to be redrawn. Think for a moment what this means. If a window has been hidden under another window, and is suddenly uncovered, it receives a WM_PAINT message, because it needs to redraw the area covered by the other window. If a window has been maximized or minimized, it receives a WM_PAINT message when restored to normal size. If a user switches back from a full-screen DOS window, all the visible windows on the desktop receive WM_PAINT messages. In short, WM_PAINT messages play a vital role in the life a window.

Note: Windows provides programmers with an enormous number of very valuable services to which DOS programmers have no access. The border, background, and title of a window are all taken care of by default. Furthermore, Windows works in the background to reliably remind every window on the desktop to redraw itself when necessary. So, although it's sometimes true that Windows demands quite a bit from its programmers, it gives a great deal back in the form of default services.

BeginPaint, EndPaint,
and Device Contexts

By now you should be ready to take a close-up look at the WM_PAINT message handler function for EasyText:

```
153: void EasyText_OnPaint(HWND hwnd)
154: {
155:    PAINTSTRUCT PaintStruct;
156:    RECT Rect;
157:
158:    HDC PaintDC = BeginPaint(hwnd, &PaintStruct);
```

```
159:
160:    TextOut(PaintDC, 10, 10, Directions, lstrlen(Directions));
161:
162:    GetClientRect(hwnd, &Rect);
163:
164:    DrawText(PaintDC, "The middle of the road", -1, &Rect,
165:            DT_SINGLELINE ¦ DT_CENTER ¦ DT_VCENTER);
166:
167:    EndPaint(hwnd, &PaintStruct);
168: }
```

To help you understand exactly what's going on here, it might help if I strip the function of everything but its most fundamental parts:

```
void EasyText_OnPaint(HWND hwnd)
{
  PAINTSTRUCT PaintStruct;

  HDC PaintDC = BeginPaint(hwnd, &PaintStruct);

  EndPaint(hwnd, &PaintStruct);
}
```

This example can serve as a template from which you can build all your paint routines. The basic elements are the calls to BeginPaint (line 158) and EndPaint (line 167), as well as to their related variables—which in this example are called PaintDC and PaintStruct.

The key role of the BeginPaint function is to give you access to a *device context* (HDC) for a window. Device contexts might be a totally new concept for some people who come from DOS. As a result, you might want to pay special attention (during this brief discussion) to one of the key concepts in Windows programming.

Device contexts form a link between your program and certain external output devices that can be attached to a computer. In particular, device contexts form the interface between your application and a printer or video card.

It's probably safe to say that if device contexts did not already exist, somebody would have to invent them. In other words, they form an essential part of any robust programming environment. Until Windows came along, all DOS programmers either consciously or unconsciously felt a lack.

Device contexts are important, because there are so many different kinds of video cards and printers in existence. For instance, there are VGA, EGA, CGA, Hercules, and who knows how many different SuperVGA cards lying in wait for unwary programmers. Printers are even more numerous and varied.

4

In the past, every single application needed its own drivers to run these different devices. WordPerfect, for instance, was famous for its wonderful printer drivers. Their existence gave the product a kind of flexibility that users loved. But of course, not every little start-up company that came down the pike could afford to develop its own set of drivers; even if they could, all that redundant effort would not make a great deal of sense.

To resolve this problem, Windows made it possible for manufacturers of hardware output devices to write drivers that can be hooked into any Windows program. The key to this whole process is the development of device contexts, which form the link between your application, a device driver, and an actual hardware device (see Figure 4.3). Their existence makes it possible for you to write one set of code that can, at least in theory, use multiple devices.

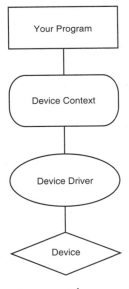

Figure 4.3. *Hardware, such as a printer or video screen, is controlled by device drivers. Windows programs talk to device drivers through a device context.*

It is quite feasible under Windows to write one set of code that will work equally well with a CGA, VGA, or EGA monitor. This can be done without you ever having to write any device-specific code. Any DOS programmer who has done serious work in the graphics world is bound to recognize that this is a very major accomplishment, even if it does come replete with a few caveats illustrated at various points in this book.

By now, you should start to understand why it is so important to begin every paint procedure with a call to BeginPaint. BeginPaint is the function that retrieves the device context for a particular window, and without the device context you aren't going to get very far when attempting to display graphics.

> **Caution:** There are several different ways to get device contexts from the system. One of the most convenient is called GetDC. To my mind, GetDC is so well-named, and so easy to use, that there is a temptation to use it in place of BeginPaint. Don't ever do this. It causes all kinds of inexplicable and undefined behavior! BeginPaint is specifically designed to be used in conjunction with WM_PAINT messages. If you try to work without it, your window is likely not to respond correctly when brought to the top from behind another window—or when it needs to be repainted.

DO   DON'T

DO use BeginPaint to retrieve a device context for a WM_PAINT message handler function.

DON'T use GetDC inside of WM_PAINT message handler functions.

DO use GetDC when you are not responding to WM_PAINT messages, but still need access to the current device context.

Just as BeginPaint is the proper way to start a paint function, EndPaint is the proper way to close it off. Be sure to encapsulate the heart of your response to every WM_PAINT message within these two functions.

BeginPaint and EndPaint both take an HWND and the address of PAINTSTRUCT as parameters. Here are the fields of a PAINTSTRUCT:

```
typedef struct tagPAINTSTRUCT {      /* ps */
   HDC  hdc;
   BOOL fErase;
   RECT rcPaint;
   BOOL fRestore;
   BOOL fIncUpdate;
   BYTE rgbReserved[16];
} PAINTSTRUCT;
```

The first field is simply a copy of the device context for the window. The second specifies whether or not the background of the window should be redrawn. The third designates the rectangle inside of which the drawing will occur. It is important to understand that this latter rectangle is not synonymous with the area of the client rectangle. The reason for this is that Windows is smart enough to tell a window exactly how much of itself needs to be redrawn. This can be important when a window in the background is half-revealed by a movement of a window in the foreground. The rcPaint field says, in effect: "Don't bother to repaint your whole surface, just paint this little section which has been revealed to the user." The remaining three fields of the PAINTSTRUCT are reserved by Windows and need not concern you in this—um—context.

TextOut and *DrawText*

The BeginPaint and EndPaint functions form bookends around the core of the paint routine:

```
TextOut(PaintDC, 10, 10, Directions, lstrlen(Directions));

GetClientRect(hwnd, &Rect);

DrawText(PaintDC, "The middle of the road", -1, &Rect,
         DT_SINGLELINE | DT_CENTER | DT_VCENTER);
```

In the EasyText program, you can examine the two most common ways of displaying text in a Windows program. The first is called TextOut (line 160), and the second, DrawText (line 164).

TextOut is the easiest to use of the two functions. All that is required is a device context, some starting coordinates, a string, and the length of the string. The most common means of determining the string length is to call on one of the C language's built-in functions, such as strlen, or Windows own lstrlen.

The higher level DrawText function takes a device context, a string, a string length, a RECT, and some flags as parameters. If you pass DRAWTEXT a NULL terminated string, you can pass -1 in the third parameter, which lets Windows calculate the length of the string. The RECT parameter designates the area inside which the string will be painted. In this case, I've used the GetClientRect function to retrieve the area of the entire client window, and then passed in three flags which instruct Windows to center the string in the RECT. Figure 4.4 illustrates how Windows continues to center to the string, regardless of what shape the window happens to assume. Notice that the string output by TextOut remains resolutely in place, regardless of the shape or size of the window.

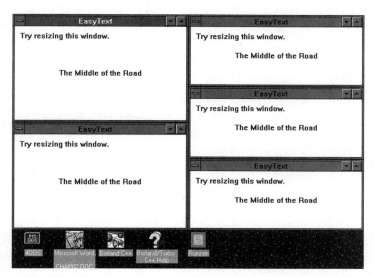

Figure 4.4. *The string output by* DrawText *always finds the center of the client area—no matter how often you drag or reshape its boundaries.*

4

Before leaving this subject, I should point out that the previous paragraphs are really only an introduction to the subject of outputting text in a Windows application. Many more facets remain to be discussed, particularly Windows incredibly powerful font functions. (See Chapter 9, "Font Basics.")

Summary

In this chapter, you had a chance to get an overview of messages, message crackers, and the WM_PAINT message handler function.

One of the most important passages in this chapter discussed the way WINDOWSX uses macros to parse the otherwise somewhat cryptic parameters passed to the WndProc. Message crackers also are important, because they help to break WndProcs up into structured code that is relatively easy to debug and to understand.

You also learned about the necessity of handling WM_DESTROY messages, and got a brief glimpse at WM_CREATE messages and the crucial role they can play in your application.

The final sections of the chapter concentrated on device contexts and the BeginPaint and EndPaint functions. You saw that text can be output to a window with either the TextOut or DrawText functions.

Q&A

1. Q: How can I remember what parameters are passed to a message handler function?

   A: It used to be possible to memorize nearly all the important aspects of a programming language. These days, however, you would need to be a true wunderkind to even begin working on such a Herculean task. My advice is not to even try to memorize the parameters of more than a very few functions. Instead, simply keep a copy of WINDOWSX.H open on your desktop, and copy the appropriate headers out of it whenever you need them. Specifically, if I want to know how to define a `Cls_OnCreate` function, I open up WINDOWSX and do a global search for `WM_CREATE`. This takes me directly to the code I need to see.

2. Q: I'm still confused about `WM_CREATE` messages. When are they sent and how often are they sent?

   A: `WM_CREATE` messages usually come cruising down the pike only once during the life of a program's main window. In particular, they are sent every time you call `CreateWindow`. As you saw in the last chapter, the call to `CreateWindow` occurs early on in `WinMain`, before the program enters the message loop. The message is sent to the window so you can get a chance to perform any initialization you might want just before a window becomes visible. Throughout this book, you will get many chances to see how to handle `WM_CREATE` messages.

3. Q: You said that `DrawText` is a higher level function than `TextOut`. What does this mean?

   A: The functionality associated with `DrawText` is more complex than the functionality associated with `TextOut`. `DrawText` knows how to format text, whereas `TextOut` usually only prints text in very simple ways. Specifically, `DrawText` knows how to center text, how to expand tabs, and how to break up text into lines that fit within a predefined rectangle. If you are interested in expanding `TextOut`'s capabilities without using `DrawText`, you might want to explore the `SetTextAlign` function.

Workshop

The Workshop provides quiz questions to help you solidify your understanding of the material covered and exercises to provide you with experience in using what you've learned. Try to understand the quiz and exercise answers before continuing on to the next chapter. Answers are provided in Appendix A.

Quiz

1. What is the purpose of the HANDLE_MSG macro?

2. Two macros are associated with most messages. The first macro calls the message handler function. What is the purpose of the second macro?

3. Name two functions that can be used to output text.

4. Besides BeginPaint, a second method was described for retrieving a handle to a device context. What function do you call when using this second method?

5. If you aren't using message crackers, how do you find out about information which is associated with a message? In other words, which parameters do you check?

6. In this chapter, the word device usually refers to a video screen or video card. What other kind of device might be important when responding to WM_PAINT messages?

7. If you don't explicitly respond to a message inside a window procedure, what happens to it?

8. Messages are really just constants. How can you find out the value of the constant associated with WM_CREATE messages?

9. What are the basic steps involved in starting a new Windows program? Do you always need to type in the whole program from scratch?

10. Describe some of the differences between a traditional DOS program and an event-oriented Windows program.

Exercises

1. Write a program that prints your name and address in the upper-left corner of a window.

2. Write a program that prints your name and address so that it will always remain centered in the middle of a window, even if that window is resized.

3. Write a program that uses both SetTextAlign and TextOut.

4. Rewrite the EasyText program without using message crackers.

5. Using your debugger, put a breakpoint at the beginning of the WM_CREATE message handler function; then, step through it when it is called.

The Mouse
and the
Keyboard

In this chapter, you will learn how to get control over the mouse and keyboard. In particular, you will see

☐ How to detect when a key has been pressed

☐ How to detect which key has been pressed

☐ How to detect if the system (Alt) key has been pressed

☐ How to track the position of the mouse

☐ How to detect mouse button presses

☐ How to detect double-clicks

In addition, you'll learn a number of tips about painting text to the screen that will complement the knowledge you picked up in the last chapter. Another subject, broached briefly, involves the proper technique for forwarding messages from a message handler function to the default window procedure.

Most of the material in this chapter isn't particularly difficult, but it is important because it covers many fundamental I/O services. When you finish this chapter, you should have a good feeling for how to write programs that can make good use of the mouse and keyboard.

A Program That Reports Mouse and Keyboard Events

Now that you've explored the window procedure and basic text output, you are ready for a brief introduction to more advanced topics, such as the keyboard and mouse. Through the good graces of the message system, Windows enables you to get immediate and relatively complete control over these two hardware devices.

To begin our exploration, type in and run the program in Listing 5.1.

 Listing 5.1. The KeyMouse program shows how to trap keyboard and mouse input.

```
1: ///////////////////////////////////////////////////////////
2: //   Program Name: KEYMOUSE.CPP
3: //   Programmer: Charlie Calvert
4: //   Description: Show how to trap keyboard and mouse input.
5: ///////////////////////////////////////////////////////////
6:
7: #define STRICT
```

```
 8: #include <windows.h>
 9: #include <windowsx.h>
10: #include <string.h>
11: #include <stdio.h>
12: #pragma warning (disable: 4068)
13: #pragma warning (disable: 4100)
14:
15: // ------------------------------------------------------------
16: // Interface
17: // ------------------------------------------------------------
18:
19: // Some variables
20: static int XVal = 10;
21: static int YVal = 30;
22: static char szAppName[] = "KeyMouse";
23: static HWND MainWindow;
24:
25: // Some procs
26: LRESULT CALLBACK _export WndProc(HWND hWindow, UINT Message,
27: WPARAM wParam, LPARAM lParam);
28: BOOL Register(HINSTANCE hInst);
29: HWND Create(HINSTANCE hInst, int nCmdShow);
30:
31: #define KeyMouse_DefProc     DefWindowProc
32: void KeyMouse_OnDestroy(HWND hwnd);
33: void KeyMouse_OnChar(HWND hwnd, UINT ch, int cRepeat);
34: void KeyMouse_OnKey(HWND hwnd, UINT vk, BOOL fDown,
35:                     int cRepeat, UINT flags);
36: void KeyMouse_OnLButtonDown(HWND hwnd, BOOL fDoubleClick,
37:                             int x, int y, UINT keyFlags);
38: void KeyMouse_OnLButtonUp(HWND hwnd, int x, int y,
39:                           UINT keyFlags);
40: void KeyMouse_OnMouseMove(HWND hwnd, int x,
41:                           int y, UINT keyFlags);
42: void KeyMouse_OnPaint(HWND hwnd);
43: void KeyMouse_OnSysKey(HWND hwnd, UINT vk,
44:                        BOOL fDown, int cRepeat, UINT flags);
45:
46:
47: // ------------------------------------------------------------
48: // Initialization
49: // ------------------------------------------------------------
50:
51: ///////////////////////////////////////////////////////////////
52: // Program entry point
53: ///////////////////////////////////////////////////////////////
54:
55: #pragma argsused
56: int PASCAL WinMain(HINSTANCE hInst, HINSTANCE hPrevInstance,
```

5

continues

Listing 5.1. continued

```
57: LPSTR   lpszCmdParam, int nCmdShow)
58: {
59:   MSG   Msg;
60:
61:   if (!hPrevInstance)
62:       if (!Register(hInst))
63:        return FALSE;
64:
65:   MainWindow = Create(hInst, nCmdShow);
66:       if(MainWindow)
67:        return FALSE;
68:   while (GetMessage(&Msg, NULL, 0, 0))
69:   {
70:       TranslateMessage(&Msg);
71:       DispatchMessage(&Msg);
72:   }
73:
74:   return Msg.wParam;
75: }
76:
77: /////////////////////////////////////////////////////////
78: // Register the window
79: /////////////////////////////////////////////////////////
80: BOOL Register(HINSTANCE hInst)
81: {
82:   WNDCLASS WndClass;
83:
84:   WndClass.style          = CS_HREDRAW ¦ CS_VREDRAW ¦ CS_DBLCLKS;
85:   WndClass.lpfnWndProc    = WndProc;
86:   WndClass.cbClsExtra     = 0;
87:   WndClass.cbWndExtra     = 0;
88:   WndClass.hInstance      = hInst;
89:   WndClass.hIcon          = LoadIcon(NULL, IDI_APPLICATION);
90:   WndClass.hCursor        = LoadCursor(NULL, IDC_ARROW);
91:   WndClass.hbrBackground  = GetStockBrush(WHITE_BRUSH);
92:   WndClass.lpszMenuName   = NULL;
93:   WndClass.lpszClassName  = szAppName;
94:
95:   return RegisterClass (&WndClass);
96: }
97:
98: /////////////////////////////////////////////////////////
99: // Create the window
100: /////////////////////////////////////////////////////////
101: HWND Create(HINSTANCE hInstance, int nCmdShow)
102: {
103:
104:   HWND hwnd = CreateWindow(szAppName, szAppName,
105:                             WS_OVERLAPPEDWINDOW,
```

```
106:              CW_USEDEFAULT, CW_USEDEFAULT,
107:              CW_USEDEFAULT, CW_USEDEFAULT,
108:              NULL, NULL, hInstance, NULL);
109:
110:   if (hwnd == NULL)
111:     return hwnd;
112:
113:   ShowWindow(hwnd, nCmdShow);
114:   UpdateWindow(hwnd);
115:
116:   return hwnd;
117: }
118:
119: // ----------------------------------------------------------
120: // WndProc and Implementation
121: // ----------------------------------------------------------
122:
123: //////////////////////////////////////////////////////////////
124: // The Window Procedure
125: //////////////////////////////////////////////////////////////
126: LRESULT CALLBACK _export WndProc(HWND hwnd, UINT Message, WPARAM
127:                                  wParam, LPARAM lParam)
128: {
129:   switch(Message)
130:   {
131:     HANDLE_MSG(hwnd, WM_DESTROY, KeyMouse_OnDestroy);
132:     HANDLE_MSG(hwnd, WM_CHAR, KeyMouse_OnChar);
133:     HANDLE_MSG(hwnd, WM_KEYDOWN, KeyMouse_OnKey);
134:     HANDLE_MSG(hwnd, WM_KEYUP, KeyMouse_OnKey);
135:     HANDLE_MSG(hwnd, WM_MOUSEMOVE, KeyMouse_OnMouseMove);
136:     HANDLE_MSG(hwnd, WM_LBUTTONDBLCLK,  KeyMouse_OnLButtonDown);
137:     HANDLE_MSG(hwnd, WM_LBUTTONDOWN, KeyMouse_OnLButtonDown);
138:     HANDLE_MSG(hwnd, WM_LBUTTONUP, KeyMouse_OnLButtonUp);
139:     HANDLE_MSG(hwnd, WM_PAINT, KeyMouse_OnPaint);
140:     HANDLE_MSG(hwnd, WM_SYSKEYUP, KeyMouse_OnSysKey);
141:     HANDLE_MSG(hwnd, WM_SYSKEYDOWN, KeyMouse_OnSysKey);
142:   default:
143:     return KeyMouse_DefProc(hwnd, Message, wParam, lParam);
144:   }
145: }
146:
147: //////////////////////////////////////////////////////////////
148: // Handle WM_DESTROY
149: //////////////////////////////////////////////////////////////
150: #pragma argsused
151: void KeyMouse_OnDestroy(HWND hwnd)
152: {
153:   PostQuitMessage(0);
154: }
155:
```

continues

Listing 5.1. continued

```
156: ////////////////////////////////////////////////////////////
157: // Handle regular keyboard hits
158: // Use if you want to trap the letter keys or number keys.
159: ////////////////////////////////////////////////////////////
160: #pragma argsused
161: void KeyMouse_OnChar(HWND hwnd, UINT ch, int cRepeat)
162: {
163:   char S[100];
164:
165:   HDC DC = GetDC(hwnd);
166:
167:   sprintf(S,
168:     "WM_CHAR ==> Ch = %c  cRepeat = %d    ", ch, cRepeat);
169:   TextOut(DC, XVal, YVal + 20, S, strlen(S));
170:
171:   ReleaseDC(hwnd, DC);
172: }
173:
174: ////////////////////////////////////////////////////////////
175: // Handle a key press
176: // Don't try to process letter or number keys here. Instead,
177: // use WM_CHAR messages.
178: ////////////////////////////////////////////////////////////
179: #pragma argsused
180: void KeyMouse_OnKey(HWND hwnd, UINT vk,
181:                     BOOL fDown, int cRepeat, UINT flags)
182: {
183:   char S[100];
184:
185:   HDC DC = GetDC(hwnd);
186:
187:   if (fDown)
188:     sprintf(S, "WM_KEYDOWN == > vk = %d  fDown = %d cRepeat = %d"
189:             " flags = %d          ", vk, fDown, cRepeat, flags);
190:   else
191:     sprintf(S, "WM_KEYUP == > vk = %d  fDown = %d cRepeat = %d "
192:             "flags = %d          ", vk, fDown, cRepeat, flags);
193:   TextOut(DC, XVal, YVal + 40, S, strlen(S));
194:
195:   ReleaseDC(hwnd, DC);
196: }
197:
198: ////////////////////////////////////////////////////////////
199: // This function is called when the left mouse button is
200: // click or when the user double-clicks the mouse
201: ////////////////////////////////////////////////////////////
202: void KeyMouse_OnLButtonDown(HWND hwnd, BOOL fDoubleClick, int x,
203:                             int y, UINT keyFlags)
204: {
```

```
205:    char S[100];
206:    HDC PaintDC = GetDC(hwnd);
207:
208:    if (fDoubleClick)
209:      sprintf(S,
210:        "WM_LBUTTONDBLCLK ==> Db = %d x = %d y = %d Flags = %d   ",
211:        fDoubleClick, x, y, keyFlags);
212:    else
213:      sprintf(S,
214:        "WM_LBUTTONDOWN ==> Db = %d x = %d y = %d Flags = %d   ",
215:        fDoubleClick, x, y, keyFlags);
216:    TextOut(PaintDC, XVal, YVal + 100, S, strlen(S));
217:
218:    ReleaseDC(hwnd, PaintDC);
219: }
220:
221: //////////////////////////////////////////////////////////////
222: // This function is called when the mouse button is released
223: //////////////////////////////////////////////////////////////
224: void KeyMouse_OnLButtonUp(HWND hwnd, int x, int y, UINT keyFlags)
225: {
226:    char S[100];
227:    HDC PaintDC = GetDC(hwnd);
228:
229:    sprintf(S, "WM_LBUTTONUP ==> x = %d y = %d F = %d    ",
230:            x, y, keyFlags);
231:    TextOut(PaintDC, XVal, YVal + 120, S, strlen(S));
232:
233:    ReleaseDC(hwnd, PaintDC);
234: }
235:
236: //////////////////////////////////////////////////////////////
237: // This function is called whenever the mouse moves
238: //////////////////////////////////////////////////////////////
239: void KeyMouse_OnMouseMove(HWND hwnd, int x, int y, UINT keyFlags)
240: {
241:    char S[100];
242:    HDC PaintDC = GetDC(hwnd);
243:
244:    sprintf(S, "WM_MOUSEMOVE ==> x = %d y = %d keyFlags = %d    ",
245:            x, y, keyFlags);
246:    TextOut(PaintDC, XVal, YVal + 80, S, strlen(S));
247:
248:    ReleaseDC(hwnd, PaintDC);
249: }
250:
251: //////////////////////////////////////////////////////////////
252: // Handle WM_PAINT messages.
253: //////////////////////////////////////////////////////////////
254: void KeyMouse_OnPaint(HWND hwnd)
```

continues

Listing 5.1. continued

```
255: {
256:    PAINTSTRUCT PaintStruct;
257:    RECT Rect;
258:    static char *Message[] =
259:    {
260:    "WM_CHAR",
261:    "WM_KEY",
262:    "WM_SYSKEY",
263:    "WM_MOUSEMOVE",
264:    "WM_MOUSEDOWN",
265:    "WM_MOUSEUP"
266:    };
267:
268:    HDC PaintDC = BeginPaint(hwnd, &PaintStruct);
269:    HFONT OldFont = SelectFont(PaintDC,
270:                    GetStockObject(OEM_FIXED_FONT));
271:
272:    GetClientRect(hwnd, &Rect);
273:    DrawText(PaintDC, "MOUSE AND KEYBOARD DEMONSTRATION", -1,
274:            &Rect, DT_CENTER);
275:    Rect.top    = 20;
276:    Rect.bottom = 40;
277:    DrawText(PaintDC,
278:            "(Try experimenting with the mouse and keyboard)",
279:            -1, &Rect, DT_CENTER);
280:
281:    SelectFont(PaintDC, OldFont);
282:
283:    for (int i = 0; i < 6; i++)
284:      TextOut(PaintDC, XVal, YVal + (20 * (i + 1)),
285:              Message[i], strlen(Message[i]));
286:
287:    EndPaint(hwnd, &PaintStruct);
288: }
289:
290: ///////////////////////////////////////////////////////////
291: // This function is called whenever the ALT key is pressed.
292: ///////////////////////////////////////////////////////////
293: void KeyMouse_OnSysKey(HWND hwnd, UINT vk, BOOL fDown,
294:                        int cRepeat, UINT flags)
295: {
296:    char S[100];
297:
298:    HDC DC = GetDC(hwnd);
299:
300:    if (fDown)
301:    {
302:      sprintf(S,"WM_SYSKEYDOWN == > "
303:              "vk = %d  fDown = %d cRepeat = %d flags = %d        ",
304:              vk, fDown, cRepeat, flags);
305:      TextOut(DC, XVal, YVal + 60, S, strlen(S));
```

```
306:    FORWARD_WM_SYSKEYDOWN(hwnd, vk, cRepeat, flags,
307:                          KeyMouse_DefProc);
308:  }
309:  else
310:  {
311:    sprintf(S, "WM_SYSKEYUP == > "
312:            " vk = %d  fDown = %d cRepeat = %d flags = %d        ",
313:              vk, fDown, cRepeat, flags);
314:    TextOut(DC, XVal, YVal + 60, S, strlen(S));
315:    FORWARD_WM_SYSKEYUP(hwnd, vk, cRepeat, flags,
316:                        KeyMouse_DefProc);
317:  } // end if
318:
319:    ReleaseDC(hwnd, DC);
320: }
```

Listing 5.2 shows the KeyMouse definition file.

 Listing 5.2. KEYMOUSE.DEF.

```
 1: ;   KEYMOUSE.DEF
 2:
 3: NAME            KeyMouse
 4: DESCRIPTION     'KeyMouse Window'
 5: EXETYPE         WINDOWS
 6: STUB            'WINSTUB.EXE'
 7: CODE            PRELOAD MOVEABLE DISCARDABLE
 8: DATA            PRELOAD MOVEABLE MULTIPLE
 9:
10: HEAPSIZE        4096
11: STACKSIZE       5120
```

Listing 5.3 shows the Borland makefile for KeyMouse.

Listing 5.3. KEYMOUSE.MAK (Borland).

```
 1: # KEYMOUSE.MAK
 2:
 3: # macros
 4: APPNAME = KeyMouse
 5: INCPATH = C:\BC\INCLUDE
 6: LIBPATH = C:\BC\LIB
 7: FLAGS = -H -ml -W -v -w4 -I$(INCPATH) -L(LIBPATH)
 8:
 9: # link
```

```
10: $(APPNAME).exe: $(APPNAME).obj $(APPNAME).def
11:   bcc $(FLAGS) $(APPNAME).obj
12:
13: # compile
14: $(APPNAME).obj: $(APPNAME).cpp
15:  bcc -c $(FLAGS) $(APPNAME).cpp
```

Listing 5.4 shows the Microsoft makefile for KeyMouse.

 Listing 5.4. KEYMOUSE.MAK (Microsoft).

```
1: # KEYMOUSE.MAK
2:
3: APPNAME = KeyMouse
4:
5: # linking
6: $(APPNAME).exe : $(APPNAME).obj $(APPNAME).def
7:   link /CO $(APPNAME), /align:16, NUL, /nod llibcew libw, $(APPNAME)
8:
9: # compiling
10: $(APPNAME).obj : $(APPNAME).cpp
11:   cl -c -AL -Ow -W4 -Zp -Zi; $(APPNAME).cpp
```

Output When KEYMOUSE.CPP is run, it produces the output seen in Figure 5.1.

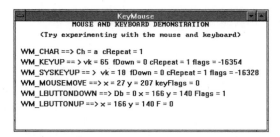

Figure 5.1. *KEYMOUSE.CPP shows the information conveyed by the most important mouse and keyboard messages.*

 This program shows how to detect when a key has been pressed; then, it shows the value of that key and a few pieces of related information. It also shows how to detect when the mouse has been moved, and if a mouse button has been pressed. In particular, it prints output to the screen, which in turn reports any

keyboard or mouse related activities that might occur on the system when this program has the focus.

Keymouse is designed to show off nine Windows messages associated with the keyboard and mouse:

Message	Result
WM_CHAR	A number or letter key was pressed.
WM_KEYDOWN	A key was pressed.
WM_KEYUP	A key was released.
WM_LBUTTONDOWN	The left mouse button was pressed.
WM_LBUTTONUP	The left mouse button was released.
WM_LBUTTONDBLCLK	The left mouse button was double-clicked.
WM_MOUSEMOVE	The mouse was moved.
WM_SYSKEYDOWN	The Alt key was pressed.
WM_SYSKEYUP	The Alt key was released.

Take a few moments to play with this program. Be careful to note the way the program reacts when you move the mouse, or press a key or key combination. Remember that whenever you press the Alt key, the system menu on the upper-left corner of the title bar is activated. Regular keyboard response won't resume until you press the Alt key again, or take some other action which changes the focus.

Note: The concept of *focus* is extremely important in Windows programming. Focused windows respond to keyboard and mouse input, whereas non-focused windows don't respond. For instance, if the File Manager or Program Manager has the focus, it responds to a press of the Alt-F key by popping open its File menu. However, if you bring the KeyMouse program to the foreground of the desktop, the Program Manager or File Manager no longer responds to the press of a keystroke. This occurs because the KeyMouse program now has the focus. You often can tell if a particular program has the focus by checking to see if its title bar is highlighted.

It's important to understand that only one window has the focus at a time. For instance, if you pop open the File menu, that newly opened menu has the focus, and the main window of the program is inactive. The same thing happens when you pop open the Run dialog from the File menu of the Program Manager. When the Run dialog has the focus, the rest of the Program Manager is inactive.

Output Outside of *WM_PAINT* Handler Functions

Before beginning a discussion of the mouse and keyboard messages listed previously, it's worth taking a look at the two different techniques used in this program for producing output. The first is visible in the KeyMouse_OnPaint function, which responds to WM_PAINT messages. This technique was explored in some detail in the last chapter, so there is no need for further commentary on this subject. However, the second technique, visible in the KeyMouse_OnChar function, deserves some thought:

```
161: void KeyMouse_OnChar(HWND hwnd, UINT ch, int cRepeat)
162: {
163:    char S[100];
164:
165:    HDC DC = GetDC(hwnd);
166:
167:    sprintf(S,
168:       "WM_CHAR ==> Ch = %c   cRepeat = %d      ", ch, cRepeat);
169:    TextOut(DC, XVal, YVal + 20, S, strlen(S));
170:
171:    ReleaseDC(hwnd, DC);
172: }
```

In just a moment, I'll talk about the actual purpose of the KeyMouse_OnChar function and about how it handles WM_CHAR messages. Before I get to that subject however, I want to make sure you understand the crucial difference between the way the KeyMouse_OnChar and the KeyMouse_OnPaint functions handle the device context. This is a point you have to get clear in your head, or you'll never get your programs to act correctly.

The first thing the KeyMouse_OnChar function does is get a device context. It does this, not by calling BeginPaint and EndPaint, but by snagging the device context with calls to GetDC (line 168) and ReleaseDC. The TextOut (line 172) method uses this device context to output information to the screen, just as the EasyText program did in the last chapter.

To understand the difference between calling GetDC and calling BeginPaint, you only need to drag another program over the KeyMouse window. If, for instance, you were to temporarily obscure the left half of the KeyMouse window, the scene visible in Figure 5.2 would greet your eyes when the KeyMouse window is again brought to the fore.

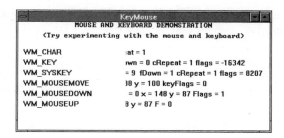

Figure 5.2. *The* KeyMouse *program with some of its information blotted out after it was temporarily obscured by another program.*

If you understand what has happened here, you are definitely getting a feel for the mechanisms employed by the Windows message system. A WM_PAINT message is sent to a window every time a portion obscured by another window is uncovered. Therefore, the title and the words on the far-left portion of the KeyMouse program are visible whenever the window is visible. However, any text painted in, say, the KeyMouse_OnChar function, won't be repainted. The reason for this, of course, is that only WM_CHAR messages are sent to the KeyMouse_OnChar method. It doesn't know, or care, if a WM_PAINT message is sent!

Note: In DOS programs, the contents of windows are frequently saved wholesale in a buffer and then restored whenever a window is brought back on top. This isn't the way Windows works. Instead, the contents of a window are restored by sending a WM_PAINT message, in response to which a window explicitly performs the acts necessary to repaint itself.

Nothing is terribly complicated about the mechanism I'm describing here. However, its import is so crucial to your understanding of Windows programming techniques, that it is almost impossible for you to contemplate it in too much depth. It's essential to understand that drawing done in response to WM_PAINT messages is always visible when a window is visible—simply because Windows ensures that WM_PAINT messages are sent at all the appropriate times. When responding to WM_PAINT messages, you should use BeginPaint and EndPaint; at all other times, you should use GetDC and ReleaseDC.

Okay. Now that you have a feeling for the difference between BeginPaint and GetDC, the next step is to tackle the WM_CHAR message. WM_CHAR messages are sent to a program whenever a user presses one of the standard keys. That is, if a user presses the A key or B key, a WM_CHAR message is sent. Notice that WM_CHAR messages are *not* sent when the user presses one of the function keys, or the arrow keys on the numeric keyboard.

The value associated with a keypress is sent to the KeyMouse_OnChar function in the ch variable, which is declared to be an unsigned integer. In other words, if the user presses the A key, ch is set to ASCII value 97, which is the letter "a". If the user holds down the Shift key while pressing A, the ASCII value 65 is sent in the ch variable. ASCII 65, of course, represents the letter "A".

If a key is pressed repeatedly between calls to WM_CHAR, the number of key presses that occurred is sent in the cRepeat variable. Although this information is usually not very important, Windows still passes it on to you in case you have some use for it.

The KeyMouse_OnChar function serves as a set piece for the virtues of WINDOWSX. If KeyMouse didn't take advantage of WINDOWSX, it would have to parse the wParam and lParam variables sent to the program's WndProc in order to determine the correct value of the keypress and the repeat count. (See Figure 5.3.) The repeat count information, for instance, is stored in the low word of lParam. The high-order word holds several pieces of information that are generally not useful to applications. As a result, the high-order word is not passed on to KeyMouse_OnChar.

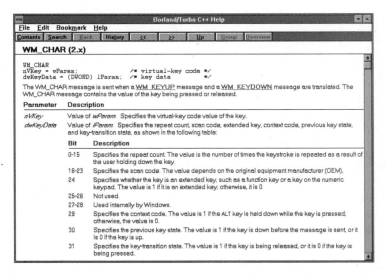

Figure 5.3. *A Borland Help Screen shows how information about keypresses is packed into* lParam *and* wParam*. Thanks to WINDOWSX, detailed understanding of this information is no longer needed.*

Before WINDOWSX came along, programmers ferreted out all this information on their own by reading the fine print in the reference manuals, and by studying the actual bits in wParam and lParam. This was a time-consuming and error-prone process—a process that could be particularly frustrating to beginners.

DO	DON'T

DO use WM_CHAR messages for reading the alpha-numeric keys. These key presses are correctly translated by Windows before the WM_CHAR message is sent. Therefore, WM_CHAR messages are an ideal way to tell if a number or letter is selected by the user.

DON'T use WM_CHAR for trying to detect whether a function key or an arrow key has been pressed.

DO use WM_KEYDOWN messages to determine whether a function key or arrow key has been pressed.

DON'T use WM_KEYDOWN messages to read alpha-numeric keys. Number keys and letter keys have not yet been properly translated when WM_KEYDOWN messages are sent; hence, you can easily misinterpret the value of the keystroke associated with a WM_KEYDOWN message. More information about WM_KEYDOWN messages is presented in the next section.

Detecting Key Presses with *WM_KEYDOWN*

As you saw earlier, the WM_CHAR message is, from the point of view of a DOS programmer, one of the simplest and most straightforward messages sent to the window procedure. The ch parameter, which is passed to the KeyMouse_OnChar message handler function, contains the value of the key pressed, as long as that key is a letter or number. The other parameters keep track of how many times that key was pressed since the last time a WM_CHAR message was sent.

To handle other keypresses, such as a left-arrow, right-arrow, or function keys, you should process the WM_KEYDOWN message.

```
180: void KeyMouse_OnKey(HWND hwnd, UINT vk,
181:                     BOOL fDown, int cRepeat, UINT flags)
182: {
```

```
183:    char S[100];
184:
185:    HDC DC = GetDC(hwnd);
186:
187:    if (fDown)
188:      sprintf(S, "WM_KEYDOWN == > vk = %d   fDown = %d cRepeat = %d"
189:              " flags = %d         ", vk, fDown, cRepeat, flags);
190:    else
191:      sprintf(S, "WM_KEYUP == > vk = %d   fDown = %d cRepeat = %d "
192:              "flags = %d         ", vk, fDown, cRepeat, flags);
193:    TextOut(DC, XVal, YVal + 40, S, strlen(S));
194:
195:    ReleaseDC(hwnd, DC);
196: }
```

Note: As you can see from the preceding code, the KeyMouse_OnKey routine is one of those rare cases in which a single message handler function is sent more than one message. The fDown parameter tells whether the message being sent is a keypress or key release, and the previous code shows that it's easy to perceive the distinction between the two simply by checking whether fDown is set to TRUE or FALSE.

Windows makes it very easy for programmers to discover when the right-arrow key, left-arrow key, or function key has been pressed. This information is packed into the message handler function's vk parameter in terms of one of a number of constants that are defined in WINDOWS.H.

The vk parameter is to the KeyMouse_OnKey function what the ch parameter is to the KeyMouse_OnChar function. In other words, if the user presses the **A** key, that value is passed to the KeyMouse_OnChar function in the ch variable. However, if the user presses—say—the left-arrow key, the VK_LEFT constant is passed to the KeyMouse_OnKey method via the vk parameter.

The VK_LEFT constant is one of several predefined constants declared in WINDOWS.H. Here, for instance, is an excerpt from that list:

```
#define VK_END          0x23
#define VK_HOME         0x24
#define VK_LEFT         0x25
#define VK_UP           0x26
#define VK_RIGHT        0x27
#define VK_DOWN         0x28
#define VK_SELECT       0x29
#define VK_PRINT        0x2A
#define VK_EXECUTE      0x2B
```

```
#define VK_SNAPSHOT          0x2C
#define VK_INSERT            0x2D
#define VK_DELETE            0x2E
#define VK_HELP              0x2F
#define VK_NUMPAD0           0x60
#define VK_NUMPAD1           0x61
#define VK_NUMPAD2           0x62
#define VK_NUMPAD3           0x63
```

You can also find this information in various reference books, or in your on line help files.

The following modified version of the KeyMouse_OnKey function shows how to detect a few of these keystrokes:

```c
void KeyMouse_OnKey(HWND hwnd, UINT vk,
                    BOOL fDown, int cRepeat, UINT flags)
{
  char S[100];

  HDC DC = GetDC(hwnd);

  switch (vk)
  {
    case VK_LEFT:
      strcpy(S, "Left arrow pressed.        ");
      break;
    case VK_RIGHT:
      strcpy(S, "Right arrow pressed.       ");
      break;
    case VK_F1:
      strcpy(S, "F1 key pressed.            ");
      break;
    case VK_F12:
      strcpy(S, "F12 key pressed.           ");
      break;
    case VK_CLEAR:
      strcpy(S, "Numeric keypad 5, NumLock off");
      break;
    case VK_NUMPAD5:
      strcpy(S, "Numeric keypad 5, NumLock on");
      break;
  default:
      strcpy(S, "Out to lunch, back in five!  ");
  }

  TextOut(DC, XVal, YVal + 40, S, strlen(S));

  ReleaseDC(hwnd, DC);
}
```

5

When examining this procedure, you might want to note the VK_CLEAR and VK_F12 constants. Capturing both of these keystrokes could be a bit complicated for DOS programmers working with certain compilers. But in Windows, this kind of information is readily available.

The System Key

In Windows, the system key is the Alt key. In other words, when you hold down the Alt key, you are holding down the system key.

Windows often gives more information than a user is ever likely to need. The KeyMouse program, for instance, traps WM_SYSKEYDOWN and WM_SYSKEYUP messages, which usually should be passed on directly to DefWndProc. The reason the messages need to be passed on is that the system keys handle a lot of default Windows keyboard behavior, such as the famous Alt-Tab keystroke that switches between applications. In cases like this, it is absolutely essential that you call the FORWARD_WM_XXX macros declared in WINDOWSX. This is shown in the following excerpt from KeyMouse_OnSysKey:

```
300:    if (fDown)
301:    {
302:        sprintf(S,"WM_SYSKEYDOWN == > "
303:            "vk = %d  fDown = %d cRepeat = %d flags = %d       ",
304:            vk, fDown, cRepeat, flags);
305:        TextOut(DC, XVal, YVal + 60, S, strlen(S));
306:        FORWARD_WM_SYSKEYDOWN(hwnd, vk, cRepeat, flags,
307:                            KeyMouse_DefProc);
308:    }
```

Even though I mentioned this issue in the last chapter, it might be worthwhile to explicitly look at the message cracker for WM_SYSKEYDOWN message, as it's declared in WINDOWSX.H:

```
/* void Cls_OnSysKey(HWND hwnd, UINT vk, BOOL fDown,
                    int cRepeat, UINT flags); */
#define HANDLE_WM_SYSKEYDOWN(hwnd, wParam, lParam, fn) \
    ((fn)((hwnd), (UINT)(wParam), TRUE,
    (int)LOWORD(lParam), (UINT)HIWORD(lParam)), 0L)
#define FORWARD_WM_SYSKEYDOWN(hwnd, vk, cRepeat, flags, fn) \
    (void)(fn)((hwnd), WM_SYSKEYDOWN, (WPARAM)(UINT)(vk),
MAKELPARAM((UINT)(cRepeat), (UINT)(flags)))
```

The key issue to focus on is the declaration of FORWARD_WM_SYSKEYDOWN macro. This is the macro responsible for passing the WM_SYSKEYDOWN message on to the default Window procedure.

I think it's inevitable that new Windows programmers occasionally will forget to pass a message on for further processing. To help remind you of the gravity of this error, you might want to try commenting out the FORWARD_WM_SYSKEYDOWN macro in KeyMouse_OnSysKey. Then, recompile and run the program. Now try pressing Alt-Tab; notice that the default behavior associated with that key combination doesn't occur. Now, remove the comments, recompile, and note that the standard behavior returns.

> **Note:** Remember that most messages you handle explicitly never get passed on to DefWindowProc. In other words, most of the time, you exit WndProc by returning directly from a message handler function and then dropping out the bottom of the function. Of course, the messages you don't directly handle are always passed on to DefWindowProc by default. In the KeyMouse_OnSysKeyDown function, however, you want to both explicitly handle the message and also pass the message on to KeyMouse_DefProc for further handling.
>
> This concept is a bit subtle, so you might want to take time to contemplate the WndProc function, and to trace in your mind the usual path a message takes when it passes through.
>
> ```
> LRESULT CALLBACK _export WndProc(HWND hwnd, UINT Message, WPARAM
>                                  wParam, LPARAM lParam)
> {
>   switch(Message)
>   {
>     HANDLE_MSG(hwnd, WM_DESTROY, KeyMouse_OnDestroy);
>     HANDLE_MSG(hwnd, WM_CHAR, KeyMouse_OnChar);
>     HANDLE_MSG(hwnd, WM_KEYDOWN, KeyMouse_OnKey);
>     HANDLE_MSG(hwnd, WM_KEYUP, KeyMouse_OnKey);
>     HANDLE_MSG(hwnd, WM_MOUSEMOVE, KeyMouse_OnMouseMove);
>     HANDLE_MSG(hwnd, WM_LBUTTONDBLCLK, KeyMouse_OnLButtonDown);
>     HANDLE_MSG(hwnd, WM_LBUTTONDOWN, KeyMouse_OnLButtonDown);
>     HANDLE_MSG(hwnd, WM_LBUTTONUP, KeyMouse_OnLButtonUp);
>     HANDLE_MSG(hwnd, WM_PAINT, KeyMouse_OnPaint);
>     HANDLE_MSG(hwnd, WM_SYSKEYUP, KeyMouse_OnSysKey);
>     HANDLE_MSG(hwnd, WM_SYSKEYDOWN, KeyMouse_OnSysKey);
>   default:
>     return KeyMouse_DefProc(hwnd, Message, wParam, lParam);
>   }
> }
> ```
>
> Remember that KeyMouse_DefProc does nothing more than call DefWindowProc!

In general, it's important to remember that erratic, inexplicable behavior in an application can sometimes be attributed to missing calls to the default window procedure. If one day you find yourself stuck in the midst of some lengthy, hair-pulling, patience-trying debugging session, you might want to consider the possibility that you've simply forgotten to pass a message on to the default window procedure for further processing.

The *WM_MOUSEMOVE* Message

There is something truly remarkable about the Windows message system. Even the simple act of moving a mouse across a window has a kind of fascination to it, especially when the coordinates being sent to the window are made visible, as they are in KeyMouse.

Stop for a moment and take a look at the WM_MOUSEMOVE message response function:

```
/////////////////////////////////////////////////////////////
// This function is called whenever the mouse moves
/////////////////////////////////////////////////////////////

239: void KeyMouse_OnMouseMove(HWND hwnd, int x, int y, UINT keyFlags)
240: {
241:     char S[100];
242:     HDC PaintDC = GetDC(hwnd);
243:
244:     sprintf(S, "WM_MOUSEMOVE ==> x = %d y = %d keyFlags = %d    ",
245:                 x, y, keyFlags);
246:     TextOut(PaintDC, XVal, YVal + 80, S, strlen(S));
247:
248:     ReleaseDC(hwnd, PaintDC);
249: }
```

The first thing to notice is what a good job the WINDOWSX message cracker does of passing on relevant information to the KeyMouse_OnMouseMove function. If you look in a reference book, you'll see that when a window procedure gets a WM_MOUSEMOVE message, information is packed into the hwnd, wParam, and lParam parameters. The latter of these parameters carries information about the column the mouse is on in its low-order word, and information about the row it's on in its high-order word. But thanks to the message crackers, this obscure information is translated into the *x* and *y* coordinates visible in the KeyMouse_OnMouseMoves header.

The KeyMouse_OnMouseMove function makes the x, y, and keyFlags parameters visible on-screen by first translating them into a string through the sprintf function, and

then by displaying them through the TextOut function. This is the same system you saw previously when studying the response to a keypress.

Sometimes, it seems to me that the WndProc function is weathering a storm of messages that come in at a rate that literally boggles the mind. You can get a feeling for how many WM_MOUSEMOVE messages are sent to the program by studying the KeyMouse_OnMouseMove function in action. Remember that every time a new set of mouse coordinates is shown on-screen, another message has been processed by the WndProc. It's as if the window procedure is walking through a blizzard of messages that descends on it in great flurries of activity.

Besides the *x* and *y* coordinates of the mouse, the other piece of information sent with every WM_MOUSEMOVE message is contained in the keyFlags argument. This parameter can have one of the following values:

Constant	Significance
MK_CONTROL	The control key is down.
MK_LBUTTON	The left mouse button is down.
MK_RBUTTON	The right mouse button is down.
MK_MBUTTON	The middle mouse button is down.
MK_SHIFT	The shift key is down.

These constants are bit flags, which means that you have to use bitwise operators to test whether they are set or not. Doing this is really very simple. For instance, if you want to test to see if the control key is pressed while the mouse is moving, all you need to do is AND keyFlags with MK_CONTROL and then test the result:

```
if ((keyFlags & MK_CONTROL) == MK_CONTROL)
  DoSomething
```

To see exactly how this process works, you might want to take the time to modify the KeyMouse_OnMouseMove function so that the text output changes colors, depending on which keys are pressed:

```
void KeyMouse_OnMouseMove(HWND hwnd, int x, int y, UINT keyFlags)
{
  char S[100];
  HDC PaintDC = GetDC(hwnd);

  sprintf(S, "WM_MOUSEMOVE ==> x = %d y = %d keyFlags = %d    ",
            x, y, keyFlags);

  if ((keyFlags & MK_CONTROL) == MK_CONTROL)
    SetTextColor(PaintDC, RGB(0, 0, 255));
  if ((keyFlags & MK_LBUTTON) == MK_LBUTTON)
    SetTextColor(PaintDC, RGB(0, 255, 0));
```

5

```
    if ((keyFlags & MK_RBUTTON) == MK_RBUTTON)
      SetTextColor(PaintDC, RGB(255, 0, 0));
    if ((keyFlags & MK_SHIFT) == MK_SHIFT)
      SetTextColor(PaintDC, RGB(255, 0, 255));

    TextOut(PaintDC, XVal, YVal + 80, S, strlen(S));

    ReleaseDC(hwnd, PaintDC);
}
```

The modified `KeyMouse_OnMouseMove` function is capable of really showing off the powers inherent in the Windows message system. The line associated with the `WM_MOUSEMOVE` message smoothly changes colors as the mouse buttons and Control and Shift keys are pressed.

Note: In the process of modifying the `KeyMouse_OnMove` function, I've introduced the `SetTextColor` and `RGB` API calls. These two calls are used over and over again in Windows programs. As a result, you might want to take a few moments to get a feeling for how they work.

The `RGB` macro returns a 4-byte value that designates a color. The color to be returned is defined by the three parameters passed to the macro, each of which can have a value from 0 to 255.

If the third parameter is set to 255, and the others to 0, the resulting color will be dark blue. If the first parameter is set to 255, and the others to 0, the resulting color will be red. The middle parameter controls the amount of green in the color returned by the `RGB` macro.

In the fourth example of the previous function, both the blue and the red are turned on all the way, resulting in a deep purple. If you wanted to produce a gray color, you could set all three values to 127. Setting them all to 0 produces a deep black, and setting them all to 255 produces white. If you turn on green and red simultaneously, you produce a bright yellow. With just a few minutes of experimentation, you should begin to get a feeling for all the interesting combinations that can be produced with this powerful macro.

The `SetTextColor` function is easier to understand than the `RGB` macro, because it does nothing more than its name implies. That is, it sets the text color output with the device context passed to it. In other words, it "copies" the result of the `RGB` function into the device context.

Processing Button Selections and Double-Clicks

The KeyMouse program uses the KeyMouse_OnLButtonDown and KeyMouse_OnLButtonUp functions to record button presses. These functions work very much like the other routines presented in this chapter, so you shouldn't have much trouble with them.

It's easier to understand what happens when a button is released, than it is to understand what happens when a button is pressed. Therefore start with the KeyMouse_OnLButtonUp function:

```
224: void KeyMouse_OnLButtonUp(HWND hwnd, int x, int y, UINT keyFlags)
225: {
226:    char S[100];
227:    HDC PaintDC = GetDC(hwnd);
228:
229:    sprintf(S, "WM_LBUTTONUP ==> x = %d y = %d F = %d    ",
230:            x, y, keyFlags);
231:    TextOut(PaintDC, XVal, YVal + 120, S, strlen(S));
232:
233:    ReleaseDC(hwnd, PaintDC);
234: }
```

All in all, nothing could be much simpler than this little fellow. Its purpose, of course, is simply to let the user know where the mouse was when the user released the left mouse button. This is accomplished through the tried-and-true method of snagging hold of the DC and then using it to print information to the screen.

Handling button presses is a bit more complex, however, because it is necessary to distinguish between ordinary button presses and button presses that are really double-clicks. Fortunately, Windows has a system which makes it relatively easy to distinguish between these two conditions.

If you want to process double-clicks on the left or right mouse button, you must begin by setting the window style to CS_DBLCLKS. This is done in the Register method:

```
84: win.style = CS_HREDRAW | CS_VREDRAW | CS_DBLCLKS;
```

In this case, you can see that the style associated with the window class now contains three flags—the third of which informs Windows that this class wants to be informed when the user double-clicks the mouse in its client area.

The message sent when the user double-clicks the left mouse button is WM_LBUTTONDBLCLK, but the appropriate WINDOWSX message cracker forwards this information on to the same message handler function that processes WM_LBUTTONDOWN messages.

Note: As a rule, message crackers enable each individual message to have its own message handler function. But in a few cases, similar to the WM_LBUTTONDBLCLK message, WINDOWSX sends more than one message to a single function. This process is illustrated in several locations in the previous example program, most notably the in the WM_KEYDOWN, (lines 188 and 191) and WM_LBUTTONDOWN message handler functions (lines 210 and 214). You should remember, however, that message handler functions that receive more than one message are the very rare exceptions to the rule. Most of the time, each message has its own message handler function.

Take the time to study exactly how the KeyMouse_OnLButtonDown function works:

```
202: void KeyMouse_OnLButtonDown(HWND hwnd, BOOL fDoubleClick, int x,
203:                             int y, UINT keyFlags)
204: {
205:   char S[100];
206:   HDC PaintDC = GetDC(hwnd);
207:
208:   if (fDoubleClick)
209:     sprintf(S,
210:       "WM_LBUTTONDBLCLK ==> Db = %d x = %d y = %d Flags = %d  ",
211:       fDoubleClick, x, y, keyFlags);
212:   else
213:     sprintf(S,
214:       "WM_LBUTTONDOWN ==> Db = %d x = %d y = %d Flags = %d  ",
215:       fDoubleClick, x, y, keyFlags);
216:   TextOut(PaintDC, XVal, YVal + 100, S, strlen(S));
217:
218:   ReleaseDC(hwnd, PaintDC);
219: }
```

After getting hold of the device context, the function checks to see whether this is a normal keypress or a double-click. In the latter case, the fDoubleClick parameter will be set to TRUE. In these cases, the function prints out a string stating that a WM_LBUTTONDBLCLK message has been sent; the function also informs the user about the current coordinates and flag settings.

Of course, if no double-click has occurred, the user is told that a WM_LBUTTONDOWN message has just come down the pike. The function then lays out the current state of all the parameters, including the *x* and *y* coordinates the mouse was at when the button press occurred.

As I hinted earlier, Windows programs respond to changes in their environment similar to the way a well-driven car responds to highway signs, or to curves in the road.

In other words, Windows makes sure that a program is sent plenty of information about its environment. The job of the programmer is to teach a program how to respond to these messages. In this chapter, you've seen that a Windows program can respond to a blizzard of keyboard and mouse messages, and still stays on the road—handling exactly as it should.

Summary

In this chapter, you dug beneath the surface of a Windows program to see how keyboard and mouse messages are handled.

In particular, you got a look at GetDC, ReleaseDC, RGB, and the SetTextColor functions. You also were introduced to a slew of Windows constants, such as VK_CLEAR, WM_LBUTTONDBLCLK, and MK_CONTROL. Obviously, most people are never going to be able to memorize all these identifiers, so you must learn how to use the reference books and online help services available to you. Don't try to memorize the constants; instead memorize the places where you can find them.

Of course, some messages are so important that you should always have them in mind. Messages that fit in this category include WM_PAINT, WM_KEYDOWN, WM_CHAR, WM_MOUSEMOVE, and WM_LBUTTONDOWN. These easy-to-comprehend messages prove their usefulness again and again when you are programming Windows applications.

Overall, it most definitely doesn't take a genius to see that the Windows message system works. It gives programmers the kind of control over the computer's hardware that DOS programmers often longed in vain to achieve. So, take the time to linger over the riches revealed in this chapter. But don't dally too long, because this stuff is nothing compared to the exciting graphics-specific code you'll see in the next chapter.

5

Q&A

1. Q: I'm still not clear about the differences between WM_KEYDOWN and WM_CHAR messages. Why does the latter even exist?

   A: The key point to remember is that WM_KEYDOWN messages occur whenever a key is pressed. However, when this message is sent to a window procedure, Windows has not yet translated the keystroke. As a result, it's easy to become confused about exactly which key has been pressed. WM_CHAR messages, however, are an ideal place to find out about which alpha-numeric key the user has pressed.

2. Q: What is the difference between the BeginPaint and GetDC functions?

A: The BeginPaint and EndPaint functions are only used when responding to WM_PAINT messages. Because WM_PAINT messages are sent to a window whenever it needs to be updated, anything painted to the screen (with a DC retrieved by BeginPaint) is always visible when the window is visible. The GetDC function, however, can be called at virtually any time during the life of an application. As a result, it gives you considerably more flexibility than the BeginPaint function does; but anything painted to the screen with a DC, obtained by GetDC, lasts only until the window is covered up by some other object (such as a window or dialog).

Workshop

The Workshop provides quiz questions to help you solidify your understanding of the material covered and exercises to provide you with experience in using what you've learned. Try to understand the quiz and exercise answers before continuing on to the next chapter. Answers are provided in Appendix A.

Quiz

1. Name two messages that are sent to the KeyMouse_OnLButtonDown function.

2. What are the VK constants?

3. What is the CS_DBLCLKS style, and when and where do you use it?

4. What color is produced if all three parameters to RGB are set to zero?

5. How can you test to see if the MK_CONTROL bit has been set in a keyFlags parameter?

6. What is another name for the System key?

7. How can you pass a message on from a message handler function to DefWndProc?

8. Where does the focus go when you press the system key when the KeyMouse programming is running?

9. On the whole, which function do you think gets called more often, KeyMouse_OnKey or KeyMouse_OnChar?

10. What would happen if you forgot to call ReleaseDC after calling GetDC in the KeyMouse_OnMouseMove function?

Exercises

1. Use `sprintf` to help you create a program that writes out the coordinates at which the user clicks the left and right mouse buttons—and which prints these coordinates at the location where the button-down event occurred.

2. Use the `SetTextColor` function and `RGB` macro to print out the word Red in red, the word Green in green, and the word Blue in blue.

5

Introduction to Resources

This chapter presents an introduction to resources. Resources enable you to encapsulate visible and logical elements of your program, such as menus, string tables, and bitmaps inside special files that can be linked into your program. The end result is a simple and flexible way to add powerful features to your code.

A number of specific techniques are discussed in this chapter, including

- ☐ Creating resource scripts
- ☐ Using the resource compiler
- ☐ Creating menus
- ☐ Creating icons
- ☐ Creating custom cursors
- ☐ Creating user-defined resources

By the end of the day, you should feel that you understand what resources are and how they can be used to enhance your programs. However, this chapter is really only part one in a two-part process. The second part, presented on Day 7, will greatly expand your knowledge of resources by showing you how to use bitmaps, dialogs, and string tables.

To ensure that you get plenty of hands-on experience, I have included a program called EMERSON.CPP that uses a menu, dialog, bitmap, string table, user-defined resource, a custom icon, and a custom cursor. This program is developed slowly throughout the course of this chapter and the next. My goals are to start with fairly simple resources in this chapter and explore more complex, in-depth issues in the next chapter.

By the end of this two-step process, you should begin to feel that you can create the kind of powerful and flexible programs for which Windows is renowned. In other words, these two chapters help you make the transition from beginner to intermediate status.

So What Are Resources Anyway?

Resources represent one of the most important aspects of Windows programming. These special files enable you to easily add features to your program, in much the same way you can add a clock, stereo, or a pair of fuzzy dice to a new car. The point is that these are plug-and-play features that you can add without having to do a great deal of coding.

This is not to say that resources don't require any work on your part. If you add a new stereo to your car, you have to go through the process of installing the stereo. In the same way, if you add a bitmap or an icon to your program, you have to install the new feature. This requires some work, but it isn't as difficult as the process you would have to go through if you were starting from scratch.

There is no set limit to the number of different types of resources that can be added to a program. However, at this stage in the history of Windows, resources usually refer to menus, dialogs, bitmaps, icons, string tables, fonts, cursors, and perhaps one or two other tools.

Just so a common terminology is available, it might be worthwhile to take a moment to define each of the major resources being used in Windows programs:

☐ *Menus* usually appear along the top of a main window; they give the user verbal or iconic options for manipulating the features of a program. It is increasingly common to see programmers making use of pop-up menus that float freely on the desktop.

☐ *Dialogs* are special windows that usually contain edit boxes, buttons, radio buttons, check boxes, and other controls that enable the user to enter data or select features.

☐ *Bitmaps* are graphical objects, such as photographs, pictures, or drawings that can be painted onto a window or dialog. These files have a predefined format and usually end with a .BMP extension.

☐ *Icons* are very much like bitmaps, but they always have a predefined size. When a program is minimized, its icon is usually visible on the bottom of the screen.

☐ A *string table* is a list of strings kept in an easy-to-use format. Though they have many uses, Windows programs frequently store lists of error messages in string tables.

☐ *Fonts* are the character sets used to draw text or symbols on-screen. The complex world of fonts is explored next week, in Chapters 9, 10, and 11.

☐ *Cursors* show where the mouse is located on-screen. The arrow cursor, hourglass cursor, and I-beam cursor are frequently used in Windows, but you can create any type of cursor you want, and display it at any time during the life of your program. Figure 6.1 shows icon and menu resources in a Windows environment.

6

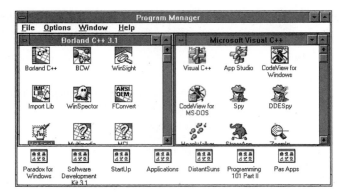

Figure 6.1. *Icon and menu resources play big parts in the Windows environment.*

The previously listed items are only the most common types of resources. Many other types have been created, and will be created in the future. In fact, some companies sell libraries of custom resources. The point is that Windows resources are designed to be extensible tools; they are limited only by the imagination of Windows programmers.

This book doesn't spend much time exploring custom resources, because that subject can become very involved. However, the Emerson program shows you how to create a very simple custom resource that consists solely of one long string. The string is displayed on-screen as a poem. Although this is an elementary example, it should serve to show you the possibilities waiting to be tapped by inventive programmers.

Most Windows programmers enjoy resources. In fact, if this is a new subject for you, you are in for a very nice surprise. Resources give your application a great deal of power while demanding only minimal effort on your part.

Furthermore, this overview of resources marks the beginning of a freewheeling exploration of the many special features available to Windows programmers. Because you already know how to perform basic coding chores, this book now focuses on an exploration of the many powerful features available to you. A good deal of creative thought went into the design of the Windows environment and into the programming heritage from which it sprang. Be prepared to reap the harvest!

Resource Scripts

There are several different ways to create resources. Perhaps the simplest and most powerful methods are achieved through the use of Borland's Resource Workshop (WORKSHOP.EXE) and Microsoft's App Studio (APSTUDIO.EXE). Both are

first-rate tools that enable you to create menus, dialogs, and bitmaps simply by drawing them on-screen with a mouse.

Although the App Studio and the Resource Workshop are helpful and easy-to-use, this book works mostly with resource scripts, which also are known as RC or DLG files. I use these scripts because they adopt themselves well to a written medium, such as a book.

After being created, these scripts can be run through a special compiler, made by either Microsoft or Borland, in order to produce binary resource files (which have a .RES extension). Both the Microsoft and Borland visual programming tools mentioned can produce either .RES files or .RC files. As a result, I sometimes find myself switching back and forth between editing resources visually with the Resource Workshop, and editing them manually, as text files. You might want to experiment so you can find which techniques work best for you. To compare the results of your visual programming experiments with the samples presented here in the text, simply view the textual .RC or .DLG files you have created.

The Emerson Program: Part I

By now, I imagine you're ready to take a look at the Emerson program's source code. So, without further adieu, I'll cut straight to the good stuff. When working with this program, don't forget to start by copying the files used in making WINDOW1.EXE to a new subdirectory. Go through the files, and change the words "Window1" to "Emerson" and rename the files from WINDOW1.* to EMERSON.*.

Taking these steps will save you a good deal of time and will familiarize you with proper Windows coding technique. In other words, you aren't supposed to start each program from scratch. Instead, it's expected that you'll copy blocks of code from one program to the next. Don't think of this as cheating; think of it as proper Windows programming technique!

Listing 6.1 shows the code for the first version of the Emerson program. You'll see a full implementation of the code in the next chapter.

Listing 6.1. The Emerson program shows you how to utilize resources.

```
1: // ======================================================
2: // Program Name: EMERSON
3: // Programmer: Charlie Calvert
4: // Description: Part 1 of 2 part exploration of resources
```

continues

Listing 6.1. continued

```
 5: // =========================================================
 6:
 7: #define STRICT
 8: #include <windows.h>
 9: #include <windowsx.h>
10: #pragma hdrstop
11: #include "Emerson.h"
12: #pragma warning (disable : 4068)
13: #pragma warning (disable : 4100)
14:
15: static char szAppName[] = "Emerson";
16: static HINSTANCE hInstance;
17: static HANDLE hResource;
18:
19: int ScrollWidth;
20: int MaxLines  = 21;
21: int Start = 33;
22: int TextHeight;
23: int PageSize;
24: int nPosition = 0;
25:
26: // ===============================================
27: // INITIALIZATION
28: // ===============================================
29:
30: /////////////////////////////////////////////////
31: // The WinMain function is the program entry point.
32: // Register the Window, Create it, enter the Message Loop.
33: // If either of the first two steps fail, then quit
34: /////////////////////////////////////////////////
35: #pragma argsused
36: int PASCAL WinMain(HINSTANCE hInst, HINSTANCE hPrevInstance,
37:                    LPSTR  lpszCmdParam, int nCmdShow)
38: {
39:   MSG  Msg;
40:
41:   if (!hPrevInstance)
42:     if (!Register(hInst))
43:       return FALSE;
44:
45:   if (!Create(hInst, nCmdShow))
46:     return FALSE;
47:
48:   while (GetMessage(&Msg, NULL, 0, 0))
49:   {
50:      TranslateMessage(&Msg);
51:      DispatchMessage(&Msg);
52:   }
53:
54:   return Msg.wParam;
```

```
 55: }
 56:
 57:
 58: ////////////////////////////////////////////////
 59: //Register Window
 60: ////////////////////////////////////////////////
 61: BOOL Register(HINSTANCE hInst)
 62: {
 63:    WNDCLASS WndClass;
 64:
 65:    WndClass.style          = CS_HREDRAW | CS_VREDRAW;
 66:    WndClass.lpfnWndProc    = WndProc;
 67:    WndClass.cbClsExtra     = 0;
 68:    WndClass.cbWndExtra     = 0;
 69:    WndClass.hInstance      = hInst;
 70:    WndClass.hIcon          = LoadIcon(hInst, "Icon");
 71:    WndClass.hCursor        = LoadCursor(hInst, "Cursor");
 72:    WndClass.hbrBackground  = GetStockBrush(WHITE_BRUSH);
 73:    WndClass.lpszMenuName   = "Menu";
 74:    WndClass.lpszClassName  = szAppName;
 75:
 76:    return RegisterClass (&WndClass);
 77: }
 78:
 79: ////////////////////////////////////////////////
 80: // Create the window and show it.
 81: ////////////////////////////////////////////////
 82: BOOL Create(HINSTANCE hInst, int nCmdShow)
 83: {
 84:
 85:    hInstance = hInst;
 86:
 87:    HWND hwnd = CreateWindow(szAppName, szAppName,
 88:                             WS_OVERLAPPEDWINDOW,
 89:                             CW_USEDEFAULT, CW_USEDEFAULT,
 90:                             CW_USEDEFAULT, CW_USEDEFAULT,
 91:                             NULL, NULL, hInst, NULL);
 92:
 93:    if (hwnd == NULL)
 94:      return FALSE;
 95:
 96:    ShowWindow(hwnd, nCmdShow);
 97:    UpdateWindow(hwnd);
 98:
 99:    return TRUE;
100: }
101:
102: //=================================================
103: // IMPLEMENTATION
104: //=================================================
105:
```

6

continues

Listing 6.1. continued

```
106: /////////////////////////////////////////////
107: // The window proc helps control the program at runtime
108: /////////////////////////////////////////////
109: LRESULT CALLBACK __export WndProc(HWND hwnd, UINT Message,
110:                                   WPARAM wParam, LPARAM lParam)
111: {
112:   switch(Message)
113:   {
114:     HANDLE_MSG(hwnd, WM_CREATE, Emerson_OnCreate);
115:     HANDLE_MSG(hwnd, WM_DESTROY, Emerson_OnDestroy);
116:     HANDLE_MSG(hwnd, WM_COMMAND, Emerson_OnCommand);
117:     HANDLE_MSG(hwnd, WM_PAINT, Emerson_OnPaint);
118:     default: return Emerson_DefProc(hwnd, Message, wParam, lParam);
119:   }
120: }
121:
122: /////////////////////////////////////////////
123: // Create Window
124: // Load the Bitmap from resource
125: /////////////////////////////////////////////
126: #pragma argsused
127: BOOL Emerson_OnCreate(HWND hwnd, CREATESTRUCT FAR* lpCreateStruct)
128: {
129:   hResource = LoadResource(hInstance,
130:             FindResource(hInstance, "Brahma", "TEXT"));
131:   return TRUE;
132: }
133:
134: /////////////////////////////////////////////
135: // Destructor
136: // Delete Bitmap from memory
137: /////////////////////////////////////////////
138: #pragma argsused
139: void Emerson_OnDestroy(HWND hwnd)
140: {
141:   FreeResource(hResource);
142:   PostQuitMessage(0);
143: }
144:
145:
146: /////////////////////////////////////////////
147: //  The Emerson Dialog Procedure controls the dialog
148: /////////////////////////////////////////////
149: #pragma argsused
150: void Emerson_OnCommand(HWND hwnd, int id, HWND hwndCtl,
151:                        UINT codeNotify)
151: {
152:   switch(id)
153:   {
154:     case CM_ABOUT:
```

```
155:        NotYetAvailable(hwnd);
156:        break;
157:
158:      case CM_BITMAP:
159:        NotYetAvailable(hwnd);
160:        break;
161:
162:      case CM_BRAHMIN:
163:        NotYetAvailable(hwnd);
164:        break;
165:
166:      case CM_WOODNOTES:
167:        NotYetAvailable(hwnd);
168:        break;
169:
170:      case CM_SEASHORE:
171:        NotYetAvailable(hwnd);
172:        break;
173:    }
174: }
175:
176: //////////////////////////////////////////////////////
177: // Handle WM_PAINT
178: // Paint a bunch of copies of TheBitmap
179: //////////////////////////////////////////////////////
180: void Emerson_OnPaint(HWND hwnd)
181: {
182:    PAINTSTRUCT PaintStruct;
183:    char far *Poem;
184:    RECT Rect;
185:
186:    HDC PaintDC = BeginPaint(hwnd, &PaintStruct);
187:
188:    Poem = (char far *)LockResource(hResource);
189:    GetClientRect(hwnd, &Rect);
190:    Rect.left += 10;
191:    Rect.top += 10;
192:    DrawText(PaintDC, Poem, -1, &Rect, DT_EXTERNALLEADING);
193:    GlobalUnlock(hResource);
194:
195:    EndPaint(hwnd, &PaintStruct);
196: }
197:
198: /////////////////////////////////////////////////
199: // NotYetAvailable
200: /////////////////////////////////////////////////
201: void NotYetAvailable(HWND hwnd)
202: {
203:    MessageBox(hwnd, "Not yet available", "Under Construction",
                   MB_OK);
204: }
```

Listing 6.2 lists the Emerson header file.

Listing 6.2. EMERSON.H.

```
 1: // ================================================
 2: // Name: EMERSON.H
 3: // Programmer: Charlie Calvert
 4: // Description: Header file for EMERSON.CPP
 5: // ================================================
 6: #define CM_ABOUT 101
 7: #define CM_BITMAP 201
 8: #define CM_BRAHMIN 202
 9: #define CM_WOODNOTES 203
10: #define CM_SEASHORE 204
11:
12: // Macros
13: #define max(a,b)    (((a) > (b)) ? (a) : (b))
14: #define min(a,b)    (((a) < (b)) ? (a) : (b))
15:
16: // The Emerson Class
17: #define Emerson_DefProc    DefWindowProc
18: BOOL Emerson_OnCreate(HWND hwnd, CREATESTRUCT FAR* lpCreateStruct);
19: void Emerson_OnDestroy(HWND hwnd);
20: void Emerson_OnCommand(HWND hwnd, int id, HWND hwndCtl,
                           UINT codeNotify);
21: void Emerson_OnPaint(HWND hwnd);
22:
23: // Some procs
24: BOOL Register(HINSTANCE hInstance);
25: BOOL Create(HINSTANCE hInstance, int nCmdShow);
26: LRESULT CALLBACK __export WndProc(HWND hWindow, UINT Message,
                                      WPARAM wParam,
27: LPARAM lParam);
28: void NotYetAvailable(HWND hwnd);
```

Listing 6.3 lists the Emerson resource file.

Listing 6.3. EMERSON.RC.

```
 1: #include <windows.h>
 2: #include "Emerson.h"
 3:
 4: /*   The Emerson Menu     */
 5: Menu MENU
 6: BEGIN
 7:   POPUP "Poems"
 8:   BEGIN
 9:     MENUITEM "Bitmap", CM_BITMAP
10:     MENUITEM "Brahmin", CM_BRAHMIN
```

```
11:    MENUITEM "Woodnotes", CM_WOODNOTES
12:    MENUITEM "SeaShore", CM_SEASHORE
13:  END
14:  MENUITEM "&About", CM_ABOUT
15: END
16:
17:
18: /*   The Emerson Icon     */
19: Icon ICON "Emerson.ico"
20:
21: /*   The Emerson Poem     */
22: Brahma TEXT Brahma.txt
23:
24: /*   The Emerson Cursor   */
25: Cursor CURSOR "emerson.cur"
```

EMERSON.ICO (32X32)   *EMERSON.CUR (32X32)*

Listing 6.4 is the Emerson text file.

 Listing 6.4. A text file that contains the Emerson poem.

```
1: Brahma
2: by Ralph Waldo Emerson
3:
4: If the red slayer think he slays
5:   Or if the slain think he is slain,
6: They know not well the subtle ways
7:   I keep and pass and turn again.
8:
9: Far or forget to me is near;
10:   Shadow and sunlight are the same;
11: The vanished gods to me appear;
12:   And one to me are shame and fame.
13:
14: They reckon ill who leave me out
15:   When me they fly, I am the wings;
16: I am the doubter and the doubt,
17:   And I the hymn the Brahmin sings.
18:
19: The strong gods pine for my abode,
```

continues

Listing 6.4. continued

```
20:    And pine in vain the sacred Seven;
21: But thou, meek lover of the good!
22:    Find me, and turn thy back on heaven.
```

Listing 6.5 lists the Emerson definition file.

Type   **Listing 6.5. EMERSON.DEF.**

```
1: ;   EMERSON.DEF
2: NAME              Emerson
3: DESCRIPTION       'Emerson example'
4: EXETYPE           WINDOWS
5: STUB              'WINSTUB.EXE'
6: CODE              PRELOAD MOVEABLE DISCARDABLE
7: DATA              PRELOAD MOVEABLE MULTIPLE
8: HEAPSIZE          4096
9: STACKSIZE         8192
```

Listing 6.6 lists the Borland Emerson makefile.

Type   **Listing 6.6. EMERSON.MAK (Borland).**

```
1: # EMERSON.MAK
2:
3: APPNAME = Emerson
4: INCPATH = C:\BC\INCLUDE
5: LIBPATH = C:\BC\LIB
6: CFLAGS = -H -ml -W -v -w4 -I$(INCPATH) -L$(LIBPATH)
7:
8: # linking
9: $(APPNAME).exe: $(APPNAME).Obj $(APPNAME).Def $(APPNAME).Res
10:   bcc $(CFLAGS) $(APPNAME).obj
11:   brc $(APPNAME).res
12:
13: # compiling
14: $(APPNAME).obj: $(APPNAME).cpp
15:   bcc -c $(CFLAGS) $(APPNAME).cpp
16:
17: # resource
18: $(APPNAME).res: $(APPNAME).rc
19:   brc -r -i$(INCPATH) $(APPNAME).rc
```

Listing 6.7 lists the Microsoft Emerson makefile.

Listing 6.7. EMERSON.MAK (Microsoft).

```
 1: #-------------------
 2: # EMERSON.MAK
 3: #-------------------
 4:
 5: APPNAME = Emerson
 6:
 7: #-------------------
 8: # linking
 9: #-------------------
10: $(APPNAME).exe : $(APPNAME).obj $(APPNAME).def $(APPNAME).res
11:    link /CO $(APPNAME), /align:16, NUL, /nod llibcew libw, $(APPNAME)
12:    rc $(APPNAME).res
13:
14: #-------------------
15: # compile
16: #-------------------
17: $(APPNAME).obj : $(APPNAME).cpp
18:    cl -c -AL -GA -Ow -W4 -Zp -Zi $(APPNAME).cpp
19:
20: #-------------------
21: # Compile
22: #-------------------
23: $(APPNAME).res: $(APPNAME).rc
24:    rc -r $(APPNAME).rc
25:
26: =======================================================
```

Output
In this version, the main window of the Emerson program has a custom cursor and consists of a single poem, as shown in Figure 6.2. A simple menu is at the top of the program. If you select any of the Emerson menu options, you are informed that the program is not yet complete. When you minimize the Emerson program, it displays a custom icon.

Looking Ahead

Analysis
The key to understanding resources is the RC file, which is listed in its entirety in the previous code listings. Most of the rest of this chapter is devoted to analyzing that file, and to seeing how you can use its pieces in your program. In particular, I do the following:

- [ ] Describe the resource compilers

- [ ] Take a reasonably in-depth look at menus

- [ ] Devote a few paragraphs to the program's icon
- [ ] Devote a few more to its cursor
- [ ] Wind up the chapter by talking about displaying a custom resource

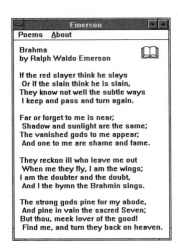

Figure 6.2. *The EMERSON.EXE program. The book in the upper-right corner of the main window is the program's cursor.*

In the next chapter, I include an exploration of dialogs, bitmaps, and string resources.

The subject matter included in this chapter (and the next) is hardly an exhaustive exploration of resources, but it should be enough to get you started working with these useful tools. As this book progresses, other important facts about resources are explored in a natural way, when the subject arises.

Using the Resource Compiler

When learning about resources, the place to begin is with an overview of the resource compiler, which can be used to compile RC scripts. Of course, if you are using Borland's or Microsoft's tools, you don't normally have to go to the DOS prompt and explicitly run the resource compiler. This is a chore the IDE performs for you. However, it's still important for you to understand that this stage exists. You also should know how to perform the task if it ever becomes necessary. Some readers might prefer to compile from the DOS prompt. In this case, it's important to know how to use a resource compiler.

The key point to remember is that after you've completed an RC file, you can compile it from the command line using Microsoft's Resource Compiler (RC.EXE) or the Borland Resource Compiler (BRC.EXE). The commands for using either compiler are essentially identical, but I've chosen to give examples of how to use Microsoft's tool. Borlanders can follow along by putting a "b" in front of the letters "rc."

Here is the syntax to use when you want to compile an .RC file into a .RES file:

```
rc -r -ic:\bc\include emerson.rc
```

If all goes well, you should have a file called EMERSON.RES. If you wind up with a bunch of error messages, you might want to compare your work again with the file listing shown previously.

While I'm on the subject, I'll list the most important options available to you while using the resource compiler. Suppose you have a precompiled executable file, called EMERSON.EXE, to which you want to add a resource. To do so, you need only type the following at the DOS prompt:

```
rc EMERSON.RC EMERSON.EXE
```

Or, if the RES file already exists, you can type

```
rc EMERSON.RES EMERSON.EXE
```

It turns out that in both of these examples, it isn't necessary to enter the name of the executable file, because it shares the same name as the resource. As a result, you could type either

```
rc EMERSON.RC
```

or

```
rc EMERSON.RES
```

in lieu of the first two examples.

Of course, most of the time you'll probably not be using the resource compiler directly from the command line; you'll be calling it from the IDE, or from a project file or makefile (such as the Microsoft EMERSON.MAK text file used to generate EMERSON.EXE). A quick glance at this makefile reveals that it contains syntax not included in the makefile from Chapter 2, "Building Projects, Creating Windows," and Chapter 3, "A Standard Windows Program."

Most significant are the explicit rules for compiling the resource itself. Notice that at the bottom of the file, I've passed the -r parameter to the resource compiler, thereby instructing it to build a RES file without combining it with an executable file. The

6

opposite approach is taken in the linking phase, which combines EMERSON.EXE with EMERSON.RC. In that case, you omit the -r parameter.

Note: Borland users take the exact same approach to adding resource logic to their makefiles. In other words, a quick comparison of the Borland and Microsoft makefiles for the Emerson program reveals that both companies use the exact same syntax when adding resources to a project. Hurrah!

Before plunging into a description of menus, I probably ought to make a brief reference to the include statements at the top of the RC file:

```
1: #include <windows.h>
2: #include "Emerson.h"
```

The EMERSON.H header file at the top of EMERSON.RC is brought in solely because it contains, among other things, the following constant:

```
#define CM_ABOUT    101
```

This constant is linked to the Emerson menu choice, which brings up the program's dialog. The constant quite literally is sent to the program's main window procedure as part of a message whenever the Emerson menu item is chosen. Your job, as a programmer, is to teach the Emerson program to respond properly when the number arrives at the WndProc.

You also should know that it's often necessary to include WINDOWS.H at the top of a resource script. This is done because various constants need to be accessed by the resource compiler. For instance, if you do not include WINDOWS.H in the RC file, Microsoft's compiler gives you the following message at compile time:

```
ABOUT.RC(18): error RW2001: undefined keyword: DS_MODALFRAME
```

The error won't occur when using BRC, because Borland's tool already knows about the definitions in WINDOWS.H. As a result, Borland users don't need to include the file in their resources, or wait for it to be compiled during each build.

Creating a Simple Menu

Here is the code that creates the menu for the Emerson program:

```
 5: Menu MENU
 6: BEGIN
 7:   POPUP "Poems"
 8:   BEGIN
 9:     MENUITEM "Bitmap", CM_BITMAP
10:     MENUITEM "Brahmin", CM_BRAHMIN
11:     MENUITEM "Woodnotes", CM_WOODNOTES
12:     MENUITEM "SeaShore", CM_SEASHORE
13:   END
14:   MENUITEM "&About", CM_ABOUT
15: END
```

EMERSON.RC obviously contains code that isn't going to be understood by a C compiler. Instead, it can be compiled by either RC.EXE or BRC.EXE.

Though written in a language you haven't seen before, the code for EMERSON.RC is simple enough that it shouldn't cause you any serious problems. The script begins by supplying both the name and the type of the resource to be used, as shown in line 5. This line says the resource is a menu, and its name is "Menu." The menu can have almost any name. For instance, the following line also is valid:

```
ABOUT_MENU MENU
```

In the `Register` function, Emerson passes the menu name to the `WndClass` structure. The name is your handle to this resource:

```
WndClass.lpszMenuName    = "Menu";
```

This line of code associates a menu with the program's main window. You don't need to do anything else to make the menu appear. The rest is handled internally by Windows, without any assistance on your part.

Sometimes, programmers prefer to save memory by assigning a number to a menu instead of a written name:

```
125 MENU
BEGIN
    MENUITEM "Emerson", CM_ABOUT
END
```

Doing things this way forces you to take a slightly different approach to the `Register` function. For instance, if you had associated the number 125 with your menu, you could load it with the following line of code:

```
WndClass.lpszMenuName    = "#125";
```

6

Programmers sometimes accidentally associate a numeric identifier with a resource, even when they are trying to use a string as an identifier. In other words, they do something like this in their resource script:

```
#define MYMENU 125

MYMENU MENU
BEGIN
  MENUITEM "Emerson", CM_ABOUT
END
```

Then, they accidentally try to associate the string MYMENU with the appropriate field in the WndClass structure:

```
WndClass.lpszMenuName   = "MYMENU";
```

This isn't going to work, because no such string is associated with a menu in the resource file. To correct the problem, you could write

```
WndClass.lpszMenuName = MAKEINTRESOURCE(MYMENU);
```

The MAKEINTRESOURCE macro converts numeric identifiers into something Windows resources management facilities can understand. If you want to know more about MAKEINTRESOURCE, you can look it up in WINDOWS.H.

The act of naming a menu is one of those situations in which the number of options Windows gives you can make a relatively trivial operation appear difficult. But remember, to create a menu you need to do the following:

☐ Give a name to a menu resource.

☐ Assign that name to the appropriate field of the WndClass structure.

All this other stuff about numeric identifiers and MAKEINTRESOURCE is just icing on the cake. You don't have to use any of that unless you are desperate to save memory. My advice (even in those circumstances) is to think twice, or even three times, before abandoning the clarity of the string-based menu-naming technique.

Designing Menus

So far, you have seen how to name a menu and how to make it appear on the screen. The next step is to see how to design the body of the menu. I'll talk about what takes place between the begin...end pair in the body of a menu definition.

The menu for the Emerson program consists of two separate parts, as shown in Figure 6.3.

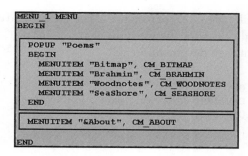

Figure 6.3. *The first part of the Emerson menu is a popup; the second a lone menu item.*

If the pop-up menu were removed from the Emerson program, the resource file for the menu would be very simple:

```
Menu MENU
BEGIN
     MENUITEM "About", CM_ABOUT
END
```

These few lines of code produce the menu shown in Figure 6.4.

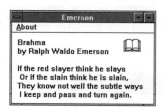

Figure 6.4. *A close-up of a simplified version of the menu from the Emerson program.*

The following line of code defines the appearance of the very simple menu shown in Figure 6.4:

```
MENUITEM "About", CM_ABOUT
```

MENUITEM is a single entry in a menu, whereas POPUP is an entire window (such as the pop-up list that appears when you open the File menu in many major applications). After the MENUITEM declaration, the actual string to be shown in the menu is spelled out in quotes; finally, the constant to be associated with the menu item is declared.

This is a very simple language. For instance, if you want to add extra items to the menu, you can insert additional lines between the begin...end pair, and define constants to be associated with each new menu item:

```
/* EMERSON1.RC */
#define CM_DIALOG1 101;
#define CM_DIALOG2 102;
#define CM_DIALOG3 103;

MENU_1 MENU
BEGIN
     MENUITEM "Dialog1", CM_DIALOG1
     MENUITEM "Dialog2", CM_DIALOG2
     MENUITEM "Dialog3", CM_DIALOG3
END
```

This new resource file would create a menu like the one shown in Figure 6.5.

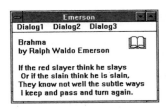

Figure 6.5. *The menu created by a modified version of EMERSON1.RC.*

DO   DON'T

DO take a moment to notice the range of constants defined in the previous example file. The first item is defined as 101, but it could just as easily have been any positive unsigned integer. I chose 101 from force of habit.

DO choose integer values between 1 and 64K for the constants used in your menus. It's best to avoid integers less than 256 (0x100), because sometimes they can have a different significance in a Windows program.

DO associate an identifier with each menu item. For instance, I have associated CM_DIALOG1, CM_DIALOG2, and CM_DIALOG3 with the menu items in the previous example. These names can make coding easier, make your code easier to read, and help you avoid dumb mistakes.

DON'T use the same number twice, unless you are absolutely sure you know what you are doing. If you try to use the same number for two different menu items, trouble is bound to ensue.

When a particular menu item is selected by the user, the constant associated with that menu item is sent to the program's WndProc. Both the menu item and its associated constant arrive packaged in the form of a WM_COMMAND messages. As a result, they are handled by Emerson_OnCommand:

```
150: void Emerson_OnCommand(HWND hwnd, int id, HWND hwndCtl, UINT
                            codeNotify)
151: {
152:   switch(id)
153:   {
154:     case CM_ABOUT:
155:       NotYetAvailable(hwnd);
156:       break;
157:
158:     case CM_BITMAP:
159:       NotYetAvailable(hwnd);
160:       break;
161:
162:     case CM_BRAHMIN:
163:       NotYetAvailable(hwnd);
164:       break;
165:
166:     case CM_WOODNOTES:
167:       NotYetAvailable(hwnd);
168:       break;
169:
170:     case CM_SEASHORE:
171:       NotYetAvailable(hwnd);
172:       break;
173:   }
174: }
```

As you can see, a simple case statement enables the Emerson program to deal with each menu item. At this stage in the program's development, the response to menu selection is simply to pop up a MessageBox stating that the feature hasn't been implemented. The details of this implementation are filled in during the course of the next chapter.

6

Note: If you aren't using WINDOWSX, you can look in the wParam argument sent to WndProc to determine the ID of the selected menu item. This is the same value passed on in the id field of Cls_OnCommand.

Pop-up menus are the standard drop-down menus you see at the top of most programs, such as the File menu at the top of your compiler.

The following bit of code produces the pop-up menu shown in Figure 6.6:

```
POPUP "Poems"
BEGIN
  MENUITEM "Bitmap", CM_BITMAP
  MENUITEM "Brahmin", CM_BRAHMIN
  MENUITEM "Woodnotes", CM_WOODNOTES
  MENUITEM "SeaShore", CM_SEASHORE
END
```

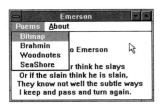

Figure 6.6. *A pop-up menu is activated when you click the menu bar. It's really just a window with text in it.*

As you can see, a pop-up menu consists of a title line that is visible on the menu bar, and a set of menu items grouped together between a begin...end pair. The menu items are what you see when the pop-up menu is activated. Note that each menu item is associated with a constant defined in EMERSON.H. These constants are sent to the program's WndProc when a menu selection is made by the user.

Right now, I'm not going to go into any more depth about how menus are put together. If you want a more detailed description, you can skip ahead to Chapter 17, "Menus and Icons in Depth," where the subject of menus is broached a second time (and in more depth).

Adding an Icon and a Cursor to EMERSON.CPP

The only sensible way to create an icon is to use a tool, such as the App Studio or the Resource Workshop. While working with either of these tools, the actual act of creating an icon is reduced to the enjoyable job of drawing a picture with the mouse.

Note: Let's face it: drawing an icon doesn't demand the same kind of intellectual rigor that's inherent in even relatively simple programming chores. As a result, I'm not going to explain how to use the Resource Workshop or App Studio to perform this chore. Most readers will probably be able to figure that out with no more than a quick glance at their manuals.

This does not mean, however, that it's not important to take the time to create effective icons. The point is that even if you are the type of obsessive workaholic who insists on working yourself to the edge of utter distraction ever single day of your life, that is, even if you are an ordinary programmer, you need to set aside time to enjoy yourself while you are engaged in the essential job of creating icons. If you don't, people won't respect your application. Users put incredible weight on seemingly trivial details—such as the appearance of icons.

After you create your icon, you can add it to your project through a simple two-step process:

☐ Add the following line to your RC file:

```
Emerson ICON "Emerson.ico"
```

☐ In your Register method, set the `WndClass.hIcon` field to your icon with this line of code:

```
WndClass.hIcon = LoadIcon(hInst, "Emerson");
```

Take a moment to compare the preceding line from the Register method to the line used in Chapters 3, 4, and 5:

```
WndClass.hIcon = LoadIcon(NULL, IDI_APPLICATION);
```

The differences here stem from the fact that the latter example loads a predefined Windows resource, and the former example loads a custom resource.

When loading a custom icon, set the first field of LoadIcon to the HInstance of the program that contains the Icon resource; set the second field to the name of the icon. In most cases, the program that contains the icon you want to use is the current program, so all you need to do is pass in the global HINSTANCE from your app.

When loading a predefined Windows resource, set the first field of LoadIcon to NULL and then specify the appropriate resource identifier in the second field. As mentioned earlier, predefined Windows resources are listed in WINDOWS.H:

```
#define IDI_APPLICATION    MAKEINTRESOURCE(32512)
#define IDI_HAND           MAKEINTRESOURCE(32513)
#define IDI_QUESTION       MAKEINTRESOURCE(32514)
#define IDI_EXCLAMATION    MAKEINTRESOURCE(32515)
#define IDI_ASTERISK       MAKEINTRESOURCE(32516)
```

If you think about it, the differences between these two approaches are not nearly as arbitrary as they might seem. Normally, you have to specify the HINSTANCE of the application where the icon resource resides. Built-in Windows resources, however, don't really belong to any application. They are just part of the system. As a result, you don't need to pass in an HINSTANCE; instead, you can pass in NULL!

After the previous explanation of creating icons, it's easy to move on to a discussion of cursors. Once again, you should start by carefully defining the cursor in the Resource Workshop.

Note: With the Emerson program, I was able to "borrow" my cursor from the image of a book found in the WingDings font (that comes with Windows). I used the Charmap program, from the Windows subdirectory, to locate the symbol I wanted to use. I copied the selected symbol into the Write program and used the font manipulation there to make it the size I wanted for my cursor. Then, I pushed the Print Screen button to copy the current screen into the Windows clipboard. The next steps were to paste the contents of the clipboard into the Paintbrush program, and to use the tools there to cut and paste the image into a small bitmap, which I again stored in the clipboard. The final steps were to paste this image into the Resource Workshop cursor tool and save my work.

> Phew! It sounds pretty complicated when I describe it like that! However, the whole process took only a few minutes, whereas it undoubtedly would have taken me several hours to create the image on my own.
>
> One reason I tell you this story is that it shows the way Windows apps can work together to create a new kind of tool, with functionality that transcends the capabilities of any one application.

After you created your cursor, you can link it into your application through the Register function. You can do this with the following line of code:

```
WndClass.hCursor = LoadCursor(hInst, "Cursor");
```

Once again, you should compare this line with the methods shown in earlier chapters:

```
WndClass.hCursor = LoadCursor(NULL, IDC_ARROW);
```

Clearly, the same rules that dictate the loading of an icon also dictate the loading of cursors.

DO   DON'T

DO pass the program's HINSTANCE as the first parameter to LoadCursor or LoadIcon if you are loading a custom cursor or custom icon.

DON'T pass the program's HINSTANCE to LoadCursor or LoadIcon if you are loading a system resource defined by one of the constants in WINDOWS.H.

That's all there is to it. From a technical standpoint, it's simple to add an icon or cursor to your program! However, icons and cursors have additional features that are a bit complex. These include drawing icons in a dialog, painting icons on a window, or switching cursors at runtime. Because these are more advanced, and less frequently used, I describe them in Chapter 17.

User-Defined Resources

I said earlier that you can create your own types of resources if you so desire. In the Emerson program, this technique is used to make a resource out of a text file.

6

This stunt is possible, because Windows enables programmers to store raw data in a resource file. This data can assume any shape or format that you might find useful. When you load this resource into your program, all Windows needs to do is retrieve a pointer to this data through the LoadResource function. After it turns over the pointer, Windows washes its hands of the whole episode and lets you do what you want with the binary data it gave you.

In effect, this means that anything you can store in memory can be placed in a resource file and retrieved through the LoadResource command. This obviously opens up an incredible range of possibilities for programmers who are willing to do a little creative work.

In this particular case, I don't want to get involved in anything very fancy, so Emerson uses a simple text resource, containing a poem that can be easily loaded from disk and displayed on-screen. By now, it should come as no surprise to hear that this whole process is started by defining the resource in an RC file.

To define the resource, simply type a text file and save it to disk. After creating the file, you can instruct Windows to store it in a .RES file by entering the following line in EMERSON.RC:

```
Brahma TEXT Brahma.txt
```

This line follows the same format you saw when defining a cursor, bitmap, or icon in a resource file. In other words

- [ ] Give the resource a name, which in this case is Brahma.

- [ ] Give the resource a type. I have called this type TEXT, because it explains what kind of resource I have created. I could just as easily, however, have used the word POEM, or the word FOOBAR. The point is only that the type is a unique identifier that I can reference again inside my program.

- [ ] The final step is to list the name of the file I want to include in my program. Obviously, Windows treats this file as nothing more than an array of binary data. It doesn't care what is inside the file.

These steps assure that after compiling the Emerson program, the resulting executable file contains a copy of the Brahma poem. The only chore left, then, is to load the poem from disk and into memory.

This is done by calling LoadResource and FindResource in response to a WM_CREATE message:

```
hResource = LoadResource(hInstance,
           FindResource(hInstance, "Brahma", "TEXT"));
```

By now, the previous lines should be pretty much self-explanatory. The program simply passes in the HINSTANCE of the executable file that contains the resource, and then tells FindResource the name of the resource and its type. FindResource literally scans through the executable file to find the resource. After locating the resource, FindResource passes the resource's handle to LoadResource, which then physically moves the object into memory.

Note: In its literature, Microsoft states that LoadIcon and LoadCursor both call LoadResource and FindResource. In other words, the process described does little more than explicitly perform chores normally carried out by higher level functions.

After you load the resource, you need to lock down the memory involved before you use it:

```
Poem = (char far *)LockResource(hResource);
```

As you can see, the Emerson program also typecasts the pointer returned by LoadResource. As a result of the typecast, the code now directly addresses the binary data returned by LockResource as if it were a string. Of course, this works out fine, because the data could indeed be thought of as nothing more than a long string saved into a text file.

The Emerson program is now free to draw the string to the screen so that the user can view the poem. This is a two-step process that involves first obtaining the dimensions of the main window, and then calling DrawText to fill the window with the poem.

After the text is displayed, the program is free to unlock the data and go on about its business:

```
GlobalUnlock(hResource);
```

The act of unlocking the memory doesn't mean that the object has been destroyed. It only means that the memory is no longer locked down.

To completely free the resource, you need to explicitly call FreeResource, most likely in response to the WM_DESTROY message:

```
FreeResource(hResource)
```

It turns out, however, that this isn't absolutely necessary, because the memory will automatically be deallocated when the program ends.

Custom Resources: Additional Thoughts

The last section is really just a *five-minute intro* to a fairly complex subject. I'm going to add a few more comments in this section, but you needn't get too bogged down in this material if it doesn't interest you. I present it mainly because some readers might be curious.

When a program is first loaded into memory, its resources are not necessarily loaded along with it. This is possible because the format for executables has been completely redefined since the days DOS was king. These files are now based on what is called the New Executable (NE) format. One of the features of this new type of file is the ability to coexist with, and to offer support for, resources.

If, for some reason, you don't want the Brahma poem to remain on disk after the executable is loaded, you could specifically mark it PRELOAD:

```
Brahma TEXT PRELOAD FIXED Brahma.txt
```

As a result, it will be loaded into memory when the program is loaded into memory. That is, it will be *preloaded* before the call to LoadResource.

Most of the time, however, memory considerations tempt programmers to keep resources on disk until they explicitly load them. The Emerson program loads the resources into memory by calling first FindResource and then LoadResource. This doesn't mean, however, that the resource is now permanently ensconced in memory. Windows regards resources as DISCARDABLE unless they are explicitly marked as FIXED, per the previous example.

DISCARDABLE objects can be shuffled off to the hard disk if Windows feels that other dynamic objects have more significance. If the Brahma resource is discarded, it must be laboriously reloaded back into memory when LockResource is called. The logic for doing this is built into LockResource, and the result of the function guarantees that the Brahma resource won't be moved or discarded until you call either UnlockResource or GlobalUnlock. In other words, if LoadResource is called, and it finds that the Brahma resource has been discarded, the program first reloads the Brahma resource from disk, and then locks it in place. While locked, it can't be moved or shuffled back onto disk. This is a useful state of affairs, but not one that you want to prevail for a lengthy period of time. As a result, it's important to call GlobalUnlock as soon as possible after locking a resource and displaying it on-screen.

Hopefully, this discussion clears up the difference between calling `GlobalUnlock` and calling `FreeResource`. The former call only gives Windows permission to move or discard the memory, whereas `FreeResource` explicitly tells Windows to deallocate the memory associated with the resource.

There is one final twist to this tale, which I might as well relate (now that I've gone this far). As you know, Windows can load multiple copies of a program into memory. It doesn't, however, normally load multiple copies of a program's resources into memory. In other words, if three copies of the Emerson program are in memory, they all use the same copy of the Brahma custom resource. To accommodate this situation, Windows increments a flag when `LoadResource` is called, and then decrements a flag when `FreeResource` is called. The memory for any particular resource is never really freed until a call to `FreeResource` decrements this flag back to zero. Therefore, the resource is available as long as a copy of the Emerson program is in memory.

As you can tell from the last few paragraphs, a good deal is going on behind-the-scenes that wasn't covered in my *five-minute intro* to custom resources. I want to stress, however, that you don't need to understand all of this in order to simply use a basic custom `TEXT` resource in your program. I've included this additional information for two related reasons:

1. Some people never really feel comfortable with a technique until they have not only a mechanical understanding of a subject, but also a conceptual understanding.

2. If I'm going to give a real introduction to resources, I need to pull back the curtain a little bit so you can see the little man behind-the-scenes who tweaks the levers and pushes the buttons. Until you meet him, you haven't really had a thorough tour of the premises.

Summary

This chapter presented an introduction to resources. You saw that resources are visual or logical elements that can be added to a program through a series of usually straightforward steps. You also learned that resources are defined in an RC file, compiled into a .RES file, and finally merged with the program's executable file.

Menus were among the resources specifically covered. You learned how to assign a constant to a particular menu item, and saw that when a menu item is selected, these constants are sent to the `WndProc` in the form of a `WM_COMMAND` message. You saw that inside of the `Emerson_OnCommand` function each of these constants can be responded to in turn.

During the discussion of icons and cursors, you learned about the difference between resources that belong to the system, and resources that are loaded from a disk. You saw that in the former case, you can specify NULL as the first parameter to LoadResource or LoadIcon. In the latter case, you saw that the program's HINSTANCE is required in the first parameter.

The last two sections in this chapter covered custom resources. That discussion ended with an overview of how Windows handles the memory associated with a resource.

The next chapter, "Advanced Resources: Bitmaps and Dialogs," continues this discussion by examining bitmaps, dialogs, and string resources. See you there!

Q&A

1. Q: I'm confused by all these different compilers. What exactly are the differences among RC.EXE, BRC.EXE, WORKSHOP.EXE, APSTUDIO.EXE, and my compiler?

   A: In the beginning, there was only one compiler, which was used "simply" to compile your C source code. When the idea of adding resources came along, Microsoft built RC.EXE, which can compile RC files and add them to a New Executable type file. BRC is simply Borland's clone of the Microsoft tool. After people had been working with resources for a while, it became clear that their creation could be greatly simplified by enabling programmers to simply draw their elements on the screen. Hence, tools like the Resource Workshop and App Studio were born. To make these tools more powerful, compiler makers gave them the capability to either call RC.EXE, or to perform the same chores that RC.EXE performs. To bring things full circle, I should perhaps add that all of this activity regarding resources is separate from the chores performed by your basic C or C++ compiler.

2. Q: What's the difference between UnlockResource and GlobalUnlock?

   A: UnlockResource is really just a macro that calls GlobalUnlock to do the real work. GlobalUnlock is most often used with the functions GlobalAlloc, GlobalLock, and GlobalFree. These functions are used for allocating memory, similar to the way that DOS C compilers use the malloc function to allocate memory. When using GlobalAlloc, it traditionally has been necessary to lock the memory before using it—just as you need to lock down a custom resource before using it.

3. Q: So who is this Emerson dude, anyway?

   A: Ralph Waldo Emerson, a native of New England, was born in 1803 and
   died in 1882. Early in his life, he was a minister in the Unitarian Church,
   but later became one of the foremost proponents of transcendentalism. He is
   remembered most often for his essays, but some people also have found
   value in his poetry. Walt Whitman regarded Emerson as a major influence.

Workshop

The Workshop provides quiz questions to help you solidify your understanding of the
material covered and exercises to provide you with experience in using what you've
learned. Try to understand the quiz and exercise answers before continuing on to the
next chapter. Answers are provided in Appendix A.

Quiz

1. How do you tell the resource compiler (RC.EXE) to convert the
   EMERSON.RC file into a .RES file?

2. How do you tell the resource compiler to combine EMERSON.RES and
   EMERSON.EXE into one file?

3. In the following statement, what is the significance of the term CM_ABOUT?

   ```
   MENUITEM "About", CM_ABOUT
   ```

4. What is the difference between a pop-up menu and a menu item?

5. What is the first parameter passed to LoadIcon?

6. When a WM_COMMAND message is sent to a Window, after a menu selection,
   which parameter of the WndProc holds the menu item id?

7. What is the difference between FindResource and LoadResource?

8. What is the difference between GlobalUnlock and FreeResource?

9. What is a New Executable file?

10. Can resources be stored in a DLL?

Exercises

1. Using custom resources to store the text, write a program that displays its own WinMain procedure in its main window.

2. Write a program that can use custom resources to display two different pieces of text. Enable the user to switch back and forth between these two pieces of text by selecting different items from the menu.

Advanced
Resources:
Bitmaps and
Dialogs

This chapter presents an overview of three sophisticated resources: dialogs, bitmaps, and string tables. Though string tables are fairly easy to use, both dialogs and bitmaps can be heady topics, because they involve the allocation and deallocation of relatively complex system resources.

Specifically, this chapter covers

☐ Creating and using dialogs

☐ Creating and using bitmaps

☐ Creating and using string tables

☐ Creating and using scrollbars

☐ An overview of the inner workings of the Emerson program

I introduce scrollbars in this chapter, primarily because the Emerson program needs them. You should note, however, that scrollbars are not resources, but controls. The whole subject of controls is discussed in-depth during Week 2.

The core of this chapter focuses on bitmaps and dialogs. Given sufficiently complex circumstances, both subjects could be expanded to fill several chapters' worth of material. My goal is to give you the basic knowledge you need to pop up dialogs and display bitmaps. During the next few chapters, you will get plenty of opportunity to practice these techniques. The early part of Week Three contains tips about the more advanced aspects of both subjects.

Emerson2

The first order of business is to get the Emerson2 program on the table for all to see. This program is a continuation and completion of the program started in the last chapter. The big difference is that Emerson2 uses string tables to store text, whereas the first Emerson program used custom resources.

Well, without further comment, see Listing 7.1 for the code.

Listing 7.1. Example program with string table, dialog, and bitmap.

```
1: // ==============================================
2: // Program Name: EMERSON2
3: // Programmer: Charlie Calvert
4: // Description: Example program with string table,
5: //              dialog, and bitmap
6: // ==============================================
```

```
 7:
 8: #define STRICT
 9: #include <windows.h>
10: #include <windowsx.h>
11: #pragma hdrstop
12: #include <string.h>
13: #include "Emerson2.h"
14: #pragma warning (disable : 4100)
15: #pragma warning (disable : 4068)
16: static char szAppName[] = "Emerson2";
17: static HINSTANCE hInstance;
18:
19: int MaxLines  = 21;
20: int Start = 32;
21: int TextHeight;
22: int PageSize = 10;
23: int nPosition = 0;
24: BOOL DrawBitmaps = TRUE;
25:
26: // ================================================
27: // INITIALIZATION
28: // ================================================
29:
30: //////////////////////////////////////////////////
31: // The WinMain function is the program entry point.
32: //////////////////////////////////////////////////
33: #pragma argsused
34: int PASCAL WinMain(HINSTANCE hInst, HINSTANCE hPrevInstance,
35:                    LPSTR  lpszCmdParam, int nCmdShow)
36: {
37:   MSG  Msg;
38:
39:   if (!hPrevInstance)
40:     if (!Register(hInst))
41:       return FALSE;
42:
43:   if (!Create(hInst, nCmdShow))
44:     return FALSE;
45:
46:   while (GetMessage(&Msg, NULL, 0, 0))
47:   {
48:     TranslateMessage(&Msg);
49:     DispatchMessage(&Msg);
50:   }
51:
52:   return Msg.wParam;
53: }
54:
55:
```

continues

Listing 7.1. continued

```
56: /////////////////////////////////////////////
57: // Register Window
58: /////////////////////////////////////////////
59: BOOL Register(HINSTANCE hInst)
60: {
61:   WNDCLASS WndClass;
62:
63:   WndClass.style         = CS_HREDRAW | CS_VREDRAW;
64:   WndClass.lpfnWndProc   = WndProc;
65:   WndClass.cbClsExtra    = 0;
66:   WndClass.cbWndExtra    = 0;
67:   WndClass.hInstance     = hInst;
68:   WndClass.hIcon         = LoadIcon(hInst, "Emerson2");
69:   WndClass.hCursor       = LoadCursor(NULL, IDC_ARROW);
70:   WndClass.hbrBackground = GetStockBrush(WHITE_BRUSH);
71:   WndClass.lpszMenuName  = "MENU_1";
72:   WndClass.lpszClassName = szAppName;
73:
74:   return RegisterClass (&WndClass);
75: }
76:
77: /////////////////////////////////////////////
78: // Create the window and show it.
79: /////////////////////////////////////////////
80: BOOL Create(HINSTANCE hInst, int nCmdShow)
81: {
82:
83:   hInstance = hInst;
84:
85:   HWND hwnd = CreateWindow(szAppName, szAppName,
86:                             WS_OVERLAPPEDWINDOW | WS_VSCROLL,
87:                             CW_USEDEFAULT, CW_USEDEFAULT,
88:                             CW_USEDEFAULT, CW_USEDEFAULT,
89:                             NULL, NULL, hInst, NULL);
90:
91:   if (hwnd == NULL)
92:     return FALSE;
93:
94:   ShowWindow(hwnd, nCmdShow);
95:   UpdateWindow(hwnd);
96:
97:   return TRUE;
98: }
99:
100: //=================================================
101: // IMPLEMENTATION
102: //=================================================
103:
```

```
104: ///////////////////////////////////////////////
105: // The window proc helps control the
106: // program while it is running
107: ///////////////////////////////////////////////
108: LRESULT CALLBACK __export WndProc(HWND hwnd, UINT Message,
109:                                   WPARAM wParam, LPARAM lParam)
110: {
111:   switch(Message)
112:   {
113:     HANDLE_MSG(hwnd, WM_CREATE, Emerson_OnCreate);
114:     HANDLE_MSG(hwnd, WM_DESTROY, Emerson_OnDestroy);
115:     HANDLE_MSG(hwnd, WM_COMMAND, Emerson_OnCommand);
116:     HANDLE_MSG(hwnd, WM_KEYDOWN, Emerson_OnKey);
117:     HANDLE_MSG(hwnd, WM_PAINT, Emerson_OnPaint);
118:     HANDLE_MSG(hwnd, WM_VSCROLL, Emerson_OnVScroll);
119:     default:
120:        return Emerson_DefProc(hwnd, Message, wParam, lParam);
121:   }
122: }
123:
124: ///////////////////////////////////////////////
125: // Create Window
126: // Load the Bitmap from resource
127: ///////////////////////////////////////////////
128: #pragma argsused
129: BOOL Emerson_OnCreate(HWND hwnd, CREATESTRUCT FAR* lpCreateStruct)
130: {
131:   TEXTMETRIC TextMetrics;
132:
133:   TheBitmap = LoadBitmap(hInstance, "Bitmap");
134:   if (!TheBitmap)
135:   {
136:     MessageBox(hwnd, "No Bitmap", "Fatal Error", MB_OK);
137:     return FALSE;
138:   }
139:
140:   HDC PaintDC = GetDC(hwnd);
141:   GetTextMetrics(PaintDC, &TextMetrics);
142:   ReleaseDC(hwnd, PaintDC);
143:   TextHeight = TextMetrics.tmHeight +
144:                TextMetrics.tmExternalLeading;
145:
146:   SetScrollRange(hwnd, SB_VERT, 0,
147:                  MaxLines - Start, FALSE);
148:
149:   return TRUE;
150: }
151:
```

continues

Listing 7.1. continued

```
152: /////////////////////////////////////////////
153: // Destructor: Delete Bitmap from memory
154: /////////////////////////////////////////////
155: #pragma argsused
156: void Emerson_OnDestroy(HWND hwnd)
157: {
158:   DeleteBitmap(TheBitmap);
159:   PostQuitMessage(0);
160: }
161:
162: /////////////////////////////////////////////
163: //  The Emerson2 Dialog Procedure controls the dialog
164: /////////////////////////////////////////////
165: #pragma argsused
166: void Emerson_OnCommand(HWND hwnd, int id,
167:                         HWND hwndCtl, UINT codeNotify)
168: {
169:   switch(id)
170:   {
171:     case CM_ABOUT:
172:     {
173:       FARPROC AboutBox =
174:           MakeProcInstance((FARPROC)AboutDlgProc, hInstance);
175:       DialogBox(hInstance, "About",
176:                 hwnd, (DLGPROC)AboutBox);
177:       FreeProcInstance(AboutBox);
178:       break;
179:     }
180:
181:     case CM_BRAHMIN:
182:       Start = 32;
183:       MaxLines = 22;
184:       InvalidateRect(hwnd, NULL, TRUE);
185:       DrawBitmaps = FALSE;
186:       break;
187:
188:     case CM_WOODNOTES:
189:       Start = 0;
190:       MaxLines = 32;
191:       InvalidateRect(hwnd, NULL, TRUE);
192:       DrawBitmaps = FALSE;
193:       break;
194:
195:     case CM_SEASHORE:
196:       Start = 64;
197:       MaxLines = 37;
198:       InvalidateRect(hwnd, NULL, TRUE);
199:       DrawBitmaps = FALSE;
200:       break;
201:
```

```
202:      case CM_DRAWBITMAPS:
203:        DrawBitmaps = TRUE;
204:        InvalidateRect(hwnd, NULL, TRUE);
205:        break;
206:   }
207: }
208:
209: /////////////////////////////////////////////
210: // Handle WM_KEYDOWN to aid in scrolling poems
211: /////////////////////////////////////////////
212: #pragma argsused
213: void Emerson_OnKey(HWND hwnd, UINT vk, BOOL fDown, int cRepeat,
                        UINT flags)
214: {
215:   switch(vk)
216:   {
217:     case VK_HOME:
218:       SendMessage(hwnd, WM_VSCROLL, SB_TOP, 0L);
219:       break;
220:
221:     case VK_DOWN:
222:       SendMessage(hwnd, WM_VSCROLL, SB_LINEDOWN, 0L);
223:       break;
224:
225:     case VK_UP:
226:       SendMessage(hwnd, WM_VSCROLL, SB_LINEUP, 0L);
227:       break;
228:   }
229: }
230:
231: /////////////////////////////////////////////
232: // Handle WM_PAINT: Paint TheBitmap and poems
233: /////////////////////////////////////////////
234: void Emerson_OnPaint(HWND hwnd)
235: {
236:   PAINTSTRUCT PaintStruct;
237:   SIZE L;
238:   int NumImages = 15;
239:   char S[101];
240:   int Y = 0;
241:
242:   HDC PaintDC = BeginPaint(hwnd, &PaintStruct);
243:
244:
245:   if (DrawBitmaps)
246:   {
247:     HDC BitmapDC = CreateCompatibleDC(PaintDC);
248:     HBITMAP OldBitmap = SelectBitmap(BitmapDC, TheBitmap);
249:     for (int i = 0; i < NumImages; i++)
250:       for (int j = 0; j < NumImages; j++)
```

continues

7

Listing 7.1. continued

```
251:          BitBlt(PaintDC, i * 66, j * 66, 64, 64,
252:                 BitmapDC, 0, 0, SRCCOPY);
253:    SelectBitmap(BitmapDC, OldBitmap);
254:    DeleteDC(BitmapDC);
255:  }
256:  else
257:  {
258:    HPEN APen = CreatePen(PS_NULL, 0, 0);
259:    HPEN SavePen = SelectPen(PaintDC, APen);
260:    for (int i = nPosition; i < MaxLines; i++)
261:    {
262:      LoadString(hInstance, i + Start, S, 100);
263:      TextOut(PaintDC, 1, Y, S, strlen(S));
264:      GetTextExtentPoint(PaintDC, S, strlen(S), &L);
265:      if (L.cx == 0)
266:        Rectangle(PaintDC, 1, Y, 400, Y + 1 + TextHeight);
267:      else
268:        Rectangle(PaintDC, L.cx, Y,
269:                  L.cx + 200, Y + 1 + TextHeight);
270:      Y += TextHeight;
271:    }
272:    Rectangle(PaintDC, 1, Y, 400, Y + 1 + 400);
273:    SelectPen(PaintDC, SavePen);
274:    DeleteObject(APen);
275:  }
276:  EndPaint(hwnd, &PaintStruct);
277: }
278:
279: ///////////////////////////////////////////////
280: // Handle WM_VSCROL: Aid in scrolling poems
281: ///////////////////////////////////////////////
282: #pragma argsused
283: void Emerson_OnVScroll(HWND hwnd, HWND hwndCtl, UINT code, int pos)
284: {
285:  switch(code)
286:  {
287:    case SB_TOP:
288:      nPosition = 0;
289:      break;
290:
291:    case SB_BOTTOM:
292:      nPosition = MaxLines;
293:      break ;
294:
295:    case SB_LINEUP:
296:      if (nPosition > 0) nPosition -= 1 ;
297:      break ;
298:
299:    case SB_LINEDOWN:
300:      if (nPosition < MaxLines) nPosition += 1 ;
301:      break ;
```

```
302:
303:      case SB_PAGEUP:
304:        nPosition -= PageSize;
305:        break ;
306:
307:      case SB_PAGEDOWN:
308:        nPosition += PageSize;
309:        break ;
310:
311:      case SB_THUMBPOSITION:
312:        nPosition = pos;
313:        break;
314:    }
315:    nPosition = max(0, min (nPosition, MaxLines - 1)) ;
316:    SetScrollPos (hwnd, SB_VERT, nPosition, TRUE) ;
317:    InvalidateRect (hwnd, NULL, FALSE);
318: }
319: // -----------------------------------------
320: // Emerson Dialog
321: // -----------------------------------------
322:
323: /////////////////////////////////////////////
324: //   The Emerson Dialog Procedure
325: /////////////////////////////////////////////
326: #pragma argsused
327: BOOL CALLBACK _export AboutDlgProc(HWND hDlg, UINT Message,
328:                                    WPARAM wParam, LPARAM lParam)
329: {
330:    switch(Message)
331:    {
332:      case WM_INITDIALOG:
333:        return TRUE;
334:
335:      case WM_COMMAND:
336:        if (LOWORD(wParam) == IDOK ||
337           LOWORD(wParam) == IDCANCEL)
338:        {
339:          EndDialog(hDlg, IDOK);
340:          return TRUE;
341:        }
342:        break;
343:    }
344:    return FALSE;
345: }
```

Listing 7.2 shows the Emerson2 header file.

Type   Listing 7.2. EMERSON2.H.

```
 1: // ================================================
 2: // Name: EMERSON2.H
 3: // Programmer: Charlie Calvert
 4: // Description: Header file for EMERSON2.CPP
 5: // ================================================
 6: #define CM_ABOUT 101
 7: #define CM_DRAWBITMAPS 201
 8: #define CM_BRAHMIN 202
 9: #define CM_WOODNOTES 203
10: #define CM_SEASHORE 204
11:
12: // Macros
13: #define max(a,b)    (((a) > (b)) ? (a) : (b))
14: #define min(a,b)    (((a) < (b)) ? (a) : (b))
15:
16: // The Emerson Class
17: #define Emerson_DefProc     DefWindowProc
18: BOOL Emerson_OnCreate(HWND hwnd,
19:                       CREATESTRUCT FAR* lpCreateStruct);
20: void Emerson_OnDestroy(HWND hwnd);
21: void Emerson_OnCommand(HWND hwnd, int id,
22:                        HWND hwndCtl, UINT codeNotify);
23: void Emerson_OnKey(HWND hwnd, UINT vk, BOOL fDown, int cRepeat,
24:                    UINT flags);
24: void Emerson_OnPaint(HWND hwnd);
25: void Emerson_OnVScroll(HWND hwnd, HWND hwndCtl,
26:                        UINT code, int pos);
27:
28: // Variables
29: HBITMAP TheBitmap;
30:
31:
32: // Some Procs
33: BOOL Register(HINSTANCE hInstance);
34: BOOL Create(HINSTANCE hInstance, int nCmdShow);
35: LRESULT CALLBACK __export WndProc(HWND hWindow,
36:                 UINT Message, WPARAM wParam, LPARAM lParam);
37: BOOL CALLBACK _export AboutDlgProc(HWND hDlg, UINT Message,
38:                        WPARAM wParam, LPARAM lParam);
```

Listing 7.3 shows the Emerson2 resource file.

Type **Listing 7.3. EMERSON2.RC.**

```
 1: /* The Emerson2 RC file */
 2: #include <windows.h>
 3: #include "Emerson2.h"
 4:
 5: /* The Bitmap reference */
 6: Bitmap BITMAP "Bitmap.bmp"
 7:
 8: /*    The Emerson2 Menu      */
 9: MENU_1 MENU
10: BEGIN
11:    POPUP "Poems"
12:      BEGIN
13:        MENUITEM "Bitmaps", CM_DRAWBITMAPS
14:         MENUITEM "Brahmin", CM_BRAHMIN
15:        MENUITEM "Woodnotes", CM_WOODNOTES
16:        MENUITEM "SeaShore", CM_SEASHORE
17:      END
18:
19:    MENUITEM "&About", CM_ABOUT
20: END
21:
22:
23: /*    The About Dialog    */
24: About DIALOG 18, 18, 141, 58
25: STYLE DS_MODALFRAME | WS_POPUP | WS_CAPTION | WS_SYSMENU
26: CAPTION "About Dialog"
27: BEGIN
28:    PUSHBUTTON "Ok", IDOK, 5, 39, 132, 12,
29:                 WS_CHILD | WS_VISIBLE | WS_TABSTOP
30:    CTEXT "Emerson Example", -1, 1, 9, 140, 8,
31:                 WS_CHILD | WS_VISIBLE | WS_GROUP
32:    CTEXT "Copyright (c) World Community, Inc.",
33:          -1, 1, 23, 140, 10,
34:          WS_CHILD | WS_VISIBLE | WS_GROUP
35: END
36:
37: /*    The Emerson2 Icon    */
38: About ICON "Emerson2.ico"
39:
40: /*    The String Table    */
41: STRINGTABLE
42: BEGIN
43:      0, "Woodnotes (Part 1)"
44:      1, "by Ralph Waldo Emerson"
45:      2, ""
46:      3, "When the pine tosses its cones"
47:      4, "To the song of its waterfall tones,"
```

continues

Listing 7.3. continued

```
48:       5, "Who speeds to the woodland walks?"
49:       6, "To birds and trees who talks?"
50:       7, "Caesar of his leafy Rome,"
51:       8, "There the poet is at home."
52:       9, "He goes to the river-side,--"
53:      10, "Not hook nor line hath he;"
54:      11, "He stands in the meadows wide,--"
55:      12, "Nor gun nor scythe to see."
56:      13, "Sure some god his eye enchants:"
57:      14, "What he knows nobody wants,"
58:      15, "In the wood he travels glad,"
59:      16, "Without better fortune had,"
60:      17, "Melancholy without bad."
61:      18, "Knowledge this man prizes best"
62:      19, "Seems fantastic to the rest:"
63:      20, "Pondering shadows, colors, clouds,"
64:      21, "Grass-buds and caterpillar-shrouds,"
65:      22, "Boughs on which the wild bees settle,"
66:      23, "Tints that spot the violet's petal,"
67:      24, "Why nature loves the number five,"
68:      25, "And why the star-form she repeats:"
69:      26, "Lover of all things alive,"
70:      27, "Wonderer at all he meets,"
71:      28, "Wonderer chiefly at himself,"
72:      29, "Who can tell him what he is?"
73:      30, "Or how meet in human elf"
74:      31, "Coming and past eternities?"
75:      32, "Brahma"
76:      33, "by Ralph Waldo Emerson"
77:      34, ""
78:      35, "If the red slayer think he slays"
79:      36, "  Or if the slain think he is slain,"
80:      37, "They know not well the subtle ways"
81:      38, "  I keep and pass and turn again."
82:      39, ""
83:      40, "Far or forget to me is near;"
84:      41, "  Shadow and sunlight are the same;"
85:      42, "The vanished gods to me appear;"
86:      43, "  And one to me are shame and fame."
87:      44, ""
88:      45, "They reckon ill who leave me out"
89:      46, "  When me they fly, I am the wings;"
90:      47, "I am the doubter and the doubt,"
91:      48, "  And I the hymn the Brahmin sings."
92:      49, ""
93:      50, "The strong gods pine for my abode,"
94:      51, "  And pine in vain the sacred Seven;"
95:      52, "But thou, meek lover of the good!"
96:      53, "  Find me, and turn thy back on heaven."
97:      64, "SeaShore"
```

```
 98:       65, " by Ralph Waldo Emerson"
 99:       66, ""
100:       67, "I heard or seemed to hear the chiding Sea"
101:       68, "Say, Pilgrim, why so late and slow to come?"
102:       69, "Am I not always here, thy summer home?"
103:       70, "Is not my voice thy music, morn and eve?"
104:       71, "My breath thy healthful climate in the heats,"
105:       72, "My trouch thy antidote, my bay thy bath?"
106:       73, "Was ever couch magnificent as mine?"
107:       74, "Lie on the warm rock-ledges, and there learn"
108:       75, "A little hut suffices like a town."
109:       76, "I make your sculptured architecture vain,"
110:       77, "Vain beside mine. I drive my wedges home,"
111:       78, "And carve the coastwise mountain into caves."
112:       79, "Lo! here is Rome and Nineveh and Thebes,"
113:       80, "Karnak and Pyramid and Giant's Stairs"
114:       81, "Half piled or prostrate; and my newest slab"
115:       82, "Older than all thy race."
116:       83, ""
117:       84, "Behold the Sea,"
118:       85, "The opaline, the plentiful and strong,"
119:       86, "Yet beautiful as is the rose in June,"
120:       87, "Fresh as the trickling rainbow of July;"
121:       88, "Sea full of food, the nourisher of kinds,"
122:       89, "Purger of earth, and medicine of men;"
123:       90, "Creating a sweet climate by my breath,"
124:       91, "Washing out harms and griefs from memory,"
125:       92, "And, in my mathematic ebb and flow,"
126:       93, "Giving a hint of that which changes not."
127:       94, "Rich are the sea-gods: -- who gives gifts but they?"
128:       95, "They grope the sea for pearls, but more than pearls:"
129:       96, "They pluck Force thence, and give it to the wise."
130:       97, "For every wave is wealth to Daedalus,"
131:       98, "Wealth to the cunning artist who can work"
132:       99, "This matchless strength. Where shall he find, O waves!"
133:       100, "A load your Atlas shoulders cannot lift?"
134: END
```

BITMAP.BMP (64X64)   *EMERSON2.ICO (32X32)*

Listing 7.4 shows the Emerson2 module definition file.

Listing 7.4. **EMERSON2.DEF.**

```
1: ;   EMERSON2.DEF
2: NAME            Emerson2
3: DESCRIPTION     'Emerson2 example'
4: EXETYPE         WINDOWS
5: STUB            'WINSTUB.EXE'
6: CODE            PRELOAD MOVEABLE DISCARDABLE
7: DATA            PRELOAD MOVEABLE MULTIPLE
8: HEAPSIZE        4096
9: STACKSIZE       8192
```

Listing 7.5 shows the Borland makefile for Emerson2.

Listing 7.5. **EMERSON2.MAK (Borland).**

```
1: # EMERSON2.MAK
2:
3: APPNAME = Emerson2
4: INCPATH = C:\BC\INCLUDE
5: LIBPATH = C:\BC\LIB
6: CFLAGS = -H -ml -W -v -w4 -I$(INCPATH) -L$(LIBPATH)
7:
8: # linking
9: $(APPNAME).exe: $(APPNAME).Obj $(APPNAME).Def $(APPNAME).Res
10:    bcc $(CFLAGS) $(APPNAME).obj
11:    brc $(APPNAME).res
12:
13: # compiling
14: $(APPNAME).obj: $(APPNAME).cpp
15:    bcc -c $(CFLAGS) $(APPNAME).cpp
16:
17: # resource
18: $(APPNAME).res: $(APPNAME).rc
19:    brc -r -i$(APPNAME).rc
```

Listing 7.6 shows the Microsoft makefile for Emerson2.

 Listing 7.6. EMERSON2.MAK (Microsoft).

```
 1: #--------------------
 2: # EMERSON2.MAK for Microsoft
 3: #--------------------
 4:
 5: APPNAME = Emerson2
 6:
 7: #--------------------
 8: # linking
 9: #--------------------
10: $(APPNAME).exe : $(APPNAME).obj $(APPNAME).def $(APPNAME).res
11:    link /CO $(APPNAME), /align:16, NUL, /nod llibcew libw, $(APPNAME)
12:    rc $(APPNAME).res
13:
14: #--------------------
15: # compile
16: #--------------------
17: $(APPNAME).obj : $(APPNAME).cpp
18:    cl -c -AL -Gsw GA -Ow -W4 -Zp -Zi $(APPNAME).cpp
19:
20: #--------------------
21: # Compile
22: #--------------------
23: $(APPNAME).res: $(APPNAME).rc
24:    rc -r $(APPNAME).rc
```

Output
At start-up time, the background of the Emerson program consists of a single bitmap printed multiple times across the window, as shown in Figure 7.1. At the top of the program is a simple menu. If you select the About menu option, a dialog stating information about the program appears on the screen. The Options menu enables you to display either the bitmap pattern or one of three different poems by Ralph Waldo Emerson. When you minimize the Emerson program, it displays a custom icon.

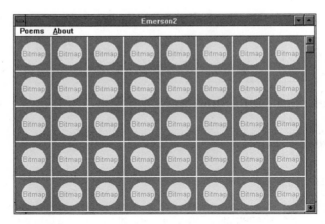

Figure 7.1. *EMERSON.EXE shown as it appears on-screen with its menu, dialog, and resource.*

What Am I Supposed to Do with All These Files?

You've probably noticed that the source code for the Emerson project has grown to include eight different files: EMERSON.CPP, EMERSON.BMP, EMERSON.H, EMERSON.RC, EMERSON.DEF, EMERSON.ICO, EMERSON.CUR, and EMERSON.MAK. Phew!

The idea that so many different files belong to a single project takes a little getting used to. The thing to do is to relax and take things one step at a time.

There is nothing unusual about making use of such a wide variety of files in a single Windows program. To help you get a grasp of this ragtag menagerie, I've made up a copy of an often-shown schematic diagram depicting the various files which make up a typical Windows executable file. This diagram is shown in Figure 7.2.

This picture, in and of itself, doesn't really convey much new information. Use it to help organize your thoughts. If you want, you can take a look at this diagram now, and then refer back to it later when you have a better feeling for the way Windows programming works.

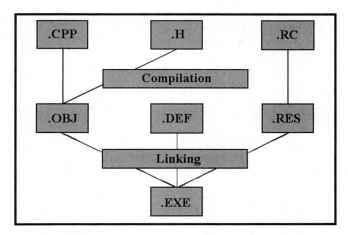

Figure 7.2. *A hierarchical diagram depicting the various portions of a Windows executable program.*

DO   **DON'T**

DO use abstractions to help organize your ideas. Think in terms of objects, structured programs, and modules. When you want to hold the whole ball of wax in your hand, think in terms of a project file or a makefile. The ability to handle abstract concepts is not a trivial gift. Take advantage of it!

Of course, you can switch back to the other mode when your boss, mother, husband, friend, and so on comes by to see what you're doing. Then, you can lay all the pieces out in front of them and let them *ooh* and *ahh* over your work. You don't have to tell them that it's really not as complex as it seems!

DON'T become overwhelmed by the mere presence of so many files. Much of the complexity is merely numerical, not technical. In other words, taken one at a time, none of the previous files are difficult to understand. However, if you try to hold all the balls up in the air at once, the task begins to seem a bit daunting. The solution is to divide and conquer! This isn't just a cliché, it's a slogan to live by!

Creating the Dialog

In the last chapter, you saw how to create the menu, icon, and cursor to be used with EMERSON2.CPP. The next step is to create the dialog, which is a considerably more complex operation. I'm going to spend several pages going over this material, because I feel that a good Windows programmer ought to have a thorough understanding of this process.

Using a dialog involves three steps:

1. Define the dialog in a resource file.

2. Create code to pop up the dialog on-screen.

3. Create a dialog procedure to handle the user's input while the dialog is running. You can think of a dialog procedure as being a window procedure for dialogs, although, in fact, they are distinct entities. When added to EMERSON2.RC, the definition of the dialog looks like this:

```
23: /*   The About Dialog    */
24: About DIALOG 18, 18, 141, 58
25: STYLE DS_MODALFRAME | WS_POPUP | WS_CAPTION | WS_SYSMENU
26: CAPTION "About Dialog"
27: BEGIN
28:    PUSHBUTTON "Ok", IDOK, 5, 39, 132, 12,
29:                WS_CHILD | WS_VISIBLE | WS_TABSTOP
30:    CTEXT "Emerson Example", -1, 1, 9, 140, 8,
31:                WS_CHILD | WS_VISIBLE | WS_GROUP
32:    CTEXT "Copyright (c) World Community, Inc.",
33:            -1, 1, 23, 140, 10,
34:            WS_CHILD | WS_VISIBLE | WS_GROUP
35: END
```

If you want to create the dialog using a visual tool, you should aim to create something that looks like the image seen in Figure 7.3. Remember that the About dialog is simply another resource added to EMERSON2.RC. You don't need to start another project in order to create the dialog. It can be part of the original resource file. If at any time you have trouble re-creating the image using visual tools, edit the dialog as text and copy in the preceding code exactly as it appears.

When examining the source code for the About dialog, you should note that the first line includes a name for the dialog, followed by the declaration of its type and its dimensions. The next line ORs together four constants defined in WINDOWS.H:

☐ DS_MODALFRAME: Creates a dialog box with a frame that works well with the WS_CAPTION and WS_SYSMENU styles.

☐ WS_POPUP: Microsoft defines the WS_POPUP style by saying it creates a pop-up window. In addition, you should understand that windows with the WS_POPUP style can roam all over the desktop, and may be owned by a window other than the desktop.

☐ WS_CAPTION: Creates a dialog that has a title bar across the top.

☐ WS_SYSMENU: Creates a dialog with the system menu icon in the upper-left corner of the caption bar.

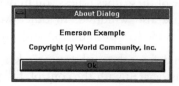

Figure 7.3. *The About dialog consists of a push button with an ID of 1 (IDOK) and two static text items.*

I discuss these constants in more depth in Chapter 14. For now, you can experiment with them by omitting one or more from the Emerson program's dialog, and by viewing the results on-screen.

Note: The About dialog runs in the *modal state*. To understand what this means, simply run the Emerson2 program, pop up the dialog, and then try to select the main window (or one of the menu items from the main window). You'll find that you can't do this, because the dialog now has a lock on the program's focus. This is typical modal behavior. The dialog is, in effect, telling the user: "Deal with me before you try to do anything else with this program." In other words, you must close this dialog before you can continue using the program.

The opposite of a modal dialog is the less commonly used *modeless* dialog. When a modeless dialog is on-screen, you can access its features and the features of the main program. You'll get a chance to work with these dialogs during Week 2, when you look at the WinSize program.

After the style of the About dialog is declared, the caption is defined:

```
CAPTION "About Dialog"
```

The caption appears in the title, or *caption bar*, at the top of the dialog. If you leave the caption statement out altogether, the bar will be blank. Of course, no text will appear if you don't use the WS_CAPTION style when defining the dialog.

The dialog definition ends with a few lines of code declared between a begin..end pair. These lines define the dialog's push button and its two lines of text. You won't be able to make sense of these lines unless you understand that the push button and both text controls are also windows. In other words, the dialog box has three subwindows placed inside it: a push button and two static controls:

☐ The line which defines the push button takes seven parameters. The first is the text to be associated with the control, followed by the control's ID, bounding rectangle, and style. The bounding rectangle is defined by four numbers. The first is the *X* position, the second the *Y* position, the third the control's *width*, and the fourth its *height*.

☐ Because the static controls containing the text are also windows, it should come as no surprise to hear that they take the same parameters as the pushbutton. By default, static controls have no border.

Note: It can take awhile to get comfortable with the idea that pushbuttons and static controls are windows. When first introduced to the Windows programming environment, I thought it got its name from the big windows on-screen in which programs ran. I was thinking, I suppose, of the Program Manager as one window and my compiler as a second window. It took me awhile to grasp that any one program can be made of multiple windows.

For instance, complex visual tools, such as the App Studio or Resource Workshop, might have 20, 30, or even more windows visible at one time. One lesson to be learned from this is that you shouldn't be afraid to add subwindows to your programs in order to make them easier to use. Creating a few windows on the desktop is not particularly expensive to the environment. If you need them, use them.

The menu in the EMERSON2.RC file uses a constant called CM_ABOUT, which is defined in EMERSON2.H. However, the IDOK identifier associated with the button in this dialog is defined in WINDOWS.H—which is included at the top of the RC file. The following excerpt from WINDOWS.H shows where IDOK is declared, and also features a series of related constants often associated with buttons in dialogs:

```
/* Standard dialog button IDs */
#define IDOK              1
#define IDCANCEL          2
#define IDABORT           3
#define IDRETRY           4
#define IDIGNORE          5
#define IDYES             6
#define IDNO              7
```

Note: Borland users should notice that both BRC and the Workshop already know about WINDOWS.H. As a result, they don't need to include WINDOWS.H at the top of the EMERSON.RC text file. Readers who are using other compilers, however, may not be able to compile the resource unless WINDOWS.H is included.

The only thing I need to add is that static text items are often given IDs of -1. This is done because static text items usually exist as inert objects on the desktop. Given the fact that there is rarely a need to communicate with them, there is also no need to have a unique ID which identifies them.

Popping Up a Dialog

Now that the dialog has been created, the next step is to pop it up on the desktop. This is another seemingly "magic" Windows programming process that involves a number of steps that might not be entirely intuitive to you at first.

I've broken down this discussion of popping up a dialog into three sections:

1. The first is the one you are currently reading. It gives a brief overview of the code which makes the dialog resources visible to a user.

2. The second section is a meditation on the MakeProcInstance function.

3. The third section describes the DialogBox and AboutDialogProc functions. The latter is similar to a WndProc, except that it is associated with a dialog instead of a window.

As I mentioned in the last chapter, when the user selects the About menu item, it sends a WM_COMMAND message to the program's window procedure. After the message crackers are through parsing the WndProcs parameters, the ID associated with the chosen menu item is sent to the About_OnCommand function:

```
void About_OnCommand(HWND hwnd, int id, HWND hwndCtl, UINT codeNotify)
{
  switch(id)
  {
    case CM_ABOUT:
    {
      FARPROC AboutBox = MakeProcInstance((FARPROC)AboutDlgProc,
                                          hInstance);
      DialogBox(hInstance, "ABOUT", hwnd, (DLGPROC)AboutBox);
      FreeProcInstance(AboutBox);
      break;

      case CM_DRAWBITMAPS:
      etc...
    }
  }
}
```

All the menu selections in a program are associated with WM_COMMAND messages. As a result, Cls_OnCommand can become a quite lengthy and complex function governed by a long and very hairy switch statement. In the bad old days before WINDOWSX, programmers would embed this long switch statement in the midst of the even longer switch statement comprising the body of a WndProc. What a mess!

By now, it should be clear that a CM_ABOUT identifier, attached to WM_COMMAND message, comes cruising down the pike every time the user selects the About menu item. The program responds to this message by popping up the About dialog. As you can see, the first step in popping up the dialog is to call MakeProcInstance. This subject is complex enough that I've decided to treat it in its own section.

All About *MakeProcInstance*

MakeProcInstance needs to be called so the function passed to it can have access to the data in your application. It does this by creating a small chunk of code that binds the program's data segment to the dialog procedure.

This is simple enough to say, but a bit more difficult to understand. In fact, the whole subject of what MakeProcInstance does can be a bit confusing. As a result, it might be helpful to start by telling a little allegorical (and somewhat whimsical) science fiction story.

I've mentioned before that Windows consists of a series of primitive objects. For just a moment, you might want to exercise your imagination by thinking of these objects as planetary systems in a far away galaxy. In this case, one planet, called Windows, is the head of a very big and powerful empire. The other planet, called Emerson, is a smaller and less powerful colony of the Windows empire.

Sometimes, it's necessary for Windows to send an emissary, or message carrier, to Emerson with an important message. When the message carrier gets to Emerson, he doesn't know anything about that planet's language or culture. As a result, there is a communication problem.

The solution is to call on the wise old hacker `MakeProcInstance`, known to his friends as Chief Handshake. Chief Handshake knows how to hack the Emerson `DataSegement`, which is in effect a computerized library full of cultural information about the planet Emerson. Handshake gives the emissary links to the `DataSegment`. It turns out that once the message carrier is linked to the `DataSegment`, he can overcome the cultural differences between the Windows empire and the Emerson colony. As a result, he is able to deliver his message in a way that can be understood.

The point of this peculiar little tale is that Windows and the Emerson program exist in two different areas of memory that need to be reconciled. This job is done by `MakeProcInstance`, which in effect tells where the Emerson program's data segment is located. When Windows calls the dialog procedure, it is possible for the dialog procedure to get access to the Emerson program's data segment, which in turn makes it possible for the two objects to communicate.

It might be helpful to take a look at this same issue from a slightly more technical perspective.

A dialog procedure is associated with the About dialog, just as a Windows procedure is associated with the main window. You know that window procedures are called by Windows itself. In other words, it isn't your program that calls `WndProc`; it's Windows. In the same way, the About dialog procedure is not called by your program; it's called by Windows.

The key fact to grasp is that the dialog procedure in effect "belongs" to Windows when being called by Windows. However, Windows and your program don't share the same data segment. Unless the `MakeProcInstance` function gives access to Emerson's data segment, the dialog procedure won't have access to the variables, functions, and constants associated with your program.

7

Because of the job it performs, you might want to think of MakeProcInstance as the Handshake procedure. The Handshake procedure creates a small snatch of prelude code for your program's dialog procedure. This prelude code acquaints Windows with your program's data segment. It introduces them, enabling them to shake hands and start talking.

Note: Programmers who have worked with Interrupt Service Routines (ISRs) are familiar with the phenomena previously described. DOS calls an ISR, but unless you take special precautions, the ISR won't have access to your program's data segment. To resolve this problem, programmers often hide the data segment of their program inside their program's code segment. Because the ISR also resides in your program's code segment, it's possible to retrieve the data segment and access your program's data. This isn't the same way Windows handles the problem, but the challenges involved are similar.

Before leaving this subject, it's worth pointing out that every call to MakeProcInstance needs to be balanced with a call to FreeProcInstance. The FreeProcInstance function frees the dialog procedure from the data segment and deallocates resources expended by MakeProcInstance.

The *DialogBox* and the *AboutDlgProc*

After the MakeProcInstance hand-shaking business is out of the way, the next step is to call DialogBox. This call is directly parallel to the CreateWindow procedure in a program's initialization. I'll extend this idea: you also can draw a very loose and entirely theoretical parallel between the RegisterClass function and the act of defining a dialog in an RC file.

A quick glance at the Emerson2 program's dialog procedure helps underline the very close analogy between the WndProc function and the AboutDlgProc:

```
327: BOOL CALLBACK _export AboutDlgProc(HWND hDlg, UINT Message,
328:                                     WPARAM wParam, LPARAM lParam)
329: {
330:    switch(Message)
331:    {
```

```
332:     case WM_INITDIALOG:
333:       return TRUE;
334:
335:     case WM_COMMAND:
336:       if (LOWORD(wParam) == IDOK ||
337:             LOWORD(wParam) == IDCANCEL)
338:       {
339:         EndDialog(hDlg, TRUE);
340:         return TRUE;
341:       }
342:       break;
343:   }
344:   return FALSE;
345: }
```

Both the WndProc and AboutDlgProc are never called directly by your program. Instead, they are both sent messages by the system, and they both use a switch statement to process these messages.

One of the important points to grasp is that the message loop associated with your main window is superseded by another loop (internal to Windows) during the life of the AboutDlgProc. In effect, what happens is that the code associated with your main window is in limbo while the About dialog runs. You can imagine a sort of dead space between the call to DialogBox and the call to FreeProcInstance; this decouples the dialog procedure from Windows:

```
DialogBox(hInstance, "ABOUT", hwnd, (DLGPROC)AboutBox);
// Dead Space, a void while another message loop runs //
FreeProcInstance(AboutBox);
```

As I mentioned earlier, the dialog procedures in this book don't use message crackers. As a result, the AboutDlgProc closely resembles an old-fashioned, pre-WINDOWSX WndProc, replete with a potentially endless switch statement.

Fortunately, the switch statement in the Emerson AboutDlgProc is very close to a minimal dialog procedure. Most of it consists of a response to IDOK or IDCANCEL messages. The IDOK messages sent to the dialog originate in the OK button, defined in the EMERSON2.RC file. IDCANCEL messages are sent when the user double-clicks the system menu icon (located in the upper-left corner of the dialog).

What you've seen is a rough sketch of the way dialogs are handled in a Windows program. There is, of course, more to the story than I've told here. As usual, however, I introduce you to the big themes, and then come back later and show you how the details are put together. This way, each chapter won't overwhelm you with a mass of information too complicated to absorb in one reading.

7

I know that even in this simplified overview, dialogs can still be a bit tricky to grasp. As a result, it might be helpful to take another quick look at the main points:

☐ First, define the dialog in a RC file, either by editing it as text, or by using a tool like the App Studio or Resource Workshop.

☐ Call MakeProcInstance in order to bind the program's data segment to the dialog procedure.

☐ Call DialogBox in order to create the dialog as a "physical entity" in the Windows environment.

☐ Respond to messages sent from Windows to the dialog's window procedure.

☐ Call FreeProcInstance in order to restore Windows to the state it was in before the call to MakeProcInstance.

This list can serve as a kind of guide, or recipe, for creating dialogs.

BMPs: An Aesthetic Interlude

The next resource to be explored is the bitmap shown in Figure 7.4. You can create this bitmap using the Windows Paintbrush program or any other tool which produces BMP files. You don't need to imitate the BMP exactly, although you'll probably want to make your image the same size, which is 64 pixels in width by 64 pixels in height. However, within those simple guidelines, you should feel free to either copy the previous resource as nearly as possible, or improvise any sort of design which strikes your fancy.

If you are editing the RC file as text, you only need to add a single line to the top of the EMERSON.RC file:

```
Bitmap BITMAP "Bitmap.bmp"
```

That's all you need to do to create a bitmap. Like creating icons, this is a very simple step from a purely intellectual perspective. From an aesthetic perspective, however, creating bitmaps can be very challenging. Many programmers wisely decide to hire outside talent to produce the artwork for their programs.

At any rate, when you have some kind of a bitmap sketched, you need to take the steps to show it on-screen. Like the act of creating a dialog, this can prove to be a bit tricky. As a result, I've put the description of the whole process in its own section.

Figure 7.4. *A suggested bitmap for use in the Emerson program.*

The Emerson Program Paints a Bitmap

The act of loading a bitmap into memory is very much like loading an icon, cursor, or custom resource. The following fragment of code from the Emerson_OnCreate function shows the whole process, including error checking:

```
133:    TheBitmap = LoadBitmap(hInstance, "Bitmap");
134:    if (!TheBitmap)
135:    {
136:      MessageBox(hwnd, "No Bitmap", "Fatal Error", MB_OK);
137:      return FALSE;
138:    }
```

The LoadBitmap API function needs two parameters. The first is the Instance of the executable file, or DLL, which contains the bitmap to be loaded. Remember that the hInstance variable is declared globally in the Emerson program. It assigns a value during the program's Create function. The second parameter to LoadBitmap is the name of the bitmap.

Because LoadBitmap might fail, it's important to check to see that the bitmap handle, declared in the EMERSON.H file, hasn't been set to zero. If the resource's handle is zero, Emerson_OnCreate returns FALSE, which causes the program to fail. If you want to see how this works, you can modify the second parameter to LoadBitmap, so that it reads Batmap (or something like that). In such a case, the bitmap won't be loaded, and the program will fail.

7

DO   **DON'T**

DO remember to call `LoadBitmap` before you try to use a bitmap in your program. Just including it in your RC file is not enough.

DON'T forget to balance every call to `LoadBitmap` with a call to `DeleteObject` or `DeleteBitmap`. In the Emerson program, the call to `DeleteBitmap` occurs in response to the `WM_DESTROY` message. `DeleteBitmap` is a type compatible WINDOWSX macro that encapsulates the functionality of `DeleteObject`.

After loading the bitmap, EMERSON2.CPP displays it multiple times in response to a `WM_PAINT` message:

```
247:    HDC BitmapDC = CreateCompatibleDC(PaintDC);
248:    HBITMAP OldBitmap = SelectBitmap(BitmapDC, TheBitmap);
249:    for (int i = 0; i < NumImages; i++)
250:      for (int j = 0; j < NumImages; j++)
251:        BitBlt(PaintDC, i * 66, j * 66, 64, 64,
252:               BitmapDC, 0, 0, SRCCOPY);
253:    SelectBitmap(BitmapDC, OldBitmap);
254:    DeleteDC(BitmapDC);
```

To see exactly what is going on here, I'll show you how the heart of this function would look if the bitmap were to be displayed only one time:

```
HDC BitmapDC = CreateCompatibleDC(PaintDC);
HBITMAP OldBitmap = SelectBitmap(BitmapDC, TheBitmap);
BitBlt(PaintDC, 0, 0, 64, 64, BitmapDC, 0, 0, SRCCOPY);
SelectBitmap(BitmapDC, OldBitmap);
DeleteDC(BitmapDC);
```

This code creates a second device context compatible with the window's device context. The bitmap to be displayed must first be selected into this second device context before it can be shown, or *blitted* to the screen. The screen itself, of course, is represented by a device context called `PaintDC`.

The `SelectObject` function "selects" an object into a given device context. `SelectObject` always returns the object that previously inhabited the device context. In this example, I copy `TheBitmap` into `BitmapDC`, and then carefully save the `OldBitmap` in a variable created specifically for that purpose. After the bitmap has been displayed, I carefully copy `OldBitmap` back into the device context and then delete the entire DC.

DO	**DON'T**

DO remember to copy the bitmap into its own, specially created device context.

DO remember to save the old bitmap in a variable.

DON'T forget to copy this old bitmap back into the device context.

It might be helpful to take another look at device contexts, first introduced in Chapter 4, "Messages, WINDOWSX, and Painting Text." I sometimes think of a device context as a pool of water with various objects suspended in it. Every object in the pool takes on a special look, appropriate to the context and resulting from the refractory properties of the water. Think of plunging your hand into a mountain lake. Because your hand is now being seen in a new context, it becomes larger and somehow distorted by the process.

Pretend there is only room for a certain number of objects in this pool. If you want to insert a new one, you must first remove an old one. When you are through, be sure to swap the old one back. It's important to the pond's ecology!

I'll be explicit about how this analogy works:

A bitmap copied into a device context for a standard VGA screen is seen in terms of a 640X480, 16-color VGA screen. This is different from the way it would look on a CGA screen. You see a bitmap in a new context when you copy it onto a VGA screen, just as your hand is seen in a new context when you plunge it into a pool of water.

When you call `SelectObject`, you are introducing a new element into the device context, that is, into the pool of water. Because there is only room for x number of items in the device context, one has to be removed before a new one can be copied in. When you are through with the new item, remove it, and then replace it with the original item.

Note: The act of copying items in and out of a device context is accomplished by the `SelectObject` function. WINDOWSX supplies type-compatible alternatives to `SelectObject` with names like `SelectBitmap` and `SelectPen`. If you use them, you avoid having to perform annoying typecasts. You should, however, feel free to use either call, depending on your tastes.

You are now ready to learn about the BitBlt function, pronounced "bit blit." BitBlt performs the chore of actually painting the bitmap on the screen.

I like to think of the name BitBlt as standing for "bit blast," because it quickly blasts the bitmap onto the screen. Authorities from Microsoft, however, state that it stands for *bit block transfer*. Regardless, the BitBlt function takes no less than nine parameters:

- ☐ The first parameter is a device context representing the screen (see the following explanation).

- ☐ The next four parameters define the place in the client window where the bitmap appears.

- ☐ The next parameter is a compatible device context holding an in-memory copy of the bitmap. This device context is what gets blasted onto the screen, or rather, into the device context which represents the screen.

- ☐ The next two parameters define the *X* and *Y* positions inside the original bitmap. In other words, if the original bitmap were 128 pixels-by-128 pixels in size, and you wanted to show only a section 64 pixels-by-64 pixels in size, you would use these parameters to specify where that 64-by-64 block begins.

- ☐ The final parameter defines the logical operation to be performed when the bitmap is transferred to the screen.

It turns out that there are at least 15 different operations that can be selected using the last parameter to BitBlt. Most of the time, you simply use SRCCOPY, which paints the bitmap on the screen, or other device context. In the next chapter, and in other places in this book, you'll see that other options are available:

BLACKNESS	Produces black output
DSTINVERT	Inverts the destination bitmap
MERGECOPY	Uses the AND operator to combine source and pattern
MERGEPAINT	Uses OR to combine the inverted source and destination
NOTSRCCOPY	Inverts source before copying it to its destination
NOTSRCERASE	Inverts the result of combining destination and source
PATCOPY	Copies the pattern to the destination bitmap

PATINVERT	Uses the XOR operator to combine source and pattern
PATPAINT	Uses OR to combine inverted source and pattern
SRCAND	Uses the AND operator to combine source and pattern
SRCCOPY	Copies the source bitmap to the destination bitmap
SRCERASE	Inverts destination and combines with source using AND
SRCINVERT	Uses XOR to combine source and destination
SRCPAINT	Uses OR to combine the destination and source
WHITENESS	Produces white output

If these options don't make much sense to you, don't sweat it. I'm supplying them mostly so hot graphics jockeys from the DOS world will see what a rich set of alternatives is available to Windows programmers.

Perhaps it will be helpful if I am frank here and state that the act of blitting bitmaps to the screen left me somewhat baffled when I first started writing Windows code. After all, the entire life cycle of a bitmap involves seven discreet steps:

1. Load the bitmap.
2. Create a compatible DC.
3. Select the bitmap into the DC.
4. BitBlt the compatible DC into the windows DC.
5. Select the old bitmap into the compatible DC.
6. Delete the compatible DC.
7. Delete the bitmap.

Furthermore, it's important that you understand that these seven steps aren't merely a "suggested course of action." In fact, a minor slip-up on even one of the seven steps outlined can set in motion a slow but sure process that will inevitably deplete Windows of the resources it needs to run. In particular, it's absolutely essential that you do not forget to call SelectObject or to delete a DC.

If you do fail to clean up after using a bitmap, the computer's *system resources* get depleted. When this happens, Windows starts to fall apart bit-by-bit, in a manner somewhat similar to the collapse of the computer HAL near the end of *2001: A Space*

Odyssey. In particular, you might notice that bitmaps lose their colors, menus or text disappear, and eventually the whole machine freezes up. To keep track of how many system resources you have available, you can view the About box visible in either the Program or File Manager.

Note: Somehow, I've gotten through this whole description of bitmaps without ever mentioning the Windows Graphics Device Interface (GDI). The *GDI* is a subset of Windows designed to handle graphics programming. All the GDI functions are contained in a special DLL called GDI.EXE. When you want to show a bitmap on-screen, use GDI functions, such as `BitBlt`. In fact, when you use a device context, you are using a GDI function. In the Windows world, GDI is the gateway to graphics. (Day 18, "GDI and Metafiles," features an in-depth look at the GDI.)

String Tables

String tables are one of the simplest of all resources to use. They are very valuable, because they are memory efficient. The key point to remember is that string resources are loaded into memory 16 items at a time. You can have a string resource containing hundreds of lines of text; but if you need access to only a subset of those items, the whole list of strings won't have to be loaded into memory at the same time.

To create a string resource, you can simply add a few lines of text to your RC file. Following is a complete definition of a string resource:

```
STRINGTABLE
BEGIN
  0, "Woodnotes (Part 1)"
  1, "by Ralph Waldo Emerson"
END
```

Each executable file can contain only one string table, so you don't need to give the string table a name. Instead, you can simply declare its type, and then directly define the strings themselves. The strings each are given a unique number, and all of them are encased inside a `begin..end` pair.

Because strings are loaded into memory 16 items at a time, you should begin each block of strings on appropriate boundaries. For instance, the first set of strings might reside between 0 and 15, or 0 and 31. The next set would start at number 16, 32, or 48.

Loading strings into memory is simple. All you need do is call LoadString. LoadString takes four parameters:

☐ The first is the hInstance of the executable file or DLL that contains the string resource.

☐ The second is the unique number associated with a string.

☐ The third parameter is a buffer to hold the contents of the string to be loaded.

☐ The fourth parameter designates the length of the string buffer used in the third parameter.

Note: Two asides should be mentioned in conjunction with the second and third parameters to LoadString.

1. You can declare constant identifiers to be used with the second parameter. For instance, I could have declared a constant called CM_WOODNOTES_TITLE, and set it equal to zero. Then, I could have used this identifier instead of the number zero to retrieve the poem's title.

2. It's usually not a good idea to declare an array to hold an in-memory copy of the contents of a string table. The whole point of string tables is to keep the strings out of memory and on disk whenever possible. Therefore, Emerson holds all the strings in only one small buffer, being sure to write each of them to the screen as soon as they are retrieved.

The scheme for displaying the poems from the Emerson program is encapsulated primarily in the WM_COMMAND and WM_PAINT functions. In responding to the first message, the Emerson program learns which poem the user wants to view. In responding to the second message, the user actually displays the appropriate strings on-screen.

Here is an excerpt from the Emerson_OnCommand function:

```
181:    case CM_BRAHMIN:
182:        Start = 32;
183:        MaxLines = 22;
184:        InvalidateRect(hwnd, NULL, TRUE);
185:        DrawBitmaps = FALSE;
186:        break;
```

7

If the user wants to see the Brahma poem, a CM_BRAHMIN identifier is attached to a WM_COMMAND message. In response, the Emerson program sets two integer variables to the beginning and ending offsets of the Brahma poem in the program's string table:

```
Start = 32;
MaxLines = 22;
```

The next step is to force Windows to send a WM_PAINT message to the Emerson program. This is done by calling the highly valuable InvalidateRect function.

The essence of handling the WM_PAINT message is simply to call LoadString to get hold of each string that needs to be displayed, and then to paint that string to the screen with TextOut. To do this, all Emerson need to do is enter a FOR loop that iterates from Start to (Start + Maxlines). The actual implementation, however, is complicated by the presence of scrollbars, as explained in the next section.

To summarize, a string table is a very simple, very powerful device that enables you to display huge chunks of text with only minimal costs, in terms of memory usage. Many programmers use string tables to store lists of error strings to be displayed by their programs.

Scrollbars

The Emerson program's scrollbars enable the user to scroll through a long poem that can't be shown completely in a single window.

To understand how Emerson's scrollbars work, you need to concentrate on the variable called nPosition. nPosition tells Emerson what line in a poem is currently at the top of the screen. For instance, if a poem is 50 lines long, and the user has scrolled the first 20 lines above the top of the screen, nPosition would be set to 20. If the first line of the poem is at the top of the screen, nPosition would be set to 0.

The value of nPosition is changed whenever the user presses an arrow key, or whenever the user clicks the scrollbar.

Adding scrollbars to a program is an easy, three-step process:

1. Create the Scrollbar by using the WS_VSCROLL style in the program's Create function:

```
HWND hwnd = CreateWindow(szAppName, szAppName,
                         WS_OVERLAPPEDWINDOW | WS_VSCROLL,
                         CW_USEDEFAULT, CW_USEDEFAULT,
                         CW_USEDEFAULT, CW_USEDEFAULT,
                         NULL, NULL, hInst, NULL);
```

2. Call `SetScrollRange` with the `SB_VERT` flag. The third and fourth parameters to this function designate the range over which the program will need to be able to scroll:

```
SetScrollRange(hwnd, SB_VERT, 0,
                    MaxLines - Start, FALSE);
```

3. The final step is to respond to `WM_VSCROLL` messages, which are sent whenever the user clicks the scrollbar.

Here is a greatly simplified `Emerson_OnVScroll` function:

```
void Emerson_OnVScroll(HWND hwnd, HWND hwndCtl, UINT code, int pos)
{
  switch(code)
  {
    case SB_LINEUP:
      if (nPosition > 0) nPosition -= 1 ;
      break ;

    case SB_LINEDOWN:
      if (nPosition < MaxLines) nPosition += 1 ;
      break ;

    case SB_THUMBPOSITION:
      nPosition = pos;
      break;
  }
  nPosition = max(0, min (nPosition, MaxLines)) ;
  SetScrollPos (hwnd, SB_VERT, nPosition, TRUE) ;
  InvalidateRect (hwnd, NULL, FALSE);
}
```

If the user clicks the arrow at the top of the scrollbar, an `SB_LINEUP` flag is sent along with a `WM_VSCROLL` message. In response, Emerson decrements `nPosition` by one, then sets the scroll box with a call to `SetScrollPos`. The scroll box is the little square "thumb" shown in Figure 7.5. The final step is to call `InvalidateRect`, so the poem on-screen is repositioned to reflect the user's request.

These same basic steps are repeated, with some minor variations, if the user clicks the arrow at the bottom of the scrollbar (`SB_LINEDOWN`), or if the user drags the thumb with the mouse (`SB_THUMBPOSITION`). The result is that the scrollbar enables you to give the user some control over a program's output.

7

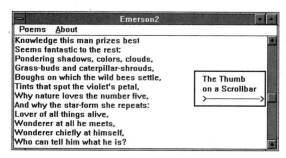

Figure 7.5. *The "thumb" on a scrollbar.*

Note: In response to WM_VSCROLL messages, Emerson calls InvalidateRect. In doing so, it passes FALSE in the third parameter, which designates whether or not to repaint the main window's surface. Had it passed TRUE, the entire screen would have been repainted every time the user clicked the scrollbar. This results in an ugly blinking pattern on-screen, which is annoying to the user and humiliating to the programmer.

To avoid this, the Emerson program goes through a number of elaborate convolutions in response to a WM_PAINT message. These gymnastics ensure that only a reasonably small portion of the screen gets repainted after a call to Emerson_OnVScroll. Therefore, the poem scrolls up and down smoothly and quickly enough to satisfy most users. An excellent alternative to the method I use here is provided by the ScrollWindow function.

The code I've provided paints a series of rectangles over the old text (so the old text doesn't appear when the poem scrolls). To make this work, I try to ensure that each rectangle is reasonably small. Because the Rectangle function, by default, uses a black pen to draw the outline of a rectangle, I needed to replace this pen with a NULL pen:

```
HPEN APen = CreatePen(PS_NULL, 0, 0);
HPEN SavePen = SelectPen(PaintDC, APen);


// Draw the text and block out old text with rectangles.

SelectPen(PaintDC, SavePen);
DeleteObject(APen);
```

Whenever the user clicks the scrollbar, a WM_VSCROLL message gets sent to the main window. But what happens when the user presses the up arrow or down arrow?

Well, the Emerson program can respond easily enough to this kind of input simply by handling WM_KEYDOWN messages. A press of the down arrow, for instance, results in a WM_KEYDOWN message with the VK_DOWN flag set. Emerson responds to this keypress by creating its own WM_VSCROLL message:

```
221:     case VK_DOWN:
222:        SendMessage(hwnd, WM_VSCROLL, SB_LINEDOWN, 0L);
223:        break;
```

The SendMessage function recalls the WndProc, this time with a WM_VSCROLL message accompanied by the SB_LINEDOWN flag. Now the program can handle this message exactly as it would handle a mouse click on the down arrow portion of the scrollbar!

The only thing left to say about using scrollbars is that the TextHeight variables need to be set to a specific value when the main window gets a WM_CREATE message:

```
140:    HDC PaintDC = GetDC(hwnd);
141:    GetTextMetrics(PaintDC, &TextMetrics);
142:    ReleaseDC(hwnd, PaintDC);
143:    TextHeight = TextMetrics.tmHeight +
144:                     TextMetrics.tmExternalLeading;
```

This code begins by calling GetDC to get the device context to the main window. The HDC is needed in the call to GetTextMetrics, which retrieves a struct of type TEXTMETRIC containing information about the main window's default font. Two fields of the TEXTMETRIC struct are used to calculate the height of the font used to display the poem. This height is used when calculating where to display each line of text on-screen in the WM_PAINT method. Specifically, it's used to calculate *Y*, which is passed as the third parameter to TextOut.

Okay. That wraps up the discussion of scrollbars and brings you to the end of this chapter. This is also the end of the discussion of the Emerson program (which has occupied us for two chapters).

Summary

Day 7 has introduced you to dialogs, bitmaps, string tables, and scrollbars. In particular, you learned about

- ☐ Creating dialogs with resource scripts

- ☐ Using the MakeProcInstance function to bind the program's data segment to a dialog procedure

- ☐ Calling `DialogBox` to create a dialog

- ☐ Calling `FreeProcInstance` to detach a program's data segment from a dialog procedure

- ☐ Creating bitmaps

- ☐ Copying bitmaps into a compatible device context

- ☐ Blasting the bitmap from one device context onto another so it can be seen on-screen

- ☐ Preserving the original state of a device context and freeing bitmaps from memory

- ☐ Creating string tables

- ☐ Loading and reading string tables

- ☐ Managing string table resources

- ☐ Creating scrollbars with the `WS_VSCROLL` style

- ☐ Responding to `WM_VSCROLL` messages

Remember that this chapter contains only an introduction to dialogs and bitmaps. Both subjects are covered again in several different places throughout this book. In particular, in Chapter 16, "Advanced Dialogs: Getting and Setting Data," there is an in-depth discussion of dialog boxes. In Chapter 18, "GDI and Metafiles," there is an in-depth treatment of bitmaps.

Though you've had a fairly complete introduction to resources, I discuss this subject again in Chapter 17, "Menus and Icons in Depth." There, you'll get a chance to review certain advanced aspects of this large subject.

Once again, my goal is to introduce you to the basics of a topic before exploring it again during a second pass. If I hit you with everything at once, you might be overwhelmed. Analogies: a student gets introduced to James Joyce's *Ulysses* and a *Dick and Jane* book on the same day or learns geometry and calculus at the same time. My goal is to take one step at a time.

Q&A

1. **Q:** I still don't understand the relationship between the GDI and bitmaps. Can you go over that again?

   A: The people who created Windows tried to think in terms of discreet modules, or "objects." Eventually, it became clear that almost everything related to graphics needed to be treated in its own discreet category—which programmers called the Graphics Device Interface (GDI). More specifically, all calls that use a device context are by definition part of the GDI. If you look in your ..Windows\System subdirectory, you'll find a file called GDI.EXE. This DLL contains all the calls that are part of the Graphics Device Interface.

2. **Q:** Tell me more about dialogs.

   A: Dialogs are used either to display information, as in the About dialog box in this program, or to get information from the user. Many programs contain dialog boxes that pop up just long enough to get the user's name, or to ask the user to select one of several different choices. Most of these latter kinds of dialogs are modal, because the program often needs the user's input before it can continue. For instance, when you save a piece of source code, a dialog box is displayed to enable you to enter the name of the file where your source will be saved. This is usually a modal dialog box, because the program can't proceed until you specify a name or cancel the outline procedure. *Modal* dialogs are created by calls to `DialogBox`, whereas *Modeless* dialogs are created by calls to `CreateDialog`.

Workshop

The Workshop provides quiz questions to help you solidify your understanding of the material covered and exercises to provide you with experience in using what you've learned. Try to understand the quiz and exercise answers before continuing on to the next chapter. Answers are provided in Appendix A.

Quiz

1. What function is used to launch a modal dialog?

2. Trick question: What messages are sent to the program's main window when

3. What message is sent to the WndProc when a menu item is chosen?

4. Every call to MakeProcInstance must be balanced by a call to _____?

5. Every call to LoadBitmap must be balanced by a call to _____?

6. If you have strings stored in a string table, how do you retrieve them so the program can display them on-screen.

7. What message gets sent when a user clicks the scrollbar?

8. What is the TEXTMETRIC structure and where is it defined?

9. When you click the OK button in the About dialog, what message is generated and where is it sent?

10. What does the Emerson program have to call MakeProcInstance?

Exercises

1. The Emerson program creates a default background by repainting a single bitmap 15 times in the *X* and *Y* directions. Optimize the program so that it only paints the minimum number of bitmaps needed to fill the main window, regardless of how large or small the user makes the program.

2. Add a scrollbar to the Emerson program that handles horizontal scrolling.

The following program, called SysInfo, brings together many of the ideas discussed during Week 1. SysInfo displays information about the current state of the GDI heap, the USER heap, and the Global Heap.

This is the first version of a program that will be expanded a little bit at the end of each week. Eventually, you'll end up with a program that can tell you a considerable amount about the state of your system in terms of the internal memory managed by Windows. This program will run under Windows 3.1, but not under Windows NT.

Listing R1.1 shows the SysInfo source file.

Type   Listing **R1.1. SYSINFO.CPP.**

```
1: /////////////////////////////////////////////////
2: //   Program Name: SYSINFO.CPP
3: //   Programmer: Charlie Calvert
4: //   Description: What I did on my system's vacation
5: //   Date: 08/09/93
6: /////////////////////////////////////////////////
7:
8: #define STRICT
9: #include <windows.h>
10: #include <windowsx.h>
11: #include <toolhelp.h>
12: #include <stdio.h>
13: #include <string.h>
14: #include "SysInfo.h"
15:
16: #pragma warning (disable: 4068)
17: #pragma warning (disable: 4100)
18:
19: // ----------------------------------------
20: // Interface
21: // ----------------------------------------
22:
23: static char szAppName[] = "SysInfo";
24: static HWND MainWindow;
25: static HINSTANCE hInstance;
26:
27: // ----------------------------------------
28: // Initialization
29: // ----------------------------------------
30:
31: /////////////////////////////////////////////
32: // Program entry point
33: /////////////////////////////////////////////
34: #pragma argsused
35: int PASCAL WinMain(HINSTANCE hInst, HINSTANCE hPrevInstance,
36:                    LPSTR  lpszCmdParam, int nCmdShow)
37: {
38:   MSG  Msg;
39:
```

```
40:   if (!hPrevInstance)
41:     if (!Register(hInst))
42:       return FALSE;
43:
44:   MainWindow = Create(hInst, nCmdShow);
45:   if (MainWindow)
46:      return FALSE;
47:   while (GetMessage(&Msg, NULL, 0, 0))
48:   {
49:      TranslateMessage(&Msg);
50:      DispatchMessage(&Msg);
51:   }
52:
53:   return Msg.wParam;
54: }
55:
56: ////////////////////////////////////////////
57: // Register the window
58: ////////////////////////////////////////////
59: BOOL Register(HINSTANCE hInst)
60: {
61:   WNDCLASS WndClass;
62:
63:   WndClass.style          = CS_HREDRAW | CS_VREDRAW;
64:   WndClass.lpfnWndProc    = WndProc;
65:   WndClass.cbClsExtra     = 0;
66:   WndClass.cbWndExtra     = 0;
67:   WndClass.hInstance      = hInst;
68:   WndClass.hIcon          = LoadIcon(NULL, IDI_APPLICATION);
69:   WndClass.hCursor        = LoadCursor(NULL, IDC_ARROW);
70:   WndClass.hbrBackground  = GetStockBrush(WHITE_BRUSH);
71:   WndClass.lpszMenuName   = "MENU_1";
72:   WndClass.lpszClassName  = szAppName;
73:
74:   return RegisterClass (&WndClass);
75: }
76:
77: ////////////////////////////////////////////
78: // Create the window
79: ////////////////////////////////////////////
80: HWND Create(HINSTANCE hInst, int nCmdShow)
81: {
```

continues

Listing R1.1. continued

```
82:    hInstance = hInst;
83:
84:    HWND hWindow = CreateWindow(szAppName, szAppName,
85:                        WS_OVERLAPPEDWINDOW,
86:                        CW_USEDEFAULT, CW_USEDEFAULT,
87:                        CW_USEDEFAULT, CW_USEDEFAULT,
88:                        NULL, NULL, hInstance, NULL);
89:
90:    if (hWindow == NULL)
91:      return hWindow;
92:
93:    ShowWindow(hWindow, nCmdShow);
94:    UpdateWindow(hWindow);
95:
96:    return hWindow;
97: }
98:
99: // -------------------------------------
100: // WndProc and Implementation
101: // -------------------------------------
102:
103: ////////////////////////////////////////
104: // The Window Procedure
105: ////////////////////////////////////////
106: LRESULT CALLBACK _export WndProc(HWND hWindow, UINT Message,
107:                                  WPARAM wParam, LPARAM lParam)
108: {
109:    switch(Message)
110:    {
111:      HANDLE_MSG(hWindow, WM_DESTROY, SysInfo_OnDestroy);
112:      HANDLE_MSG(hWindow, WM_COMMAND, SysInfo_OnCommand);
113:      HANDLE_MSG(hWindow, WM_PAINT, SysInfo_OnPaint);
114:      default:
115:        return SysInfo_DefProc(hWindow, Message,
116:                               wParam, lParam);
116:    }
117: }
118:
119: ////////////////////////////////////////
120: // Handle WM_DESTROY
121: ////////////////////////////////////////
```

```
122: #pragma argsused
123: void SysInfo_OnDestroy(HWND hwnd)
124: {
125:   PostQuitMessage(0);
126: }
127:
128: #pragma argsused
129: void SysInfo_OnCommand(HWND hwnd, int id,
130:                        HWND hwndCtl, UINT codeNotify)
131: {
132:   switch(id)
133:   {
134:     case CM_ABOUT:
135:       FARPROC AboutBox =
136:         MakeProcInstance((FARPROC)AboutDlgProc, hInstance);
137:       DialogBox(hInstance, "About", hwnd, (DLGPROC)AboutBox);
138:       FreeProcInstance(AboutBox);
139:       break;
140:   }
141: }
142:
143: //////////////////////////////////////////
144: // Handle WM_PAINT
145: //////////////////////////////////////////
146: void SysInfo_OnPaint(HWND hwnd)
147: {
148:   HDC PaintDC;
149:   PAINTSTRUCT PaintStruct;
150:   SYSHEAPINFO Info;
151:   char S[100];
152:
153:   Info.dwSize = sizeof(SYSHEAPINFO);
154:   SystemHeapInfo(&Info);
155:   DWORD FreeSpace = GetFreeSpace(0) / 1024;
156:
157:   PaintDC = BeginPaint(hwnd, &PaintStruct);
158:   sprintf(S, "Percent free in the USER heap: %d",
159:           Info.wUserFreePercent);
160:   TextOut(PaintDC, 10, 10, S, strlen(S));
161:   sprintf(S, "Percent free in the GDI heap: %d",
162:           Info.wGDIFreePercent);
163:   TextOut(PaintDC, 10, 35, S, strlen(S));
```

continues

Listing R1.1. continued

```
164:    sprintf(S, "Kilobytes free on Global heap: %ld", FreeSpace);
165:    TextOut(PaintDC, 10, 60, S, strlen(S));
166:    EndPaint(hwnd, &PaintStruct);
167: }
168:
169: // ---------------------------------------------
170: // SysInfo Dialog
171: // ---------------------------------------------
172:
173: /////////////////////////////////////////////////
174: //   The SysInfo Dialog Procedure
175: /////////////////////////////////////////////////
176: #pragma argsused
177: BOOL CALLBACK AboutDlgProc(HWND hDlg, WORD Message,
178:                              WPARAM wParam, LPARAM lParam)
179: {
180:    switch(Message)
181:    {
182:      case WM_INITDIALOG:
183:        return TRUE;
184:
185:      case WM_COMMAND:
186:        if (wParam == IDOK ¦¦ wParam == IDCANCEL)
187:        {
188:          EndDialog(hDlg, TRUE);
189:          return TRUE;
180:        }
181:        break;
182:    }
183:    return FALSE;
184: }
```

Listing R1.2 shows the SYSINFO header file.

 Listing R1.2. The SYSINFO.H.

```
1: /////////////////////////////////////////////////
2: //  Program Name: SYSINFO.H
```

```
 3: //  Programmer: Charlie Calvert
 4: //  Description: What I did on my system's vacation
 5: //  Date: 08/09/93
 6: /////////////////////////////////////////////////
 7:
 8: #define CM_ABOUT 101
 9:
10: // Declarations for class SysInfo
11: #define SysInfo_DefProc      DefWindowProc
12: void SysInfo_OnDestroy(HWND hwnd);
13: void SysInfo_OnCommand(HWND hwnd, int id,
14:                         HWND hwndCtl, UINT codeNotify);
15: void SysInfo_OnPaint(HWND hwnd);
16:
17: // Funcs
18: BOOL Register(HINSTANCE hInst);
19: HWND Create(HINSTANCE hInst, int nCmdShow);
20: LRESULT CALLBACK _export WndProc(HWND hWindow, UINT Message,
21:                                  WPARAM wParam, LPARAM lParam);
22: BOOL CALLBACK AboutDlgProc(HWND hDlg, WORD Message,
23:                            WPARAM wParam, LPARAM lParam);
```

Listing R1.3 shows the SYSINFO resource file.

Type   **Listing R1.3. SYSINFO.RC.**

```
 1: /////////////////////////////////////////////////
 2: //  Module Name: SYSINFO.RC
 3: //  Programmer: Charlie Calvert
 4: //  Description: Resource File
 5: //  Date: 08/09/93
 6: /////////////////////////////////////////////////
 7:
 8: #include <windows.h>
 9: #include "SysInfo.h"
10:
11: MENU_1 MENU
12: BEGIN
```

continues

Listing R1.3. continued

```
13:    MENUITEM "About", CM_ABOUT
14: END
15:
16: About DIALOG 18, 18, 141, 58
17: STYLE DS_MODALFRAME ¦ WS_POPUP ¦ WS_CAPTION ¦ WS_SYSMENU
18: CAPTION "About Dialog"
19: BEGIN
20:    CTEXT "What I Did on My System's Vacation",
21:           -1, 1, 9, 140, 8, WS_CHILD ¦ WS_VISIBLE ¦ WS_GROUP
22:    CTEXT "Copyright (c) Hackers Delight, Inc.",
23:           -1, 1, 23, 140, 10, WS_CHILD ¦ WS_VISIBLE ¦ WS_GROUP
24:    PUSHBUTTON "Ok", IDOK, 5, 39, 132, 12,
25:           WS_CHILD ¦ WS_VISIBLE ¦ WS_TABSTOP
26: END
```

Listing R1.4 shows the definition file for SysInfo.

Listing R1.4. SYSINFO.DEF.

```
 1: ;SysInfo.Def
 2:
 3: NAME        SysInfo
 4: DESCRIPTION 'SysInfo Vacation (c) 1993 by Charles Calvert'
 5: EXETYPE     WINDOWS
 6: STUB        'WINSTUB.EXE'
 7: CODE        PRELOAD MOVEABLE DISCARDABLE
 8: DATA        PRELOAD MOVEABLE MULTIPLE
 9:
10: HEAPSIZE    4096
11: STACKSIZE   5120
```

Listing R1.5 shows the Borland SYSINFO makefile.

Listing R1.5. SYSINFO.MAK (Borland).

```
 1: # SYSINFO.MAK
 2:
```

```
 3: # macros
 4: APPNAME = SysInfo
 5: INCPATH = C:\BC\INCLUDE
 6: LIBPATH = C:\BC\LIB
 7: FLAGS = -ml -W -v -w4 -I$(INCPATH) -L(LIBPATH)
 8:
 9: # link
10: $(APPNAME).exe: $(APPNAME).obj $(APPNAME).def $(APPNAME).res
11:    bcc $(FLAGS) $(APPNAME).obj
12:    brc $(APPNAME).res
13:
14: # compile
15: $(APPNAME).obj: $(APPNAME).cpp
16:    bcc -c $(FLAGS) $(APPNAME).cpp
17:
18:$(APPNAME).res: $(APPNAME).rc
19:   brc -r -I$(INCPATH) $(APPNAME).rc
```

Listing R1.6 shows the Microsoft SYSINFO makefile.

Type   Listing R1.6. **SYSINFO.MAK (Microsoft).**

```
 1: # SYSINFO.MAK for Microsoft
 2:
 3: APPNAME = SysInfo
 4: LIBS = llibcew libw toolhelp
 5:
 6: # linking
 7: $(APPNAME).exe : $(APPNAME).obj $(APPNAME).def $(APPNAME).res
 8:    link $(APPNAME), /align:16, NUL, /nod $(LIBS), $(APPNAME)
 9:    rc $(APPNAME).res
10:
11:
12: # compile
13: $(APPNAME).obj : $(APPNAME).cpp
14:    cl -AL -c -Gsw -Ow -W4 -Zp  $(APPNAME).cpp
15:
16:
17: # Compile
```

continues

Listing R1.6. continued

```
18: $(APPNAME).res: $(APPNAME).rc
19:  rc -r $(APPNAME).rc
```

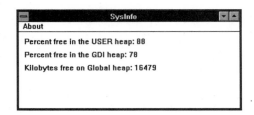

Figure R1.1. *The SysInfo program shows the state of the User, GDI and Global heap.*

As with all the programs in this book, SysInfo should be compiled in the large memory model. The SysInfo program has a main window that contains some text that describes system memory and a dialog that tells the user about the program. It responds directly to WM_DESTROY, WM_COMMAND, and WM_PAINT messages. The resource for the file contains only a simple dialog and menu. The menu sends a WM_ABOUT message to SysInfo_OnCommand, which responds by popping up the dialog.

The code that pops up the dialog, shown on lines 136-138, calls MakeProcInstance to set up the memory for the dialog procedure, then calls DialogBox to create the dialog, and finally frees the allocated memory associated with the dialog box by calling FreeProcInstance. This is a little three step dance that Windows programs perform on a regular basis.

At the very bottom of the program you can see the dialog procedure itself, which is an example of the minimal effort needed to effectively handle a dialog. All it really does is respond to IDOK and IDCANCEL messages by shutting down the dialog with a call to EndDialog (line 177):

```
BOOL CALLBACK AboutDlgProc(HWND hDlg, WORD Message,
                           WPARAM wParam, LPARAM lParam)
{
  switch(Message)
  {
    case WM_INITDIALOG:
```

```
        return TRUE;

    case WM_COMMAND:
      if (wParam == IDOK || wParam == IDCANCEL)
      {
        EndDialog(hDlg, TRUE);
        return TRUE;
      }
      break;
  }
  return FALSE;
}
```

The other significant portion of the program is the response to WM_PAINT (line 153):

```
Info.dwSize = sizeof(SYSHEAPINFO);
SystemHeapInfo(&Info);
DWORD FreeSpace = GetFreeSpace(0) / 1024;


PaintDC = BeginPaint(hwnd, &PaintStruct);
sprintf(S, "Percent free in the USER heap: %d",
        Info.wUserFreePercent);
TextOut(PaintDC, 10, 10, S, strlen(S));
sprintf(S, "Percent free in the GDI heap: %d",
        Info.wGDIFreePercent);
TextOut(PaintDC, 10, 35, S, strlen(S));
sprintf(S, "Kilobytes free on Global heap: %ld", FreeSpace);
TextOut(PaintDC, 10, 60, S, strlen(S));
EndPaint(hwnd, &PaintStruct);
```

The basic structure of this message function handler should be familiar to you by now. The code first calls BeginPaint in order to retrieve a valid device context, and then uses TextOut to paint the text to the screen. When the function is done, it cleans up by making a call to EndPaint.

The unfamiliar code in SysInfo_OnPaint involves calls to SystemheapInfo and GetFreeSpace.

Of these two functions, the latter is the simpler to understand. It is a standard Windows API call that retrieves information about the amount of free space available on the heap. On many systems, the number you see in this space is likely to be very large, so the program makes it a bit more comprehensible by dividing it by 1,024. This lets SysInfo report on the number of kilobytes available, rather than the number of bytes.

The SystemHeapInfo function is part of the ToolHelp DLL that ships with Windows 3.1. This useful function retrieves information about the local heap associated with USER.EXE and GDI.EXE. Like ToolHelp itself, User and GDI are both DLLs that ship with Windows. They contain many routines that you call throughout the life of a Windows program. For instance, all the GDI routines (such as BitBlt or TextOut) are found in GDI.EXE. (If this doesn't make complete sense yet, don't worry. The whole subject comes up again when you read Chapter 20, which focuses on DLLs.)

You can use SysInfo whenever you are working with GDI functions. If you see the numbers associated with the GDI heap going down little by little, and never coming back up, you know you have a memory leak and need to recheck your code. In other words, the SysInfo program can be used to help you debug your code.

In fact, the ToolHelp DLL is designed to be an aid to programmers who want to get a peek beneath the surface of the Windows environment. This collection of functions is explored further in the next two versions of this program. For now, all you need to know is that ToolHelp contains many routines that can be used to explore the state of the system's internal memory structures. You can use it to see how your program is interacting with Windows.

That's all there is to say about SYSINFO.CPP. It's a relatively straightforward Windows program that performs a very useful function.

One week ago, code like this might have looked utterly unfamiliar to you. Now it should be starting to make some sense and taking on the appearance of an old friend. Congratulations—you are on your way to becoming a real Windows programmer! This is no small accomplishment. Give yourself a pat on the back and then get back in there and start hacking!

2

The major goal of the first week was to help you feel comfortable with writing standard Windows programs and to show you the power at your fingertips by exposing you to resources. Now that you have your sea legs, it's time to set sail and start exploring Windows in earnest.

Where You're Going

Week Two focuses on window controls, fonts, and window classes. The programs you produce will become increasing powerful—and increasingly complex.

The first additions to be added to your toolkit are fonts. This turns out to be a surprisingly large subject. Fonts give you a thorough introduction to some of the impressive data structures, which are free for the asking in the Windows operating environment. As you explore the LOGFONT and TEXTMETRIC structures, you'll learn that Windows is a storehouse of information about the capabilities of the system on which it is running.

Sometimes the information that the operating system can send to a program comes in the form of a long list of complex data structures. To make this whole process manageable, Windows enables you to set up special functions, named *callbacks*, designed specifically to process lists of data. Callbacks are surrounded by an almost magical aura, and mastering them is one of the fine arts of Windows programming.

After you start learning how to mine the available resources, you can find some way to present them to the user. This is where window controls enter the scene.

Window controls form the interface between the user and a program's data. When the user needs to utilize a program's capabilities, he or she does so with window controls. When a programmer wants to display information to the user, the tool of choice is a window control.

Your exposure to window controls comes replete with an advanced course in the Windows messaging system. When programmers want to communicate with a control, such as a list box or a combo, they do so by sending a message to the control. Conversely, when the user manipulates a control, a program finds out about this action by sampling the messages that are sent to its window procedure or procedures.

By the time you begin to master Windows formidable array of data structures, callbacks, and controls, you'll be well into the thick of the fray. To help you manage the multiplicity of available options, the designers of Windows have supplied you with a wide array of easy to use WINDOWSX macros. Present in WINDOWSX is a purity of logic and a nicety of design that can help you comprehend and deftly overcome the challenges you face.

The last chapter in Week Two loops back to take a second look at the process of launching a window (as originally explained during Week 1). This second pass over the subject allows you to peer deep beneath the surface of a Windows program so that you can learn how to fine-tune its appearance and behavior. As you learn to manipulate the various elements of the WNDCLASS structure, you should feel that you're finally taking control of the environment in which you program.

Good programmers have an insatiable curiosity about the tools with which they work—and about the operating system in the midst of which they labor. People who have caught fire, who really want to learn, will find that Week 2 is loaded with valuable information and eye-opening tips. So gird your loins, tighten your suspenders, trim your sails, or do whatever it is you do when you are getting ready for some serious work. Week 2 is a cornucopia of knowledge—be prepared to have some fun (especially on Day 8, when you are introduced to the Snake program). When finished, you can move on to Week 3, where you will find the really good material about multimedia and graphics.

A First Look
at Snako

Now that you have made a few voyages across the deep space separating DOS from the world of Windows programming, you deserve to relax for a bit with the first cut of a Windows program called Snake. The Snake program is a graphics-oriented take on a famous game that's been available since before PCs existed.

The code seen here reappears in a different guise in Chapter 21, "Snako for Windows." There, it is developed into something that might appeal to the rich palette of today's gamers.

This chapter is a review of Week 1 and a reward for all your hard work. I also introduce a few new concepts. In particular, you will learn about

- Creating and using timers
- Creating child windows
- Animation
- XORing bitmaps to the screen
- Dividing code into modules

This material can be approached in a more relaxed manner than some of the other material you've seen and will see in this book. However, many concepts, notably child windows and modularization, are very important. Getting some extra experience with bitmaps also should stand you in good stead. So, be prepared to have some fun, to review some old ideas, and to pick up a few new ones. Let's go!

The Promised Bonus Program

This first version of the Snake program, called Snake1, is designed to excite the imagination of people who enjoy games. My goal is to provide you with a functioning set of tools from which you can design your own game. At the same time, I want to give you a toy that is at least somewhat interesting in and of itself.

Hopefully, the potential of the Snake1 program will incite you to get involved in a little hands-on programming. Lots of improvements can be made to this program, and no one's better suited to implement them than yourself. If this code intrigues you, play around with it some. Add a few features; make a few optimizations. There is no better way to learn how to program than to get plenty of hands-on experience!

Note: The fact that games are entertaining doesn't make them trivial from a programmer's point of view. In fact, the best games are constructed by top-notch technicians whose techniques are studied by programmers at places such as NASA. Game programming includes a lot of cutting-edge technology and requires extremely refined skills.

I'll start by showing you the source so you can get the first version of Snake up and running. (See Listing 8.1.) Remember, the point of this exercise is not only to teach you something new, but also to let you flex your newly found muscle by hiking across some already familiar portions of the Windows programming landscape.

 Listing 8.1. The Snake1 program lets you have some fun while getting experience working with bitmaps and timers.

```
 1: // ==========================================================
 2: // Program Name: SNAKE1.CPP
 3: // Programmer: Charlie Calvert
 4: // Description: Game with bitmaps, key handling and timer
 5: // ==========================================================
 6:
 7: #define STRICT
 8: #include <windows.h>
 9: #include <windowsx.h>
10: #pragma hdrstop
11: #include <stdlib.h>
12: #pragma warning (disable : 4100)
13: #pragma warning (disable : 4068)
14: #include "snake1.h"
15: #include "grunt.h"
16:
17: // statics
18: static char szAppName[] = "Snake";
19: static char szGameName[] = "GameWindow";
20: static HWND MainWindow;
21: static HWND hGameWindow;
22:
23: // Shared variables
24: int Size = 32;
25: int StartCol;
26: int StartRow;
27: int MaxCols;
28: int MaxRows;
29: div_t NumXSects, NumYSects;
30:
```

continues

Listing 8.1. continued

```
31: // Variables
32: HINSTANCE hInstance;
33: HBITMAP Head, Body, OneHundred;
34:
35: //-------------------------------------------------------
36: // Setup
37: //-------------------------------------------------------
38:
39: //////////////////////////////////////////////
40: // WinMain
41: //////////////////////////////////////////////
42: #pragma argsused
43: int PASCAL WinMain(HINSTANCE hInst, HINSTANCE hPrevInstance,
44:                    LPSTR  lpszCmdParam, int nCmdShow)
45: {
46:   MSG  Msg;
47:
48:   if (!hPrevInstance)
49:     if (!Register(hInst))
50:       return FALSE;
51:
52:   if (!(MainWindow = Create(hInst, nCmdShow)))
53:     return FALSE;
54:
55:   while (GetMessage(&Msg, NULL, 0, 0))
56:   {
57:     TranslateMessage(&Msg);
58:     DispatchMessage(&Msg);
59:   }
60:   return Msg.wParam;
61: }
62:
63: //////////////////////////////////////////////
64: // Save hInstance, Create window, Show window maximized
65: //////////////////////////////////////////////
66: HWND Create(HINSTANCE hInst, int nCmdShow)
67: {
68:   hInstance = hInst;
69:
70:   HWND hWindow = CreateWindow(szAppName,
71:                              "A Snake and its Tail",
72:                              WS_OVERLAPPEDWINDOW,
73:                              CW_USEDEFAULT, CW_USEDEFAULT,
74:                              CW_USEDEFAULT, CW_USEDEFAULT,
75:                              NULL, NULL, hInst, NULL);
76:
77:   if (hWindow == NULL)
78:     return hWindow;
79:
```

```
80:    nCmdShow = SW_SHOWMAXIMIZED;
81:
82:    ShowWindow(hWindow, nCmdShow);
83:    UpdateWindow(hWindow);
84:
85:    return hWindow;
86: }
87:
88: ////////////////////////////////////////
89: // Register window
90: ////////////////////////////////////////
91: ATOM Register(HINSTANCE hInst)
92: {
93:    WNDCLASS WndClass;
94:
95:    WndClass.style          = CS_HREDRAW | CS_VREDRAW;
96:    WndClass.lpfnWndProc    = WndProc;
97:    WndClass.cbClsExtra     = 0;
98:    WndClass.cbWndExtra     = 0;
99:    WndClass.hInstance      = hInst;
100:   WndClass.hIcon          = LoadIcon(NULL, IDI_APPLICATION);
101:   WndClass.hCursor        = LoadCursor(NULL, IDC_ARROW);
102:   WndClass.hbrBackground  = GetStockBrush(GRAY_BRUSH);
103:   WndClass.lpszMenuName   = NULL;
104:   WndClass.lpszClassName  = szAppName;
105:
106:   RegisterClass (&WndClass);
107:
108:   WndClass.style          = CS_HREDRAW | CS_VREDRAW;
109:   WndClass.lpfnWndProc    = GameWndProc;
110:   WndClass.hIcon          = 0;
111:   WndClass.hCursor        = LoadCursor(NULL, IDC_ARROW);
112:   WndClass.hbrBackground  = GetStockBrush(WHITE_BRUSH);
113:   WndClass.lpszClassName  = szGameName;
114:
115:   return RegisterClass (&WndClass);
116: }
117:
118: //---------------------------------------
119: // The Implementation
120: //---------------------------------------
121:
122: ////////////////////////////////////////
123: // WndProc
124: ////////////////////////////////////////
125: LRESULT CALLBACK __export WndProc(HWND hWindow, UINT Message,
126:                                   WPARAM wParam, LPARAM lParam)
127: {
128:    switch(Message)
129:    {
```

continues

Listing 8.1. continued

```
130:      HANDLE_MSG(hWindow, WM_CREATE, Snake_OnCreate);
131:      HANDLE_MSG(hWindow, WM_DESTROY, Snake_OnDestroy);
132:    default:
133:       return Snake_DefProc(hWindow, Message, wParam,lParam);
134:    }
135: }
136:
137: /////////////////////////////////////////
138: // WM_CREATE
139: /////////////////////////////////////////
140: #pragma argsused
141: BOOL Snake_OnCreate(HWND hwnd, CREATESTRUCT FAR*
142: lpCreateStruct)
143: {
144:   Head = LoadBitmap(hInstance, "Head");
145:   if (!Head)
146:   {
147:     MessageBox(hwnd, "No head", "Fatal Error", MB_OK);
148:     return FALSE;
149:   }
150:
151:   Body = LoadBitmap(hInstance, "Body");
152:   if (!Body)
153:   {
154:     MessageBox(hwnd, "No body", "Fatal Error", MB_OK);
155:     return FALSE;
156:   }
157:
158:   OneHundred = LoadBitmap(hInstance, "Hundred");
159:   if (!OneHundred)
160:   {
161:     MessageBox(hwnd, "No OneHundred", "Fatal Error", MB_OK);
162:     return FALSE;
163:   }
164:
165:   int CXFull = GetSystemMetrics(SM_CXSCREEN);
166:   NumXSects = div(CXFull, Size);
167:   MaxCols = (NumXSects.quot - 1) * Size;
168:   int BordWidth = CXFull - MaxCols;
169:   div_t StartC = div(BordWidth, 2);
170:   StartCol = StartC.quot;
171:
172:   int CYFull = GetSystemMetrics(SM_CYFULLSCREEN);
173:   NumYSects = div(CYFull, Size);
174:   MaxRows = (NumYSects.quot - 1) * Size;
175:   BordWidth = CYFull - MaxRows;
176:   StartC = div(BordWidth, 2);
177:   StartRow = StartC.quot;
178:
```

```
179:
180:    hGameWindow = CreateWindow("GameWindow", "A",
181:                        WS_CHILD | WS_VISIBLE,
182:                        StartCol, BORDERSIZE, MaxCols, MaxRows,
183:                        hwnd, NULL, hInstance, NULL);
184:
185:    return TRUE;
186: }
187:
188: ///////////////////////////////////////
189: // WM_DESTROY
190: ///////////////////////////////////////
191: #pragma argsused
192: void Snake_OnDestroy(HWND hWindow)
193: {
194:    if (Head) DeleteObject(Head);
195:    if (Body) DeleteObject(Body);
196:    if (OneHundred) DeleteObject(OneHundred);
197:    PostQuitMessage(0);
198: }
```

Listing 8.2 shows the Snake1 header file.

 Listing 8.2. SNAKE1.H.

```
1: ///////////////////////////////////////
2: // Module Name: Snake1.h
3: // Programmer: Charlie Calvert
4: // Description: Header file with procs
5: ///////////////////////////////////////
6:
7: // Class Snake
8: #define Snake_DefProc      DefWindowProc
9: BOOL Snake_OnCreate(HWND hWindow, CREATESTRUCT FAR* lpCreateStruct);
10: void Snake_OnDestroy(HWND hWindow);
11:
12:
13: // Procs
14: HWND Create(HINSTANCE hInst, int nCmdShow);
15: ATOM Register(HINSTANCE hInst);
16: BOOL SetUpWindow(HWND hWindow);
17: LRESULT CALLBACK __export WndProc(HWND, UINT,
18:                                      WPARAM, LPARAM);
```

Listing 8.3 shows the Grunt source code.

Listing 8.3. GRUNT.CPP.

```
 1: // ============================================================
 2: // Module Name: GRUNT.CPP
 3: // Programmer: Charlie Calvert
 4: // Description: Do the grunt work of moving the snake
 5: // ============================================================
 6:
 7: #define STRICT
 8: #include <windowsx.h>
 9: #define hdrstop
10: #include <string.h>
11: #include <stdlib.h>
12: #include "grunt.h"
13: #pragma warning (disable : 4100)
14: #pragma warning (disable : 4068)
15:
16: // local variables
17: BOOL NewSect;
18: static int VK_p = 112;
19: static int SnakeTimer = 1;
20: static long TotalClicks = 0;
21: static int Sections;
22: static int NumPrizes;
23: static TPrize Prizes[MAXPRIZES];
24: static TSectInfo SectInfo[MAXSECTIONS];
25: TTurn TurnList[25];
26: int NumTurns;
27:
28: // Global variables
29: extern div_t NumXSects;
30: extern div_t NumYSects;
31: extern int Size;
32: extern int MaxCols;
33: extern int MaxRows;
34: extern HBITMAP Head, Body, OneHundred;
35:
36: ///////////////////////////////////////////
37: // GameWndProc
38: ///////////////////////////////////////////
39: LRESULT CALLBACK __export GameWndProc(HWND hWindow, UINT Message,
40:                                         WPARAM wParam, LPARAM lParam)
41: {
42:   switch(Message)
43:   {
44:     HANDLE_MSG(hWindow, WM_CREATE, Game_OnCreate);
45:     HANDLE_MSG(hWindow, WM_CHAR, Game_OnChar);
46:     HANDLE_MSG(hWindow, WM_KEYDOWN, Game_OnKey);
47:     HANDLE_MSG(hWindow, WM_PAINT, Game_OnPaint);
48:     HANDLE_MSG(hWindow, WM_TIMER, Game_OnTimer);
49:     default:
```

```
50:          return Game_DefProc(hWindow, Message, wParam,lParam);
51:    }
52: }
53:
54: //////////////////////////////////////
55: // WM_CREATE
56: //////////////////////////////////////
57: #pragma argsused
58: BOOL Game_OnCreate(HWND hwnd, CREATESTRUCT FAR* lpCreateStruct)
59: {
60:    if (!SetTimer(hwnd, SnakeTimer, 125, NULL))
61:    {
62:      MessageBox(hwnd, "No Timers Available", "Snake Info", MB_OK);
63:      return FALSE;
64:    }
65:
66:    NumPrizes = 0;
67:    InitializeSections();
68:
69:    return TRUE;
70: }
71:
72: //////////////////////////////////////
73: // WM_DESTROY
74: //////////////////////////////////////
75: void Game_OnDestroy(HWND hWindow)
76: {
77:    KillTimer(hWindow, SnakeTimer);
78: }
79:
80: //////////////////////////////////////
81: // WM_CHAR
82: //////////////////////////////////////
83: #pragma argsused
84: void Game_OnChar(HWND hWindow, UINT ch, int cRepeat)
85: {
86:    if (ch == VK_p)
87:      KillTimer(hWindow, SnakeTimer);
88: }
89:
90: //////////////////////////////////////
91: // WM_KEYDOWN
92: //////////////////////////////////////
93: #pragma argsused
94: void Game_OnKey(HWND hWindow, UINT vk,
95:                 BOOL fDown, int cRepeat, UINT flags)
96: {
97:    switch(vk)
98:    {
99:      case VK_DOWN: GetOldDir(Down); break;
```

continues

Listing 8.3. continued

```
100:     case VK_UP: GetOldDir(Up); break;
101:     case VK_LEFT: GetOldDir(Left); break;
102:     case VK_RIGHT: GetOldDir(Right); break;
103:   }
104:   MoveBitmap(hWindow);
105: }
106:
107: /////////////////////////////////////////
108: // WM_PAINT
109: /////////////////////////////////////////
110: void Game_OnPaint(HWND hWindow)
111: {
112:   PAINTSTRUCT PaintStruct;
113:
114:   HDC DC = BeginPaint(hWindow, &PaintStruct);
115:
116:   HDC PicDC = CreateCompatibleDC(DC);
117:
118:   // Draw Head
119:   HBITMAP OldBmp = SelectBitmap(PicDC, Head);
120:   BitBlt(DC, SectInfo[0].Col, SectInfo[0].Row,
121:           Size, Size, PicDC, 0, 0, SRCINVERT);
122:   SelectObject(PicDC, OldBmp);
123:
124:   // Draw Body
125:   OldBmp = SelectBitmap(PicDC, Body);
126:   for (int i = 1; i <= Sections; i++)
127:     BitBlt(DC, SectInfo[i].Col, SectInfo[i].Row,
128:             Size, Size, PicDC, 0, 0, SRCINVERT);
129:
130:   SelectObject(PicDC, OldBmp);
131:   DeleteDC(PicDC);
132:
133:   EndPaint(hWindow, &PaintStruct);
134:
135:   SectInfo[0].DirChange = FALSE;
136: }
137:
138: /////////////////////////////////////////
139: // WM_TIMER
140: /////////////////////////////////////////
141: #pragma argsused
142: void Game_OnTimer(HWND hwnd, UINT id)
143: {
144:   HBITMAP SaveBmp;
145:
146:   SetFocus(hwnd);
147:
148:   if (id == SnakeTimer)
149:   {
```

```
150:        MoveBitmap(hwnd);
151:        TotalClicks++;
152:
153:        if ((TotalClicks % 10) == 0)
154:        {
155:          SetSections();
156:          SetPrizes();
157:
158:          HDC PaintDC = GetDC(hwnd);
159:          HDC PicDC = CreateCompatibleDC(PaintDC);
160:
161:          NewSect = TRUE;
162:
163:          // Paint new prize
164:          SaveBmp = SelectBitmap(PicDC, OneHundred);
165:          BitBlt(PaintDC, Prizes[NumPrizes].Col,
166:            Prizes[NumPrizes].Row, 32, 32, PicDC, 0, 0, SRCINVERT);
167:          SelectObject(PicDC, SaveBmp);
168:
169:          DeleteDC(PicDC);
170:          ReleaseDC(hwnd, PaintDC);
171:      }
172:    }
173: }
174:
175: //-------------------------------------
176: // The Implementation
177: //-------------------------------------
178:
179: /////////////////////////////////////////
180: // Called by MoveBitmap
181: // Keeps track of internal Col and Row
182: // for each section of snake
183: /////////////////////////////////////////
184: void SetColRow(void)
185: {
186:   int i;
187:
188:   for (i = 0; i <= Sections; i++)
189:   {
190:     SectInfo[i].OldCol = SectInfo[i].Col;
191:     SectInfo[i].OldRow = SectInfo[i].Row;
192:
193:     switch(SectInfo[i].Dir)
194:     {
195:       case Up: SectInfo[i].Row -= Size; break;
196:       case Down: SectInfo[i].Row += Size; break;
197:       case Left: SectInfo[i].Col -= Size; break;
198:       case Right: SectInfo[i].Col += Size; break;
199:     }
```

continues

Listing 8.3. continued

```
200:    }
201:
202:    for (i = Sections; i > 0; i—)
203:    {
204:      if (SectInfo[i - 1].DirChange)
205:      {
206:        SectInfo[i].DirChange = TRUE;
207:        SectInfo[i].Dir = SectInfo[i - 1].Dir;
208:        SectInfo[i - 1].DirChange = FALSE;
209:      }
210:    }
211: }
212:
213: //////////////////////////////////////
214: // Called by MoveBitmap
215: // Keeps track of which section of
216: // snake will turn next
217: //////////////////////////////////////
218: void SetNewTurnSection(void)
219: {
220:    for (int i = 1; i <= Sections; i++)
221:    {
222:      if (TurnList[NumTurns].SectChangeDir[i] == TRUE)
223:      break;
224:    }
225:    TurnList[NumTurns].SectChangeDir[i] = FALSE;
226:    i++;
227:    TurnList[NumTurns].SectChangeDir[i] = TRUE;
228: }
229:
230: //////////////////////////////////////
231: // Make a noise and set constants
232: // when a collision occurs
233: //////////////////////////////////////
234: void Boom(HWND hwnd)
235: {
236:    memset(SectInfo, 0, sizeof(SectInfo));
237:    Sections = 0;
238:    NumPrizes = 0;
239:    for (int i = 0; i < 10; i++)
240:      MessageBeep(-1);
241:    InitializeSections();
242:    InvalidateRect(hwnd, NULL, TRUE);
243: }
244:
245: //////////////////////////////////////
246: // Erase prizes
247: //////////////////////////////////////
248: void WhiteOut(HWND hwnd, int i)
249: {
```

```
250:    HDC PaintDC = GetDC(hwnd);
251:    HDC MemDC = CreateCompatibleDC(PaintDC);
252:
253:    HBITMAP SaveBmp = SelectBitmap(MemDC, OneHundred);
254:    BitBlt(PaintDC, Prizes[i].Col,
255:           Prizes[i].Row, 32, 32, MemDC, 0, 0, SRCINVERT);
256:    SelectObject(MemDC, SaveBmp);
257:
258:    DeleteDC(MemDC);
259:    ReleaseDC(hwnd, PaintDC);
260: }
261:
262: /////////////////////////////////////
263: //
264: /////////////////////////////////////
265: void CheckForCollision(HWND hwnd)
266: {
267:
268:    if (SectInfo[0].Col < 0) Boom(hwnd);
269:    if (SectInfo[0].Row < 0) Boom(hwnd);
270:    if (SectInfo[0].Col + Size > MaxCols) Boom(hwnd);
271:    if (SectInfo[0].Row + Size > MaxRows) Boom(hwnd);
272:
273:    // See if Snake hit his own tail
274:    for (int i = 1; i <= Sections; i++)
275:      if (SectInfo[i].Col == SectInfo[0].Col &&
276:          SectInfo[i].Row == SectInfo[0].Row)
277:        Boom(hwnd);
278:
279:    // Erase a prize when he hits it
280:    for (i = 0; i <= NumPrizes; i++)
281:    {
282:      if (Prizes[i].Exists)
283:      {
284:        if ( ((SectInfo[0].Row >= Prizes[i].Row) &&
285:             (SectInfo[0].Row <= Prizes[i].Row + (Size - 1))) &&
286:           ((SectInfo[0].Col >= Prizes[i].Col) &&
287:             (SectInfo[0].Col <= Prizes[i].Col + (Size - 1))) )
288:        {
289:          Prizes[i].Exists = FALSE;
290:          WhiteOut(hwnd, i);
291:        }
292:      }
293:    }
294: }
295:
296: /////////////////////////////////////
297: // Init procedure at start of game
298: /////////////////////////////////////
299: void InitializeSections()
300: {
```

continues

255

Listing 8.3. continued

```
301:    int i, StartCol, StartRow;
302:
303:    Sections = 5;
304:    StartCol = Size * 3;
305:    StartRow = Size * 3;
306:
307:    for (i = 0; i <= Sections; i++)
308:    {
309:      SectInfo[i].Dir = Right;
310:      SectInfo[i].DirChange = FALSE;
311:      SectInfo[i].Col = StartCol - (Size * i);
312:      SectInfo[i].Row = StartRow;
313:      SectInfo[i].OldCol = SectInfo[i].Col;
314:      SectInfo[i].OldRow = SectInfo[i].Row;
315:    }
316:    NewSect = FALSE;
317: }
318:
319: ////////////////////////////////////////
320: //
321: ////////////////////////////////////////
322: void GetOldDir(TDir NewDir)
323: {
324:    TurnList[NumTurns].Dir = NewDir;
325:    TurnList[NumTurns].SectChangeDir[1] = TRUE;
326:
327:    SectInfo[0].OldDir = SectInfo[0].Dir;
328:    SectInfo[0].Dir = NewDir;
329:    SectInfo[0].DirChange = TRUE;
330:    TurnList[0].TurnCol = SectInfo[0].Col;
331:    TurnList[0].TurnRow = SectInfo[0].Row;
332: }
333:
334: ////////////////////////////////////////
335: // Draw the Snake
336: ////////////////////////////////////////
337: void MoveBitmap(HWND hwnd)
338: {
339:    SetColRow();
340:
341:    HDC DC = GetDC(hwnd);
342:    HDC PicDC = CreateCompatibleDC(DC);
343:
344:    CheckForCollision(hwnd);
345:
346:    // Paint head
347:    HBITMAP OldBmp = SelectBitmap(PicDC, Head);
348:    BitBlt(DC, SectInfo[0].OldCol, SectInfo[0].OldRow,
349:           Size, Size, PicDC, 0, 0, SRCINVERT);
```

```
350:    BitBlt(DC, SectInfo[0].Col, SectInfo[0].Row,
351:           Size, Size, PicDC, 0, 0, SRCINVERT);
352:    SelectObject(PicDC, OldBmp);
353:
354:    // Paint body
355:    OldBmp = SelectBitmap(PicDC, Body);
356:    BitBlt(DC, SectInfo[1].Col, SectInfo[1].Row,
357:           Size, Size, PicDC, 0, 0, SRCINVERT);
358:    BitBlt(DC, SectInfo[Sections].Col, SectInfo[Sections].Row,
359:           Size, Size, PicDC, 0, 0, SRCINVERT);
360:
361:    // If he grew
362:    if (NewSect)
363:    {
364:      BitBlt(DC, SectInfo[Sections].Col, SectInfo[Sections].Row,
365:             Size, Size, PicDC, 0, 0, SRCINVERT);
366:      NewSect = FALSE;
367:    }
368:
369:    SelectObject(PicDC, OldBmp);
370:
371:    SectInfo[0].DirChange = FALSE;
372:
373:    DeleteDC(PicDC);
374:    ReleaseDC(hwnd, DC);
375:
376:    SetNewTurnSection();
377: }
378:
379: ///////////////////////////////////////
380: //
381: ///////////////////////////////////////
382: void SetPrizes(void)
383: {
384:    NumPrizes++;
385:
386:    Prizes[NumPrizes].Exists = TRUE;
387:    Prizes[NumPrizes].Row = (rand() % NumYSects.quot) * Size;
388:    Prizes[NumPrizes].Col = (rand() % NumXSects.quot) * Size;
389: }
390:
391: ///////////////////////////////////////
392: //
393: ///////////////////////////////////////
394: void SetSections(void)
395: {
396:    Sections++;
397:
398:    SectInfo[Sections].Dir = SectInfo[Sections - 1].Dir;
399:    SectInfo[Sections].DirChange = FALSE;
```

continues

257

Listing 8.3. continued

```
400:
401:   switch (SectInfo[Sections].Dir)
402:   {
403:     case Left:
404:     {
405:       SectInfo[Sections].Col = SectInfo[Sections - 1].Col + Size;
406:       SectInfo[Sections].Row = SectInfo[Sections - 1].Row;
407:       break;
408:     }
409:
410:     case Right:
411:     {
412:       SectInfo[Sections].Col = SectInfo[Sections - 1].Col - Size;
413:       SectInfo[Sections].Row = SectInfo[Sections - 1].Row;
414:       break;
415:     }
416:
417:     case Up:
418:     {
419:       SectInfo[Sections].Col = SectInfo[Sections - 1].Col;
420:       SectInfo[Sections].Row = SectInfo[Sections - 1].Row + Size;
421:       break;
422:     }
423:
424:     case Down:
425:     {
426:       SectInfo[Sections].Col = SectInfo[Sections - 1].Col;
427:       SectInfo[Sections].Row = SectInfo[Sections - 1].Row - Size;
428:       break;
429:     }
430:   } // end switch
431: }
432:       SectInfo[Sections].OldCol = SectInfo[Sections - 1].Col;
433:       SectInfo[Sections].OldRow = SectInfo[Sections - 1].Row;
```

Listing 8.4 shows the Grunt header file.

Type   **Listing 8.4. GRUNT.H.**

```
1: ////////////////////////////////////////////
2: // Module Name: GRUNT.H
3: // Programmer: Charlie Calvert
4: // Description: Do the work of moving the snake
5: ////////////////////////////////////////////
6: #include <windows.h>
7: #include <windowsx.h>
8:
```

```
 9: #define BORDERSIZE 15
10: #define MAXSECTIONS 1024
11: #define MAXPRIZES 512
12:
13: // Type definitions
14: enum TDir {Left, Right, Up, Down};
15:
16: struct TSectInfo
17: {
18:   BOOL DirChange;
19:   TDir Dir, OldDir;
20:   int SecNum;
21:   int Row, Col;
22:   int OldRow, OldCol;
23: };
24:
25: struct TTurn
26: {
27:   TDir Dir;
28:   BOOL SectChangeDir[256];
29:   int TurnCol, TurnRow;
30: };
31:
32: struct TPrize
33: {
34:   BOOL Exists;
35:   int Value;
36:   int Col, Row;
37: };
38:
39:
40: // Class Game
41: #define Game_DefProc      DefWindowProc
42: BOOL Game_OnCreate(HWND hWindow,
43:                     CREATESTRUCT FAR* lpCreateStruct);
44: void Game_OnDestroy(HWND hWindow);
45: void Game_OnChar(HWND hWindow, UINT ch, int cRepeat);
46: void Game_OnKey(HWND hWindow, UINT vk,
47:                 BOOL fDown, int cRepeat, UINT flags);
48: void Game_OnPaint(HWND hWindow);
49: void Game_OnTimer(HWND hWindow, UINT id);
50:
51: // Procs
52: LRESULT CALLBACK __export GameWndProc(HWND, UINT,
53:                                       WPARAM, LPARAM);
54: void InitializeSections();
55: void GetOldDir(TDir NewDir);
56: void MoveBitmap(HWND hWindow);
57: void SetSections(void);
58: void SetPrizes(void);
```

Listing 8.5 lists the Snake1 resource file.

 Listing 8.5. SNAKE1.RC.

```
1: // SNAKE1.RC
2: Body    BITMAP "body.bmp"
3: Head    BITMAP "head.bmp"
4: Hundred BITMAP "hundred.bmp"
```

BODY.BMP (32x32)   *HEAD.BMP (32x32)*   *HUNDRED.BMP (32x32)*

Listing 8.6 shows the Snake1 definition file.

 Listing 8.6. SNAKE1.DEF.

```
1: ; SNAKE1.DEF
2: NAME        SNAKE1
3: DESCRIPTION    'Snake1'
4: EXETYPE        Windows
5: STUB        'WINSTUB.EXE'
6: CODE        PRELOAD MOVEABLE DISCARDABLE
7: DATA        PRELOAD MOVEABLE MULTIPLE
8: HEAPSIZE  4096
9: STACKSIZE 5120
```

Listing 8.7 shows the Snake1 makefile for Borland compilers.

 Listing 8.7. SNAKE1.MAK (Borland).

```
1: # SNAKE1.MAK
2:
3: APPNAME = Snake1
4: INCPATH = C:\BC\INCLUDE
5: LIBPATH = C:\BC\LIB
6: FLAGS = -H -ml -W -v -w4 -I$(INCPATH) -L$(LIBPATH)
```

```
 7:
 8: # linking
 9: $(APPNAME).exe: $(APPNAME).obj Grunt.obj $(APPNAME).def
     $(APPNAME).res
10: bcc $(FLAGS) $(APPNAME).obj GRUNT.OBJ
11: brc $(APPNAME).res
12:
13: # compiling
14: $(APPNAME).obj: $(APPNAME).cpp
15:   bcc -c $(FLAGS) $(APPNAME).cpp
16:
17: # compiling
18: GRUNT.OBJ: GRUNT.CPP
19:   bcc -c $(FLAGS) GRUNT.CPP
20:
21: # resource
22: $(APPNAME).res: $(APPNAME).rc
23:   brc -r -i$(INCPATH) $(APPNAME).rc
```

Listing 8.8 shows the Snake1 makefile for Microsoft compilers.

Type   **Listing 8.8. SNAKE1.MAK (Microsoft).**

```
 1: # SNAKE1.MAK
 2:
 3: APPNAME = Snake1
 4:
 5: # linking
 6: $(APPNAME).exe : $(APPNAME).obj GRUNT.OBJ $(APPNAME).def
 7:   link $(APPNAME) Grunt, /align:16, NUL, /nod slibcew libw,
          $(APPNAME)
 8:
 9:   rc $(APPNAME)
10:
11: # compiling
12: $(APPNAME).obj : $(APPNAME).cpp
13:   cl -c -AL -GA -Ow -W4 -Zp  $(APPNAME).cpp
14:
15: # compiling
16: GRUNT.OBJ : GRUNT.CPP
17:   cl -c -AL -GA -Ow -W4 -Zp  GRUNT.CPP
18:
19: # compiling
20: $(APPNAME).res : $(APPNAME).rc
21:   rc -r $(APPNAME).rc
```

The game starts by showing a short snake moving slowly across the screen. (See Figure 8.1.) The direction the snake moves can be controlled with the arrow keys. The object of the game is to keep the snake from running into the sides of the playing field, or into its ever-lengthening body. For variety, special little bonus bitmaps appear on-screen from time to time. The snake is hungry and likes to eat these bonus bitmaps. You should steer the snake near them whenever possible.

To complete the code, you need to generate the three bitmaps shown below the source. All three bitmaps should be 32x32 pixels.

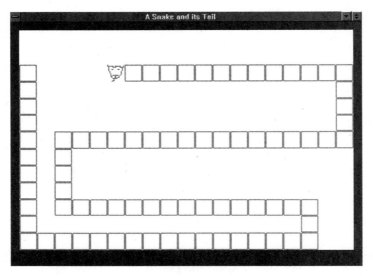

Figure 8.1. *The snake winds its way across the playing field.*

The Child Window

Snake1 has, not one, but two windows. The main window is visible only as a small gray border stretching around the outside of the playing field. The central playing field for the game is actually a child window called GameWindow. GameWindow exists primarily to simplify the mathematics in Snake1. The issue is that all three bitmaps used in the game are 32x32 pixels in size. As a result, it would be useful if the dimensions of the game board were a multiple of 32 and couldn't be resized. To achieve these goals, Snake1 maximizes its main window, and then pops up a child window with X and Y dimensions, evenly divisible by 32.

Maximizing a window on startup is very simple. All you need to do is set nCmdShow to the proper constant, as defined in WINDOWS.H:

```
nCmdShow = SW_SHOWMAXIMIZED;
ShowWindow(hWindow, nCmdShow);
```

After the main window is maximized, Snake1 creates the GameWindow in response to a WM_CREATE message. Creation is a three-step process:

1. Register the window.

2. Calculate the window's dimensions.

3. Call CreateWindow to make the window visible to the user.

In principle, creating a child window is no different than creating the main window of the program. The steps involved are identical; you register the window and then create it.

You've seen these steps many times in this book. However, I'll step through the process with you, so there won't be any questions about what is happening. The idea of creating child windows is crucially important in Windows, and it's essential that you understand it. If the ideas come a little slowly to you, don't worry. This material is covered again and again in various guises throughout this book.

Snake1 registers the GameWindow in the same place that it registers its main window. If you look at the Register method, you'll see that it registers class Snake1, and then registers a second window called GameWindow:

```
 19: static char szGameName[] = "GameWindow";

... /* Code to define class main window Snake1 */

106:    RegisterClass (&WndClass);
    /* Now register the game window */

109:    WndClass.lpfnWndProc      = GameWndProc;
110:    WndClass.hIcon            = 0;
111:    WndClass.hCursor          = LoadCursor(NULL, IDC_ARROW);
112:    WndClass.hbrBackground    = GetStockBrush(WHITE_BRUSH);
113:    WndClass.lpszClassName    = szGameName;
114:
115:    return RegisterClass (&WndClass);
```

It's not necessary to redefine all the fields of the WNDCLASS structure. Instead, many of them can be carried over unchanged from one class to the next. One field that has to be redefined, however, is the lpfnWndProc variable (line 109) designating the window procedure. The WndProc is the place where the behavior associated with a window is defined. Because GameWindow is the program's playing field, it's obviously going to have a lot of specialized behavior associated with it. That behavior is defined in its own separate module, called Grunt. Grunt is explained in the next section. Figure 8.2 shows where the GameWindow is placed.

Okay. So far, you've seen the Snake1 program register the GameWindow. The next step is to create the window by calling CreateWindow. Snake1 performs this action in response to the WM_CREATE message.

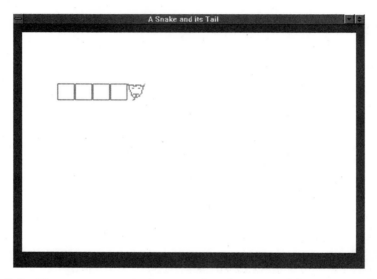

Figure 8.2. *The* GameWindow *sits on top and in the center of the main window.*

All the previous programs in this book have passed CW_USEDEFAULT in the four parameters used to declare a window's dimensions. In this case, however, Snake1 specifically calculates the dimensions passed to CreateWindow.

The calculations are necessary because the program runs on a wide variety of platforms. Sometimes, the screen is 640x480; other times, it's 1024x768 or 800x600. Because there's no way to know the dimensions ahead of time, calculations must be made at runtime.

To find out about the current platform, Snake1 calls the GetSystemMetrics function. When passed SM_CXSCREEN and SM_CYSCREEN as arguments, GetSystemMetrics reports the dimensions (in pixels) of the current screen. Snake1 uses this information to calculate the largest comfortable playing field that can be created on the current screen. It saves the results in global variables called MaxCols, MaxRows, and StartCol. Following is the code that calculates MaxCols:

```
int CXFull = GetSystemMetrics(SM_CXSCREEN);
NumXSects = div(CXFull, Size);
MaxCols = (NumXSects.quot - 1) * Size;
  etc...
```

After Snake knows the GameWindow's optimum size, it is free to create it:

```
hGameWindow = CreateWindow("GameWindow", "A",
                    WS_CHILD | WS_VISIBLE,
                    StartCol, BORDERSIZE, MaxCols, MaxRows,
                    hwnd, NULL, hInstance, NULL);
```

You've seen code like this in the Create function of every full-scale Windows program shown in this book. It should be completely familiar, except for a few slight variations.

> **Note:** The third argument to CreateWindow contains WS_CHILD OR'd together with WS_VISIBLE. All the previous code in this book passed WS_OVERLAPPEDWINDOW in this position. Unlike WS_OVERLAPPENDWINDOW, WS_CHILD windows don't have a border, caption bar, minimize box, maximize box, or system menu. In other words, WS_CHILD is a simpler, more modest style than WS_OVERLAPPEDWINDOW.
>
> The addition of the WS_VISIBLE style enables you to create a window without explicitly calling ShowWindow or UpdateWindow. Programmers frequently use this style with ChildWindows, but not with the main window of a program.
>
> At this stage in the book, you shouldn't spend too much time worrying about window styles. You will, however, explore the subject in-depth in Chapter 12, "Window Controls and Control Message APIs."

Okay. The last few paragraphs outlined the steps needed to create a child window. This is material that has already been covered in considerable depth in earlier chapters. I've gone through it again just to help orient you, to help you see the main points in the clearest possible terms.

Remember, all you need to do is

☐ Register the window.

☐ Call CreateWindow to bring the window into existence.

When you're done, the only step left is to maintain your creation by tending to its window procedure. Snake1 handles this process in the Grunt module.

The Grunt Module

It turns out that the GameWindow gives three big benefits:

1. It provides a nice symmetrical board to play on, with dimensions evenly divisible by 32.

2. It isolates all the tricky calculations for running the snake in a single module.

3. It demonstrates how to create a stand-alone module that can be joined to a larger Windows program.

The first benefit was discussed in-depth in the last section. The second benefit helps simplify programming chores, eliminate bugs, and aid in program maintenance. In other words, it gives the benefits accrued whenever programmers use good structured programming techniques. The third benefit of GRUNT.CPP is that it shows you how to create a multimodule Windows program.

Snake1 isn't a particularly large program, but the techniques used in creating the Grunt module can serve as a guide showing you how to organize your own large Windows program. Figure 8.3 gives a conceptual picture demonstrating how modules can be linked to form a larger program.

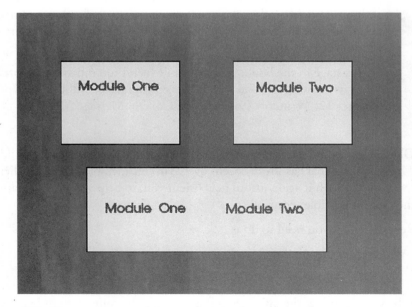

Figure 8.3. *Two or more modules can be joined together to form a larger program.*

You can turn to this code to see how to declare external variables that can be shared between modules, and how to call a function located in a separate module. More importantly, you can see how to build a .CPP file around a single window, so that both the window and the module exist as parallel, easily identifiable entities. This is the central tenet of structured programming and the kernel idea from which object-oriented programming sprang.

The rules for splitting a program into modules aren't that different in Windows than they are in DOS. The basic idea is to create header files for each of your modules, and then to declare shared types and functions in those header files. If you decide that you need to declare a global variable, you can use the extern keyword to make it available in more than one module, just as you would in DOS.

DO   DON'T

When creating modules to be linked into your main program:

DO create a header file for each module you want to share.

DON'T place anything except compiler directives, type declarations, and function declarations in the header file.

DO place global variables to be shared between the module and the main program inside the .CPP source files, rather than in header files.

DO place the keyword extern in front of global variables that must be referenced outside of the module in which they are defined. For example, the variables MaxCols and MaxRows are referenced both in the main module and in the Grunt module. As a result, they are defined in the SNAKE1.CPP file, and then referenced with the extern keyword in the GRUNT.CPP file:

```
extern int MaxCols;
extern int MaxRows;
```

Considerably more can be said about creating large, multimodule programs. However, this material is covered in considerable depth in basic C++ programming books. Rather than repeat that material here, I'll try to stick to the subject matter at hand, which is Windows programming.

Perhaps you have noticed that the code in the Grunt module can be divided into two main sections. At the top is the GameWndProc. Referenced in the window procedure, and implemented directly beneath it, are the `Game_OnCreate`, `Game_OnDestroy`, `Game_OnPaint`, `Game_OnChar`, `Game_OnKey`, and `Game_OnTimer` functions. Together, this code makes up the top half of the `Grunt` module.

Note: None of the code in the `Grunt` module is ever called directly from SNAKE1.CPP. Instead, SNAKE1.CPP creates the `GameWindow` in response to a `WM_CREATE` message (line 141). Then, `Game_OnXXX` functions are called by Windows, primarily in response to `WM_TIMER` messages (line 366) and `WM_KEYDOWN` messages (line 318).

The bottom half of the `Grunt` module contains the routines after which the module is named. This code does the dirty work of calculating where the snake should move next and testing to see whether it has collided with anything. These are not message handler functions, so their naming convention doesn't follow the `Game_OnXXX` format. Instead, they have simple utilitarian names such as `MoveBitmap` and `CheckForCollisions`.

The Timer

The engine that drives the Snake program depends on a Windows message called `WM_TIMER`.

Timers are devices that send `WM_TIMER` messages to a window at relatively even intervals. As you know, most of the messages sent to a window are generated by some action on the part of the user. However, timers keep putting along without any input from the user or the programmer.

Note: I say that timers come at "relatively" even intervals, because the DOS/Windows message-based environment can't be counted on to send messages at absolutely regular intervals! Don't imagine that it can, and don't waste time wishing it were so. If you need to find more precise timers, you can look at the multimedia timers, found in MMSYSTEM.H. (Although these timers aren't directly discussed in this book, you'll get a chance to explore other multimedia features on Day 20.)

Handling timers is usually a relatively simple operation that has three parts.

1. The first step is to initialize the timer with a call to SetTimer.

2. The second step is to respond to WM_TIMER messages in the Cls_OnTimer message handler function.

3. The last step is to free the timer resources when you're through with the timer. This is accomplished by calling KillTimer.

Snake1 performs the initialization of the timer in the Game_OnCreate function:

```
284:    if (!SetTimer(hwnd, SnakeTimer, 125, NULL))
285:    {
286:      MessageBox(hwnd, "No Timers Available", "Snake Info", MB_OK);
287:      return FALSE;
288:    }
```

The SetTimer function takes four parameters.

☐ The first parameter is the HWND of the window with which the timer is associated.

☐ The second parameter is a unique ID associated with the timer.

☐ The third parameter is the interval, in milliseconds, at which you want WM_TIMER messages to be sent to your window.

☐ The fourth parameter is the name of an optional callback procedure, which Windows can call in lieu of sending WM_TIMER messages to your window. As you can see, the Snake program opts to pass NULL in this fourth parameter. This is because programmers rarely need to work with a timer callback.

After the timer is initialized, the Snake program simply responds to WM_TIMER messages:

```
void Snake_OnTimer(HWND hWindow, UINT id)
{
  MoveBitMap(hWindow);
  TotalClicks++;
  if ((TotalClicks % 10) == 0)
  {
    SetSections();
    SetPrizes();
    ...
    /* additional code for adding sections to snake etc...  */
  }
}
```

In this program, WM_TIMER messages come cruising down the pike approximately every 150 milliseconds. If you want the snake to move faster, you can create a timer that sends a message every 75 milliseconds, 25 milliseconds, and so forth.

Timers are system resources, similar to bitmaps and icons. As a result, you must be careful to check that a call to SetTimer succeeds; you also must be sure to destroy timers when you are through with them. The proper way to destroy a timer is by calling KillTimer, passing it the HWND (of the window to which the timer belongs), and passing it the ID of the timer itself:

```
KillTimer(hWindow, SnakeTimer);
```

If you forget to destroy a timer, the system might run out of timers; as a result, applications (yours and others) on the system will be left high and dry, with no alternative but to pop up a series of embarrassing message boxes informing the user that the program can't run correctly because of a lack of timers.

DO   **DON'T**

DO balance every call to SetTimer with a call to KillTimer.

DON'T ever quit an application that uses a timer without first destroying that timer.

DON'T create any more timers than you absolutely have to use.

Now that you understand how timers work, I'm going to give only a very brief overview of the Snake_OnTimer function. If you want more details, start up the debugger, start setting breakpoints, and in general, be prepared to get your hands a bit dirty.

The main function of Snake_OnTimer is to call the MoveBitMap procedure, which paints the snake to the screen. However, as you can see, Snake_OnTimer includes extra logic for adding a new section to the snake once every 10 times the WM_TIMER message is sent. As a result, the snake keeps getting longer and longer, and the user finds it more and more difficult to steer the snake safely across the screen.

Some of the logic for painting the snake is duplicated in the Snake_OnPaint function. This is done only because it might be necessary to repaint the screen if it becomes covered up for some reason.

Painting the Snake

Whenever the code in Snake "blits" an image to the screen, it does so by using the SRCINVERT constant in the last parameter passed to BitBlt. As a result, these images are XOR'd to the screen. This is an easy way to achieve a certain kind of animation that leaves the area beneath the blitted image intact.

When you XOR an image to the screen, you can erase it simply by XORing the same image a second time in the same place. In other words, the first time you XOR an image to the screen you make it visible; the second time you make it invisible. This process doesn't disturb any images residing beneath the image blitted to the screen.

The key to animating an object is to blit it to the screen, erase it, move it forward a bit, blit it again, erase it, move it forward again, and so on (for as long as you want to create the illusion of movement).

At this point in the book, I don't want to burden you with additional information about XORing bitmaps or about the subtleties of the BitBlt function. I cover that information in detail in Chapter 18, "GDI and MetaFiles."

You should note , however, that the use of SRCINVERT always reverses the colors of any bitmap you create. As a result, you might want to have two copies of the bitmaps used in this program. The first copy would be in the normal colors you want to use in the game; the second copy would be an inverted version for use with the RC file. When the inverted version is blitted to the screen with SRCINVERT, the bitmap will appear as you originally drew it. Most Windows paint programs include a feature for inverting bitmaps.

Most of the rest of the program simply involves standard C++ coding practices and a review of subject matter that was covered earlier in this book. If you are having trouble picking up on the logic of this program, the key point to understand is that each section of the snake is a complete entity that knows its current and previous location and direction.

Whenever the head of the snake turns, a chain effect is set, whereby the news that a move was made is passed down the snake's body from section to section. In other words, when a WM_TIMER message is sent, each section takes on the state that the section preceding it in line had when the last WM_TIMER message was sent. The actual passing on of the information is done in the SetColRow function. The end result is that the "news" of a turn is passed down the line from the head to the tail. This algorithm is exercised religiously, even though only the first and last sections of the snake's body are painted in response to each WM_TIMER message.

Hopefully, you'll find that the Snake program is an enjoyable and instructive experience. I've tried to make it intriguing enough so that you'll be drawn in by its charms—and in the process start to take to heart some of the lessons presented in the last few chapters.

Examples and explanations that illustrate fundamental programming principles can only take you so far. If you want to really learn how to program a particular language or environment, you have to start writing some code on your own. Adding additional features to the Snake program would be a good place to start.

Summary

The main purposes of this chapter are to let you have some fun and to give you some hands-on experience. Along the way, several new issues were introduced. In particular, you saw how to

- ☐ Create timers by calling `SetTimer` and how to destroy them by calling `KillTimer`
- ☐ How to respond to `WM_TIMER` messages
- ☐ How to create a child window
- ☐ How to place a window in a separate module and call it from the main body of a program

Don't underestimate this knowledge just because it's given to you in the form of a game. If you take it to heart, it will help you make the exciting transition from Windows programming neophyte to Windows programming guru!

Q&A

1. Q: Why should you automatically maximize the main window of the Snake program? Doesn't this act negate the benefits of a multitasking environment?

    A: This is a philosophical or aesthetic question rather than a technical issue. My rationale for maximizing the window is simply that you can't properly multitask a game like this anyway, because the snake will run into a wall if it's left unattended for more than a few moments. Given those circumstances, a whole class of problems can be avoided by simply assuming that anyone playing Snake will want to give it their whole attention. If the user is

going to be totally focused on one window, why not make the window as big as possible? Secondly, maximizing the window enables the Snake program to avoid the difficult (insane?) calculations that would be involved if the playing field were resized at runtime!

2. Q: I thought Windows wasn't meant to be a gaming environment. Doesn't the Snake program violate the basic spirit of Windows?

A: Every copy of Windows ships with at least two games built into it. The designers of this environment definitely did not mean to exclude gamers. However, there is some truth to the idea that DOS games perform better than Windows games. This is because DOS programmers have complete control over the machine. Yet, the Snake program shows that reasonably fast graphics can be done inside the Windows environment. Certainly, Windows gives game programmers a big leg up because of its powerful, built-in graphics support. In the long run, however, I think it's important to realize that no one programming environment has a monopoly on all the most sought after virtues. Right now, the best of all possible worlds probably would be one in which users and programmers had easy access to both DOS and Windows. Say what?

Workshop

The Workshop provides quiz questions to help you solidify your understanding of the material covered and exercises to provide you with experience in using what you've learned. Try to understand the quiz and exercise answers before continuing on to the next chapter. Answers are provided in Appendix A.

Quiz

1. What two steps are necessary to create a child window?

2. Why is `RegisterClass` called twice in the `Register` function of Snake1?

3. What is the name of the window procedure for the child window in Snake1?

4. Why doesn't the `Game_OnDestroy` function call `PostQuitMessage`?

5. How do you create a timer?

6. How can the Snake program be sure that `KillTimer` will be called before the program ends?

7. What constant do you use if you want to XOR a bitmap to the screen?

8. How can you find out how many pixels are needed to fill a single row on the screen of a computer?

9. Use your reference books or the online help to find 10 pieces of information that can be retrieved using the `GetSystemMetrics` function.

10 What's the purpose of the `Game_OnChar` message handler function?

Exercises

1. Have some fun, use your imagination, and add the features you feel are missing from the Snake program!

2. In the next few chapters, you'll learn a lot about dialogs and window controls. If you enjoy games, use some of these techniques to add spice to the Snake program. In other words, make the Snake program an ongoing project.

Font Basics

In this chapter, you'll see how fonts are created in the Windows environment. In particular, the following subjects are covered:

☐ Creating fonts with the API calls `CreateFontIndirect`, `CreateFont`, and `GetStockObject`

☐ Getting information about the current font by calling `GetTextMetrics` and `GetTextFace`

☐ Using and analyzing the `LOGFONT` structure

☐ Using and analyzing the `TEXTMETRIC` structure

☐ Rotating a font

☐ Deleting fonts with `DeleteObject`

The point of this chapter is to give you a solid working knowledge of fonts that should hold you in good stead throughout most normal programming projects.

Chapter 10, "Windows Controls," is dedicated primarily to an exploration of Window controls. However, it also continues the theme of this chapter by allowing you to enumerate the fonts on your system with a callback function.

Font Madness Arrives on the PC!

Not long after Windows 3.0 came out, I was freelancing, picking up various kinds of work—some of it programming and some of it just hell-for-leather consulting. One of the jobs I landed involved working for a graphics designer. He had a shop filled with expensive printers, scanners, Macs and—now that Windows was out—a few PCs.

I did technically straightforward tasks for him, such as cleaning up his WIN.INI file and cutting redundant calls out of his AUTOEXEC.BAT. A more technical part of my job involved satisfying his passionate interest in fonts.

People in the Mac world have, of course, been working with fonts for years. Because these resources were part of his business, all his Macs were loaded down with an incredible range of fonts. His goal was to match that diversity by arming his PCs with even more fonts. Not just five, or ten fonts—but twenty, thirty, maybe forty or more fonts. He was very serious about his business, and people paid him good money for his trouble.

Unfortunately, Windows was new to him, and he didn't have the time to master all the details. What he needed was someone who could sort all those fonts for him, and more importantly, find out how he could get access to all of them from inside of PageMaker, CorelDraw, and Word for Windows.

Unfortunately, the DOS world had done nothing to prepare me for his challenge. For years, I stared at the same old DOS character set. When it came to fonts, I had the aesthetic sense of a duck-billed platypus. I didn't know Times from Courier, bold from italic, or WingDing from Symbol. I was utterly unaware of most of the aesthetic distinctions that lay very much at the heart of this guy's business.

Through hard work and good fortune, I eventually got most of the fonts straightened out. But it was a challenge. I just hadn't understood what a complicated and subtle subject I had stumbled across.

Over the years, I've always been grateful for that experience, not only because it taught me a lot, but because it showed me how passionately some people care about fonts. It's a subject which can arouse intense sentiments. My advice to new Windows programmers is to get a good grasp of this subject. If all else fails, you should simply give your users access to all the fonts on the system, letting them choose which ones they want in any particular situation. The point is, you never know when you will stumble across someone who really cares about this subject.

Anyway, fonts are fun. They even can add flare to routine programs. As a result, I explore this subject in some depth over the next several chapters.

The Simple Font Program

You now should be ready to take a look at the first font example, SimpFont (see Listing 9.1). It shows you one very simple and straightforward way to create a font.

 Listing 9.1. The Simpfont program explores methods for creating and manipulating fonts.

```
 1: /////////////////////////////////////////////////
 2: //   Program Name: SIMPFONT.CPP
 3: //   Programmer: Charlie Calvert
 4: //   Description: SimpFont windows program
 5: //   Date: 3/20/93
 6: /////////////////////////////////////////////////
 7:
 8: #define STRICT
 9: #include <windows.h>
```

continues

Listing 9.1. continued

```
10: #include <windowsx.h>
11: #pragma hdrstop
12: #include <stdio.h>
13: #include <stdlib.h>
14: #include <string.h>
15: #include "simpfont.h"
16: #include "fontstr.h"
17: #pragma warning (disable: 4068)
18:
19: // variables
20: static char szAppName[] = "SimpFont";
21: static HWND MainWindow;
22: static HINSTANCE hInstance;
23: static LOGFONT LogFont;
24: static HFONT TheFont;
25: static char aFaceName[80];
26: TEXTMETRIC TextMets;
27: char * FontChoice[] = {"New Times Roman", "Arial",
28:                        "Symbol", "StockFont"};
29: enum TChoice {Roman, Swiss, Symbol, StockFont};
30: TChoice Choice;
31:
32: // ----------------------------------
33: // Initialization
34: // ----------------------------------
35:
36: ///////////////////////////////////////
37: // Program entry point
38: ///////////////////////////////////////
39: #pragma argsused
40: int PASCAL WinMain(HINSTANCE hInst, HINSTANCE hPrevInstance,
41:                    LPSTR  lpszCmdParam, int nCmdShow)
42: {
43:   HWND hWindow;
44:   MSG  Msg;
45:
46:   if (!hPrevInstance)
47:     if (!Register(hInst))
48:       return FALSE;
49:
50:   if (!(MainWindow = Create(hInst, nCmdShow)))
51:     return FALSE;
52:
53:   while (GetMessage(&Msg, NULL, 0, 0))
54:   {
55:     TranslateMessage(&Msg);
56:     DispatchMessage(&Msg);
57:   }
58:
```

```
59:     return Msg.wParam;
60: }
61:
62: //////////////////////////////////////
63: // Register the window
64: //////////////////////////////////////
65: BOOL Register(HINSTANCE hInst)
66: {
67:    WNDCLASS WndClass;
68:
69:    WndClass.style          = CS_HREDRAW | CS_VREDRAW;
70:    WndClass.lpfnWndProc    = WndProc;
71:    WndClass.cbClsExtra     = 0;
72:    WndClass.cbWndExtra     = 0;
73:    WndClass.hInstance      = hInst;
74:    WndClass.hIcon          = LoadIcon(NULL, IDI_APPLICATION);
75:    WndClass.hCursor        = LoadCursor(NULL, IDC_ARROW);
76:    WndClass.hbrBackground  = GetStockBrush(WHITE_BRUSH);
77:    WndClass.lpszMenuName   = "Menu";
78:    WndClass.lpszClassName  = szAppName;
79:
80:    return RegisterClass (&WndClass);
81: }
82:
83: //////////////////////////////////////
84: // Create the window
85: //////////////////////////////////////
86: HWND Create(HINSTANCE hInst, int nCmdShow)
87: {
88:
89:    hInstance = hInst;
90:
91:    HWND hWindow = CreateWindow(szAppName, szAppName,
92:                     WS_OVERLAPPEDWINDOW,
93:                     CW_USEDEFAULT, CW_USEDEFAULT,
94:                     CW_USEDEFAULT, CW_USEDEFAULT,
95:                     NULL, NULL, hInstance, NULL);
96:
97:    if (hWindow == NULL)
98:      return hWindow;
99:
100:   ShowWindow(hWindow, nCmdShow);
101:   UpdateWindow(hWindow);
102:
103:   return hWindow;
104: }
105:
106: // -------------------------------------
107: // WndProc and Implementation
108: // -------------------------------------
109:
```

continues

Listing 9.1. continued

```
110: //////////////////////////////////////
111: // The Window Procedure
112: //////////////////////////////////////
113: LRESULT CALLBACK _export WndProc(HWND hWindow, UINT Message,
114:                                  WPARAM wParam, LPARAM lParam)
115: {
116:   switch(Message)
117:   {
118:     HANDLE_MSG(hWindow, WM_DESTROY, SimpFont_OnDestroy);
119:     HANDLE_MSG(hWindow, WM_CREATE, SimpFont_OnCreate);
120:     HANDLE_MSG(hWindow, WM_COMMAND, SimpFont_OnCommand);
121:     HANDLE_MSG(hWindow, WM_PAINT, SimpFont_OnPaint);
122:     default:
123:       return SimpFont_DefProc(hWindow, Message, wParam, lParam);
124:   }
125: }
126:
127: //////////////////////////////////////
128: // Get a new font, specify Escapement
129: //////////////////////////////////////
130: HFONT GetFont(int Escapement, char * Name)
131: {
132:   memset(&LogFont, 0, sizeof(LOGFONT));
133:
134:   LogFont.lfHeight        = 37;
135:   LogFont.lfWeight        = 400;
136:   LogFont.lfEscapement    = Escapement;
137:   LogFont.lfItalic        = 1;
138:   LogFont.lfUnderline     = 1;
139:   LogFont.lfOutPrecision  = OUT_STROKE_PRECIS;
140:   LogFont.lfClipPrecision = CLIP_STROKE_PRECIS;
141:   LogFont.lfQuality       = DEFAULT_QUALITY;
142:   strcpy(LogFont.lfFaceName, Name);
143:
144:   if (TheFont != 0) DeleteObject(TheFont);
145:
146:   TheFont = CreateFontIndirect(&LogFont);
147:
148:   return TheFont;
149: }
150:
151: //////////////////////////////////////////////
152: // Handle WM_DESTROY
153: //////////////////////////////////////////////
154: #pragma argsused
155: void SimpFont_OnDestroy(HWND hwnd)
156: {
157:   if (TheFont != 0) DeleteObject(TheFont);
158:   PostQuitMessage(0);
159: }
160:
```

```
161: /////////////////////////////////////////////
162: // Handle WM_CREATE
163: /////////////////////////////////////////////
164: #pragma argsused
165: BOOL SimpFont_OnCreate(HWND hwnd, CREATESTRUCT FAR* lpCreateStruct)
166: {
167:   GetFont(0, "New Times Roman");
168:   return TRUE;
169: }
170:
171: /////////////////////////////////////////////
172: // Handle WM_COMMAND
173: /////////////////////////////////////////////
174: #pragma argsused
175: void SimpFont_OnCommand(HWND hwnd, int id, HWND hwndCtl,
176:                          UINT codeNotify)
176: {
177:   char S[500];
178:
179:   switch (id)
180:   {
181:     case CM_INFO:
182:       GetFontString(S, TextMets, aFaceName);
183:       MessageBox(hwnd, S, "Font Info", MB_OK);
184:       break;
185:
186:     case CM_ROMAN:
187:       Choice = Roman;
188:       InvalidateRect(hwnd, NULL, TRUE);
189:       break;
190:
191:     case CM_SWISS:
192:       Choice = Swiss;
193:       InvalidateRect(hwnd, NULL, TRUE);
194:       break;
195:
196:     case CM_SYMBOL:
197:       Choice = Symbol;
198:       InvalidateRect(hwnd, NULL, TRUE);
199:       break;
200:
201:     case CM_ANSI_FIXED_FONT:
202:       if (TheFont != 0) DeleteObject(TheFont);
203:       TheFont = GetStockFont(ANSI_FIXED_FONT);
204:       Choice = StockFont;
205:       InvalidateRect(hwnd, NULL, TRUE);
206:       break;
207:
208:     case CM_ANSI_VAR_FONT:
209:       if (TheFont != 0) DeleteObject(TheFont);
```

continues

Listing 9.1. continued

```
210:        TheFont = GetStockFont(ANSI_VAR_FONT);
211:        Choice = StockFont;
212:        InvalidateRect(hwnd, NULL, TRUE);
213:        break;
214:
215:      case CM_DEVICE_DEFAULT_FONT:
216:        if (TheFont != 0) DeleteObject(TheFont);
217:        TheFont = GetStockFont(DEVICE_DEFAULT_FONT);
218:        Choice = StockFont;
219:        InvalidateRect(hwnd, NULL, TRUE);
220:        break;
221:
222:      case CM_OEM_FIXED_FONT:
223:        if (TheFont != 0) DeleteObject(TheFont);
224:        TheFont = GetStockFont(OEM_FIXED_FONT);
225:        Choice = StockFont;
226:        InvalidateRect(hwnd, NULL, TRUE);
227:        break;
228:
229:      case CM_SYSTEM_FONT:
230:        if (TheFont != 0) DeleteObject(TheFont);
231:        TheFont = GetStockFont(SYSTEM_FONT);
232:        Choice = StockFont;
233:        InvalidateRect(hwnd, NULL, TRUE);
234:        break;
235:
236:      case CM_SYSTEM_FIXED_FONT:
237:        if (TheFont != 0) DeleteObject(TheFont);
238:        TheFont = GetStockFont(SYSTEM_FIXED_FONT);
239:        Choice = StockFont;
240:        InvalidateRect(hwnd, NULL, TRUE);
241:        break;
242:   }
243: }
244:
245: ///////////////////////////////////////////////
246: // Handle WM_PAINT changing the color, and rotating the font
247: ///////////////////////////////////////////////
248: void SimpFont_OnPaint(HWND hwnd)
249: {
250:   PAINTSTRUCT PaintStruct;
251:   HFONT OldFont;
252:
253:   HDC PaintDC = BeginPaint(hwnd, &PaintStruct);
254:
255:   if (Choice == StockFont)
256:   {
257:     OldFont = SelectFont(PaintDC, TheFont);
258:     GetTextFace(PaintDC, sizeof(aFaceName),
259:                 (LPSTR) aFaceName);
```

```
260:      GetTextMetrics(PaintDC, &TextMets);
261:      SetTextColor(PaintDC, RGB(rand() % 255,
262:                     rand() % 255, rand() % 255));
263:      TextOut(PaintDC, 10, 10, aFaceName, strlen(aFaceName));
264:      TextOut(PaintDC, 10, 30, "Stock Fonts", 11);
265:      TextOut(PaintDC, 10, 50, "Ten Letters", 11);
266:      SelectFont(PaintDC, OldFont);
267:    }
268:    else
269:    {
270:      for (int i = 0; i <= 3; i++)
271:      {
272:        TheFont = GetFont(900 * i, FontChoice[Choice]);
273:        OldFont = SelectFont(PaintDC, TheFont);
274:        SetTextColor(PaintDC, RGB(rand() % 255,
275:                       rand() % 255, rand() % 255));
276:        TextOut(PaintDC, 200, 200, "Ahoy!" , 5);
277:        GetTextFace(PaintDC, sizeof(aFaceName),
278:                      (LPSTR) aFaceName);
279:        GetTextMetrics(PaintDC, &TextMets);
280:        SelectFont(PaintDC, OldFont);
281:      }
282:      TextOut(PaintDC, 10, 10, aFaceName, strlen(aFaceName));
283:    }
284:
285:    EndPaint(hwnd, &PaintStruct);
286: }
```

Listing 9.2 shows the Simpfont header file.

Type **Listing 9.2. SIMPFONT.H.**

```
 1: ////////////////////////////////////////////
 2: //   Program Name: SIMPFONT.H
 3: //   Programmer: Charlie Calvert
 4: //   Description: SimpFont windows program
 5: //   Date: 6/12/93
 6: ////////////////////////////////////////////
 7:
 8: #define CM_INFO 100
 9: #define CM_ROMAN 101
10: #define CM_SWISS 102
11: #define CM_SYMBOL 103
12:
13: #define CM_ANSI_FIXED_FONT    201
14: #define CM_ANSI_VAR_FONT 202
15: #define CM_DEVICE_DEFAULT_FONT      203
```

continues

Listing 9.2. continued

```
16: #define CM_OEM_FIXED_FONT 204
17: #define CM_SYSTEM_FONT    205
18: #define CM_SYSTEM_FIXED_FONT 206
19:
20: // Declarations for class SimpFont
21: #define SimpFont_DefProc     DefWindowProc
22: BOOL SimpFont_OnCreate(HWND hwnd, CREATESTRUCT FAR* lpCreateStruct);
23: void SimpFont_OnDestroy(HWND hwnd);
24: void SimpFont_OnCommand(HWND hwnd, int id, HWND hwndCtl,
                            UINT codeNotify);
25: void SimpFont_OnPaint(HWND hwnd);
26:
27: // Procs
28: LRESULT CALLBACK _export WndProc(HWND hWindow, UINT Message,
29:                                  WPARAM wParam, LPARAM lParam);
30: BOOL Register(HINSTANCE hInst);
31: HWND Create(HINSTANCE hInst, int nCmdShow);
32: BOOL CALLBACK InfoDlgProc(HWND hDlg, WORD Message,
33:                                  WPARAM wParam, LPARAM lParam);
```

Listing 9.3 shows the Fontstr source file.

Listing 9.3. FONTSTR.CPP.

```
 1: ////////////////////////////////////////////
 2: //   Module Name: FONTSTR.CPP
 3: //   Programmer: Charlie Calvert
 4: //   Description: Simpfont program font analysis
 5: //   Date: 6/12/93
 6: ////////////////////////////////////////////
 7:
 8: #define STRICT
 9: #include <windows.h>
10: #include <windowsx.h>
11: #include <string.h>
12: #include <stdio.h>
13:
14: // variables
15: TEXTMETRIC TextMetrics;
16: static char TheFaceName[80];
17:
18: // procs
19: char * GetType(char * S);
20: char * GetFamily(char * S);
21: char * GetCharSet(char * S);
22:
```

```
23: char * GetFontString(char * S, TEXTMETRIC TextMetric,
                          char * FaceName)
24: {
25:   char szType[99], szFamily[99], szCharSet[99];
26:
27:   TextMetrics = TextMetric;
28:   strcpy(TheFaceName, FaceName);
29:
30:   GetType(szType);
31:   GetFamily(szFamily);
32:   GetCharSet(szCharSet);
33:
34:   sprintf(S, "Font: %s \n Height: %d \n "
35:              "Ascent: %d \n Descent: %d \n "
36:              "AveCharW: %d \n MaxCharW: %d \n "
37:              "Weight: %d \n Italic: %hd \n "
38:              "Underlined: %d \n"
39:              "%s \n %s \n %s ",
40:   TheFaceName,
41:   TextMetrics.tmHeight,
42:   TextMetrics.tmAscent,
43:   TextMetrics.tmDescent,
44:   TextMetrics.tmAveCharWidth,
45:   TextMetrics.tmMaxCharWidth,
46:   TextMetrics.tmWeight,
47:   TextMetrics.tmItalic,
48:   TextMetrics.tmUnderlined,
49:   szType, szFamily, szCharSet);
50:
51:   return S;
52: }
53:
54: char * GetType(char * S)
55: {
56:   strcpy(S, "Font Type: ");
57:   if ((TextMetrics.tmPitchAndFamily & TMPF_FIXED_PITCH) == 0)
58:   strcat(S, "Default <> ");
59:   if ((TextMetrics.tmPitchAndFamily & TMPF_FIXED_PITCH) ==
60:         TMPF_FIXED_PITCH)
61:   strcat(S, "Fixed <> ");
62:   if ((TextMetrics.tmPitchAndFamily & TMPF_VECTOR) ==
63:         TMPF_VECTOR)
64:   strcat(S, "Vector <> ");
65:   if ((TextMetrics.tmPitchAndFamily & TMPF_TRUETYPE) ==
66:         TMPF_TRUETYPE)
67:   strcat(S, "TrueType <> ");
68:   if ((TextMetrics.tmPitchAndFamily & TMPF_DEVICE) ==
69:         TMPF_DEVICE)
70:   strcat(S, "Device <> ");
71:
```

continues

Listing 9.3. continued

```
 72:    if (strlen(S) > 11)
 73:      S[strlen(S) - 3] = '\0';
 74:
 75:    return S;
 76: }
 77:
 78: char * GetFamily(char * S)
 79: {
 80:    int R = TextMetrics.tmPitchAndFamily & 0XF0;
 81:    strcpy(S, "Family: ");
 82:    if (R == FF_DONTCARE) strcat(S, "Don't Care or don't know");
 83:    if (R == FF_ROMAN)  strcat(S, "Roman");
 84:    if (R == FF_SWISS)  strcat(S, "Swiss");
 85:    if (R == FF_MODERN) strcat(S, "Modern");
 86:    if (R == FF_SCRIPT) strcat(S, "Script");
 87:    if (R == FF_DECORATIVE) strcat(S, "Decorative");
 88:
 89:    return S;
 90: }
 91:
 92: char * GetCharSet(char * S)
 93: {
 94:    strcpy(S, "Char Set: ");
 95:
 96:    if (TextMetrics.tmCharSet == ANSI_CHARSET)
 97:      strcat(S, "Ansi");
 98:
 99:    if (TextMetrics.tmCharSet == DEFAULT_CHARSET)
100:      strcat(S, "Default");
101:
102:    if (TextMetrics.tmCharSet == SYMBOL_CHARSET)
103:      strcat(S, "Symbol");
104:
105:    if (TextMetrics.tmCharSet == OEM_CHARSET)
106:      strcat(S, "OEM");
107:
108:    return S;
109: }
```

Listing 9.4 shows the Fontstr header file.

Type   **Listing 9.4. FONTSTR.H.**

```
1: ////////////////////////////////////////////
2: //   Module Name: FONTSTR.H
3: //   Programmer: Charlie Calvert
4: //   Description: Simpfont program font analysis
```

```
5: //  Date: 6/12/93
6: ///////////////////////////////////////////
7:
8: char * GetFontString(char * S, TEXTMETRIC TextMetric,
9:                          char * FaceName);
```

Listing 9.5 shows the definition file for SimpFont.

Listing 9.5. SIMPFONT.DEF.

```
 1: ; SIMPFONT.DEF
 2:
 3: NAME            SimpFont
 4: DESCRIPTION     'SimpFont Window'
 5: EXETYPE         WINDOWS
 6: STUB            'WINSTUB.EXE'
 7: HEAPSIZE        4096
 8: STACKSIZE       5120
 9: CODE            PRELOAD MOVEABLE DISCARDABLE
10: DATA            PRELOAD MOVEABLE MULTIPLE
```

Listing 9.6 shows the SimpFont makefile for Borland compilers.

Listing 9.6. SIMPFONT.MAK (Borland).

```
 1: # --------------------------------
 2: # SIMPFONT.MAK
 3: # --------------------------------
 4:
 5: # macros
 6: APPNAME = SimpFont
 7: INCPATH = C:\BC\INCLUDE
 8: LIBPATH = C:\BC\LIB
 9: FLAGS = -H -ml -W -v -w4 -I$(INCPATH) -L$(LIBPATH)
10:
11: # link
12: $(APPNAME).exe: $(APPNAME).obj $(APPNAME).def \
                    $(APPNAME).res FONTSTR.OBJ
13:   bcc $(FLAGS) $(APPNAME).obj FONTSTR.OBJ
14:   brc $(APPNAME).res
15:
16: # compile
17: $(APPNAME).obj: $(APPNAME).cpp
18:   bcc -c $(FLAGS) $(APPNAME).cpp
```

continues

Listing 9.6. continued

```
19:
20: # compile
21: FONTSTR.OBJ: FONTSTR.CPP
22:   bcc -c $(FLAGS) FONTSTR.CPP
23:
24: # compile
25: $(APPNAME).res: $(APPNAME).rc
26: brc -r -i$(INCPATH) $(APPNAME).rc
```

Listing 9.7 The SimpFont makefile for Microsoft compilers.

 Listing 9.7. SIMPFONT.MAK (Microsoft).

```
1: #----------------------
2: # SIMPFONT.MAK makefile,
3: # Microsoft version
4: #----------------------
5:
6: APPNAME = SimpFont
7:
8: $(APPNAME).exe : $(APPNAME).obj $(APPNAME).def \
                    fontstr.obj $(APPNAME).res
9:      link $(APPNAME) fontstr, /align:16, NUL, \
              /nod llibcew libw, $(APPNAME)
10:     rc $(APPNAME).res
11:
12: $(APPNAME).obj : $(APPNAME).cpp
13:     cl -c -AL -GA -Ow -W2 -Zp $(APPNAME).cpp
14:
15: FONTSTR.OBJ : FONTSTR.CPP
16:     cl -c -AL -GA -Ow -W2 -Zp FONTSTR.CPP
17:
18: $(APPNAME).res : $(APPNAME).rc
19:     rc -r $(APPNAME).rc
```

Output When it starts up, this program prints out a single word four times in four randomly chosen colors. Each time the word is printed, it's aligned along another one of the major axis of a circle—that is, at the 90 degree mark, the 0 degree mark, the 270 degree mark, and the 180 degree mark. The output from this program is shown in Figure 9.1. A menu at the top of the program enables you to select different fonts, including three TrueType fonts and all of the stock fonts on the system. The display of the stock fonts is less interesting than the TrueType display, because it can't be rotated.

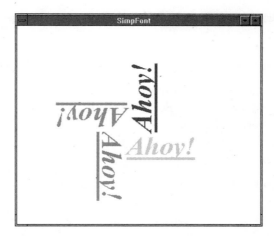

Figure 9.1. *The output from the SIMPFONT.CPP program shows how text can be rotated around a 360 degree arc.*

The SimpFont program is important, because it shows you how to create stock fonts, normal fonts, and TrueType fonts. This is knowledge every Windows programmer can't afford to do without.

> **Note:** TrueType fonts appeared the first time in Windows 3.1. They give the user high-quality letters, both on-screen and on a printer. In addition, they enable the programmer to port a font from one location to another. That is, TrueType fonts can be moved from the screen to the printer with a minimal loss of quality. Furthermore, they can be moved with a document from one system to another, through a technique (not discussed in this book) called embedding.

Getting Started with Fonts

Fonts tend to have complicated lives. In general, they move through six phases:

1. They're designed by filling out a big structure called a `LOGFONT`.

2. They're created by calling `CreateFontIndirect`.

3. They're copied into a device context with `SelectFont` or `SelectObject`.

4. They're shown to the screen with `TextOut` or `DrawText`.

5. They're copied back out of the device context.

6. They're deleted from the system with a call to `DeleteObject`.

Clearly, this is a fairly complex process. My goal is to make it comprehensible to you by explaining it in simple terms. Furthermore, I'll let the SimpFont program illustrate this process in considerable depth. By the end of the chapter, this whole subject should be old hat. You'll know what Windows fonts are and know how to create them. So let's get started!

The key function in the SimpFont program is called `GetFont`. This is where TrueType fonts are created:

```
130: HFONT GetFont(int Escapement, char * Name)
131: {
132:   memset(&LogFont, 0, sizeof(LOGFONT));
133:
134:   LogFont.lfHeight       = 37;
135:   LogFont.lfWeight       = 400;
136:   LogFont.lfEscapement   = Escapement;
137:   LogFont.lfItalic       = 1;
138:   LogFont.lfUnderline    = 1;
139:   LogFont.lfOutPrecision  = OUT_STROKE_PRECIS;
140:   LogFont.lfClipPrecision = CLIP_STROKE_PRECIS;
141:   LogFont.lfQuality      = DEFAULT_QUALITY;
142:   strcpy(LogFont.lfFaceName, Name);
143:
144:   if (TheFont != 0) DeleteObject(TheFont);
145:
146:   TheFont = CreateFontIndirect(&LogFont);
147:
148:   return TheFont;
149: }
```

The `GetFont` procedure has four parts:

1. The procedure first uses the `memset` function to zero out the `LOGFONT` structure.

2. Then, it fills out various fields of the `LOGFONT` structure.

3. Next, it checks to see if a variable called `TheFont` already holds the handle to a valid font. If it does, that font is deleted.

4. Finally, `GetFont` makes the font itself by calling `CreateFontIndirect`.

This process, or one very much like it, is what you'll usually go through when you want to create a font. One exception to this rule is when you want a stock font. Stock fonts are easy to obtain, as you will see a bit later in this chapter.

For now, though, I want to concentrate on the GetFont function. The key, obviously enough, to the whole function is the traumatic LOGFONT structure, which has enough fields in it to host an entire football league. Anyway, it's complex enough to warrant its own section.

The Logical Fonts Section

Normally, when you write text to the screen in Windows, you use the *system font*. This is a nice reliable tool, that meets most day-to-day needs. However, there are times when you want to add more spice to a program and use fonts that can make your code more versatile, attractive, and appealing.

The key to this whole topic is the following somewhat daunting logical font structure, or LOGFONT (as it is called in WINDOWS.H):

```
typedef struct tagLOGFONT {
    int    lfHeight;
    int    lfWidth;
    int    lfEscapement;
    int    lfOrientation;
    int    lfWeight;
    BYTE   lfItalic;
    BYTE   lfUnderline;
    BYTE   lfStrikeOut;
    BYTE   lfCharSet;
    BYTE   lfOutPrecision;
    BYTE   lfClipPrecision;
    BYTE   lfQuality;
    BYTE   lfPitchAndFamily;
    BYTE   lfFaceName[LF_FACESIZE];
} LOGFONT;
```

If you want to create a font in Windows, you need to fill out a few fields in the preceding record and pass the record to a function called CreateFontIndirect.

Note: You can pass this same list of fields to a function called CreateFont. It takes 14 parameters, all with the same names and the same import as the fields in the CreateFontIndirect function. Because they each have their advantages, it's really a toss-up as to which of the two functions you use.

The existence of `CreateFont` and `CreateFontIndirect` makes creating fonts very simple—in principle. The problem, of course, is knowing how to fill out the fields in the `LOGFONT` structure. The good news is that if you want, you can simply pass zero to all but the first and last fields and then let Windows choose default values for the rest. The following call to `CreateFont` shows how this can be done.

```
hfont = CreateFont(25, 0, 0, 0, 0, 0, 0, 0,
                       0, 0, 0, 0, 0, "Arial");
```

If you are using `CreateFontIndirect`, you can simply use `memset` to zero out the fields (as shown in the `GetFont` procedure).

The problem with this system, however, is that Windows frequently fails to fill out the missing fields with values that you would think appropriate. As a result, you can ask for an Arial font and end up with a Script font, and vice versa.

So, the best way to create a particular font is often to fill out at least four or five of the `LOGFONT` fields with specific values. To help you get an idea of how to proceed, I've provided the following list, which should give at least a minimal introduction to all the `LOGFONT` fields. For now, you'll probably just want to glance through it. You can study this subject in more detail after you have the first example up and running. Once again, the point is not to memorize all these fields, but to know of their existences and purposes, and to know where you can look them up.

`lfHeight`	The height of the font. If the number is negative, the internal leading is ignored.
`lfWidth`	The width of the font. You can set this to 0 if you want Windows to calculate an appropriate width for you.
`lfEscapement`	The angle at which the font is printed. 0 is normal, 900 is straight up, 1800 is upside down and backwards, and 2700 is straight down. TrueType fonts can hit all these positions and the positions in between. (See Figures 9.1 and 9.2.)
`lfOrientation`	Not implemented at this time, but someday it should affect the angle at which individual characters are printed.
`lfWeight`	The weight of the font, in increments of 100, starting at 0 and ending at 900. Entering 0 enables Windows to pick a default weight.

	700 is usually the number associated with bold print.
lfItalic	Set to 0 for normal and 1 (nonzero) for italic.
lfUnderline	Set to 0 for normal and 1 (nonzero) for underlined.
lfStrikeOut	Set to 0 for normal and 1 (nonzero) if you want a line drawn through the center of the font—as if it were crossed out.
lfCharSet	The characters used by the font:

ANSI_CHARSET	0
DEFAULT_CHARSET	1
SYMBOL_CHARSET	2
SHIFTJIS_CHARSET	128
OEM_CHARSET	255

The most common value for lfCharSet is 0. Although DEFAULT_CHARSET make seem like a safe and intuitive option, it's best to avoid it on most occasions.

lfOutPrecision	Specifies how precisely the font mapper tries to match your request. You can force the system to always use a TrueType font by choosing OUT_TT_ONLY_PRECIS.
lfClipPrecision	Dictates how Windows clips a font that runs off the edge of Window or that's partially covered by another Window. CLIP_STROKE_PRECIS usually works fine.
lfQuality	Dictates how closely the font matches your request for height, width, underline, and so forth. If you choose DEFAULT_QUALITY, Windows tries to synthesize a font to meet your request. If you choose PROOF_QUALITY, Windows might ignore your request in favor of a more aesthetically pleasing, precise, and well-formed font. DRAFT_QUALITY is somewhere in between the other two.

lfPitchAndFamily	Helps guide Windows toward a choice if the exact typeface requested isn't available. For instance, if you want New Times Roman, but the font isn't available on the system, choosing FF_ROMAN helps Windows find a good substitute. You can OR the family value with VARIABLE_PITCH, DEFAULT_PITCH, or FIXED_PITCH, depending on your needs.
lfFaceName	The name of the font you want to use.

As you can see, the people who put Windows together take the subject of fonts extremely seriously—as indeed they should. Typesetting is a long, time-honored tradition, and now this entire art form is being moved from the printed page to the computer screen.

DO / DON'T

DO take the time to experiment with some of the values used in the LOGFONT structure from the GetFont function. For instance, if you increase the value of the lfWeight field, you get a thicker, heavier font. If you increase the lfHeight field, the font gets bigger. If you set the lfItalic field to zero, the font is no longer italicized.

DON'T, however, squander time figuring out ways to create all the fonts available on your system. In the next two chapters, I show you how to easily generate a wide range of fonts. After you have a means of automatically producing fonts, you can use the debugger or the code I provide to find out what values Windows has assigned to a particular LOGFONT structure. You can then copy those values to your own code and outfit your program with any fonts you might need.

Rotating a Font

In SimpFont, I've filled out the LOGFONT fields with sample values, choosing nice, hefty values for the height and weight and turning on the italic and underline features by setting them to nonzero values.

The field that SimpFont takes special control over is called lfEscapement. As mentioned in the previous list, this field dictates the angle at which the text appears on-screen. For instance, a value of zero prints the text in standard fashion from left to right, whereas 900, 1,800, and 2,700 move the text around the arcs of a circle in a counter-clockwise procession (as shown in Figure 9.2).

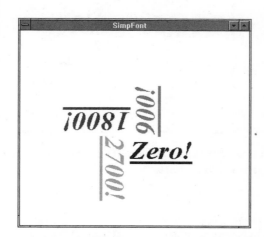

Figure 9.2. *This version of the SimpFont program illustrates the effect of passing specific numeric values in the lfEscapement field.*

By the way, Microsoft really outdid themselves by finding such an esoteric name for this field. An escapement is part of a mechanical device, such as a watch or typewriter. The escapement enables a wheel or notched bar to move forward one step at a time, and only when instructed.

Figure 9.3 shows the escapement circle broken into ninths.

Creating a Font

After you fill out the fields of the LOGFONT structure, you're nearly ready to call CreateFontIndirect. Before making the call, however, be sure to check to see if an old font needs to be deleted:

```
if (TheFont != 0) DeleteObject(TheFont);
```

Figure 9.3. *It's possible to take the SimpFont example somewhat further by breaking the "escapement" circle into ninths.*

Note: There's no way to overemphasize the importance of the call to `DeleteObject`. It's crucially important not to accidentally leave a resource, such as a font or a bitmap, in memory! Doing so will slowly but surely deplete the system resources and eventually bring Windows to its knees!

In the end, nearly any dedicated programmer can start creating fonts, bitmaps, and other resources. The hard part is cleaning up after yourself! I'm not simply being compulsive here. It's actually very difficult to be sure that all the system resources are cleaned up at the end of a program's run.

Remember that if you have the SDK, you can use the Debug version of Windows to help you track this sort of thing down. If you have the necessary tools, for heaven's sake get the Debug kernel up and running. It's a great educational tool.

While on the subject, I'll point out the `WM_DESTROY` message handler function, which deletes the font before the program closes:

```
DeleteObject(TheFont);
```

Whatever you do, don't forget to delete your resources! I may sound a bit like a broken record when I'm emphasizing this point, but at least I'm stuck on an important, nay, highly significant groove. Sabe?

After all the excitement leading up to it, the actual call to `CreateFontIndirect` comes as something of a let down:

```
TheFont = CreateFontIndirect(&LogFont);
```

That's all there is to it. You just pass one parameter in and get the font back out on the other end.

So, creating fonts is simple, no? Okay, so it's not really so simple. In the next two chapters I show you ways to make this process a bit easier, or at least more manageable.

Stock Fonts

Now that you know how to make fonts with `CreateFont` and `CreateFontIndirect`, I'll take a moment to show you how to create a font with a call to `GetStockObject`, or its WINDOWSX type-specific macro, `GetStockFont`:

```
201:    case CM_ANSI_FIXED_FONT:
202:        if (TheFont != 0) DeleteObject(TheFont);
203:        TheFont = GetStockFont(ANSI_FIXED_FONT);
204:        Choice = StockFont;
205:        InvalidateRect(hwnd, NULL, TRUE);
206:        break;
207:
```

This code is an excerpt from the `SimpFont_OnCommand` function. It gets called when the user selects a menu item indicating his or her desire to see the `ANSI_FIXED_FONT`.

As you can see, SimpFont first checks to see if `TheFont` variable already addresses a valid font. If it does, the font is deleted. The next step is the call to `GetStockFont`.

To obtain a stock font, pass in a constant that is defined in WINDOWS.H, such as `ANSI_FIXED_FONT` or `OEM_FIXED_FONT`. All the available stock fonts are used in the SimpFont program. In fact, one of the program's goals is to give you a good look at the stock fonts on your system.

After SimpFont has a handle to a stock font, it sets a global enumerated variable called `Choice` to the value `StockFont`. As shown in the next section, the `SimpFont_OnPaint` function checks this value to see what information needs to be painted to the screen. The final step (in the previous code) is the call to `InvalidateRect`, which asks Windows to send a `WM_PAINT` message to the main window.

As you can see, creating stock fonts is very simple—so simple, in fact, that they seem a bit mysterious to programmers. At times, it's as if stock fonts come out of nowhere, as if they were created by magic. But, of course, this is not the case.

Stock fonts are predefined resources that are yours simply for the asking. In other words, you can create these same fonts by calling `CreateFontIndirect`, with the appropriately filled out `LOGFONT` structure. The great virtue of stock fonts, however, is that they are easy to obtain because the `LOGFONT` structure has already been filled out for you. The drawback, of course, is that you don't have much control over what the system gives you.

Note: When running SimpFont, notice that each stock font has a particular face name that reveals the raw material from which Windows created the font. For instance, the `ANSI_FIXED_FONT` is a just a particular version of the standard courier font. (See Figure 9.4.)

If this font is close to what you need, but not quite on target, use the SimpFont program to find out how to fill a `LOGFONT` with the appropriate values. Then, create the font and begin to experiment with it. Change fields in the `LOGFONT` structure until you have exactly what you need.

Figure 9.4. *The SimpFont program can tell you what formula Windows used to create a stock font.*

WM_PAINT Messages Call the Tune!

When the user selects a new stock font or normal font from the SimpFont menu, the program calls InvalidateRect to coax Windows into sending a WM_PAINT message to the program. The response to these messages forms a crucial portion of the program's logic.

Step back a moment and think about what has happened. In the previous sections, you learned how to create a font. This section shows you how to paint a font on-screen. This is a three-step process.

1. Select the font into the device context and save a copy of the old font.

2. Call a procedure, such as TextOut or DrawText, which actually paints the font on-screen.

3. Preserve system resources by copying the old font back into the device context.

Now that you have an overview of what goes on, take a look at a specific example, as illustrated by the SimpFont program.

SimpFont_OnPaint features the traditional calls to BeginPaint and EndPaint. In between is code for painting both TrueType fonts and stock fonts. I treat each of these subjects separately, acting as if each were encapsulated in its own WM_PAINT message handler. The SimpFont program actually combines both sets of code into one function and examines the Choice variable to decide which part to call at any one moment.

Here is a stripped down version of how SimpFont paints TrueType fonts:

```
void SimpFont_OnPaint(HWND hwnd)
{
  PAINTSTRUCT PaintStruct;
  HFONT OldFont;

  HDC PaintDC = BeginPaint(hwnd, &PaintStruct);

  for (int i = 0; i <= 3; i++)
  {
    TheFont = GetFont(900 * i, FontChoice[Choice]);
    OldFont = SelectFont(PaintDC, TheFont);
    SetTextColor(PaintDC, RGB(rand() % 255,
                rand() % 255, rand() % 255));
```

```
  TextOut(PaintDC, 200, 200, "Ahoy!" , 5);
  SelectFont(PaintDC, OldFont);
}
TextOut(PaintDC, 10, 10, aFaceName, strlen(aFaceName));

EndPaint(hwnd, &PaintStruct);
}
```

`SimpFont_OnPaint` starts by creating the font with a call to `GetFont`. When making this call, SimpFont need only pass in a font name, along with the value associated with the `lfEscapement` field. This latter argument ensures that the font is printed at each of the points of the compass.

Note the vitally important calls to `SelectFont`, which is a WINDOWSX macro that calls `SelectObject`. At the beginning of the function, `SelectFont` copies the font to the device context. At the end, it copies it back out again. In this case, the device context happens to be the screen, but the process is similar when sending fonts to the printer.

The call to `SetTextColor` is straightforward enough for most purposes. I've complicated it here by throwing in the `Rand` function, which generates random numbers. If you strip that out, however, the call is reduced to something like the following compound statement:

```
SetTextColor(PaintDC, RGB(0, 0, 255));
```

The big difference, of course, is that in the SimpFont version, each of the fields of the RGB macro contain numbers generated by the `Rand` function. These randomly chosen numbers define the colors of the font.

> **Note:** As an experiment, try covering and uncovering the window numerous times in succession. Doing so forces a series of calls to the `WM_PAINT` message handler function. Each call produces a new random set of values to be passed to the `SetTextColor` API routine. If you only cover a small part of the window at a time, you can see exactly how the `BeginPaint` and `EndPaint` functions conspire to handle updating only the portions of the screen that have been hidden. This is the type of feature you might not want in a shipping product, but it's an ideal teaching tool. If you want to eliminate it, simply remove the calls to `Rand`.

The call to `TextOut` remains static through all four iterations of `SimpFont_OnPaint`'s loop.

```
TextOut(PaintDC, 200, 200, "Ahoy!" , 5);
```

The font rotation and hue changes occur because of the variables passed to
CreateFontIndirect and SetTextColor.

<table>
<tr><td>**DO**</td><td>**DON'T**</td></tr>
</table>

DO use CreateFontIndirect and SetTextColor to change the qualities of
the font.

DON'T worry about how Windows actually paints the font.

DON'T try to optimize code by writing directly to video memory, or by
tweaking the algorithm used to draw shapes on-screen. These techniques
belong to the DOS world. Instead,

DO things the Windows way. Windows programmers aren't dealing with
hardware, they're dealing with abstract concepts, such as fonts or device
contexts. To change the appearance of a font, change the objects associated with it. After you design the font, it will, in effect, display itself on-
screen without your help (and in a manner beyond your control).

The SimpFont_OnPaint function also handles painting stock fonts to the screen. Here's
an abbreviated version of the code:

```
OldFont = SelectFont(PaintDC, TheFont);
GetTextFace(PaintDC, sizeof(aFaceName),
            (LPSTR) aFaceName);
GetTextMetrics(PaintDC, &TextMets);
TextOut(PaintDC, 10, 10, aFaceName, strlen(aFaceName));
SelectFont(PaintDC, OldFont);
```

As you can see, stock fonts are painted to the screen in the same way as the other fonts.
That's because they are really normal fonts, with their LOGFONT structure predefined
by Windows!

Besides the calls to TextOut, and the standard SelectFont two-step dance, the portions
of the previous code that stand out most clearly are the calls to GetTextMetrics and
GetTextFace. GetTextFace snags the name of the current font installed in a device
context. The SimpFont program paints this font name to the screen, so you can see
whether or not your system is actually capable of producing the font you requested.

The call to GetTextMetrics can't be explained so easily. In fact, I'll treat this call in its
own section.

301

GetTextMetrics and the *FontStr* Module

When you create a font, you usually fill out a LOGFONT (or its equivalent fields) in a CreateFont call. You need to perform this operation in reverse when getting this information back from the system.

Windows provides detailed information about the current font through the GetTextMetrics call, and the TEXTMETRIC structure that it retrieves. The TEXTMETRIC structure tells you how big the font is, whether it's underlined or italicized, what pitch and family it has, and so on.

Not to be outdone by the LOGFONT structure, the TEXTMETRIC structure includes no less than 20 fields! This proliferation of minutia enables you to learn more than you most likely ever wanted to know about the current font:

```
typedef struct tagTEXTMETRIC {  /* tm */
    int  tmHeight;
    int  tmAscent;
    int  tmDescent;
    int  tmInternalLeading;
    int  tmExternalLeading;
    int  tmAveCharWidth;
    int  tmMaxCharWidth;
    int  tmWeight;
    BYTE tmItalic;
    BYTE tmUnderlined;
    BYTE tmStruckOut;
    BYTE tmFirstChar;
    BYTE tmLastChar;
    BYTE tmDefaultChar;
    BYTE tmBreakChar;
    BYTE tmPitchAndFamily;
    BYTE tmCharSet;
    int  tmOverhang;
    int  tmDigitizedAspectX;
    int  tmDigitizedAspectY;
} TEXTMETRIC;
```

SimpFont wrestles with the TEXTMETRIC structure in an isolated module called FontStr. FontStr returns most of the TEXTMETRIC fields in a single string. This module is designed so it can be easily linked to another program, as you'll see in the next chapter.

The core of FontStr is the GetFontString function. It contains the following straightforward, but lengthy, call to sprintf:

```
sprintf(S, "Font: %s \n Height: %d \n "
           "Ascent: %d \n Descent: %d \n "
           "AveCharW: %d \n MaxCharW: %d \n "
           "Weight: %d \n Italic: %hd \n "
           "Underlined: %d \n"
           "%s \n %s \n %s ",
           TheFaceName,
           TextMetrics.tmHeight,
           TextMetrics.tmAscent,
           TextMetrics.tmDescent,
           TextMetrics.tmAveCharWidth,
           TextMetrics.tmMaxCharWidth,
           TextMetrics.tmWeight,
           TextMetrics.tmItalic,
           TextMetrics.tmUnderlined,
           szType, szFamily, szCharSet);
```

As you can see from Figure 9.5, most of the information from the TEXTMETRIC structure is transferred into a single string. This string is returned to the WM_COMMAND handler function in the program's main module and displayed through a call to the MessageBox function:

```
// user selects FontInfo menu item.
case CM_INFO:
  GetFontString(S, TextMets, aFaceName);
  MessageBox(hwnd, S, "Font Info", MB_OK);
  break;
```

GetFontString is the only function exported by the FontStr module.

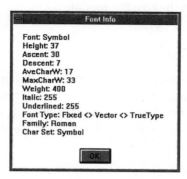

Figure 9.5. *The SimpFont program pops up a Message box relating important information about the currently selected font.*

The parts of the FontStr module described so far are fairly straightforward. The tricky sections involve deciphering the contents of the tmPitchAndFamily and the tmCharSet fields:

☐ The four low-order bits of `tmPitchAndFamily` describe the type of font, which can be one of the following values:

`TMPF_FIXED_PITCH:`	A fixed-pitch font
`TMPF_VECTOR:`	A vector or TrueType font
`TMPF_TRUETYPE:`	A TrueType font
`TMPF_DEVICE:`	A device font

Many times, a font combines one or more of these values.

☐ The four high-order bits can be ANDed together with the hexadecimal value `0xF0`, and then used to determine the current font family. Common font families include Roman, Swiss, Script, and Modern.

☐ The `tmCharSet` field is set to one of the following values:

`ANSI_CHARSET`	0
`DEFAULT_CHARSET`	1
`SYMBOL_CHARSET`	2
`SHIFTJIS_CHARSET`	128
`OEM_CHARSET`	255

Extracting this information from a `TEXTMETRIC` structure is the job of the following functions, all found in the `FontStr` module:

```
char * GetType(char * S);
char * GetFamily(char * S);
char * GetCharSet(char * S);
```

The `GetType` function uses `BitWise` operations to find the current font type. The `GetFamily` function uses the hex value `F0` to determine the font family, and the `GetCharSet` functions retrieves the current `CharSet`. If you want to understand these functions in-depth, you should crank up the debugger and start stepping through them one line at a time.

Note: Although SimpFont doesn't use it, I should probably also mention the `GetDeviceCaps` routine. It enables you to ask Windows what capabilities are associated with a particular device, such as a video screen or printer. You can use this function to discover whether the device can, for instance, print very large fonts, clip fonts, or stroked fonts.

> You should keep both the GetDeviceCaps and GetTextMetrics functions
> in mind, because no serious work with fonts can be conducted without
> them. The whole subject of printing fonts will be addressed during
> Week 3.

Summary

Day 9 has been dedicated to a discussion of fonts. This is a big topic, so I have made no attempt to be exhaustive. Instead, I've tried to introduce the main ideas in a relatively simple and straightforward manner.

In particular, you saw that the life of a typical font can have six parts:

1. Design it by filling out the LOGFONT structure.

2. Create it with CreateFontIndirect.

3. Copy it into a device context with a call to SelectFont or SelectObject.

4. Display the font by calling TextOut or DrawText.

5. Select the old font back into the device context with SelectFont or SelectObject.

6. Destroy the font by calling DeleteObject.

   For example:

   ```
   if (theFont != 0) DeleteObject(TheFont);
   memset(&LogFont, 0, sizeof(LOGFONT));
   LogFont.ifHeight              = 45;
   strcpy(LogFont.lfFaceName, "Arial");
   TheFont = CreateFontIndirect(&LogFont);
   OldFont = SelectFont(PaintDC, TheFont);
   TextOut(PaintDC, 10, 10, 'hello', 50;
   SelectFont(PaintDC, OldFont);
   ```

   See the FontEasy example on the sample disk for further guidance.

If, at any time, you want to get information about the current font, you can do so by calling GetTextMetrics and by examining the TEXTMETRIC structure.

Though neither of the next two chapters focuses exclusively on fonts, they do include useful information about them. The next chapter, for instance, focuses on retrieving all the currently available fonts from the system through a callback function. In Chapter 18, "GDI and Metafiles," you'll see how to use common dialogs to view and retrieve any font currently available on the system.

Q&A

1. Q: What is a font family?

   A: Windows usually work with one of five different font families: Decorative, Modern, Roman, Script, or Swiss. Each family has its own traits. The Swiss family, for instance, has no serifs. Serifs are the little strokes at the bottom of an F, R, and T, or the strokes that you see on the ends of an S and Z. The Roman family, on the other hand, has serifs. Typefaces in the Modern family have constant stroke widths. It's as if they were made from a pipe that never varies in width. The Swiss and Roman families, on the other hand, have varying stroke widths. That's all I can say on this subject in this context, but if you want more information, many books about fonts are available—the best of which might not even mention the subject of computers.

1. Q: I still don't understand TrueType fonts and stock fonts. Please explain.

   A: A stock font is simply a predefined font. Nothing at all is unusual about it except for the fact that Windows declared its dimensions ahead of time. TrueType fonts, on the other hand, are Microsoft's answer to PostScript fonts. As a rule, they have a higher quality and a greater degree of flexibility than the other fonts that come with Windows.

Workshop

The Workshop provides quiz questions to help you solidify your understanding of the material covered and exercises to provide you with experience in using what you've learned. Try to understand the quiz and exercise answers before continuing on to the next chapter. Answers are provided in Appendix A.

Quiz

1. What functions can produce TrueType fonts?

2. What functions produce stock fonts?

3. What is a TrueType font?

4. What is a stock font?

5. How can you find out the name of the current font?

6. How can you find out the size of the current font?

7. What is the face name of the DEVICE_DEFAULT_FONT on your system?

8. What is the face name of the SYSTEM_FONT on your system?

9. How do you copy a font into a device context?

10. What is contained in the four low-order bits of the tmPitchAndFamily field?

Exercises

1. Round out the GetFontString function so that it reports on all of the fields from a TEXTMETRIC structure.

2. Try creating a Script font. Hint: On most systems, the key to this process is setting the LOGFONT lfCharSet field to OEM_CHARSET. See if this works on your system.

Window Controls

M T W R F S

This chapter begins an exploration of a program called FontsExp, that displays all the fonts on the system. FontsExp uses a number of small subwindows called controls. These controls form an interface that enables the user to interact with the program.

The examination of FontsExp is divided into two sections. The first section, included in this chapter, studies the various Window controls introduced in the FontsExp program. In particular, it includes an examination of

- Static controls, used primarily to display text that the user can't edit
- List boxes, used to display lists of one line strings that can be scrolled by the user
- Edit controls, which enable the user to edit a string
- Check boxes, which are like the tiny boxes on a ballot or school quiz; if an X is in the box, the item is selected. Otherwise, it's either gray or blank.

The second section, included in Chapter 11, "Talking to Controls, Using the `EnumFontFamilies` Callback," presents an explanation of how to communicate with controls and how to use a callback function to retrieve the fonts available on the system. In particular, that section shows

- How to use `SendMessage` and `PostMessage`
- How to communicate with list boxes and check boxes
- How to create user-defined messages
- How to call `EnumFontFamilies`

The material covered in these two chapters is very important, because controls form a key part of the Windows operating environment. In fact, controls are so important, I address the subject again on Days 12 and 13.

Understanding Controls and Messages

Controls are interface elements (or interface tools) that help present information to the user in a clear and easily comprehensible manner.

It's possible to imagine a parallel between a window (or a series of windows) and the control panel for a stereo, tape recorder, or radio. When seen this way, visual tools, such as buttons, radio buttons and check boxes are like knobs or buttons on a stereo.

Just as a button turns a stereo on and off and a knob adjusts its volume, controls manage the flow of events inside a computer.

Interface elements, such as controls, become very important when you are wrestling with large quantities of information. For instance, my friend at the graphics designer shop had a large number of fonts on his machine. A simple written list of these fonts got to be as overwhelming as the list of fields in a big Windows structure. What people need is some sort of visual interface that can present these fonts to them in a readily comprehensible fashion. In your programs, you shouldn't just list the names of fonts, you should show users what the fonts look like. Let your users explore any particular font in detail. The FontsExp program shows one way to go about doing this.

Readers, writers, and users—all of us—need a way to grasp the vast amount of information that comes streaming at us in this confusing—and fascinating—information age. Windows controls are about presenting information to people. They're about interface design. Overall, they're one of the most important elements of the inspired vision that drives GUI environments such as Windows.

The Font Display

You can get started with controls by taking a look at an actual example showing how to manipulate the elements of a Windows interface. The window FontsExp creates is shown in Figure 10.1.

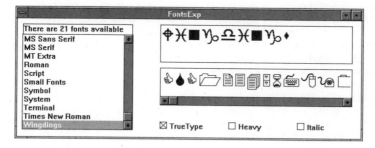

Figure 10.1. *The FontsExp program enables you to iterate through all the fonts on the system.*

The visual front end of the FontsExp program bears a slight resemblance to the view you see when you pop up a Fonts common dialog. (Common dialogs are explored in Chapter 18, "GDI and Metafiles.") From a programmer's perspective, however, FontsExp is a very different type of program. It takes you inside the world of Windows fonts, letting you control how, where, and with what degree of detail fonts are presented to the user.

You can build on the knowledge, presented in the next few pages, to expand the FontsExp program into a world-class tool that many Windows users would love to have at their disposal. As always in the world of programming, there are plenty of opportunities. So, without further ado, you can move on to the code shown in Listing 10.1.

Listing 10.1. The FontsExp program demonstrates techniques for using fonts and controls.

```
 1: //////////////////////////////////////////////////////////
 2: //   Program Name: FONTSEXP.CPP
 3: //   Programmer: Charlie Calvert
 4: //   Description: FontsExp windows program
 5: //   Date: 06/20/93
 6: //////////////////////////////////////////////////////////
 7:
 8: #define STRICT
 9: #include <windows.h>
10: #include <windowsx.h>
11: #pragma hdrstop
12: #include <string.h>
13: #include "FontsExp.h"
14: #include "fontstr.h"
15: #pragma warning (disable: 4068)
16: // --------------------------------------------------------
17: // Interface
18: // --------------------------------------------------------
19:
20: static char szAppName[] = "FontsExp";
21: static HWND MainWindow;
22: static HINSTANCE hInstance;
23: static TEXTMETRIC TextMetrics;
24: char aTextFace[80];
25:
26: // --------------------------------------------------------
27: // Initialization
28: // --------------------------------------------------------
29:
30: //////////////////////////////////////////////////////////
31: // Program entry point
32: //////////////////////////////////////////////////////////
33: #pragma argsused
34: int PASCAL WinMain(HINSTANCE hInst, HINSTANCE hPrevInstance,
35:                     LPSTR  lpszCmdParam, int nCmdShow)
36: {
37:   MSG  Msg;
38:
```

```
39:    if (!hPrevInstance)
40:      if (!Register(hInst))
41:        return FALSE;
42:
43:    MainWindow = Create(hInst, nCmdShow);
44:    if (MainWindow)
45:      return FALSE;
46:    while (GetMessage(&Msg, NULL, 0, 0))
47:    {
48:        TranslateMessage(&Msg);
49:        DispatchMessage(&Msg);
50:    }
51:
52:    return Msg.wParam;
53: }
54:
55: //////////////////////////////////////////////////////////
56: // Register the window
57: //////////////////////////////////////////////////////////
58: BOOL Register(HINSTANCE hInst)
59: {
60:    WNDCLASS WndClass;
61:
62:    WndClass.style          = CS_HREDRAW | CS_VREDRAW;
63:    WndClass.lpfnWndProc    = WndProc;
64:    WndClass.cbClsExtra     = 0;
65:    WndClass.cbWndExtra     = 0;
66:    WndClass.hInstance      = hInst;
67:    WndClass.hIcon          = LoadIcon(NULL, IDI_APPLICATION);
68:    WndClass.hCursor        = LoadCursor(NULL, IDC_ARROW);
69:    WndClass.hbrBackground  = GetStockBrush(WHITE_BRUSH);
70:    WndClass.lpszMenuName   = "Menu";
71:    WndClass.lpszClassName  = szAppName;
72:
73:    return RegisterClass (&WndClass);
74: }
75:
76: //////////////////////////////////////////////////////////
77: // Create the window
78: //////////////////////////////////////////////////////////
79: HWND Create(HINSTANCE hInst, int nCmdShow)
80: {
81:
82:    hInstance = hInst;
83:
84:    HWND hwnd = CreateWindow(szAppName, szAppName,
85:                             WS_OVERLAPPEDWINDOW,
86:                             CW_USEDEFAULT, CW_USEDEFAULT,
87:                             CW_USEDEFAULT, CW_USEDEFAULT,
88:                             NULL, NULL, hInst, NULL);
```

10

continues

Listing 10.1. continued

```
 89:
 90:   if (hwnd == NULL)
 91:     return hwnd;
 92:
 93:   ShowWindow(hwnd, nCmdShow);
 94:   UpdateWindow(hwnd);
 95:
 96:   return hwnd;
 97: }
 98:
 99: // ---------------------------------------------------------
100: // WndProc and Implementation
101: // ---------------------------------------------------------
102:
103: ///////////////////////////////////////////////////////////
104: // The Window Procedure
105: ///////////////////////////////////////////////////////////
106: LRESULT CALLBACK _export WndProc(HWND hwnd, UINT Message,
107:                                  WPARAM wParam, LPARAM lParam)
108: {
109:   FONTENUMPROC lpfnEnumProc;
110:   ENUMSTRUCT EnumStruct;
111:   char S[100];
112:
113:   switch(Message)
114:   {
115:     case WM_STARTFONTS:
116:     {
117:       HDC DC = GetDC(hwnd);
118:       lpfnEnumProc =
             (FONTENUMPROC)MakeProcInstance((FARPROC)FontCallBack,
119:                                     hInstance);
120:       EnumStruct.Count = 0;
121:       EnumStruct.hWindow = hFontList;
122:       EnumFontFamilies(DC, NULL, lpfnEnumProc,
123:                        (LONG)&EnumStruct);
124:       FreeProcInstance((FARPROC)lpfnEnumProc);
125:
126:       ReleaseDC(hwnd, DC);
127:
128:       wsprintf(S, "There are %d fonts available",
129:               EnumStruct.Count);
130:       SetWindowText(hNumFonts, S);
131:
132:       SetFocus(hFontList);
133:       SendMessage(hFontList, LB_SETCURSEL, 0, 0);
134:       ShowTheFont(hwnd);
135:       return 1;
136:     }
137:
```

```
138:     case WM_NEWFONT:
139:     {
140:       if (TheFont != 0)
141:         DeleteObject(TheFont);
142:       TheLogFont = (LPLOGFONT)lParam;
143:       TheFont = CreateFontIndirect(TheLogFont);
144:       return 1;
145:     }
146:
147:     HANDLE_MSG(hwnd, WM_COMMAND, FontsExp_OnCommand);
148:     HANDLE_MSG(hwnd, WM_CREATE, FontsExp_OnCreate);
149:     HANDLE_MSG(hwnd, WM_DESTROY, FontsExp_OnDestroy);
150:     default:
151:       return FontsExp_DefProc(hwnd, Message, wParam, lParam);
152:   }
153: }
154:
155: ////////////////////////////////////////////////////////////
156: // Handle WM_CREATE
157: ////////////////////////////////////////////////////////////
158: #pragma argsused
159: BOOL FontsExp_OnCreate(HWND hwnd, CREATESTRUCT FAR* lpCreateStruct)
160: {
161:   static char *Titles[] = { "TrueType" , "Heavy", "Italic" };
162:
163:   hFontList = CreateWindow("listbox", NULL,
164:                     WS_CHILD | WS_VISIBLE | LBS_STANDARD,
165:                     9, 30, 201, 180, hwnd, HMENU(ID_LISTBOX),
166:                     hInstance, NULL);
167:
168:   hNumFonts = CreateWindow("static", NULL,
169:                       WS_CHILD | WS_VISIBLE | WS_BORDER,
170:                       10, 10, 200, 20, hwnd, HMENU(-1),
171:                       hInstance, NULL);
172:
173:   hFontName = CreateWindow("static", NULL,
174:                       WS_CHILD | WS_VISIBLE | WS_BORDER,
175:                       260, 10, 350, 70, hwnd, HMENU(-1),
176:                       hInstance, NULL);
177:   hAlphaEdit = CreateWindow("edit", NULL,
178:                     WS_CHILD | WS_VISIBLE | WS_BORDER | WS_HSCROLL |
179:                     ES_LEFT | ES_AUTOHSCROLL | ES_MULTILINE,
180:                     260, 90, 350, 70, hwnd, HMENU(-1),
181:                     hInstance, NULL);
182:
183:   for (int i = 0; i < 3; i++)
184:     ButtonWindows[i] = CreateWindow("button", Titles[i],
185:                           WS_CHILD | WS_VISIBLE | BS_CHECKBOX,
186:                           260 + (i * 125), 180, 100, 35, hwnd,
187:                           HMENU(-1), hInstance, NULL);
```

continues

Listing 10.1. continued

```
188:
189:    TheFont = 0;
190:
191:    PostMessage(hwnd, WM_STARTFONTS, 0, 0);
192:
193:    return TRUE;
194: }
195:
196: /////////////////////////////////////////////////////////
197: // Handle WM_DESTROY
198: /////////////////////////////////////////////////////////
199: #pragma argsused
200: void FontsExp_OnDestroy(HWND hwnd)
201: {
202:    if (TheFont != 0)
203:       DeleteObject(TheFont);
204:    PostQuitMessage(0);
205: }
206:
207: /////////////////////////////////////////////////////////
208: // Handle WM_COMMAND
209: /////////////////////////////////////////////////////////
210: #pragma argsused
211: void FontsExp_OnCommand(HWND hwnd, int id, HWND hwndCtl,
                              UINT codeNotify)
212: {
213:    char S[500];
214:
215:    switch (id)
216:    {
217:      case ID_LISTBOX:
218:        if (codeNotify == LBN_SELCHANGE)
219:          ShowTheFont(hwnd);
220:        break;
221:
222:      case CM_INFO:
223:        GetFontString(S, TextMetrics, aTextFace);
224:        MessageBox(hwnd, S, "Info", MB_OK);
225:        break;
226:    }
227: }
228:
229: /////////////////////////////////////////////////////////
230: // ShowTheFont
231: /////////////////////////////////////////////////////////
232: void ShowTheFont(HWND hwnd)
233: {
234:    FONTENUMPROC lpfnEnumProc;
235:    char lpszBuffer[150];
236:    ENUMSTRUCT EnumStruct;
```

```
237:    HFONT SaveIt;
238:
239:    char Alpha[] = {"1234567890abcdefghijklmnopqrstuvwxyz"
240:                    "ABCDEFGHIJKLMNOPQRSTUVWXYZ"};
241:
242:    HDC DC = GetDC(hwnd);
243:
244:    int Index = SendMessage(hFontList, LB_GETCURSEL, 0, 0);
245:    SendMessage(hFontList, LB_GETTEXT, Index, LPARAM(lpszBuffer));
246:    lpfnEnumProc = (FONTENUMPROC)MakeProcInstance(
247:                    (FARPROC)DescribeFontCallBack, hInstance);
248:    EnumStruct.Count = 0;
249:    EnumStruct.hWindow = hwnd;
250:    EnumFontFamilies(DC, lpszBuffer, lpfnEnumProc,(LONG)&EnumStruct);
251:    FreeProcInstance((FARPROC)lpfnEnumProc);
252:
253:    if (TheFont != 0)
254:      SaveIt = SelectFont(DC, TheFont);
255:    GetTextMetrics(DC, &TextMetrics);
256:    HandleMetrics(TextMetrics);
257:    GetTextFace(DC, 150, aTextFace);
258:    if (TheFont != 0)
259:      SelectFont(DC, SaveIt);
260:
261:    ReleaseDC(hwnd, DC);
262:
263:    SendMessage(hFontName, WM_SETTEXT, 0, LPARAM(&lpszBuffer));
264:    SendMessage(hFontName, WM_SETFONT, WPARAM(TheFont), 0);
265:
266:    SendMessage(hAlphaEdit, WM_SETTEXT, 0, LPARAM(&Alpha));
267:    SendMessage(hAlphaEdit, WM_SETFONT, WPARAM(TheFont), 0);
268: }
269:
270: ///////////////////////////////////////////////////////
271: // HandleMetrics
272: ///////////////////////////////////////////////////////
273: void HandleMetrics(TEXTMETRIC TextMetrics)
274: {
275:
276:    if ((TextMetrics.tmPitchAndFamily & TMPF_TRUETYPE) ==
             TMPF_TRUETYPE)
277:      SendMessage(ButtonWindows[0], BM_SETCHECK, 1, 0L);
278:    else
279:      SendMessage(ButtonWindows[0], BM_SETCHECK, 0, 0L);
280:
281:    if ((TextMetrics.tmWeight) > 600)
282:      SendMessage(ButtonWindows[1], BM_SETCHECK, 1, 0L);
283:    else
284:      SendMessage(ButtonWindows[1], BM_SETCHECK, 0, 0L);
285:
```

continues

Listing 10.1. continued

```
286:    if (TextMetrics.tmItalic)
287:      SendMessage(ButtonWindows[2], BM_SETCHECK, 1, 0L);
288:    else
289:      SendMessage(ButtonWindows[2], BM_SETCHECK, 0, 0L);
290:
291: }
292:
293:
294: //////////////////////////////////////////////////////////
295: // FontCallback
296: //////////////////////////////////////////////////////////
297: #pragma argsused
298: int CALLBACK FontCallBack(LPENUMLOGFONT lpnlf,
299:                           LPNEWTEXTMETRIC lpntm,
300:                           int FontType, ENUMSTRUCT FAR * lpData)
301: {
302:   SendMessage(lpData->hWindow, LB_ADDSTRING, 0,
303: LPARAM(lpnlf->elfLogFont.lfFaceName));
304:   lpData->Count++;
305:   return 1;
306: }
307:
308: //////////////////////////////////////////////////////////
309: // DescribeFontCallback
310: //////////////////////////////////////////////////////////
311: #pragma argsused
312: int CALLBACK DescribeFontCallBack(LPENUMLOGFONT lpnlf,
313:                                   LPNEWTEXTMETRIC lpntm,
314:                                   int FontType,
                                      ENUMSTRUCT FAR * lpData)
315: {
316:   SendMessage(lpData->hWindow, WM_NEWFONT, 0,
                  LPARAM(&lpnl >elfLogFont));
317:   return 1;
318: }
```

Listing 10.2 shows the header file for FontsExp.

Type   Listing 10.2. FONTSEXP.H.

```
1: //////////////////////////////////////////////////
2: //   Program Name: FONTSEXP.H
3: //   Programmer: Charlie Calvert
4: //   Description: FontsExp windows program
5: //   Date: 06/20/93
6: //////////////////////////////////////////////////
```

```
 7:
 8: // constants
 9: #define WM_STARTFONTS (WM_USER + 0)
10: #define WM_NEWFONT (WM_USER + 1)
11:
12: #define ID_LISTBOX 1
13: #define CM_INFO 101
14:
15:
16: // Types
17: typedef struct
18: {
19:    int Count;
20:    HWND hWindow;
21: }ENUMSTRUCT;
22:
23: // Declarations for class FontsExp
24: #define FontsExp_DefProc     DefWindowProc
25: BOOL FontsExp_OnCreate(HWND hwnd, CREATESTRUCT FAR* lpCreateStruct);
26: void FontsExp_OnDestroy(HWND hwnd);
27: void FontsExp_OnCommand(HWND hwnd, int id, HWND hwndCtl,
                            UINT codeNotify);
28:
29: // Variables
30: HWND hFontList;
31: HWND hAlphaEdit;
32: HWND hTrueType;
33: HWND hNumFonts;
34: HWND hFontName;
35: static HFONT TheFont;
36: static LPLOGFONT TheLogFont;
37: HWND ButtonWindows[3];
38:
39: // Procs
40: LRESULT CALLBACK _export WndProc(HWND hwnd, UINT Message,
41:                                  WPARAM wParam, LPARAM lParam);
42: BOOL Register(HINSTANCE hInst);
43: HWND Create(HINSTANCE hInst, int nCmdShow);
44: void HandleMetrics(TEXTMETRIC TextMetrics);
45: void ShowTheFont(HWND hwnd);
46: BOOL CALLBACK _export FontCallBack(LPENUMLOGFONT lpnlf,
47:                     LPNEWTEXTMETRIC lpntm,
48:                     int FontType, ENUMSTRUCT FAR * lpData);
49: int CALLBACK _export DescribeFontCallBack(LPENUMLOGFONT lpnlf,
50:                     LPNEWTEXTMETRIC lpntm,
51:                     int FontType, ENUMSTRUCT FAR * lpData);
```

Listing 10.3 shows the source file for FontStr.

 Listing 10.3. FONTSTR.CPP.

```
1: ///////////////////////////////////////////////
2: //   Program Name: FONTSTR.CPP
3: //   Programmer: Charlie Calvert
4: //   Description: Create description of a font
5: //   Date: 06/20/93
6: ///////////////////////////////////////////////
7:
8: #define STRICT
9: #include <windows.h>
10: #include <windowsx.h>
11: #include <string.h>
12: #include <stdio.h>
13:
14:
15: // variables
16: TEXTMETRIC TextMetrics;
17: static char TheFaceName[80];
18:
19: // procs
20: char * GetType(char * S);
21: char * GetFamily(char * S);
22: char * GetCharSet(char * S);
23:
24: char * GetFontString(char * S, TEXTMETRIC TextMetric,
                          char * FaceName)
25: {
26:   char szType[99], szFamily[99], szCharSet[99];
27:
28:   TextMetrics = TextMetric;
29:   strcpy(TheFaceName, FaceName);
30:
31:   GetType(szType);
32:   GetFamily(szFamily);
33:   GetCharSet(szCharSet);
34:
35:   sprintf(S, "Font: %s \n Height: %d \n "
36:              "Ascent: %d \n Descent: %d \n "
37:              "AveCharW: %d \n MaxCharW: %d \n "
38:              "Weight: %d \n Italic: %hd \n "
39:              "Underlined: %d \n"
40:              "%s \n %s \n %s ",
41:   TheFaceName,
42:   TextMetrics.tmHeight,
43:   TextMetrics.tmAscent,
44:   TextMetrics.tmDescent,
45:   TextMetrics.tmAveCharWidth,
```

```
46:    TextMetrics.tmMaxCharWidth,
47:    TextMetrics.tmWeight,
48:    TextMetrics.tmItalic,
49:    TextMetrics.tmUnderlined,
50:    szType, szFamily, szCharSet);
51:
52:    return S;
53: }
54:
55: char * GetType(char * S)
56: {
57:    strcpy(S, "Font Type: ");
58:
59:    if ((TextMetrics.tmPitchAndFamily & TMPF_FIXED_PITCH) ==
60:        TMPF_FIXED_PITCH)
61:    strcat(S, "Fixed <> ");
62:    if ((TextMetrics.tmPitchAndFamily & TMPF_VECTOR) == TMPF_VECTOR)
63:    strcat(S, "Vector <> ");
64:    if ((TextMetrics.tmPitchAndFamily & TMPF_TRUETYPE) ==
          TMPF_TRUETYPE)
65:    strcat(S, "TrueType <> ");
66:    if ((TextMetrics.tmPitchAndFamily & TMPF_DEVICE) == TMPF_DEVICE)
67:    strcat(S, "Device <> ");
68:
69:    if (strlen(S) > 11)
70:      S[strlen(S) - 3] = '\0';
71:
72:    return S;
73: }
74:
75: char * GetFamily(char * S)
76: {
77:    int R = TextMetrics.tmPitchAndFamily & 0XF0;
78:    strcpy(S, "Family: ");
79:    if (R == FF_DONTCARE)
80:      strcat(S, "Don't Care or don't know");
81:    if (R == FF_ROMAN)
82:      strcat(S, "Roman");
83:    if (R == FF_SWISS)
84:      strcat(S, "Swiss");
85:    if (R == FF_MODERN)
86:      strcat(S, "Modern");
87:    if (R == FF_SCRIPT)
88:      strcat(S, "Script");
89:    if (R == FF_DECORATIVE)
90:      strcat(S, "Decorative");
91:
92:    return S;
93: }
94:
```

continues

Listing 10.3. continued

```
 95: char * GetCharSet(char * S)
 96: {
 97:   strcpy(S, "Char Set: ");
 98:
 99:   if (TextMetrics.tmCharSet == ANSI_CHARSET)
100:     strcat(S, "Ansi");
101:   if (TextMetrics.tmCharSet == DEFAULT_CHARSET)
102:     strcat(S, "Default");
103:   if (TextMetrics.tmCharSet == SYMBOL_CHARSET)
104:     strcat(S, "Symbol");
105:   if (TextMetrics.tmCharSet == OEM_CHARSET)
106:     strcat(S, "OEM");
107:
108:   return S;
109: }
```

Listing 10.4 shows the header file for FontStr.

 Listing 10.4. FONTSTR.H.

```
1: /////////////////////////////////////////////////
2: //   Program Name: FontStr.h
3: //   Programmer: Charlie Calvert
4: //   Description: FontsExp windows program header
5: //   Date: 06/20/93
6: /////////////////////////////////////////////////
7: char * GetFontString(char * S, TEXTMETRIC TextMetric,
8:                      char * FaceName);
```

Listing 10.5 shows the resource file for FontsExp.

 Listing 10.5. FONTSEXP.RC.

```
1: #include "fontsexp.h"
2: menu MENU
3: BEGIN
4:   MENUITEM "Info", CM_INFO
5: END
```

Listing 10.6 shows the definition file for FontsExp.

Listing 10.6. FONTSEXP.DEF.

```
 1: ; FONTSEXP.DEF
 2:
 3: NAME            FontsExp
 4: DESCRIPTION     'FontsExp Window'
 5: EXETYPE         WINDOWS
 6: STUB            'WINSTUB.EXE'
 7: CODE            PRELOAD MOVEABLE DISCARDABLE
 8: DATA            PRELOAD MOVEABLE MULTIPLE
 9:
10: HEAPSIZE        4096
11: STACKSIZE       5120
```

Listing 10.7 shows the Borland makefile for FontsExp.

Listing 10.7. FONTSEXP.MAK (Borland).

```
 1: # FONTSEXP.MAK
 2:
 3: # macros
 4: APPNAME = FontsExp
 5: INCPATH = C:\BC\INCLUDE
 6: LIBPATH = C:\BC\LIB
 7: FLAGS = -H -ml -W -v -w4 -I$(INCPATH) -L$(LIBPATH)
 8:
 9: # link
10: $(APPNAME).exe: $(APPNAME).obj $(APPNAME).def FONTSTR.OBJ
      $(APPNAME).res
11:   bcc $(FLAGS) $(APPNAME).obj FONTSTR.OBJ
12:   brc $(APPNAME).res
13:
14: # compile
15: $(APPNAME).obj: $(APPNAME).cpp
16:   bcc -c $(FLAGS) $(APPNAME).cpp
17:
18: # compile
19: FONTSTR.OBJ: FONTSTR.CPP
20:   bcc -c $(FLAGS) FONTSTR.CPP
21:
22: # compile
23: $(APPNAME).res: $(APPNAME).rc
24:   brc -r i$(INCPATH) $(APPNAME).rc
```

Listing 10.8 shows the Microsoft makefile for FONTSEXP.

 Listing 10.8. FONTSEXP.MAK(Microsoft).

```
 1: #-----------------------
 2: # FONTSEXP.MAK makefile,
 3: # Microsoft version
 4: #-----------------------
 5: FONTSEXP.EXE : FONTSEXP.OBJ FONTSEXP.DEF FONTSTR.OBJ  FONTSEXP.RES
 6:   link /CO fontsexp fontstr, /align:16, NUL, /nod llibcew libw,
      fontsexp
 7:
 8:     rc FONTSEXP.RES
 9:
10: FONTSEXP.OBJ : FONTSEXP.CPP
11:     cl -c -AL -GA -Ow -W2 -Zp -Zi FONTSEXP.CPP
12:
13: FONTSTR.OBJ : FONTSTR.CPP
14:     cl -c -AL -GA -Ow -W2 -Zp -Zi FONTSTR.CPP
15:
16: FONTSEXP.RES : FONTSEXP.RC
17:     rc -r FONTSEXP.RC
```

 The FontsExp program creates a window and populates it with static controls, edit controls, check boxes, and list boxes. It uses these controls to enable the user to display a series of fonts. The FontInfo menu choice lets the user view information about the current font. See Figure 10.2.

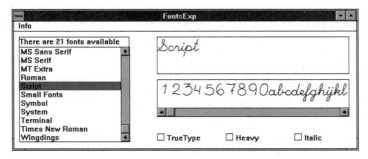

Figure 10.2. *The FontExp program, displaying the system font in its list box and the Script font in an edit and static control.*

Now that you've seen the code, it's time to rev up your engines and pay special attention to the rest of this chapter. Most Windows programmers work with controls on a daily basis. Understand them thoroughly, and you'll be well on your way to creating powerful, robust programs that users love.

Static Controls

When you want to create a static control, all you need to do is call CreateWindow. Static controls are the easiest controls to utilize. Here are the minimum steps involved:

☐ Call CreateWindow.

☐ Fill in the first field of CreateWindow, called lpszClassname, with the word "static."

☐ Fill in the third field, called dwStyle, with the WS_CHILD and WS_VISIBLE styles, and any others you might need to add, such as SS_LEFT or SS_SIMPLE.

☐ Specify the control's dimensions.

☐ Fill in the program's hwndParent field with the HWND from the main window.

☐ Give the control a unique ID by filling in the hMenu field with a predefined constant.

☐ Use SetWindowText to fill the control with a string.

As you'll see, there are a few other factors to keep in mind, but these steps form the core ideas used when creating static controls. In fact, you can use these steps as a template for creating all window controls. In other words, all controls are created by calls to CreateWindow, with special attention being paid to the fields previously outlined. Because of their importance, I discuss these fields in detail over the next few paragraphs. Figure 10.3 shows the FontsExp program with two static controls.

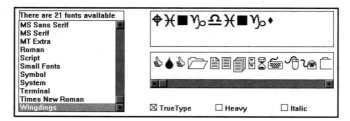

Figure 10.3. *The FontsExp program uses two static controls.*

Following are the calls that create the two static controls in the FontsExp program:

```
168:    hNumFonts = CreateWindow("static", NULL,
169:                             WS_CHILD | WS_VISIBLE | WS_BORDER,
170:                             10, 10, 200, 20, hwnd, HMENU(-1),
171:                             hInstance, NULL);
172:
173:    hFontName = CreateWindow("static", NULL,
174:                        WS_CHILD | WS_VISIBLE | WS_BORDER,
175:                        260, 10, 350, 70, hwnd, HMENU(-1),
                            hInstance, NULL);
176:
```

As you can see, this code looks like the routines used to create a main window, except that there's no need to first register a class. The reason for this omission is simply that the "static" class has been preregistered for you.

Note: The fact that a static control is just a preregistered window is such an important point that I want to take a moment to emphasize it.

In this book, you have learned how to create a number of different windows that behave in a particular way. You did this by filling out their WNDCLASS structure with values of your own choosing, and then writing message response functions called from a window procedure. In the process, you created several classes of potentially reusable windows that behave in various, predefined ways.

This is exactly what has already been done for you with the static, list box, combo box, button, and scrollbar classes. Microsoft has already registered these classes and defined how they will respond to certain messages. The GameWindow class from the Snake1 program, for instance, has a certain defined behavior stemming from the structure of its WNDCLASS and WndProc. The same is true of the static class.

You have been calling CreateWindow regularly since the second chapter. When creating child window controls, however, you need to take special note of a few key points. The next few paragraphs outline those points for you while showing you how to create a static control.

The dwStyle field (line 169) of CreateWindow ORs together WS_CHILD, WS_VISIBLE, and WS_BORDER. The first and last styles simply tell Windows that this is a child window with a border. The WS_VISIBLE style is a nifty little flag that requests Windows to call the ShowWindow function. In past chapters, most calls to CreateWindow have been followed by calls to ShowWindow and UpdateWindow:

```
ShowWindow(hwnd, nCmdShow);
UpdateWindow(hwnd);
```

If you use the WS_VISIBLE style, this isn't necessary, because Windows does the dirty work for you.

The next set of fields you need be concerned with are those that define the size of the border surrounding the static control. When CreateWindow is being called for a main window, these fields are usually filled with CW_USEDEFAULT constants. With list boxes, however, you should explicitly fill in these fields with the actual dimensions you want associated with your list box.

The next step is to fill out the hwndParent parameter to CreateWindow. Controls are child windows, and children need parents. In this case, of course, the parent is the main window.

Another field you need to be aware of is the ninth, called hMenu (line 165). This is where you normally designate the menu to be associated with a window. Because static controls don't have menus, this field is available as a place to specify an ID number to be associated with a window.

The ID number you pick can prove important later when you set up a line of communication between a control and its parent window. As a result, if you decide to specify a value in this field, you should pick a unique ID number for each control. This is especially true for controls that are embedded in dialogs. In those cases, the ID number is the only link between a dialog and a control.

Because programmers develop a lot of these ID constants in their programs, they've fallen into the habit of using #defines to act as mnemonics:

```
#define MYLISTBOX 101
#define MYBUTTON 102
#define MYWHATHAVEYOU 103
```

Notice that you need to typecast the ID number to an HMENU value before the program will compile.

> **Note:** The FontsExp program usually communicates with a control through its HWND, which is carefully saved after every call to CreateWindow. This technique is easy to use when working with controls embedded in windows. Inside of dialogs, however, it's simpler to use an ID.

To make static controls useful objects, all you need to do is place a bit of text in them with the SetWindowText call:

```
SetWindowText(hNumFonts, S);
```

hNumFonts is the handle to a window, and *S* is the string that appears in the static control.

Static controls are the simplest controls you're likely to use in a Windows program. Of course, nothing in Windows is ever devoid of syntactical verbosity. For instance, there are a number of changes you can run on static texts; you can change their border and color, or use them to seat icons or bitmaps.

Following are some of the valid styles that can be OR'd into the dwStyle field of a static control:

SS_BLACKRECT	SS_BLACKFRAME
SS_GRAYRECT	SS_GRAYFRAME
SS_WHITERECT	SS_WHITEFRAME
SS_LEFT	SS_RIGHT
SS_CENTER	SS_ICON

Feel free to experiment with these styles. Take special note, however, of the simple examples I've included in the FontsExp program. They can remain as an image of what lies at the heart of every control—an ordinary window with something painted inside it.

> **Note**: In this example program, a great deal goes on in the WM_CREATE message function handler. It's the place in which all the controls used in the program are created. This, of course, only makes sense. In fact, the idea of creating controls in response to a WM_CREATE message really defines

what the message is all about. A WM_CREATE message is sent to a window specifically to say: "Hey, wake up there; it's time for you to create all your child windows and to do any other initialization you deem necessary!"

List Boxes

Of particular interest in the context of the current chapter is the code for creating list box controls:

```
163:    hFontList = CreateWindow("listbox", NULL,
164:                    WS_CHILD | WS_VISIBLE | LBS_STANDARD,
165:                    9, 30, 201, 180, hwnd, HMENU(ID_LISTBOX),
166:                    hInstance, NULL);
```

List boxes are rectangular windows that present the user with an array of items to select. A list box and a static control are shown in Figure 10.4.

Figure 10.4. *A static control with a string in it. Immediately beneath it is a list box filled with font names.*

In the list box, the most important field is the third, in which you can define the style of the class:

```
WS_CHILD | WS_VISIBLE | LBS_STANDARD,
```

By this time, I'm sure it won't come as a surprise to you to learn that the LBS_STANDARD flag is part of another lengthy array of options. This is the Windows way of doing things. Good Windows programmers eventually develop a kind of love/hate relationship with these tables full of options and possibilities. After all, each list may be a bit confusing, but it also contains numerous tidbits that can be used to spice up your program.

Because Borland and Microsoft have already provided you with several copies of this list, I'll show you only the ones programmers are likely to use on a regular basis:

LBS_MULTIPLESEL	User can select more than one item at a time
LBS_EXTENDEDSEL	Enables multiple items to be selected by using the Shift key and the mouse or special key combinations
LBS_NOTIFY	When turned off, the parent window doesn't know whether the user has clicked or double-clicked a string
LBS_STANDARD	The standard list box with a border, and with LBS_NOTIFY turned on
LBS_OWNERDRAW	The style you need if you want to display bitmaps, or other nonstandard items in a list box
LBS_USETABSTOPS	To use for multiple columns in a single list box
LBS_WANTKEYBOARDINPUT	Enables the programmer to pick up on keyboard input when the list box has the focus

Of these items, the two most important are LBS_STANDARD and LBS_MULTIPLESEL. Multiple selection list boxes work like the windows in the File Manager; they let you select multiple items at one time. Of course, they don't have all the capabilities of the windows in the File Manager, but they do enable multiple selections.

In your day-to-day programming life, creating a list box will prove to be a trivial task that you can accomplish in just a few moments. Simply cut and paste the call from another program, or copy the CreateWindow call from your main window. Then, change a few of the fields. There's really nothing to it.

The subject of communicating with a list box can become fairly involved. Therefore, I'll postpone any in-depth discussion of the topic until the next chapter.

For now, a few simple examples should suffice. If you want to add a string to a list box, you can do so by sending it an LB_ADDSTRING message:

```
char * MyString[] = "Sambo";
SendMessage(hListBox, LB_ADDSTRING, 0, LPARAM(MyString));
```

Conversely, you can retrieve a string from a list box by first getting the index of the currently selected item with an LB_GETCURSEL message:

```
int Index = SendMessage(hFontList, LB_GETCURSEL, 0, 0);
```

Use the index to retrieve the string by using an LB_GETTEXT message:

```
SendMessage(hFontList, LB_GETTEXT, Index, LONG(lpszBuffer));
```

This material is being presented here mostly as a reference tool. For now, don't spend too much time worrying about the actual process involved in communicating with list boxes. The whole topic is reintroduced and explained in-depth in the next chapter.

Check Boxes

Following are the calls that create all three of the check boxes used in this program:

```
static char *Titles[] = {"TrueType" , "Heavy", "Italic"};

for (int i = 0; i < 3; i++)
  ButtonWindows[i] = CreateWindow("button", Titles[i],
                     WS_CHILD | WS_VISIBLE | BS_CHECKBOX,
                     260  + (i * 125), 180, 100, 35,
                     hwnd, HMENU(-1), hInstance, NULL);
```

To create a check box you should specify the "button" class name and use the BS_CHECKBOX style. The preceding example also shows how to use constant arrays and for loops to create a series of three controls—techniques you'll probably use on many occasions.

Note: *Check boxes* are little square bordered windows with a name attached to them, as shown in Figure 10.4. If the bordered window has an X in it, that item is selected; otherwise, it's not selected. In most cases, users click a check box with a mouse to select or deselect an option. FontsExp, however, sends messages to select or deselect a check box, and the user never interacts with the box directly.

Figure 10.5 shows check boxes in the list box of the FontsExp program. If you use the arrow keys to move the highlight bar up and down the list, the check boxes blink on and off like Christmas lights.

Figure 10.5. *A selected check box has an X in it, whereas unselected check boxes are blank.*

I'm sure you've already guessed that the BS_CHECKBOX style is only one of many different possible styles that can be associated with a button control. This versatile class is one that Windows programmers rely on time and time again. Take a careful look at the following button styles:

BS_CHECKBOX	Creates a check box
BS_DEFPUSHBUTTON	Has a heavy black border and is chosen by default when the user presses the Enter key
BS_GROUPBOX	Brings a group of controls together into a group
BS_3STATE	Can be grayed as well as checked and unchecked
BS_AUTO3STATE	Responds automatically to being selected
BS_AUTOCHECKBOX	Responds when the user selects it
BS_AUTORADIOBUTTON	Responds when the user selects it
BS_LEFTTEXT	Text on the left, not the right side of a check box or radio button
BS_OWNERDRAW	Lets the programmer define the appearance of a button
BS_PUSHBUTTON	Standard button
BS_RADIOBUTTON	When placed in a group, the user usually only can select one of these at a time

This list shows that buttons are very versatile tools. At first, you might not even make the connections among standard OK buttons, check boxes, and radio buttons. However, all these tools belong to the same class, and you should learn to think of them as being closely related.

Communicating with check boxes can be a fairly delicate matter. For now, I'll only state that you can use the BM_SETCHECK messages to perform the most important aspects of the job. The key point to remember is that passing 1 in the WM_PARAM field sets the check, whereas passing 0 clears the check mark:

```
SendMessage(ButtonWindows[0], BM_SETCHECK, 1, 0L);
```

If you want to query a check box as to the state of its button, use BM_GETCHECK:

```
SendMessage(ButtonWindows[0], BM_GETCHECK, 0, 0L);
```

Because I don't want to overwhelm you with too much material in one day, I'll delay any in-depth discussion of this topic until the next chapter. There, you'll see how FontsExp uses messages to control and query check boxes.

Edit Controls

The FontsExp program also makes use of an edit control, shown in Figure 10.6. Edit controls are used for getting input from a user through the keyboard, as in a text editor. In fact, edit controls can be used to create small text editors that can handle a few pages of text at a time.

Figure 10.6. *The edit control, with its scrollbar, displays the ever-useful WingDings font.*

In this particular program, you might never type in the edit control; you might prefer to simply scroll its text back and forth. However, it's easy to see how a user might want to look at a particular combination of letters, so I've designed the program to respond to that contingency. Notice, however, that this is the only part of the program that requires any typing skills. Windows is a long way from the DOS prompt!

The call to initialize the edit control uses six different styles OR'd together to form the third parameter:

```
177:    hAlphaEdit = CreateWindow("edit", NULL,
178:               WS_CHILD | WS_VISIBLE | WS_BORDER | WS_HSCROLL |
179:               ES_LEFT | ES_AUTOHSCROLL | ES_MULTILINE,
180:               260, 90, 350, 70, hwnd, HMENU(-1),
181:               hInstance, NULL);
```

DO add the WS_BORDER style if you want the control to be outlined in black. Scrollbars are handled automatically by list boxes. You can add this feature to your edit controls simply by using the WS_HSCROLL style.

DON'T confuse this style with either the ES_AUTOHSCROLL or ES_AUTOVSCROLL styles. These two styles let the user scroll text into view if it is hidden behind the right or bottom edge of a control.

I'm sure the astute reader has already prepared him or herself for another long list of identifiers. So, without further delay, here are the edit control styles:

ES_AUTOHSCROLL	Automatically scrolls horizontally
ES_AUTOVSCROLL	Automatically scrolls vertically
ES_CENTER	Centers the text
ES_LEFT	Aligns text on the left margin
ES_LOWERCASE	Converts text to lowercase
ES_MULTILINE	Uses multiple lines
ES_NOHIDESEL	Forces Windows to keep the text highlighted, even if you set the focus to another control. (If you highlight a text fragment, Windows will normally not preserve the selection after the control loses focus.)
ES_OEMCONVERT	Helps preserve characters outside the range of normal letters and numbers
ES_PASSWORD	Helps prevent other users from seeing what is being typed into an edit control
ES_READONLY	Uses the edit control only for viewing text
ES_RIGHT	Aligns text on the right margin
ES_UPPERCASE	Sets all input to uppercase

| ES_WANTRETURN | Treats carriage returns normally, rather than sending them on to the default button |

This list is invaluable. Countless Windows programmers have spent hours trapping WM_KEYDOWN messages to handle carriage returns, or to create edit controls appropriate for handling passwords. Don't become one of these poor, overworked programmers. Instead, take a careful look at these styles so you don't have to reinvent the proverbial wheel!

Communicating with edit controls is a fairly simple process. To insert text into an edit control, call SetWindowText, just as you do with a static control:

```
SetWindowText(hAlphaEdit, S);
```

To retrieve text from an edit control, call GetWindowText:

```
GetWindowText(hAlphaEdit, S, sizeof(S));
```

With GetWindowText, the first parameter is the HWND of the edit control; the second is a buffer to hold the string displayed in the control; the third is the maximum number of bytes the string can hold.

In the next chapter, you'll see that the SendMessage function provides an alternative to this technique. For instance, the following call passes the string Alpha to an edit control:

```
SendMessage(hAlphaEdit, WM_SETTEXT, 0, LPARAM(&Alpha));
```

Don't worry if this last call still looks a bit obscure to you. It is explored in-depth in the next chapter.

Besides WM_SETTEXT, edit controls also respond to a series of messages that enable you to directly manipulate their text. Most of these messages involve relatively advanced Windows programming issues, but you should at least be aware of their existence. Here is a small sample:

EM_CANUNDO	Checks whether an operation can be undone
EM_GETMODIFY	Checks whether contents have changed
EM_GETRECT	Gets control's coordinates
EM_GETSEL	Gets position of current selection
EM_LIMITTEXT	Limits text in an edit control
EM_REPLACESEL	Replaces current selection
EM_SETPASSWORDCHAR	Sets password character

EM_SETREADONLY	Sets the read-only state
EM_SETSEL	Selects text
EM_UNDO	Undoes the preceding operation

Summary

In this chapter, you had a chance to become acquainted with Windows controls. You saw that these tools can be used to form an interactive interface between your program and a user.

This chapter covered the creation of four controls:

1. Static controls

2. List boxes

3. Check boxes

4. Edit controls

Because you've also looked at scrollbars, you have knowledge of five different controls.

When creating window controls, the most important step is to fill in the first field of CreateWindow, called lpszClassName, with the class name of a control. For instance, if you want to create an edit control, copy the word *edit* into lpszClassName. Other controls are created by copying in one of the following words: *static, scrollbar, list box,* or *button.*

This chapter also presented an in-depth discussion of the various styles used to define the behavior of a control. For instance, you saw that the ES_CENTER style centers text in an edit control, and the BS_CHECKBOX style converts an ordinary button into a check box.

Q&A

1. Q: You showed us so many different window styles in this chapter. How are we ever supposed to keep up with all this information?

   A: Don't bother memorizing all the styles shown in this chapter. Instead, just absorb the fact that every control has a set of styles that can be used to fine tune, or even radically change, its appearance and behavior. Another

helpful point is that the styles associated with each of the controls begin with a particular set of letters. For instance, edit control styles all begin with ES. To help you understand how this works, here is a list of letters associated with each of the major control types:

Button	BS
Combo box	CBS
Edit	ES
List box	LBS
Static	SS

2. Q: I still don't understand this business of communicating with a style through an ID or an HWND. What gives?

A: Windows is monolithic in size, but it's also extremely flexible. Controls are designed so you can communicate with them either through their HWND or ID. When a control is embedded in a window it's simplest to communicate with it through an HWND. Dialogs have a slightly different relationship with their controls, so it's easiest to communicate with a dialog's controls through their ID. Whether you use an HWND or an ID, the key point is that you have a unique handle associated with a control.

Workshop

The Workshop provides quiz questions to help you solidify your understanding of the material covered and exercises to provide you with experience in using what you've learned. Try to understand the quiz and exercise answers before continuing on to the next chapter. Answers are provided in Appendix A.

Quiz

1. What single function can be used to create all the controls listed in this chapter?

2. Why don't you need to register the class of a static control?

3. How do you designate the parent of a control?

4. You can communicate with a control through its HWND or its _____?

5. How do you specify the ID of a control?

6. What logical operation is used to specify the style of a control?

7. Other than `PostMessage` and `SendMessage`, what two commands can be used to place or retrieve a string in an edit control or static control?

8. Why are list boxes and check boxes called controls?

9. What control is the `EM_SETSEL` message associated with, and what is its function?

10. How can you tell if a check box is selected?

Exercises

1. Write a small program with a single static control. Every time the user clicks the left mouse button, have the text in the edit control change.

2. Create a program with a single list box and a single edit control. Design the program so that the text in the edit control will be transferred to the list box when the user clicks the left mouse button.

Talking to Controls, Using the *EnumFontFamilies* Callback

Today, you'll use the debugger to see how Windows communicates with list boxes, edit controls, static controls, and buttons. You'll also learn more about the `SendMessage` and `PostMessage` functions, which enable you to place your own messages (or standard Windows messages) into the message queue.

A third topic explored in this chapter involves enumerating the fonts on the system. This is accomplished through the `EnumFontFamilies` function and the `EnumFontFamilies` callback. Because of the presence of a callback, this chapter also includes another brief look at `MakeProcInstance`.

Specifically, this chapter covers

- ☐ The FontsExp program
- ☐ Creating user-defined messages
- ☐ The `SendMessage` function
- ☐ The `PostMessage` function
- ☐ Using the callback function, `EnumFontFamilies`
- ☐ Communicating with list boxes
- ☐ Communicating with check boxes

This chapter continues the exploration of the FontsExp program, so there aren't any new code listings. But that doesn't mean you get a free ride. Instead of spending time getting a new program up and running, I want you to concentrate on learning how to use the debugger. The material presented in this chapter is quite challenging, and you might not ever totally understand how it works unless you take the time to watch it execute in your debugger. Throughout the chapter, I make several references to the debugger, and how you can use it to explore this program. Take those references seriously, they're important!

A Brief History of *WM_STARTFONTS*

From a purely conceptual point of view, this chapter covers fairly complex material. The theme for the day is communication, specifically the way Windows communicates with messages and callbacks.

Note: The tricky stuff in this chapter is here because I regard it as absolutely essential information. Sending and posting messages is one of the most common jobs performed by Windows programmers. A book like this has to contain a clear description of how messages work. Without a fairly detailed knowledge of their inner workings, you'll never really understand what your job as a programmer is all about. Callback functions are used less frequently, but they play a vital roll in the Windows paradigm. Take your time going through this chapter.

The agenda is as follows:

☐ Learn about a user-defined message called WM_STARTFONTS.

☐ Trace WM_STARTFONTS from the moment of its conception until it sets off two calls to EnumFontFamilies, thereby causing messages to be sent that fill up the list box and other visual elements of the FontsExp program.

Each step on the agenda is explained methodically, starting from point one and working to the end. The narrative flow is provided by the life history of WM_STARTFONTS. In other words, the chapter starts by describing the declaration of WM_STARTFONTS, then follows through by describing how the message is sent and processed. My theory is that if you watch a message from the moment it's defined, until it's finally delivered and processed, you'll get a complete overview of the subject—without any major gaps or omissions.

Delivering the Mail

Before starting the discussion of WM_STARTFONTS, it might be helpful to take just a moment to pick up the thread from the last chapter. On Day 10, you had a detailed look at the WM_CREATE method response function for the FontsExp program. In the process, you learned how to create edit controls, static controls, list boxes, and check boxes with the CreateWindow procedure.

I didn't mention one command in FontsExp_OnCreate; that's the call to PostMessage:

```
PostMessage(hwnd, WM_STARTFONTS, 0, 0);
```

To understand how PostMessage works, it's best to start out by defining messages from a new, and hopefully elucidating, perspective. WM_STARTFONTS is a user-defined message sent to tell the main window that it's time to fill up the list box and other controls with the names and descriptions of all the fonts on the system. There are two differences between user-defined messages and other messages:

☐ User-defined messages are declared by the programmer, whereas normal Windows messages are declared in WINDOWS.H, or in other header files that come with the system.

☐ User-defined messages normally have only local scope. This means that they can be defined for one class only.

More specifically, user-defined messages are calculated in terms of a constant called WM_USER, which is defined in WINDOWS.H.

```
/* NOTE: All messages below 0x0400 are RESERVED by Windows */
#define WM_USER         0x0400
```

As you can see, the comment in WINDOWS.H specifies that messages below 1024 (0X400) are reserved for internal use by Windows.

The WM_STARTFONTS message is defined in FONTSEXP.H:

```
#define WM_STARTFONTS (WM_USER + 0)
```

The preceding line of code simply states that WM_STARTFONTS should be assigned a number which will enable Windows to recognize it as a message of local import. By definition, it is intended specifically for the FontsExp class. To define additional messages, simply add 1 to the value of WM_STARTFONTS:

```
#define WM_STARTFONTS          (WM_USER + 0)
#define WM_NEWFONT             (WM_USER + 1)
```

and so on.

Of course, the WM_STARTFONTS message isn't the only message on the system which is assigned to hex value 400. In fact, the following messages, from WINDOWS.H, each have the same offset:

```
#define BM_GETCHECK            (WM_USER+0)
#define EM_GETSEL              (WM_USER+0)
#define CB_GETEDITSEL          (WM_USER+0)
#define DM_GETDEFID            (WM_USER+0)
#define STM_SETICON            (WM_USER+0)
```

This duplication of constants doesn't lead to confusion, because these messages are always sent to a particular window—designated by the HWND in the first parameter to PostMessage or SendMessage:

```
HWND hMainWindow, hCheckBox;  // Handles to windows
PostMessage(hMainWindow, WM_STARTFONTS, 0, 0L);
SendMessage(hCheckBox, BM_GETCHECK, 0, 0L);
```

This call states explicitly that WM_STARTFONTS is being sent to the program's main window. If it were accidentally sent to a check box, Windows would cheerfully ignore all the fonts on your system and return the state of the check box.

There are times when you need to create a message that is sent across the desktop to more than one application. To do that, call RegisterWindowMessage, which returns a unique message (defined at runtime) to be used by your applications.

DO   DON'T

DO use WM_USER as an offset for messages that are going to be sent only to one class.

DON'T try to send these messages between applications.

DO use the RegisterWindowMessage function to assign numbers to messages that will be sent between applications.

SendMessage and *PostMessage*

Now that you know how WM_STARTFONTS is declared, you're ready to take a look at PostMessage and SendMessage. These are two of the more interesting API calls. They perform functions that appear to be quite similar, but are in fact quite different. They should occupy separate, but adjacent, living quarters in your imagination.

The basic purpose of both SendMessage and PostMessage is to tell a particular window to perform a task. The SendMessage function does this by explicitly calling the window procedure associated with the HWND in its parameter list. SendMessage doesn't return from that window procedure until the window has processed the message in question.

The PostMessage function, however, doesn't explicitly call a window procedure. Instead, it posts a message to the application's message queue and immediately returns. Every application has a message queue that will, by default, handle up to eight messages at a time. Messages are retrieved from the queue by the GetMessage function. If you glance at FontsExp's WinMain function, you can see that after GetMessage is called, a message is passed on to the window procedure with the DispatchMessage function. What it all boils down to is that SendMessage delivers a message directly to a window procedure, whereas PostMessage just plops a message into a queue. In other words, SendMessage is the express route, and PostMessage is the slower, more laid-back way to deliver the mail. (See Figure 11.1.)

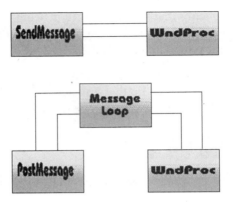

Figure 11.1. `SendMessage` *delivers a message directly to a window procedure, whereas* `PostMessage` *takes a more roundabout route.*

DO	**DON'T**

DO use `SendMessage` when time is of the essence, that is, when you want to be sure a message is processed before the `SendMessage` call ends.

DON'T use `SendMessage` if you can possibly put off processing the message.

DO remember that `SendMessage` won't return until its message has been processed.

DON'T forget that `PostMessage` returns immediately, enabling your program to continue to be processed sequentially, at least until the message is delivered (or until some other event takes over the processor).

In this particular case, FontsExp uses `PostMessage` for two reasons. The first is that there is no immediate need to process the message; the second reason is that the creation of the window should end before the `WM_STARTFONTS` message is processed.

How can FontsExp be sure that the creation of the window will be completed before the message is processed? To understand the reasoning, simply trace through the steps involved in starting a Windows application.

Start the debugger and place a breakpoint at the first call to `CreateWindow`. Next, start stepping through the program from the beginning, after `WinMain` is called. The first step is the call to `RegisterWindow`. Then, there are the calls to `CreateWindow`, `ShowWindow`, `UpdateWindow`, and `GetMessage`.

Note: Because you might be using any one of a number of different compilers, I can't describe exactly how to use your debugger. If you are not yet familiar with your debugger, you should take the time to learn about it by reading your compiler's documentation. Think of it as a trade off: there's no new code in this chapter, so you should spend your free time getting acquainted with your debugger and stepping through the FontsExp program. Believe me, it will be well worth it!

The WM_STARTFONTS message is posted at the end of a WM_CREATE message handler function. WM_CREATE messages are sent during the call to CreateWindow. This means that a window will finish creation, be shown, and be updated before GetMessage ever has a chance to pull the WM_STARTFONTS message out of the application queue.

Here's another view of the whole process:

1. Register the window.

2. Call CreateWindow. This is the stage at which a window handles WM_CREATE messages. This is also when the WM_STARTFONTS message is posted.

3. Show and update the window.

4. Start the message loop. It's during this stage that the WM_STARTFONTS message is actually passed on to WndProc.

I'm discussing this topic in-depth, because the whole idea of sending and posting messages is a crucial part of the life of a Windows application. Furthermore, you won't really understand what's being said in the rest of this chapter unless you first understand, at least in general terms, how SendMessage and PostMessage work.

Enumerating the System Fonts

In the last section, you saw the mail being delivered. You saw the posting of the WM_STARTFONTS message, and then saw it through to its address in the WndProc procedure. After the post office has done its job, the next step is to process the message in the body of the WndProc. To follow this with your debugger, place a breakpoint on the line that begins with lpfnEnumProc. Now run the FontsExp program again from the beginning, and continue until you reach the breakpoint in WM.STARTFONTS.

```
case WM_STARTFONTS:
{
  HDC DC = GetDC(hwnd);
```

```
lpfnEnumProc = (FONTENUMPROC)MakeProcInstance(
                (FARPROC)FontCallBack, hInstance);
EnumStruct.Count = 0;
EnumStruct.hWindow = hFontList;
EnumFontFamilies(DC, NULL,
                lpfnEnumProc, (LONG)&EnumStruct);
FreeProcInstance((FARPROC)lpfnEnumProc);

ReleaseDC(hwnd, DC);

wsprintf(S, "There are %d fonts available",
        EnumStruct.Count);
SetWindowText(hNumFonts, S);

SetFocus(hFontList);
SendMessage(hFontList, LB_SETCURSEL, 0, 0);
ShowTheFont(hwnd);
return 1;
}
```

The goal of this code is to enumerate through the system fonts. It asks the system: "What fonts do you have available?" The system answers back, "Arial, New Times Roman, Script" (and so on). This process becomes somewhat complex, primarily because its windows (not the FontsExp program) that knows which fonts are available. Therefore, the FontsExp program has to find a way to ask Windows which fonts are available on the system.

The solution is to set up an address for Windows to mail the information to, and then to simply wait at that address while Windows iterates through all the available fonts. Each time a font is found, Windows sends a letter to the proper address in FontsExp. It's just like ordering something from the Land's End catalog. You send something in the mail and wait for the goodies to arrive. Anybody can do it! (See Figure 11.2.)

The first step is to set up the mailing address, which in this case happens to be a function called FontCallBack. Right now, don't worry about how this function works; just concentrate on the fact that it exists. It's a little post office box with its own address.

Here is how to tell Windows the address of the FontCallBack function:

```
lpfnEnumProc = (FONTENUMPROC)MakeProcInstance(
                (FARPROC)FontCallBack, hInstance);
```

This is a fairly nasty piece of work. But don't worry; it's not that hard to sort the syntactical wheat from the syntactical chaff in a case like this.

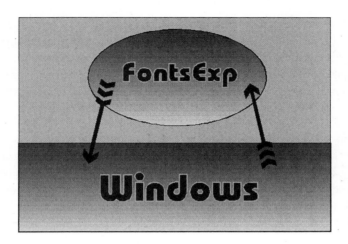

Figure 11.2. *FontsExp asks Windows what fonts are available, and Windows sends information back.*

The core call is to `MakeProcInstance`. This is the function that sets up an address for the `FontCallBack` procedure. More specifically, what actually happens is that Windows attaches a bit of prolog code to `FontCallBack`. This prolog code binds the FontsExp's data segment to the `FontCallBack` function.

Note: Setting up the `FontCallBack` procedure involves a similar process to the one you went through when you were learning how to set up a `DialogBox` procedure. All the issues are the same. The `FontCallBack` function is part of FontsExp, but it's going to be called by Windows. This means that `FontCallBack` is really a part of Windows (and not part of your application) when it is being called. As a result, the `FontCallBack` function would not normally have access to the FontsExp's data segment. One of the purposes of the call to `MakeProcInstance` is to resolve this problem through the auspices of the bit of prolog code (mentioned previously).

If, by some chance, the last few paragraphs don't make a great deal of sense to you, you should turn back to the discussion of the `DialogBox` procedure, fall back to the mailing address analogy, use the debugger to set breakpoints on the `FontCallBack` function, and keep running or stepping through the program until this process begins to make sense.

> The point is that Windows and your program need to agree on the mailing address to which the list of fonts will be delivered. The MakeProcInstance function registers the address with the postal service and makes sure a clean path of communication is available.

In order to call MakeProcInstance successfully, you should typecast the value it returns as a FONTENUMPROC. This is necessary because the EnumFontFamilies procedure, which you will read about in a moment, expects to be passed an address of type FONTENUMPROC. You should also typecast the FontCallBack procedure as a simple FARPROC. A FARPROC is really only a generic procedure type, without any specific arguments or return value. Of course, it goes without saying that all FARPROCs are assumed to be declared FAR.

Note: If you're not familiar with making typecasts, you can think of the specific one shown here like this: A Ford Mustang is a specific type of car, just as the FontCallBack function is a specific type of function; but a FARPROC is just a generic term for a procedure, just as the word vehicle or car is often used as a generic term for a Mustang. MakeProcInstance returns a generic term, and FontsExp performs a typecast so it can treat the return value as a specific type of address. It's saying: "Okay. As far as you are concerned, you're just delivering a car, but I know that this particular car is a Mustang, so I'm going to treat it that way." It's as if the guy who does the trucking just thinks: "Okay, I'm delivering a load of cars. I don't know what make they are and I don't care." However, the dealer he's delivering to knows exactly what kinds of cars are being shipped; so, he can tell his workers: "Go down to the shipping bay and pick up that Mustang that's coming in."

The next few lines look like this:

```
EnumStruct.Count = 0;
EnumStruct.hWindow = hFontList;
EnumFontFamilies(DC, NULL, lpfnEnumProc, (LONG)&EnumStruct);
```

The center of focus is the EnumFontFamilies call, which takes a device context as its first parameter. The second parameter is the name of a font family, which in this case is set to NULL. The third parameter is the address of the callback function, which is the post office box to which information will be sent. The final parameter is the address of some data which you can pass to the FontCallBack function. In many cases, you can set this last parameter to zero. However, I have filled it in here, primarily so you can see how to use it.

Feel free to pass in the address of any structure or type in this last parameter to the EnumFontFamilies function. In this specific case, I'm passing in a record that contains two fields: the first an integer and the second an HWND. I want to stress that I've customized this structure for my own purposes. If you prefer, you can pass a structure containing four strings and a float, the address of another procedure, or just plain old NULL. Any valid pointer address is fine.

The Callback Function

During the call to EnumFontFamilies, Windows sends the mail to the FontCallBack function. To see the connection here, use the debugger to set a break in FontCallBack, and then step into the EnumFontFamilies call in the WndProc. You should see the focus switch from EnumFontFamilies directly to FontCallBack:

```
int CALLBACK FontCallBack(LPENUMLOGFONT lpnlf,
                          LPNEWTEXTMETRIC lpntm,
                          int FontType, ENUMSTRUCT FAR * lpData)
{
  SendMessage(lpData->hWindow, LB_ADDSTRING, 0,
              LONG(lpnlf->elfLogFont.lfFaceName));
  return 1;
}
```

The parameters to FontCallBack are defined by the EnumFontFamProc API function. In actual practice, you might never name a routine EnumFontFamProc. Instead, this function serves as a placeholder for a name defined inside of a particular program. Obviously, in the preceding code, I substituted the name FontCallBack for EnumFontFamProc. However, when you need to look up the parameters passed to this function, you should search for EnumFontFamProc in your documentation.

The *FontCallBack* Function

```
int CALLBACK FontCallBack(LPENUMLOGFONT, LPNEWTEXTMETRIC,
int, ENUMSTRUCT FAR*)
```

The parameters passed to FontCallBack tell almost everything any programmer could ever want to know about a font:

☐ The first parameter is the LOGFONT of the font.

☐ The second parameter is the TEXTMETRIC structure.

☐ The third parameter can be used to determine if the font is a TrueType font, or if it is meant to be displayed on a screen, a printer, neither, or both.

☐ The last parameter is the user-defined data passed in when EnumFontFamilies was called.

Between them, the first two parameters hold structures containing some thirty different fields that detail the characteristics of the font. (Use your debugger to examine these fields.)

Example:
```
int CALLBACK FontCallBack(LPENUMLOGFONT, lpnlf, LPNEWTEXTMETRIC 1pntm,
                          int FontType, enumstruct far * lpdata)
{
SendMessage (lpData->hWindow, LP_ADDSTRING, 0, LONG
            (1pnlf>elfLogFont.1fFaceName));
return 1;
}
```

In this particular case, 90 percent of the data passed to FontCallBack is simply ignored. The only real area of interest is the 1fFaceName field of the LOGFONT structure. This data is promptly sent off to the list box where it is displayed for the user's perusal. The process of sending the message to a list box is described in the next section.

Immediately after being sent off, the next piece of mail comes flying in (airmail as it were), courtesy of Windows itself. Once again, FontCallBack bundles up the font name and sends it off to the list box to be displayed. This whole process is continued until there are no more fonts left to iterate or the callback returns 0.

When the call to EnumFontFamilies returns, the programmer must be careful to free the prolog code allocated by MakeProcInstance:

```
FreeProcInstance((FARPROC)lpfnEnumProc);
```

You should also remember to free the device context used during the call to EnumFontFamilies:

```
ReleaseDC(hwnd, DC);
```

Well, there you have it. You've just seen a rough outline of how to enumerate the fonts on the system through a callback. There were seven steps involved:

☐ Write a callback procedure.

☐ Get a device context.

☐ Call MakeProcInstance to create a link between your program and Windows proper.

☐ Call EnumFontFamilies and wait for Windows to send the font information to your callback.

☐ Process the information sent to your callback.

☐ Use FreeProcInstance to free the prolog code allocated by MakeProcInstance.

☐ Release the DC.

These outlined steps are all good and well in and of themselves. However, nothing described so far does anything to fill the user in on what has taken place. In order to give the call a visual element, FontsExp must first communicate directly with visual controls such as list boxes, check boxes, and edit and static controls.

Talking to a List Box

One of the most important parts of the `FontCallBack` function is the call to `SendMessage`:

```
SendMessage(lpData->hWindow, LB_ADDSTRING, 0,
            LONG(lpnlf->elfLogFont.lfFaceName));
```

This function actually sends the names of the enumerated fonts to the list box so the user can peruse them at his or her leisure.

You already know that `SendMessage` delivers a notice directly to a particular `WndProc`, which in this case happens to be the window procedure of the list box. What's new here, though, is the `LB_ADDSTRING` message:

☐ `LB_ADDSTRING` is one of nearly 40 predefined messages that can be sent to a list box. If you look up `LB_ADDSTRING` in your reference materials, you'll see that when this message is sent, the following occurs.

☐ Windows expects the third parameter (`WPARAM`) of `SendMessage` or `PostMessage` to be set to zero.

☐ The fourth parameter is set to the address of the string that's going to be added to the list box. Because the fourth parameter of the `SendMessage` function is an `LPARAM`, it's necessary to typecast the string before sending it.

Following is a list of some of the more commonly used messages sent to a list box:

`LB_ADDSTRING`	Adds a string
`LB_DELETESTRING`	Deletes a string
`LB_DIR`	Adds a list of filenames
`LB_GETCOUNT`	Gets the number of items
`LB_GETCURSEL`	Gets the index of a selected item
`LB_GETSEL`	Gets the selection state of an item
`LB_GETSELCOUNT`	Gets the number of selected items

LB_GETTEXT	Gets a string
LB_GETTEXTLEN	Gets the length of a string
LB_RESETCONTENT	Removes all items
LB_SELECTSTRING	Selects a matching string in a list box
LB_SELITEMRANGE	Selects consecutive items in a list box
LB_SETCOLUMNWIDTH	Sets the width of columns in a list box
LB_SETCURSEL	Selects an indexed string in a list box
LB_SETSEL	Selects a string in a multiple-selection list box
LB_SETTOPINDEX	Ensures that an item is visible
LB_SETTABSTOPS	Sets Tab stops

Note: In the FontsExp example, I used SendMessage to communicate with a control. In WINDOWSX, however, there is a set of macros declared, which can somewhat simplify this whole procedure. For instance, instead of sending an LB_ADDSTRING message, WINDOWSX lets you use the following macro:

```
#define ListBox_AddString(hwndCtl, lpsz)
```

which is defined like this:

```
((int)(DWORD)SendMessage((hwndCtl), LB_ADDSTRING,

                  0, (LPARAM)(LPCSTR)(lpsz)))
```

For many people, WINDOWSX macros are easier to use than the SendMessage function. However, in this book, I occasionally use SendMessage for two different reasons.

☐ I feel it's important that you understand how the WINDOWSX macros actually work. WINDOWSX is fine, but you shouldn't use it unless you understand the foundation on which it rests.

☐ You really should be thoroughly familiar with how to use SendMessage, because you will encounter a great deal of code that's dependent on it.

I frequently use the WINDOWSX macros rather than SendMessage. I prefer WindowsX because it is elegant, and readily portable to Win32.

After the `FontCallBack` function has been sent the name of all the fonts on the system, the program needs to fill the static control above the list box (line 128 of FONTEXP.CPP):

```
wsprintf(S, "There are %d fonts available", EnumStruct.Count);
SetWindowText(hNumFonts, S);
```

Notice that these lines of code are still part of the response to the `WM_STARTFONTS` message. They use the `Count` field, which was incremented every time `FontCallBack` was sent a new piece of mail. (See Figure 11.3.)

Figure 11.3. *The list box and its static text after they have been filled with information about the fonts on the system.*

The next step in the program is to set the focus on the list box; then, highlight the first item in the box. (Use the debugger to step through lines 132 and 133, which, by the way, are *still* part of the response to `WM_STARTFONT`:

```
SetFocus(hFontList);
SendMessage(hFontList, LB_SETCURSEL, 0, 0);
```

This call to `SetFocus` is very important. A list box can respond when a user manipulates the arrow keys. However, this process won't work unless the list box has the focus, and unless it is selected. To select a list box, call `SetFocus` with the `HWND` of the control as the sole parameter. This has the same effect as actually clicking the control with the mouse.

Selecting an item in a list box is a straightforward process. All you need to do is send the list box an `LB_SETCURSEL` message and the index of the item to highlight. The message itself instructs the list box to highlight a particular item. The index of the item to highlight is specified in `WPARAM`. Because the index is zero-based, a value of zero in `WPARAM` instructs the list box to highlight the first item in the list.

Showing the Font

At this point, you've had a look at all the calls initiated by the WM_STARTFONTS message, except for the call to ShowTheFont. The ShowTheFont function takes care of all the controls except the list box and static control immediately above it. More specifically, it displays the name of the currently selected font in a big static control, shows a selection of characters from that font in the scrollable edit control, and sets the check boxes to their appropriate values. (See Figure 11.4.)

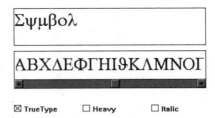

Figure 11.4. *These controls are handled by the* ShowTheFont *function.*

Note: The ShowTheFont function is called, not only at the beginning of the program in response to WM_STARTFONTS message, but also every time the user selects a different font in the list box. In other words, the list box gets filled only one time—at program creation. ShowTheFont, however, gets called every time the user asks that another font be displayed.

Following is the code for ShowTheFont. Take the time to step through the code with your debugger while you follow the discussion.

```
void ShowTheFont(HWND hwnd)
{
  FONTENUMPROC lpfnEnumProc;
  char lpszBuffer[150];
  ENUMSTRUCT EnumStruct;
  HFONT SaveIt;

  char Alpha[] = {"1234567890abcdefghijklmnopqrstuvwxyz"
                  "ABCDEFGHIJKLMNOPQRSTUVWXYZ"};

  HDC DC = GetDC(hwnd);

  int Index = SendMessage(hFontList, LB_GETCURSEL, 0, 0);
```

```
    SendMessage(hFontList, LB_GETTEXT, Index, LONG(lpszBuffer));
    lpfnEnumProc = (FONTENUMPROC)MakeProcInstance(
                   (FARPROC)DescribeFontCallBack, hInstance);
    EnumStruct.Count = 0;
    EnumStruct.hWindow = hwnd;
    EnumFontFamilies(DC, lpszBuffer, lpfnEnumProc,
                   (LONG)&EnumStruct);
    FreeProcInstance((FARPROC)lpfnEnumProc);

    if (TheFont != 0)
      SaveIt = SelectFont(DC, TheFont);
    GetTextMetrics(DC, &TextMetrics);
    HandleMetrics(TextMetrics);
    GetTextFace(DC, 150, aTextFace);
    if (TheFont != 0)
      SelectFont(DC, SaveIt);

    ReleaseDC(hwnd, DC);

    SendMessage(hFontName, WM_SETTEXT, 0, LONG(&lpszBuffer));
    SendMessage(hFontName, WM_SETFONT, WPARAM(TheFont), 0);

    SendMessage(hAlphaEdit, WM_SETTEXT, 0, LONG(&Alpha));
    SendMessage(hAlphaEdit, WM_SETFONT, WPARAM(TheFont), 0);
}
```

The function starts by getting the name of the currently selected font from the list box.
To do this, it must first find the index of the selected item, and then ask for the string
associated with that item number.

Note: When retrieving an item from a list box, you usually first find out
which item the user has selected by sending a LB_GETCURSEL message.
Then, use the LB_GETTEXT message to retrieve the string:

```
int Index = SendMessage(hFontList, LB_GETCURSEL, 0, 0);
SendMessage(hFontList, LB_GETTEXT, Index, LONG(lpszBuffer));
```

The LB_GETCURSEL message should have both the WPARAM and the LPARAM
of the SendMessage function set to zero. The LB_GETTEXT message, on the
other hand, expects the index of the string to be in the WPARAM argument,
and a buffer to hold the string in LPARAM. The buffer in LPARAM must be
long enough to hold the string and the NULL terminator. If you need to
get the length of a particular string, send an LB_GETTEXTLEN message.

Of course, the first time these messages are sent, the selected item will be
the first item in the list box. However, this function gets called over and

over again throughout the life of a program as shown in the next section. On later occasions, the user will most likely select a different item than the one set by default at the beginning of the program.

The Return of *EnumFontFamilies*

The next step is a second call to `EnumFontFamilies`. This time, the name of a font (that you want to know about) is passed in the second parameter. The mailing address, or callback, is named `DescribeFontCallback`:

```
#pragma argsused
int CALLBACK DescribeFontCallBack(LPENUMLOGFONT lpnlf,
                                  LPNEWTEXTMETRIC lpntm,
                                  int FontType, ENUMSTRUCT FAR * lpData)
{
  SendMessage(lpData->hWindow, WM_NEWFONT, 0,
              LONG(&lpnlf->elfLogFont));
  return 1;
}
```

During the previous call to `EnumFontFamilies`, the callback procedure was called once for every font on the system. This time, however, `DescribeFontCallBack` is called only once. The purpose of the first set of calls is to get the name of all the fonts on the system. The purpose of the second call is to get detailed information about a specific font, specified in the second parameter of `EnumFontFamilies`.

Note: Obviously, it would have been possible to only call `EnumFontFamilies` once in this program. That is, I could have iterated through the fonts once and maintained a linked list or dynamic array containing all the information about each font on the system. I opted not to take this route for the following reasons:

☐ I want to give you working examples demonstrating two different ways to call `EnumFontFamiles`.

☐ I want to avoid complicating the code and wasting memory by introducing an extraneous data structure, such as a linked list or dynamic array.

> ☐ I want to avoid duplicating available resources. If the information is directly available from Windows, why should a programmer bother to keep a separate list for his or her own program?
>
> Considerations such as these are typical of the kinds of factors Windows programmers need to keep in mind when designing their programs.

The DescribeFontCallBack function, invoked by EnumFontFamilies, uses the SendMessage procedure to inform the main program about the information it has received. This time, the message sent is called WM_NEWFONT, and it is sent back directly to the main window, rather than to a list box.

The information packaged along with the WM_NEWFONT message is a LOGFONT. You should note that the dimensions of the font are chosen by Windows, and that this program makes no attempt to change them.

Back in the WndProc, the response to the WM_NEWFONT message is simply to use the packaged LOGFONT to create a new font for the main window:

```
case WM_NEWFONT:
{
  if (TheFont != 0)
    DeleteObject(TheFont);
  TheLogFont = (LPLOGFONT)lParam;
  TheFont = CreateFontIndirect(TheLogFont);
  return 1;
}
```

Notice that the code carefully deletes any existing font. Then, it typecasts the lParam to get hold of the LOGFONT and calls CreateFontIndirect to create a new font. The font itself is stored in a global variable. After the SendMessage function is processed, the code returns to the ShowTheFont function.

Tip: Set debugger breakpoints on both the DescribeFontCallBack and the WM_NEWFONT case statements and then step through the program several times until you understand the relationship between the two code fragments. This is quintessential Windows programming—take the time to understand how it works!

Working with Check Boxes

Now that you have a copy of the new font available, show it to the user and display some information about the font.

The program first calls `GetTextMetric`, which provides all kinds of information about the font, including whether or not it is a TrueType font, whether it's italicized, and what its current weight is. This structure is shunted off to `HandleMetrics`, which sets the check boxes to reflect the state of this information:

```
void HandleMetrics(TEXTMETRIC TextMetrics)
{

    if ((TextMetrics.tmPitchAndFamily &
        TMPF_TRUETYPE) == TMPF_TRUETYPE)
      SendMessage(ButtonWindows[0], BM_SETCHECK, 1, 0L);
    else
      SendMessage(ButtonWindows[0], BM_SETCHECK, 0, 0L);

    if ((TextMetrics.tmWeight) > 600)
      SendMessage(ButtonWindows[1], BM_SETCHECK, 1, 0L);
    else
      SendMessage(ButtonWindows[1], BM_SETCHECK, 0, 0L);

    if (TextMetrics.tmItalic)
      SendMessage(ButtonWindows[2], BM_SETCHECK, 1, 0L);
    else
      SendMessage(ButtonWindows[2], BM_SETCHECK, 0, 0L);

}
```

Notice that the BM_SETCHECK message always takes zero as its last parameter. You should set WPARAM to 1 to set the check, and 0 to erase the check. Once again, no one expects you to remember how to use the BM_SETCHECK message. All that's important is that you know it exists, and that you know how to look up the information. If remembering all these bits of information comes to you easily, that's fine. But don't waste time struggling to remember all these details. Just know how to look them up when you need them.

The last few calls in ShowTheFont send the information to the two edit controls with the WM_SETTEXT message, which wants a string buffer sent in the last parameter. After sending the font to the control, set the font with the WM_SETFONT message. You'll probably want to take a close look at those two SendMessage calls, because they perform an important task that you might want to utilize in your own programs.

Anyway, the FontsExp program wouldn't be nearly as useful, or as much fun, if the text on-screen wasn't written in the current font.

Hit Me with the Highlights!

Take a moment to review the steps of the ShowTheFont function (if possible, follow along with your debugger):

☐ Query the list box to find the currently selected font name.

☐ Send the font name to Windows with EnumFontFamilies.

☐ Windows returns an associated LOGFONT structure from DescribeFontCallBack.

☐ Use the LOGFONT to create a global font.

☐ Use the font's TEXTMETRIC to retrieve a few bits of detailed information for the user's perusal.

None of these steps are particularly difficult to perform. You just need to remember what has to be done, and then go about doing it in a logical, straightforward manner.

Note: Focus for a moment on just one segment of this process:

☐ FontExp calls EnumFontFamiles.

☐ EnumFontFamiles calls Windows.

☐ Windows sends information to the callback procedure.

☐ The callback function sends a message to the main window.

☐ The main window creates a copy of the font.

As you've seen by using the debugger, the logic outlined here is radically different from the sequential programming that goes on in most DOS programs. Messages are flying all over the place, data segments are being patched up with prolog code, and the instruction pointer is flying from one part of you program to the next.

This is a classic example of what event-oriented programming is all about. Grasp these concepts, cup them in the palms of your hands, and examine them one by one. See how they all fit together and admire their complexity.

Don't waste time trying to decide whether this system is better or worse than the one familiar from command-line environments. That's an interesting topic in and of itself, but it's not the theme of this book. For now, concentrate on how Windows does things. It's a fascinating process, and it's not over yet, as you'll see in the next section.

The Return of *ShowTheFont*

Before I close this chapter, I want to turn your attention to the WM_COMMAND message function handler, which receives a message every time the user selects another item on the list box. To follow along with the debugger, set a breakpoint on the ShowTheFont function (line 219) of FontExpOnCommand:

```
void FontsExp_OnCommand(HWND hwnd, int id, HWND hwndCtl, UINT
codeNotify)
{
  char S[500];

  switch (id)
  {
    case ID_LISTBOX:
      if (codeNotify == LBN_SELCHANGE)
        ShowTheFont(hwnd);
      break;

    case CM_INFO:
      GetFontString(S, TextMetrics, aTextFace);
      MessageBox(hwnd, S, "Info", MB_OK);
      break;
  }
}
```

The code checks to see whether the id parameter is set to ID_LISTBOX and whether the message being sent signifies that the selection in the list box has changed. If both statements are true, ShowTheFont is called. As mentioned, ShowTheFont knows how to set the controls in the window to exhibit an example and a description of the current font.

It's quite typical of Windows to make it so very easy to find out whether or not a selection has changed in a list box. Information about things the user has done almost always comes to you free of charge, courtesy of the people at Microsoft. However, it's also typical of Windows to make it fairly difficult for you to send information back

to the user. Windows is such an ornate and powerful tool, that creating an effective interface can sometimes be a little bit tricky.

Finally, you should notice that this program calls the GetFontString function (which was developed back on Day 9). This function displays additional information about the current font. I include it here, because it's useful to the user, and because it illustrates how simple it is to share a module between two different Windows programs.

Summary

Whew! Well, you've covered a lot of ground in this chapter. You've learned about communicating with static controls, list boxes, check boxes, and edit controls. You've had another look at fonts and learned how to put them at your absolute beck and call with the EnumFontFamilies and GetTextMetrics calls.

By now, you should be getting the sense that you have the ability to completely control your presentation of textual materials. You know all about LOGFONTs, TEXTMETRICs, and the EnumFontFamilies callbacks. This knowledge should help you convey written information to users with all the punch and flash you could ever desire.

I'm aware that some of the information about controls came at you fairly fast and furious. Don't worry; rather than racing on to another topic, I'm going to slow the pace here a bit. In the next chapter, you'll get a second look at Windows controls, and get a chance to see how they can be used to manipulate directory information. You can turn to Appendix C for an overview of window controls.

Q&A

1. Q: I still really don't understand the EnumFontFamProc. Please explain this more.

   A: When you work with callbacks, one of the key things you need to know is how to set up the mailbox to which information will be mailed. Not just any mailbox will do. There has to be one with a particular set of characteristics. More specifically, Windows expects the function that sends information to have a certain number of arguments of a particular type. The EnumFontFamProc function defines what those types are, so you'll know how to set up the mailbox. The actual name, EnumFontFamProc, is just a place-holder reserving space for the name you want to give to the function. You can call it virtually anything you want.

2. Q: You've given me two long lists of constants associated with list boxes. I can't make sense of them all. What gives?

   A: In the last chapter, I listed the *styles* you can apply to list boxes. You can pass list box styles (LBS), such as LBS_STANDARD or LBS_MULTIPLESEL, to CreateWindow when you want to design a particular type of list box. However, when you want to communicate with a list box, use the list box messages (LB) that are listed in this chapter—LB_GETSEL, LB_GETTEXT, and LB_SETSEL. Obviously, there's not much of an advantage in trying to memorize all the different messages that can be sent to a control. Instead, you should remember that there are two types of constants associated with each control. One type helps define its style and appearance. These types are used with CreateWindow. The second type helps you communicate with a control. These constants are used with SendMessage or PostMessage. For me, the best way to keep track of these messages is either through the online help, or by browsing through WINDOWS.H.

3. Q: Why is the second parameter to EnumFontFamilies empty the first time you call it, and filled the second?

   A: This question lies very much at the heart of this chapter. When you call EnumFontFamilies with the second parameter blank, the function enumerates all the fonts on the system, taking care to create a sample LOGFONT for each type. When you fill in the lpszFamily parameter, Windows retrieves information about a particular font. In both cases, the sample fonts retrieved are designed by Windows. If you want, you can study the actual LOGFONT structure that Windows creates either inside a debugger, or inside the FontsExp program.

Workshop

The Workshop provides quiz questions to help you solidify your understanding of the material covered and exercises to provide you with experience in using what you've learned. Try to understand the quiz and exercise answers before continuing on to the next chapter. Answers are provided in Appendix A.

Quiz

1. How can you tell Windows to give a particular control the focus?

2. What is the difference between PostMessage and SendMessage?

3. What do you think the letters BM, in BM_SETCHECK, stand for?

4. How can you find out what to do with the WPARAM and LPARAM portions of an LB_GETTEXT message?

5. What is a callback?

6. What's the purpose of the prolog code created by MakeProcInstance?

7. Every call to MakeProcInstance must be matched by a call to _____?

8. How do you create a message with a unique identifier?

9. If a particular window class has only one user-defined message, what numerical value normally is associated with it?

10. What happens if you send a BM_GETCHECK message to the main window of the FontsExp program?

Exercises

1. Use the information retrieved by FontsExp to create a program that writes two strings to the screen, one using the New Times Roman font, and the second using WingDings. Hard code valid LOGFONTs for these fonts into your program.

2. Add additional static controls to the FontsExp program that displays the currently selected text's height and weight.

Window Controls and the Control Message API

M T W R F S

My primary purpose in this chapter is to give you additional exposure to window controls. In particular, you will get

☐ An introduction to radio buttons and group boxes

☐ A demonstration of how to use the control message APIs in lieu of the `SendMessage` function

☐ Code demonstrating how to tab back and forth between window controls

☐ Code showing how to group controls together

☐ Code showing how to create a simple Windows shell

☐ A brief introduction to the `WM_PARENTNOTIFY` message

The example program for this chapter, FileBox, enables the user to examine the contents of a subdirectory, change subdirectories, and launch another program. It can be used as a rudimentary substitute for the Program Manager.

Once again, the discussion of this program will be spread over two chapters. Day 13 will be devoted to four primary topics:

☐ Subclassing, a technique for changing the default behavior of a control

☐ An introduction to push buttons

☐ Using special properties of list boxes to aid in file management

☐ Controlling the size of a window with `WM_GETMINMAXINFO` messages

Creating a Windows Shell

When designing the FileBox program, my primary goal was to produce a program that demonstrates how to use window controls. In particular, I wanted to show how to subclass a window control, and how to use push buttons, radio buttons, and some advanced features of list boxes.

Of course, it's always nice to spice up these example programs by giving them some additional functionality. One interesting trait of the FileBox program is that it can be used as a clumsy substitute for the Program Manager, or for other Windows shells such as the Norton Desktop.

It's helpful for programmers to understand exactly what the Program Manager does. It's a programmer's job to peer beneath the surface of the operating environment to see how things actually work. Of course, the layers of mystery can only be peeled off one at a time, but seeing through the facade presented by the Program Manager is definitely one important step. Figure 12.1 shows the FileBox program as a Windows shell.

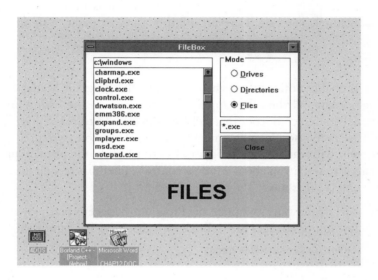

Figure 12.1. *The FileBox program functioning as a Windows shell.*

To use the FileBox program as a Windows shell, open the SYSTEM.INI file, in the Windows subdirectory, and change the line

```
shell=progman.exe
```

so that it reads like this:

```
shell=c:\bw\filebox\filebox.exe
```

where c:\bw\filebox is the path to your copy of the FileBox program.

The next time you start Windows, the FileBox program will pop up instead of the Program Manager. Now all you need do is iterate through the subdirectories on the hard drive until you find an executable file that you want to run. Double-click the filename, and it will start up just as a file starts up when you double-click its icon in the Program Manager.

> **Note:** In this discussion, I'm assuming that you are running either Win3.1 or Win3.0 for DOS. If you are running either Windows NT, the FileBox program probably won't work for you as a Program Manager substitute. You can, however, still run it as an ordinary Windows program.

You've probably noticed that when you close the Program Manager, it sends out messages asking all the other applications to close. In the listing for the FileBox program, I don't include code that will reproduce this feature. I omit it, because I don't want you to be accidentally shutting down the whole system every time you experiment with the FileBox program. In other words, the primary purpose of this program is to teach you about window controls. FileBox's second life as a Windows shell is only a side show.

At any rate, if you want to imitate the Program Manager's behavior at closing time, make a few minor changes to FileBox's `WM_CLOSE` message handler function:

```
void FileBox_OnClose(HWND hwnd)
{
  if (MessageBox(hwnd, "Exit Windows?", "FileBox",
      MB_ICONQUESTION ¦ MB_OKCANCEL) == IDOK)
    {
      if (ExitWindows(0, 0))
        DestroyWindow(hwnd);
    }
}
```

All the magic is in the call to `ExitWindows`.

Syntax

The *ExitWindows* function

```
BOOL ExitWindows(DWORD, UNIT)
```

The `ExitWindows` function is used to shut down the Windows operating environment. It takes two parameters:

```
DWORD dwReturnCode;      /* return or restart code   */
UINT reserved;           /* reserved; must be zero   */
```

This same call can be used to restart Windows, or to reboot your system and then restart Windows. This functionality is utilized by programmers who want to change the environment after letting users modify drivers or other portions of the system.

To give ExitWindows this capability, pass one of the following constants in the first parameter:

EW_REBOOTSYSTEM   Terminate system and restart.

EW_RESTARTWINDOWS   Terminate Windows and restart.

Example:

```
if (ExitWindows(0, 0))
DestroyWindow(hwnd);
```

Before showing you the code for FileBox, I'll mention that it's a bit like the first version of the Snake program, because it's designed to pique your interest, to titillate. Only the most rudimentary functionality is built into the FileBox program. If you want to create a Windows shell that's tailor-made for your own needs, FileBox can show you how to get started. There is no better way to learn how to program Windows than to actually sit down and design and implement your own programs.

The Code

Now that the preliminaries are out of the way, you can safely afford to have some serious fun with a little bit of code that actually does something at least potentially useful. Listing 12.1 provides the source code.

Listing 12.1. The FileBox program can be used as a Windows shell.

```
 1: /////////////////////////////////////////////////
 2: //   Program Name: FILEBOX.CPP
 3: //   Programmer: Charlie Calvert
 4: //   Description: FileBox windows program
 5: //   Date: 06/28/93
 6: /////////////////////////////////////////////////
 7:
 8: #define STRICT
 9: #include <windows.h>
10: #include <windowsx.h>
11: #pragma warning (disable: 4068)
12: #pragma hdrstop
13: #include <direct.h>
14: #include <string.h>
15: #include "filebox.h"
16: // ---------------------------------------------
17: // Interface
```

continues

Listing 12.1. continued

```
18: // -------------------------------------------
19:
20: // Variables
21: static char szAppName[] = "FileBox";
22: static HWND MainWindow;
23: static HINSTANCE hInstance;
24:
25: char *ButtonText[] = {"&Drives", "D&irectories", "&Files"};
26: char *BmpName[] = {"DRIVES", "DIRS", "FILES"};
27: WORD DirShowVal[] = {DDL_DRIVES ¦ DDL_EXCLUSIVE, DDL_DIRECTORY
28:                        ¦ DDL_EXCLUSIVE, DDL_ARCHIVE};
29: HWND hControl[8];
30: HBITMAP Bmp[3];
31: HWND PathWin;
32: FARPROC lpfnNewEditProc;
33: char FilesWildCard[100];
34:
35: // ----------------------------------------------------------
36: // Initialization
37: // ----------------------------------------------------------
38:
39: /////////////////////////////////////////////////////////////
40: // Program entry point
41: /////////////////////////////////////////////////////////////
42: #pragma argsused
43: int PASCAL WinMain(HINSTANCE hInst, HINSTANCE hPrevInstance,
44:                    LPSTR  lpszCmdParam, int nCmdShow)
45: {
46:   MSG  Msg;
47:
48:
49:   if (!hPrevInstance)
50:     if (!Register(hInst))
51:       return FALSE;
52:
53:   SetMessageQueue(20);
54:
55:   MainWindow = Create(hInst, nCmdShow);
56:   if (MainWindow)
57:     return FALSE;
58:   while (GetMessage(&Msg, NULL, 0, 0))
59:   {
60:     if (!IsDialogMessage(MainWindow, &Msg))
61:     {
62:       TranslateMessage(&Msg);
63:       DispatchMessage(&Msg);
64:     }
65:   }
66:   return Msg.wParam;
```

```
67: }
68:
69: /////////////////////////////////
70: // Register the window
71: /////////////////////////////////
72: BOOL Register(HINSTANCE hInst)
73: {
74:   WNDCLASS WndClass;
75:
76:   WndClass.style         = CS_HREDRAW | CS_VREDRAW;
77:   WndClass.lpfnWndProc   = WndProc;
78:   WndClass.cbClsExtra    = 0;
79:   WndClass.cbWndExtra    = 0;
80:   WndClass.hInstance     = hInst;
81:   WndClass.hIcon         = LoadIcon(NULL, IDI_APPLICATION);
82:   WndClass.hCursor       = LoadCursor(NULL, IDC_ARROW);
83:   WndClass.hbrBackground = GetStockBrush(WHITE_BRUSH);
84:   WndClass.lpszMenuName  = NULL;
85:   WndClass.lpszClassName = szAppName;
86:
87:   return RegisterClass (&WndClass);
88: }
89:
90: ////////////////////////////////////////////////////////
91: // Create the window
92: ////////////////////////////////////////////////////////
93: HWND Create(HINSTANCE hInst, int nCmdShow)
94: {
95:
96:   hInstance = hInst;
97:
98:   HWND hwnd = CreateWindow(szAppName, szAppName,
99:                     WS_OVERLAPPED | WS_CAPTION | WS_SYSMENU |
100:                    WS_MINIMIZEBOX | WS_THICKFRAME,
101:                    CW_USEDEFAULT, CW_USEDEFAULT,
102:                    CW_USEDEFAULT, CW_USEDEFAULT,
103:                    NULL, NULL, hInst, NULL);
104:
105:   if (hwnd == NULL)
106:     return hwnd;
107:
108:   ShowWindow(hwnd, nCmdShow);
109:   UpdateWindow(hwnd);
110:
111:   return hwnd;
112: }
113:
114: // --------------------------------------------------------
115: // WndProc and Implementation
```

continues

Listing 12.1. continued

```
116: // ------------------------------------------------------
117:
118: //////////////////////////////////////////////////////////
119: // The Window Procedure
120: //////////////////////////////////////////////////////////
121: LRESULT CALLBACK _export WndProc(HWND hwnd, UINT Message,
122:                                  WPARAM wParam, LPARAM lParam)
123: {
124:   switch(Message)
125:   {
126:     HANDLE_MSG(hwnd, WM_CREATE, CopyAll_OnCreate);
127:     HANDLE_MSG(hwnd, WM_DESTROY, FileBox_OnDestroy);
128:     HANDLE_MSG(hwnd, WM_CLOSE, FileBox_OnClose);
129:     HANDLE_MSG(hwnd, WM_COMMAND, FileBox_OnCommand);
130:     HANDLE_MSG(hwnd, WM_GETMINMAXINFO, FileBox_OnGetMinMaxInfo);
131:     HANDLE_MSG(hwnd, WM_PAINT, FileBox_OnPaint);
132:     HANDLE_MSG(hwnd, WM_PARENTNOTIFY, FileBox_OnParentNotify);
133:     HANDLE_MSG(hwnd, WM_RBUTTONDOWN, FileBox_OnRButtonDown);
134:     default:
135:        return FileBox_DefProc(hwnd, Message, wParam, lParam);
136:   }
137: }
138:
139: //////////////////////////////////////////////////////////
140: // Create the Callback procedures
141: //////////////////////////////////////////////////////////
142: void MakeCallBackProcs()
143: {
144:   lpfnNewEditProc =
145:     MakeProcInstance(FARPROC(NewEditProc), hInstance);
146:
147:   OldEditProc = (WNDPROC)SetWindowLong(hControl[ID_EDIT],
148:                           GWL_WNDPROC, LONG(lpfnNewEditProc));
149: }
150:
151: //////////////////////////////////////////////////////////
152: // Handle WM_Create
153: //////////////////////////////////////////////////////////
154: #pragma argsused
155: BOOL CopyAll_OnCreate(HWND hwnd, CREATESTRUCT FAR* lpCreateStruct)
156: {
157:
158:   for (int i = 0; i < 3; i++)
159:   {
160:     Bmp[i] = LoadBitmap(hInstance, BmpName[i]);
161:     if (!Bmp[i])
162:     {
163:       MessageBox(hwnd, "No Bitmap", "Fatal Error", MB_OK);
```

```
164:       return FALSE;
165:     }
166:   }
167:
168:   hControl[ID_FILELIST] = CreateWindow("listbox", NULL,
169:                   WS_CHILD | WS_VISIBLE |
170:                   LBS_STANDARD | WS_TABSTOP,
171:                   15, 30, 220, 180, hwnd, HMENU(ID_FILELIST),
172:                   hInstance, NULL);
173:
174:   hControl[ID_GROUP] = CreateWindow("button", "Mode",
175:                   WS_CHILD | WS_VISIBLE | BS_GROUPBOX,
176:                   250, 2, 131, 122, hwnd, HMENU(ID_GROUP),
177:                   hInstance, NULL);
178:
179:
180:   hControl[ID_DRIVES] = CreateWindow("button",
181:                   ButtonText[ID_DRIVES],
182:                   WS_CHILD | WS_VISIBLE | WS_GROUP | BS_AUTORADIOBUTTON |
183:                   WS_TABSTOP | WS_GROUP,
184:                   270, 25 + (0 * 30), 95, 30, hwnd,
185:                   HMENU(ID_DRIVES + 100), hInstance, NULL);
186:
187:   for (i = 1; i < 3; i++)
188:     hControl[i] = CreateWindow("button", ButtonText[i],
189:                   WS_CHILD | WS_VISIBLE | BS_AUTORADIOBUTTON,
190:                   270, 25 + (i * 30), 95, 30, hwnd,
191:                   HMENU(i + 100), hInstance, NULL);
192:
193:   hControl[ID_EDIT]  = CreateWindow("edit", "*.exe",
194:                   WS_CHILD | WS_VISIBLE | WS_BORDER|
195:                   WS_TABSTOP | WS_GROUP,
196:                   250, 130, 131, 25, hwnd, HMENU(ID_EDIT),
197:                   hInstance, NULL);
198:
199:   hControl[ID_CLOSE] = CreateWindow("button", "Close",
200:                   WS_CHILD | WS_VISIBLE | BS_PUSHBUTTON |
201:                   WS_TABSTOP | WS_GROUP,
202:                   250, 161, 131, 45, hwnd, HMENU(ID_CLOSE),
203:                   hInstance, NULL);
204:
205:   PathWin  = CreateWindow("static", NULL,
206:                   WS_CHILD | WS_VISIBLE | WS_BORDER,
207:                   14, 10, 222, 20, hwnd,
208:                   HMENU(ID_PATHS),  hInstance, NULL);
209:
210:   DlgDirList(hwnd, "*.*", ID_FILELIST,
211:            ID_PATHS, DirShowVal[DirShowType]);
212:
213:   MakeCallBackProcs();
```

12

continues

Listing 12.1. continued

```
214:
215:    Button_SetCheck(hControl[0], TRUE);
216:    SetFocus(hControl[ID_FILELIST]);
217:
218:    strcpy(FilesWildCard, "*.exe");
219:
220:    return TRUE;
221: }
222:
223: ///////////////////////////////////////////////////////
224: // Handle WM_DESTROY
225: ///////////////////////////////////////////////////////
226: #pragma argsused
227: void FileBox_OnDestroy(HWND hwnd)
228: {
229:    for (int i = 0; i < 3; i++)
230:      DeleteBitmap(Bmp[i]);
231:
232:    SetWindowLong(hControl[ID_EDIT], GWL_WNDPROC,
233:                  LONG(OldEditProc));
234:    FreeProcInstance(lpfnNewEditProc);
235:    PostQuitMessage(0);
236: }
237:
238: ///////////////////////////////////////////
239: // Handle WM_CLOSE
240: ///////////////////////////////////////////
241: void FileBox_OnClose(HWND hwnd)
242: {
243:    if (MessageBox(hwnd, "Do you want to exit?", "FileBox",
244:        MB_ICONQUESTION | MB_OKCANCEL) == IDOK)
245:      DestroyWindow(hwnd);
246: }
247:
248: ///////////////////////////////////////////
249: // SetListbox
250: ///////////////////////////////////////////
251: #pragma argsused
252: void SetListbox(HWND hwnd)
253: {
254:    RECT R;
255:    char WildCard[150];
256:
257:    if (DirShowType == FILEMODE)
258:      strcpy(WildCard, FilesWildCard);
259:    else
260:      strcpy(WildCard, "*.*");
261:
262:    ListBox_ResetContent(hControl[ID_FILELIST]);
263:    ListBox_Dir(hControl[ID_FILELIST], DirShowVal[DirShowType],
```

```
264:                 WildCard);
265:
266:    R.left = 14;
267:    R.top = 220;
268:    R.right = 14 + BMPX;
269:    R.bottom = 220 + BMPY;
270:    InvalidateRect(hwnd, &R, FALSE);
271: }
272:
273:
274: ////////////////////////////////////////////////////////
275: // Handle MouseClick on listbox for DIR or DRIVE change
276: ////////////////////////////////////////////////////////
277: #pragma argsused
278: void HandleMouseClick(HWND hwnd, int id, HWND hwndCtl,
                              UINT codeNotify)
279: {
280:    char Buffer[100];
281:
282:    DlgDirSelect(hwnd, Buffer, ID_FILELIST);
283:    DlgDirList(hwnd, Buffer, ID_FILELIST, ID_PATHS,
284:               DirShowVal[DirShowType]);
285: }
286:
287:
288: ////////////////////////////////////////////////////////
289: // Handle WM_COMMAND
290: ////////////////////////////////////////////////////////
291: #pragma argsused
292: void FileBox_OnCommand(HWND hwnd, int id, HWND hwndCtl,
                              UINT codeNotify)
293: {
294:    char S[150], lpszBuffer[150];
295:
296:    switch(id)
297:    {
298:      case ID_DRIVES + 100:
299:        DirShowType = DRIVEMODE;
300:        SetListbox(hwnd);
301:        break;
302:
303:      case ID_DIRS + 100:
304:        DirShowType = DIRMODE;
305:        SetListbox(hwnd);
306:        break;
307:
308:      case ID_FILES + 100:
309:        DirShowType = FILEMODE;
310:        SetListbox(hwnd);
311:        break;
```

continues

Listing 12.1. continued

```
312:
313:     case ID_FILELIST:
314:       if (codeNotify == LBN_DBLCLK)
315:       {
316:         if (DirShowType != FILEMODE)
317:           HandleMouseClick(hwnd, id, hwndCtl, codeNotify);
318:         else
319:         {
320:           int index = ListBox_GetCurSel(hControl[ID_FILELIST]);
321:           _getdcwd(0, S, 125);
322:           ListBox_GetText(hControl[ID_FILELIST], index,
323:                           lpszBuffer);
324:           strcat(S, "\\");
325:           strcat(S, lpszBuffer);
326:           WinExec(S, SW_SHOWNORMAL);
327:         }
328:       }
329:       break;
330:
331:     case ID_CLOSE:
332:       SendMessage(hwnd, WM_CLOSE, 0, 0);
333:       break;
334:   }
335: }
336:
337: /////////////////////////////////////
338: // Handle WM_GetMinMaxInfo
339: /////////////////////////////////////
340: #pragma argsused
341: void FileBox_OnGetMinMaxInfo(HWND hwnd,
342:                                MINMAXINFO FAR* lpMinMaxInfo)
342: {
343:   lpMinMaxInfo->ptMaxSize.x = XSIZE;
344:   lpMinMaxInfo->ptMaxSize.y = YSIZE;
345:   lpMinMaxInfo->ptMaxPosition.x = 100;
346:   lpMinMaxInfo->ptMaxPosition.y = 100;
347:   lpMinMaxInfo->ptMinTrackSize.x = XSIZE;
348:   lpMinMaxInfo->ptMinTrackSize.y = YSIZE;
349:   lpMinMaxInfo->ptMaxTrackSize.x = XSIZE;
350:   lpMinMaxInfo->ptMaxTrackSize.y = YSIZE;
351: }
352:
353: void HandleRightButton(HWND hwnd)
354: {
355:   switch(DirShowType)
356:   {
357:     case DRIVEMODE:
358:       Button_SetCheck(hControl[1], TRUE);
359:       Button_SetCheck(hControl[0], FALSE);
```

```
360:        Button_SetCheck(hControl[2], FALSE);
361:        DirShowType = DIRMODE;
362:        break;
363:
364:      case DIRMODE:
365:        Button_SetCheck(hControl[2], TRUE);
366:        Button_SetCheck(hControl[0], FALSE);
367:        Button_SetCheck(hControl[1], FALSE);
368:        DirShowType = FILEMODE;
369:        break;
370:
371:      default:
372:        Button_SetCheck(hControl[0], TRUE);
373:        Button_SetCheck(hControl[1], FALSE);
374:        Button_SetCheck(hControl[2], FALSE);
375:        DirShowType = DRIVEMODE;
376:    }
377:    SetListbox(hwnd);
378: }
379:
380: ////////////////////////////////////////
381: // Handle WM_PAINT
382: ////////////////////////////////////////
383: void FileBox_OnPaint(HWND hwnd)
384: {
385:   PAINTSTRUCT PaintStruct;
386:   HBITMAP OldBmp;
387:
388:   HDC PaintDC = BeginPaint(hwnd, &PaintStruct);
389:   HDC BltDC = CreateCompatibleDC(PaintDC);
390:
391:   OldBmp = SelectBitmap(BltDC, Bmp[DirShowType]);
392:   BitBlt(PaintDC, 14, 220, BMPX, BMPY, BltDC, 0, 0, SRCCOPY);
393:
394:   SelectBitmap(BltDC, OldBmp);
395:   DeleteDC(BltDC);
396:   EndPaint(hwnd, &PaintStruct);
397: };
398:
399: ////////////////////////////////////////
400: // Handle WM_PARENTNOTIFY
401: ////////////////////////////////////////
402: #pragma argsused
403: void FileBox_OnParentNotify(HWND hwnd, UINT msg,
404:                             HWND hwndChild, int idChild)
405: {
406:   if (msg == WM_RBUTTONDOWN)
407:     HandleRightButton(hwnd);
408: }
409:
```

continues

Listing 12.1. continued

```
410: /////////////////////////////////////
411: // Handle WM_RBUTTONDOWN
412: /////////////////////////////////////
413: #pragma argsused
414: void FileBox_OnRButtonDown(HWND hwnd, BOOL fDoubleClick,
415:                                  int x, int y, UINT keyFlags)
416: {
417:   HandleRightButton(hwnd);
418: }
419:
420: // -----------------------------------------------------------
421: // The SubClassed WNDPROCS
422: // -----------------------------------------------------------
423:
424: void SetNewWildCard(HWND hwnd)
425: {
426:   char Buffer[150];
427:
428:   GetWindowText(hwnd, Buffer, sizeof(Buffer));
429:   strcpy(FilesWildCard, Buffer);
430:   if (DirShowType == FILEMODE)
431:     SetListbox(MainWindow);
432: }
433:
434: /////////////////////////////////////
435: // SubClassing for RadioButtons
436: /////////////////////////////////////
437: LRESULT CALLBACK NewEditProc(HWND hwnd, UINT Message,
438:                                  WPARAM wParam, LPARAM lParam)
439: {
440:   switch(Message)
441:   {
442:     case WM_GETDLGCODE:
443:       return DLGC_WANTALLKEYS;
444:
445:     case WM_KEYDOWN:
446:       switch (wParam)
447:       {
448:         case VK_RETURN:
449:           SetNewWildCard(hwnd);
450:           SetFocus(hControl[ID_CLOSE]);
451:           break;
452:
453:         case VK_TAB:
454:           int State = GetKeyState(VK_SHIFT);
455:           if (State >> 8)
456:             SetFocus(hControl[DirShowType]);
457:           else
458:             SetFocus(hControl[ID_CLOSE]);
459:           break;
```

```
460:        }
461:
462:        break;
463:
464:      case WM_KILLFOCUS:
465:        SetNewWildCard(hwnd);
466:        break;
467:
468:      case WM_SETFOCUS:
469:        Edit_SetSel(hwnd, 0, -1);
470:        break;
471:    }
472:
473:    return
474:      CallWindowProc(OldEditProc, hwnd, Message, wParam, lParam);
475: }
```

Listing 12.2 shows the FileBox header file.

Type

Listing 12.2. FILEBOX.H.

```
 1: /////////////////////////////////////////////////
 2: // Module: FILEBOX.H
 3: // Programmer: Charlie Calvert
 4: // Date 06/25/93
 5: /////////////////////////////////////////////////
 6:
 7: // Constants
 8: #define ID_DRIVES 0
 9: #define ID_DIRS 1
10: #define ID_FILES 2
11: #define ID_CLOSE 3
12: #define ID_FILELIST 4
13: #define ID_GROUP 5
14: #define ID_EDIT 6
15: #define ID_PATHS 7
16:
17: #define BMPX 365
18: #define BMPY 100
19:
20: #define XSIZE 403
21: #define YSIZE 360
22:
23: // Types
24: enum TCurMode {DRIVEMODE, DIRMODE, FILEMODE};
25:
26: // Declarations for class FileBox
```

continues

Listing 12.2. continued

```
27: #define FileBox_DefProc     DefWindowProc
28: BOOL CopyAll_OnCreate(HWND hwnd,
29:                         CREATESTRUCT FAR* lpCreateStruct);
30: void FileBox_OnDestroy(HWND hwnd);
31: void FileBox_OnClose(HWND hwnd);
32: void FileBox_OnCommand(HWND hwnd, int id,
33:                         HWND hwndCtl, UINT codeNotify);
34: void FileBox_OnGetMinMaxInfo(HWND hwnd,
35:                         MINMAXINFO FAR* lpMinMaxInfo);
36: void FileBox_OnPaint(HWND hwnd);
37: void FileBox_OnParentNotify(HWND hwnd, UINT msg,
38:                         HWND hwndChild, int idChild);
39: void FileBox_OnRButtonDown(HWND hwnd, BOOL fDoubleClick,
40:                         int x, int y, UINT keyFlags);
41:
42: // Funcs
43: LRESULT CALLBACK _export WndProc(HWND hWindow, UINT Message,
44:                             WPARAM wParam, LPARAM lParam);
45: LRESULT CALLBACK _export NewEditProc(HWND hWindow, UINT Message,
46:                             WPARAM wParam, LPARAM lParam);
47: void HandleRightButton(HWND hwnd);
48: BOOL Register(HINSTANCE hInst);
49: HWND Create(HINSTANCE hInst, int nCmdShow);
50: TCurMode DirShowType;
51: WNDPROC OldEditProc;
```

Listing 12.3 is shows the FileBox resource file.

Listing 12.3. FILEBOX.RC.

```
1: DRIVES BITMAP "DRIVE.BMP"
2: FILES BITMAP "FILES.BMP"
3: DIRS BITMAP "DIRS.BMP"
```

Listing 12.4 shows the FileBox definition file.

DRIVES.BMP (365×100)

FILES.BMP (365×100)

FILES

DIRS.BMP (365×100)

DIRECTORIES

 Listing 12.4. FILEBOX.DEF.

```
 1: ; FILEBOX.DEF
 2:
 3: NAME          FileBox
 4: DESCRIPTION   'FileBox Window'
 5: EXETYPE       WINDOWS
 6: STUB          'WINSTUB.EXE'
 7: HEAPSIZE      4096
 8: STACKSIZE     5120
 9: CODE          PRELOAD MOVEABLE DISCARDABLE
10: DATA          PRELOAD MOVEABLE MULTIPLE
```

Listing 12.5 is the Borland makefile for FileBox.

 Listing 12.5. FILEBOX.MAK (Borland).

```
 1: # -----------------
 2: # FILEBOX.MAK
 3: # -----------------
 4:
 5: # macros
 6: APPNAME = FileBox
 7: INCPATH = C:\BC\INCLUDE
 8: LIBPATH = C:\BC\LIB
```

continues

Listing 12.5. continued

```
 9: FLAGS = -H -ml -W -v -w4 -I$(INCPATH) -L$(LIBPATH)
10:
11: # link
12: $(APPNAME).exe: $(APPNAME).obj $(APPNAME).def $(APPNAME).res
13:   bcc $(FLAGS) $(APPNAME).obj
14:   rc $(APPNAME).res
15:
16: # compile
17: $(APPNAME).obj: $(APPNAME).cpp
18:   bcc -c $(FLAGS) $(APPNAME).cpp
19:
20: # resource
21: $(APPNAME).res: $(APPNAME).rc
22:   rc -r -i$(INCPATH) $(APPNAME).rc
```

Listing 12.6 shows the Microsoft makefile for FileBox.

Type   Listing 12.6. FILEBOX.MAK (Microsoft).

```
 1: # ----------------------
 2: # FILEBOX.MAK
 3: # ----------------------
 4:
 5: # macros
 6: APPNAME = FileBox
 7: LINKFLAGS = /align:16, NUL, /nod slibcew libw
 8: FLAGS = -c -AL -GA -Ow -W3 -Zp
 9:
10: # ----------------------
11: # link
12: # ----------------------
13: $(APPNAME).exe : $(APPNAME).obj $(APPNAME).def $(APPNAME).res
14:   link $(APPNAME), $(LINKFLAGS), $(APPNAME)
15:   rc $(APPNAME).res
16:
17: # ----------------------
18: # compile
19: # ----------------------
20: $(APPNAME).obj : $(APPNAME).cpp
21:   cl $(FLAGS) $(APPNAME).cpp
22:
23: # ----------------------
24: # resource
25: # ----------------------
26: $(APPNAME).res: $(APPNAME).rc
27:   rc -r $(APPNAME).rc
```

The following are the bitmaps used in FileBox.

> DRIVES.BMP
> FILES.BMP
> DIRECTORIES.BMP

Output

When you run this program, you see an image like that shown in Figure 12.2. In the upper-right corner of the window is a set of three radio buttons inside a group box. Click one of these radio buttons, and the display changes to show the currently available directories, drives, or files. You can also switch between these three settings (or modes) by clicking the right mouse button on any portion of the program. When the Files option isn't selected, you can iterate through the currently available drives and directories with the left mouse button. Double-click an executable file to start. At all times, the currently selected mode is displayed at the bottom of the screen in large letters. An edit control on the right middle of the screen enables you to specify a new file mask. Enter any value, and then press Enter or Tab in order to see the new file listing.

Analysis

A good way to get started with this program is to discuss its use of the control message API. The control message API is a set of WINDOWSX macros that can be used instead of calls to `SendMessage` and `PostMessage`. These macros are spread throughout the program, and help make the code easier to understand and maintain.

The `SendMessage` and `PostMessage` interfaces for controls that you saw in the last two chapters aren't particularly self-explanatory. They're visually cumbersome and force the programmer to perform a number of awkward typecasts.

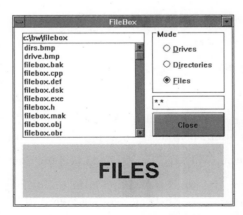

Figure 12.2. *The FileBox program displays information about the contents of a subdirectory.*

Note: Other alternatives to the SendMessage interface include object-oriented frameworks, such as Borland's Object Windows Library (OWL) and Microsoft's Foundation Classes (MFC). These extensive code bases can be quite elegant at times, and they certainly have attracted many intelligent and well-spoken adherents.

Certainly, real object-oriented programming has a number of advantages, but it doesn't always meld perfectly with Windows. The problem is that the Windows API is a procedural code base. It isn't object-oriented in the strict sense of the word. As a result, the two paradigms fail to connect at certain key junctures.

As someone who has made extensive use of OWL, I've come to believe that it's difficult to take proper advantage of it—unless you first have a thorough understanding of the underlying API. In other words, good OWL programmers, by definition, must have an in-depth knowledge of the material presented in this book. MFC and OWL are useful tools, but you can't truly understand them unless you thoroughly comprehend the Windows API code base on which they stand.

You've already seen how WINDOWSX can be used to create order out of the rambling case statements in window procedures. An equally neat trick is performed by the control message APIs.

For instance, this line of code

```
SendMessage(hwndCtl, LB_ADDSTRING, 0, (LPARAM)lpszBuffer);
```

can be considerably simplified by using the control message API:

```
ListBox_AddString(hwndCtl, lpszBuffer);
```

Note: Right now, the control message API is not listed in the Borland or Microsoft online help files. Three possible solutions involve

☐ Printing WINDOWSX.H and keeping the list by your desk

☐ Using the Annotate feature of the online help system to add these listings to your help system (see Figure 12.3). (This alternative would be especially attractive in big shops.)

☐ Creating your own WINDOWSX help file

Figure 12.3 shows the Annotate feature of the help system.

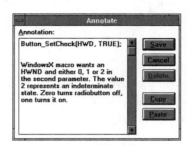

Figure 12.3. *Using the Annotate feature of the help system to document WINDOWSX features.*

Overall, the control message API provides an excellent alternative to the SendMessage interface. It's not only considerably simpler to use, but it also can work with the STRICT compiler directive to harness the power of type-checking. This helps you create good, clean code the first time around.

Unlike the SendMessage interface, the control message API is fully compatible with Win32. This means that using it can be a big help when you need to tweak your code so that it runs under Windows NT or Win32s. In this day and age, most experienced programmers are very anxious to adopt any coding methods that can make their programs more portable.

Before getting into specific examples of how the control message API is used in FILEBOX.CPP, I'll give you a better feeling for the program's overall structure. But don't worry, calls to the control message API appear throughout this chapter and the next. I'll discuss each in turn—as we come to them.

Creating Radio Buttons

The WM_CREATE message handler function in FileBox looks a lot like its counterpoint in the FontExp program. Its fundamental task is to create a series of controls that interface with the user throughout the life of the program.

Four of the most important of those controls are a set of three radio buttons surrounded by a group box. The next few paragraphs describe how they work. Here are the main points you need to master:

☐ Both radio buttons and group boxes belong to the button class. The key to creating them is to assign them the right style, such as BS_RADIOBUTTON or BS_GROUPBOX.

☐ The BS_AUTORADIOBUTTON style enables radio buttons to automatically handle mouse clicks.

☐ Radio buttons should be arranged under the aegis of a single group box. You should use the WS_GROUP style to ensure that only one item inside a group box can be selected at a time.

☐ Group boxes are primarily visual tools. The functionality associated with the controls inside a group box is the result of using the WS_GROUP and WS_TABSTOP styles, and has nothing to do with whether or not a group box is present.

☐ Users want to be able to tab between controls in a window. The IsDialogMessage function automatically gives you this behavior with only minimal work on your part.

Radio buttons (shown in Figure 12.4) enable the user to select one of several different mutually exclusive options. For instance, it's possible to select drives, directories, or files. You can't, however, select two options simultaneously, such as drives and directories. Nor can you select all three at once.

Throughout the next two chapters, I refer to each of these mutually exclusive options as different *modes*. In other words, the user can be in File mode, Directory mode, or Drive mode. When you're in File mode, you can view and manipulate the currently available files. When you're in Drive mode, you can view and manipulate the currently available drives, and so on.

Figure 12.4. *The radio buttons in the FileBox program are mutually exclusive: you can select only one at a time.*

The group box, which encloses a set of radio buttons, shows the user which sets of radio buttons are meant to work together as a unit. In some programs, you might find the need to have several group boxes on one screen, each containing a set of mutually exclusive options. The message to the user is that he or she can choose one option from each group box.

Note: When you are coding dialogs, Windows supplies built-in behavior that helps to enforce the preceding rules. Inside a window, however, you need to call `IsDialogMessage` to ensure that radio buttons and other controls respond to keypresses as the user expects. The built-in mouse behavior, however, remains intact whether you are in a window or in a dialog.

I've decided to tackle `IsDialogMessage`, `WS_TABSTOP`, and the whole subject of tabbing through controls in the next section. My goal is to allow you to view the subject of tabbing in isolation so you can better grasp its importance.

Here is the code which creates the radio buttons and their encompassing group box:

```
hControl[ID_GROUP] = CreateWindow("button", "Mode",
                    WS_CHILD | WS_VISIBLE | BS_GROUPBOX,
                    250, 2, 131, 122, hwnd, HMENU(ID_GROUP),
                    hInstance, NULL);


hControl[ID_DRIVES] = CreateWindow("button",
                    ButtonText[ID_DRIVES],
                    WS_CHILD | WS_VISIBLE | BS_AUTORADIOBUTTON |
                    WS_TABSTOP | WS_GROUP,
                    270, 25 + (0 * 30), 95, 30, hwnd,
                    HMENU(ID_DRIVES), hInstance, NULL);

for (i = 1; i < 3; i++)
    hControl[i] = CreateWindow("button", ButtonText[i],
                    WS_CHILD | WS_VISIBLE | BS_AUTORADIOBUTTON,
                    270, 25 + (i * 30), 95, 30, hwnd, HMENU(i),
                    hInstance, NULL);
```

You can see that the radio buttons belong to the "button" class. To differentiate one type of button from another, FileBox ORs an appropriate constant, such as `BS_AUTORADIOBUTTON` or `BS_RADIOBUTTON`, into `CreateWindow`'s style field.

The distinction between the `BS_RADIOBUTTON` and `BS_AUTORADIOBUTTON` styles is that buttons with the latter style automatically respond when the user clicks them. This response includes displaying a *selected* radio button, as well as deselecting any other radio buttons in the current group.

If you look at the main listings for the FileBox program, you see that both the first of the radio buttons, and the Close push button, make use of the WS_GROUP style. When you turn this style on, it informs Windows that this and any following controls should be treated as a group. The end of the group is marked by the appearance of the next control that uses the WS_GROUP style. In particular, the three radio buttons are treated as one group, and the next group begins with the push button labeled "Close." This behavior occurs because the first radio button and the push button are both assigned the WS_GROUP style.

The behavior associated with a particular group is twofold:

1. Only one member of a group of radio buttons can be selected at a time.

2. You can tab from this group to the next group in a single step without having to tab through each of the intervening radio buttons.

Note that the group box, which encloses the radio buttons, is also a member of the "button" class. This fact is somewhat counterintuitive, because group boxes don't look like buttons.

The function of group boxes is simply to enclose a set of controls in order to *group* them together logically by giving the user a visual hint as to their purpose. Group boxes lack the underlying complexity inherent in most features of the Windows programming environment. One keeps poking at them, expecting them to yield some hitherto unknown secret. It's a bit frustrating to have them remain so spare and immutable. The explanation for this atypical simplicity is that a group box's primary purpose is visual! It's not meant to do anything; it just informs the user about which controls are meant to be treated as a unit.

It's now time to move on to a description of IsDialogMessage and its relationship to the WS_TABSTOP and WS_GROUP styles.

IsDialogMessage and Tabbing

The theme of the last few paragraphs is the importance of treating a set of radio buttons as a single group of controls. This simple act makes life considerably easier for the user. If he or she wants to select a particular option, there is no need to first turn one radio button on, and then go back and turn another off. Instead, the buttons work together in a logical and intuitive manner.

So far so good. The catch here is that I've been talking totally in terms of mouse clicks. The user also expects to be able to navigate through the program with the keyboard.

All the careful grouping of controls, discussed in the last few paragraphs, only applies to users armed with a mouse. Taming the keyboard is an entirely different issue.

When you are designing a modal dialog, Windows provides excellent support for the basic functionality associated with keyboards. In other words, you can automatically tab between controls, shift-tab backwards through controls, and select different radio buttons with the arrow keys. Inside a dialog, you don't have to do anything special to get this behavior. But all this functionality is turned off inside a window. It's gone. Vanished.

To bring it back, you need to change the message loop for your entire program. Specifically, you need to add a call to `IsDialogMessage`:

```
while (GetMessage(&Msg, NULL, 0, 0))
{
  if (!IsDialogMessage(MainWindow, &Msg))
  {
    TranslateMessage(&Msg);
    DispatchMessage(&Msg);
  }
}
```

Compare the preceding code with the standard message loop from the previous programs in this book:

```
while (GetMessage(&Msg, NULL, 0, 0))
{
  TranslateMessage(&Msg);
  DispatchMessage(&Msg);
}
```

The logic added to the FileBox program simply states that any dialog messages sent to FileBox should be handled separately, and shouldn't be passed on to `TranslateMessage` and `DispatchMessage`.

The phrase "dialog messages" is really just a euphemism for "keyboard messages." `IsDialogMessage` grabs hold of any key presses the user makes and processes them separately. As a result, FileBox enables you to tab through controls and to use the arrow keys to select radio buttons.

The last piece in this puzzle is the `WS_TABSTOP` style, which is OR'd into certain key controls in the FileBox program. Giving a control this style informs Windows that the user needs to be capable of tabbing to this control. It's equally important to know when to omit this style, because there are some controls you don't want the user to have to tab through every time he or she is trying to move the focus. In particular, you should only apply the `WS_TABSTOP` style to the first control in a group of radio buttons.

12

DO remember that the IsDialogMessage is useless to you if you forget to use the proper styles with your controls. IsDialogMessage, WS_TABSTOP, and WS_GROUP all need to work together to give the user access to your program's interface.

DON'T underestimate the extreme importance of the IsDialogMessage function. This one call adds a great deal of functionality to your program at the price of only a minimal amount of work. It may not seem so important now, but a time will come when you'll absolutely need this function. Don't forget it!

Any control you want to tab to should have the WS_TABSTOP style. The first control in any set of controls should be assigned the WS_GROUP style. The end of the set is marked by assigning the first control of the next set the WS_GROUP style.

Using Radio Buttons to Switch Modes

Now that you've got a feeling for the whole subject of grouping controls, and of tabbing between controls, it's time to dig a little deeper into the FileBox program. In particular, you'll learn how the program responds when the user clicks a radio button or selects it with the keyboard.

The FileBox program uses two different techniques for changing among the File, Directory, and Drive modes.

☐ The first technique involves responding to radio button selections with the mouse or arrow keys.

☐ The second technique involves responding to clicks to the right mouse button.

The next few paragraphs concentrate on the first technique. The second technique is discussed partially in this chapter and partially in the next.

IsDialogMessage and the BS_AUTORADIOBUTTON style conspire to make radio buttons extremely easy to use. All you really have to do is set up some code in the WM_COMMAND message handler function and then wait around for the user to select a radio button. In the FileBox program, the code looks like this:

```
case ID_DRIVES:
  DirShowType = DRIVEMODE;
  SetListbox(hwnd);
  break;

case ID_DIRS:
  DirShowType = DIRMODE;
  SetListbox(hwnd);
  break;

case ID_FILES:
  DirShowType = FILEMODE;
  SetListbox(hwnd);
  break;
```

If the user selects the Drive radio button, an enumerated variable, called `DirShowType`, is set to `DRIVEMODE`, and the `SetListBox` function is called. A discussion of the `SetListBox` function and the various global variables used in this program is included in the next chapter. For now, you need only note that this same process is repeated when the File or Directory radio buttons are selected.

Clearly, it's a cinch to write the code that handles mouse clicks on the radio buttons. The only time this code is likely to cause you any trouble is if you forget to set the `WS_GROUP` style at the beginning of each group, or if you forget that radio buttons keep you informed of their state (with `WM_COMMAND` messages). Keep these two ideas in mind, and you can spice your programs up with these nifty little controls any time you want.

In the last few paragraphs, you've learned about radio buttons and group boxes and about how they are created. Here are the key points to remember:

☐ Radio buttons and group boxes are buttons created with the `BS_RADIOBUTTON` or `BS_GROUPBOX` style.

☐ The `BS_AUTORADIOBUTTON` style enables radio buttons to automatically handle mouse clicks.

☐ Use the `WS_GROUP` style to arrange radio buttons under the aegis of a single group box.

☐ Group boxes are primarily visual tools.

☐ The `IsDialogMessage` function provides built-in tabbing between controls.

12

Put Your Right-Button Down!

The right mouse button is often neglected in Windows programming. For some reason, it's simply ignored, and the remarkable potential therein remains entirely untapped.

Needless to say, situations like this are grand opportunities. They're just waiting for someone to come along and take advantage of them. In an attempt to show what can be done with the right mouse button, I've thrown in the following code:

```
void HandleRightButton(HWND hwnd)
{
  switch(DirShowType)
  {
    case DRIVEMODE:
      Button_SetCheck(hControl[1], TRUE);
      Button_SetCheck(hControl[0], FALSE);
      Button_SetCheck(hControl[2], FALSE);
      DirShowType = DIRMODE;
      break;

    case DIRMODE:
      Button_SetCheck(hControl[2], TRUE);
      Button_SetCheck(hControl[0], FALSE);
      Button_SetCheck(hControl[1], FALSE);
      DirShowType = FILEMODE;
      break;

    default:
      Button_SetCheck(hControl[0], TRUE);
      Button_SetCheck(hControl[1], FALSE);
      Button_SetCheck(hControl[2], FALSE);
      DirShowType = DRIVEMODE;
  }
  SetListbox(hwnd);
}


/////////////////////////////////////
// Handle WM_RBUTTONDOWN
/////////////////////////////////////
#pragma argsused
void FileBox_OnRButtonDown(HWND hwnd, BOOL fDoubleClick,
                           int x, int y, UINT keyFlags)
{
  HandleRightButton(hwnd);
}
```

The preceding code iterates through the program's possible modes when the user clicks the right mouse button. Complications arise, because it's necessary to keep the radio buttons in sync with the changes that are taking place.

Handling radio buttons this way is considerably more complicated than just responding to clicks directly on a button. The big difference is that the work performed as a result of the BS_AUTORADIOBUTTON style is no longer kicking in automatically. Instead, the FileBox program has to explicitly change the settings of the radio buttons.

For instance, if the user clicks the right mouse button while the program is in DRIVEMODE, the Drive radio button is turned off by a call to the Button_SetCheck macro. Then, the Directory radio button is turned on, and DirShowType is set to DIRMODE. Just to be sure all goes smoothly, the program sends a probably redundant call to ensure that the Drive radio button is turned off. A similar process occurs when the program is in DIRMODE or FILEMODE.

The syntax involved in this process is considerably simplified by the use of the message control API. These WINDOWSX macros are so intuitive that there is little need for me to explain how they work. However, it can't hurt to go through the process one time, just to be sure you've got your message control ducks all lined up in a neat, comprehensible row.

The Button_SetCheck macro fronts for the BM_SETCHECK message. If you were calling SendMessage directly, your code would look like this:

```
SendMessage(RadioBtns[0], BM_SETCHECK, WPARAM(TRUE), 0L);
SendMessage(RadioBtns[1], BM_SETCHECK, WPARAM(FALSE), 0L);
SendMessage(RadioBtns[2], BM_SETCHECK, WPARAM(FALSE), 0L);
```

WINDOWSX simplifies these calls by enabling you to write the following:

```
Button_SetCheck(RadioBtns[0], TRUE);
Button_SetCheck(RadioBtns[1], FALSE);
Button_SetCheck(RadioBtns[2], FALSE);
```

The actual macro definition in WINDOWSX.H for Button_SetCheck looks like this:

```
#define Button_SetCheck(hwndCtl, check)
((void)SendMessage((hwndCtl), BM_SETCHECK, (WPARAM)(int)(check), 0L))
```

The macro simply calls SendMessage, being careful to properly typecast the user's request to turn the button on or off. Needless to say, a value of 0 in WPARAM turns the radio button off, whereas a value of 1 turns it on.

It's unfortunate that the message control API isn't listed in the online help by either Microsoft or Borland. Nevertheless, it's worthwhile going through a little extra effort to use it in your program. Remember, the message control API has several advantages:

☐ It has an intuitive, easy-to-use syntax.

☐ It provides strong type-checking, at the same time alleviating the need to make potentially error-prone typecasts.

☐ It provides compatibility with WIN32 code that isn't necessarily available when you use SendMessage directly.

WM_PARENTNOTIFY Messages

There is one last important point to be made about the way FileBox handles right mouse clicks. A problem arises when the user clicks the right mouse button on one of the buttons or on the list box. Trouble occurs because the WM_RBUTTONDOWN message generated by Windows is absorbed by the control. Fortunately, the folks at Microsoft anticipated situations like this, and so they created the WM_PARENTNOTIFY message, which is sent to a control's parent in the event a control receives one of the following messages:

```
WM_CREATE
WM_DESTROY
WM_LBUTTONDOWN
WM_MBUTTONDOWN
WM_RBUTTONDOWN
```

The result is that the controls can become "semi-transparent" when the user clicks them with the right mouse button. Messages that would have been lost are piggy-backed on WM_PARENTNOTIFY messages, thereby informing the main window of what has happened.

It's easy to respond to a WM_PARENTNOTIFY message:

```
void FileBox_OnParentNotify(HWND hwnd, UINT msg,
                            HWND hwndChild, int idChild)
{
  if (msg == WM_RBUTTONDOWN)
    HandleRightButton(hwnd);
}
```

Summary

The primary focuses of this chapter are radio buttons and the control message API. In particular, you learned about

☐ How to create a Windows shell

☐ How to create radio buttons

☐ How to communicate with radio buttons through the `Button_SetCheck` macro

☐ Arranging radio buttons in groups with the `WS_GROUP` and `WS_TABSTOP` styles

☐ Using the control message API to talk to list boxes or radio buttons

☐ Using `IsDialogMessage` to handle keystrokes in a window

So far, you've heard only part of the tale to be told about the FileBox program. The second half of the story involves push buttons, list boxes, and window subclassing. You can read all about those subjects in the next chapter.

Q&A

Q: I still don't understand `IsDialogMessage`. What's it all about, anyway?

A: The act of tabbing between controls or selecting radio buttons with the arrow keys seems so intuitive to a user that it's easy to start to take it for granted. The process itself, however, must be taken care of manually, by literally setting the focus from one control to the next at the appropriate time. Fortunately, Windows has internal logic that knows how to handle this type of situation. To take advantage of this logic, all you need to do is call `IsDialogMessage`. From that point on, Windows handles everything for you by actually tracking the keyboard messages and setting the focus accordingly.

Workshop

The Workshop provides quiz questions to help you solidify your understanding of the material covered and exercises to provide you with experience in using what you've learned. Try to understand the quiz and exercise answers before continuing on to the next chapter. Answers are provided in Appendix A.

Quiz

1. What command can be used to automatically reboot the system and restart Windows?

2. What does the `IsDialogMessage` function do, and where in your program should you place it?

3. Group boxes belong to what class? How about radio buttons?

4. Where can you find a list of the control message API calls?

5. What standard WM_XXX message corresponds to the Button_SetCheck macro?

6. How can you get a radio button to automatically respond to button clicks?

7. What is the purpose of a group box?

8. How do you mark the beginning and end of a group of controls?

9. What is the difference between the WS_GROUP and WS_TABSTOP styles?

10. How can you check to see if a call to WinExec has succeeded, and what should you do if it fails?

Exercises

1. Create a program that uses two sets of radio buttons. Set them up so you can tab between groups and select one radio button from each group.

2. Add a menu to the top of the FileBox Windows shell with the following items listed in it:

   Calendar
   Clock
   Control Panel
   DOS Prompt
   File Manager
   Notepad
   Write

   When the user selects any of these items, launch the appropriate program. Remember that the best way to launch a DOS box is to start DOSPRMPT.PIF.

3. Pop up a message box that will report when a call to WinExec fails. Use the return code from WinExec to post an informative message for the user.

Subclassing
Window
Controls

After covering some fairly straightforward material on push buttons, the WM_GETMINMAXINFO message, and list boxes, this chapter launches into an in-depth discussion of subclassing. This important technique represents the crucial last brick in the edifice of knowledge you are constructing around the subject of window controls.

Subclassing enables you to alter the behavior of a control by temporarily taking over its window procedure. As you will see, the end result is that you can modify a list box, push button, or other control so that it does exactly what you want.

As a special bonus, the end of this chapter contains a relatively short program that demonstrates how you can subclass a window that belongs to an entirely different program. This admittedly rather esoteric technique enables you to reach into other programs, or into the inner workings of Windows itself, and change the behavior of another programmer's code.

Here's a sketch of the major subjects covered in this chapter:

☐ An overview of push buttons

☐ WM_CLOSE messages and the DestroyWindow function

☐ A look at the WM_GETMINMAXINFO message

☐ A second look at list boxes, concentrating on their capability to display directory information with DlgDirList and DlgDirSelect

☐ An explanation about how a program iterates through the available drives or directories when the list box is clicked

☐ Extensive examples of how to subclass a Window

☐ A discussion about how to read from and write to initialization (.INI) files

☐ An explanation about how to create menus on the fly

Working with Push Buttons

Now, you need to pick up the narrative thread, more or less, where it was set down at the end of the last chapter. Specifically, the focus was on the new controls found in the FileBox program. The next tool up for discussion is the gray shaded push button, which users can select with the mouse.

Even the most inexperienced users can figure out how to shut down the FileBox program; all they have to do is click the big Close button (shown in Figure 13.1).

The classic push button controls are almost as emblematic of Windows as an icon or the standard overlapped window. You've probably seen these types of buttons a thousand times before, and if you decide to make a go of this Windows programming business, you'll most likely create a few thousand more of them.

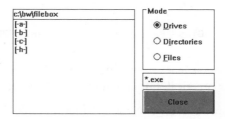

Figure 13.1. *The FileBox's push button is nestled into the bottom-right corner of this group of controls.*

Here's the code from the `FileBox_OnCreate` function (from Listing 12.1 of the previous chapter) that creates the Close button:

```
199: hControl[ID_CLOSE] = CreateWindow("button", "Close",
200:                 WS_CHILD | WS_VISIBLE | BS_PUSHBUTTON |
201:                 WS_TABSTOP | WS_GROUP,
202:                 250, 138, 131, 70, hwnd, HMENU(ID_CLOSE),
203:                 hInstance, NULL);
```

The effort involved in creating push buttons is almost non-existent compared to the functionality and elegance they bring to your program. To create the same visual effect in a typical DOS program would take many more lines of code and considerable planning.

Note: The key points in the previous call to `CreateWindow` are simple:

☐ Designate the button class in the `lpszClassName` parameter of `CreateWindow` (line 199).

☐ Add `BS_PUSHBUTTON` style to the `dwStyle` field (line 200).

☐ Designate the button's coordinates (line 202).

☐ Typecast the `HMENU` field to assign the button an ID (line 203).

By now, this should be a very familiar process, requiring only minimal thought and effort.

13

It's just as simple to respond to a push button as it is to create one. The actual process is very similar to responding to a menu selection. That is, you set up camp in the `Cls_OnCommand` function and wait for Windows to send a `WM_COMMAND` message with the ID of your button attached. For instance, here is a very simple response to the selection of a push button:

```
case ID_CLOSE:
  MessageBox(hwnd, "Close Button pushed", "Beep", MB_OK);
  break;
```

This code pops up a `MessageBox` informing the user that he or she has pushed the Close button. It's not very practical, but certainly nothing could be simpler.

The actual code from `FileBox_OnCommand` function looks like this:

```
331: case ID_CLOSE:
332:   SendMessage(hwnd, WM_CLOSE, 0, 0);
333:   break;
```

The FileBox program relays the user's choice to a separate portion of the program by sending it a `WM_CLOSE` message (line 332). A `WM_CLOSE` message will shut down an application.

Remember that this program can be used as a Windows shell. Whenever you close the Windows shell, it shuts down all the other applications on the desktop and then enables Windows itself to shut down. This obviously is a fairly major event, and so you want to double check with the user to make sure that is indeed his or her intention.

A complication occurs because there are two different ways to close the FileBox application. You can click the Close button or use the system icon in the upper-left corner of the program. The system menu, of course, doesn't send `ID_CLOSE` messages to `FileBox_OnCommand`. Instead, it results in a `WM_CLOSE` message being sent to the main window.

Note: The system icon is added to a window by ORing in the `WS_SYSMENU` style to the third field of `CreateWindow`. You can, of course, close an application by either double-clicking this icon or selecting close from it's menu.

Because the system menu's behavior is built into Windows, the FileBox program opts to go along with this prearranged scheme. It sends its own `WM_CLOSE` message, and then responds to both the system menu's and the Close button's messages with the following code:

```
void FileBox_OnClose(HWND hwnd)
{
 if (MessageBox(hwnd, "Do you want to exit?", "FileBox",
      MB_ICONQUESTION ¦ MB_OKCANCEL) == IDOK)
    DestroyWindow(hwnd);
}
```

Calling `DestroyWindow` on an application's main window is all that needs to be done to shut down a program. This one call deactivates a window, disposes its menu and its child windows, flushes its queue, destroys its timers, disconnects it from the rest of the system, and sets the focus elsewhere. It goes without saying that `DestroyWindow` also sends a `WM_DESTROY` message to your main window.

If you don't override a window's default response to a `WM_CLOSE` message, it automatically calls `DestroyWindow`. FileBox doesn't really change the main window's response to a `WM_CLOSE` message—the end result is still a call to `DestroyWindow`. What the FileBox program does differently is prompt the user to confirm the action before carrying it through.

DO

DON'T

When you want to shut down an application:

DO close an application by sending a `WM_CLOSE` message or by calling `DestroyWindow` directly.

DON'T ever try to call `Cls_OnDestroy` directly, and don't ever try to close a Window by sending it a `WM_DESTROY` message.

Restricting the Size of a Window

Unlike all the other examples you have seen in this book, the FileBox program can't be resized by a user pulling on its borders. Also, this program doesn't change size, even when you maximize it. This behavior, which is somewhat reminiscent of a dialog, is achieved by responding to the `WM_GETMINMAXINFO` message:

```
341:void FileBox_OnGetMinMaxInfo(HWND hwnd,
342:                            MINMAXINFO FAR* lpMinMaxInfo)
343: {
344:    lpMinMaxInfo->ptMaxSize.x = XSIZE;
345:    lpMinMaxInfo->ptMaxSize.y = YSIZE;
346:    lpMinMaxInfo->ptMaxPosition.x = 100
```

```
347:    lpMinMaxInfo->ptMaxPosition.y = 100
348:    lpMinMaxInfo->ptMinTrackSize.x = XSIZE;
349:    lpMinMaxInfo->ptMinTrackSize.y = YSIZE;
350:    lpMinMaxInfo->ptMaxTrackSize.x = XSIZE;
351:    lpMinMaxInfo->ptMaxTrackSize.y = YSIZE;
352: }
```

This message handler function receives two parameters:

☐ A copy of the HWND with which it's associated (line 341)

☐ A MINMAXINFO structure (line 342)

MINMAXINFO has six fields, each declared to be of type POINT. A POINT structure usually is used to designate a location on-screen. It has two fields of type integer: the first called x, and the second called y. See Table 13.1 for the MINMAXINFO structure fields.

Table 13.1. The fields of the MINMAXINFO structure.

ptReserved	Not used
ptMaxSize	How big the window will be when it's maximized
ptMaxPosition	Where the upper-left corner of the window should be positioned when the window is maximized
ptMinTrackSize	The smallest size the window can be when the user tries to resize it by pulling on its borders
ptMaxTrackSize	The largest size the window can be when the user tries to resize it by pulling on its borders

The WM_GETMINMAXINFO message comes cruising down the pike when the window is being created (or at the approximate time the WM_CREATE message gets sent).

Note: If you don't use WINDOWSX, you need to typecast the WndProc's LPARAM to type MINMAXINFO when responding to the WM_MINMAXINFO message. From that point on, your approach could be very similar to that of the code in FILEBOX.CPP.

When trying to control the size of a main window, programmers often mistakenly try to manipulate the x, y, nWidth, and nHeight field passed to CreateWindow. As a rule, that's a mistake. It's best to pass CW_USEDEFAULT in those parameters. The real way to

control the size and shape of a main window is by handling WM_GETMINMAXINFO messages. This isn't a hard and fast rule, but certainly, rather than directly modifying the coordinates passed to CreateWindow, you should consider responding to WM_GETMINMAXINFO messages.

Well, that's all there is to say about the WM_GETMINMAXINFO message. Technically, it's not very challenging, but in it's proper place, it can prove to be invaluable.

Directory Magic

FILEBOX.EXE fills the program's list box with the names of files, directories, or drives. This seemingly complicated task is greatly simplified by a few simple Window's API functions called DlgDirList and DlgDirSelect.

In and of themselves, neither of these functions are particularly hard to use. However, the FileBox program interacts with these functions through the use of global constants called DirShowType and DirShowVal. Both constants help make the program considerably easier to read and maintain. In the next few pages, you'll read about the new API calls and about the techniques for using them. The goal is to see how to avoid creating hopelessly confusing spaghetti code that even you won't be able to understand three months from now.

To get started, take a look at a fragment that appears just before the end of the WM_CREATE message handler function:

```
DlgDirList(hwnd, "*.*", ID_FILELIST,
           ID_PATHS, DirShowVal[DirShowType]);
```

The DlgDirList API call fills a list box with information about a particular drive or subdirectory. For instance, it can fill a list box with a list of the currently available files, drives, and subdirectories. See Table 13.2 for the parameters passed to DlgDirList.

Table 13.2. The parameters passed to DlgDirList.

HWND hwndDlg	Handle of the window or dialog containing the list box
LPSTR lpszPath	Wildcards designating the files to be shown
int idListBox	ID of the list box
int idStaticPath	ID of the static control for currently selected files(s)
UINT uFileType	Identifier designating the types of files to show

When calling `DlgDirList`, start by placing the ID of the appropriate list box in `DlgDirList`'s third parameter. Then, fill in the other parameters with information about the files or directories you want to display. Don't forget that `DlgDirList` automatically fills in a static control with the name of the currently selected file. All you need to do is hand over the ID of the control in `DlgDirList`'s fourth parameter. See Table 13.3 for `DlgDirLists`'s fifth parameter constants.

Table 13.3. The fifth parameter to `DlgDirList` consists of one or more constants that specify exactly what should be shown in the listbox.

`DDL_READWRITE`	Read-write data files
`DDL_READONLY`	Read-only files
`DDL_HIDDEN`	Hidden files
`DDL_SYSTEM`	System files
`DDL_DIRECTORY`	Directories
`DDL_ARCHIVE`	Archives
`DDL_POSTMSGS`	Posts messages to the application, not the dialog
`DDL_DRIVES`	Drives
`DDL_EXCLUSIVE`	Excludes normal files and lists only files of the specified type

If you pass in `DDL_READWRITE` in the fifth parameter of a call to `DlgDirList`, it fills up the designated list box with a list of files that have their read and write attributes set. If you send in the `DDL_DRIVES` identifier, you'll see all the normal files, and a list of drives. If you want to see only drives, pass in `DDL_DRIVES` OR'd together with `DDL_EXCLUSIVE`.

In the FileBox program, a constant array is set up to designate each of three types of displays generated by the application:

```
WORD DirShowVal[] = {DDL_DRIVES | DDL_EXCLUSIVE,
                     DDL_DIRECTORY | DDL_EXCLUSIVE,
                     DDL_ARCHIVE};
```

`DirShowVal` is always set to one of the three modes displayed in its declaration. For instance, if the user selects the Files radio button, `DirShowVal` is set to `DDL_ARCHIVE`, which ensures that all the normal files in the current directory are shown. If the user

chooses Directories, `DirShowVal` is set to `DDL_DIRECTORY ¦ DDL_EXCLUSIVE`, which shows only a list of the currently available subdirectories.

To manage this, FileBox relies on the locally declared `DirShowType` variable, which is of type `TCurMode`:

```
enum TCurMode {DRIVEMODE, DIRMODE, FILEMODE};
TCurMode DirShowType;
```

The interaction of these different variables ensures that the call to `DlgDirList` always generates either a list of normal files, a list of directories, or a list of drives, depending on the current value of `DirShowType`.

One portion of the program can set the current value of `DirShowType` to either `DRIVEMODE`, `DIRMODE`, or `FILEMODE`:

```
DirShowType = FILEMODE;
```

Now, whenever you need to call `DlgDirList`, you can pass in the correct constants by indexing into the `DirShowVal` array:

```
DirShowVal[DirShowType]
```

The final call looks like this:

```
DlgDirList(hwnd,"*.*", ID_FILELIST,
           ID_PATHS, DirShowVal[DirShowType]);
```

There are, of course, other ways to handle this type of situation. I've shown you this one because it helps to simplify a type of coding chore that comes up frequently in Windows programming.

> **Note:** Some people are confused by the constants that are spread throughout Windows code like confetti. In the case of `DlgDirList`, this confusion is compounded because only recent documents use the standard Windows declared constants rather than raw numbers.
>
> The basic principle behind the constants is simply to declare a set of flags that have a certain meaning. This is really a very simple idea, no more complex than a child's game. Kids, for instance, love to set up codes that govern behavior. "If I say the number one, you turn to the left; if I say the number two, you turn to the right." That kind of thing. Very simple, very straightforward.

13

At any rate, the actual constants used with the `DlgDirList` function are defined in WINDOWS.H:

```
/* DlgDirList, DlgDirListComboBox flags values */
#define DDL_READWRITE       0x0000
#define DDL_READONLY        0x0001
#define DDL_HIDDEN          0x0002
#define DDL_SYSTEM          0x0004
#define DDL_DIRECTORY       0x0010
#define DDL_ARCHIVE         0x0020
#define DDL_POSTMSGS        0x2000
#define DDL_DRIVES          0x4000
#define DDL_EXCLUSIVE       0x8000
```

These can be translated into kid-talk like this: "If I say value one, you show me read-only files; if I say two, you show me the hidden files." It's an extremely simple system, complicated only slightly by the addition of logical operators.

In the declaration for the `DirShowVal` array, the `DDL_DIRECTORY` and the `DDL_EXCLUSIVE` values are OR'd together. This is done by writing:

```
DDL_DIRECTORY ¦ DDL_EXCLUSIVE
```

which is exactly the same thing as writing:

```
0x0010 ¦ 0x8000
```

There is no significant difference between the statements. For that matter, I could just as easily have written `0x8010`, which is what the two values OR'd together look like.

The problem, of course, is that writing `0x8010` isn't very intelligible to people who are trying to decipher the code several months or years later. So, Windows uses predeclared constants. It's not always the world's most aesthetically pleasing system, but it is very practical.

Before moving on, it might be helpful for me to sum up this section of the chapter:

☐ The `DlgDirList` function fills a list box with a list of files, directories, drives, and so forth.

☐ `DlgDirList` takes five parameters, all of which are fairly easy to handle under normal circumstances.

☐ FileBox's mode is specified by one of three sets of identifiers passed in
`DlgDirList uFileType` parameter.

☐ To track these identifiers, the FileBox program sets up two global variables
called `DirShowType` and `DirShowVal`.

Changing Drives and Directories

The next (and final) step is to see how FileBox responds when the user starts clicking
the list box. In other words, you need to see how the FileBox program iterates through
subdirectories and enables the user to run a particular program.

If a user clicks a directory or drive name in the list box, a message is sent to the
`WM_COMMAND` message handler function. The following code is activated:

```
case ID_FILELIST:
  if (codeNotify == LBN_DBLCLK)
  {
    if (DirShowType != FILEMODE)
      HandleMouseClick(hwnd, id, hwndCtl, codeNotify);
    else
    {
      int index = ListBox_GetCurSel(hControl[ID_FILELIST]);
      _getdcwd(0, S, 125);
      ListBox_GetText(hControl[ID_FILELIST], index,
                      lpszBuffer);
      strcat(S, "\\");
      strcat(S, lpszBuffer);
      WinExec(S, SW_SHOWNORMAL);
    }
  }
  break;
```

FileBox checks to see if the user has double-clicked the list box. If the user has, the
program does one of two things—depending on whether or not the user is in file
mode. If the user is viewing a list of files, the program tries to call `WinExec` to launch
the selected filename. If the user is in drive mode or directory mode, the
`HandleMouseClick` function is called:

```
#pragma argsused
void HandleMouseClick(HWND hwnd, int id, HWND hwndCtl, UINT codeNotify)
{
  char Buffer[100];
```

13

```
DlgDirSelect(hwnd, Buffer, ID_FILELIST);
DlgDirList(hwnd, Buffer, ID_FILELIST,
           ID_PATHS, DirShowVal[DirShowType]);
}
```

The `DlgDirSelect` function retrieves the file the user clicked. If a directory or drive is selected, `DlgDirSelect` strips off the encasing brackets and/or hyphens and returns a valid directory or drive listing. Pass this value to `DlgDirList`, and Windows automatically changes to the specified drive or directory.

The point is that Windows does the dirty work of parsing file names and changing directories, but also it protects both the programmer and the user from the ugly stuff that used to take place at the DOS prompt. The goal is to try to produce a more intuitively obvious interface to the dark and obscure hardware that is always lurking just below the surface. People tend to love their machines, but they don't necessarily want to have to open up the hood and get their hands dirty. Functions, such as `DlgDirList`, help smooth the way; they help make computers more intelligible to humans.

Of course, some people want to open up the hood and have a peak at what is going on underneath. For those intrepid souls, I've stuck in the following function:

```
void SetListbox(HWND hwnd)
{
  RECT R;

  ListBox_ResetContent(BoxWin);
  ListBox_Dir(BoxWin, DirShowVal[DirShowType], "*.*");

  R.left = 14;
  R.top = 220;
  R.right = 14 + BMPX;
  R.bottom = 220 + BMPY;
  InvalidateRect(hwnd, &R, FALSE);
}
```

These first two lines of code, which utilize the control message API, perform pretty much the same task as `DlgDirList`. The `ListBox_ResetContent` function clears the listbox, and the `ListBox_Dir` macro fills it with the appropriate information from the current subdirectory.

The thing these functions don't do, of course, is change the directory. However, the `SetListbox` function doesn't need to change directories, because it's called only when the user switches from file mode to directory mode, or from directory mode to drive mode (and so forth). As a result, at this point in the program, you don't have to change directories or drives.

The `ListBox_ResetContent` macro fronts for the `LB_RESETCONTENT` message. Before the advent of WINDOWSX, list boxes were always cleared with the following line of code:

```
SendMessage(BoxWin, LB_RESETCONTENT, 0, 0L);
```

By now, you probably are catching on to the way these control message macros get their names. As a result, it should come as no surprise that the `ListBox_Dir` function fronts for the `LB_DIR` message. For instance, here is a typical `SendMessage` call that utilizes `LB_DIR`:

```
SendMessage(BoxWin, LB_DIR, DDL_DRIVES | DDL_EXCLUSIVE,
            LPARAM(lpszBuffer));
```

In this example, the `lpszBuffer` might hold a string, such as *.* or *.EXE. FileBox uses the WINDOWSX macros and a few other tricks to simplify the call so that it looks like this:

```
ListBox_Dir(BoxWin, DirShowVal[DirShowType], "*.*");
```

It's still not a paradigm of syntactical clarity, but it's much easier to read.

Note: You might also want to pick up on the call to `InvalidateRect`, which lies at the bottom of the `SetListbox` function. `InvalidateRect`, you'll remember, causes a `WM_PAINT` message to be sent to a window. This is one of the rare cases in which you might want to use the second parameter of this API call. Passing a `RECT` in this parameter forces Windows to redraw only a defined portion of your window. The two reasons for passing a `RECT` are

1. It saves clock cycles.
2. It prevents unsightly blinking when the program is redrawn.

Introduction to Subclassing Window Controls

In the last few chapters you've had a look at all the major controls:

check boxes	edits
group boxes	list boxes
push buttons	radio buttons
scrollbars	statics

13

By now, you should have a feeling for how crucial these tools are to the construction of any useful Windows program. Use them well and you can create programs that are easy to use and easy to understand.

However, there is one fairly serious catch. The problem is that controls remain black boxes to programmers. We can't know how they work internally, because Microsoft has never published their source code. Furthermore, there are times when we need to slightly alter their behavior so that they will fit seamlessly into our programs.

Obviously, I wouldn't introduce this topic unless Microsoft had provided a solution to the problem. That solution is called *subclassing*. Subclassing a window control isn't technically difficult, but it does require that programmers grasp a few important new concepts.

Here's what you need to know:

☐ Just like a dialog or window, every control has a window procedure that dictates its behavior.

☐ The address of a control's window procedure is stored in memory, and it can be retrieved and/or replaced.

☐ If you replace the window procedure of a control with the address of one of your own functions, you can get first crack at any messages sent to a control.

☐ After you've seen a particular message, you can either pass it on to the control's original window procedure or swallow it so that it disappears without a trace. In either case, you can respond to the message in a manner of your own choosing, thereby changing the predefined behavior of a control.

That's all there is to it. Overall, this is a fairly simple procedure, somewhat akin to the process you go through when creating dialogs or callbacks. In other words, the key steps involve calling MakeProcInstance and setting up a "mailing address" to which Windows can send messages.

Note: In a book like this, there is little need for discussion about subclassing a control. My goals are to show you the tools at hand and to give you examples of how they are supposed to work under normal, or even ideal, circumstances. In the real world, however, programmers tend to encounter "exceptions" to the rules almost as often as they encounter "normal" circumstances. As a result, subclassing controls is something

SAMS
Sams
Learning
Center
SAMS
PUBLISHING

programmers tend to do on a regular basis. In other words, this is another
important topic, and you probably should take the time necessary to
properly master this material.

Subclassing Controls: The Particulars

Now that you understand what subclassing is all about, it's time to start talking about
a specific example. The FileBox program subclasses its edit control. It needs to do this
for five partially interrelated reasons:

☐ It needs to handle WM_KILLFOCUS messages so it can check to see if the edit
   control needs to tell the list box that the user has changed the file mask (see
   Figure 13.2).

☐ It needs to handle WM_GETDLGCODE messages.

☐ It needs to handle the Enter key in a particular manner.

☐ It needs to restore the normal tabbing behavior it lost when it responded to
   WM_GETDLGCODE.

☐ It needs to highlight the text in the edit control every time it receives the
   focus, that is, when it receives a WM_SETFOCUS message.

Figure 13.2. *Residing just above the program's push button, FileBox's edit control
contains a file mask.*

The previous list represents a fairly tangled web of ideas that quite accurately reflect
the kind of challenge you should expect from a real-world Windows programming
project. The only way out of this particular weave of problems is to start subclassing
like mad. Don't worry if all of this doesn't quite make sense to you yet. This is a
difficult problem, and the exact details may not become clear to you until you've
studied it under the debugger from several different angles.

To begin researching this problem, you might want to look at the WM_GETDLGCODE message, which interacts in some interesting ways with IsDialogMessage. As explained in the last chapter, IsDialogMessage grabs certain key presses and handles them for you, thereby providing your program with important built-in functionality, such as automatic tabbing between controls. The trade-off here is that IsDialogMessage forces you to relinquish control over those key presses that are being handled by Windows. In particular, unless the edit control specifically designates otherwise (when responding to WM_GETDLGCODE messages), IsDialogMessage decides that edit controls don't really need to see the Enter key.

What if you want to respond to presses of the Enter key? Well, the answer is that you have to handle WM_GETDLGCODE messages by returning DLGC_WANTALLKEYS:

```
case WM_GETDLGCODE:
  return DLGC_WANTALLKEYS;
```

Unfortunately, the saga isn't quite over, because the DLGC_WANTALLKEYS message effectively eliminates the built-in IsDialogMessage tabbing behavior for the program's edit control. This means that the FileBox program needs to explicitly restore proper tabbing for edit controls. The best way it can do that is through subclassing.

If all this seems a bit confusing and complicated, that's because it *is* confusing and complicated. You're not looking at the type of prime real estate that the designers of Windows would want to show off to just anyone. Instead, you're examining the territory where the best Windows programmers earn their stripes.

What's been established so far is that the edit control in the FileBox program needs to be subclassed so that it can handle certain messages in a particular manner. In other words, the default behavior for edit controls just isn't good enough in these circumstances. As a result, you have to dig deep to learn how to alter that behavior. Here's how it works:

When you create a WNDCLASS structure in a register function, or when you pass information in with CreateWindow call, Windows saves your work in the local heap of a dynamic link library called USER.EXE. By making calls to a series of functions with names like SetWindowLong and SetClassLong, you can retrieve or replace most of this information.

Because controls are really just windows with their own WNDCLASS structures and their own internal data, there is no reason why you can't turn to Windows and ask for the address of their window procedure. When you have it, you can replace it with one of your own.

When you want to subclass a window control, start with the following two-step process:

☐ Create memory for a window procedure by calling MakeProcInstance.

☐ Swap that window procedure into the place formerly occupied by Microsoft's window procedure.

Here's how the whole thing looks when you write code to subclass an edit control:

```
FARPROC lpfnNewEdit;
WNDPROC OldListProc;
HWND hEdit;

lpfnNewEdit = MakeProcInstance(FARPROC(NewEditProc), hInstance);
OldEditProc = (WNDPROC)SetWindowLong(hEdit, GWL_WNDPROC,
                                     LONG(lpfnNewList));
```

lpfnNewEdit is a pointer variable designed to point at the new window procedure supplied by FileBox. The OldEditProc variable, on the other hand, can be used to store the address of the old window procedure designed by Microsoft.

FileBox allocates prolog code for the new procedure by calling MakeProcInstance. It passes the address of the new procedure to Windows and saves the address of the old window procedure. This is done by calling SetWindowLong.

The next step is to design the new window procedure, which looks like this:

```
LRESULT CALLBACK NewEditProc(HWND hwnd, UINT Message,
                             WPARAM wParam, LPARAM lParam)
{
  switch(Message)
  {
    case WM_GETDLGCODE:
      return DLGC_WANTALLKEYS;

    case WM_KEYDOWN:
      ...                      // Code to handle tabbing
      break;

    case WM_KILLFOCUS:
      SetNewWildCard(hwnd);
      break;

    case WM_SETFOCUS:
      Edit_SetSel(hwnd, 0, -1);
      break;
  }
  return
    CallWindowProc(OldEditProc, hwnd, Message, wParam, lParam);
}
```

13

The declaration for NewEditProc looks exactly like the declaration for any other window procedure. It takes all the same parameters and returns exactly the same values. It's just like the FileBox's main window procedure, only it's used for an edit control.

The switch statement that forms the body for the window procedure, is exactly like the switch statement you might see in the main window's WNDPROC, or in a dialog box procedure.

In fact, the only difference between this window procedure and a normal window procedure is that it ends by referencing the CallWindowProc function, rather than DefWndowProc:

```
return CallWindowProc(OldEditProc,hwnd,Message,wParam,lParam);
```

Needless to say, the mission of CallWindowProc is to pass a message to the original window procedure. It's able to do this because you specifically pass the address of the original window procedure in the first parameter.

DO   DON'T

DO remember to pass messages to the original window procedure if you want them to be processed normally.

You **DON'T** have to pass on any messages that you don't want the control to process. For instance, many programmers subclass edit controls, and then simply neglect to pass on any non-numeric input. The result is an edit control that forces the user to type numbers and refuses to acknowledge any attempts to type letters. If you need an edit control to act like this, you can get one by subclassing.

As usual, the last step in this process is to clean up. In FileBox, this takes place in response to the WM_DESTROY message:

```
SetWindowLong(hEdit, GWL_WNDPROC, LONG(OldEditProc));
FreeProcInstance(lpfnNewEdit);
```

The call to SetWindowLong takes three parameters. The first is the handle to the window you want to change; the second is a constant designating an offset into the data located in USER.EXE's local heap; the third is the function you want to insert into memory.

After FileBox replaces the window procedure it so unceremoniously borrowed, the final step is to destroy the one it created. There! Now everything is back the way its was before FileBox came on the scene.

You might want to take a moment to consider what has happened here. The key points to absorb are as follows:

☐ The FileBox program needed to change the default behavior of its edit control.

☐ In order to do this, it had to swap the address of its own custom-made window procedure into the USER.EXE's local heap, and get back the address of the old window procedure.

☐ It handled certain messages, as it saw fit, and passed the others directly to the old window procedure.

☐ When finished, the FileBox program carefully cleaned up after itself by putting the old window procedure back where it found it. FileBox then called `FreeProcInstance` on the address of its own custom-made window procedure.

Hopefully, you can see why subclassing has a little aura of magic around it. It's exciting territory that you can really have some fun with—if you are so inclined.

I also should mention that the subclassing shown here is specific to a particular window. It's possible to subclass an entire class of controls so all the versions of that control (that appear in any program) exhibit behavior that you define. For obvious reasons, this is something you wouldn't normally want to do, and as a result I don't cover it in this book.

13

Bonus Program: Subclassing the Windows Desktop!

To round out this chapter, I've prepared a short example program called MenuAid that shows how to subclass a window, that isn't part of your current program.

MenuAid hooks into the desktop window, which forms the backdrop on which the Windows shell appears when you first boot the computer. MenuAid's sole task, when subclassing the desktop window, is to respond to right mouse clicks by sending a message back to its own main window procedure. When the main window receives this message, it pops up a menu of available programs. If the user selects an item from this menu, MenuAid runs the selected program. The end result is that the user can access a list of available programs by clicking the right mouse button on the desktop (see Figure 13.3).

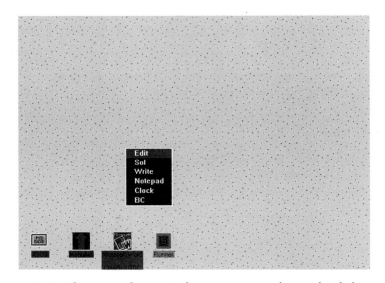

Figure 13.3. *The iconized MenuAid program responds to right-clicks on the Windows desktop by popping up a menu.*

The idea for this program was suggested by Dave Wilhelm, a veteran C and Pascal programmer who works in Borland tech support. I decided to hack my own version for this book because it's an interesting program that serves a useful purpose. My thanks, and hats off to Dave Wilhelm—he's an excellent programmer, and it's very generous of him to share his idea with us.

Listing 13.1 shows the code to the MenuAid program. Have fun with it!

Listing 13.1. The MenuAid program shows how to subclass the Windows desktop.

```
1: ///////////////////////////////////////////////
2: //   Program Name: MENUAID.CPP
3: //   Programmer: Charlie Calvert
4: //   Thanks: Dave Wilhelm
5: //   Description: MenuAid windows program
6: //   Date: 07/04/93
7: ///////////////////////////////////////////////
```

```
 8:
 9: #define STRICT
10: #include <windows.h>
11: #include <windowsx.h>
12: #include <string.h>
13:
14: // ----------------------------------------------------------
15: // Interface
16: // ----------------------------------------------------------
17:
18: #define CM_EDIT 1
19: #define WM_SPECIAL (WM_USER + 0x100)
20: #define ID_LISTBOX 102
21: #define CM_UPDATE 103
22: #define XSIZE 223
23: #define YSIZE 253
24:
25: LRESULT CALLBACK _export WndProc(HWND hwnd, UINT Message,
26:                                       WPARAM wParam, LPARAM  lParam);
27: LRESULT CALLBACK _export NewDesktopProc(HWND hWindow, UINT Message,
28: WPARAM wParam, LPARAM lParam);
29: BOOL Register(HINSTANCE hInst);
30: HWND Create(HINSTANCE hInst, int nCmdShow);
31: HMENU NewMenu(void);
32:
33: // Declarations for class MenuAid
34: #define MenuAid_DefProc     DefWindowProc
35: BOOL MenuAid_OnCreate(HWND hwnd,
36:                     CREATESTRUCT FAR* lpCreateStruct);
37: void MenuAid_OnDestroy(HWND hwnd);
38: void MenuAid_OnCommand(HWND hwnd, int id,
39:                     HWND hwndCtl, UINT codeNotify);
40: void MenuAid_OnGetMinMaxInfo(HWND hwnd,
41:                     MINMAXINFO FAR* lpMinMaxInfo);
42:
43: static char szAppName[] = "MenuAid";
44: static char IniName[] = "MenuAid.Ini";
45: static HWND MainWindow, DeskWnd, hListBox;
46: static HINSTANCE hInstance;
47: WNDPROC OldDesk;
48: FARPROC lpfnNewProc;
49: HMENU Float;
50: static int ItemsInMenu = 1;
51:
52: // -----------------------------
53: // Initialization
54: // -----------------------------
55:
56: /////////////////////////////////////
57: // Program entry point
58: /////////////////////////////////////
```

continues

417

Listing 13.1. continued

```
59: #pragma argsused
60: int PASCAL WinMain(HINSTANCE hInst, HINSTANCE hPrevInstance, LPSTR
61:                    lpszCmdParam, int nCmdShow)
62: {
63:   MSG  Msg;
64:
65:   if (!hPrevInstance)
66:     if (!Register(hInst))
67:       return FALSE;
68:
69:   MainWindow = Create(hInst, nCmdShow);
70:   if (MainWindow)
71:     return FALSE;
72:   while (GetMessage(&Msg, NULL, 0, 0))
73:   {
74:       TranslateMessage(&Msg);
75:       DispatchMessage(&Msg);
76:   }
77:
78:   return Msg.wParam;
79: }
80:
81: ////////////////////////////////
82: // Register the window
83: ////////////////////////////////
84: BOOL Register(HINSTANCE hInst)
85: {
86:   WNDCLASS WndClass;
87:
88:   WndClass.style          = CS_HREDRAW | CS_VREDRAW;
89:   WndClass.lpfnWndProc    = WndProc;
90:   WndClass.cbClsExtra     = 0;
91:   WndClass.cbWndExtra     = 0;
92:   WndClass.hInstance      = hInst;
93:   WndClass.hIcon          = LoadIcon(hInst, "MenuAid");
94:   WndClass.hCursor        = LoadCursor(NULL, IDC_ARROW);
95:   WndClass.hbrBackground  = GetStockBrush(LTGRAY_BRUSH);
96:   WndClass.lpszMenuName   = NULL;
97:   WndClass.lpszClassName  = szAppName;
98:
99:    return RegisterClass (&WndClass);
100: }
101:
102: ////////////////////////////////
103: // Create the window
104: ////////////////////////////////
105: HWND Create(HINSTANCE hInst, int nCmdShow)
106: {
107:    hInstance = hInst;
```

```
108:    DWORD Style = WS_OVERLAPPEDWINDOW & ~WS_MAXIMIZEBOX;
109:
110:    HWND hwnd = CreateWindow(szAppName, szAppName,
111:                    Style & ~WS_THICKFRAME,
112:                    CW_USEDEFAULT, CW_USEDEFAULT,
113:                    CW_USEDEFAULT, CW_USEDEFAULT,
114:                    NULL, NULL, hInst, NULL);
115:
116:    if (hwnd == NULL)
117:      return hwnd;
118:
119:    nCmdShow = SW_SHOWMINIMIZED;
120:
121:    ShowWindow(hwnd, nCmdShow);
122:    UpdateWindow(hwnd);
123:
124:    return hwnd;
125: }
126:
127: // ----------------------------------------------------------
128: // WndProc and Implementation
129: // ----------------------------------------------------------
130:
131: ////////////////////////////////////
132: // The Window Procedure
133: ////////////////////////////////////
134: LRESULT CALLBACK _export WndProc(HWND hwnd, UINT Message,
135:                                    WPARAM wParam, LPARAM lParam)
136: {
137:    switch(Message)
138:    {
139:      case WM_SPECIAL:
140:        POINT P = MAKEPOINT(lParam);
141:        Float = NewMenu();
142:        TrackPopupMenu(Float, TPM_LEFTALIGN,
143:                        P.x, P.y, 0, hwnd, NULL);
144:        return 0;
145:
146:      HANDLE_MSG(hwnd, WM_CREATE, MenuAid_OnCreate);
147:      HANDLE_MSG(hwnd, WM_DESTROY, MenuAid_OnDestroy);
148:      HANDLE_MSG(hwnd, WM_COMMAND, MenuAid_OnCommand);
149:      HANDLE_MSG(hwnd, WM_GETMINMAXINFO, MenuAid_OnGetMinMaxInfo);
150:      default:
151:        return MenuAid_DefProc(hwnd, Message, wParam, lParam);
152:    }
153: }
154:
155: void FillListBox(HWND hwnd)
156: {
157:    int Temp, Total = 0;
158:    const int Size = 1024;
```

continues

Listing 13.1. continued

```
159:   char Buffer[Size];
160:
161:   ListBox_ResetContent(hwnd);
162:   ListBox_AddString(hwnd, "Edit");
163:
164:   int Len = GetPrivateProfileString("Files", NULL, "",
165:                                   Buffer, Size, IniName);
166:   while(Len > Total)
167:   {
168:     ListBox_AddString(hwnd, Buffer);
169:     Temp = strlen(Buffer) + 1;
170:     Total += Temp;
171:     memmove(Buffer, &Buffer[Temp], Size - Total);
172:   }
173: }
174:
175: ////////////////////////////////
176: // Handle WM_DESTROY
177: ////////////////////////////////
178: #pragma argsused
179: BOOL MenuAid_OnCreate(HWND hwnd, CREATESTRUCT FAR* lpCreateStruct)
180: {
181:   Float = NULL;
182:
183:   DeskWnd = GetDesktopWindow();
184:   lpfnNewProc =
185:     MakeProcInstance(FARPROC(NewDesktopProc), hInstance);
186:   OldDesk = (WNDPROC)SetWindowLong(DeskWnd,
187:                                   GWL_WNDPROC, LONG(lpfnNewProc));
188:
189:   hListBox = CreateWindow("ListBox", NULL,
190:                 WS_CHILD ¦ WS_VISIBLE ¦ LBS_NOTIFY ¦ WS_BORDER,
191:                 10, 10, 200, 200, hwnd,
192:                 HMENU(ID_LISTBOX), hInstance, NULL);
193:
194:   FillListBox(hListBox);
195:
196:   HMENU TheMenu = CreateMenu();
197:   HMENU AMenu = CreatePopupMenu();
198:   AppendMenu(AMenu, MF_STRING, CM_EDIT, "Edit");
199:   AppendMenu(AMenu, MF_STRING, CM_UPDATE, "Update");
200:   AppendMenu(TheMenu, MF_ENABLED ¦ MF_POPUP,
201:             (UINT) AMenu, "&File");
202:   SetMenu(hwnd, TheMenu);
203:
204:   Float = NewMenu();
205:
206:   return TRUE;
207: }
```

```
208:
209: ////////////////////////////////////
210: // Handle WM_DESTROY
211: ////////////////////////////////////
212: #pragma argsused
213: void MenuAid_OnDestroy(HWND hwnd)
214: {
215:   SetWindowLong(DeskWnd, GWL_WNDPROC, LONG(OldDesk));
216:   FreeProcInstance(lpfnNewProc);
217:   DestroyMenu(Float);
218:   PostQuitMessage(0);
219: }
220:
221: ////////////////////////////////////
222: // Launch
223: ////////////////////////////////////
224: void FAR Launch(int id)
225: {
226:   char FileName[50];
227:   char Buffer[200];
228:
229:   if (GetMenuString(Float, id, FileName,
230:                       sizeof(FileName), MF_BYCOMMAND) > 0)
231:     if (GetPrivateProfileString("Files", FileName, "",
232:                       Buffer, sizeof(Buffer), IniName) > 0)
233:       WinExec(Buffer, SW_SHOWNORMAL);
234: }
235:
236: ////////////////////////////////////
237: // Handle WM_COMMAND
238: ////////////////////////////////////
239: #pragma argsused
240: void MenuAid_OnCommand(HWND hwnd, int id, HWND hwndCtl,
241:                         UINT codeNotify)
241: {
242:   const int Size = 250;
243:   char Buffer[Size];
244:   char Buffer2[Size];
245:
246:   if((id > CM_EDIT) && (id <= ItemsInMenu))
247:     Launch(id);
248:   else
249:     switch(id)
250:       {
251:         case CM_EDIT:
252:           GetWindowsDirectory(Buffer, Size);
253:           strcpy(Buffer2, Buffer);
254:           strcat(Buffer2, "\\notepad.exe ");
255:           strcat(Buffer2, Buffer);
256:           strcat(Buffer2, "\\MenuAid.Ini");
257:           WinExec(Buffer2, SW_SHOWNORMAL);
```

13

continues

Listing 13.1. continued

```
258:            break;
259:
260:        case ID_LISTBOX:
261:          if(codeNotify == LBN_DBLCLK)
262:          {
263:              int Index = ListBox_GetCurSel(hListBox);
264:              SendMessage(hwnd, WM_COMMAND, Index + 1, 0L);
265:          }
266:          break;
267:
268:        case CM_UPDATE:
269:          FillListBox(hListBox);
270:          Float = NewMenu();
271:          break;
272:      }
273: }
274:
275: ////////////////////////////////////////
276: // Handle WM_GetMinMaxInfo
277: ////////////////////////////////////////
278: #pragma argsused
279: void MenuAid_OnGetMinMaxInfo(HWND hwnd,
280:                             MINMAXINFO FAR* lpMinMaxInfo)
281: {
282:   lpMinMaxInfo->ptMaxSize.x = XSIZE;
283:   lpMinMaxInfo->ptMaxSize.y = YSIZE;
284:   lpMinMaxInfo->ptMaxPosition.x = 100;
285:   lpMinMaxInfo->ptMaxPosition.y = 100;
286:   lpMinMaxInfo->ptMinTrackSize.x = XSIZE;
287:   lpMinMaxInfo->ptMinTrackSize.y = YSIZE;
288:   lpMinMaxInfo->ptMaxTrackSize.x = XSIZE;
289:   lpMinMaxInfo->ptMaxTrackSize.y = YSIZE;
290: }
291:
292: ////////////////////////////////////////
293: // NewMenu
294: ////////////////////////////////////////
295: HMENU NewMenu(void)
296: {
297:   int Temp, Total = 0;
298:   const int Size = 1024;
299:   char Buffer[Size];
300:   ItemsInMenu = 2;
301:
302:   if (Float) DestroyMenu(Float);
303:   int Len = GetPrivateProfileString("Files", NULL, "",
304:                                     Buffer, Size, IniName);
305:
306:   Float = CreatePopupMenu();
```

```
307:    AppendMenu(Float, MF_STRING, 1, "Edit");
308:
309:    while(Len > Total)
310:    {
311:      AppendMenu(Float, MF_ENABLED | MF_STRING,
312:                 ItemsInMenu, Buffer);
313:      Temp = strlen(Buffer) + 1;
314:      Total += Temp;
315:      memmove(Buffer, &Buffer[Temp], Size - Total);
316:      ItemsInMenu++;
317:    }
318:
319:    return Float;
320: }
321:
322: ////////////////////////////////////
323: // NewDesktopProc
324: ////////////////////////////////////
325: LRESULT CALLBACK NewDesktopProc(HWND hwnd, UINT Message, WPARAM
326:                                 wParam, LPARAM lParam)

327: {
328:    if (Message == WM_RBUTTONDOWN)
329:      PostMessage(MainWindow, WM_SPECIAL, 0, lParam);
330:
331:    return CallWindowProc(OldDesk, hwnd, Message, wParam, lParam);
332: }
```

Listing 13.2 shows the definition file for MenuAid.

 Listing 13.2. MENUAID.DEF.

```
 1: ; MENUAID.DEF
 2:
 3: NAME           MenuAid
 4: DESCRIPTION    'MenuAid Window'
 5: EXETYPE        WINDOWS
 6: STUB           'WINSTUB.EXE'
 7: CODE           PRELOAD MOVEABLE
 8: DATA           PRELOAD MOVEABLE MULTIPLE
 9:
10: HEAPSIZE       4096
11: STACKSIZE      25120
```

13

Listing 13.3 shows the resource file for MenuAid.

Listing 13.3. **MENUAID.RC.**

```
1: // MENUAID.RC
2: MenuAid ICON "MENUAID.ICO"
```

MENUAID.ICO (32X32)

Listing 13.4 shows the Borland makefile for MenuAid.

 Listing 13.4. **MENUAID.MAK (Borland).**

```
 1: # MENUAID.MAK
 2:
 3: # macros
 4: APPNAME = MenuAid
 5: INCPATH = C:\BC\INCLUDE
 6: LIBPATH = C:\BC\LIB
 7: FLAGS = -H -ml -W -v -w4 -I$(INCPATH) -L$(LIBPATH)
 8:
 9: # link
10: $(APPNAME).exe: $(APPNAME).obj $(APPNAME).def $(APPNAME).res
11:    bcc $(FLAGS) $(APPNAME).obj
12:    rc $(APPNAME).res
13: # compile
14: $(APPNAME).obj: $(APPNAME).cpp
15:    bcc -c $(FLAGS) $(APPNAME).cpp
16:
17: # compile
18: $(APPNAME).res: $(APPNAME).rc
19:    rc -r -i$(INCPATH) $(APPNAME).rc
```

Listing 3.5 shows the Microsoft makefile for MenuAid.

 Listing 13.5. **MENUAID.MAK (Microsoft).**

```
1: # MENUAID.MAK
2:
3: # macros
4: APPNAME = MenuAid
5:
```

```
 6: LINKFLAGS = /align:16, NUL, /nod llibcew libw
 7: FLAGS = -c -AL -Gw -Ow -W3 -Zp
 8:
 9: # link
10: $(APPNAME).exe : $(APPNAME).obj $(APPNAME).def $(APPNAME).res
11:    link $(APPNAME), $(LINKFLAGS), $(APPNAME)
12:    rc $(APPNAME).res
13:
14: # compile
15: $(APPNAME).obj: $(APPNAME).cpp
16:    cl -c $(FLAGS) $(APPNAME).cpp
17:
18: # compile
19: $(APPNAME).res: $(APPNAME).rc
20:    rc -r $(APPNAME).rc
```

Figure 13.4. *By default, MenuAid appears on the desktop in iconized form; it looks like this if you open the icon.*

This program enables you to launch applications either by clicking files in a list box or by selecting items from a floating menu. The menu can be reached by clicking the right mouse button anywhere on the desktop window. This program first appears in a minimized state. You can leave it that way if you want, or you can pop it open to reveal a list box containing the same list of files displayed in the program's floating menu. (See Figure 13.4.) The list of programs you can run is kept in a file called MENUAID.INI, which should be stored in the Windows subdirectory. The Edit option, in the program's menu, enables you to modify this file at any time in order to change the available files.

MenuAid in Brief

The code for the MenuAid program has been carefully tested, and should run without a hitch on your system. However, before you proceed, I'll warn you that subclassing the Windows desktop can be a rather delicate operation. As a result, you should be sure to save your work before you try it.

I'm not going to spend a lot of time discussing this program. In particular, I'm going to leave it up to you to discover how this program subclasses the desktop. This is secret bonus territory here, and you have to do your own spelunking. (Hint: check out the first three calls in `MenuAid_OnCreate`, starting on line 179.)

There are, however, two important techniques used in this program that everyone should know about:

- ☐ MenuAid shows how to create menus dynamically at runtime.
- ☐ It also shows you how to read the contents of an initialization file, which in this case is called MENUAID.INI.

In the next two sections, I'll discuss both of these issues.

Working with Initialization Files

Windows programs store information in initialization files, all of which have an .INI extension. These files come in two flavors. The first is a small (but important) set of one called WIN.INI. You can access the contents of this file with the following functions:

`GetProfileString:`	Retrieves a string from WIN.INI
`GetProfileInt:`	Retrieves an integer value from WIN.INI
`WriteProfileString:`	Writes a string to WIN.INI

Here are two excerpts from the WIN.INI file on my computer:

```
[SoundBlaster]
Port=220
Int=7
DMA=1

[PDOXWIN]
WORKDIR=C:\PDOXWIN\WORKING
PRIVDIR=C:\PDOXWIN\PRIVATE
```

If one of the drivers for my soundblaster card wants to know which port to use, it can access the information with `GetProfileInt`. If Paradox for Windows wants to know my current working directory, it can access the information by calling `GetProfileString`. Either piece of information can be changed by calling `WriteProfileString`.

The problem with this scheme is that any one Windows machine can have hundreds of programs, all of which might want to store initialization data. Before long, the WIN.INI file becomes even more unmanageable than it was when you first loaded Windows. The remedy for this situation is the following set of calls, which can be used to read or write information from a "private" initialization file bearing any name you choose:

`GetPrivateProfileString:`	Retrieves a string from an .INI file.
`GetPrivateProfileInt:`	Retrieves an integer from an .INI file.
`WritePrivateProfileString:`	Writes a string to an .INI file.

The MenuAid program uses `GetPrivateProfileString` to read information from MENUAID.INI, which is stored in the Windows subdirectory. The format for MENUAID.INI looks like this:

```
[Files]
<FileName>=<PathToFile>
```

The key parts of this file can be described as follows:

☐ The word Files represents the title of the only section in the initialization file.

☐ The word Filename represents an entry that appears in the program's menu.

☐ The string `PathToFile` informs MenuAid where to find the program the user wants to run.

To help you understand how this simple format works in practice, take a look at Figure 13.5.

Given the initialization file (previously shown), the first entry in the program's menu starts up the famous Windows Solitaire game. Specifically, if the user selects Sol from the program's floating menu, MenuAid can retrieve the location of the solitaire program by making the following call:

```
if (GetPrivateProfileString("Files", FileName, "",
              Buffer, sizeof(Buffer), IniName) > 0)
```

13

Figure 13.5. *Selecting Edit from the floating menu pops up the Notepad with an editable copy of MENUAID.INI.*

After MenuAid retrieves the path to the program that the user wants to run, it passes the information to WinExec, which launches the program. If you would like to study this process in more depth, take a look at the Launch procedure in the program's source code.

GetPrivateProfileString

```
int GetPrivateProfileString(LPCSTER, LPCSTR, LPCSTR,
                            LPSTR, INT, LPCSTR)
```

GetPrivateProfileString	Takes six parameters:
LPCSTR lpszSection:	The address of a section in the file
LPCSTR lpszEntry:	The address of an entry, such as Sol
LPCSTR lpszDefault:	A default string to return on failure
LPSTR lpszReturnBuffer:	A buffer to hold a reply
int cbReturnBuffer:	Size of the buffer that holds the reply
LPCSTR lpszFilename:	Initialization file, such as MENUAID.INI

Use the GetPrivateProfileString function to return information from an initialization file other than WIN.INI. Just pass in the name of the file, the name of the section in the file, and the name of the entry you want to read. In return, GetPrivateProfileString retrieves your entry. If the function can't find your entry, it returns the default string you specify in the fourth parameter.

Example:

```
GetPrivateProfileString("Files", FileName,"",
                Buffer, sizeof(Buffer), IniName)
```

You should know that the MenuAid program also uses the GetPrivateProfilestring to return a list of all the entries in the MENUAID.INI file:

```
int Len = GetPrivateProfileString("Files", NULL, "",
                                  Buffer, Size, IniName);
```

Called this way, `GetPrivateProfileString` returns a list of all the entries in the Files section of MENUAID.INI. Each entry is null terminated. The MenuAid program contains a function called `NewMenu` that demonstrates one possible technique for parsing this kind of buffer.

Dynamic Menus

The second technique that you can study in the MenuAid program involves the creation of dynamic menus. This process enables you to create menus on the fly. This is something that the MenuAid program has to do, because it never knows what might be in the MENUAID.INI file.

Strictly for teaching purposes, I also build the program's main menu from scratch at runtime. This is a technique you might need to use in your own programs, although it's less likely you'll need to build a floating menu from scratch at runtime.

Here's how it works:

```
HMENU TheMenu = CreateMenu();
HMENU AMenu = CreatePopupMenu();
AppendMenu(AMenu, MF_STRING, CM_EDIT, "Edit");
AppendMenu(AMenu, MF_STRING, CM_UPDATE, "Update");
AppendMenu(TheMenu, MF_ENABLED | MF_POPUP,
          (UINT) AMenu, "&File");
SetMenu(hwnd, TheMenu);
```

As you can see, the program first creates a basic menu by calling `CreateMenu`, and then creates a pop-up menu by calling `CreatePopUpMenu`. These calls each return an `HMENU`, which is a handle to a menu.

After FileBox creates the menu, it fills in its contents by calling `AppendMenu`. Notice that `AppendMenu` is also used to add the pop-up menu to the main menu.

13

Syntax

AppendMenu

```
BOOL AppendMenu(HMENU, UINT, UINT, LPCSTR)
```

AppendMenu takes four parameters:

`HMENU hmenu`	Menu to which items are appended
`UINT fuFlags`	Flags, such as `MF_STRING` or `MF_DISABLED`
`UINT idNewItem`	An ID that is sent with `WM_COMMAND`
`LPCSTR lpNewItem`	The string or data to be shown

Use the AppendMenu function to add a new item to the bottom of an existing menu. The state of the item can be specified in the second parameter.

Example:

```
AppendMenu(AMenu, MF_STRING, CM_EDIT, "Edit")
```

After you've created the menu for your program, you can display it to the user by calling SetMenu.

One of the more interesting aspects of the MenuAid program is the call to TrackPopupMenu. This function creates a floating menu that responds to mouse clicks by sending WM_COMMAND messages to a window specified in its first parameter. In MenuAid, this menu is displayed outside the client area. However, you can program a floating menu to pop up when the user clicks the right mouse button on any window.

TrackPopupMenu has seven arguments:

`HMENU hmenu;`	Pops up menu to be displayed
`UINT fuFlags;`	Flags, such as TPM_RIGHTALIGN
`int x;`	X, or column coordinate
`int y;`	Y, or row coordinate
`int nReserved;`	Reserved
`HWND hwnd;`	Window in which to send WM_COMAND messages (owner)
`const RECT FAR *lprc`	Rectangle the user can click without dismissing the menu

As a rule, nothing is tricky about working with menus. Windows covers this territory very thoroughly; by and large, they've done an excellent job providing tools that are easy to use (from both the programmer's and the user's point of view).

If you want to place bitmaps inside a menu, however, the subject does get a bit more complicated. You'll see how to do this in Chapter 18, "GDI and Metafiles." In that chapter, you can look at a number of issues involving advanced menu programming.

Summary

This chapter gave you a fairly thorough introduction to subclassing.

You also had a look at

☐ The WM_GETMINMAXINFO message

☐ Creating menus on the fly

☐ Creating push buttons

☐ Reading and manipulating initialization files

☐ The DlgDirList and DlgDirSelect functions

You should sit back and congratulate yourself on getting through the material about controls. Like Bob Dylan, you probably feel you need a dump truck to unload your head—though I doubt he was thinking about computers when he wrote that line! At any rate, why don't you kick back for awhile and celebrate by just taking it easy? In fact, if you've got the true hard-core, compulsive programmer's habit, you might want to sit down and write a little program that displays all the controls you've learned about in the last four chapters. Right?

Not!

Q&A

1. Q: I still don't understand the relationship between IsDialogMessage and WM_GETDLGCODE. Please explain.

   A: The crux of the matter is that IsDialogMessage translates certain key strokes, such as Tab and Shift-Tab, so that they result in the next control, or group of controls, being selected. However, IsDialogMessage sends out WM_GETDLGCODE messages to all the controls in its purvue. If any of them respond with DLGC_WANTALLKEYS, all keystrokes can get through to that specific control. FileBox needs to find a middle ground between these two extremes. To get that kind of control, you need to subclass.

2. Q: Tell me more about when I should and shouldn't pass messages to CallWindowProc.

   A: The NewEditProc function changes the behavior of edit controls primarily by responding in a particular way to certain messages. For instance, when selected it receives a WM_FOCUS message and responds by highlighting the

13

contents of the edit control. An equally powerful technique is to simply swallow any messages that come into a control. For instance, if you don't want the user to delete anything typed in an edit control, you can refuse to pass on any Backspace or arrow key messages. This is a place where passive aggression can pay off in a big way!

Workshop

The Workshop provides quiz questions to help you solidify your understanding of the material covered and exercises to provide you with experience in using what you've learned. Try to understand the quiz and exercise answers before continuing on to the next chapter. Answers are provided in Appendix A.

Quiz

1. When calling CreateWindow, what styles are used to distinguish a push button from a radio button?

2. What WINDOWSX macro can you use in place of the LB_DIR message?

3. Name 10 macros from the control message API that can be used to manipulate list boxes?

4. What field of a WNDPROC function contains the MINMAXINFO structure when a WM_GETMINMAXINFO message is sent?

5. If you want a window to be a certain shape and size, why is it sometimes better to respond to WM_GETMINMAXINFO messages rather than change the coordinates in the arguments to CreateWindow?

6. What API call is used to replace the window function of a control with one of your own functions?

7. Find the WINDOWSX macro used in the FileBox program to highlight the text in the edit control.

8. How can you create a floating menu?

9. What's the difference between GetPrivateProfileString and GetProfileString?

10. What message gets sent every time InvalidateRect is called? What does the second parameter of InvalidateRect do?

Exercises

1. In FileBox, comment out the reference to `CallWindowProc` from the `NewEditProc` function and then run the program. What happens?

2. Modify the edit control so the user can't type in any illegal file characters (such as a space).

Stylish Windows

It's time to take a more in-depth look at the process of creating and registering windows. In particular, this chapter explores

☐ How to change the style of a window

☐ How to create child windows and pop-up windows

☐ How to use `GetClassWord` and `SetClassWord` to change the style of a window

☐ How to use `GetWindowWord` and `SetWindowWord` to take advantage of the `cbWndExtra` field of the `WNDCLASS` structure

Throughout this chapter, the text focuses on the WinStyle program that displays 10 different child windows, each with a different combination of window styles.

Putting on the Style

You may have already surmised that it wasn't merely coincidence that Microsoft named its new operating environment—ahem—Windows. Almost every programming technique discussed so far has revolved in one way or another around the creation, destruction, or maintenance of windows. Considerably more, however, is to be said about this topic.

In particular, you've not yet had a chance to learn more than a few basic concepts about pop-up and child windows. To create additional space for displaying information or to get input from the user, these handy little tools can be spawned by the main window of a program. Like the program's main window, each of these children can be given a particular window style so that its appearance and functionality can be adopted to the purposes at hand. Figure 14.1 illustrates how changing the style field can affect the appearance of a child window.

Tip: If you click on the mouse on any of the child windows, a messagebox will appear. Inside the messagebox you will find a list of the window styles that were used to create that particular child window.

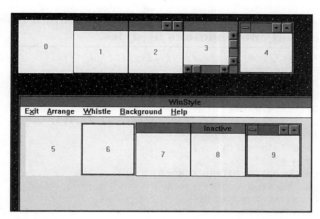

Figure 14.1. *The WinStyle program displays 10 child windows.*

The ten children of the WinStyle program stand in two groups. The first of these groups exists outside the physical bounds of the main window, whereas the second group lines up in a row in the window's client area. The first set of windows all have the WS_POPUP style associated with them, whereas the second set uses the WS_CHILD style. The lesson to be learned here is simple:

☐ WS_CHILD windows can't be moved outside the bounds of a window.

☐ WS_POPUP windows, on the other hand, can be moved anywhere on the desktop.

The style field of a CreateWindow call can be manipulated to request windows that differ radically from one another in appearance. For instance, some of the child windows in the WinStyle program have borders; others don't. Some have title bars, and some have scroll bars. Some windows with title bars don't have minimize boxes or maximize boxes; others do. In fact, the WinStyle program produces a wide range of windows, each of which has its own unique traits.

One of the key capabilities of the child windows in the WinStyle program is that they all can display their window styles as text shown inside of MessageBoxes. If you want to know how to make a child window show on-screen, all you have to do is click it once. It tells you what combination of styles were used in its creation.

Before you read any more about the WinStyle program, you should get the program up and running (see Listing 14.1) on your own machine so you can take it through its paces.

Listing 14.1. The WinStyle program demonstrates window styles and combinations of styles.

```
 1: ////////////////////////////////////////////////////////
 2: //   Program Name: WINSTYLE.CPP
 3: //   Programmer: Charlie Calvert
 4: //   Description: WinStyle windows program
 5: //   Date: 04/03/93
 6: ////////////////////////////////////////////////////////
 7: #define STRICT
 8: #include <windows.h>
 9: #include <windowsx.h>
10: #pragma warning (disable:4068)
11: #pragma hdrstop
12: #include <string.h>
13: #include <stdlib.h>
14: #include "winstyle.h"
15: // ------------------------------------------------------
16: // Interface
17: // ------------------------------------------------------
18:
19: static char szAppName[] = "WinStyle";
20: static char szChildName[] = "StyleChild";
21: static HWND MainWindow;
22: static HINSTANCE hInstance;
23:
24:
25: // ------------------------------------------------------
26: // Initialization
27: // ------------------------------------------------------
28:
29: ////////////////////////////////////////////////////////
30: // Program entry point
31: ////////////////////////////////////////////////////////
32: #pragma argsused
33: int PASCAL WinMain(HINSTANCE hInst, HINSTANCE hPrevInstance,
34:                    LPSTR lpszCmdParam, int nCmdShow)
35: {
36:   MSG  Msg;
37:
38:   if (!hPrevInstance)
39:     if (!Register(hInst))
40:       return FALSE;
41:
42:   MainWindow = Create(hInst, nCmdShow);
43:   if (MainWindow)
44:     return FALSE;
45:   while (GetMessage(&Msg, NULL, 0, 0))
46:   {
47:      TranslateMessage(&Msg);
48:      DispatchMessage(&Msg);
49:   }
```

```
50:
51:    return Msg.wParam;
52: }
53:
54: /////////////////////////////////////////////////////////
55: // Register the window
56: /////////////////////////////////////////////////////////
57: BOOL Register(HINSTANCE hInst)
58: {
59:    WNDCLASS WndClass;
60:
61:    WndClass.style            = CS_HREDRAW | CS_VREDRAW;
62:    WndClass.lpfnWndProc      = WndProc;
63:    WndClass.cbClsExtra       = 0;
64:    WndClass.cbWndExtra       = 0;
65:    WndClass.hInstance        = hInst;
66:    WndClass.hIcon            = LoadIcon(NULL, IDI_APPLICATION);
67:    WndClass.hCursor          = LoadCursor(NULL, IDC_ARROW);
68:    WndClass.hbrBackground    = NULL;
69:    WndClass.lpszMenuName     = "MENU_1";
70:    WndClass.lpszClassName    = szAppName;
71:
72:    BOOL Result = RegisterClass (&WndClass);
73:
74:    if (!Result)
75:       return FALSE;
76:
77:    WndClass.lpfnWndProc      = ChildWndProc;
78:    WndClass.cbWndExtra       = sizeof(WORD);
79:    WndClass.hIcon            = NULL;
80:    WndClass.hCursor          = LoadCursor(NULL, IDC_IBEAM);
81:    WndClass.lpszMenuName     = NULL;
82:    WndClass.lpszClassName    = szChildName;
83:
84:    return RegisterClass (&WndClass);
85:
86: }
87:
88: /////////////////////////////////////////////////////////
89: // Create the window
90: /////////////////////////////////////////////////////////
91: HWND Create(HINSTANCE hInst, int nCmdShow)
92: {
93:
94:    hInstance = hInst;
95:
96:    HWND hWindow = CreateWindow(szAppName, szAppName,
97:                      WS_CAPTION | WS_MINIMIZEBOX | WS_THICKFRAME,
98:                      10, 150, CW_USEDEFAULT, CW_USEDEFAULT,
99:                      NULL, NULL, hInst, NULL);
100:
```

continues

Listing 14.1. continued

```
101:    if (hWindow == NULL)
102:       return hWindow;
103:
104:    ShowWindow(hWindow, nCmdShow);
105:    UpdateWindow(hWindow);
106:
107:    return hWindow;
108: }
109:
110: // ------------------------------------------------------
111: // WndProc and Implementation
112: // ------------------------------------------------------
113:
114: //////////////////////////////////////////////////////////
115: // The Window Procedure
116: //////////////////////////////////////////////////////////
117: LRESULT CALLBACK _export WndProc(HWND hwnd, UINT Message,
118:                                  WPARAM wParam, LPARAM lParam)
119: {
120:    switch(Message)
121:    {
122:       HANDLE_MSG(hwnd, WM_CREATE, WinStyle_OnCreate);
123:       HANDLE_MSG(hwnd, WM_DESTROY, WinStyle_OnDestroy);
124:       HANDLE_MSG(hwnd, WM_COMMAND, WinStyle_OnCommand);
125:       default:
126:          return WinStyle_DefProc(hwnd, Message, wParam, lParam);
127:    }
128: }
129:
130:
131: //////////////////////////////////////////////////////////
132: // ArrangeWinds
133: //////////////////////////////////////////////////////////
134: void ArrangeWinds(HWND hwnd)
135: {
136:    RECT R;
137:
138:    int j = 0;
139:
140:    for (int i = 0; i < 9; i++)
141:    {
142:       MoveWindow(ChildWindows[i], 10 + (j * 100),
143:                  10, 100, 100, TRUE);
144:       if (i == 4)
145:          j = 0;
146:       else
147:          j++;
148:    }
149:
150:    GetWindowRect(hwnd, &R);
```

```
151:
152:    MoveWindow(ChildWindows[i],
153:              R.left + 10 +
154:              GetSystemMetrics(SM_CXFRAME) + (j * 100),
155:              R.top + GetSystemMetrics(SM_CYCAPTION) +
156:              GetSystemMetrics(SM_CYFRAME) +
157:              GetSystemMetrics(SM_CYMENU) +
158:              10, 100, 100, TRUE);
159: }
160:
161: ////////////////////////////////////////////////////////////
162: // Handle WM_Create
163: ////////////////////////////////////////////////////////////
164: #pragma argsused
165: BOOL WinStyle_OnCreate(HWND hwnd, CREATESTRUCT FAR* lpCreateStruct)
166: {
167:
168:    Pattern1 = LoadBitmap(hInstance, "PATTERN1");
169:    if (!Pattern1)
170:      MessageBox(hwnd, "No Pattern", "Error", MB_OK);
171:
172:    Pattern2 = LoadBitmap(hInstance, "PATTERN2");
173:    if (!Pattern2)
174:      MessageBox(hwnd, "No Pattern", "Error", MB_OK);
175:
176:    Pattern3 = LoadBitmap(hInstance, "PATTERN3");
177:    if (!Pattern2)
178:      MessageBox(hwnd, "No Pattern", "Error", MB_OK);
179:
180:    hPurpleHaze = CreateSolidBrush(RGB(127, 255, 255));
181:
182:    SetClassWord(hwnd, GCW_HBRBACKGROUND, (WORD)hPurpleHaze);
183:
184:
185:    for (WORD i = 0; i < 9; i ++)
186:    {
187:      ChildWindows[i] = CreateWindow(szChildName, NULL, Styles[i],
188:                        0,0,0,0, hwnd, NULL, hInstance, NULL);
189:    }
190:
191:    ChildWindows[i] = CreateWindow(szChildName, NULL, Styles[i],
192:                      0, 0, 0, 0, NULL, NULL, hInstance, NULL);
193:
194:
195:    hPurpleHaze = CreateSolidBrush(RGB(255, 255, 127));
196:
197:    SetClassWord(ChildWindows[0], GCW_HBRBACKGROUND,
198:                 (WORD)hPurpleHaze);
199:
200:    for (i = 0; i < 10; i++)
201:      SetWindowWord(ChildWindows[i], 0, i);
```

continues

Listing 14.1. continued

```
202:
203:    ArrangeWinds(hwnd);
204:
205:    SetWindowText(ChildWindows[8], "Inactive");
206:    return TRUE;
207: }
208:
209: //////////////////////////////////////////////////////////
210: // Handle WM_DESTROY
211: //////////////////////////////////////////////////////////
212: #pragma argsused
213: void WinStyle_OnDestroy(HWND hwnd)
214: {
215:    HBRUSH OldBrush;
216:
217:    DeleteObject(Pattern1);
218:    DeleteObject(Pattern2);
219:    DeleteObject(Pattern3);
220:
221:    OldBrush = (HBRUSH)GetClassWord(hwnd, GCW_HBRBACKGROUND);
222:    SetClassWord(hwnd, GCW_HBRBACKGROUND,
223:                 (WORD)GetStockObject(WHITE_BRUSH));
224:    DeleteBrush(OldBrush);
225:
226:    PostQuitMessage(0);
227: }
228:
229: //////////////////////////////////////////////////////////
230: // Handle WM_COMMAND
231: //////////////////////////////////////////////////////////
232: #pragma argsused;
233: void WinStyle_OnCommand(HWND hwnd, int id, HWND hwndCtl,
234:                                 UINT codeNotify)
235:    HBRUSH OldBrush;
236:
237:    switch (id)
238:    {
239:      case CM_ARRANGE:
240:        ArrangeWinds(hwnd);
241:
242:      case CM_WHISTLE:
243:        SetFocus(ChildWindows[9]);
244:        break;
245:
246:      case CM_RED:
247:        OldBrush = (HBRUSH)GetClassWord(hwnd, GCW_HBRBACKGROUND);
248:        hPurpleHaze = CreateSolidBrush(RGB(255, 127, 127));
249:        SetClassWord(hwnd, GCW_HBRBACKGROUND, (WORD)hPurpleHaze);
250:        DeleteBrush(OldBrush);
```

```
251:        InvalidateRect(hwnd, NULL, TRUE);
252:        break;
253:
254:    case CM_GREEN:
255:        OldBrush = (HBRUSH)GetClassWord(hwnd, GCW_HBRBACKGROUND);
256:        hPurpleHaze = CreateSolidBrush(RGB(127, 255, 127));
257:        SetClassWord(hwnd, GCW_HBRBACKGROUND, (WORD)hPurpleHaze);
258:        DeleteBrush(OldBrush);
259:        InvalidateRect(hwnd, NULL, TRUE);
260:        break;
261:
262:    case CM_BLUE:
263:        OldBrush = (HBRUSH)GetClassWord(hwnd, GCW_HBRBACKGROUND);
264:        hPurpleHaze = CreateSolidBrush(RGB(127, 127, 255));
265:        SetClassWord(hwnd, GCW_HBRBACKGROUND, (WORD)hPurpleHaze);
266:        DeleteBrush(OldBrush);
267:        InvalidateRect(hwnd, NULL, TRUE);
268:        break;
269:
270:    case CM_SPECIAL1:
271:        OldBrush = (HBRUSH)GetClassWord(hwnd, GCW_HBRBACKGROUND);
272:        hPurpleHaze = CreatePatternBrush(Pattern1);
273:        SetClassWord(hwnd, GCW_HBRBACKGROUND, (WORD)hPurpleHaze);
274:        DeleteBrush(OldBrush);
275:        InvalidateRect(hwnd, NULL, TRUE);
276:        break;
277:
278:    case CM_SPECIAL2:
279:        OldBrush = (HBRUSH)GetClassWord(hwnd, GCW_HBRBACKGROUND);
280:        hPurpleHaze = CreatePatternBrush(Pattern2);
281:        SetClassWord(hwnd, GCW_HBRBACKGROUND, (WORD)hPurpleHaze);
282:        DeleteBrush(OldBrush);
283:        InvalidateRect(hwnd, NULL, TRUE);
284:        break;
285:
286:    case CM_SPECIAL3:
287:        OldBrush = (HBRUSH)GetClassWord(hwnd, GCW_HBRBACKGROUND);
288:        hPurpleHaze = CreatePatternBrush(Pattern3);
289:        SetClassWord(hwnd, GCW_HBRBACKGROUND, (WORD)hPurpleHaze);
290:        DeleteBrush(OldBrush);
291:        InvalidateRect(hwnd, NULL, TRUE);
292:        break;
293:
294:    case CM_EXIT:
295:        SendMessage(ChildWindows[9], WM_CLOSE, 0, 0);
296:
297:        OldBrush = (HBRUSH)GetClassWord(ChildWindows[0],
298:                                         GCW_HBRBACKGROUND);
299:        SetClassWord(ChildWindows[0], GCW_HBRBACKGROUND,
300:                    (WORD)GetStockObject(WHITE_BRUSH));
301:        DeleteBrush(OldBrush);
```

continues

14

443

Listing 14.1. continued

```
302:
303:        DestroyWindow(hwnd);
304:        break;
305:
306:      case CM_HELP:
307:        MessageBox(hwnd,
308:                   "Click on child windows to see their style",
309:                   "Help", MB_OK | MB_ICONASTERISK);
310:        break;
311:   }
312: }
313:
314:
315: // --------------------------------------------------------
316: // The StyleChild
317: // --------------------------------------------------------
318:
319: ////////////////////////////////////////////////////////////
320: // The Window Procedure
321: ////////////////////////////////////////////////////////////
322: LRESULT CALLBACK _export ChildWndProc(HWND hwnd, UINT Message,
323:                                       WPARAM WParam, LPARAM lParam)
324: {
325:   switch(Message)
326:   {
327:     HANDLE_MSG(hwnd, WM_LBUTTONDOWN, StyleChild_OnLButtonDown);
328:     HANDLE_MSG(hwnd, WM_PAINT, StyleChild_OnPaint);
329:     default:
330:       return StyleChild_DefProc(hwnd, Message, wParam, lParam);
331:   }
332: }
333:
334: ////////////////////////////////////////////////////////////
335: // Handle WM_LBUTTONDOWN
336: ////////////////////////////////////////////////////////////
337: #pragma argsused
338: void StyleChild_OnLButtonDown(HWND hwnd, BOOL fDoubleClick,
339:                               int x, int y, UINT keyFlags)
340: {
341:   char szNum[100];
342:
343:   WORD i = GetWindowWord(hwnd, 0);
344:   wsprintf(szNum, "Number: %d", i);
345:   MessageBox(hwnd, szStyles[i], szNum,
346:              MB_OK | MB_ICONINFORMATION);
347: }
348:
349: ////////////////////////////////////////////////////////////
350: // Respond WM_PAINT
351: ////////////////////////////////////////////////////////////
```

```
352: void StyleChild_OnPaint(HWND hwnd)
353: {
354:   PAINTSTRUCT PaintStruct;
355:   HDC PaintDC;
356:   char lpszBuffer[100];
357:   RECT R;
358:
359:   WORD i = GetWindowWord(hwnd, 0);
360:   wsprintf(lpszBuffer, "%d", i);
361:
362:   PaintDC = BeginPaint(hwnd, &PaintStruct);
363:
364:   SetTextColor(PaintDC, RGB(0, 0, 255));
365:   SetBkMode(PaintDC, TRANSPARENT);
366:   GetClientRect(hwnd, &R);
367:   DrawText(PaintDC, lpszBuffer, -1, &R,
368:            DT_SINGLELINE | DT_CENTER | DT_VCENTER);
369:
370:   EndPaint(hwnd, &PaintStruct);
371: }
```

Listing 14.2 shows the header file for WinStyle.

 Listing 14.2. WINSTYLE.H.

```
 1: ////////////////////////////////////////////////////////////
 2: //   Program Name: WINSTYLE.H
 3: //   Programmer: Charlie Calvert
 4: //   Description: WinStyle windows program
 5: //   Date: 04/03/93
 6: ////////////////////////////////////////////////////////////
 7:
 8: // Const
 9: #define CM_ARRANGE  1
10: #define CM_WHISTLE  2
11: #define CM_EXIT 3
12: #define CM_HELP 4
13: #define CM_BLUE     101
14: #define CM_RED 102
15: #define CM_GREEN 103
16: #define CM_SPECIAL1 104
17: #define CM_SPECIAL2 105
18: #define CM_SPECIAL3 106
19:
20: DWORD Styles[] = { WS_POPUP | WS_VISIBLE,
21:                    WS_POPUP | WS_VISIBLE | WS_CAPTION,
22:                    WS_POPUP | WS_VISIBLE | WS_CAPTION |\
23:                      WS_MINIMIZEBOX | WS_MAXIMIZEBOX,
```

continues

14

445

Listing 14.2. continued

```
24:                         WS_POPUP ¦ WS_VISIBLE ¦ WS_CAPTION ¦\
25:                          WS_HSCROLL ¦ WS_VSCROLL,
26:                         WS_OVERLAPPEDWINDOW ¦ WS_VISIBLE,
27:                         WS_CHILDWINDOW ¦ WS_VISIBLE,
28:                         WS_CHILDWINDOW ¦ WS_VISIBLE ¦ WS_THICKFRAME,
29:                         WS_CHILDWINDOW ¦ WS_VISIBLE ¦ WS_BORDER ¦\
30:                          WS_CAPTION,
31:                         WS_CHILDWINDOW ¦ WS_VISIBLE ¦ WS_CAPTION ¦\
32:                          WS_DISABLED,
33:                         WS_OVERLAPPEDWINDOW ¦ WS_VISIBLE
34:                    };
35:
36: char *szStyles[] = { "WS_POPUP ¦ WS_VISIBLE",
37:                      "WS_POPUP ¦ WS_VISIBLE ¦ WS_CAPTION",
38:                      "WS_POPUP ¦ WS_VISIBLE ¦ WS_CAPTION ¦\
39:                       WS_MINIMIZEBOX ¦ WS_MAXIMIZEBOX",
40:                      "WS_POPUP ¦ WS_VISIBLE ¦ WS_CAPTION ¦\
41:                       WS_HSCROLL ¦ WS_VSCROLL",
42:                      "WS_OVERLAPPEDWINDOW ¦ WS_VISIBLE",
43:                      "WS_CHILDWINDOW ¦ WS_VISIBLE",
44:                      "WS_CHILDWINDOW ¦ WS_VISIBLE ¦\
45:                       WS_THICKFRAME",
46:                      "WS_CHILDWINDOW ¦ WS_VISIBLE ¦ WS_BORDER ¦\
47:                       WS_CAPTION",
48:                      "WS_CHILDWINDOW ¦ WS_VISIBLE ¦ WS_CAPTION ¦\
49:                       WS_DISABLED",
50:                      "WS_OVERLAPPEDWINDOW ¦ WS_VISIBLE"
51:                    };
52:
53: // Declarations for class WinStyle
54: #define WinStyle_DefProc     DefWindowProc
55: BOOL WinStyle_OnCreate(HWND hwnd,
                           CREATESTRUCT FAR* lpCreateStruct);
56: void WinStyle_OnDestroy(HWND hwnd);
57: void WinStyle_OnCommand(HWND hwnd, int id, HWND hwndCtl,
58:                         UINT codeNotify);
59:
60: #define StyleChild_DefProc    DefWindowProc
61: void StyleChild_OnPaint(HWND hwnd);
62: void StyleChild_OnLButtonDown(HWND hwnd, BOOL fDoubleClick,
63:                               int x, int y, UINT keyFlags);
64:
65: // Variables
66: HWND ChildWindows[10];
67: HBRUSH hPurpleHaze;
68: HBITMAP Pattern1, Pattern2, Pattern3;
69:
70: // Parent Procs
71: LRESULT CALLBACK _export WndProc(HWND hWindow, UINT Message,
72:                                  WPARAM wParam, LPARAM lParam);
```

```
73: BOOL Register(HINSTANCE hInst);
74: HWND Create(HINSTANCE hInst, int nCmdShow);
75:
76: // Child Procs
77: LRESULT CALLBACK _export ChildWndProc(HWND hwnd, UINT Message,
78:                                        WPARAM wParam, LPARAM lParam);
```

Listing 14.3 shows the resource file for WinStyle.

 Listing 14.3. WINSTYLE.RC.

```
1: #include "winstyle.h"
2:
3: MENU_1 MENU
4: BEGIN
5:      MENUITEM "E&xit", CM_EXIT
6:      MENUITEM "&Arrange", CM_ARRANGE
7:      MENUITEM "&Whistle", CM_WHISTLE
8:      POPUP "&Background"
9:      BEGIN
10:        MENUITEM "&Blue", CM_BLUE
11:        MENUITEM "&Red", CM_RED
12:        MENUITEM "&Green", CM_GREEN
13:        MENUITEM "&Special_1", CM_SPECIAL1
14:        MENUITEM "&Special_2", CM_SPECIAL2
15:        MENUITEM "&Special_3", CM_SPECIAL3
16:      END
17:      MENUITEM "&Help", CM_HELP
18: END
19:
20: PATTERN1 BITMAP "PATTERN1.BMP"
21: PATTERN2 BITMAP "PATTERN2.BMP"
22: PATTERN3 BITMAP "PATTERN3.BMP"
```

PATTERN1.BMP (8X8)   *PATTERN2.BMP (8X8)*   *PATTERN3.BMP (8X8)*

Listing 14.4 shows the Borland makefile for WinStyle.

Listing 14.4. WINSTYLE.MAK (Borland).

```
1: # WINSTYLE.MAK
2:
3: # macros
4: APPNAME = WinStyle
5: INCPATH = C:\BC\INCLUDE
6: FLAGS = H ml -W -v -w4 -I$(INCPATH)
7:
8: # link
9: $(APPNAME).exe: $(APPNAME).obj $(APPNAME).def $(APPNAME).res
10:    bcc $(FLAGS) $(APPNAME).obj
11:    rc $(APPNAME).res
12:
13: # compile
14: $(APPNAME).obj: $(APPNAME).cpp
15:    bcc -c $(FLAGS) $(APPNAME).cpp
16:
17: # resource
18: $(APPNAME).res: $(APPNAME).rc
19:    rc -r -i$(APPNAME).rc
```

Listing 14.5 shows the Microsoft makefile for WinStyle.

 Listing 14.5. WINSTYLE.MAK (Microsoft).

```
1: #-------------------
2: # WINSTYLE.MAK
3: #-------------------
4:
5: APPNAME = WinStyle
6:
7: #-------------------
8: # link
9: #-------------------
10: $(APPNAME).exe : $(APPNAME).obj $(APPNAME).def $(APPNAME).res
11:    link $(APPNAME), /align:16, NUL, /nod llibcew libw, $(APPNAME)
12:    rc $(APPNAME).res
13:
14: #-------------------
15: # compile
16: #-------------------
17: $(APPNAME).obj : $(APPNAME).cpp
18:    cl -c AL GA -Ow -W3 -Zp $(APPNAME).cpp
19:
20: #-------------------
21: # resource
22: #-------------------
23: $(APPNAME).res: $(APPNAME).rc
24:    rc -r $(APPNAME).rc
```

Output This program creates a series of child and pop-up windows that illustrate how the style field of CreateWindow can be used to control the appearance of a window. Notice that half the descendants of the main window have the WS_POPUP style and can roam freely on the desktop. The other half have the WS_CHILD style and are restricted to the main window's client area. To see exactly what style is associated with a particular window, click it with the mouse. The menu for the program demonstrates that all of the descendants created in this program can be controlled by the main window. That is, the main window is the parent; the others are the children and must do its bidding.

Creating the Child Windows

As has been the case in the last couple chapters, you need to focus on the WM_CREATE message handler function if you want to get a feeling for how this program works. The code to concentrate on looks like this:

```
static char szChildName[] = "StyleChild";

...

   for (WORD i = 0; i < 9; i ++)
   {
     ChildWindows[i] = CreateWindow(szChildName,NULL,
                       Styles[i], 0, 0, 0, 0, hwnd,
                       NULL, hInstance, NULL);
   }

   ChildWindows[i] = CreateWindow(szChildName,
                     NULL, Styles[i], 0, 0, 0, 0,
                     NULL, NULL, hInstance, NULL);
```

What you have here is nothing more than a couple more calls to the CreateWindow function. In this case, you can see that the window class is set to a name of my own choosing, called StyleChild, rather than to one of the predefined windows classes, such as button or list boxes.

Because this class wasn't preregistered by Windows, the WinClass program is forced to register it. There are no hard and fast rules as to where the best place might be for registering a window class. A rule of thumb is to register any big class in a separate module, and to register small classes in the same register function as the main window. In other words, if you have a big class with a long complicated WndProc, you might move it into its own module so you can get a good clear look at exactly what kind of beast you're wrestling with. This is purely a matter of taste however, and programmers should feel free to develop or adopt any style that suits them (or their bosses!).

14

> **Note:** A bit of confusion can stem from the fact that programmers tend to
> refer to any descendant of a window as a child window. In other words,
> there is the technical term WS_CHILD, and there are the more colloquial
> terms, such as child or children.

At any rate, the StyleChild class is just a little fellow that would probably end up
looking a bit out of place if it was isolated in a separate module. So I've hidden the
registration code away in the Register function:

```
BOOL Register(HINSTANCE hInst)
{
  WNDCLASS WndClass;

  WndClass.style           = CS_HREDRAW | CS_VREDRAW;
  WndClass.lpfnWndProc     = WndProc;
  WndClass.cbClsExtra      = 0;
  WndClass.cbWndExtra      = 0;
  WndClass.hInstance       = hInst;
  WndClass.hIcon           = LoadIcon(NULL, IDI_APPLICATION);
  WndClass.hCursor         = LoadCursor(NULL, IDC_ARROW);
  WndClass.hbrBackground   = NULL;
  WndClass.lpszMenuName    = "MENU_1";
  WndClass.lpszClassName   = szAppName;

  BOOL Result = RegisterClass (&WndClass);

  if (!Result)
    return FALSE;

  WndClass.lpfnWndProc     = ChildWndProc;
  WndClass.cbWndExtra      = sizeof(WORD);
  WndClass.hIcon           = NULL;
  WndClass.hCursor         = LoadCursor(NULL, IDC_IBEAM);
  WndClass.lpszMenuName    = NULL;
  WndClass.lpszClassName   = szChildName;

  return RegisterClass (&WndClass);

}
```

The first half of this code is just like every other Register function you have seen so
far, except the hbrBackground field is set to NULL. This enables WinStyle to utilize a
a custom-made background, generated in the WinStyle_OnCreate function.

The real center of attraction in the Register function is the registration of the
StyleChild class. There, four of the fields from the WinStyle class are reused, whereas
the other six are redefined.

In particular, you might notice that StyleChild has its own WndProc and its own cursor. To see the cursor in action, load the program and move the mouse over one of the active child windows (such as window five). You'll see the cursor change from the arrow shape to the I-beam shape.

Alert readers have probably also noticed that the cbWndExtra field is allocated two bytes, which is the size of a WORD in the DOS Windows environment. All that's going on here is that Windows is being told to set aside two bytes of memory every time a new window of the StyleChild class is created. This memory is reserved for any purpose that might cross a programmer's mind. Windows will never touch that space. It is reserved for the programmer.

In this particular case, all WinStyle does with this extra memory is fill it with the number associated with each window. In other words, the first window has a zero in this field, the second a one, the third a two, and so on. Then, during the child window's paint procedure, WinStyle gets the number back out of memory and paints it on-screen.

I'm getting ahead of myself here. For now, it's probably best to stay focused on the WM_CREATE message handler.

All the windows, except one, are created in a single loop. What sets the last window apart from the others is that it has no parent. Because of this, it can be hidden completely behind the main window—the user might entirely forget its existence. Because there might be a need to call the window to the fore, I've set things up so that all the user needs to do is "whistle", and the window will pop up from wherever it might be hiding. This is done with the good graces of the SetFocus function. If you haven't done so already, make a note of this one, as SetFocus is a procedure you are likely to want to call fairly often:

```
case CM_WHISTLE:
  SetFocus(ChildWindows[9]);
  break;
```

Syntax

The *SetFocus* Function

HWND SetFocus(HWND)

HWND hwnd: The handle of the window that is to receive the focus.

On success, SetFocus returns the HWND of the window that last had the focus. The function returns NULL on failure.

SetFocus is very easy to use; pass the handle of the window you want to focus in its sole parameter. The result is that the referenced window is brought to the fore, and further input from the keyboard is directed to it. This is especially easy to do in the WinStyle program, because it carefully saves the handles to all the child windows in an array. If you don't happen to have the HWND of a window or control available, you can usually retrieve it with a call to GetWindow or GetDlgItem.

Example:

```
SetFocus(MyWindow);
```

As you probably noticed, when calling CreateWindow for its children, WinStyle sets their dimensions to zero. It assigns zero to the x, y, nwidth, and nheight fields. This is done, in part, because the calculations for their correct locations is somewhat convoluted. As a result, I store these long lines of code in a separate function where they can be clearly seen. More importantly, this code can be called more than once. Every time the user chooses Arrange from the main menu, all the windows hurry back to the place they started. The key point is that the code for arranging the windows needs to be called both during program creation and when the Arrange menu item is selected. Therefore, it finds a home in its own function:

```
void ArrangeWinds(HWND hwnd)
{
  RECT R;

  int j = 0;

  for (int i = 0; i < 9; i++)
  {
    MoveWindow(ChildWindows[i], 10 + (j * 100),
              10, 100, 100, TRUE);
    if (i == 4)
      j = 0;
    else
      j++;
  }

  GetWindowRect(hwnd, &R);

  MoveWindow(ChildWindows[i],
             R.left + 10 +
             GetSystemMetrics(SM_CXFRAME) + (j * 100),
             R.top + GetSystemMetrics(SM_CYCAPTION) +
             GetSystemMetrics(SM_CYFRAME) +
             GetSystemMetrics(SM_CYMENU) +
             10, 100, 100, TRUE);
}
```

This code serves as an introduction to the nifty MoveWindow routine that will probably prove useful for you on numerous occasions.

Syntax

The *MoveWindow* Function

```
BOOL MoveWindow(HWND, int, int, int, int, BOOL)

HWND hwnd; /* Window handle */
int nLeft; /* x coordinate */
int nTop;        /* y coordinate */
int nWidth; /* width of window  */
int nHeight;        /* height of window  */
BOOL fRepaint;        /* repaint flag  */
```

The MoveWindow call is very straightforward. Place the HWND of the window you want to move in its first parameters, and place the rectangle you want the window to occupy in the last four parameters. In other words, MoveWindow not only changes the location of the upper-left corner of the window in question, it also changes the location of the lower-right corner. As a result, both the location and the size of a window can be changed at the same time. Don't let that last one slip by undigested; when you need to change the location, size, or shape of a dialog or window, you can do so with MoveWindow. (If MoveWindow doesn't quite suit your needs, additional control is given by a function called SetWindowPos.)

Example:

```
MoveWindow(hMyWindow, 0, 0, 100, 100, TRUE)
```

What you must watch out for with the MoveWindow call is the fact that the position of a child window is defined by the coordinates of its owner, whereas the position of a pop-up window is defined by its position on-screen. In each case, the position 0,0 is regarded as the upper-left corner of the coordinate system. However, in the client coordinate system, 0,0 is usually the upper-left corner of a window; in the screen system, it's usually the upper-left corner of the screen.

Note: In the WinStyle program, windows zero and five have the exact same coordinates, but they are located in entirely different places on the screen. The same is true for windows one and six, two and seven, and three and eight. The difference between each set of windows is that pop-up windows use screen coordinates, and child windows use client coordinates.

This distinction keeps reappearing throughout many different fragments of Windows code. For instance, the GetClientRect and GetWindowRect calls differ; the first retrieves the coordinates of a window relative to its own dimensions, whereas the latter returns a window's coordinates

14

relative to its position on-screen. In other words, `GetClientRect` always returns `0,0` as the upper-left corner of a window.

If that were the end of the matter, the whole subject of the Windows coordinate system could be dismissed in only a few sentences. However, it happens that the location `0,0` is not—in actual point of fact—always defined as the upper-left corner of a screen or window. Yes, even this seemingly sacrosanct screen coordinate can be changed when a programmer decides to set the window or viewport origin by calling the Windows API functions `SetViewportOrg` and `SetWindowOrg`. Chapter 18, "GDI and Metafiles," discusses these powerful calls.

To test whether you really understand some of the basics of the Windows coordinate system, take a look at the call that defines the location of the last of the child window, which is called—in a sort of coincidental, off-the-cuff John Lennon tribute—window number nine. This window, as you recall, doesn't have a parent, and it isn't a child window. As a result, its dimensions are defined in screen coordinates.

However, I wanted to place it with the group of child windows so you could see that it can be hidden behind the main window. This is a trait unique to parentless windows. Its siblings always reside in front of their parent.

Take a good close look at the call that sets the dimensions of window number nine:

```
RECT R;

    ...

GetWindowRect(hwnd, &R);

MoveWindow(ChildWindows[i],
           R.left + 10 + (j * 100) +
           GetSystemMetrics(SM_CXFRAME),
           R.top + GetSystemMetrics(SM_CYCAPTION) +
           GetSystemMetrics(SM_CYFRAME) +
           GetSystemMetrics(SM_CYMENU) +
           10, 100, 100, TRUE);
```

The code starts by getting the screen-based coordinates of the program's main window. Now, both window number nine and its parent are defined in terms of their location on-screen. Ten is added to this location, and the presence of the four child windows is taken into account by multiplying *j* times the width of each of those windows.

However, that's not the end of the story. Before the preferred location of the parentless window can be calculated, the width of the `WindowFrame` must also be taken into account. To get the width of the window frame, the WinStyle program makes a call to `GetSystemMetrics`, and passes in the constant `SM_CXFRAME`. In short, the program asks Windows to return the width of this, and every other window's, left-hand border.

This same type of calculation must be performed before the location of the top of window number nine can be calculated correctly. In particular, WinStyle calls `GetSystemMetrics` to retrieve the height of the frame at the top of the window, the height of the caption, and the height of the menu bar. All this data is added to the screen coordinate for the top of its parent and then it's incremented by ten.

> **Note**: All the normal child windows don't need to take into account the height of the menu bar or the caption. All they need to know is that the menu bar and caption are located ten pixels from the top of the client area of the window to which they belong. In other words, the menu bar, caption, and frame are never considered to be part of the client area of a window.

It has taken me quite awhile to explain this funny business about screen coordinates and client coordinates, `GetWindowRect` and `GetClientRect`. However, I think it's worth pointing out that no portion of this coordinate system, in and of itself, is particularly complicated. If the accumulated weight of all these bits of information becomes a bit overwhelming at times, slow down and take things one step at a time. Just go slowly, take the time to reason things out, and you'll find that Windows isn't really that difficult to program.

What Windows programming takes is dedication, not raw intelligence. You have to want to do this. If you don't want it, for heaven's sake just put this book down and go outside and enjoy yourself. The big secret is that good Windows code is written by programming wonks. You have to be at least fifty percent propeller-head or you'll let yourself in for untold miseries!

You Need a Lot of Class If You Want to Do It with Style

This is probably as good a time as any to finally do some serious talking about the actual window styles. Here are the styles of the ten child windows:

1. `WS_POPUP ¦ WS_VISIBLE`

2. `WS_POPUP ¦ WS_VISIBLE ¦ WS_CAPTION`

3. WS_POPUP ¦ WS_VISIBLE ¦ WS_CAPTION ¦ WS_MINIMIZEBOX ¦ WS_MAXIMIZEBOX

4. WS_POPUP ¦ WS_VISIBLE ¦ WS_CAPTION ¦ WS_HSCROLL ¦ WS_VSCROLL

5. WS_OVERLAPPEDWINDOW ¦ WS_VISIBLE

6. WS_CHILDWINDOW ¦ WS_VISIBLE

7. WS_CHILDWINDOW ¦ WS_VISIBLE ¦ WS_THICKFRAME

8. WS_CHILDWINDOW ¦ WS_VISIBLE ¦ WS_BORDER ¦ WS_CAPTION

9. WS_CHILDWINDOW ¦ WS_VISIBLE ¦ WS_CAPTION ¦ WS_DISABLED

10. WS_OVERLAPPEDWINDOW ¦ WS_VISIBLE

The first four windows all have the WS_POPUP style. As a result, they use screen coordinates instead of client coordinates. Also, they can move outside their parents' boundaries, whereas the child windows aren't allowed to stray too far from the nest.

The first four windows all have the WS_POPUP style (see Figures 14.2, 14.3, and 14.4).

Figure 14.2. *Pop-up window number one uses the* WS_VISIBLE *and the* WS_CAPTION *style.*

Notice also that the fifth and the tenth windows have exactly the same style. The difference between them is that one has a parent window and the other does not. In other words, the eighth field of the fifth window contains the HWND of WinStyle's main window, and the eighth field of the tenth child window is set to NULL.

The WS_OVERLAPPEDWINDOW constant is really a combination of the following six styles:

```
WS_OVERLAPPED
WS_CAPTION
WS_SYSMENU
WS_THICKFRAME
WS_MINIMIZEBOX
WS_MAXIMIZEBOX
```

The makers of Windows created the WS_OVERLAPPEDWINDOW style because the six constants are frequently grouped together. They just figured everyone would get tired

of writing the same six words over and over again; so they developed a shorthand. Let's give the developers a hand—they done good!

Most of the styles are fairly self explanatory. An exception is child window nine, which has the WS_DISABLED style attached to it. Disabled windows are totally inert. You can't manipulate them with the mouse or the keyboard.

Figure 14.3. *The third pop-up window uses the* WS_VISIBLE, WS_CAPTION, WS_HSCROLL *and,* WS_VSCROLL *styles.*

Note: Besides using the WS_DISABLED style, a common method of creating disabled windows is to call EnableWindow. This API function takes two parameters: the HWND of the window you want to disable and a BOOL set to FALSE. Calling this function with the second parameter set to TRUE reenables the window.

Anyway, the whole purpose of the WinStyle program is to define the styles visually, through a program. You can see for yourself that some of them have borders, some have minimize boxes, and so on. To see exactly how a particular visual effect was created, just click the window.

This is the way the world's headed. Our textbooks are going to become increasingly interactive. Writers won't have to explain everything anymore; they can just show you by saying: "Hey, why don't you just pop up the program and take a look? Just click one of the child windows and you'll see what I mean!"

Figure 14.4. *The fourth pop-up window uses the classic* WS_OVERLAPPEDWINDOW *style in conjunction with* WS_VISIBLE.

Note: The styles for this program are stored in an array, similar to the way the file attributes for DlgDirList were stored in an array for the code in the last chapter. As I explained in some depth on Day 13, this technique of storing lists of identifiers or constants in arrays can help simplify your code. It's a technique all Windows programmers should master.

A Little Bit of Background

By now, you've had a look at the main elements of the WinStyle program. You know the difference between child and pop-up windows (illustrated by their opposite coordinate systems), and you know how to change the appearance of a window by altering its style. With these ideas under your belt, you're free to move on to an examination of how to change the background of a window. While studying this technique, you get a chance to master the SetWindowLong API function (which was introduced in the last chapter).

The following two lines of code alter the background of the WinStyle class:

```
hPurpleHaze = CreateSolidBrush(RGB(127, 255, 255));
SetClassWord(hwnd, GCW_HBRBACKGROUND, (WORD)hPurpleHaze);
```

To get a good feeling for what is going on here, start by taking a look at the following excerpt from the Register function:

```
WndClass.hIcon        = LoadIcon(NULL, IDI_APPLICATION);
WndClass.hCursor      = LoadCursor(NULL, IDC_ARROW);
WndClass.hbrBackground = NULL;
WndClass.lpszMenuName = "MENU_1";
```

This, of course, is the place where some of the primary traits of this program's main window are defined. In particular, you might notice that this program has an hbrBackground field that's set to NULL.

In order to fill this field, the WinStyle program calls SetClassWord, passes it an HWND, a constant, and the handle to a brush. In the past, all the brushes used in this book were obtained through calls to GetStockObject. The PurpleHaze brush, however, was created through a call to CreateSolidBrush.

The *CreateSolidBrush* Function

CreateSolidBrush takes a single parameter that defines the color of the brush you want to create. In this particular case, WinStyle defines a light cyan as the color for the brush. Of course, this choice makes it appear that this brush isn't very aptly named. However, during its youth, the WinStyle program was considerably more flamboyant than it is now. If you want to restore some of its youthful vigor, try passing RGB the following parameters:

```
hPurpleHaze = CreateSolidBrush(RGB(255, 100, 255));
```

Whew! That brings back some memories, doesn't it? But as they say, if you can remember the sixties, you sure missed out on an awful lot of fun! Unfortunately, not all of it was such good clean fun.

Besides passing SetClassWord an HWND and a brush, the WinStyle program also passes in the GCW_HBRBACKGROUND constant. If you look up this constant in your reference manuals, you'll see that it has a value of -10.

SetClassWord enables you to alter the values you specified when you called the Register function. In particular, if you passed a value of 0 in the second parameter, you would have access to the cbClsExtra field of the WNDCLASS structure. However, WinStyle passes in -10, which takes you back five 16-bit words back to the HBRBACKGROUND field. Don't use this type of arithmetic to try to create your own constants for accessing different parts of the WNDCLASS structure. Instead, use the predefined constants you find in your docs.

It's important for you to remember that the CreateSolidBrush function uses up some of the GDI resources available from the Windows environment. When the program shuts down, it must give these resources back (or bite the very hand that feeds it). As a result, the WinStyle_OnDestroy function includes the following code:

```
215:    HBRUSH OldBrush;

221:    OldBrush = (HBRUSH)GetClassWord(hwnd, GCW_HBRBACKGROUND);
222:    SetClassWord(hwnd, GCW_HBRBACKGROUND,
223:                 (WORD)GetStockObject(WHITE_BRUSH));
224:    DeleteBrush(OldBrush);
```

The GetClassWord function is the SetClassWord function in reverse. WinStyle uses GetClassWord to retrieve the brush from the User heap (where the WNDCLASS structure is stored). After WinStyle has the brush again, you would think it could proceed to delete it. However, this isn't the case. The problem is that after the brush is first retrieved, it still belongs to the system—the Windows operating environment!

14

To free the brush from the system, WinStyle gives Windows another brush in its stead. This brush is just a stock object, which means it belongs to the system anyway. Now that Windows is happy, WinStyle can proceed to delete the brush it created earlier. I know you've seen this kind of logic before in this book, but I reiterate it here because it's so important—and so very easy to forget. This is a place programmers can carelessly introduce bugs into their program that can take hours, or even days, to track down.

Changing Brushes in Midstream

If you choose the Background option from the program's main menu, you see the menu box shown in Figure 14.5.

Figure 14.5. *When selected, the Background menu option reveals six different choices.*

To create the Background menu box, you need to include the following code in WINSTYLE.RC:

```
POPUP "&Background"
    BEGIN
      MENUITEM "&Blue", CM_BLUE
      MENUITEM "&Red", CM_RED
      MENUITEM "&Green", CM_GREEN
      MENUITEM "&Special_1", CM_SPECIAL1
      MENUITEM "&Special_2", CM_SPECIAL2
      MENUITEM "&Special_3", CM_SPECIAL3
    END
```

This pop-up menu box contains six different menu items. When the user selects any of these items, a WM_COMMAND message is sent to the WndProc.

If the user chooses the Blue menu item, for instance, the WinStyle program executes the following code from the WinStyle_OnCommand function:

```
262:    case CM_BLUE:
263:        OldBrush = (HBRUSH)GetClassWord(hwnd, GCW_HBRBACKGROUND);
264:        hPurpleHaze = CreateSolidBrush(RGB(127, 127, 255));
265:        SetClassWord(hwnd, GCW_HBRBACKGROUND, (WORD)hPurpleHaze);
```

```
266:        DeleteBrush(OldBrush);
267:        InvalidateRect(hwnd, NULL, TRUE);
268:        break;
```

This code is closely related to what you saw earlier in the WM_DESTROY message handler function. Specifically, WinStyle first gloms onto the old brush from the User heap. Then, it creates a new brush and feeds the hungry maw of Windows with it (with the SetClassWord function). The next step is to delete the recently liberated brush; then, coerce Windows into showing the resulting change by forcing a repaint with the InvalidateRect function.

A slight variation on this theme is played out when the user chooses the Special_2 menu option. In this case, one of the program's three bitmaps is turned into a brush—thanks to the good graces of the CreatePatternBrush API function:

```
278:      case CM_SPECIAL2:
279:        OldBrush = (HBRUSH)GetClassWord(hwnd, GCW_HBRBACKGROUND);
280:        hPurpleHaze = CreatePatternBrush(Pattern2);
281:        SetClassWord(hwnd, GCW_HBRBACKGROUND, (WORD)hPurpleHaze);
282:        DeleteBrush(OldBrush);
283:        InvalidateRect(hwnd, NULL, TRUE);
284:        break;
```

Take a moment to be sure you are absorbing this information. The key fact to remember is that Windows can convert a bitmap into a brush! The brush, however, should be exactly 8x8 pixels in size, as shown in Figure 14.6.

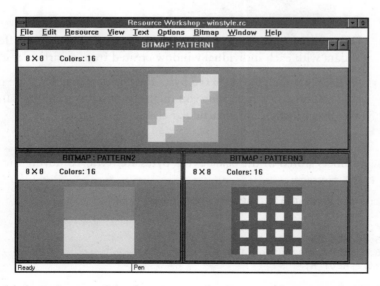

Figure 14.6. *A close-up of the three 8x8 pixel patterns used to create the WinStyle "Special" backgrounds.*

461

After you create a brush through this mechanism, Windows paints it repeatedly so that it fills in the entire background of a window. The second background, shown in Figure 14.6, for example, could be used to punish users who refuse to follow your carefully laid-down rules. You should, however, promise to replace it with a more copacetic background if they'll agree to be good. You might also notice that the background used in Special_3 should be familiar to all users of Borland's solemn, but elegant, "chiseled steel" dialog boxes.

Using the *cbWndExtra* Bytes

The last little trick performed by the WinStyle program involves those two bytes it sets aside in the cbWndExtra field during the Register function. As mentioned, those bytes are filled, during WinStyle_OnCreate, with the number which is to be associated with each of the child windows:

```
200:    for (i = 0; i < 10; i++)
201:        SetWindowWord(ChildWindows[i], 0, i);
```

Notice that in this case, WinStyle uses the SetWindowWord function rather than the SetClassWord function. The difference is that SetClassWord focuses on the cbWndExtra bytes rather than the cbClassExtra bytes.

DO   **DON'T**

DO use the cbWndExtra bytes when you want to associate a different set of data with each individual window created from a particular class.

DON'T use the cbClassExtra bytes for this purpose. They are primarily used on those rare occasions you might want to associate the same data with every instance of a particular class.

The numbers stored in the cbWndExtra bytes are retrieved during the response to a WM_PAINT message:

```
352: void StyleChild_OnPaint(HWND hwnd)
353: {
354:    PAINTSTRUCT PaintStruct;
355:    HDC PaintDC;
356:    char lpszBuffer[100];
357:    RECT R;
```

```
358:
359:    WORD i = GetWindowWord(hwnd, 0);
360:    wsprintf(lpszBuffer, "%d", i);
361:
362:    PaintDC = BeginPaint(hwnd, &PaintStruct);
363:
364:    SetTextColor(PaintDC, RGB(0, 0, 255));
365:    SetBkMode(PaintDC, TRANSPARENT);
366:    GetClientRect(hwnd, &R);
367:    DrawText(PaintDC, lpszBuffer, -1, &R,
368:            DT_SINGLELINE | DT_CENTER | DT_VCENTER);
369:
370:    EndPaint(hwnd, &PaintStruct);
371:
```

As you can see, WinStyle snatches the cbWndExtra bytes with the GetWindowWord function, translates them into a string, and pastes them up on the child windows for all to see.

Note that the every instance of the StyleChild class shares this same Paint method. As a result, they all paint their number in the middle of their screen.

The final note of interest here is that the StyleChild_OnPaint method calls on the DrawText method (rather than the TextOut) method to display its little message on-screen. The DT_SINGLELINE, DT_CENTER, and DT_VCENTER constants, discussed earlier in this book, are defined in your reference materials. The key point to remember is that the DT_VCENTER constant, which positions text in the vertical center of the screen, won't work unless used in conjunction with DT_SINGLELINE. Once again, don't try to memorize all these facts right away. Instead, just look 'em up when you need to use 'em.

Summary

This whole chapter has been a meditation on window styles and the uses of the WNDCLASS structure. In particular, you learned about the GetClassWord and GetWindowWord functions, and about their cousins SetClassWord and SetWindowWord. You also had a good look at child and pop-up windows and a little tour of the ever-useful MoveWindow function. All this information should come in handy many times throughout your Windows programming career.

Q&A

1. Q: When I call SetClassWord or SetClassLong, what exactly is being changed?

   A: When you call RegisterClass, Windows allocates memory for your WNDCLASS structure and copies it into that memory. It also zeros out the cbClassExtra and cbWndExtra fields. This means that after the call to RegisterWindow, an actual copy of the WNDCLASS structure is in memory. SetClassWord and GetClassWord enable you to reach into memory and change the attributes of that structure. Note that this is only going to automatically affect windows created after the change was made.

2. Q: I still don't understand the difference between cbClassExtra and cbWndExtra. Please explain this.

   A: Each window has its own cbWndExtra bytes, whereas there's only one copy of the cbClassExtra bytes—regardless of how many windows of this class currently are on the desktop. When WinStyle is executed, it registers the WinStyle and the StyleChild window classes. The first is the program's main window; the second is the class used when creating all the child windows. The StyleChild class is registered once, but there are nine instances of this class created by the program. Each of these nine instances has its own style fields and its own cbWndExtra field. In other words, Windows sets aside memory for one copy of the StyleChild WNDCLASS, but it sets additional memory aside for each instance of the class that is created through a call to CreateWindow. That means the WinStyle program has one copy of the cbClassExtra field and at least nine copies of the cbWndExtra field. It's important to note, however, that some of the fields from the WNDCLASS structure are copied into each of the memory structures—allocated when each instance of the child window is created.

Workshop

The Workshop provides quiz questions to help you solidify your understanding of the material covered and exercises to provide you with experience in using what you've learned. Try to understand the quiz and exercise answers before continuing on to the next chapter. Answers are provided in Appendix A.

Quiz

1. What is the difference between a child window and a pop-up window?

2. What is the difference between GetClientRect and GetWindowRect?

3. What is the purpose of the WS_OVERLAPPEDWINDOW style, and what other styles are associated with it?

4. What two calls can you use to make a window shrink to one-half its current size?

5. How can you find the width of the border on a window that has the WS_THICKFRAME style?

6. How can you disable a window?

7. Every single time, without exception, that you successfully call CreateSolidBrush, you also have to make another call. What is that call?

8. What is the difference between GetClassWord and GetWindowWord?

9. What is the purpose of GCW_HBRBACKGROUND?

10. Who decides how many extra bytes a window has, and what general types of purposes can they have?

Exercises

1. Use the ShowWindow function to create a child window without using the WS_VISIBLE style.

2. Use the cbWndExtra field of WNDCLASS to store a string that names each of the child windows (in this program) that has a caption. When the user clicks one of those windows, have the string appear in the caption.

14

You've learned a lot in Week 2, and that new knowledge can be used to improve and update the SysInfo project that was started at the end of Week 1. The new additions enable the program to use ToolHelp functions to retrieve lists of the classes, modules, and tasks in memory on the system at runtime.

Listing R2.1 shows the SysInfo source file.

Type   Listing R2.1. **SYSINFO.CPP.**

```
1: /////////////////////////////////////////////
   //////
2: //   Program Name: SYSINFO.CPP
3: //   Programmer: Charlie Calvert
4: //   Description: My system's vacation
          version 2
5: //   Date: 08/11/93
6: /////////////////////////////////////////////
   //////
7:
```

continues

Listing R2.1. continued

```
 8: #define STRICT
 9: #include <windows.h>
10: #include <windowsx.h>
11: #include <toolhelp.h>
12: #include <stdio.h>
13: #include <string.h>
14: #include "SysInfo.h"
15:
16: #pragma warning (disable: 4068)
17: #pragma warning (disable: 4100)
18:
19: // -----------------------------------------
20: // Interface
21: // -----------------------------------------
22:
23: static char szAppName[] = "SysInfo";
24: static HWND MainWindow;
25: static HINSTANCE hInstance;
26: static HWND hListBox;
27: // -----------------------------------------
28: // Initialization
29: // -----------------------------------------
30:
31: /////////////////////////////////////////////
32: // Program entry point
33: /////////////////////////////////////////////
34: #pragma argsused
35: int PASCAL WinMain(HINSTANCE hInst, HINSTANCE hPrevInstance,
36:                    LPSTR  lpszCmdParam, int nCmdShow)
37: {
38:   MSG  Msg;
39:
40:   if (!hPrevInstance)
41:     if (!Register(hInst))
42:       return FALSE;
43:
44:   MainWindow = Create(hInst, nCmdShow);
45:   if (MainWindow)
46:     return FALSE;
47:   while (GetMessage(&Msg, NULL, 0, 0))
```

```
48:    {
49:        TranslateMessage(&Msg);
50:        DispatchMessage(&Msg);
51:    }
52:
53:    return Msg.wParam;
54: }
55:
56: /////////////////////////////////////////
57: // Register the window
58: /////////////////////////////////////////
59: BOOL Register(HINSTANCE hInst)
60: {
61:    WNDCLASS WndClass;
62:
63:    WndClass.style        = CS_HREDRAW ¦ CS_VREDRAW;
64:    WndClass.lpfnWndProc      = WndProc;
65:    WndClass.cbClsExtra    = 0;
66:    WndClass.cbWndExtra       = 0;
67:    WndClass.hInstance        = hInst;
68:    WndClass.hIcon         = LoadIcon(NULL, IDI_APPLICATION);
69:    WndClass.hCursor        = LoadCursor(NULL, IDC_ARROW);
70:    WndClass.hbrBackground  = GetStockBrush(WHITE_BRUSH);
71:    WndClass.lpszMenuName      = "MENU_1";
72:    WndClass.lpszClassName  = szAppName;
73:
74:    return RegisterClass (&WndClass);
75: }
76:
77: /////////////////////////////////////////
78: // Create the window
79: /////////////////////////////////////////
80: HWND Create(HINSTANCE hInst, int nCmdShow)
81: {
82:    hInstance = hInst;
83:
84:    HWND hWindow = CreateWindow(szAppName, szAppName,
85:                    WS_OVERLAPPEDWINDOW,
86:                    CW_USEDEFAULT, CW_USEDEFAULT,
87:                    CW_USEDEFAULT, CW_USEDEFAULT,
88:                    NULL, NULL, hInstance, NULL);
89:
```

continues

Listing R2.1. continued

```
90:    if (hWindow == NULL)
91:      return hWindow;
92:
93:    ShowWindow(hWindow, nCmdShow);
94:    UpdateWindow(hWindow);
95:
96:    return hWindow;
97: }
98:
99: // -------------------------------------
100: // WndProc and Implementation
101: // -------------------------------------
102:
103: ///////////////////////////////////////////
104: // The Window Procedure
105: ///////////////////////////////////////////
106: LRESULT CALLBACK _export WndProc(HWND hWindow, UINT Message,
107:                                  WPARAM wParam, LPARAM lParam)
108: {
109:   switch(Message)
110:   {
111:     HANDLE_MSG(hWindow, WM_CREATE, SysInfo_OnCreate);
112:     HANDLE_MSG(hWindow, WM_DESTROY, SysInfo_OnDestroy);
113:     HANDLE_MSG(hWindow, WM_COMMAND, SysInfo_OnCommand);
114:     HANDLE_MSG(hWindow, WM_PAINT, SysInfo_OnPaint);
115:     default: return SysInfo_DefProc(hWindow, Message,
116:                                     wParam, lParam);
116:   }
117: }
118:
119: ///////////////////////////////////////
120: // Handle WM_CREATE
121: ///////////////////////////////////////
122: #pragma argsused
123: BOOL SysInfo_OnCreate(HWND hwnd,
                           CREATESTRUCT FAR* lpCreateStruct)
124: {
125:   hListBox = CreateWindow("listbox", szAppName,
126:                    WS_CHILD | WS_VISIBLE | LBS_STANDARD,
127:                    300, 10, 200, 180,
```

```
128:                          hwnd, NULL, hInstance, NULL);
129:
130:     CreateWindow("button", "Class",
131:                          WS_CHILD | BS_PUSHBUTTON | WS_VISIBLE,
132:                          10, 210, 130, 30,
133:                          hwnd, HMENU(CM_CLASS), hInstance, NULL);
134:
135:     CreateWindow("button", "Module",
136:                          WS_CHILD | BS_PUSHBUTTON | WS_VISIBLE,
137:                          190, 210, 130, 30,
138:                          hwnd, HMENU(CM_MODULE), hInstance, NULL);
139:
140:     CreateWindow("button", "Task",
141:                          WS_CHILD | BS_PUSHBUTTON | WS_VISIBLE,
142:                          370, 210, 130, 30,
143:                          hwnd, HMENU(CM_TASK), hInstance, NULL);
144:
145:     return TRUE;
146: }
147:
148:
149: //////////////////////////////////
150: // Handle WM_DESTROY
151: //////////////////////////////////
152: #pragma argsused
153: void SysInfo_OnDestroy(HWND hwnd)
154: {
155:     PostQuitMessage(0);
156: }
157:
158: //////////////////////////////////
159: // Handle WM_CREATE
160: //////////////////////////////////
161: #pragma argsused
162: void SysInfo_OnCommand(HWND hwnd, int id,
163:                        HWND hwndCtl, UINT codeNotify)
164: {
165:     switch(id)
166:     {
167:       case CM_ABOUT:
168:         FARPROC AboutBox =
169:           MakeProcInstance((FARPROC)AboutDlgProc, hInstance);
```

continues

471

Listing R2.1. continued

```
170:          DialogBox(hInstance, "About", hwnd, (DLGPROC)AboutBox);
171:          FreeProcInstance(AboutBox);
172:          break;
173:
174:       case CM_CLASS:
175:          SetClassContents();
176:          break;
177:
178:       case CM_MODULE:
179:          SetModuleContents();
180:          break;
181:
182:       case CM_TASK:
183:          SetTaskContents();
184:          break;
185:    }
186: }
187:
188: void SystemOutLine(HDC PaintDC, int Y)
189: {
190:    int len;
191:    int YInc = 25;
192:    char S[100];
193:    DWORD dwFlags;
194:
195:    dwFlags = GetWinFlags();
196:
197:    len = sprintf(S, "This is an %s system.",
198:       (dwFlags & WF_CPU286) ? "80286" :
199:       (dwFlags & WF_CPU386) ? "80386" :
200:       (dwFlags & WF_CPU486) ? "80486" : "unknown");
201:    TextOut(PaintDC, 10, Y + YInc, S, len);
202:
203:    len = sprintf(S, "A coprocessor is %s ",
204:       (dwFlags & WF_80x87) ? "present" : "not present");
205:    TextOut(PaintDC, 10, Y + 2 * YInc, S, len);
206:
207:    len = sprintf(S, "Mode: %s",
208:       (dwFlags & WF_ENHANCED) ? "Enhanced" : "Standard");
209:    TextOut(PaintDC, 10, Y + 3 * YInc, S, len);
```

```
210:
211:    len = sprintf(S, "Paging is %s",
212:        (dwFlags & WF_PAGING) ? "available" : "unavailable");
213:    TextOut(PaintDC, 10, Y +  4 * YInc, S, len);
214: }
215:
216: ////////////////////////////////////////
217: // Handle WM_PAINT
218: ////////////////////////////////////////
219: void SysInfo_OnPaint(HWND hwnd)
220: {
221:    HDC PaintDC;
222:    PAINTSTRUCT PaintStruct;
223:    SYSHEAPINFO Info;
224:    char S[100];
225:
226:    Info.dwSize = sizeof(SYSHEAPINFO);
227:    SystemHeapInfo(&Info);
228:    DWORD FreeSpace = GetFreeSpace(0) / 1024;
229:
230:    PaintDC = BeginPaint(hwnd, &PaintStruct);
231:    sprintf(S, "Percent free in the USER heap: %d",
232:            Info.wUserFreePercent);
233:    TextOut(PaintDC, 10, 10, S, strlen(S));
234:    sprintf(S, "Percent free in the GDI heap: %d",
235:            Info.wGDIFreePercent);
236:    TextOut(PaintDC, 10, 35, S, strlen(S));
237:    sprintf(S, "Kilobytes free on Global heap: %ld", FreeSpace);
238:    TextOut(PaintDC, 10, 60, S, strlen(S));
239:
240:    SystemOutLine(PaintDC, 60);
241:
242:    EndPaint(hwnd, &PaintStruct);
243: }
244:
245: // ------------------------------------------------
246: // SysInfo Dialog
247: // ------------------------------------------------
248:
249: ////////////////////////////////////////////////////
250: // The SysInfo Dialog Procedure
251: ////////////////////////////////////////////////////
```

continues

Listing R2.1. continued

```
252: #pragma argsused
253: BOOL CALLBACK AboutDlgProc(HWND hDlg, WORD Message,
254:                                 WPARAM wParam, LPARAM lParam)
255: {
256:   switch(Message)
257:   {
258:     case WM_INITDIALOG:
259:       return TRUE;
260:
261:     case WM_COMMAND:
262:       if (wParam == IDOK || wParam == IDCANCEL)
263:       {
264:         EndDialog(hDlg, TRUE);
265:         return TRUE;
266:       }
267:       break;
268:   }
269:   return FALSE;
270: }
271:
272: //////////////////////////////////////////////////
273: // SetClassContents
274: //////////////////////////////////////////////////
275: BOOL SetClassContents(void)
276: {
277:   CLASSENTRY Class;
278:   BOOL Result;
279:
280:   ListBox_ResetContent(hListBox);
281:   Class.dwSize = sizeof(CLASSENTRY);
282:   ClassFirst(&Class);
283:   ListBox_AddString(hListBox, Class.szClassName);
284:   while (Result)
285:   {
286:     Result = ClassNext(&Class);
287:     ListBox_AddString(hListBox, Class.szClassName);
288:   }
289:   return TRUE;
290: }
291:
```

```
292: ////////////////////////////////////////
293: // SetModuleContents
294: ////////////////////////////////////////
295: #pragma argsused
296: BOOL SetModuleContents(void)
297: {
298:   MODULEENTRY Module;
299:   BOOL Result;
300:
301:   ListBox_ResetContent(hListBox);
302:   Module.dwSize = sizeof(MODULEENTRY);
303:   ModuleFirst(&Module);
304:   ListBox_AddString(hListBox, Module.szModule);
305:   while (Result)
306:   {
307:     Result = ModuleNext(&Module);
308:     ListBox_AddString(hListBox, Module.szModule);
309:   }
310:   return TRUE;
311: }
312:
313: ////////////////////////////////////////
314: // SetTaskContents
315: ////////////////////////////////////////
316: BOOL SetTaskContents(void)
317: {
318:   TASKENTRY Task;
319:   BOOL Result;
320:
321:   ListBox_ResetContent(hListBox);
322:   Task.dwSize = sizeof(TASKENTRY);
323:   TaskFirst(&Task);
324:   ListBox_AddString(hListBox, Task.szModule);
325:   while (Result)
326:   {
327:     Result = TaskNext(&Task);
328:     ListBox_AddString(hListBox, Task.szModule);
329:   }
330:   return TRUE;
331: }
```

Listing R2.2 shows the SysInfo header file.

 Listing R2.2. SYSINFO.H.

```
 1: /////////////////////////////////////////////////
 2: //   Program Name: SYSINFO.H
 3: //   Programmer: Charlie Calvert
 4: //   Description: My system's vacation version 2
 5: //   Date: 08/11/93
 6: /////////////////////////////////////////////////
 7:
 8: #define CM_ABOUT 101
 9: #define CM_CLASS 102
10: #define CM_TASK 103
11: #define CM_MODULE 104
12:
13: #define ID_CLASSLISTBOX 103
14: #define ID_MODULELISTBOX 104
15: #define ID_TASKLISTBOX 105
16:
17: // Declarations for class SysInfo
18: #define SysInfo_DefProc     DefWindowProc
19: BOOL SysInfo_OnCreate(HWND hwnd, CREATESTRUCT FAR*
20:                          lpCreateStruct);
22: void SysInfo_OnDestroy(HWND hwnd);
22: void SysInfo_OnCommand(HWND hwnd, int id,
23:                          HWND hwndCtl, UINT codeNotify);
24: void SysInfo_OnPaint(HWND hwnd);
25:
26: // Funcs
27: BOOL Register(HINSTANCE hInst);
28: HWND Create(HINSTANCE hInst, int nCmdShow);
29: LRESULT CALLBACK _export WndProc(HWND hWindow, UINT Message,
30:                                  WPARAM wParam, LPARAM lParam);
31: BOOL CALLBACK AboutDlgProc(HWND hDlg, WORD Message,
32:                                  WPARAM wParam, LPARAM lParam);
33: BOOL SetClassContents(void);
34: BOOL SetModuleContents(void);
35: BOOL SetTaskContents(void);
```

Listing R2.3 shows the SysInfo resource file.

Type Listing **R2.3. SYSINFO.RC.**

```
 1: //////////////////////////////////////////////////
 2: //  Module Name: SYSINFO.RC
 3: //  Programmer: Charlie Calvert
 4: //  Description: Resource File for version 2
 5: //  Date: 08/11/93
 6: //////////////////////////////////////////////////
 7:
 8: #include <windows.h>
 9: #include "SysInfo.h"
10:
11: MENU_1 MENU
12: BEGIN
13:   MENUITEM "About", CM_ABOUT
14: END
15:
16: About DIALOG 18, 24, 141, 58
17: STYLE DS_MODALFRAME ¦ WS_POPUP ¦ WS_CAPTION ¦ WS_SYSMENU
18: CAPTION "About Dialog"
19: BEGIN
20:     CTEXT "What I Did on My System's Vacation", -1, 1, 9, 140,
21:        8, WS_CHILD ¦ WS_VISIBLE ¦ WS_GROUP
22:     CTEXT "Copyright (c) 1993 Hackers, Inc.", -1, 1, 23, 140,
23:        10, WS_CHILD ¦ WS_VISIBLE ¦ WS_GROUP
24:     PUSHBUTTON "Ok", IDOK, 5, 39, 132, 12,  WS_CHILD ¦
25:        WS_VISIBLE ¦ WS_TABSTOP
26: END
27:
28:
29: ClassList DIALOG 38, 30, 212, 127
30: STYLE DS_MODALFRAME ¦ WS_POPUP ¦ WS_CAPTION ¦ WS_SYSMENU
31: CAPTION "Classes"
32: BEGIN
33:     CONTROL "", ID_CLASSLISTBOX, "LISTBOX", 37: LBS_STANDARD ¦
34:        WS_CHILD ¦ WS_VISIBLE, 23, 9, 166, 90
35:     PUSHBUTTON "Ok", IDOK, 5, 107, 201, 14, 40: WS_CHILD ¦
36:        WS_VISIBLE ¦ WS_TABSTOP
38: END
```

continues

Listing R2.3. continued

```
39:
41: TaskList DIALOG 18, 18, 141, 127
42: STYLE DS_MODALFRAME ¦ WS_POPUP ¦ WS_CAPTION ¦ WS_SYSMENU
43: CAPTION "Tasks"
44: BEGIN
45:     CONTROL "", ID_TASKLISTBOX, "LISTBOX", 49: LBS_STANDARD ¦
46:       WS_CHILD ¦ WS_VISIBLE, 21, 9, 99, 90
47:     PUSHBUTTON "Ok", IDOK, 6, 107, 128, 14, 52: WS_CHILD ¦
48:       WS_VISIBLE ¦ WS_TABSTOP
50: END
51:
53: ModuleList DIALOG 18, 18, 141, 127
54: STYLE DS_MODALFRAME ¦ WS_POPUP ¦ WS_CAPTION ¦ WS_SYSMENU
55: CAPTION "Modules"
56: BEGIN
57:     CONTROL "", ID_MODULELISTBOX, "LISTBOX",
58:       WS_CHILD ¦ WS_VISIBLE, 21, 9, 99, 90
59:     PUSHBUTTON "Ok", IDOK, 6, 107, 128, 14, 64: WS_CHILD ¦
60:       WS_VISIBLE ¦ WS_TABSTOP
61:     LBS_STANDARD ¦
62: END
```

Listing R2.4 shows the SysInfo definition file.

 Listing R2.4. SYSINFO.DEF.

```
1: ; SYSINFO.DEF
2:
3: NAME           SysInfo
4: DESCRIPTION    'SysInfo Vacation (c) 1993
                   by Charles Spence Calvert'
5: EXETYPE        WINDOWS
6: CODE           PRELOAD MOVEABLE DISCARDABLE
7: DATA           PRELOAD MOVEABLE MULTIPLE
8: HEAPSIZE       4096
9: STACKSIZE      5120
```

Listing R2.5 shows the Borland SysInfo makefile.

Listing R2.5. SYSINFO.MAK (Borland).

```
 1: # SYSINFO.MAK
 2:
 3: # macros
 4: APPNAME = SysInfo
 5: INCPATH = C:\BC\INCLUDE
 6: LIBPATH = C:\BC\LIB
 7: FLAGS = -ml -W -v -w4 -I$(INCPATH) -L(LIBPATH)
 8:
 9: # link
10: $(APPNAME).exe: $(APPNAME).obj $(APPNAME).def $(APPNAME).res
11:    bcc $(FLAGS) $(APPNAME).obj
12:    brc $(APPNAME).res
13:
14: # compile
15: $(APPNAME).obj: $(APPNAME).cpp
16:    bcc -c $(FLAGS) $(APPNAME).cpp
17:
18: $(APPNAME).res: $(APPNAME).rc
19:    brc -r -I$(INCPATH) $(APPNAME).rc
```

Listing R2.6 shows the Microsoft makefile for SysInfo.

Listing R2.6. SYSINFO.MAK (Microsoft).

```
 1: # SYSINFO.MAK for Microsoft
 2:
 3: APPNAME = SysInfo
 4: LIBS = llibcew libw toolhelp
 5:
 6: # linking
 7: $(APPNAME).exe : $(APPNAME).obj $(APPNAME).def $(APPNAME).res
 8:    link $(APPNAME), /align:16, NUL, /nod $(LIBS), $(APPNAME)
 9:    rc $(APPNAME).res
10:
11: # compile
```

continues

Listing R2.6. continued

```
12: $(APPNAME).obj : $(APPNAME).cpp
13:    cl -AL -c -Gsw -Ow -W4 -Zp  $(APPNAME).cpp
14:
15: # Compile
16: $(APPNAME).res: $(APPNAME).rc
17:    rc -r $(APPNAME).rc
```

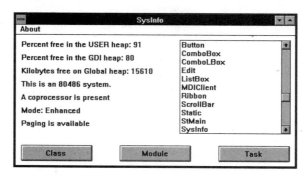

Figure R2.1. *The SysInfo program displays a list of class names currently in memory.*

By now, you should be aware that Windows stores a great deal of information in memory. This information usually can be made available to a program simply by calling a function or setting up a callback. In this particular case, SysInfo obtains information about classes, modules, and tasks with a set of ToolHelp functions called ClassFirst, TaskFirst, ModuleFirst, ClassNext, TaskNext, and ModuleNext. Anyone who has used the popular RTL functions FindFirst and FindNext should be familiar with the way these functions work.

SysInfo also reports on the current processor, whether the machine is in standard or enhanced mode, whether a coprocessor is present, and whether or not paging is enabled. These last set of facts are retrieved from the system by calling a single function called GetWinFlags.

To display the information it obtains, the SysInfo program uses TextOut, a list box, and three push buttons. TextOut is used to display information retrieved with GetWinFlags, whereas the push button and list box are enlisted to encapsulate the data from the ToolHelp functions.

By this time, you should be familiar with the process of creating list boxes and buttons as SysInfo does in SysInfo_OnCreate. The series of calls to CreateWindow, which are made in response to a WM_CREATE message, are absolutely standard, and contain no surprises.

The real work of retrieving information about classes, tasks, and modules can be illustrated by looking at the SetClassContents function:

```
BOOL SetClassContents(void)
{
  CLASSENTRY Class;
  BOOL Result;

  ListBox_ResetContent(hListBox);
  Class.dwSize = sizeof(CLASSENTRY);
  ClassFirst(&Class);
  ListBox_AddString(hListBox, Class.szClassName);
  while (Result)
  {
    Result = ClassNext(&Class);
    ListBox_AddString(hListBox, Class.szClassName);
  }
  return TRUE;
}
```

The first thing SysInfo does after the user selects the class button is ensure that the program's list box is empty and ready for input. This is accomplished with a call to the WINDOWSX macro called ListBox_ResetContent. This macro takes a single parameter designating the list box's HWND.

SysInfo then calls ClassFirst, passing it a single parameter of type CLASSENTRY. Here's the way the CLASSENTRY struct is defined in TOOLHELP.H:

```
typedef struct tagCLASSENTRY
{
    DWORD dwSize;
    HMODULE hInst;                 /* This is really an hModule */
    char szClassName[MAX_CLASSNAME + 1];
    WORD wNext;
} CLASSENTRY;
```

The first field in the CLASSENTRY struct needs to be set to the size of the structure itself before it's passed to ClassFirst. This is done, in part, to keep your code compatible with any future releases of Windows that might change some portion of this structure.

In return for filling out the first field of the CLASSENTRY struct and passing it in with ClassFirst, Windows returns the name of the first class in its list of classes. SysInfo gloms on to this information, which is kept in the szClassName variable, and passes it to the list box with the aid of another WINDOWSX macro called ListBox_AddString.

After the first string is in place, SysInfo goes to the well a second time with a call to ClassNext. In return for these efforts, Windows returns the name of the next class on its internal lists. The process is repeated until all the classes in the system have been enumerated; this is signaled by ClassNext returning zero.

That's all you need to do to retrieve information about the available classes on the system. The process for retrieving modules and tasks is nearly identical. However, there are slight changes in naming conventions and some fairly major changes in the shape of the structure passed in to Windows. Once you understand how the classes on the system are retrieved, you should have no trouble grasping the nearly identical code for retrieving tasks and modules.

Obtaining information from Windows with the GetWinFlags function is also a fairly straightforward process. GetWinFlags requires no parameters. It returns a 32-bit value that contains a series of flags specifying information about the current system. The flags are demonstrated in the SysInfo program and listed separately in your documentation or in the online help. To use these flags, simply test to see which ones are set with the bitwise logical AND operator:

```
len = sprintf(S, "This is an %s system.",
  (dwFlags & WF_CPU286) ? "80286" :
  (dwFlags & WF_CPU386) ? "80386" :
  (dwFlags & WF_CPU486) ? "80486" : "unknown");
TextOut(PaintDC, 10, Y + YInc, S, len);
```

Here, you can see that SysInfo (using code taken nearly verbatim from the online help) checks to see if the current system is a 286, 386, or 486. After it finds the answer, SysInfo paints the answer to the screen for the user's benefit.

That's all I'm going to say about SysInfo for now. The program is growing into a valuable tool that offers considerable insight into the inner workings of the Windows environment. Most of its prowess stems from the existence of the ToolHelp DLL, which Microsoft added to Windows with the release of version 3.1. At the end of Week 3, SysInfo is expanded even further, giving a more detailed look at the current system.

3

Many of the secrets of Windows programming have already been revealed to you in the pages of this book. You know the basic facts about windows, window procedures, resources, dialogs, controls, callbacks, the GDI, WINDOWSX, and event-oriented programming. Not all these techniques have been easy to master; however, by now they should be familiar topics, which you can call upon when you want to create your own attractive, easy to use programs.

Where You're Going

Week 3 introduces advanced material on four fundamental programming issues: dialogs, menus, icons, and the GDI. You already know the basics about these topics, but there is much additional information that you should thoroughly comprehend if you want to become truly knowledgeable about Windows. You'll also learn about three advanced topics: the multiple document interface

(MDI), dynamic link libraries (DLLs), and multimedia programming. There will, of course, be a host of related topics that are covered in conjunction with these major themes.

Anyone familiar with the Windows environment realizes what an important role dialogs play in many of the best designed programs. To further your knowledge of this subject, the first two chapters in Week 3 focus on placing controls inside dialogs, as well as the art of setting and getting data from these controls. Other important dialog-related subjects involve changing the color of dialogs, differences between modal and modeless dialogs, common dialogs, and dynamic changes of the appearance of dialogs at runtime. When finished with these chapters, you'll be able to use dialogs to communicate with users in a natural, intuitive manner.

Menus have been featured in most of the programs presented in this book. However, a number of advanced menuing techniques still need to be covered before you can take full advantage of these powerful and flexible resources. On Day 17, you'll learn about the system menu, nesting menus, and creating user draw menus. In addition, you'll learn how to make the interface to your program more intuitive through the creative use of cursors, icons, and accelerators. Accelerators enable you to add *hot keys* to your program that give users immediate access to important features.

You've already learned a lot about significant GDI concepts, such as bitmaps, "bitblitting," "stretchblitting," and device contexts. However, I've talked little about classical GDI graphics per se—that is, the art of drawing geometric shapes to the screen and saving them into files. On Day 18, you'll create a dynamic Windows paint program. It will enable you to use the mouse to draw colorful geometric figures and to save your designs in a compact, easy to use metafile. The featured program shows how to use the mouse to "rubber band" a flexible outline that previews the shape to be drawn.

Day 19 continues the exploration of the GDI and introduces MDI applications. Both the Borland and Microsoft IDEs are MDI applications. That is, they are single applications that host a series of tilable and cascadable windows that act as discreet entities. The GDI has many powerful features. It also presents the reader with a number of subtle programming techniques that need to be mastered. When finished, you'll have cultivated a skill that is absolutely necessary in the development of certain types of applications.

The last two chapters in the book feature longer programs that should prove entertaining and challenging. Day 20 presents a multimedia application that plays CD ROMS, MIDI files, and WAVE files with the message-based portion of the media control interface (MCI). In addition, the program also shows you how to record WAVE files. With a little work, the multimedia program presented in this book can be developed into a significant application that would be appealing to a wide range of consumers.

Day 20 also shows how to create dynamic link libraries (DLLs) and how to use a dialog as the main window of your program. DLLs are a particularly important programming technique. Fortunately, they are also relatively easy to master. DLLs will give you an insight into the structure of the entire Windows environment, because the Windows API itself is stored inside of these powerful binary files.

Day 21 returns to the Snake program and presents you with code that should prove entertaining and fun to use. If you want, you can use Snako as the starting point for your own games; or just play around with it while celebrating the completion of all your hard work.

By the time you finish Week 3, you'll have been introduced to all the major topics involved in Windows programming, and to many of the fine points that turn good Windows programmers into highly valued experts. Along the way, you'll be exposed to some very exciting technology that represents the cutting edge of contemporary computing.

Dialog Boxes and Mapping Modes

In this lesson, you'll learn about dialog boxes and the variations you can run on the Windows coordinate system.

In particular, you will learn about

☐   Modal dialog boxes

☐   Modeless dialog boxes

☐   Mapping modes

☐   Logical coordinates

This chapter introduces a program called WINSIZE.CPP, which demonstrates both how to create and run dialogs, and also how to manipulate six of the coordinate systems available to Windows programmers. The actual act of creating modal and modeless dialogs is also covered in this chapter. Controlling the color of the dialog and manipulating the data displayed in it are subjects covered in the next chapter.

This chapter is arranged so that most of the material on mapping modes occurs in its first half, and most of the material on dialogs occurs in the second half.

Coordinating the Coordinates

As shown in Figure 15.1, the WinSize program has two dialogs for displaying data; it also has a main window, in which geometric figures can be drawn. The smaller of the two dialogs, the Size dialog, shows the coordinates of the main window when the program is using any of six different mapping modes.

Mapping modes are ways of describing the units of measurement used to define a window's coordinates. For instance, by default a program uses the MM_TEXT mapping mode, which depends on the convention that each unit of measurement in a window is equivalent to one pixel.

Note: A pixel is the smallest visible unit that can be manipulated on a screen. For instance, if a program takes over the entire screen and renders it completely black except for one tiny point in the upper left-hand corner of the screen, that single point would be a pixel. Though they are not demonstrated in the WinSize program, Windows provides routines, called SetPixel and GetPixel, for manipulating the screen on this level.

The standard VGA screen has 640 pixels running from left to right, and 480 pixels running from top to bottom. SuperVGA modes are typically either 800X600 pixels or 1024X768 pixels.

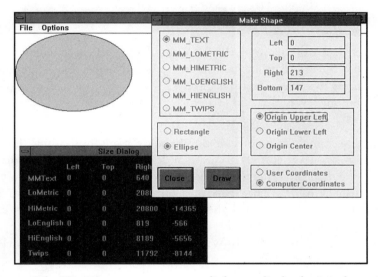

Figure 15.1. *The WinSize program uses two dialogs to display basic information about the Windows coordinate system.*

Because screens can have a variable number of pixels on them, programmers sometimes want to abandon the MM_TEXT coordinate system and use a more stable unit of measurement in its place. In an attempt to give the programmer what he or she seeks, the Windows environment provides several logical coordinate systems.

Note: The physical coordinate system on a monitor is always measured in pixels. These are units which have an actual, physical presence on-screen. The monitor and computer think of the coordinate system on-screen as being a reflection of the number of pixels in any particular area. As humans, though, we might think: "OK, look down about three inches from the top of the screen." Or maybe: "About twenty millimeters from the left of the screen, there's a small red line...." When people map these human measurement systems on top of the screen's physical system, it's called creating a *logical* mapping mode. The real bottom line, however, is always the physical pixels on the screen.

Rather than working in pixels, the Windows logical coordinate systems (in theory) measure the screen in inches, millimeters, and twips. Twips are units used when measuring typefaces. More specifically, a twip is one-twentieth of a point, and a point is about one seventy-second of an inch. Therefore, a twip is 1/20 * 1/72, or 1/1440 of an inch.

These seemingly very precise numbers are a bit misleading, however, because Windows is never entirely accurate in describing anything other than the MM_TEXT mapping mode. In other words, Windows always knows exactly how many pixels are on-screen or inside of a particular area, but it can't always determine exactly how large an inch or a millimeter might be on a particular system. Part of the reason for this is that a hardware device, such as a monitor, will never reveal its size to the software running on a system. That is, Windows can't tell the difference between a 14-inch or 15-inch monitor.

The *SetMapMode* Function

Syntax

```
int SetMapMode(HDC, int)
```

The command to change the mapping mode is very simple. All you do is select the mapping mode you want to use in the current device context:

The SetMapMode function takes two parameters. The first is the current device context, and the second is one of the fnMapMode constants (defined later in this section). The function returns the previous mapping mode. (See lines 188, 205, and 301 in WINSIZE.CPP.)

Example:

```
SetMapMode(PaintDC, MM_TEXT);
```

The *GetMapMode* Function

```
int GetMapMode(HDC);
```

This easy-to-use GetMapMode function retrieves the current mapping mode from a device context. The device context you want to know about serves as the sole argument to this function. GetMapMode returns one of the fnMapMode constants listed in Table 15.1.

Example:

```
int CurrentMappingMode = GetMapMode(PaintDC);
```

where the returned value is once again one of the fnMapMode constants.

Table 15.1. Here is a table outlining the six major mapping systems.

Mapping mode	Logical units	Physical unit	X++	Y++
MM_TEXT	1	Device pixel	Right	Down
MM_HIENGLISH	1000	1 inch	Right	Up
MM_HIMETRIC	100	1 millimeter	Right	Up
MM_LOENGLISH	100	1 inch	Right	Up
MM_LOMETRIC	10	1 millimeter	Right	Up
MM_TWIPS	1440	1 inch	Right	Up

This table shows that each unit in the MM_HIENGLISH mapping system is .001 inches in size, whereas each unit in the MM_HIMETRIC system is .01 mm in size. In all cases, except the MM_TEXT mapping mode, the X values by default get larger as you move to the right, and the Y values by default get larger as you move up the screen.

One way to get a handle on these ideas is to think of the MM_TEXT coordinate system as being arranged like the words on a page. That is, you start reading in the upper left-hand corner, move to the right, and then move down. The other mapping modes are more like the standard Cartesian grid, with the (0,0) point being located in the upper left-hand corner of the screen, and the screen itself being a portion of the bottom right-hand quadrant of the grid. These concepts are demonstrated in Figures 15.2 and 15.3.

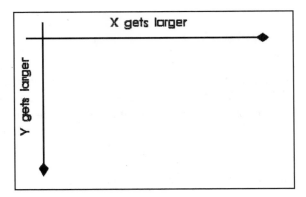

Figure 15.2. *The* MM_TEXT *mapping mode, by default, has coordinates that increase when you move down or to the right.*

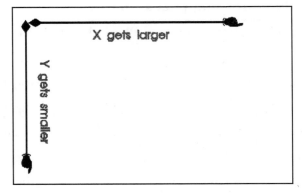

Figure 15.3. *The* MM_HIENGLISH *mapping mode treats the screen as if it were part of the bottom right-hand quadrant of a Cartesian grid.*

GDI and Device Coordinates

After you get a feeling for the six mapping modes, the next thing to grasp is that the origin from which the Windows coordinates are calculated can be moved around the screen to any location you choose. The easiest way to do this is with the SetViewportOrg command (see the following in-depth explanation). The following code fragment moves the viewpoint origin to its default position in the upper left-hand corner of a window:

```
SetViewportOrg(PaintDC, 0, 0);
```

The next set of commands moves the origin to the center of the screen, as shown in Figure 15.4:

```
GetClientRect(hwnd, &Rect);
SetViewportOrg(PaintDC, Rect.right / 2, Rect.bottom / 2);
```

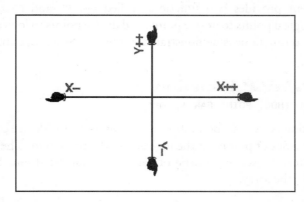

Figure 15.4. *The Windows coordinates look like this when you use the* MM_HIENGLISH *mapping mode and move the origin to the center of the screen.*

So What's All This Business About the GDI?

Lying just beneath the surface of this subject is one of the most important ideas in Windows programming. The entire field of creating graphics output in Windows is subsumed under a single heading called the Graphics Device Interface (GDI). As a rule, GDI commands work with an HDC, that is, with a device context. And finally (here's the kicker), device contexts always work with some particular type of mapping mode. (The GDI is discussed further in Day 18, "GDI and Metafiles.")

Just to make sure this idea is clear in your mind, let's turn the coin over and look at it from the opposite side. Logical coordinates are always associated with GDI objects, that is, with device contexts. This means that non-GDI commands, such as GetClientRect or GetWindowRect, never return logical coordinates. These commands don't utilize an HDC, and they aren't GDI commands. Therefore, they don't retrieve information in logical coordinates. They always deal in pixels.

This same detachment from the GDI coordinate system is demonstrated by the Windows messaging system. For instance, WM_SIZE, WM_MOVE, and WM_LBUTTONDOWN messages always send device coordinates rather than logical coordinates, because they are not part of the GDI.

Because of this disparity between logical and device coordinates, the Windows environment provides two functions, called LPtoDP and DPtoLP, which quickly translate logical points to device points and device points to logical points. The latter of these two functions is demonstrated in the WinSize program.

The *DPtoLP* Function

```
BOOL DPtoLP(HDC, POINT FAR *, int)
```

This function converts a point or series of points on the device coordinate system to a point or series of points on the logical coordinate system. The first parameter is a device context, the second an array of points to be translated, and the third the number of points in the array.

Example:

```
RECT SizeData;
DPtoLP(PaintDC, (LPPOINT)&SizeData, 2);
```

The preceding code follows a pattern mirrored throughout the WinSize program, because it uses a RECT structure rather than a POINT structure. This is done because DPtoLP is often used to translate values returned from GetClientRect or GetWindowRect. RECT structures, of course, are really just two contiguous POINT structures. (See lines 189 and 301 in WINSIZE.CPP.)

Advanced Mapping Concepts

Windows programmers have adopted a rather confusing terminology, which makes a distinction between viewport coordinates and window coordinates. When using this terminology, the device or viewport coordinates are always measured in pixels. Window coordinates, however, are measured in terms of whatever logical units are associated with the current mapping mode, such as inches, millimeters, or twips.

The *SetViewportOrg* Function

```
DWORD SetWindowOrg(HDC, int, int);
DWORD SetViewportOrg(DC, int, int);
```

`SetViewportOrg` sets the origin for the device coordinate system.

`SetWindowOrg` sets the origin for the logical coordinate system.

Both functions take three parameters:

☐ The first is a device context: `HDC`.

☐ The second is a signed integer specifying the X origin for the coordinate system.

☐ The third is a signed integer specifying the Y origin for the coordinate system.

The function returns the coordinates of the previous origin, with the X coordinates in the low word and the Y coordinates in the high word.

Examples:

```
SetViewportOrg(PaintDC, 100, 100);
SetWindowOrg(PaintDC, 100, 100);
```

You should refer to the source, or read the rest of this section referring to these examples to see more practical examples of how to call these functions. (See lines 211, 215, and 219.)

Passing the same coordinates to `SetViewportOrg` and `SetWindowOrg` often yields radically different results, depending on the current mapping mode. Because the window origin is calculated in terms of the viewport origin, the following calls will move the viewport origin to the center of the screen, and then move the window origin to the right and down, relative to the new viewport origin:

```
GetClientRect(hwnd, &Rect);
SetViewportOrg(PaintDC, Rect.right / 2, Rect.bottom / 2);
SetWindowOrg(PaintDC, -Rect.right / 2, -Rect.bottom / 2);
```

DO   DON'T

DO feel free to change window and device coordinates at the same time you use these later mapping modes.

DON'T change window and viewport coordinates at the same time, unless you are absolutely certain you can see your way through to some very clearly defined "logical" destination. The one notable exception is with two mapping modes not discussed in this book, called `MM_ISOTROPIC` and `MM_ANISOTROPIC`.

Before You Move On

It's perhaps worth mentioning that I'm well aware that the stuff I've been talking about in the last few pages can lead to a serious meltdown of certain essential neural centers. So instead of turning up the juice, I'll just leave you with a taste of the possibilities inherent in this system, and let the young at heart and adventuresome of spirit pursue these matters to whatever extremes they deem necessary. This is not to imply that I don't find this subject both important and intriguing—only that this book isn't the right place to pursue it in detail. Anyway, the WinSize program demonstrates these ideas better than they could possibly be explained in words.

Speaking of the WinSize program (see Listing 15.1), it's time for you to get it up and running. Pay close attention, because this program contains tricks that you'll use over and over again when hacking Windows.

Listing 15.1. WINSIZE.CPP.

```
 1: /////////////////////////////////////////////////////
 2: // WINSIZE.CPP — What Size is the Window?
 3: // programmer: Charlie Calvert
 4: // date: 3/26/93
 5: /////////////////////////////////////////////////////
 6: #define STRICT
 7: #include <windows.h>
 8: #include <windowsx.h>
 9: #pragma hdrstop
10: #include <stdio.h>
11: #include <stdlib.h>
12: #include <string.h>
13: #include "winsize.h"
14: #pragma warning (disable: 4068)
15:
16: // -------------------------------------------------
17: // Setup
18: // -------------------------------------------------
19:
20: static char szAppName[] = "WinSize";
21: static HWND MainWindow;
22: static HINSTANCE hInstance;
23:
24: /////////////////////////////////////////////////////
25: // Program entry point
26: /////////////////////////////////////////////////////
27: #pragma argsused
28: int PASCAL WinMain(HINSTANCE hInst, HINSTANCE hPrevInstance,
29:                    LPSTR  lpszCmdParam, int nCmdShow)
```

15

```
30: {
31:   MSG   Msg;
32:
33:   hInstance = hInst;
34:
35:   if (!hPrevInstance)
36:     if (!Register(hInst))
37:       return FALSE;
38:
39:   MainWindow = Create(hInst, nCmdShow);
40:   if (MainWindow)
41:     return FALSE;
42:   while (GetMessage(&Msg, NULL, 0, 0))
43:   {
44:       TranslateMessage(&Msg);
45:       DispatchMessage(&Msg);
46:   }
47:
48:   return Msg.wParam;
49: }
50:
51: /////////////////////////////////////////////////////////
52: // Register the window
53: /////////////////////////////////////////////////////////
54: BOOL Register(HINSTANCE hInst)
55: {
56:   WNDCLASS WndClass;
57:
58:   WndClass.style           = CS_HREDRAW ¦ CS_VREDRAW;
59:   WndClass.lpfnWndProc     = WndProc;
60:   WndClass.cbClsExtra      = 0;
61:   WndClass.cbWndExtra      = 0;
62:   WndClass.hInstance       = hInst;
63:   WndClass.hIcon           = LoadIcon(NULL, IDI_APPLICATION);
64:   WndClass.hCursor         = LoadCursor(NULL, IDC_ARROW);
65:   WndClass.hbrBackground   = GetStockBrush(WHITE_BRUSH);
66:   WndClass.lpszMenuName    = "MENU";
67:   WndClass.lpszClassName   = szAppName;
68:
69:   return RegisterClass (&WndClass);
70: }
71:
72: /////////////////////////////////////////////////////////
73: // Create the window
74: /////////////////////////////////////////////////////////
75: HWND Create(HINSTANCE hInst, int nCmdShow)
76: {
77:   HWND hWindow = CreateWindow(szAppName, szAppName,
78:                               WS_OVERLAPPEDWINDOW,
```

continues

Listing 15.1. continued

```
79:                          CW_USEDEFAULT, CW_USEDEFAULT,
80:                          CW_USEDEFAULT, CW_USEDEFAULT,
81:                          NULL, NULL, hInst, NULL);
82:
83:    if (hWindow == NULL)
84:       return hWindow;
85:
86:    ShowWindow(hWindow, nCmdShow);
87:    UpdateWindow(hWindow);
88:
89:    return hWindow;
90: }
91:
92: //------------------------------------------------------------
93: // The Implementation
94: //------------------------------------------------------------
95:
96: //------------------------------------------------------------
97: // The WndProc
98: //------------------------------------------------------------
99:
100: LRESULT CALLBACK _export WndProc(HWND hwnd, UINT Message,
101:                                  WPARAM wParam, LPARAM lParam)
102: {
103:    switch (Message)
104:    {
105:      HANDLE_MSG(hwnd, WM_COMMAND, WinSize_OnCommand);
106:      HANDLE_MSG(hwnd, WM_CREATE, WinSize_OnCreate);
107:      HANDLE_MSG(hwnd, WM_PAINT, WinSize_OnPaint);
108:      HANDLE_MSG(hwnd, WM_SIZE, WinSize_OnSize);
109:      HANDLE_MSG(hwnd, WM_DESTROY, WinSize_OnDestroy);
110:      default:
111:         return WinSize_DefProc(hwnd, Message, wParam, lParam);
112:    }
113: }
114:
115: /////////////////////////////////////////
116: // Handle WM_CREATE
117: /////////////////////////////////////////
118: #pragma argsused
119: BOOL WinSize_OnCreate(HWND hwnd, CREATESTRUCT FAR*
120: lpCreateStruct)
121: {
122:    HINSTANCE hIn;
123:
124:    hIn = lpCreateStruct->hInstance;
125:
126:    lpfnSizeBox = MakeProcInstance((FARPROC)SizeBoxProc, hIn);
127:
```

```
128:    BlueBrush = CreateSolidBrush(RGB(0, 255, 255));
129:    GreenBrush = CreateSolidBrush(RGB(255, 255, 127));
130:    return TRUE;
131: }
132:
133: /////////////////////////////////
134: // Handle WM_DESTROY
135: /////////////////////////////////
136: #pragma argsused
137: void WinSize_OnDestroy(HWND hwnd)
138: {
139:    DeleteObject(BlueBrush);
140:    DeleteObject(GreenBrush);
141:    FreeProcInstance(lpfnSizeBox);
142:    PostQuitMessage(0);
143: }
144:
145: /////////////////////////////////
146: // WM_COMMAND
147: /////////////////////////////////
148: #pragma argsused
149: void WinSize_OnCommand(HWND hwnd, int id, HWND hwndCtl,
150:                        UINT codeNotify)
151: {
152:    switch(id)
153:    {
154:      case CM_SIZEBOX:
155:        if (hSizeBox == 0)
156:        {
157:          hSizeBox = CreateDialog(hInstance, "SizeDialog",
158:                              hwnd,(DLGPROC)lpfnSizeBox);
159:          InvalidateRect(hwnd, NULL, FALSE);
160:        }
161:        break;
162:
163:      case CM_MAKESHAPE:
164:        lpfnMakeShape = MakeProcInstance((FARPROC)MakeShapeProc,
165:                                         hInstance);
166:        DialogBox(hInstance, "MakeShape",
167:                  hwnd,(DLGPROC)lpfnMakeShape);
168:        FreeProcInstance(lpfnMakeShape);
169:        InvalidateRect(hwnd, NULL, FALSE);
170:        break;
171:
172:      case CM_EXIT:
173:        DestroyWindow(hwnd);
174:        break;
175:    }
176: }
177:
```

continues

499

Listing 15.1. continued

```
178: ///////////////////////////////
179: //  If the Size Dialog is open, this will fill it in with
180: //  the size of the window as expressed in each of the
181: //  different mapping modes
182: ///////////////////////////////
183: void FillSizeBox(HWND hwnd, HDC PaintDC)
184: {
185:   TSIZEDATA    SizeData;
186:   for (int i = 0; i < 6; i++)
187:   {
188:     SetMapMode(PaintDC, Modes[i]);
189:     GetClientRect(hwnd, &SizeData[i]);
190:     DPtoLP(PaintDC, (LPPOINT)&SizeData[i], 2);
191:   }
192:   SendMessage(hSizeBox, WM_SETDATA, 0, (long)&SizeData);
193: }
194:
195: ///////////////////////////////
196: // WM_PAINT
197: ///////////////////////////////
198: void WinSize_OnPaint(HWND hwnd)
199: {
200:   RECT          Rect;
201:   HDC           PaintDC ;
202:   PAINTSTRUCT   ps ;
203:
204:   PaintDC = BeginPaint (hwnd, &ps) ;
205:   SetMapMode (PaintDC, Modes[ModeCase]);
206:   GetClientRect(hwnd, &Rect);
207:
208:   switch (OriginMode)
209:   {
210:     case ORG_UPLEFT :
211:       SetViewportOrg(PaintDC, 0, 0);
212:       break;
213:
214:     case ORG_LOWLEFT:
215:       SetViewportOrg(PaintDC, 0, Rect.bottom);
216:       break;
217:
218:     case ORG_CENTER:
219:       SetViewportOrg(PaintDC,Rect.right/2,Rect.bottom / 2);
220:       break;
221:   }
222:
223:   HBRUSH OldBrush = SelectBrush(PaintDC, BlueBrush);
224:
225:   switch (Shape)
226:   {
227:     case RECTANGLE:
```

```
228:         Rectangle(PaintDC, RLeft, RTop, RRight, RBottom);
229:         break;
230:
231:     case CIRCLE:
232:         Ellipse(PaintDC, RLeft, RTop, RRight, RBottom);
233:         break;
234:   }
235:   SelectObject(PaintDC, OldBrush);
236:
237:   if (hSizeBox != 0)
238:     FillSizeBox(hwnd, PaintDC);
239:
240:   EndPaint (hwnd, &ps) ;
241: }
242:
243: /////////////////////////////////
244: // WM_SIZE
245: /////////////////////////////////
246: #pragma argsused
247: void WinSize_OnSize(HWND hwnd, UINT state, int cx, int cy)
248: {
249:   HDC PaintDC = GetDC(hwnd);
250:   if (hSizeBox != 0)
251:     FillSizeBox(hwnd, PaintDC);
252:   ReleaseDC(hwnd, PaintDC);
253: }
254:
255: /////////////////////////////////
256: // MakeShape Dialog
257: /////////////////////////////////
258: void SetRectText(HWND hwnd)
259: {
260:   char S[45];
261:   HWND ParentWindow;
262:
263:   ParentWindow = GetWindow(hwnd, GW_OWNER);
264:   InvalidateRect(ParentWindow, NULL, TRUE);
265:   sprintf(S, "%d", RLeft);
266:   SendDlgItemMessage(hwnd, ID_RLEFT, WM_SETTEXT, 0, (long)S);
267:   sprintf(S, "%d", RRight);
268:   SendDlgItemMessage(hwnd, ID_RRIGHT, WM_SETTEXT, 0, (long)S);
269:   sprintf(S, "%d", RTop);
270:   SendDlgItemMessage(hwnd, ID_RTOP, WM_SETTEXT, 0, (long)S);
271:   sprintf(S, "%d", RBottom);
272:   SendDlgItemMessage(hwnd, ID_RBOTTOM, WM_SETTEXT, 0, (long)S);
273: }
274:
275: /////////////////////////////////
276: // GetUserCords
277: /////////////////////////////////
```

continues

Listing 15.1. continued

```
278: void GetUserCords(HWND hwnd)
279: {
280:   char S[100];
281:
282:   GetWindowText(GetDlgItem(hwnd, ID_RLEFT), S, 100);
283:   RLeft = atoi(S);
284:   GetWindowText(GetDlgItem(hwnd, ID_RTOP), S, 100);
285:   RTop = atoi(S);
286:   GetWindowText(GetDlgItem(hwnd, ID_RRIGHT), S, 100);
287:   RRight = atoi(S);
288:   GetWindowText(GetDlgItem(hwnd, ID_RBOTTOM), S, 100);
289:   RBottom = atoi(S);
290: }
291:
292: /////////////////////////////////
293: // MakeShape
294: /////////////////////////////////
295: void MakeShape(HWND hDlg)
296: {
297:   RECT R;
298:
299:   GetClientRect(GetParent(hDlg), &R);
300:   HDC DC = GetDC(GetParent(hDlg));
301:   SetMapMode(DC, Modes[ModeCase]);
302:   DPtoLP(DC,(LPPOINT)&R, 2);
303:   ReleaseDC(GetParent(hDlg), DC);
304:
305:   switch (OriginMode)
306:   {
307:     case ORG_CENTER:
308:       RLeft = -(R.right / 3);
309:       RTop = -(R.bottom / 3);
310:       RRight = (R.right / 3);
311:       RBottom = (R.bottom / 3);
312:       break;
313:
314:     case ORG_LOWLEFT:
315:       RBottom = -(R.bottom / 3);
316:       RLeft = R.left / 3;
317:       RTop = R.top / 3;
318:       RRight = R.right / 3;
319:       break;
320:
321:     case ORG_UPLEFT:
322:       RLeft = R.left / 3;
323:       RTop = R.top / 3;
324:       RRight = R.right / 3;
325:       RBottom = R.bottom / 3;
326:       break;
327:   }
328: }
```

```
329:
330:
331: /////////////////////////////////
332: // DoDraw
333: /////////////////////////////////
334: void DoDraw(HWND hwnd)
335: {
336:    if (UseCompCords)
337:      MakeShape(hwnd);
338:    SetRectText(hwnd);
339: }
340:
341: /////////////////////////////////
342: // DoRectCommand
343: /////////////////////////////////
344: BOOL DoRectCommand(HWND hwnd, WORD wParam)
345: {
346:    switch(wParam)
347:    {
348:      case ID_DRAW:
349:        GetUserCords(hwnd);
350:        InvalidateRect(GetParent(hwnd), NULL, TRUE);
351:        return TRUE;
352:
353:      case ID_RTEXT:
354:        ModeCase = TEXT;
355:        DoDraw(hwnd);
356:        return TRUE;
357:
358:      case ID_RLOMETRIC:
359:        ModeCase = LOMETRIC;
360:        DoDraw(hwnd);
361:        return TRUE;
362:
363:      case ID_RHIMETRIC:
364:        ModeCase = HIMETRIC;
365:        DoDraw(hwnd);
366:        return TRUE;
367:
368:      case ID_RLOENGLISH:
369:        ModeCase = LOENGLISH;
370:        DoDraw(hwnd);
371:        return TRUE;
372:
373:      case ID_RHIENGLISH:
374:        ModeCase = HIENGLISH;
375:        DoDraw(hwnd);
376:        return TRUE;
377:
```

continues

Listing 15.1. continued

```
378:        case ID_RTWIPS:
379:          ModeCase = TWIPS;
380:          DoDraw(hwnd);
381:          return TRUE;
382:
383:        case ID_ORGUPLEFT:
384:          GetUserCords(hwnd);
385:          OriginMode = ORG_UPLEFT;
386:          DoDraw(hwnd);
387:          return TRUE;
388:
389:        case ID_ORGLOWLEFT:
390:          GetUserCords(hwnd);
391:          OriginMode = ORG_LOWLEFT;
392:          DoDraw(hwnd);
393:          return TRUE;
394:
395:        case ID_ORGCENTER:
396:          GetUserCords(hwnd);
397:          OriginMode = ORG_CENTER;
398:          DoDraw(hwnd);
399:          return TRUE;
400:
401:        case ID_USERCORDS:
402:          GetUserCords(hwnd);
403:          UseCompCords = FALSE;
404:          return TRUE;
405:
406:        case ID_COMPCORDS:
407:          UseCompCords = TRUE;
408:          return FALSE;
409:
410:        case ID_RECT:
411:          Shape = RECTANGLE;
412:          DoDraw(hwnd);
413:          return TRUE;
414:
415:        case ID_CIRCLE:
416:          Shape = CIRCLE;
417:          DoDraw(hwnd);
418:          return TRUE;
419:
420:        case IDOK:
421:        case IDCANCEL:
422:          {
423:            EndDialog(hwnd, TRUE);
424:            return TRUE;
425:          }
426:      }
427:    return FALSE;
428: }
```

```
429:
430: ///////////////////////////////
431: // MakeShapeProc
432: ///////////////////////////////
433: #pragma argsused
434: BOOL CALLBACK _export MakeShapeProc(HWND hwnd, WORD Msg, WORD
435: wParam, LONG lParam)
436: {
437:   switch(Msg)
438:   {
439:     case WM_INITDIALOG:
440:       SendDlgItemMessage(hwnd, ID_RTEXT, BM_SETCHECK, 1, 0L);
441:       SendDlgItemMessage(hwnd, ID_RECT, BM_SETCHECK, 1, 0L);
442:       SendDlgItemMessage(hwnd, ID_ORGUPLEFT, BM_SETCHECK, 1, 0L);
443:       SendDlgItemMessage(hwnd, ID_COMPCORDS, BM_SETCHECK, 1, 0L);
444:       return TRUE;
445:
446:     case WM_COMMAND:
447:       return (!DoRectCommand(hwnd, wParam));
448:
449:     case WM_CTLCOLOR:
450:       switch(HIWORD(lParam))
451:       {
452:         case CTLCOLOR_STATIC:
453:         case CTLCOLOR_BTN:
454:         case CTLCOLOR_EDIT:
455:           /* Set text to white and background to green */
456:           SetTextColor((HDC)wParam, RGB(0, 127, 0));
457:           SetBkMode((HDC)wParam, TRANSPARENT);
458:           return (BOOL) GreenBrush;
459:
460:         case CTLCOLOR_DLG:
461:           return (BOOL) GreenBrush;
462:       }
463:       return (BOOL) NULL;
464:   }
465:   return FALSE;
466: }
467:
468: //-------------------------------------------------
469: // SizeBoxProc Dialog
470: //-------------------------------------------------
471: #pragma argsused
472: BOOL CALLBACK _export SizeBoxProc(HWND hDlg, WORD Msg, WORD
473:                                   wParam, LONG lParam)
474: {
475:   TSIZEDATA SizeData;
476:   void *lpSizeData;
477:   char S[20];
478:   int i;
```

continues

505

Listing 15.1. continued

```
479:
480:    int Indexs[] = {2100, 2200, 2300, 2400, 2500, 2600};
481:
482:    switch(Msg)
483:    {
484:      case WM_CLOSE:
485:        DestroyWindow(hDlg);
486:        hSizeBox = 0;
487:        return TRUE;
488:
489:      case WM_CTLCOLOR:
490:        switch(HIWORD(lParam))
491:          {
492:            case CTLCOLOR_STATIC:
493:              SetTextColor((HDC)wParam, RGB(255, 0, 0));
494:              SetBkMode((HDC)wParam, TRANSPARENT);
495:              return (BOOL) GetStockObject(BLACK_BRUSH);
496:
497:             case CTLCOLOR_DLG:
498:               return (BOOL) GetStockObject(BLACK_BRUSH);
499:          }
500:         return (BOOL) NULL;
501:
502:      case WM_SETDATA:
503:        lpSizeData = (void *)lParam;
504:        memcpy(SizeData, lpSizeData, sizeof(TSIZEDATA));
505:        for (i = 0; i < 6; i++)
506:          {
507:          sprintf(S, "%d", SizeData[i].left);
508:          SendDlgItemMessage(hDlg, Indexs[i] + 1,
509:                             WM_SETTEXT, 0, long(S));
510:          sprintf(S, "%d", SizeData[i].right);
511:          SendDlgItemMessage(hDlg, Indexs[i] + 2,
512:                             WM_SETTEXT, 0, long(S));
513:          sprintf(S, "%d", SizeData[i].top);
514:          SendDlgItemMessage(hDlg, Indexs[i] + 3,
515:                             WM_SETTEXT, 0, long(S));
516:          sprintf(S, "%d", SizeData[i].bottom);
517:          SendDlgItemMessage(hDlg, Indexs[i] + 4,
518:                             WM_SETTEXT, 0, long(S));
519:          }
520:        return TRUE;
521:    }
522:    return FALSE;
523: }
```

Listing 15.2 is the WinSize header file.

Type Listing 15.2. **WINSIZE.H.**

```
 1: ///////////////////////////////////
 2: // WINSIZE.H
 3: // Programmer: Charlie Calvert
 4: // Date: 7/15/93
 5: ///////////////////////////////////
 6:
 7: // Constants
 8: #define WM_SETDATA      (WM_USER + 1)
 9: #define CM_EXIT         101
10: #define CM_SIZEBOX      1000
11: #define CM_MAKESHAPE    1001
12: #define RECTSIZE        2000
13: #define ID_MMLEFT       2101
14: #define ID_MMRIGHT      2102
15: #define ID_MMTOP        2103
16: #define ID_MMBOTTOM     2104
17: #define ID_LMLEFT       2201
18: #define ID_LMRIGHT      2202
19: #define ID_LMTOP        2203
20: #define ID_LMBOTTOM     2204
21: #define ID_HMLEFT       2301
22: #define ID_HMRIGHT      2302
23: #define ID_HMTOP        2303
24: #define ID_HMBOTTOM     2304
25: #define ID_LELEFT       2401
26: #define ID_LERIGHT      2402
27: #define ID_LETOP        2403
28: #define ID_LEBOTTOM     2404
29: #define ID_HELEFT       2501
30: #define ID_HERIGHT      2502
31: #define ID_HETOP        2503
32: #define ID_HEBOTTOM     2504
33: #define ID_TLEFT        2601
34: #define ID_TRIGHT       2602
35: #define ID_TTOP         2603
36: #define ID_TBOTTOM      2604
37: #define ID_RTEXT        3101
38: #define ID_RLOMETRIC    3102
39: #define ID_RHIMETRIC    3103
40: #define ID_RLOENGLISH   3104
41: #define ID_RHIENGLISH   3105
42: #define ID_RTWIPS       3106
43: #define ID_RISOTROPIC   3107
44: #define ID_RANSITROPIC  3108
45: #define ID_RLEFT        3110
```

continues

Listing 15.2. continued

```
46: #define ID_RRIGHT        3111
47: #define ID_RTOP          3112
48: #define ID_RBOTTOM       3113
49: #define ID_DRAW          3115
50: #define ID_COMPCORDS     3117
51: #define ID_USERCORDS     3118
52: #define ID_ORGUPLEFT     3120
53: #define ID_ORGLOWLEFT    3121
54: #define ID_ORGCENTER     3122
55: #define ID_RECT          4001
56: #define ID_CIRCLE        4002
57:
58: // Types
59: typedef RECT TSIZEDATA[6];
60: enum TModeCase {TEXT, LOMETRIC, HIMETRIC, LOENGLISH,
61:                 HIENGLISH, TWIPS, ISOTROPIC, ANSITROPIC};
62: enum TOriginMode {ORG_UPLEFT, ORG_LOWLEFT, ORG_CENTER};
63: enum TShape {RECTANGLE, CIRCLE};
64: int Modes[] = {MM_TEXT, MM_LOMETRIC, MM_HIMETRIC,
65:                MM_LOENGLISH, MM_HIENGLISH, MM_TWIPS,
66:                MM_ISOTROPIC, MM_ANISOTROPIC};
67:
68: // Declarations for class Generic
69: #define WinSize_DefProc    DefWindowProc
70: BOOL WinSize_OnCreate(HWND hwnd,
71:                       CREATESTRUCT FAR* lpCreateStruct);
72: void WinSize_OnDestroy(HWND hwnd);
73: void WinSize_OnCommand(HWND hwnd, int id,
74:                        HWND hwndCtl, UINT codeNotify);
75: void WinSize_OnPaint(HWND hwnd);
76: void WinSize_OnSize(HWND hwnd, UINT state, int cx, int cy);
77:
78: // Variables
79: FARPROC lpfnSizeBox;
80: FARPROC lpfnMakeShape;
81: HBRUSH BlueBrush, GreenBrush;
82: HWND hSizeBox;
83: TModeCase ModeCase = TEXT;
84: TOriginMode OriginMode = ORG_UPLEFT;
85: int RLeft = 10;
86: int RTop = 10;
87: int RRight = 100;
88: int RBottom = 100;
89: TShape Shape;
90: BOOL UseCompCords = TRUE;
91:
92: // procs
93: LRESULT CALLBACK _export WndProc(HWND hwnd, UINT Message,
94:                                  WPARAM wParam, LPARAM lParam);
95: BOOL Register(HINSTANCE hInst);
```

```
 96: HWND Create(HINSTANCE hInst, int nCmdShow);
 97: BOOL CALLBACK _export MakeShapeProc(HWND hWindow, WORD Msg,
 98:                                     WORD wParam, LONG lParam);
 99: BOOL CALLBACK _export SizeBoxProc(HWND hWindow, WORD Msg,
100:                                     WORD wParam, LONG lParam);
```

Listing 15.3 shows the WinSize resource file.

Listing 15.3. WINSIZE.RC.

```
 1: ////////////////////////////////////////////////////////
 2: // WINSIZE.RC — What Size is the window?
 3: // programmer: Charlie Calvert
 4: // date: 7/15/93
 5: ////////////////////////////////////////////////////////
 6: #include "WinSize.h"
 7: #include "Windows.h"
 8:
 9: ////////////////////////////////////////////////////////
10: // I've defined the following styles in order to make the
11: // code that follows at least somewhat more readable.
12: // This is not necessarily a programming technique, but rather
13: // something I've done to make the book more legible.
14: ////////////////////////////////////////////////////////
15: #define STY_STANDARD WS_CHILD ¦ WS_VISIBLE ¦ WS_GROUP
16: #define STY_GRPCHILD BS_GROUPBOX ¦ WS_CHILD ¦ WS_VISIBLE
17: #define STY_RTEXT SS_RIGHT ¦ WS_CHILD ¦ WS_VISIBLE ¦ WS_GROUP
18: #define STY_AUTRAD\
19:         BS_AUTORADIOBUTTON ¦ WS_CHILD ¦ WS_VISIBLE ¦ WS_TABSTOP
20: #define STY_STATLEFT\
21:         ES_LEFT ¦ WS_CHILD ¦ WS_VISIBLE ¦ WS_BORDER ¦ WS_TABSTOP
22: #define STY_AUTRADGRP\
23:         BS_AUTORADIOBUTTON ¦ WS_CHILD ¦ WS_VISIBLE ¦\
24:         WS_GROUP ¦ WS_TABSTOP
25:
26: Menu MENU
27: BEGIN
28:   POPUP "File"
29:   BEGIN
30:     MENUITEM "E&xit", CM_EXIT
31:   END
32:   POPUP "Options"
33:   BEGIN
34:     MENUITEM "Size Dialog", CM_SIZEBOX
35:     MENUITEM "Make Shape", CM_MAKESHAPE
36:   END
37: END
```

continues

Listing 15.3. continued

```
38:
39: SizeDialog DIALOG 16, 18, 170, 100
40: STYLE WS_POPUP ¦ WS_CAPTION ¦ WS_SYSMENU ¦ WS_VISIBLE
41: CAPTION "Size Dialog"
42: BEGIN
43:   LTEXT "MMText", -1, 7, 17, 40, 9, STY_STANDARD
44:   LTEXT "LoMetric", -1, 7, 30, 40, 9, STY_STANDARD
45:   LTEXT "HiMetric", -1, 7, 45, 40, 9, STY_STANDARD
46:   LTEXT "LoEnglish", -1, 7, 59, 40, 9, STY_STANDARD
47:   LTEXT "HiEnglish", -1, 7, 73, 40, 9, STY_STANDARD
48:   LTEXT "Twips", -1, 7, 87, 40, 9, STY_STANDARD
49:   CONTROL "", ID_MMLEFT, "STATIC", STY_STATLEFT, 42, 16, 27, 11
50:   CONTROL "", ID_MMRIGHT, "STATIC", STY_STATLEFT, 105, 16, 27, 11
51:   CONTROL "", ID_MMTOP, "STATIC", STY_STATLEFT, 74, 16, 27, 11
52:   CONTROL "", ID_MMBOTTOM, "STATIC", STY_STATLEFT, 138,16, 27, 11
53:   CONTROL "", ID_LMLEFT, "STATIC", STY_STATLEFT, 42, 30, 27, 11
54:   CONTROL "", ID_LMRIGHT, "STATIC", STY_STATLEFT, 105, 30, 27, 11
55:   CONTROL "", ID_LMTOP, "STATIC", STY_STATLEFT, 74, 30, 27, 11
56:   CONTROL "", ID_LMBOTTOM, "STATIC", STY_STATLEFT, 138,30, 27, 11
57:   CONTROL "", ID_HMLEFT, "STATIC", STY_STATLEFT, 42, 45, 27, 11
58:   CONTROL "", ID_HMRIGHT, "STATIC", STY_STATLEFT, 105, 45, 27, 11
59:   CONTROL "", ID_HMTOP, "STATIC", STY_STATLEFT, 74, 45, 27, 11
60:   CONTROL "", ID_HMBOTTOM, "STATIC", STY_STATLEFT, 138,45, 27, 11
61:   CONTROL "", ID_LELEFT, "STATIC", STY_STATLEFT, 42, 59, 27, 11
62:   CONTROL "", ID_LERIGHT, "STATIC", STY_STATLEFT, 105, 59, 27, 11
63:   CONTROL "", ID_LETOP, "STATIC", STY_STATLEFT, 74, 59, 27, 11
64:   CONTROL "", ID_LEBOTTOM, "STATIC", STY_STATLEFT, 138,59, 27, 11
65:   CONTROL "", ID_HELEFT, "STATIC", STY_STATLEFT, 42, 73, 27, 11
66:   CONTROL "", ID_HERIGHT, "STATIC", STY_STATLEFT, 105, 73, 27, 11
67:   CONTROL "", ID_HETOP, "STATIC", STY_STATLEFT, 74, 73, 27, 11
68:   CONTROL "", ID_HEBOTTOM, "STATIC", STY_STATLEFT, 138,73, 27, 11
69:   CONTROL "", ID_TLEFT, "STATIC", STY_STATLEFT, 42, 87, 27, 11
70:   CONTROL "", ID_TRIGHT, "STATIC", STY_STATLEFT, 105, 87, 27, 11
71:   CONTROL "", ID_TTOP, "STATIC", STY_STATLEFT, 74, 87, 27, 11
72:   CONTROL "", ID_TBOTTOM, "STATIC", STY_STATLEFT, 138, 87, 27, 11
73:   LTEXT "Left", -1, 42, 6, 16, 8, STY_STANDARD
74:   LTEXT "Top", -1, 74, 6, 16, 8, STY_STANDARD
75:   LTEXT "Right", -1, 105, 6, 25, 8, STY_STANDARD
76:   LTEXT "Bottom", -1, 138, 7, 25, 7, STY_STANDARD
77: END
78:
79: MakeShape DIALOG 18, 18, 190, 162
80: STYLE WS_POPUP ¦ WS_CAPTION ¦ WS_SYSMENU ¦ WS_VISIBLE
81: CAPTION "Make Shape"
82: BEGIN
83:   CONTROL "MM_TEXT",ID_RTEXT,"BUTTON",STY_AUTRADGRP,10,8,66,10
84:   CONTROL "MM_LOMETRIC", ID_RLOMETRIC, "BUTTON", STY_AUTRAD,
85:           10, 21, 66, 10
86:   CONTROL "MM_HIMETRIC", ID_RHIMETRIC, "BUTTON", STY_AUTRAD,
87:           10, 34, 66, 10
88:   CONTROL "MM_LOENGLISH", ID_RLOENGLISH, "BUTTON", STY_AUTRAD,
```

```
 89:            10, 47, 66, 10
 90:    CONTROL "MM_HIENGLISH", ID_RHIENGLISH, "BUTTON", STY_AUTRAD,
 91:            10, 60, 66, 10
 92:    CONTROL "MM_TWIPS", ID_RTWIPS, "BUTTON", STY_AUTRAD,
 93:            10, 73, 66, 10
 94:    EDITTEXT ID_RLEFT, 124, 10, 52, 12, STY_STATLEFT
 95:    EDITTEXT ID_RTOP, 124, 24, 52, 12, STY_STATLEFT
 96:    EDITTEXT ID_RRIGHT, 124, 38, 52, 12, STY_STATLEFT
 97:    EDITTEXT ID_RBOTTOM, 124, 52, 52, 12, STY_STATLEFT
 98:    CONTROL "Origin Upper Left",
 99:            ID_ORGUPLEFT, "BUTTON", STY_AUTRADGRP, 95, 81, 84, 10
100:    CONTROL "Origin Lower Left",
101:            ID_ORGLOWLEFT, "BUTTON", STY_AUTRAD, 95, 95, 84, 10
102:    CONTROL "Origin Center",
103:            ID_ORGCENTER, "BUTTON", STY_AUTRAD, 95, 108, 84, 10
104:    CONTROL "User Coordinates",
105:            ID_USERCORDS, "BUTTON", STY_AUTRADGRP, 95, 133, 84, 12
106:    CONTROL "Computer Coordinates",
107:            ID_COMPCORDS, "BUTTON", STY_AUTRAD, 95, 144, 84, 10
108:    PUSHBUTTON "Close", IDOK, 5, 134, 33, 21,
109:            WS_CHILD | WS_VISIBLE | WS_TABSTOP
110:    PUSHBUTTON "Draw", ID_DRAW, 48, 134, 33, 21
111:    RTEXT "Left", -1, 94, 12, 25, 8, STY_RTEXT
112:    RTEXT "Right", -1, 94, 40, 25, 8, STY_RTEXT
113:    RTEXT "Top", -1, 94, 26, 25, 8, STY_RTEXT
114:    RTEXT "Bottom", -1, 94, 54, 25, 8, STY_RTEXT
115:    CONTROL "", 3116, "button", STY_GRPCHILD, 90, 128, 94, 27
116:    CONTROL "", 3119, "button", STY_GRPCHILD, 90, 74, 94, 49
117:    CONTROL "", 3107, "button", STY_GRPCHILD, 5, 88, 77, 35
118:    CONTROL "Rectangle",ID_RECT,"BUTTON",STY_AUTRADGRP,11,95,66,10
119:    CONTROL "Ellipse",ID_CIRCLE,"BUTTON",STY_AUTRAD,11,109,66,10
120:    CONTROL "", 3108, "button", STY_GRPCHILD, 91, 1, 90, 69
121:    CONTROL "", 3109, "button", STY_GRPCHILD, 7, 1, 74, 85
122: END
```

Listing 15.4 shows the WinSize definition file.

Listing 15.4. WINSIZE.DEF.

```
1: ; WinSize.def
2: NAME           WinSize
3: DESCRIPTION    'Mapping Modes Info'
4: EXETYPE        WINDOWS
5: STUB           'WINSTUB.EXE'
6: CODE           PRELOAD MOVEABLE DISCARDABLE
7: DATA           PRELOAD MOVEABLE MULTIPLE
8: HEAPSIZE       4096
9: STACKSIZE      8192
```

Listing 15.5 shows the Borland makefile for WinSize.

Type   **Listing 15.5. WINSIZE.MAK (Borland).**

```
 1: # ----------------------
 2: # WINSIZE.MAK
 3: # ----------------------
 4:
 5: # macros
 6: APPNAME = WinSize
 7: INCPATH = C:\BC\INCLUDE
 8:LIBPATH = C:\BC\LIB
 9: FLAGS   = -H -ml -W -v -w4 -I$(INCPATH) -L$(LIBPATH)
10:
11: # link
12: $(APPNAME).exe: $(APPNAME).obj $(APPNAME).def $(APPNAME).res
13:    bcc $(FLAGS) $(APPNAME).obj
14:    brc $(APPNAME).res
15:
16: # compile
17: $(APPNAME).obj: $(APPNAME).cpp
18:    bcc -c $(FLAGS) $(APPNAME).cpp
19:
20: # resource
21: $(APPNAME).res: $(APPNAME).rc
22:    brc -r -i$(INCPATH) $(APPNAME).rc
```

Listing 15.6 shows the Microsoft makefile for WinSize.

Type   **Listing 15.6. WINSIZE.MAK (Microsoft).**

```
 1: #-------------------
 2: # WINSIZE.MAK
 3: #-------------------
 4:
 5: # Link
 6: WINSIZE.EXE : WINSIZE.OBJ WINSIZE.DEF WINSIZE.RES
 7:    link WinSize, /align:16, NUL, /nod llibcew libw, WinSize
 8:    rc WINSIZE.RES
 9:
10: # Compile
11: WINSIZE.OBJ : WINSIZE.CPP
12:    cl -c -AL -GA -Ow -W3 -Zp  WINSIZE.CPP
```

```
13:
14: # Compile
15: WINSIZE.RES: WINSIZE.RC
16:    rc -r WINSIZE.RC
```

 Figure 15.5 shows the WinSize program and its dialogs.

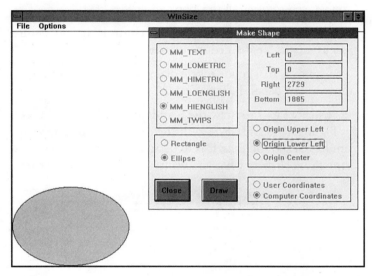

Figure 15.5. *Output you might see during a typical run of the WinSize program.*

The WinSize program draws a rectangle or an ellipse in a window. It also lets you open two dialogs: the Make Shape dialog (Figure 15.6) and the Size dialog (Figure 15.7). The Size dialog reports on the size of the entire window when measured in any of the following mapping modes: MM_TEXT, MM_HIENGLISH, MM_LOENGLISH, MM_HIMETRIC, MM_LOMETRIC, or MM_TWIPS. The Make Shape dialog enables you to change the type of shape being shown, and its dimensions. It also enables you to change the mapping mode and the viewpoint origin. If you use the Make Shape dialog to change the dimensions of a shape, select user coordinates from the dialog; then, enter the new values in the edit controls at the upper right-hand corner of the dialog. Click the Draw button to see the result. Remember, if you then change the origin, the shape might be moved off the screen. The primary purpose of the Computer Coordinates option is to force the computer to automatically calculate coordinates that will place the shape so it will be visible to the user.

513

Dialogs: Overview and Review

Before discussing the inner workings of the WinSize program, there are a few key points about dialogs that need to be emphasized:

- [ ] Dialogs are just a special form of a window.

- [ ] All dialogs have a dialog procedure associated with them. This dialog procedure is really just a minor variation on the standard window procedures you've seen so often in this book.

- [ ] As a rule, dialogs are populated with controls that are defined in RC files, just as menus are defined in RC files.

- [ ] The controls that reside inside dialogs are identical to the window controls discussed in detail during Week 2.

- [ ] It's usually easier to draw the first draft of a dialog (such as the ones shown in Figures 15.6 and 15.7) with the Resource Workshop, App Studio, or similar visual tool, than it is to design it strictly with code. When you've got something close to what you want, use the method that seems simplest.

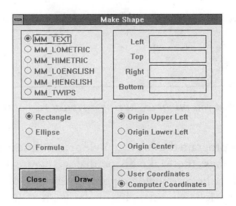

Figure 15.6. *The Make Shape dialog. The simplest way to create a dialog like this is with a visual tool.*

At this stage in the game, it might be easiest for you to think of dialogs as existing primarily so programmers can have an easy way to manipulate window controls. In other words, you can pop into the Resource Workshop or App Studio and design the interface for a dialog in just a few minutes. Then, you can pop the newly created dialog

on-screen with just a few relatively simple calls. When you're done, you have an easy way of carrying on a conversation, or "dialog," with a user.

	Left	Top	Right	Bottom
MMText	0	0	744	438
LoMetric	0	0	2790	-1643
HiMetric	0	0	27900	-16425
LoEnglish	0	0	1098	-647
HiEnglish	0	0	10984	-6467
Twips	0	0	15817	-9312

Size Dialog

Figure 15.7. *When the modeless Size Dialog is on-screen, you can still use the main window's menu.*

Let me add a clarification by stating that the preceding paragraph represents an oversimplification. During real-life programming adventures, dialogs can end up serving a number of very diverse purposes (besides those already listed). The goal of the last paragraph is not to give you a definitive description of dialogs, but to provide you with a starting point or foundation upon which your understanding of dialogs can be built.

Note: On Days 12 and 13, you learned about setting the WS_GROUP style for the first radio button inside a group. This same process must be implemented inside of dialogs, as shown in WINSIZE.RC. Also, the WS_TABSTOP style is set for all the controls in the Make Shape dialog that a user might want to reach with the Tab key.

Understanding Modal and Modeless Dialogs

The remainder of this chapter is dedicated to showing you the differences between creating modal dialogs, such as the Make Shape dialog, and modeless dialogs, such as the Size dialog. These are the two main categories of dialogs, and as a result, all Windows programmers need to understand what these terms mean.

The key points to grasp about modal and modeless dialogs are as follows:

- ☐ Modal dialogs "disable" the rest of a program so that the users can't do anything else until they make a selection from the current dialog and close it.

- ☐ Modeless dialogs are a lot like windows created with the WS_CHILD style. They float on top of the main window and let the user access the other features of the program.

- ☐ Both kinds of dialogs are created by calling MakeProcInstance to allocate a stub for the dialog procedure. Then, either CreateDialog (modeless) or DialogBox (modal) is called to launch the dialog.

- ☐ When you are all done, call FreeProcInstance to clean up the allocated memory.

All four of these points are clarified in the next few paragraphs. In particular, you'll see that although modal and modeless dialogs are created through similar calls, some specific differences in implementation are very important.

If you haven't done so already, pop up the WinSize program and start experimenting with the two dialogs. After some time, you'll probably notice that you have access to the program's main menu when the Size dialog is up, but you can't access it when the Make Shape dialog is on-screen. This is because the Make Shape dialog is a modal dialog, and the Size dialog is a modeless dialog.

Modal dialog boxes usually don't prevent you from changing from one application to another. In other words, if you are using the Make Shape dialog, you can switch to the File Manager or Program Manager, but you can't use the main menu of the WinSize program. The only exception to this rule is on the rare occasion you might use a system modal dialog box. System modal dialogs only enable the user to work inside of one dialog, and don't let the user switch to any other program.

In this particular case, the Size dialog is modeless, because the user needs to be able to watch the figures in the dialog change when he or she tugs at the borders surrounding the WinSize program. The issue here is that the Size dialog shows the dimensions of the main window as measured in several different mapping modes. When someone changes the size of the main window, the numbers in the Size dialog change. If the Size dialog were modal, it wouldn't be possible to bear witness to this effect.

Coding Modal and Modeless Dialogs

Although the actual implementations of modal and modeless dialogs are quite similar in principle, there are a number of specific differences in the ways they are created. To see the nature of these differences, you need to turn to the WinSize_OnCreate function.

As you've seen demonstrated in previous chapters, WM_CREATE message response methods can be quite complex when a program has a lot of controls in its main window. The WinSize program, however, takes a relatively straightforward approach to the initialization of its main window, primarily because the dialogs are created in the WinSize_OnCommand function. At any rate, here's what WinSize does with WM_CREATE messages:

```
BOOL WinSize_OnCreate(HWND hwnd,
                      CREATESTRUCT FAR* lpCreateStruct)
{
  HINSTANCE hIn;

  hIn = lpCreateStruct->hInstance;

  lpfnSizeBox = MakeProcInstance((FARPROC)SizeBoxProc, hIn);

  BlueBrush = CreateSolidBrush(RGB(0, 255, 255));
  GreenBrush = CreateSolidBrush(RGB(255, 255, 127));
  return TRUE;
}
```

Note: It happens that the CREATSTRUCT, piggybacking on top of the WM_CREATE message, contains a copy of the program's HINSTANCE. In previous chapters, the code in this book generally used a globally declared HINSTANCE variable. The code fragment (preceding this note) shows an alternative method of accessing the program's HINSTANCE. It's particularly useful if you want to move a Cls_OnCreate function outside the scope of your main module, without engaging in the dubious practice of declaring variables global to more than one module.

The call to MakeProcInstance (in the previous code) results in the initialization of the lpfnSizeBox variable, which is used when it's time to create the Size dialog. The issues involved here are nearly the same as those encountered on Day 11 (when you saw that MakeProcInstance was called prior to EnumFontFamilies). That is, you need to bind the data segment of the WinSize program to the window procedure for the Size dialog. As a result, even though Size dialog's window procedure is called by Windows, it still has access to the program's variables.

I'm not going to go any further than to point out that the stub for the Size dialog's window procedure is allocated in response to the WM_CREATE message, but calling MakeProcInstance on the Make Shape's dialog procedure is delayed until later in the program's history. The exact reason for these divergent courses of action will become clear in the next few paragraphs.

Now it's time to take a look at the portion of the WM_COMMAND message handler function where the two dialog boxes are actually launched. Needless to say, either of the following code fragments are called only after the user has made a selection from the program's menu:

```
case CM_SIZEBOX:
   if (hSizeBox == 0)
   {
     hSizeBox = CreateDialog(hInstance, "Options", hwnd,
                        (DLGPROC)lpfnSizeBox);
     InvalidateRect(hwnd, NULL, FALSE);
   }
   break;

case CM_MAKESHAPE:
   lpfnMakeShape = MakeProcInstance((FARPROC)MakeShapeProc,
                               hInstance);
   DialogBox(hInstance, "MakeShape", hwnd,
           (DLGPROC)lpfnMakeShape);
   FreeProcInstance(lpfnMakeShape);
   InvalidateRect(hwnd, NULL, FALSE);
   break;
```

(This code starts on line 154 of WINSIZE.CPP.) CM_SIZEBOX messages get sent to the program whenever the Size dialog option is selected from the menu, and CM_MAKESHAPE messages get sent whenever the user selects the Make Shape option from the menu.

As you can see, the WinSize program reacts differently to CM_SIZEBOX messages than it does to CM_MAKESHAPE messages. This is because Modal dialog boxes are created by calls to the DialogBox function, whereas Modeless dialogs are created by calls to the CreateDialog function. Furthermore, the call to the DialogBox procedure doesn't end until the user has closed the Make Shape dialog. This is why it's possible to call MakeProcInstance, DialogBox, and FreeProcInstance in quick succession:

```
lpfnMakeShape = MakeProcInstance((FARPROC)MakeShapeProc,
                            hInstance);
```

```
DialogBox(hInstance, "MakeShape", hwnd,
        (DLGPROC)lpfnMakeShape);
FreeProcInstance(lpfnMakeShape);
```

It's okay for `FreeProcInstance` to deallocate the memory for the dialog box procedure, because the Make Shape dialog has already been closed by the time `FreeProcInstance` is called.

The same isn't true of the `CreateDialog` procedure. This is why the WinSize program calls `MakeProcInstance` for the Size dialog in response to a `WM_CREATE` message, and why it destroys the allocated thunk while processing the `WM_DESTROY` message. The point here is that there is no way to know when the user is likely to close the Size dialog, so the `lpfnSizeBox` variable can only be safely destroyed after the user has closed the main window.

Furthermore, it's necessary to check the value of the `hSizeBox` variable before making any calls to `CreateDialog`:

```
if (hSizeBox == 0)
{
hSizeBox = CreateDialog(hInstance, "Options", hwnd,
(DLGPROC)lpfnSizeBox);
InvalidateRect(hwnd, NULL, FALSE);
}
```

This is done to ensure that the user doesn't end up crowding the screen with a whole series of instances of the Size dialog. The same thing isn't necessary with the Make Shape dialog, because the user can't get at the menu while a modal dialog is on-screen. Without access to the menu, the user won't be able to send more `CM_MAKESHAPE` messages to the `WndProc`.

The key point in the creation of each dialog is the moment when the address of its dialog procedures is passed to `MakeProcInstance`. In return for this effort, the program receives a properly fixed-up pointer. With the modal dialog, the address of the `MakeShapeProc` is called `lpfnMakeShape`. With the modeless dialog, the address of `SizeBoxProc` is passed to `MakeProcInstance`, and the returned pointer is called `lpfnSizeBox`.

As you know, both of these procedures (whose addresses are passed to `MakeProcInstance`) are really just special types of window procedures, which in their most simplified form look like this:

```
BOOL CALLBACK GenericDialogProc(HWND hDlg, WORD Message,
                                WPARAM wParam, LPARAM lParam)
{
  switch(Message)
```

```
{
  case WM_INITDIALOG:
    return TRUE;

  case WM_COMMAND:
    if (wParam == IDOK || wParam == IDCANCEL)
    {
      EndDialog(hDlg, TRUE);
      return TRUE;
    }
    break;
  }
  return FALSE;
}
```

As you can see, dialogs can be closed by calls to EndDialog.

Note: It's important to see that dialog box procedures aren't identical to window procedures. First, dialog box procedures return a BOOL rather than an LRESULT. That is, dialog box procedures don't include calls to DefWindowProc. Instead, they simply return TRUE or FALSE. Another significant difference is that dialog box procedures process WM_INITDIALOG messages rather than WM_CREATE messages.

A glance at the source for WinSize reveals that both the MakeShapeProc and the SizeBoxProc are considerably more complicated than the code fragment (previously listed). The extra code inside these functions is used primarily to change their color, and to set and retrieve data from their controls. The actual details of that process will be discussed in the next chapter.

Summary

In this chapter, you learned about the Windows coordinate system, and about creating modal and modeless dialogs. Specifically, you learned that

☐ There are eight logical mapping modes. Only the one called MM_TEXT has at least a quasi-direct relationship to the physical device coordinates, which are pixels.

☐ The strictly logical coordinate systems, such as MM_LOENGLISH are useful to programmers, but are still not entirely precise.

- [ ] There are two different types of dialogs, called modal and modeless.

- [ ] Modal dialogs take over the focus of a program until the user closes them.

- [ ] Modeless dialogs give the user the freedom to return at any time to the program's main menu, or to any other available features.

In the next chapter, you'll see how to communicate with both modal and modeless dialog boxes. In particular, you'll see how to transfer data into a dialog, and how to get the data back out again to see if the user has changed it.

The next chapter also includes a utility to be used when designing the playing board for the Snako program. The utility fits into the theme of the next chapter, because it makes heavy use of dialog boxes.

Q&A

1. Q: I still don't understand why anyone would ever want to change the mapping mode of a window. What gives?

   A: There are several different reasons for changing mapping modes, but one of the most important is the fact that device coordinates change radically from system to system. People running one of your programs in high-resolution super VGA modes might have 1024 pixels on the X axis, whereas the next person might have only 640 pixels on the X axis. If you define your main window to be 400X300 pixels, it will be nearly half the size on the second system as on the first. One way to reconcile these differences is to switch to the MM_LOENGLISH mapping mode and define your main window as being four inches wide and three inches tall. Now your window will be approximately the same size, regardless of what type of system your users own.

2. Q: Why does WinSize call MakeProcInstance in response to WM_CREATE, and FreeProcInstance in response to WM_DESTROY?

   A: It's important to understand that the decision to do things this way is not in any sense arbitrary. Each call to MakeProcInstance must be matched by one (and only one) call to FreeProcInstance; it's crucial that FreeProcInstance is not called while the dialog is on-screen. The only way to guarantee that things will work out this way is to call MakeProcInstance on the SizeBoxProc right at the very beginning of the program's life, and to free this memory only after the user has decided to destroy the main window. Other plans might accidentally enable calls to `FreeProcInstance` while the dialog is on-screen, or even worse, try to launch the dialog without calling `MakeProcInstance`.

Workshop

The Workshop provides quiz questions to help you solidify your understanding of the material covered and exercises to provide you with experience in using what you've learned. Try to understand the quiz and exercise answers before continuing on to the next chapter. Answers are provided in Appendix A.

Quiz

1. What is a mapping mode?

2. What is a pixel?

3. On a 14-inch monitor in standard VGA mode, is the fundamental unit of the `MM_LOMETRIC` mapping mode larger or smaller than a pixel?

4. What is a Viewpoint origin?

5. What is the difference between logical coordinates and device coordinates?

6. What is the difference between `SetWindowOrg` and `SetViewportOrg`?

7. What is the primary difference between modal and modeless dialogs?

8. What function is used to create a modal dialog?

9. What function is used to create a modeless dialog?

10. What are two differences between dialog procedures and window procedures?

Exercises

1. Before calling `CreateDialog`, the WinSize program checks to see if `hSizeBox` is set to `NULL`. Try removing this line of code and then recompile. What happens if you choose Size dialog in the menu three times in succession?

2. Convert the Size dialog into a modal dialog. What are the advantages and disadvantages of this new arrangement?

Advanced Dialogs: Getting and Setting Data

Today, you'll learn how to control the color of dialogs and how to set and retrieve data from their controls. Also included in this chapter is an example of how to stretch and shrink bitmaps before you "blit" them to the screen.

Specifically, this chapter contains information about

☐ `SendDlgItemMessage` and `GetDlgItem`

☐ `WM_CTLCOLOR` messages

☐ Using `StretchBlt` to shrink or expand a bitmap before painting it on-screen

Much of this chapter focuses on the WinSize program, which was introduced on Day 15. A new program, called Mapper, is presented near the end of this chapter. Mapper is part of the Snake project (which was introduced on Day 8 and which will be completed on Day 21). The Mapper program is presented in this chapter because its two dialogs fit in well with the current theme of dialogs and their controls.

Setting Data in the Size Dialog

When the Size dialog (see Figure 16.1) from the WinSize program appears on-screen, it lists the current coordinates of the main window when measured in the MM_TEXT, MM_LOMETRIC, MM_HIMETRIC, MM_LOENGLISH, MM_HIENGLISH, and MM_TWIPS mapping systems. This section contains a description of how the WinSize program calculates that information and how it displays it inside the dialog.

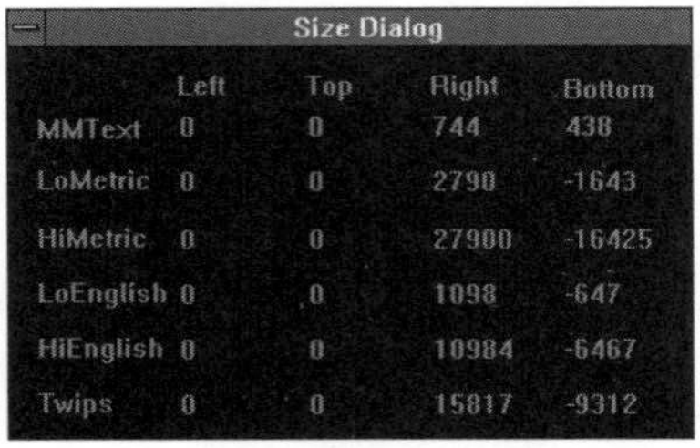

	Left	Top	Right	Bottom
MMText	0	0	744	438
LoMetric	0	0	2790	-1643
HiMetric	0	0	27900	-16425
LoEnglish	0	0	1098	-647
HiEnglish	0	0	10984	-6467
Twips	0	0	15817	-9312

Figure 16.1. *The Size dialog lists the coordinates of the current window.*

In brief outline form, the steps are as follows:

☐ The actual calculations are performed in a tight loop that calls `SetMapMode`, `GetClientRect`, and `DPtoLP` in quick succession.

☐ The results of the calculations are placed in an array and then sent in the form of a message to the Size dialog.

☐ The Size dialog places this information in its static controls with a series of calls to SendDlgItemMessage.

The next few paragraphs review each of these steps, revealing exactly how they work.

As you recall from looking at the response to the user-defined CM_SIZEBOX message, the modeless Size dialog is created by a call to CreateDialog. Immediately after this call, WinSize executes an InvalidateRect function call, which ensures that a WM_PAINT message is sent to the main window. (The WinSize_OnPaint function is listed on lines 197-240 of WINSIZE.CPP.)

The are four major steps to using the WinSize_OnPaint function:

☐ Copy the user-selected mapping mode into the current device context.

☐ Copy the user-selected viewport origin into the current device context.

☐ Draw the user-selected shape (whether it's a square or an ellipse).

☐ If the Size dialog is on-screen, fill it with the appropriate data.

You have already had a look at how the mapping mode and the viewport origin are set in a Window with calls to SetMapMode and SetViewPortOrg. Drawing a rectangle or an ellipse is, for the most part, a simple matter of defining a RECT that encompasses the particular shape. This subject is covered in-depth in Chapter 18, "GDI and MetaFiles."

This leaves only the fourth part of the WinSize_OnPaint function, which is not executed unless the Size dialog has been created and is made visible on-screen:

```
if (hSizeBox != 0)
  FillSizeBox(hwnd, PaintDC);
```

hSizeBox is the HWND of the Size Dialog. If hSizeBox is not zero, the non-API FillSizeBox procedure is called, and the Size dialog is filled with the window's coordinates (see Figure 16.1.)

The FillSizeBox procedure (line 182) gets passed the main window's HWINDOW and a handle to the current device context:

```
void FillSizeBox(HWND hwnd, HDC PaintDC)
{
  TSizeData    SizeData;
  for (int i = 0; i < 6; i++)
  {
    SetMapMode(PaintDC, Modes[i]);
    GetClientRect(hwnd, &SizeData[i]);
    DPtoLP(PaintDC, (LPPOINT)&SizeData[i], 2);
  }
```

```
    SendMessage(hSizeBox, WM_SETDATA, 0, (long)&SizeData);
}
```

This code fragment shows how WinSize iterates through the six mapping modes (discussed in Chapter 15, "Dialog Boxes and Mapping Modes"). It does so by referencing the following enumerated type, which contains a list of the relevant constants.

```
int Modes[] = {MM_TEXT, MM_LOMETRIC, MM_HIMETRIC,
               MM_LOENGLISH, MM_HIENGLISH, MM_TWIPS};
```

The first of the six times `SetMapMode` is called, the `MM_TEXT` constant is used; the second time, the `MM_LOMETRIC` is brought on stage, followed by `MM_HIMETRIC`, and so on.

After the mapping mode is set, the window's current location, expressed in *device coordinates*, is copied into a structure of type `TSizeData`:

```
typedef RECT TSizeData[6];
```

`TSizeData` is an array of our old friend `RECT`, which is just a structure used to define the coordinates of a rectangle by specifying the points comprising its upper-left and lower-right corners.

Of course, the purpose of the Size dialog is to give the window's dimensions, not in device coordinates, but in logical coordinates. As a result, a call is made to the `DPtoLP` function, which translates device points to logical points.

Making the Data Visible

At this stage of the game, the WinSize program has the numbers it wants to display. The only thing left to do is to get the numbers out where the viewer can see them.

This is accomplished by first sending the numbers to the Size dialog's window procedure:

```
SendMessage(hSizeBox, WM_SETDATA, 0, (long)&SizeData);
```

Sending information to a dialog is exactly like sending information to a control. There are no new techniques to learn and no new concepts to grasp. The only portion of this code that might be confusing is the typecast in the last parameter. There, WinSize opts to treat the address of the `SizeData` array as a 4-byte `long`.

Of course, the `WM_SETDATA` message is a user-defined message, so it's up to the WinSize program to respond to it (line 501):

```
case WM_SETDATA:
  lpSizeData = (void *)lParam;
  memcpy(SizeData, lpSizeData, sizeof(TSizeData));
  for (i = 0; i < 6; i++)
    {
    sprintf(S, "%d", SizeData[i].left);
    SendDlgItemMessage(hDlg, Indexs[i] + 1,
                        WM_SETTEXT, 0, long(S));
    sprintf(S, "%d", SizeData[i].right);
    SendDlgItemMessage(hDlg, Indexs[i] + 2,
                        WM_SETTEXT, 0, long(S));
    sprintf(S, "%d", SizeData[i].top);
    SendDlgItemMessage(hDlg, Indexs[i] + 3,
                        WM_SETTEXT, 0, long(S));
    sprintf(S, "%d", SizeData[i].bottom);
    SendDlgItemMessage(hDlg, Indexs[i] + 4,
                        WM_SETTEXT, 0, long(S));
    }
  return TRUE;
```

In this case, WinSize must battle with the Windows messaging system without the protecting armor of the WINDOWSX macros. As a result, it's necessary to perform the aesthetically embarrassing task of converting the data referenced by LPARAM into something that can be readily utilized:

```
TSIZEDATA lpSizeData = (void *)lParam;
memcpy(SizeData, lpSizeData, sizeof(TSizeData));
```

The code casts LPARAM as a pointer and then copies the data addressed by the pointer into a variable of type TSizeData.

Now that WinSize has the data in usable form, it converts it into a string and sends it to the static controls on the dialog's surface:

```
sprintf(S, "%d", SizeData[i].left);
SendDlgItemMessage(hDlg, Indexs[i] + 1,
                        WM_SETTEXT, 0, long(S));
```

This code introduces the SendDlgItemMessage function, which acts as a convenient alternative to the SendMessage function. The problem with SendMessage is that it requires an HWND before it can send a message to a control. Obviously, it would be very complicated to keep track of the HWND for each control in a dialog. SendDlgItemMessage lightens the programmer's burden by enabling him or her to use a control's ID in lieu of its HWND.

The *SendDlgItemMessage*

```
SendDlgItemMessage(HWND, int, UINT, WPARAM, LPARAM);
```

Here are the parameters to `SendDlgItemMessage`:

HWND hwndDlg;	HWND of dialog box containing the control
int idDlgItem;	ID of the control
UINT uMsg;	Message sent to the control
WPARAM wParam;	2-byte parameter
LPARAM lParam;	4-byte parameter

Use the `SendDlgItemMessage` function to send a message to a control located inside a dialog. This function requires the HWND of the dialog and the ID of the control in its first two parameters. After that, everything is exactly the same as with `SendMessage`. In other words, the next three parameters are the message itself, and then the standard WPARAM and LPARAM fields. There's nothing tricky about `SendDlgItemMessage`—it's simply a convenient way to call `SendMessage` when you are working with the controls of a dialog.

Example:

```
SendDlgItemMessage(hDlg, ID_CONTROL, WM_SETTEXT, 0, long(S));
```

It's important to understand the close relationship between the `SendMessage` and `SendDlgItemMessage` calls. For instance, the following two calls are entirely equivalent:

```
SendMessage(GetDlgItem(hDlg,Indexs[i] + 1),WM_SETTEXT,0,long(S));
SendDlgItemMessage(hDlg, Indexs[i] + 1, WM_SETTEXT, 0, long(S));
```

`SendDlgItemMessage` lets you sidestep the call to `GetDlgItem` (see following explanation). Otherwise, it's exactly the same as `SendMessage`.

The *GetDlgItem* Function

```
GetDlgItem(HWND, int);
```

`GetDlgItem` can be used to snag the HWINDOW of any control that happens to catch your fancy. It's a function programmers often overlook until the crucial moment in which it becomes absolutely vital to their program; then, they simply have to have it.

Here are the parameters to `GetDlgItem`:

HWND hwndDlg;	HWND of the dialog which owns the control
int idControl;	The ID of the control

The return value, of course, is the HWND of the control.

Example:

```
GetDlgItem(hDlg, ID_CONTROL);
```

For setting text in a dialog—that's the end of the story. It's been such a short story primarily because the idea of sending a message has been one of the primary themes of this book. By now, the SendMessage, PostMessage, and SendDlgItemMessage functions should be old hat.

To make the code in this section work, WinSize had to

☐ Create a dialog by calling MakeProcInstance and CreateDialog

☐ Fill out an array with calls to GetMapMode, GetClientRect, and DPtoLP

☐ Send the array to a dialog with SendMessage

☐ Unpackage the array with a typecast

☐ Send the individual portions of the array to the appropriate control through SendDlgItemMessage

Master this process and digest it so thoroughly that it becomes second nature; then, you can begin to lay serious claim to being a real Windows programmer. In fact, you are laying one of the key stepping stones that will enable you to advance from intermediate level to the beginnings of real work on advanced issues.

Of course, setting the text of controls in a dialog is only half the story. The second portion of the tale is getting the text back out. Because there is no need to get the text from the Size dialog, a discussion of this process is included in the next section (where the Make Shape dialog is the center of focus).

Theory: A Modal Dialog Talks to Its Parent

The Make Shape dialog is a modal dialog that does something a bit unusual: it interacts quite frequently with the program's main window. Specifically, you can change the shape of the figures on the main window by pushing buttons on the modal Make Shape dialog. This demonstrates that a modal dialog isn't isolated from its parent window, or from any other part of a program.

This is an important point, and I want to repeat it from a slightly different angle. Modal dialogs prevent users from manipulating the main body of a program. For instance, users can't get at the main menu of a program while a modal dialog is on-screen. This same restriction doesn't hold true for programmers. Nothing prevents programmers from sending messages from a dialog to the main body of a program. In other words, from the programmer's point of view, the lines of communication are still wide open—at least in one direction.

Using the linear paradigm, programmers got used to the idea that instruction A would be executed before instruction B, and that C would be executed before instruction D. This orderly progression made it possible for DOS programmers to step through their programs from beginning to end with the debugger. As you've probably noticed by now, the same thing isn't possible in a Windows program. Instead, you must place breakpoints on sections of code you want to examine and then wait until the relevant line is executed and the breakpoint takes effect.

In the WinSize program, the `DialogBox` procedure is called; while it's executing, the `WinSize_OnPaint` and `FillSizeBox` routines may be executed. As you'll see in a few moments, this is accomplished by sending a message from the dialog box procedure to the main window. The end effect is that WinSize has access to most of the functionality associated with its main window, even while the "modal" `DialogBox` procedure is executing.

Note: To the uninitiated, a process like this appears to be Windows magic. You're at point D in your program, the `DialogBox` procedure. Suddenly, you skip to point B, the `WinSize_OnPaint` procedure, and then to the `FillSizeBox` procedure, and then back to point D again. (Use the debugger to see how this works.) Whether this newly found freedom is a blessing or a curse is a question that must be answered by each individual user. Some people enjoy it, some don't. It's up to you.

Practice: Getting Data from the Make Shape Dialog

The Make Shape dialog enables the user to take control of the WinSize program. It's a pilot seat from which the user can "steer" the program in whatever direction seems appropriate.

The first order of business in the Make Shape dialog procedure is to initialize the radio buttons on the dialogs surface:

```
case WM_INITDIALOG:
  SendDlgItemMessage(hwnd, ID_RTEXT, BM_SETCHECK, 1, 0L);
  SendDlgItemMessage(hwnd, ID_RECT, BM_SETCHECK, 1, 0L);
  SendDlgItemMessage(hwnd, ID_ORGUPLEFT, BM_SETCHECK, 1, 0L);
  SendDlgItemMessage(hwnd, ID_COMPCORDS, BM_SETCHECK, 1, 0L);
  return TRUE;
```

By now, this type of code should be quite familiar. The goal is simply to set the default button for each of the major groups on-screen. This is accomplished by sending BM_SETCHECK messages to each of the appropriate controls. Nothing could be simpler.

The heart of the Make Shape dialog procedure is its response to WM_COMMAND messages. Because this is a long and involved process, WinSize handles it in a separate function called DoRectCommand.

The DoRectCommand function (line 343) features a lengthy case statement that executes whenever the user selects one of the push buttons or radio buttons on the dialog's surface. For instance, if the user selects the Draw button, the following code is executed:

```
case ID_DRAW:
  GetUserCords(hwnd);
  InvalidateRect(GetParent(hwnd), NULL, TRUE);
  return TRUE;
```

As you might recall, the edit controls in the Make Shape dialog can be manipulated by the user whenever he or she wants to specify a new set of coordinates for the shape shown on the main window. The purpose of these lines of code is to get the coordinates from the dialog's edit controls and to use these coordinates to describe the size of a shape drawn in the main window's client area.

The GetUserCords function demonstrates one way to retrieve data from edit controls in a dialog (line 277):

```
void GetUserCords(HWND hwnd)
{
  char S[100];

  GetWindowText(GetDlgItem(hwnd, ID_RLEFT), S, 100);
  RLeft = atoi(S);
  GetWindowText(GetDlgItem(hwnd, ID_RTOP), S, 100);
  RTop = atoi(S);
  GetWindowText(GetDlgItem(hwnd, ID_RRIGHT), S, 100);
  RRight = atoi(S);
  GetWindowText(GetDlgItem(hwnd, ID_RBOTTOM), S, 100);
  RBottom = atoi(S);
}
```

16

In this particular case, WinSize uses `GetWindowText` rather than a `SendDlgItemMessage` call accompanied by a `WM_GETTEXT` message. I'm showing you this choice so you'll have a wide range of options.

The GetWindowText Function

`int GetWindowText(HWND, LPSTR, int)`

The actual call to `GetWindowText` is very simple. The function requires only three parameters:

☐ The first parameter is the `HWND` of the control containing the text.

☐ The second parameter is a string to hold the information in the control.

☐ The last parameter is the longest possible length of the string.

Example:

`GetWindowText(hControl, MyStr, 100);`

After the text has been retrieved from the control, it's translated into numeric form and used in `WinSize_OnPaint` to describe the `RECT`. A rectangle or ellipse is drawn inside the `RECT`.

Once again, the experience you've had in this book allows me to outline this relatively complex process in a few short paragraphs. Naturally, this doesn't mean that getting data from dialogs is not an extremely important part of windows programming. The issue is that you've already seen an in-depth description of how to transfer data in and out of an edit control static text, push button, radio button, or other control. None of the principles involve change in any significant way because you're working with a dialog instead of a window.

What it all boils down to is that working with dialogs is simply a matter of common sense. For instance, if you want to display a street address from a database in a dialog, here are the steps you would follow:

☐ Read the address out of a text or binary file and place it inside a structure.

☐ Send this structure to a dialog, just as you sent an array to the dialog in the last section.

☐ Use `SetWindowText` or `SendDlgItemMessage` to set each individual field of the structure in a separate edit control.

☐ Wait until the user presses a button signaling that he or she is finished editing or viewing the address.

- ☐ Retrieve the text from the edit controls with `GetWindowText` or `SendDlgItemMessage`.

- ☐ Send the structure back to the main body of the program with a call to `SendMessage`.

- ☐ If the structure has changed, have the main body of the program write the new data to a disk file.

Responding to Changes in Mapping Mode

Before closing this portion of the chapter, it might be worthwhile to take a brief glance at the code that gets executed whenever the user changes mapping modes by selecting a radio button (line 352):

```
case ID_RTEXT:
  ModeCase = TEXT;
  DoDraw(hwnd);
  return TRUE;
```

The `ModeCase` variable is one of several enumerated types declared in WINSIZE.H. It's used to keep track of the user's current selections:

```
enum TModeCase {TEXT, LOMETRIC, HIMETRIC, LOENGLISH,
                HIENGLISH, TWIPS, ISOTROPIC, ANSITROPIC};
enum TOriginMode {ORG_UPLEFT, ORG_LOWLEFT, ORG_CENTER};
enum TShape {RECTANGLE, CIRCLE};
```

All the radio buttons on the dialog's surface are reflected in the values encompassed by these enumerated types. Therefore, the first order of business after a user selects a button is to set the values of the associated enumerated type. This is demonstrated (in the preceding code lines) where the enumerated variable `ModeCase` is set to `TEXT`.

The next thing to check is whether the user or the WinSize program will select the coordinates (line 333):

```
void DoDraw(HWND hwnd)
{
  if (UseCompCords)
    MakeShape(hwnd);
  SetRectText(hwnd);
}
```

If the chore is left to WinSize, the `MakeShape` procedure is called and the current device coordinates are translated into Window coordinates with calls to `GetClientRect` and `LPtoDP`. This is the same process used in the `FillSizeBox` procedure.

While still inside MakeShape (line 294), the WinSize program calculates the dimensions of the shape to be drawn:

```
case ORG_CENTER:
  RLeft = -(R.right / 3);
  RTop = -(R.bottom / 3);
  RRight = (R.right / 3);
  RBottom = (R.bottom / 3);
  break;
```

The actual size of the shape isn't important. Instead, the preceding code is designed to assure that the shape is always visible and always covers the same percentage of area in proportion to the window's total size. Also, the WinSize program makes sure that the shape covers the same area in terms of device coordinates, as long as any one particular viewpoint origin is selected. The logical coordinates, of course, change radically every time the user selects a new mapping mode. This enables the user to see the effects of the various mapping modes on the logical coordinate system.

Controlling the Color of a Dialog

It's almost time to bring the discussion of the WinSize program to a close. The only thing left to do is see how the colors for the dialog are changed.

When the Size dialog is being initialized, WinSize carefully sets up the appropriate colors for the dialog (lines 488-499). This is done by responding to WM_CTLCOLOR messages:

```
case WM_CTLCOLOR:
  switch(HIWORD(lParam))
    {
    case CTLCOLOR_STATIC:
      SetTextColor((HDC)wParam, RGB(255, 0, 0));
      SetBkMode((HDC)wParam, TRANSPARENT);
      return (BOOL) GetStockObject(BLACK_BRUSH);

    case CTLCOLOR_DLG:
      return (BOOL) GetStockObject(BLACK_BRUSH);
    }
  return (BOOL) NULL;
```

WM_CTLCOLOR messages get sent to a dialog in great flurries, one message for each of the possible controls. In the preceding case, WinSize sets static controls so they have red text on a black background. Notice the use of the SetBkMode call, which makes the background of a static text transparently reflect the color lying beneath it! In this case, the background is simply the surface of the dialog set to the color designated by the standard BLACK_BRUSH.

Note: The previous code fragments respond to the CTLCOLOR_STATIC and CTLCOLOR_DLG identifiers. Following is a complete list of these constants; they're sent to a dialog whenever one of the relevant controls needs to be updated:

CTLCOLOR_BTN	Changes the color of buttons (obsolete)
CTLCOLOR_DLG	Changes the color of dialog boxes
CTLCOLOR_EDIT	Changes the color of edit controls
CTLCOLOR_LISTBOX	Changes the color of list boxes
CTLCOLOR_MSGBOX	Changes the color of message boxes
CTLCOLOR_SCROLLBAR	Changes the color of scrollbars
CTLCOLOR_STATIC	Changes the color of static controls

The parameters, listed in the preceding note, are passed in the high word of the LPARAM that accompanies every CTL_COLOR message. The low word of the LPARAM contains the HWND of the control, which is currently being painted. This means that you can distinguish between individual controls, even when they are in the same class, thereby painting one static control red and the next green. Finally, the HDC of the control is passed in the WPARAM parameter, as shown in the previous code fragment.

The Make Shape dialog also responds to WM_CTLCOLOR messages. You might want to glance at that code, because it makes use of brushes which aren't just stock objects. When examining the code, notice that the brushes being used are created in the WM_CREATE message handler function for the main window and destroyed in the WM_DESTROY message handler.

DO   **DON'T**

DO change the color of dialogs by responding to a WM_CTLCOLOR message.

DON'T try to change the color of a dialog in the same way you change the color of a window.

DON'T expect Win32 to handle WM_CTLCOLOR exactly as the 16-bit code shown here. This is one of the few places where 16- and 32-bit code diverge.

The Mapper Program

After all the hard work you've been doing, it's time to relax with another excerpt from the Snake game (see Listing 16.1). This is a visual programming tool designed to enable programmers to quickly and easily sketch the background of a two-dimensional game board.

Listing 16.1. A program that enables you to design custom playing boards for the Snake program.

```
 1: ///////////////////////////////////////
 2: //   Program Name: MAPPER.CPP
 3: //   Programmer: Charlie Calvert
 4: //   Description: Mapper windows program
 5: //   Date: 7/18/93
 6: ///////////////////////////////////////
 7:
 8: #define STRICT
 9: #include <windows.h>
10: #include <windowsx.h>
11: #pragma hdrstop
12: #include <string.h>
13: #include <stdio.h>
14: #include <stdlib.h>
15: #include "mapper.h"
16: #pragma warning (disable: 4068)
17: #pragma warning (disable: 4100)
18: // ----------------------------------
19: // Interface
20: // ----------------------------------
21:
22: // Variables
23: static char szAppName[] = "Mapper";
24: static HWND MainWindow;
25: static HINSTANCE hInstance;
26: static FARPROC lpfnNewBitProc, lpfnArrowBox;
27: char Map[MaxY][MaxX];
28: WNDPROC StatProc1, StatProc2;
29: HBITMAP Grass, Road;
30: TDAT Dat;
31:
32: // ----------------------------------
33: // Initialization
34: // ----------------------------------
35:
36: ///////////////////////////////////////
37: // Program entry point
38: ///////////////////////////////////////
39: #pragma argsused
```

```
40: int PASCAL WinMain(HINSTANCE hInst, HINSTANCE hPrevInstance,
41:                     LPSTR  lpszCmdParam, int nCmdShow)
42: {
43:   MSG  Msg;
44:
45:   if (!hPrevInstance)
46:     if (!Register(hInst))
47:       return FALSE;
48:
49:   MainWindow = Create(hInst, nCmdShow);
50:   if (MainWindow)
51:     return FALSE;
52:   while (GetMessage(&Msg, NULL, 0, 0))
53:   {
54:       TranslateMessage(&Msg);
55:       DispatchMessage(&Msg);
56:   }
57:
58:   return Msg.wParam;
59: }
60:
61: ///////////////////////////////////////
62: // Register the window
63: ///////////////////////////////////////
64: BOOL Register(HINSTANCE hInst)
65: {
66:   WNDCLASS WndClass;
67:
68:   WndClass.style         = CS_HREDRAW ¦ CS_VREDRAW;
69:   WndClass.lpfnWndProc   = WndProc;
70:   WndClass.cbClsExtra    = 0;
71:   WndClass.cbWndExtra    = 0;
72:   WndClass.hInstance     = hInst;
73:   WndClass.hIcon         = LoadIcon(NULL, IDI_APPLICATION);
74:   WndClass.hCursor       = LoadCursor(NULL, IDC_ARROW);
75:   WndClass.hbrBackground = GetStockBrush(WHITE_BRUSH);
76:   WndClass.lpszMenuName  = NULL;
77:   WndClass.lpszClassName = szAppName;
78:
79:   return RegisterClass (&WndClass);
80: }
81:
82:
83: ///////////////////////////////////////////
84: // Create the window
85: ///////////////////////////////////////////
86: HWND Create(HINSTANCE hInst, int nCmdShow)
87: {
88:
89:   nCmdShow = SW_MAXIMIZE;
```

continues

Listing 16.1. continued

```
 90:    hInstance = hInst;
 91:
 92:    HWND hWindow = CreateWindow(szAppName, szAppName,
 93:                                    WS_POPUP,
 94:                                    CW_USEDEFAULT, CW_USEDEFAULT,
 95:                                    CW_USEDEFAULT, CW_USEDEFAULT,
 96:                                    NULL, NULL, hInstance, NULL);
 97:
 98:    if (hWindow == NULL)
 99:      return hWindow;
100:
101:    ShowWindow(hWindow, nCmdShow);
102:    UpdateWindow(hWindow);
103:
104:    return hWindow;
105: }
106:
107: // -------------------------------------
108: // WndProc and Implementation
109: // -------------------------------------
110:
111: /////////////////////////////////////////
112: // The Window Procedure
113: /////////////////////////////////////////
114: LRESULT CALLBACK _export WndProc(HWND hwnd, UINT Message,
115:                                    WPARAM wParam, LPARAM lParam)
116: {
117:    switch(Message)
118:    {
119:      case WM_DIALOG: {
120:        FARPROC OptionsBox =
121:          MakeProcInstance((FARPROC)OptionsDlgProc, hInstance);
122:          DialogBox(hInstance, "Options", hwnd, (DLGPROC)OptionsBox);
123:          FreeProcInstance(OptionsBox);
124:        return FALSE;
125:      }
126:
127:      case WM_HELP:
128:      {
129:        char *S = "MAPPER\n\n"
130:           "Use this program to design screens for SNAKO\n\n"
131:           "RSCREEN takes you one screen to the right\n"
132:           "LSCREEN takes you one screen to the left\n"
133:           "LEFT takes you one column to the left\n"
134:           "RIGHT takes you one column to the right\n"
135:           "To save a screen open the options DIALOG";
136:        MessageBox(hwnd, S, "Info",
137:                 MB_OK | MB_ICONINFORMATION);
138:        return FALSE;
```

```
139:      }
140:      HANDLE_MSG(hwnd, WM_CREATE, Mapper_OnCreate);
141:      HANDLE_MSG(hwnd, WM_DESTROY, Mapper_OnDestroy);
142:      HANDLE_MSG(hwnd, WM_LBUTTONDOWN, Mapper_OnLButtonDown);
143:      HANDLE_MSG(hwnd, WM_RBUTTONDOWN, Mapper_OnRButtonDown);
144:      HANDLE_MSG(hwnd, WM_PAINT, Mapper_OnPaint);
145:      default: return Mapper_DefProc(hwnd, Message, wParam, lParam);
146:   }
147: }
148:
149: int ReadArray(HWND hwnd)
150: {
151:   FILE * fp;
152:
153:   if ((fp = fopen("Screen.Dta", "r")) == NULL)
154:   {
155:     MessageBox(hwnd, "Can't find SCREEN.DTA" , NULL, MB_OK);
156:     return 0;
157:   }
158:
159:   fread(&Map, sizeof(Map), 1, fp);
160:   fclose(fp);
161:
162:   for (int i = 0; i < MaxY; i++)
163:     for (int j = 0; j < MaxX; j++)
164:       if (Map[i][j] != 1)
165:         Map[i][j] = 2;
166:
167:   return 1;
168: }
169:
170: /////////////////////////////////////
171: // Handle WM_CREATE
172: /////////////////////////////////////
173: #pragma argsused
174: BOOL Mapper_OnCreate(HWND hwnd, CREATESTRUCT FAR* lpCreateStruct)
175: {
176:   Grass = LoadBitmap(hInstance, "Grass");
177:   Road = LoadBitmap(hInstance, "Road");
178:
179:   if ((!Grass) ¦¦ (!Road))
180:   {
181:     MessageBox(hwnd, "Bitmaps missing!",
182:                 "Fatal", MB_OK ¦ MB_ICONSTOP);
183:     return FALSE;
184:   }
185:
186:   int X = GetSystemMetrics(SM_CXSCREEN);
187:
188:   if (X == 1024)
```

continues

Listing 16.1. continued

```
189:  {
190:    Dat.GrassX = Dat.GrassY = 32;
191:    Dat.SizeX = Dat.SizeY = 32;
192:  }
193:
194:  if (X == 800)
195:  {
196:    Dat.GrassX = Dat.GrassY = 25;
197:    Dat.SizeX = Dat.SizeY = 25;
198:  }
199:
200:  if (X == 640)
201:  {
202:    Dat.GrassX = Dat.GrassY = 20;
203:    Dat.SizeX = Dat.SizeY = 20;
204:  }
205:
206:  Dat.SPos = 0;
207:  Dat.MenuSpace = 3;
208:
209:  lpfnArrowBox =
210:    MakeProcInstance((FARPROC)ArrowDlgProc, hInstance);
211:    CreateDialog(hInstance, "Arrows", hwnd,
                     (DLGPROC)lpfnArrowBox);
212:    ReadArray(hwnd);
213:
214:  return TRUE;
215: }
216:
217: ///////////////////////////////////////
218: // Handle WM_DESTROY
219: ///////////////////////////////////////
220: #pragma argsused
221: void Mapper_OnDestroy(HWND hwnd)
222: {
223:   DeleteObject(Road);
224:   DeleteObject(Grass);
225:   FreeProcInstance(lpfnArrowBox);
226:   PostQuitMessage(0);
227: }
228:
229: ///////////////////////////////////////////////
231: // OnRButtonDown
232: ///////////////////////////////////////////////
233: #pragma argsused
234: void Mapper_OnRButtonDown(HWND hwnd, BOOL fDoubleClick,
235:                           int x, int y, UINT keyFlags)
236: {
237:   char BoxX = (x / Dat.GrassX) + Dat.SPos;
238:   char BoxY = (y / Dat.GrassY) - Dat.MenuSpace;
```

```
239:   Map[BoxY][BoxX] = 2;
240:   InvalidateRect(hwnd, NULL, FALSE);
241: }
242:
243: /////////////////////////////////////////////////
244: // OnLButtonDown
245: /////////////////////////////////////////////////
246: #pragma argsused
247: void Mapper_OnLButtonDown(HWND hwnd, BOOL fDoubleClick,
248:                                int x, int y, UINT keyFlags)
249: {
250:   char BoxX = (x / Dat.GrassX) + Dat.SPos;
251:   char BoxY = (y / Dat.GrassY) - Dat.MenuSpace;
252:   Map[BoxY][BoxX] = 1;
253:   InvalidateRect(hwnd, NULL, FALSE);
254: }
255:
256: /////////////////////////////////////////////////
257: // PAINT Bitmaps
258: // The GrassX * MenuSpace leaves room for menu
259: /////////////////////////////////////////////////
260: void PaintBitmaps(HDC PaintDC, HDC GrassDC, HDC RoadDC)
261: {
262:   for (int i = 0; i < MaxY; i++)
263:     for (int j = Dat.SPos; j < MaxX; j++)
264:       {
265:         if (Map[i][j] == 1)
266:           BitBlt(PaintDC, (j - Dat.SPos) * Dat.GrassX,
267:                   (i * Dat.GrassY) + (Dat.GrassX * Dat.MenuSpace),
268:                   Dat.GrassX, Dat.GrassY, GrassDC, 0, 0, SRCCOPY);
269:         else
270:           BitBlt(PaintDC, (j - Dat.SPos) * Dat.GrassX,
271:                   (i * Dat.GrassY) + (Dat.GrassX * Dat.MenuSpace),
272:                   Dat.GrassX, Dat.GrassY, RoadDC, 0, 0, SRCCOPY);
273:       }
274: }
275:
276: /////////////////////////////////////////////////
277: // WM_PAINT
278: /////////////////////////////////////////////////
279: void Mapper_OnPaint(HWND hwnd)
280: {
281:   PAINTSTRUCT PaintStruct;
282:   HBITMAP OldGrass, OldRoad, OldGrass1, OldRoad1;
283:
284:   HDC PaintDC = BeginPaint(hwnd, &PaintStruct);
285:
286:   HDC TGrassDC = CreateCompatibleDC(PaintDC);
287:   HDC TRoadDC = CreateCompatibleDC(PaintDC);
288:   HDC GrassDC = CreateCompatibleDC(PaintDC);
```

continues

Listing 16.1. continued

```
289:    HDC RoadDC = CreateCompatibleDC(PaintDC);
290:    HBITMAP TGrass =
291:      CreateCompatibleBitmap(PaintDC, Dat.GrassX, Dat.GrassY);
292:    HBITMAP TRoad =
293:      CreateCompatibleBitmap(PaintDC, Dat.GrassX, Dat.GrassY);
294:
295:    OldGrass = SelectBitmap(TGrassDC, Grass);
296:    OldRoad = SelectBitmap(TRoadDC, Road);
297:    OldGrass1 = SelectBitmap(GrassDC, TGrass);
298:    OldRoad1 = SelectBitmap(RoadDC, TRoad);
299:
300:    StretchBlt(GrassDC, 0, 0, Dat.GrassX, Dat.GrassY,
301:                 TGrassDC, 0, 0, BITWIDTH, BITHEIGHT, SRCCOPY);
302:    StretchBlt(RoadDC, 0, 0, Dat.GrassX, Dat.GrassY,
303:                 TRoadDC, 0, 0, BITWIDTH, BITHEIGHT, SRCCOPY);
304:
305:    PaintBitmaps(PaintDC, GrassDC, RoadDC);
306:
307:    SelectBitmap(TGrassDC, OldGrass);
308:    SelectBitmap(TRoadDC, OldRoad);
309:    SelectBitmap(GrassDC, OldGrass1);
310:    SelectBitmap(RoadDC, OldRoad1);
311:    DeleteObject(TRoad);
312:    DeleteObject(TGrass);
313:
314:    DeleteDC(GrassDC);
315:    DeleteDC(RoadDC);
316:    DeleteDC(TGrassDC);
317:    DeleteDC(TRoadDC);
318:
319:    EndPaint(hwnd, &PaintStruct);
320: }
321:
322: // ------------------------------------
323: // The Dialog procs
324: // ------------------------------------
325:
326: /////////////////////////////////////
327: // Save Array
328: /////////////////////////////////////
329: int SaveArray(HWND hwnd)
330: {
331:    FILE * fp;
332:
333:    if ((fp = fopen("screen.dta", "w+")) == NULL)
334:    {
335:      MessageBox(hwnd, "Can't save SCREEN.DTA", NULL, MB_OK);
336:      return 0;
337:    }
```

```
338:
339:    fwrite(&Map, sizeof(Map), 1, fp);
340:    fclose(fp);
341:
342:    MessageBox(hwnd, "SCREEN.DTA saved", "Success", MB_OK);
343:
344:    return 1;
345: }
346:
347: /////////////////////////////////////
348: //   The Options Dialog Procedure
349: /////////////////////////////////////
350: #pragma argsused
351: BOOL CALLBACK OptionsDlgProc(HWND hDlg, WORD Message,
352:                              WPARAM wParam, LPARAM lParam)
353: {
354:    char S[100];
355:    HWND hwnd1, hwnd2;
356:
357:    switch(Message)
358:    {
359:      case WM_DESTROY:
360:        hwnd1 = GetDlgItem(hDlg, ID_BITMAP1);
361:        hwnd2 = GetDlgItem(hDlg, ID_BITMAP2);
362:        SubclassWindow(hwnd1, StatProc1);
363:        SubclassWindow(hwnd2, StatProc2);
364:        FreeProcInstance(lpfnNewBitProc);
365:        return TRUE;
366:
367:      case WM_INITDIALOG:
368:        itoa(Dat.GrassX, S, 10);
369:        SetWindowText(GetDlgItem(hDlg, ID_XSIZE), S);
370:        itoa(Dat.GrassY, S, 10);
371:        SetWindowText(GetDlgItem(hDlg, ID_YSIZE), S);
372:
373:        itoa(MaxX, S, 10);
374:        SetWindowText(GetDlgItem(hDlg, ID_NUMX), S);
375:        itoa(MaxY, S, 10);
376:        SetWindowText(GetDlgItem(hDlg, ID_NUMY), S);
377:
378:        lpfnNewBitProc =
379:        MakeProcInstance(FARPROC(BitmapProc), hInstance);
380:        hwnd1 = GetDlgItem(hDlg, ID_BITMAP1);
381:        StatProc1 = SubclassWindow(hwnd1, lpfnNewBitProc);
382:        hwnd2 = GetDlgItem(hDlg, ID_BITMAP2);
383:        StatProc2 = SubclassWindow(hwnd2, lpfnNewBitProc);
384:        return TRUE;
385:
386:      case WM_COMMAND:
387:        switch(wParam)
```

continues

Listing 16.1. continued

```
388:        {
389:          case IDOK:
390:          case IDCANCEL:
391:            EndDialog(hDlg, TRUE);
392:            return TRUE;
393:
394:          case ID_SAVE:
395:            SaveArray(hDlg);
396:            return TRUE;
397:
398:          case ID_HELP:
399:            PostMessage(GetParent(hDlg), WM_HELP, 0, 0);
400:            return TRUE;
401:        }
402:    }
403:    return FALSE;
404: }
405:
406:
407: BOOL ExitMapper(HWND hDlg)
408: {
409:    int Result = MessageBox(hDlg, "Are you sure you want to quit?",
410:                   "Are we thinking?", MB_YESNO | MB_ICONQUESTION);
411:    if (Result == IDYES)
412:    {
413:      SendMessage(GetParent(hDlg), WM_CLOSE, 0, 0);
414:      return TRUE;
415:    }
416:    else
417:      return FALSE;
418: }
419:
420: /////////////////////////////////////
421: // HandleCommand
422: /////////////////////////////////////
423: BOOL HandleCommand(HWND hDlg, WPARAM wParam)
424: {
425:    switch(wParam)
426:    {
427:      case IDOK:
428:      case IDCANCEL:
429:        PostMessage(hDlg, WM_CLOSE, 0, 0);
430:        return TRUE;
431:
432:      case ID_RIGHT:
433:        Dat.SPos++;
434:        InvalidateRect(GetParent(hDlg), NULL, TRUE);
435:        return TRUE;
436:
```

```
437:     case ID_LEFT:
438:       Dat.SPos--;
439:       if (Dat.SPos < 0)
440:         Dat.SPos = 0;
441:       InvalidateRect(GetParent(hDlg), NULL, TRUE);
442:       return TRUE;
443:
444:     case ID_RSCREEN:
445:       if (Dat.SPos < JUMPSPACE)
446:         Dat.SPos = JUMPSPACE;
447:       else
448:         if (Dat.SPos < JUMPSPACE * 2)
449:           Dat.SPos = JUMPSPACE * 2;
450:         else
451:           if (Dat.SPos < JUMPSPACE * 3)
452:             Dat.SPos = JUMPSPACE * 3;
453:           else
454:             Dat.SPos = JUMPSPACE * 3;
455:       InvalidateRect(GetParent(hDlg), NULL, TRUE);
456:       return TRUE;
457:
458:     case ID_LSCREEN:
459:       if (Dat.SPos <= JUMPSPACE)
460:         Dat.SPos = 0;
461:       else
462:         if (Dat.SPos <= JUMPSPACE * 2)
463:           Dat.SPos = JUMPSPACE;
464:         else
465:           if (Dat.SPos <= JUMPSPACE * 3)
466:             Dat.SPos = JUMPSPACE * 2;
467:           else
468:             Dat.SPos = JUMPSPACE * 3;
469:       InvalidateRect(GetParent(hDlg), NULL, TRUE);
470:       return TRUE;
471:
472:     case ID_DIALOG:
473:       PostMessage(GetParent(hDlg), WM_DIALOG, 0, 0);
474:       break;
475:
476:     case ID_HELP:
477:       PostMessage(GetParent(hDlg), WM_HELP, 0, 0);
478:       break;
479:
480:     case ID_QUIT:
481:       ExitMapper(hDlg);
482:       return TRUE;
483:   }
484:
485:   return FALSE;
486: }
```

continues

Listing 16.1. continued

```
487:
488: /////////////////////////////////
489: //  The Bitmap Dialog Procedure
490: /////////////////////////////////
491: LRESULT CALLBACK _export BitmapProc(HWND hwnd, UINT Message,
492:                                          WPARAM wParam, LPARAM lParam)
493: {
494:   WORD id;
495:   LRESULT lResult = 0;
496:   BOOL CallOrig = TRUE;
497:   HDC PaintDC, MemDC;
498:   HBITMAP OldBitmap;
499:   PAINTSTRUCT PaintStruct;
500:
501:   id = GetWindowWord(hwnd, GWW_ID);
502:
503:   switch(Message)
504:   {
505:     BITMAP Bits;
506:
507:     case WM_PAINT:
508:       PaintDC = BeginPaint(hwnd, &PaintStruct);
509:
510:       MemDC = CreateCompatibleDC(PaintDC);
511:       switch(id)
512:       {
513:         case ID_BITMAP1:
514:           OldBitmap = SelectBitmap(MemDC, Road);
515:           break;
516:         case ID_BITMAP2:
517:           OldBitmap = SelectBitmap(MemDC, Grass);
518:           break;
519:         case ID_BITMAP3:
520:           break;
521:         case ID_BITMAP4:
522:           break;
523:       }
524:       GetObject(Grass, sizeof(BITMAP), &Bits);
525:       BitBlt(PaintDC, 1, 1, Bits.bmWidth, Bits.bmHeight,
526:             MemDC, 0, 0, SRCCOPY);
527:       SelectBitmap(MemDC, OldBitmap);
528:       DeleteDC(MemDC);
529:
530:       EndPaint(hwnd, &PaintStruct);
531:       CallOrig = FALSE;
532:       break;
533:   }
534:
535:   if (CallOrig)
```

```
536:    if (id == ID_BITMAP1)
537:      lResult = CallWindowProc(StatProc1, hwnd,
538:                                    Message, wParam, lParam);
539:    else
540:      lResult = CallWindowProc(StatProc2, hwnd,
541:                                    Message, wParam, lParam);
542:
543:   return lResult;
544: }
545:
546: //////////////////////////////////////
547: //   The Arrow Dialog Procedure
548: //////////////////////////////////////
549: #pragma argsused
550: BOOL CALLBACK ArrowDlgProc(HWND hDlg, WORD Message,
551:                              WPARAM wParam, LPARAM lParam)
552: {
553:   switch(Message)
554:   {
555:     case WM_COMMAND:
556:       return HandleCommand(hDlg, wParam);
557:
558:     case WM_CLOSE:
559:       ExitMapper(hDlg);
560:       return TRUE;
561:   }
562:   return FALSE;
563: }
```

Listing 16.2 shows the header file for Mapper.

Type   **Listing 16.2. MAPPER.H.**

```
 1: /////////////////////////////////////////
 2: //   Program Name: MAPPER.H
 3: //   Programmer: Charlie Calvert
 4: //   Description: Mapper Windows program
 5: //   Date: 07/18/93
 6: /////////////////////////////////////////
 7:
 8: // Const
 9: #define WM_DIALOG (WM_USER + 0x100)
10: #define WM_HELP (WM_USER + 0x101)
11:
12: // Arrows Dialog
13: #define ID_LEFT      150
14: #define ID_RIGHT     251
15: #define ID_DIALOG    252
16: #define ID_QUIT      253
```

continues

Listing 16.2. continued

```
17: #define ID_START    254
18: #define ID_END      255
19: #define ID_RSCREEN  256
20: #define ID_LSCREEN  257
21: #define ID_HELP     1001
22:
23: // Options dialog constants
24: #define ID_XSIZE    101
25: #define ID_YSIZE    102
26: #define ID_NUMX     103
27: #define ID_NUMY     104
28: #define ID_SAVE     105
29: #define ID_BITMAP1 120
30: #define ID_BITMAP2 121
31: #define ID_BITMAP3 122
32: #define ID_BITMAP4 123
33:
34: #define MaxY 21
35: #define MaxX 4 * 32
36:
37: #define BITHEIGHT 32
38: #define BITWIDTH 25
39:
40: #define JUMPSPACE 32
41:
42: // Types
43: struct TDAT
44: {
45:   int MenuSpace;
46:   int SizeX, SizeY;
47:   int SPos;
48:   int GrassX;
49:   int GrassY;
50: };
51:
52: // Declarations for class Mapper
53: #define Mapper_DefProc     DefWindowProc
54: BOOL Mapper_OnCreate(HWND hwnd,
55:                       CREATESTRUCT FAR* lpCreateStruct);
56: void Mapper_OnDestroy(HWND hwnd);
57: void Mapper_OnMouseMove(HWND hwnd, int x, int y, UINT keyFlags);
58: void Mapper_OnLButtonDown(HWND hwnd, BOOL fDoubleClick,
59:                           int x, int y, UINT keyFlags);
60: void Mapper_OnRButtonDown(HWND hwnd, BOOL fDoubleClick,
61:                           int x, int y, UINT keyFlags);
62: void Mapper_OnPaint(HWND hwnd);
63:
64: // Procs
65: LRESULT CALLBACK _export WndProc(HWND hwnd, UINT Message,
66:                                  WPARAM wParam, LPARAM lParam);
```

```
67: LRESULT CALLBACK _export BitmapProc(HWND hwnd, UINT Message,
68:                                 WPARAM wParam, LPARAM lParam);
69: BOOL Register(HINSTANCE hInst);
70: HWND Create(HINSTANCE hInst, int nCmdShow);
71: BOOL CALLBACK OptionsDlgProc(HWND hDlg, WORD Message,
72:                                 WPARAM wParam, LPARAM lParam);
73: BOOL CALLBACK ArrowDlgProc(HWND hDlg, WORD Message,
74:                                 WPARAM wParam, LPARAM lParam);
```

Listing 16.3 shows the resource file for Mapper.

Listing 16.3. MAPPER.RC.

```
 1: //////////////////////////////////////////////////////////////
 2: //    Program Name: MAPPER.RC
 3: //    Programmer: Charlie Calvert
 4: //    Description: Resource file for Mapper Windows program
 5: //    Date: 9/08/93
 6: //////////////////////////////////////////////////////////////
 7:
 8: #include "windows.h"
 9: #include "mapper.h"
10:
11: ROAD BITMAP "road2.bmp"
12: GRASS BITMAP "grass.bmp"
13:
14: #define STY_PUSH WS_CHILD | WS_VISIBLE | WS_TABSTOP
15: #define STY_TEXT SS_BLACKFRAME | WS_CHILD | WS_VISIBLE | WS_GROUP
16: #define STY_TEXT2 SS_LEFT | WS_CHILD | WS_VISIBLE | WS_GROUP
17:
18: Options DIALOG 37, 35, 184, 118
19: STYLE DS_MODALFRAME | WS_POPUP | WS_CAPTION | WS_SYSMENU
20: CAPTION "Options"
21: BEGIN
22:     PUSHBUTTON "Close", IDOK, 3, 98, 52, 14, STY_PUSH
23:     PUSHBUTTON "Save", ID_SAVE, 66, 98, 52, 14, STY_PUSH
24:     LTEXT "XSize:", -1, 7, 9, 22, 8, STY_TEXT2
25:     LTEXT "YSize:", -1, 6, 32, 23, 8, STY_TEXT2
26:     LTEXT "", ID_XSIZE, 30, 9, 25, 12
27:     LTEXT "", ID_YSIZE, 30, 32, 25, 12
28:     LTEXT "NumX:", -1, 7, 58, 22, 8, STY_TEXT2
29:     LTEXT "NumY:", -1, 6, 80, 23, 8, STY_TEXT2
30:     LTEXT "", ID_NUMX, 30, 58, 25, 12
31:     LTEXT "", ID_NUMY, 30, 80, 25, 12
32:     PUSHBUTTON "Help", ID_HELP, 129, 98, 52, 14, STY_PUSH
33:     CONTROL "Text", ID_BITMAP1, "STATIC", STY_TEXT, 75,15,32,32
34:     CONTROL "Text", ID_BITMAP2, "STATIC", STY_TEXT, 129,15,32,32
35:     CONTROL "Text", ID_BITMAP3, "STATIC", STY_TEXT, 129,51,32,32
```

continues

Listing 16.3. continued

```
36:     CONTROL "Text", ID_BITMAP4, "STATIC", STY_TEXT, 75,51,32,32
37:     CONTROL "", 104, "button",
38:     BS_GROUPBOX | WS_CHILD | WS_VISIBLE, 63, 3, 108, 88
39: END
40:
41: Arrows DIALOG 92, 38, 102, 75
42: STYLE WS_POPUP | WS_VISIBLE | WS_CAPTION
43: CAPTION "Directions"
44: BEGIN
45:   PUSHBUTTON "Start", ID_START, 0, 0, 34, 25, STY_PUSH
46:   PUSHBUTTON "Left", ID_LEFT, 0, 25, 34, 25, STY_PUSH
47:   PUSHBUTTON "LScreen", ID_LSCREEN, 0, 50, 34, 25, STY_PUSH
48:   PUSHBUTTON "Dialog", ID_DIALOG, 34, 0, 34, 25, STY_PUSH
49:   PUSHBUTTON "QUIT", ID_QUIT, 34, 25, 34, 25, STY_PUSH
50:   PUSHBUTTON "Help", ID_HELP, 34, 50, 34, 25, STY_PUSH
51:   PUSHBUTTON "End", ID_END, 68, 0, 34, 25, STY_PUSH
52:   PUSHBUTTON "Right", ID_RIGHT, 68, 25, 34, 25, STY_PUSH
53:   PUSHBUTTON "RScreen", ID_RSCREEN, 68, 50, 34, 25, STY_PUSH
54: END
```

ROAD2.BMP (25X32)

GRASS.BMP (25X32)

Listing 16.4 shows the definition file for Mapper.

Type   **Listing 16.4. MAPPER.DEF.**

```
1: ; MAPPER.DEF
2:
3: NAME           Mapper
4: DESCRIPTION    'Mapper Window'
5: EXETYPE        WINDOWS
6: STUB           'WINSTUB.EXE'
7: CODE           PRELOAD MOVEABLE DISCARDABLE
8: DATA           PRELOAD MOVEABLE MULTIPLE
9:
10: HEAPSIZE       4096
11: STACKSIZE      5120
```

Listing 16.5 shows the Borland makefile for Mapper.

 Listing 16.5. MAPPER.MAK (Borland).

```
 1: # Mapper.mak
 2:
 3: # macros
 4: APPNAME = Mapper
 5: INCPATH = C:\BC\INCLUDE
 6: LIBPATH = C:\BC\LIB
 7: FLAGS = -H -ml -W -v -w4 -I$(INCPATH) -L$(LIBPATH)
 8:
 9: # link
10: $(APPNAME).exe: $(APPNAME).obj $(APPNAME).def $(APPNAME).res
11:    bcc $(FLAGS) $(APPNAME).obj
12:    brc $(APPNAME).res
13:
14: # compile
15: $(APPNAME).obj: $(APPNAME).cpp
16:    bcc -c $(FLAGS) $(APPNAME).cpp
17:
18: # resource
19: $(APPNAME).res: $(APPNAME).rc
20:    brc -r -i$(INCPATH) $(APPNAME).rc
```

Listing 16.6 shows the Microsoft makefile for Mapper.

 Listing 16.6. MAPPER.MAK (Microsoft).

```
 1: #-------------------
 2: # MAPPER.MAK
 3: #-------------------
 4:
 5: APPNAME = Mapper
 6:
 7: #-------------------
 8: # linking
 9: #-------------------
10: $(APPNAME).exe : $(APPNAME).obj $(APPNAME).def $(APPNAME).res
11:    link $(APPNAME), /align:16, NUL, \
12:       /nod llibcew libw oldnames, $(APPNAME)
13:    rc $(APPNAME).res
14:
15: #-------------------
16: # compile
17: #-------------------
18: $(APPNAME).obj : $(APPNAME).cpp
```

continues

Listing 16.6. continued

```
19:    cl -c -AL -GA -Ow -W3 -Zp  $(APPNAME).cpp
20:
21: #- - - - - - - - - - - - - - - - - - -
22: # Compile
23: #- - - - - - - - - - - - - - - - - - -
24: $(APPNAME).res: $(APPNAME).rc
25   rc -r $(APPNAME).rc
```

 Figure 16.2 shows the Mapper program, which contains two dialogs. One dialog is on-screen whenever the program is in memory.

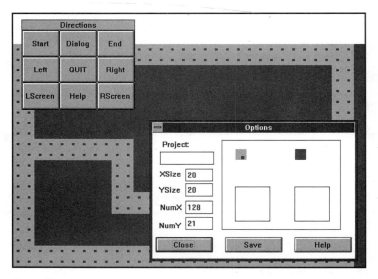

Figure 16.2. *The Mapper program.*

 The Mapper program is a utility you can use to design the playing board for the Snake program. Snake, as you might recall, is an arcade game (started in Chapter 8, "A First Look at Snako"). Chapter 21, "Snako for Windows," completes the discussion of this game.

The original version of the Snake program had an entirely blank playing field on which the Snake roved at will. The more advanced version, to be presented on Day 21, has a background consisting of a road weaving back and forth on a grassy plane, as shown in Figure 16.3. The rules of the game declare that the snake must stay on the road, and that it will die if it's accidentally steered onto the grass.

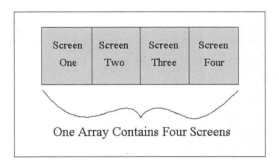

Figure 16.3. *A screen shot from the complete Snako program.*

The game consists of a series of levels; each level has a more complex pattern than the last. Furthermore, each level consists of four screens. Each time the snake erases all the dots on one screen, it is given a bridge to the next screen. When it has completed all four screens on one level, it starts again on the next level. The screens are arranged from left to right, as shown in Figure 16.4. When the snake completes the first screen in a series, it moves to the screen on its right, and so on, until a level is completed.

Screen One	Screen Two	Screen Three	Screen Four

One Array Contains Four Screens

Figure 16.4. *Four screens form each level of the Snako program.*

Each level is represented internally by an array of bitmaps 15 squares high and 100 squares wide. Here, for instance, is an excerpt from that array, showing the data necessary to represent one quarter of a level, or one screen:

```
int AnArry[15][25]  = {
  {2,2,2,2,2,2,1,1,1,1,1,1,1,1,1,1,1,1,1,1,1,1,1,1,1},
  {2,2,2,2,2,2,1,1,1,1,1,1,1,1,1,1,1,1,1,1,1,1,1,1,1},
  {1,1,1,1,2,2,1,1,1,1,1,1,1,1,1,1,1,1,1,1,2,2,2,2,2},
  {1,1,1,1,2,2,2,2,2,2,2,2,2,2,1,1,1,1,1,2,2,2,2,2,2},
  {1,1,1,1,2,2,2,2,2,2,2,2,2,2,1,1,1,1,1,1,2,2,2,1,1},
  {1,1,1,1,2,2,1,1,1,1,1,1,1,2,2,1,1,1,1,1,2,2,1,1,1},
  {1,1,1,1,2,2,1,1,1,1,1,1,1,2,2,1,1,1,1,1,2,2,1,1,1},
  {1,1,1,1,2,2,1,1,1,1,1,1,1,2,2,1,1,1,1,1,2,2,1,1,1},
  {1,1,1,1,2,2,1,1,1,1,1,1,1,2,2,2,2,2,2,2,2,2,1,1,1},
  {1,1,1,1,2,2,1,1,1,1,1,1,1,2,2,2,2,2,2,2,2,2,1,1,1},
  {1,1,1,1,2,2,1,1,1,1,1,1,1,1,1,2,2,1,1,1,1,1,1,1,1},
  {1,1,1,1,2,2,1,1,1,1,1,1,1,1,1,2,2,1,1,1,1,1,1,1,1},
  {1,1,1,1,2,2,1,1,1,1,1,1,1,1,1,2,2,1,1,1,1,1,1,1,1},
  {1,1,1,1,2,2,2,2,2,2,2,2,2,1,1,2,2,1,1,1,1,1,1,1,1},
  {1,1,1,1,2,2,2,2,2,2,2,2,2,1,1,2,2,1,1,1,1,1,1,1,1}
};
```

Any spot with a 1 might contain a bitmap depicting a square of grass, whereas any section with a 2 might contain a section of road.

If programmers work directly with arrays of numerical values, designing the screens for each playing level would be an extremely tedious, time-consuming, and error-prone process. The whole purpose of the Mapper program is to simplify this chore to the point that you can concentrate on design issues when you are constructing an array. More specifically, the Mapper program is a visual programming tool that enables you to design screens by clicking them with the mouse. For instance, a left-click of the mouse turns a square into a grass patch, and a right-click turns it into a section of road.

Note: When you work with the Mapper program, you'll find that certain features are not fully implemented. For instance, the Options dialog box contains an edit control and two static controls that are never used. It would have taken only a few moments for me to remove these visual controls, but I left them in because the Mapper program features an open-ended design. In other words, this program represents an early implementation of a more flexible tool that can be used to design the background for any game or application that has a two-dimensional background made from two or more bitmaps. In short, these external visual elements reflect internal design decisions. Specifically, I eventually want the program to be capable of processing scripts that define the elements of any number of radically different two-dimensional playing boards.

Mapper: from the Programmer's Perspective

The main purpose of the Mapper program is utilitarian. That is, it's meant primarily to be a tool for designing two-dimensional screens. However, it does contain one important new programming trick, as well as a review of several important programming techniques. Because of space considerations, I only have time to briefly mention the review issues; then, I'll go into a short description of the important new technique presented in this program.

This book has been very code-heavy. I've presented a new program in all but one chapter, and most of these programs have been fairly long. I do this because I believe examples are one of the best possible learning tools. The Mapper program gives several additional coding examples from which to learn:

☐ Mapper shows how to subclass a static control so that it can be used as a setting for displaying a bitmap on a dialog. This is an important technique utilized by many programmers. The subclassed static control resides on the Options dialog. The actual subclassed window procedure, `BitmapProc`, begins on line 475. Notice that instead of calling `SetWindowLong`, the Mapper program subclasses the window with a call to the WINDOWSX macro named `SubClassWindow`.

☐ Mapper also contains two dialogs, one modal and the other modeless. The modeless dialog, called the Arrow dialog (Figure 16.4), appears when the program is first launched. It's destroyed only when the rest of the program is closed. The Arrow dialog is interesting primarily because it serves as an alternative form of a menu. The Mapper program needs this kind of tool because there isn't room to place a menu at the top of the main window. More specifically, I designed Mapper this way because I wanted to leave open the possibility that the program would be used to design a screen that takes up the entire available display, with no room for a menu at the top.

Something New: *StretchBlt*

Like the Snake1 program presented on Day 8, the Mapper program has to be smart enough to be shown in multiple resolutions. Specifically, it "knows" about 640x480 displays, 800x600 displays, and 1024x768 displays. The resolution to this problem on Day 8 was fairly simple, but matters are more complex in this case. The problem is that the bitmaps depicting the grass and the road are both 25X32 pixels. Mapper (and Snako) must be able to have 32 of these bitmaps per column, with the left-most bitmap touching the left edge of the screen and the right-most touching the right edge of the screen. This has to be done regardless of the current screen resolution.

Of course, one solution would have been to have three different sets of bitmaps, one for each size screen. This is a reasonable solution to the problem. However, I decided against it, because it's not particularly flexible and it might require considerable work on the artist's part when Mapper is updated to work with four, six, eight, or more bitmaps at a time.

The solution Mapper utilizes involves the `StretchBlt` function, which enables you to shrink or expand a given bitmap to fit a particular set of dimensions.

Syntax

The *StretchBlt* Function

```
BOOL StretchBlt(HDC, int, int, int, int,
                HDC, int, int, int, int, DWORD)
```

The `StretchBlt` function blits a bitmap from one device context to another, while automatically stretching or shrinking the bitmap to fit the designated destination rectangle. Here is an in-depth look at the parameters:

HDC hdcDest;	The destination device context
int nXOriginDest;	The x-coordinate of the destination
int nYOriginDest;	The y-coordinate of the destination
int nWidthDest;	The width of the destination
int nHeightDest;	The height of the destination
HDC hdcSrc;	The source device context
int nXOriginSrc;	The x-coordinate of the source rectangle
int nYOriginSrc;	The y-coordinate of the source rectangle
int nWidthSrc;	The width of the source rectangle
int nHeightSrc;	The height of the source rectangle
DWORD fdwRop;	Logical raster operation (as SRCCOPY)

Example:

```
StretchBlt(PaintDC, 0, 0, 25, 25,
           MemryDC, 0, 0, 32, 32, SRCCOPY);
```

A brief examination of the `StretchBlt` call shows that it's very similar to `BitBlt`. When used in the Mapper program, however, a few curves are thrown at the programmer; these curves require a little special attention.

The big complication stems from the fact that StretchBlt is a relatively time-consuming call. The Mapper program, on the other hand, has to blit not one, but 32 * 21, or 672 bitmaps to the screen. As it turns out, the StretchBlt function requires too many clock cycles for a function that needs to be called 672 times in a row.

The solution is to stretch each of the program's two bitmaps one time, and then to blit the resulting device contexts to the screen. In other words, Mapper stretches the bitmaps into shape, and then works with these newly created bitmaps (instead of with the originals).

The following excerpts, from lines 270-297 of MAPPER.CPP, show how the Mapper OnPaint function would look if the program only handled one bitmap at a time:

```
HDC TGrassDC = CreateCompatibleDC(PaintDC);
HDC GrassDC = CreateCompatibleDC(PaintDC);

HBITMAP TGrass =
  CreateCompatibleBitmap(PaintDC, Dat.GrassX, Dat.GrassY);

OldGrass = SelectBitmap(TGrassDC, Grass);
OldGrass1 = SelectBitmap(GrassDC, TGrass);

StretchBlt(GrassDC, 0, 0, Dat.GrassX, Dat.GrassY,
           TGrassDC, 0, 0, 32, 32, SRCCOPY);

... // Code to BitBlt GrassDC to the screen 200 or so times

SelectBitmap(TGrassDC, OldGrass);
SelectBitmap(GrassDC, OldGrass1);
DeleteObject(TGrass);

DeleteDC(GrassDC);
DeleteDC(TGrassDC);
```

As you can see, Mapper starts by creating two valid device contexts with calls to CreateCompatibleDC. It then creates a compatible bitmap which can be selected into one of the device contexts. The other device context is used to hold the original bitmap.

When you are done with this stage, you have two device contexts:

☐ The first holds a blank bitmap, which has the appropriate dimensions for the current screen resolution.

☐ The second holds the original bitmap, with its predefined 25x32 dimensions still intact.

Mapper now uses `StretchBlt` to copy the original bitmap into the blank bitmap. The result is a properly sized bitmap, residing in a compatible device context. Now, Mapper is free to use this bitmap with the speedy `BitBlt` function.

Of course, when you're done, you have to go through the tedious, error-prone process of carefully deleting all the bitmaps and DCs you've created. To be sure you have done this properly, run the Debug version of Windows to verify the validity of your efforts.

Summary

The first half of this chapter focused on the techniques used to create and communicate with dialogs. In particular, you learned about the `CTLCOLOR` messages. Additional code demonstrated how to respond to button clicks and how to handle the associated messages when they're sent to a dialog procedure. The last half of the chapter introduced the Mapper program and the powerful `StretchBlt` function.

Q&A

1. Q: The Mapper program blits a bitmap into a static control on the Options dialog. How else can you display a bitmap on a dialog?

    A: By responding to `WM_PAINT` messages, you can paint the bitmap directly on the dialog's surface. This isn't always appropriate, however, because the dimensions of dialogs are calculated in a rather peculiar fashion. As a result, using static controls is often the answer. A third alternative is posed by push buttons, which can be given the `BS_OWNERDRAW` style and used in a similar fashion. Borland's Resource Workshop provides a shortcut method for using owner draw push buttons.

2. Q: In the last answer, you mentioned that dialogs use a peculiar coordinate system. What's that all about?

    A: Rather than base their dimensions on pixels, dialog boxes use a coordinate system based on a unit that is one-quarter the size of a character in the system font. This is done to guarantee dialogs will keep their relative proportions, regardless of the resolution of the current system. If, based on dialog dimensions, you want to make calculations at runtime use the `GetDialogBaseUnits` function to retrieve the size of the units and the `MapDialogRect` function to convert them to pixels.

Workshop

The Workshop provides quiz questions to help you solidify your understanding of the material covered and exercises to provide you with experience in using what you've learned. Try to understand the quiz and exercise answers before continuing on to the next chapter. Answers are provided in Appendix A.

Quiz

1. What is the difference between `SendDlgItemMessage` and `SendMessage`?

2. If all you know is the ID of a control that resides in a dialog, how can you get its `HWND`?

3. How do you convert the coordinates retrieved by `GetClientRect` into logical coordinates using the `MM_TWIPS` mapping mode?

4. If you have access to nothing but the `HWND` of the current dialog, how can you find the `HWND` of its owner?

5. Is it possible to set up lines of communication between a modal dialog and its parent? If not, why? If so, how?

6. Using a debugger, you can't step through a program in a linear fashion until it reaches a portion of the dialog procedure you want to examine. How do you get around this limitation so that you can debug a dialog proc?

7. Why does the Mapper program subclass a static control?

8. Why doesn't the Options dialog draw bitmaps directly on its own surface?

9. What is the difference between `StretchBlt` and `BitBlt`?

10. Why does Mapper have to call `CreateCompatibleBitmap`?

Exercises

1. Respond to a `WM_CTLCOLOR` message by giving the background of a dialog the Borland "chiseled steel" look (shown in the last chapter).

2. In a note at the end of the section entitled "Getting Data from the Make Shape Dialog," I describe how to use dialogs as the interface for a database of names and addresses. Create your own personal address book by implementing your own version of this database.

Menus and
Icons in Depth

Today, you'll learn about some fancy things you can do with menus, icons, cursors, and bitmaps. In particular, you'll learn

- [ ] How to create nested pop-up menus

- [ ] How to modify the system menu

- [ ] How to create owner draw menus and simple bitmap menus

- [ ] How to create and display your own cursors

- [ ] How to work with icons

- [ ] How to add accelerators to your programs that enable users to activate menu items through hot keys (such as Alt-1 or Ctrl-F1)

With the possible exception of owner draw menus, nothing in this chapter poses any serious challenge to the programmer. In fact, most of the new coding techniques you're about to see are really nothing more than fancy tricks that can add a maximum amount of pizzazz to your program with a minimal amount of effort on your part.

In order to put these techniques on display, I've thrown together a sample application that puts menus through their paces in ways that you'll hopefully find educational and at least somewhat entertaining. The program's name is MENUTEST.CPP.

Overall, you should find this chapter a bit of a respite from the intense pace of the last few chapters. Take advantage of this relatively simple material while it lasts, because tricky code is waiting just around the corner (in the next few chapters).

What's on the Menu?

By this time, you've probably found out two things:

- [ ] Most menus aren't very difficult to construct or display.

- [ ] Both Microsoft and Borland strip whatever latent difficulty there might be from menus by supplying you with powerful interactive tools. These tools churn menus out in a few relatively effortless moments.

Menus are so easy to use, however, that instead of popping up the Resource Workshop or App Studio, you might find it simpler to construct or modify menus with an editor. As a result, it's probably worthwhile to take a quick look at the naked beast itself—the code for the menu in the MenuTest program.

```
MENU_1 MENU
BEGIN
    POPUP "&File"
    BEGIN
        MENUITEM "&New", CM_NEW
        MENUITEM "&Open...", CM_OPEN
        MENUITEM "&Save", CM_SAVE
        MENUITEM "Save &as...", CM_SAVEAS
        MENUITEM SEPARATOR
        POPUP "&Print..."
        BEGIN
            MENUITEM "Print To Disk", CM_PRNDISK
            MENUITEM "Print LPT1", CM_PRNLPT1
        END

        MENUITEM "Page se&tup...", CM_PAGESETUP
        MENUITEM "P&rinter setup...", CM_PRINTERSETUP
        MENUITEM SEPARATOR
        MENUITEM "E&xit", CM_EXIT
    END

    POPUP "&Cursors"
    BEGIN
        MENUITEM "&Round Cursor\tAlt+F1", CM_ROUNDCURSOR
        MENUITEM "&Diamond Cursor\tCtrl+F2", CM_DIAMONDCURSOR
        MENUITEM "&Draw Icon\tShift+F3", CM_ICONCURSOR
    END

    POPUP "BitCursors"
    BEGIN
        MENUITEM "Item", CM_BITMENU1
        MENUITEM "Item", CM_BITMENU2
        MENUITEM "Item", CM_BITMENU3
    END

    MENUITEM "&Help", CM_HELP
END
```

Figure 17.1 shows the menu for the MenuTest programs.

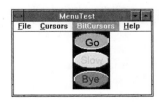

Figure 17.1. *The close-up view of the menu for the MenuTest program, with the* BitCursors *popup exposed.*

Though I briefly discussed menus earlier in this book, my basic approach to them is to let you, at your own pace and to what degree you deem necessary, pick up on their syntax. (The big exception was the quick introduction creating dynamic menus on Day 13.) The decision to treat menu creation as essentially intuitive has been predicated on the fact that the Resource Workshop and App Studio make it at least theoretically possible for you to become an excellent Windows programmer without having to write a single line of code for an RC script.

Nevertheless, it's nice to know that the syntactical backbone of menus consists primarily of the simple statements BEGIN, END, MENUITEM, and POPUP. The BEGIN and END statements are nothing but bookends that wrap around the body of an entire menu and around the body of any particular pop-up menu.

Pop-up menus, of course, are really windows that drop down to display a list of choices when they are selected. It's possible to nest two pop-up menus to appear simultaneously on-screen (see Figure 17.2).

A menu item, on the other hand, is a single item in a pop-up menu. It can also be a stand-alone item on a menu bar that, when selected, leads directly to a particular action (rather than causing a pop-up menu to appear on-screen). In Figure 17.2, the words New, Open, Save, and so forth are all menu items.

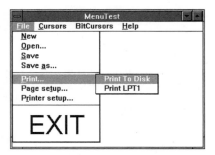

Figure 17.2. *The File menu from the MenuTest program contains nested pop-up menus and a bitmap menu item to emphasize the exit option.*

The correct way to create nested pop-up menus is simply to insert a second pop-up menu directly within the primary popup:

```
POPUP "&File"
BEGIN
    MENUITEM "&New", CM_NEW
    ...
    MENUITEM SEPARATOR
    POPUP "&Print..."
```

```
BEGIN
    MENUITEM "Print To Disk", CM_PRNDISK
    MENUITEM "Print LPT1", CM_PRNLPT1
END
...
```

This code creates a nested menu called Print. When selected, the options Print To Disk and Print LPT1 are made available to the user, as shown in Figure 17.2.

In the preceding code, you can see the statement MENUITEM SEPARATOR. These words insert a black horizontal line in the middle of a menu. SEPARATORs are menu items and can be treated exactly like any other item in a menu; that is, they can be deleted, inserted, or modified dynamically at runtime.

Before getting into the fancy stuff, I should perhaps spend a moment more talking about some of the options that can be appended onto the code for creating a menu item or pop-up menu. These optional statements enable you to perform actions such as putting a check mark in front of a menu item or graying a menu item. For instance, the following line of code produces a menu item with a check before it, as shown in Figure 17.3.

```
MENUITEM "&Round Cursor\tAlt+F1", CM_ROUNDCURSOR, CHECKED
```

The following line of code produces a checked and grayed menu item:

```
MENUITEM "&Round Cursor\tAlt+F1", CM_ROUNDCURSOR, CHECKED, GRAYED
```

Note: The \t notation inserts a TAB character into a menu. The result, shown in Figure 17.3, gives the user a very legible notification of any accelerator keys associated with a menu option. Accelerators are discussed later in this chapter.

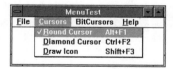

Figure 17.3. *A check mark in front of a menu item informs the reader that a particular option has been selected.*

Besides the checked and grayed options, you also can make use of the MENUBREAK and MENUBARBREAK statements, which place a particular menu item in a pop-up menu on a new line (see Figure 17.4). The MENUBARBREAK statement places a black line between each column, whereas MENUBREAK leaves only white space between each column.

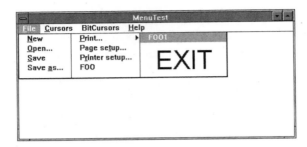

Figure 17.4. *The* MENUBARBREAK *statement creates multiple columns inside a single popup.*

Following is the code for the menu shown in Figure 17.4. You'll probably notice that I've placed two bogus items, named Foo and Foo1, into the menu in order to give it more symmetry. I've done this simply so you can get a feeling for how you can use the MENUBARBREAK statement to present lengthy columns of options in an orderly arrangement. Users can manipulate these columns with relative ease.

```
MENU_1 MENU
BEGIN
    POPUP "&File"
    BEGIN
        MENUITEM "&New", CM_NEW
        MENUITEM "&Open...", CM_OPEN
        MENUITEM "&Save", CM_SAVE
        MENUITEM "Save &as...", CM_SAVEAS,
        POPUP "&Print...", MENUBARBREAK
        BEGIN
            MENUITEM "Print To Disk", CM_PRNDISK
            MENUITEM "Print LPT1", CM_PRNLPT1
        END

        MENUITEM "Page se&tup...", CM_PAGESETUP
        MENUITEM "P&rinter setup...", CM_PRINTERSETUP
        MENUITEM "FOO", 65000
        MENUITEM "FOO1", 65001, MENUBARBREAK
        MENUITEM "E&xit", CM_EXIT
    END
```

The MenuTest Program

Now that you've had a look at the basic techniques for creating menus, it's time to explore some ways you can manipulate menus at runtime to create various effects that can make your program easier (or more fun) to use. Before going further, you should look at the code and take a few minutes to get it up and running (see Listing 17.1.)

Listing 17.1. The MenuTest program demonstrates how to use menus to create an attractive, easy-to-use interface.

```
 1: ////////////////////////////////////////////////////////
 2: //   Program Name: MENUTEST.CPP
 3: //   Programmer: Charlie Calvert
 4: //   Description: MenuTest windows program
 5: //   Date: 07/20/93
 6: ////////////////////////////////////////////////////////
 7: #define STRICT
 8: #include <windows.h>
 9: #include <windowsx.h>
10: #pragma hdrstop
11: #include "menutest.h"
12: #pragma warning (disable: 4068)
13: #pragma warning (disable: 4100)
14: // ---------------------------------------------------------
15: // Interface
16: // ---------------------------------------------------------
17: static char szAppName[] = "MenuTest";
18: static HWND MainWindow;
19: static HINSTANCE hInstance;
20: static HACCEL hAccel;
21:
22: // ---------------------------------------------------------
23: // Initialization
24: // ---------------------------------------------------------
25:
26: ////////////////////////////////////////////////////////
27: // Program entry point
28: ////////////////////////////////////////////////////////
29: #pragma argsused
30: int PASCAL WinMain(HINSTANCE hInst, HINSTANCE hPrevInstance,
31:                    LPSTR lpszCmdParam, int nCmdShow)
32: {
33:   MSG  Msg;
34:
35:   if (!hPrevInstance)
36:     if (!Register(hInst))
37:       return FALSE;
```

continues

Listing 17.1. continued

```
38:
39:    (MainWindow = Create(hInst, nCmdShow);
40:    if (MainWindow)
41:      return FALSE;
42:    while (GetMessage(&Msg, NULL, 0, 0))
43:    {
44:      if (!TranslateAccelerator(MainWindow, hAccel, &Msg))
45:      {
46:         TranslateMessage(&Msg);
47:         DispatchMessage(&Msg);
48:      }
49:    }
50:
51:    return Msg.wParam;
52: }
53:
54: ////////////////////////////////////////////////////////
55: // Register the window
56: ////////////////////////////////////////////////////////
57: BOOL Register(HINSTANCE hInst)
58: {
59:    WNDCLASS WndClass;
60:
61:    WndClass.style           = CS_HREDRAW ¦ CS_VREDRAW;
62:    WndClass.lpfnWndProc     = WndProc;
63:    WndClass.cbClsExtra      = 0;
64:    WndClass.cbWndExtra      = 0;
65:    WndClass.hInstance       = hInst;
66:    WndClass.hIcon           = LoadIcon(hInst, "ICON_1");
67:    WndClass.hCursor         = LoadCursor(NULL, IDC_ARROW);
68:    WndClass.hbrBackground   = GetStockBrush(WHITE_BRUSH);
69:    WndClass.lpszMenuName    = "MENU_1";
70:    WndClass.lpszClassName   = szAppName;
71:
72:    return RegisterClass (&WndClass);
73: }
74:
75: ////////////////////////////////////////////////////////
76: // Create the window
77: ////////////////////////////////////////////////////////
78: HWND Create(HINSTANCE hInst, int nCmdShow)
79: {
80:
81:    hInstance = hInst;
82:
83:    HWND hWindow = CreateWindow(szAppName, szAppName,
84:                    WS_OVERLAPPEDWINDOW,
85:                    CW_USEDEFAULT, CW_USEDEFAULT,
86:                    CW_USEDEFAULT, CW_USEDEFAULT,
87:                    NULL, NULL, hInst, NULL);
```

```
 88:
 89:   if (hWindow == NULL)
 90:     return hWindow;
 91:
 92:   ShowWindow(hWindow, nCmdShow);
 93:   UpdateWindow(hWindow);
 94:
 95:   return hWindow;
 96: }
 97:
 98: // -------------------------------------------------------
 99: // WndProc and Implementation
100: // -------------------------------------------------------
101:
102: ////////////////////////////////////////////////////////
103: // The Window Procedure
104: ////////////////////////////////////////////////////////
105: LRESULT CALLBACK _export WndProc(HWND hwnd, UINT Message,
106:                                  WPARAM wParam, LPARAM lParam)
107: {
108:   switch(Message)
109:   {
110:     HANDLE_MSG(hwnd, WM_CREATE, MenuTest_OnCreate);
111:     HANDLE_MSG(hwnd, WM_DESTROY, MenuTest_OnDestroy);
112:     HANDLE_MSG(hwnd, WM_COMMAND, MenuTest_OnCommand);
113:     HANDLE_MSG(hwnd, WM_DRAWITEM, MenuTest_OnDrawItem);
114:     HANDLE_MSG(hwnd, WM_LBUTTONDOWN, MenuTest_OnLButtonDown);
115:     HANDLE_MSG(hwnd, WM_MOUSEMOVE, MenuTest_OnMouseMove);
116:     HANDLE_MSG(hwnd, WM_MEASUREITEM, MenuTest_OnMeasureItem);
117:     HANDLE_MSG(hwnd, WM_PAINT, MenuTest_OnPaint);
118:     default:
119:       return MenuTest_DefProc(hwnd, Message, wParam, lParam);
120:   }
121: }
122:
123: ////////////////////////////////////////////////////////
124: // Handle WM_CREATE
125: ////////////////////////////////////////////////////////
126: #pragma argsused
127: BOOL MenuTest_OnCreate(HWND hwnd,
128:                        CREATESTRUCT FAR* lpCreateStruct)
129: {
130:   Cursor1 = LoadCursor(hInstance, "CURSOR_1");
131:   Cursor2 = LoadCursor(hInstance, "CURSOR_2");
132:   Cursor3 = LoadCursor(hInstance, "CURSOR_3");
133:
134:   Icon1 = LoadIcon(hInstance, "ICON_1");
135:
136:   Bitmap1 = LoadBitmap(hInstance, "BITMAP_1");
137:   Bitmap1a = LoadBitmap(hInstance, "BITMAP1A");
```

continues

Listing 17.1. continued

```
138:    Bitmap2 = LoadBitmap(hInstance, "BITMAP_2");
139:    Bitmap2a = LoadBitmap(hInstance, "BITMAP2A");
140:    Bitmap3 = LoadBitmap(hInstance, "BITMAP_3");
141:    Bitmap3a = LoadBitmap(hInstance, "BITMAP3A");
142:    BMPExit = LoadBitmap(hInstance, "BMPEXIT");
143:
144:    GetObject(Bitmap1, sizeof(BITMAP), &BStruct);
145:
146:    ModifyMenu(GetMenu(hwnd),
147:               CM_BITMENU1, MF_BYCOMMAND ¦ MF_OWNERDRAW,
148:               CM_BITMENU1, (LPCSTR)MAKELONG(Bitmap1, 0));
149:    ModifyMenu(GetMenu(hwnd), CM_BITMENU2,
150:               MF_BYCOMMAND ¦ MF_OWNERDRAW,
151:               CM_BITMENU2, (LPCSTR)MAKELONG(Bitmap2, 0));
152:    ModifyMenu(GetMenu(hwnd), CM_BITMENU3,
153:               MF_BYCOMMAND ¦ MF_OWNERDRAW,
154:               CM_BITMENU3, (LPCSTR)MAKELONG(Bitmap3, 0));
155:    ModifyMenu(GetMenu(hwnd), CM_EXIT,
156:               MF_BYCOMMAND ¦ MF_BITMAP,
157:               CM_EXIT, (LPCSTR)MAKELONG(BMPExit, 0));
158:
159:    HMENU SysMenu = GetSystemMenu(hwnd, FALSE);
160:
161:    DeleteMenu(SysMenu, 6, MF_BYPOSITION);
162:    DeleteMenu(SysMenu, 6, MF_BYPOSITION);
163:
164:    EditBrush = CreateSolidBrush(RGB(255, 127, 255));
165:    PaintIcon = FALSE;
166:    PaintGo = FALSE;
167:    PaintSlow = FALSE;
168:    PaintStop = TRUE;
169:
170:    hAccel = LoadAccelerators(hInstance, "MYKEYS");
171:
172:    if (hAccel == NULL)
173:      MessageBox(MainWindow, "No Accelerators", "Warning", MB_OK);
174:
175:    return TRUE;
176: }
177:
178: ///////////////////////////////////////
179: // Handle WM_DESTROY
180: ///////////////////////////////////////
181: #pragma argsused
182: void MenuTest_OnDestroy(HWND hwnd)
183: {
184:    DeleteObject(EditBrush);
185:    DeleteObject(Bitmap1);
186:    DeleteObject(Bitmap1a);
187:    DeleteObject(Bitmap2);
```

```
188:    DeleteObject(Bitmap2a);
189:    DeleteObject(Bitmap3);
190:    DeleteObject(Bitmap3a);
191:    DeleteObject(BMPExit);
192:    DestroyCursor(Cursor1);
193:    DestroyCursor(Cursor2);
194:    DestroyCursor(Cursor3);
195:    DestroyIcon(Icon1);
196:    PostQuitMessage(0);
197: }
198:
199: ////////////////////////////////////////
200: // Check menu if user selects a cursor
201: ////////////////////////////////////////
202: void CheckItem(HWND hwnd, int ID)
203: {
204:    HMENU Menu = GetMenu(hwnd);
205:    CheckMenuItem(Menu,
206:                  CM_ROUNDCURSOR, MF_BYCOMMAND | MF_UNCHECKED);
207:    CheckMenuItem(Menu,
208:                  CM_DIAMONDCURSOR, MF_BYCOMMAND | MF_UNCHECKED);
209:    CheckMenuItem(Menu,
210:                  CM_ICONCURSOR, MF_BYCOMMAND | MF_UNCHECKED);
211:    if (ID)
212:      CheckMenuItem(Menu, ID, MF_BYCOMMAND | MF_CHECKED);
213: }
214:
215: ////////////////////////////////////////
216: // Handle WM_COMMAND
217: ////////////////////////////////////////
218: #pragma argsused
219: void MenuTest_OnCommand(HWND hwnd, int id, HWND hwndCtl,
                            UINT codeNotify)
220: {
221:    FARPROC lpfnHelpBox;
222:
223:    switch(id)
224:    {
225:      case CM_NEW:
226:      case CM_OPEN:
227:      case CM_SAVE:
228:      case CM_SAVEAS:
229:      case CM_PRNDISK:
230:      case CM_PRNLPT1:
231:      case CM_PAGESETUP:
232:      case CM_PRINTERSETUP:
233:        MessageBox(hwnd, "Not yet implemented", "Info",
234:                   MB_OK | MB_ICONINFORMATION);
235:        break;
236:
```

17

continues

Listing 17.1. continued

```
237:    case CM_EXIT:
238:      DestroyWindow(hwnd);
239:      break;
240:
241:    case CM_ROUNDCURSOR:
242:      SetClassWord(hwnd, GCW_HCURSOR, (WORD)Cursor1);
243:      SetCursor(Cursor1);
244:      PaintIcon = FALSE;
245:      CheckItem(hwnd, CM_ROUNDCURSOR);
246:      break;
247:
248:    case CM_DIAMONDCURSOR:
249:      SetClassWord(hwnd, GCW_HCURSOR, (WORD)Cursor2);
250:      SetCursor(Cursor2);
251:      PaintIcon = FALSE;
252:      CheckItem(hwnd, CM_DIAMONDCURSOR);
253:      break;
254:
255:    case CM_ICONCURSOR:
256:      SetClassWord(hwnd, GCW_HCURSOR, (WORD)Cursor3);
257:      SetCursor(Cursor3);
258:      PaintIcon = TRUE;
259:      CheckItem(hwnd, CM_ICONCURSOR);
260:      break;
261:
262:    case CM_BITMENU1:
263:      PaintGo = TRUE;
264:      PaintSlow = FALSE;
265:      PaintStop = FALSE;
266:      InvalidateRect(hwnd, NULL, TRUE);
267:      break;
268:
269:    case CM_BITMENU2:
270:      PaintGo = FALSE;
271:      PaintSlow = TRUE;
272:      PaintStop = FALSE;
273:      InvalidateRect(hwnd, NULL, TRUE);
274:      break;
275:
276:    case CM_BITMENU3:
277:      PaintGo = FALSE;
278:      PaintSlow = FALSE;
279:      PaintStop = TRUE;
280:      InvalidateRect(hwnd, NULL, TRUE);
281:      SetClassWord(hwnd, GCW_HCURSOR,
282:                (WORD)LoadCursor(NULL, IDC_ARROW));
283:      SetCursor(LoadCursor(NULL, IDC_ARROW));
284:      CheckItem(hwnd, 0);
285:      PaintIcon = FALSE;
286:      break;
```

```
287:
288:     case CM_HELP:
289:       lpfnHelpBox =
290:         MakeProcInstance((FARPROC)HelpBoxProc, hInstance);
291:       DialogBox(hInstance, "HELPBOX", hwnd,
292:                 (DLGPROC)lpfnHelpBox);
293:       FreeProcInstance(lpfnHelpBox);
294:       break;
295:   }
296: }
297:
298: /////////////////////////////////////////
299: // Draw Bitmap in menu
300: /////////////////////////////////////////
301: void DrawBitmap(HDC PaintDC, HBITMAP Bitmap, int YVal)
302: {
303:   HDC MemDC;
304:   HBITMAP OldBitmap;
305:
306:   MemDC = CreateCompatibleDC(PaintDC);
307:   OldBitmap = SelectBitmap(MemDC, Bitmap);
308:   BitBlt(PaintDC, 0, YVal * BStruct.bmHeight, BStruct.bmWidth,
309:          BStruct.bmHeight, MemDC, 0, 0, SRCCOPY);
310:   SelectObject(MemDC, OldBitmap);
311:   DeleteObject(MemDC);
312: }
313:
314: /////////////////////////////////////////
315: // Handle WM_DRAWITEM
316: /////////////////////////////////////////
317: #pragma argsused
318: void MenuTest_OnDrawItem(HWND hwnd,
319:                          const DRAWITEMSTRUCT FAR* lpDrawItem)
320: {
321:   switch(lpDrawItem->itemID)
322:   {
323:     case CM_BITMENU1:
324:       if (lpDrawItem->itemState & ODS_SELECTED)
325:         DrawBitmap(lpDrawItem->hDC, Bitmap1a, 0);
326:       else
327:         DrawBitmap(lpDrawItem->hDC, Bitmap1, 0);
328:       break;
329:
330:     case CM_BITMENU2:
331:       if (lpDrawItem->itemState & ODS_SELECTED)
332:         DrawBitmap(lpDrawItem->hDC, Bitmap2a, 1);
333:       else
334:         DrawBitmap(lpDrawItem->hDC, Bitmap2, 1);
335:       break;
336:
```

continues

Listing 17.1. continued

```
337:      case CM_BITMENU3:
338:        if (lpDrawItem->itemState & ODS_SELECTED)
339:          DrawBitmap(lpDrawItem->hDC, Bitmap3a, 2);
340:        else
341:          DrawBitmap(lpDrawItem->hDC, Bitmap3, 2);
342:        break;
343:    }
344: }
345:
346: //////////////////////////////////////////
347: // Handle WM_LBUTTONDOWN
348: //////////////////////////////////////////
349: #pragma argsused
350: void MenuTest_OnLButtonDown(HWND hwnd, BOOL fDoubleClick, int x,
351:                                  int y, UINT keyFlags)
352: {
353:   if (PaintIcon)
354:   {
355:     HDC PaintDC = GetDC(hwnd);
356:     DrawIcon(PaintDC, x, y, Icon1);
357:     ReleaseDC(hwnd, PaintDC);
358:   }
359: }
360:
361: //////////////////////////////////////////
362: // Handle WM_MEASUREITEM
363: //////////////////////////////////////////
364: #pragma argsused
365: void MenuTest_OnMeasureItem(HWND hwnd, MEASUREITEMSTRUCT
366:                                  FAR* lpMeasureItem)
367: {
368:   WORD CheckWidth;
369:
370:   CheckWidth = LOWORD (GetMenuCheckMarkDimensions());
371:   switch ( lpMeasureItem->itemID )
372:   {
373:     case CM_BITMENU1:
374:     case CM_BITMENU2:
375:     case CM_BITMENU3:
376:      lpMeasureItem->itemWidth = BStruct.bmWidth - CheckWidth - 3;
377:      lpMeasureItem->itemHeight = BStruct.bmHeight - 1;
378:      break;
379:   }
380: }
381:
382: //////////////////////////////////////////
383: // Handle WM_MOUSEMOVE
384: //////////////////////////////////////////
385: void MenuTest_OnMouseMove(HWND hwnd, int x, int y, UINT keyFlags)
386: {
```

```
387:    if (((keyFlags & MK_LBUTTON) == MK_LBUTTON) && (PaintIcon))
388:    {
389:      HDC PaintDC = GetDC(hwnd);
390:      DrawIcon(PaintDC, x, y, Icon1);
391:      ReleaseDC(hwnd, PaintDC);
392:    }
393: }
394:
395: //////////////////////////////////////////
396: // Handle WM_PAINT
397: //////////////////////////////////////////
398: void MenuTest_OnPaint(HWND hwnd)
399: {
400:    PAINTSTRUCT PaintStruct;
401:    HDC PaintDC, MemDC;
402:    RECT R;
403:    HBITMAP OldBitmap;
404:
405:    PaintDC = BeginPaint(hwnd, &PaintStruct);
406:
407:    if (!PaintStop)
408:    {
409:      GetClientRect(hwnd, &R);
410:      int i = R.right / BStruct.bmWidth;
411:      int j = R.bottom / BStruct.bmHeight;
412:
413:      MemDC = CreateCompatibleDC(PaintDC);
414:
415:      if (PaintSlow)
416:        OldBitmap = SelectBitmap(MemDC, Bitmap2);
417:      else
418:        OldBitmap = SelectBitmap(MemDC, Bitmap1);
419:
420:      for (int x = 0; x <= i; x++)
421:        for (int y = 0; y <= j; y++)
422:          BitBlt(PaintDC, BStruct.bmWidth * x, BStruct.bmHeight * y,
423:            BStruct.bmWidth, BStruct.bmHeight, MemDC, 0, 0, SRCCOPY);
424:
425:      SelectObject(MemDC, OldBitmap);
426:      DeleteDC(MemDC);
427:    }
428:
429:    EndPaint(hwnd, &PaintStruct);
430: }
431:
432: // ----------------------------------------------
433: // About Box Procedure
434: // ----------------------------------------------
435: #pragma argsused
```

continues

Listing 17.1. continued

```
436:        BOOL CALLBACK HelpBoxProc(HWND hDlg, WORD Message,
                                      WPARAM wParam,
437:                                  LPARAM lParam)
438: {
439:   switch(Message)
440:   {
441:     case WM_INITDIALOG:
442:       SendDlgItemMessage(hDlg, ID_HELPEDIT,
443:                          WM_SETTEXT, 0, LPARAM(HelpStr));
444:       return TRUE;
445:
446:     case WM_CTLCOLOR:
447:       switch(HIWORD(lParam))
448:       {
449:         // Cover up background of Static control
450:         case CTLCOLOR_STATIC:
451:           return (BOOL) GetStockObject(BLACK_BRUSH);
452:
453:         case CTLCOLOR_EDIT:
454:           SetTextColor((HDC)wParam, RGB(127,127,127));
455:           return NULL;
456:
457:         case CTLCOLOR_DLG:
458:           return (BOOL) EditBrush;
459:       }
460:       return (BOOL) NULL;
461:
462:     case WM_COMMAND:
463:       if (wParam == IDOK || wParam == IDCANCEL)
464:       {
465:         EndDialog(hDlg, TRUE);
466:         return TRUE;
467:       }
468:       break;
469:   }
470:   return FALSE;
471: }
```

Listing 17.2 shows the header file for MenuTest.

Type   **Listing 17.2. MENUTEST.H.**

```
1: /////////////////////////////////////////////////////////
2: //   Program Name: MENUTEST.H
3: //   Programmer: Charlie Calvert
4: //   Description: MenuTest Windows program
5: //   Date: 04/20/93
6: /////////////////////////////////////////////////////////
```

```
 7: #define CM_NEW 101
 8: #define CM_OPEN 102
 9: #define CM_SAVE 103
10: #define CM_SAVEAS 104
11: #define CM_PRNDISK 151
12: #define CM_PRNLPT1 152
13: #define CM_PAGESETUP 105
14: #define CM_PRINTERSETUP 106
15: #define CM_EXIT 107
16:
17: #define CM_ROUNDCURSOR 201
18: #define CM_DIAMONDCURSOR 202
19: #define CM_ICONCURSOR 203
20:
21: #define CM_BITMENU1 301
22: #define CM_BITMENU2 302
23: #define CM_BITMENU3 303
24:
25: #define CM_HELP      401
26: #define ID_HELPEDIT 402
27:
28: // Constant
29: char FAR *HelpStr="Choose ROUND CURSOR or DIAMOND CURSOR to see"
30:               " new cursors. Choose DRAW ICON to draw on the"
31:               " screen. Choose GO or SLOW to set background, "
32:               " choose BYE to reset screen. The close option "
33:               " has been removed from the system menu, so exit "
34:               " using the File menu";
35:
36: // Declarations for class MenuTest
37: #define MenuTest_DefProc     DefWindowProc
38: BOOL MenuTest_OnCreate(HWND hwnd,
39:                   CREATESTRUCT FAR* lpCreateStruct);
40: void MenuTest_OnDestroy(HWND hwnd);
41: void MenuTest_OnCommand(HWND hwnd, int id,
42:                   HWND hwndCtl, UINT codeNotify);
43: void MenuTest_OnDrawItem(HWND hwnd,
44:                   const DRAWITEMSTRUCT FAR* lpDrawItem);
45: void MenuTest_OnLButtonDown(HWND hwnd, BOOL fDoubleClick,
46:                   int x, int y, UINT keyFlags);
47: void MenuTest_OnMeasureItem(HWND hwnd,
48:                   MEASUREITEMSTRUCT FAR* lpMeasureItem);
49: void MenuTest_OnMouseMove(HWND hwnd, int x,
50:                   int y, UINT keyFlags);
51: void MenuTest_OnPaint(HWND hwnd);
52:
53: // variables
54: HICON Icon1;
55: HBRUSH EditBrush;
56: HCURSOR Cursor1, Cursor2, Cursor3;
```

continues

```
57: HBITMAP Bitmap1, Bitmap1a, Bitmap2, Bitmap2a;
58: HBITMAP Bitmap3, Bitmap3a, BMPExit;
59: BITMAP BStruct;
60: BOOL PaintIcon, PaintGo, PaintSlow, PaintStop;
61:
62: // function
63: LRESULT CALLBACK _export WndProc(HWND hWindow, UINT Message,
64:                                   WPARAM wParam, LPARAM lParam);
65: BOOL Register(HINSTANCE hInst);
66: HWND Create(HINSTANCE hInst, int nCmdShow);
67: BOOL CALLBACK HelpBoxProc(HWND hDlg, WORD Message,
68:                            WPARAM wParam, LPARAM lParam);
```

Listing 17.3 shows the resource file for MenuTest.

Listing 17.3. MENUTEST.RC.

```
 1: //////////////////////////////////////////////////////////
 2: //   Program Name: MENUTEST.RC
 3: //   Programmer: Charlie Calvert
 4: //   Description: MenuTest windows program resource script
 5: //   Date: 04/28/93
 6: //////////////////////////////////////////////////////////
 7: #include "menutest.h"
 8: #include <windows.h>
 9:
10: MYKEYS ACCELERATORS
11: BEGIN
12:      VK_F1, CM_ROUNDCURSOR, VIRTKEY, ALT
13:      VK_F2, CM_DIAMONDCURSOR, VIRTKEY, CONTROL
14:      VK_F3, CM_ICONCURSOR, VIRTKEY, SHIFT
15:      "1", CM_ROUNDCURSOR, VIRTKEY, ALT
16:      "2", CM_DIAMONDCURSOR, VIRTKEY, ALT
17:      "3", CM_ICONCURSOR, VIRTKEY, ALT
18: END
19:
20: CURSOR_1 CURSOR "cursor1.cur"
21: CURSOR_2 CURSOR "cursor2.cur"
22: CURSOR_3 CURSOR "cursor3.cur"
23:
24: ICON_1 ICON "icon1.ico"
25:
26: BITMAP_1 BITMAP "iconbmp.bmp"
27: BITMAP1A BITMAP "bitmap1a.bmp"
28: BITMAP_2 BITMAP "bitmap2.bmp"
29: BITMAP2A BITMAP "bitmap2a.bmp"
30: BITMAP_3 BITMAP "bitmap3.bmp"
31: BITMAP3A BITMAP "bitmap3a.bmp"
32: BMPEXIT BITMAP "exit.bmp"
```

```
33:
34: MENU_1 MENU
35: BEGIN
36:      POPUP "&File"
37:      BEGIN
38:          MENUITEM "&New", CM_NEW
39:          MENUITEM "&Open...", CM_OPEN
40:          MENUITEM "&Save", CM_SAVE
41:          MENUITEM "Save &as...", CM_SAVEAS,
42:          MENUITEM SEPARATOR
43:          POPUP "&Print..."
44:          BEGIN
45:              MENUITEM "Print To Disk", CM_PRNDISK
46:              MENUITEM "Print LPT1", CM_PRNLPT1
47:          END
48:          MENUITEM "Page se&tup...", CM_PAGESETUP
49:          MENUITEM "P&rinter setup...", CM_PRINTERSETUP
50:        MENUITEM SEPARATOR
51:          MENUITEM "E&xit", CM_EXIT
52:      END
53:      POPUP "&Cursors"
54:      BEGIN
55:          MENUITEM "&Round Cursor\tAlt+F1", CM_ROUNDCURSOR
56:          MENUITEM "&Diamond Cursor\tCtrl+F2", CM_DIAMONDCURSOR
57:          MENUITEM "&Draw Icon\tShift+F3", CM_ICONCURSOR
58:      END
59:      POPUP "BitCursors"
60:      BEGIN
61:          MENUITEM "Item", CM_BITMENU1
62:          MENUITEM "Item", CM_BITMENU2
63:          MENUITEM "Item", CM_BITMENU3
64:      END
65:      MENUITEM "&Help", CM_HELP
66: END
67:
68: HELPBOX DIALOG 18, 18, 166, 119
69: STYLE DS_MODALFRAME | WS_POPUP | WS_CAPTION | WS_SYSMENU
70: CAPTION "Help Dialog"
71: BEGIN
72:      PUSHBUTTON "Close", IDOK, 11, 97, 144, 14
73:      CONTROL "Icon_1", -1,  "STATIC", SS_ICON | WS_CHILD |
74:              WS_VISIBLE | WS_GROUP, 137, 9, 16, 16
75:      CONTROL "Icon_1", -1, "STATIC", SS_ICON | WS_CHILD |
76:              WS_VISIBLE | WS_GROUP, 13, 9, 16, 16
77:      CONTROL "", ID_HELPEDIT, "EDIT", ES_CENTER | ES_MULTILINE |
78:              ES_READONLY | WS_CHILD | WS_VISIBLE | WS_BORDER |
79:              WS_VSCROLL | WS_TABSTOP, 6, 34, 154, 56
80: END
```

ICON1.ICO (32X32)   *CURSOR1.CUR (32X32)*   *CURSOR2.CUR (32X32)*

CURSOR3.CUR (32X32)   *ICONBMP.BMP (68X36)*   *BITMAP1A.BMP (68X36)*

BITMAP2.BMP (68X36)   *BITMAP2A.BMP (68X36)*   *BITMAP3.BMP (68X36)*

BITMAP3A.BMP (68X36)   *EXIT.BMP (128X64)*

          EXIT

Listing 17.4 shows the definition file for MenuTest.

Type   Listing 17.4. **MENUTEST.DEF.**

```
1: ; MENUTEST.DEF
2: NAME           MenuTest
3: DESCRIPTION    'MenuTest Window'
4: EXETYPE        WINDOWS
5: STUB           'WINSTUB.EXE'
6: HEAPSIZE       4096
7: STACKSIZE      5120
8: CODE           PRELOAD MOVEABLE DISCARDABLE
9: DATA           PRELOAD MOVEABLE MULTIPLE
```

Listing 17.5 shows the Borland makefile for MenuTest.

Listing 17.5. MENUTEST.MAK (Borland).

```
 1: # MENUTEST.MAK
 2:
 3: # macros
 4: APPNAME = MenuTest
 5: INCPATH = C:\BC\INCLUDE
 6: LIBPATH = C:\BC\LIB
 7: FLAGS = -H -ml -W -v -w4 -I$(INCPATH) -L$(LIBPATH)
 8:
 9: # link
10: $(APPNAME).exe: $(APPNAME).obj $(APPNAME).def $(APPNAME).res
11:   bcc $(FLAGS) $(APPNAME).obj
12:   brc menutest.res menutest.exe
13:
14: #compile
15: $(APPNAME).obj: $(APPNAME).cpp
16:   bcc -c $(FLAGS $APPNAME).cpp
17:
18: #compile
19: MenuTest.res: $(APPNAME).rc
20:   brc -r -i$(INCPATH) MenuTest.rc
```

Listing 17.6 shows the Microsoft makefile for MenuTest.

Listing 17.6. MENUTEST.MAK (Microsoft).

```
 1: # --------------------
 2: MenuTest.Mak
 3: # --------------------
 4:
 5: # --------------------
 6: # Link
 7: # --------------------
 8: MenuTest.exe : MenuTest.obj MenuTest.def MenuTest.res
 9: link MenuTest, /align:16, NUL, /nod llibcew libw, MenuTest
10: rc MenuTest.res
11:
12: # --------------------
13: # Compile
14: # --------------------
15: MenuTest.obj : MenuTest.ccp
16:   cl -c -AL -GA -Ow -W3 -Zp MenuTest.cpp
```

continues

Listing 17.6. continued

```
17:
18: # --------------------
19: # Compile
20: # --------------------
21: MenuTest.res: MenuTest.rc
22:   rc -r MenuTest.rc
```

 Figure 17.5 shows the MenuTest program.

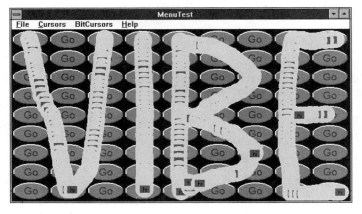

Figure 17.5. *The MenuTest program enables you to place bitmaps in menus and to paint patterns on-screen with an icon.*

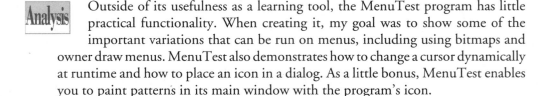 Outside of its usefulness as a learning tool, the MenuTest program has little practical functionality. When creating it, my goal was to show some of the important variations that can be run on menus, including using bitmaps and owner draw menus. MenuTest also demonstrates how to change a cursor dynamically at runtime and how to place an icon in a dialog. As a little bonus, MenuTest enables you to paint patterns in its main window with the program's icon.

To take it through its paces, select each of the menu items from the Cursors and BitCursors pop-up menus. The options from the Cursors menu change the shape of the program's cursor. The DrawCursor menu item lets you draw on the main window by pressing the left mouse button.

More on Menus

The first portion of this chapter gave an in-depth description of how to create a menu inside of an RC file. The next stage is to see what you can do with menus dynamically at runtime. Specifically, the text covers

☐ Placing a bitmap in a menu, as shown in the EXIT choice on the file menu

☐ Placing or removing a check mark in front of a menu item

☐ Creating owner draw menus that change shape and texture as the user selects individual menu items

☐ Deleting items from the system menu

Placing a Bitmap in a Menu

The key to placing a bitmap in a menu is the ModifyMenu command. This command enables you to modify the contents of an existing menu item. More specifically, it lets you change the string displayed in a menu item or entirely replace that string with a bitmap (as MenuTest does when it places the EXIT bitmap in the File menu).

The *ModifyMenu* Function

```
BOOL ModifyMenu(HMENU, UINT, UINT, UINT, LPCSTR)
```

HMENU hmenu;	Handle of the menu to modify
UINT idItem;	ID or the position of the menu item or popup
UINT fuFlags;	Multipurpose flag (see following explanation)
UINT idNewItem;	New ID of menu item
LPCSTR lpNewItem;	The new menu item, usually a string or bitmap

Most of the time, you just need to change the string or ID associated with a menu item. To do that, you need to pay special attention to the second and third fields of this function. If you pass MF_BYCOMMAND in the fuFlags field, you're telling Windows that the idItem field will be an ID. If you pass in MF_BYPOSITION, you're telling Windows that the second field is a zero-based offset from the beginning of the menu.

The third field also can be used to designate whether the `lpNewItem` argument is a string or bitmap. For instance, the following command designates the second field as an ID (rather than a position) and the last field as a string:

```
ModifyMenu(GetMenu(hwnd), CM_MYID,
        MF_BYCOMMAND ¦ MF_STRING,
        CM_MYID, (LPCSTR)"My New MenuItem");
```

The MenuTest program uses the ModifyMenu command to change the Exit option on the file menu to a bitmap:

```
ModifyMenu(GetMenu(hwnd), CM_EXIT,
        MF_BYCOMMAND ¦ MF_BITMAP,
        CM_EXIT, (LPCSTR)MAKELONG(BMPExit, 0));
```

The key portions of this call are in the third parameter, where the `MF_BITMAP` flag is placed, and the fifth parameter, where the handle to a bitmap is translated into a pointer and passed on to Windows. `BMPExit`, of course, is just a regular bitmap, designed with a paint program and loaded with a call to `LoadBitmap`.

To summarize, here's what I think about the `ModifyMenu` command: "Sometimes programmers want to delete a menu with the `DeleteMenu` command or append a menu with the `AppendMenu` command. A third alternative is to modify an existing menu with the `ModifyMenu` command." In other words, when you want to change the contents of an existing menu, use the `ModifyMenu` command.

`ModifyMenu and MF_OWNERDRAW`

The real power of the `ModifyMenu` command becomes apparent in the BitCursors pop-up menu, which features three owner draw menus, as shown in Figure 17.1. To be utterly frank, I find that after all these years, the standard Windows menu system sometimes becomes a bit of a bore, and I'm willing to do just about anything to spice it up. This is when an owner draw menu comes to the rescue. This little tool can be used to create stunning menus that can make your program stand out.

Following are the steps you take to create an owner draw menu:

☐ Call `ModifyMenu` and set the `MF_OWNERDRAW` flag.

☐ Tell Windows how large to make the pop-up menu window by responding to `WM_MEASUREITEM` messages.

☐ Respond to `WM_DRAWITEM` messages by drawing either a selected or non-selected menu item, depending on the state of the `ODS_SELECTED` flag.

The rest of this section explains these concepts in depth.

To get started with owner draw menus, just make a ModifyMenu call that looks something like this:

```
ModifyMenu(GetMenu(hwnd),
           CM_BITMENU1, MF_BYCOMMAND ¦ MF_OWNERDRAW,
           CM_BITMENU1, (LPCSTR)MAKELONG(Bitmap1, 0));
```

As you can see, this call is similar to the call to place a bitmap in a menu, except that the MF_OWNERDRAW flag is used in lieu of the MF_BITMAP flag.

Turning on the MF_OWNERDRAW flag means that the program's main window needs to start responding to WM_MEASUREITEM and WM_DRAWITEM messages. The first of these messages comes down the pike when the menu is first displayed, and gives MenuTest a chance to designate the size of the pop-up window that will hold your menu bitmaps. The second message gives MenuTest a chance to actually display the bitmap in question, a chore that must be handled explicitly by the program. (That's why they call it owner draw; the drawing is handled by the program—not by Windows.)

At first, it would seem that responding to WM_MEASUREITEM messages would be simple. As it turns out, one hang-up is that Windows sets aside a space before each menu in which a check mark can appear. (See Figure 17.3 for an example of how a check mark appears in a normal menu.)

When working with owner draw menus, however, the MenuTest program ignores the whole idea of inserting check marks. Therefore, it has to query Windows to find out how much space is set aside for check marks; it then subtracts that from the total width of the bitmap. This whole process is carried out through the auspices of the aptly named GetMenuCheckMarkDimensions function:

```
void MenuTest_OnMeasureItem(HWND hwnd,
                             MEASUREITEMSTRUCT FAR* lpMeasureItem)
{
  WORD CheckWidth;

  CheckWidth = LOWORD (GetMenuCheckMarkDimensions());
  switch ( lpMeasureItem->itemID )
  {
    case CM_BITMENU1:
    case CM_BITMENU2:
    case CM_BITMENU3:
     lpMeasureItem->itemWidth = BStruct.bmWidth - CheckWidth - 3;
     lpMeasureItem->itemHeight = BStruct.bmHeight - 1;
     break;
  }
}
```

This code, from line 350 of MENUTEST.CPP, shows how the program handles WM_MEASUREITEM messages. The first step is to get the width of the area set aside for check marks, and then to subtract that from the width of the bitmap. Windows uses this information to set the size of the window enclosing the menu items.

BStruct (see following explanation) is a BITMAP struct containing the dimensions of the current bitmap. MenuTest obtains these dimensions with a call to GetObject.

Syntax

The *GetObject* Function

```
int GetObject(HGDIOBJ, int, void FAR *)
```

HGDIOBJ hgdiobj;	Handle of the bitmap, font, brush or pen
int cbBuffer;	Size of the buffer in the third argument
void FAR* lpvObject;	Buffer to hold information retrieved by call to GetObject

When retrieving information about bitmaps, the structure used in the third parameter looks like this:

```
typedef struct tagBITMAP {   /* bm */
    int     bmType;
    int     bmWidth;
    int     bmHeight;
    int     bmWidthBytes;
    BYTE    bmPlanes;
    BYTE    bmBitsPixel;
    void FAR* bmBits;
} BITMAP;
```

Here's an example call to GetObject:

```
GetObject(Bitmap1, sizeof(BITMAP), &BStruct);
```

After MenuTest responds to WM_MEASUREITEM, the bitmap is drawn in response to WM_DRAWITEM messages. This excerpt from the MenuTest_OnDrawItem function (line 318) shows how this is done:

```
void MenuTest_OnDrawItem(HWND hwnd,
                         const DRAWITEMSTRUCT FAR *lpDrawItem)
{
  switch(lpDrawItem->itemID)
  {
    case CM_BITMENU1:
      if (lpDrawItem->itemState & ODS_SELECTED)
        DrawBitmap(lpDrawItem->hDC, Bitmap1a, 0);
      else
```

```
        DrawBitmap(lpDrawItem->hDC, Bitmap1, 0);
    break;
    ...  // Code to handle other menu items
  }
}
```

The central issue is that the menu items in question can be in one of two states, either selected or not selected. Each of these states needs to be depicted differently, as shown in Figure 17.6.

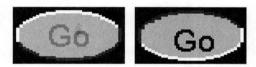

Figure 17.6. *On the left is a normal menu; on the right is a selected menu.*

Whenever the user selects a menu item, Windows politely informs MenuTest by setting the ODS_SELECTED flag. MenuTest responds by sending the appropriate bitmap to the DrawBitmap function (line 299 in MENUTEST.CPP):

```
void DrawBitmap(HDC PaintDC, HBITMAP Bitmap, int YVal)
{
  HDC MemDC;
  HBITMAP OldBitmap;

  MemDC = CreateCompatibleDC(PaintDC);
  OldBitmap = SelectBitmap(MemDC, Bitmap);
  BitBlt(PaintDC, 0, YVal * BStruct.bmHeight, BStruct.bmWidth,
         BStruct.bmHeight, MemDC, 0, 0, SRCCOPY);
  SelectObject(MemDC, OldBitmap);
  DeleteObject(MemDC);
}
```

This function is similar to a standard paint function, except that the device context is supplied directly by Windows without the user having to call either BeginPaint or GetDC.

That's all there is to it. After MenuTest has blitted the bitmap to the screen, it can forget all about its owner draw menus—at least until the next WM_DRAWITEM message comes down the pike.

Following is a quick review of the steps needed to create owner draw menus:

☐ Set the MF_OWNERDRAW flag in the fuFlags argument to ModifyMenu.

☐ Respond to WM_MEASUREITEM messages so Windows will know how large to make the pop-up menu.

☐ Respond to `WM_DRAWITEM` messages by blitting a bitmap to the screen; pay special attention to the `ODS_SELECTED` flag.

Despite the presence of a few slippery moments, working with owner draw menus isn't too complex. Hopefully, this is a feature that will be included in more programs in the near future. Certainly, I think any programmer designing a program aimed at a young audience should use owner draw menus. These menus can give a program a playful, friendly interface, which would be very appealing to children.

 Note: Owner draw menus are a classic example of how Windows puts a special burden on the programmer in order to make a program easier to use and more attractive to the user.

Modifying the System Menu

The MenuTest program removes the Close option from the system menu (see Figures 17.7 and 17.8).

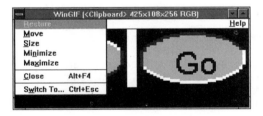

Figure 17.7. *A standard system menu.*

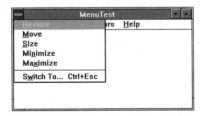

Figure 17.8. *The system menu from the MenuTest program.*

The end result of this action is to force the user to use the Exit option from the file menu, rather than exiting the program through the system menu. You should notice, for instance, that it's no longer possible to exit the program by double-clicking the system menu icon.

This code shows how to retrieve the handle to a system with a call to GetSystemMenu. You can then pass this handle to DeleteMenu. The DeleteMenu function removes entries from a menu, as explained in the following syntax box. The end result is that lines 159-162 modify the system menu in such a way that it can no longer be used to exit a program.

```
159; HMENU SysMenu = GetSystemMenu(hwnd, FALSE);
160:
161: DeleteMenu(SysMenu, 6, MF_BYPOSITION);
162: DeleteMenu(SysMenu, 6, MF_BYPOSITION);
```

This code from MenuTest_OnCreate (lines 159-162), shows how to retrieve the system menu with a call to GetSystemMenu and then delete the menu with a call to DeleteMenu.

Syntax

The *DeleteMenu* Function

```
BOOL DeleteMenu(HMENU, UINT, UINT)
```

HMENU hmenu;	Handle of the menu containing item to delete
UINT idItem;	ID or position of the item to delete
UINT fuFlags;	Flag specifying MF_BYPOSITION or MF_BYCOMMAND

The DeleteMenu call is very straightforward. The only thing you need to watch out for is that after you delete an item by position, the next item in the menu assumes the number of the item you just deleted. That's why the code shown deletes items 6 and 7 from the menu by deleting item 6 twice. In the previous example, the two items being deleted are the Close string and the menu item Separator.

Example:

```
DeleteMenu(hMenu, ID_MYMENUITEM, MF_BYCOMMAND);
```

Placing a Check Before a Menu Item

Whenever the user chooses a new cursor for the MenuTest program, a check appears in front of the newly selected option from the Cursors pop-up menu. The following code performs this action:

```
HMENU Menu = GetMenu(hwnd);
CheckMenuItem(Menu, CM_ROUNDCURSOR, MF_BYCOMMAND | MF_CHECKED);
```

As you can see, MenuTest retrieves the handle to the program's menu with a call to GetMenu, and then sends a message asking that a particular menu item be checked. By now, the details of how this type of command works should be obvious to you without any detailed explanation. However, the following flags can be sent in the third parameter of CheckMenuItem:

MF_BYCOMMAND	The second parameter is an ID.
MF_BYPOSITION	The second parameter is a zero-based position.
MF_CHECKED	Place a check mark before a menu item.
MF_UNCHECKED	Remove a check mark from a menu item.

Selecting a New Cursor

Every on-screen window has a cursor associated with it. For instance, the main window of the NotePad program uses the I-beam cursor, whereas the menu of the NotePad program uses the arrow cursor. If you open up the File | Open dialog from the NotePad program, you can watch the cursor change when you move it over the edit control in its upper-left corner.

The seemingly rather insignificant chore of setting a new cursor for a window is important, because it sends a very clear message to the user about the current state or purpose of a window. Unlike icons, cursors usually convey a great deal of very useful information to the user—often without ever quite forcing a particular thought to appear on the conscious level. That is, people instinctively seem to know to point with the arrow cursor, write with the I-beam cursor, and wait when the hourglass cursor appears. No one has to tell users the meaning of these cursors, nor do they have to consciously think about their meaning.

Note: Some people get confused about the difference between a cursor and a caret. A *cursor* is always associated with the mouse. It moves around the screen as the mouse moves. A *caret* is usually associated with a window, such as an edit control, that enables you to type in and edit information. There are a whole series of commands, not covered in this chapter, for controlling the caret. They include: CreateCaret, DestroyCaret, SetCaretBlinkTime, HideCaret, and ShowCaret. In short, a cursor is what DOS users generally call a mouse cursor, and a caret is what DOS users generally call a cursor.

There are two common ways to change the cursor in a window. The first method is to go all the way into the internals of Windows and change the structure of a window's class with `SetClassWord`:

```
SetClassWord(hwnd, GCW_HCURSOR, (WORD)Cursor1);
SetCursor(Cursor1);
```

This code uses `SetClassWord` to reach `GCW_HCURSOR` bytes into the internal Windows-owned data structure that defines the attributes of MenuTest's main window. At that location, `SetClassWord` finds the old cursor for the program's main window and replaces it with a user-defined cursor. The code then makes the new cursor visible by calling `SetCursor`. It's important to understand that this is a two-step process: change the cursor for the class and then make the new cursor visible.

Before discussing the second way of changing a cursor, I should mention that it's possible to change the cursor for a window by calling `SetCursor` alone, without reference to `SetClassWord`. However, the change is fleeting unless you have first set the cursor for the class to zero. Even then, the change only lasts until the cursor leaves the current window. Therefore, you should call `SetCursor` in conjunction with `SetClassWord`, except when they are used together in a single complex statement (see the following description).

The second technique for changing a cursor is the one used when a programmer wants to pop up the hourglass cursor while a particular process is taking place. For instance, when a complex search is being conducted in a database, programmers usually pop up an hourglass cursor and close off all other options. This way, the user is forced to wait until the search is completed.

If you want to change the cursor to an hourglass, and leave it that way until an operation is completed, call `SetCursor` and `SetCapture` in immediate succession (see the following code). When you are done, reset the cursor to its old value and call `ReleaseCapture`.

```
SetCapture(hwnd);
hCursor OldCursor = SetCursor(LoadCursor(0, IDC_HOURGLASS);
... // Perform code and/or time-intensive operation
SetCursor(OldCursor);
ReleaseCapture();
```

Typically, programmers call `SetCapture` on an inert window, such as a static text, or on a push button with an ID, such as `IDABORT` or `IDCANCEL`. If used with an inert window, the user can't do anything until ReleaseCapture is called. If used with an abort or Cancel button, the user is capable only of aborting or canceling the current operation.

The *SetCapture* Function

```
HWND SetCapture(HWND)
```

The SetCapture function takes one parameter. This parameter is the window to which you should direct all mouse input until ReleaseCapture is called. SetCapture returns the HWND of the window that previously had the focus, or returns NULL if there is no such window. ReleaseCapture takes a void argument and returns a void.

Example:

```
SetCapture(IDCANCEL);
ReleaseCapture();
```

Following is a list of the standard cursors that come with the system:

IDC_ARROW	Arrow cursor
IDC_CROSS	Similar to the X and Y axis on a Cartesian grid
IDC_IBEAM	I-beam cursor
IDC_ICON	Empty icon
IDC_SIZE	Similar to IDC_CROSS with arrows at the end of each axis
IDC_SIZENESW	Arrows pointing northeast and southwest
IDC_SIZENS	Arrows pointing north and south
IDC_SIZENWSE	Arrows pointing northwest and southeast
IDC_SIZEWE	Arrows pointing west and east
IDC_UPARROW	Big arrow pointing north
IDC_WAIT	The classic hourglass cursor

You can load any of these cursors by calling LoadCursor, with the first parameter set to zero (as previously shown).

The opposite of a system-defined cursor is a user-defined cursor. The MenuTest program displays a number of user-defined cursors. These cursors can be designed in either the Resource Workshop or the App Studio. All you need to do is make the appropriate menu selections and then start drawing with the mouse.

Given a set of predefined cursors, MenuTest loads them in response to a WM_CREATE message (Lines 130 - 132):

```
Cursor1 = LoadCursor(hInstance, "CURSOR_1");
Cursor2 = LoadCursor(hInstance, "CURSOR_2");
Cursor3 = LoadCursor(hInstance, "CURSOR_3");
```

Unlike system cursors, the Microsoft documentation states that you should call `DestroyCursor` on any custom cursors you load into a program (see lines 192-194 of MENUTEST.CPP). The debug version of Windows doesn't complain if you don't do this, but I suggest you play it safe and follow the Microsoft documentation.

That wraps up this discussion of cursors. In this section you've learned two main points:

☐ To associate a cursor permanently with a window, call both `SetClassWord` and `SetCursor`.

☐ If you want to temporarily set a cursor (during the course of an operation that can't be interrupted), call `SetCursor`; follow that with a call to `SetCapture`. When you finish, be sure to restore the original cursor and call `ReleaseCapture`.

Advanced Icons

If you pop up the Help dialog for the MenuTest program, you'll see that it contains two icons (as shown in Figure 17.9).

Figure 17.9. *The Help dialog has two imbedded icons.*

While you create the RC file for this dialog, you can give a static control the capability to house an icon. Simply assign the static control the `SS_ICON` style and supply it with the name of an icon:

```
ICON_1 ICON "icon1.ico"

CONTROL "Icon_1", -1, "STATIC",
        SS_ICON ¦ WS_CHILD ¦ WS_VISIBLE ¦ WS_GROUP,
        137, 9, 16, 16
```

Notice that this code refers to the icon by its assigned name, not by its filename. Also, the last two parameters, designating the width and height of the static text, are ignored. They're ignored because the static text box is automatically sized to fit the icon.

MenuTest's second trick with icons enables you to repeatedly paint the surface of the main window with the image of the program's icon (as shown in Figure 17.10).

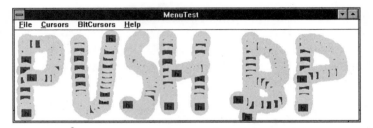

Figure 17.10. *MenuTest uses* DrawIcon *and* WM_MOUSEMOVE *messages to paint patterns on its main window.*

The following code is used to paint the icon on-screen:

```
void MenuTest_OnMouseMove(HWND hwnd, int x, int y, UINT keyFlags)
{
  if (((keyFlags & MK_LBUTTON) == MK_LBUTTON) && (PaintIcon))
  {
    HDC PaintDC = GetDC(hwnd);
    DrawIcon(PaintDC, x, y, Icon1);
    ReleaseDC(hwnd, PaintDC);
  }
}
```

Whenever the mouse is moved over the main window, the program checks to see whether the left mouse button is down and whether the Boolean PaintIcon variable is set to TRUE. If both conditions are met, MenuTest retrieves the device context of the main window and paints (with the DrawIcon function) an icon on-screen at the current mouse location.

DO	**DON'T**

DO load icons into memory with the LoadIcon call, passing zero in the first parameter if the icon is a system icon, such as IDI_APPLICATION.

DON'T forget to dispose of the memory associated with an icon by calling DestroyIcon.

Accelerators—Briefly

Finally, the issue of accelerators is up for discussion. Accelerators, or *hot keys*, enable you to define custom key combinations so a user can gain quick access to certain features of your program. For instance, the MenuTest program lets you switch cursors by pressing Alt-1, Alt-2, and Alt-3. Because you might be interested in defining more complex hot key combinations, MenuTest also accesses these same icons with Alt-F1, Ctrl-F2, and Shift-F3. Each of these latter combinations are shown to the user in the menu.

Accelerators are easy to use. To define them, just pop up the Resource Workshop or App Studio and use the custom tools they include for defining accelerators. It's also very easy to design accelerators with a word processor:

```
BEGIN
  VK_F1, CM_ROUNDCURSOR, VIRTKEY, ALT
  VK_F2, CM_DIAMONDCURSOR, VIRTKEY, CONTROL
  VK_F3, CM_ICONCURSOR, VIRTKEY, SHIFT
  "1", CM_ROUNDCURSOR, VIRTKEY, ALT
  "2", CM_DIAMONDCURSOR, VIRTKEY, ALT
  "3", CM_ICONCURSOR, VIRTKEY, ALT
END
```

Note: Typically, hot keys are defined with the Alt-key and any other number or letter key. However, the MenuTest program also provides examples of how to use the Alt, Control, and Shift keys in combination with one of the function keys.

After you've defined an accelerator table, you need to load it into memory:

```
static HACCEL  hAccel
hAccel = LoadAccelerators(hInstance, "MYKEYS");
if (hAccel == NULL)
    MessageBox(MainWindow, "No Accelerators", "Warning", MB_OK);
```

The MenuTest program performs this simple operation in response to WM_CREATE messages. However, there is an argument for moving the whole process into WinMain, because the hAccel value returned from LoadAccelerators is used in the program's message loop (see following explanation). Either course is fine. I chose to load the accelerators in MenuTest_OnCreate because I've been performing all program initialization there, and I wanted to remain consistent. (A benefit of doing all your initialization in response to WM_CREATE is that it leaves the WinMain, Create, and Register functions almost completely static from one program to the next, thereby letting you ignore them—except for a quick check of the WNDCLASS structure and the message loop.)

The final step in using accelerators is simply to add a TranslateAccelerator line to the message loop, just as you did when calling IsDialogMessage in the FileBox program:

```
while (GetMessage(&Msg, NULL, 0, 0))
{
  if (!TranslateAccelerator(MainWindow, hAccel, &Msg))
  {
    TranslateMessage(&Msg);
    DispatchMessage(&Msg);
  }
}
```

The obvious purpose of TranslateAccelerator is to handle any of the hot keys defined in your program before they are passed on to the destination window procedure with DispatchMessage. In other words, Windows checks to see if the user has pressed a hot key; if so, Windows translates the key press into a message. Otherwise, it just passes the message on directly to your main window procedure.

DO   DON'T

DO call LoadAccelerators to load accelerators into memory.

DON'T worry about disposing of accelerators. Windows handles that task internally.

Summary

Day 17 contained few surprises. Most of the code has been useful, but not particularly difficult to understand. Following is a quick review of the high points:

- [ ] You can add variety and/or flexibility to menus by nesting pop-up menus, or by using the statements SEPARATOR, MENUBARBREAK, GRAYED, CHECKED, or UNCHECKED.

- [ ] To really spice up a menu, modify it with either the MF_BITMAP or MF_OWNERDRAW styles.

- [ ] You can change the cursor associated with a window in order to clue the user to its purpose or current status.

- [ ] Icons can be placed in dialogs or painted directly on-screen.

- [ ] The keyboard interface to a program can be enhanced by using accelerators.

All this material is useful, even vital, but the only really fancy code shown in this chapter involved creating owner draw menus. Like the right mouse button, menus are a relatively wide-open field in Windows programming. Anyone willing to do a little creative work could easily come up with some very interesting innovations in this area.

Q&A

1. I still don't really understand the relationship between MF_OWNERDRAW, WM_MEASUREITEM, and WM_DRAWITEM. What's the scoop?

    When you set the MF_OWNERDRAW flag, you are in effect telling Windows that you want to handle the drawing of the menu item in question. Windows responds: "Fine, that's okay with me. Just tell me how big you want the pop-up window that's going to hold your bitmaps." You answer this question by responding to WM_MEASUREITEM messages. Now that all the preparations are complete, Windows politely sends you a WM_DRAWITEM message every time a menu item needs to be drawn or updated.

2. One more time, just so I'm sure—when I'm setting a cursor, when should I call SetCapture, and when should I call SetClassWord?

    Call SetClassWord when you want to permanently change the cursor for a window without in any other way affecting its performance. This change will stay in effect until you call SetClassWord again, or until the window in question is closed. Call `SetCapture` when you want to temporarily funnel all mouse input to one particular window, while simultaneously assuring that the cursor doesn't change—regardless of which window it is over. Typically, this kind of thing is done when you want to change the cursor to an hourglass while a lengthy processor intensive operation is taking place.

Workshop

The Workshop provides quiz questions to help you solidify your understanding of the material covered and exercises to provide you with experience in using what you've learned. Try to understand the quiz and exercise answers before continuing on to the next chapter. Answers are provided in Appendix A.

Quiz

1. The MenuTest program specifies hot keys in the menu items that are part of the Cursors pop-up menu (Figure 17.3). How does it separate these hot key assignments from the regular menu text?

2. How do you place an underline beneath a letter in a menu? What effect does this have?

3. What call needs to be inserted into a program's message loop if the program is making use of accelerators?

4. How can you tell whether a menu item is selected or not selected when you get the `WM_DRAWITEM` message?

5. Use your reference materials to specify at least seven different flags used in the third field (`fuFlags`) of the `ModifyMenu` function.

6. What's the difference between `MF_BYPOSITION` and `MF_BYCOMMAND`?

7. If you are using the `MF_BYPOSITION` flag, is the first menu item listed a zero or a one?

8. What purpose does the `SS_ICON` style serve?

9. What function must a programmer call every time he or she calls `SetCapture`? (Hint: the answer isn't `SetCursor`!)

10. How can you obtain the dimensions of a bitmap at runtime?

Exercises

1. Create a user draw menu that beeps and/or changes the background color of the main window every time the user focuses it with the arrow keys. (Extra credit: Animate an owner draw menu!)

2. Demonstrate how to use the SetCursor and SetCapture functions to globally change the cursor to an hourglass. Keep the change in effect until the user clicks the left mouse button on the program's main window.

GDI and
Metafiles

Today, you'll learn more about the GDI. The source code for this chapter demonstrates how to create the rudiments of a simple paint program that can be used to draw colorful shapes and display metafiles. In particular, you'll learn

☐ How to work with the basic GDI commands for creating geometrical shapes, such as lines, ellipses, and rectangles

☐ How to enable users to draw these shapes on-screen using the "rubber band" technique that previews what a shape will look like while a user is forming it with the mouse. From the user's perspective, this is the same technique used to grab the border of a window and resize it with the mouse.

☐ How to display two different kinds of metafiles

☐ How to create, draw, and save standard metafiles

☐ How to load and save files using common dialogs

The theme of this chapter is working with geometric shapes—on-screen, in memory, and when you save them to disk as metafiles. Metafiles offer alternatives to the slow, disk-intensive operations that you need to initiate when working with bitmaps. When working with bitmaps, the coin of the realm is the pixel, and each pixel must be defined and mapped out in detail. When working with metafiles, the bottom line is a geometric shape, such as a line, rectangle, polygon, or ellipse. Though there are some trade-offs involved, this can prove to be a quicker, more flexible, and much less disk-intensive way of working with an image.

Working with Shapes

The code for today's program centers around the GDI calls that enable you to draw geometric figures (see Table 18.1). These are the same types of figures that you find in DOS graphics libraries, such as the Borland BGI.

Table 18.1. Some important functions that draw figures.

Function Name	Output
Chord	Arcs with ends tied together by a straight line
Ellipse	Circles or ellipses
Pie	Pie-shaped figures

Function Name	Output
Polygon	Triangles, or any figures with two or more points connected by straight lines
Rectangle	Squares or rectangles
RoundRect	Squares or rectangles with rounded corners

The WM_PAINT response function, from the program which generated this figure, is shown in Listing 18.1. An example of each of the shapes from Listing 18.1 is shown in Figure 18.1. FIGS.CPP is included on this book's disk; if you want to create the program by hand, you can add Figs_OnPaint to a standard GENERIC.CPP project.

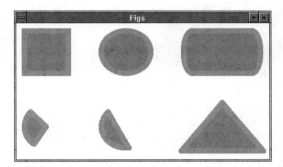

Figure 18.1. *Seated from left to right, starting on the top row: Fred Rectangle, Joyce Ellipse, Leslie RoundRect, Sarah Pie, Robin Chord, and Jed Polygon.*

Listing 18.1. This excerpt from FIGS.CPP demonstrates how to draw the six most common geometric shapes.

Type

```
1: void Figs_OnPaint(HWND hwnd)
2: {
3:   HDC PaintDC;
4:   PAINTSTRUCT PaintStruct;
5:
6:   PaintDC = BeginPaint(hwnd, &PaintStruct);
7:
8:   HBRUSH GreenBrush = CreateSolidBrush(RGB(0, 255, 63));
9:   HPEN RedPen = CreatePen(PS_INSIDEFRAME, 10, RGB(255, 0, 0));
10:   HBRUSH OldBrush = SelectBrush(PaintDC, GreenBrush);
11:   HPEN OldPen = SelectPen(PaintDC, RedPen);
12:
```

continues

Listing 18.1. continued

```
13:    Rectangle(PaintDC, 10, 10, 100, 100);
14:    Ellipse(PaintDC, 150, 10, 250, 100);
15:    RoundRect(PaintDC, 300, 10, 450, 100, 40, 80);
16:    Pie(PaintDC, 10, 150, 100, 240, 10, 150, 50, 200);
17:    Chord(PaintDC, 150, 150, 250, 240, 150, 150, 200, 200);
18:
19:    const int NumPoints = 3;
20:
21:    POINT P[NumPoints];
22:    P[0].x = 300;
23:    P[0].y = 240;
24:    P[1].x = 375;
25:    P[1].y = 150;
26:    P[2].x = 450;
27:    P[2].y = 240;
28:
29:    Polygon(PaintDC, P, NumPoints);
30:
31:    SelectBrush(PaintDC, OldBrush);
32:    SelectPen(PaintDC, OldPen);
33:    DeleteObject(RedPen);
34:    DeleteObject(GreenBrush);
35:
36:    EndPaint(hwnd, &PaintStruct);
37: }
```

Whenever you create any of the shapes shown in Figure 18.1, they're filled with the current brush and outlined with the current pen. To emphasize this fact, I created a brush and pen for Figs_OnPaint and copied it into the program's device context.

The brush shown in Figure 18.2 was created with the CreateHatchBrush function, which can take any of the following constants in its first parameter:

HS_BDIAGONAL	Diagonal hatch (45 degrees left to right)
HS_CROSS	Hatch with horizontal and vertical lines
HS_DIAGCROSS	Cross hatch
HS_FDIAGONAL	Diagonal hatch marks right to left
HS_HORIZONTAL	Horizontal lines
HS_VERTICAL	Vertical lines

Of course, if you use CreateHatchBrush, rather than CreateSolidBrush, you get hatch-marked shapes, as shown in Figure 18.2.

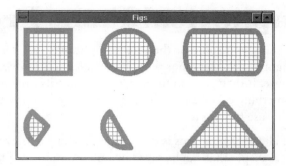

Figure 18.2. *A rectangle, ellipse, roundrect, pie, chord, and polygon all filled in with a solid brush.*

The pen used in Figs_OnPaint is bright red; it's also ten pixels thick. Thick pens can give your figures weight and substance.

Syntax

The *CreatePen* Function

```
HPEN CreatePen(int, int, COLORREF)
```

int fnPenStyle;	The pen's style
int nWidth;	The pen's width
COLORREF clrref;	The pen's color

When you're creating a pen, you can use any of the following styles in the first parameter:

PS_SOLID	A solid line
PS_DASH	A dashed line if the pen width is 1
PS_DOT	A dotted line if the pen width is 1
PS_DASHDOT	Line with dashes and dots if pen width is 1
PS_DASHDOTDOT	Line with dash and two dots if width is 1
PS_NULL	A null, or blank pen
PS_INSIDEFRAME	Line inside the frame of a closed shape

The second parameter is the pen's width measured in logical units. The third parameter is a COLORREF, which is a 32-bit value, usually created with the RGB macro.

There isn't really a whole lot more to say about creating basic geometric shapes using the GDI. The operations involved are very simple and usually quite trouble-free.

A Metaphorical Paint Program

In order to show you some of the interesting things that can be done with these geometric figures, the Metaphor program enables you to dynamically draw shapes with the mouse. It then goes on to show that it's possible to save collections of these shapes in something called a metafile. A metafile can be played back at will by using several easy-to-use functions.

The basis of all CAD programs is the idea of breaking a drawing down into a series of geometrical shapes that can be saved in a file. A number of fancy paint programs, such as CorelDRAW!, also base much of their output on a similar scheme. In fact, CorelDRAW! enables you to export its drawings as metafiles.

The Metaphor program is a starting point, but with a little patience and perseverance, you can convert it into a very powerful paint program. See Listing 18.2 for the code.

Listing 18.2. The Metaphor program enables the user to create and display metafiles that contain lists of geometric shapes.

```
 1: //////////////////////////////////////////////////////////
 2: //  File Name: METAPHOR.CPP
 3: //  Programmer: Charlie Calvert
 4: //  Description: Meta windows program
 5: //  Date: 4/17/93
 6: //////////////////////////////////////////////////////////
 7: #define STRICT
 8: #include <windows.h>
 9: #include <windowsx.h>
10: #pragma hdrstop
11: #include <string.h>
12: #include <direct.h>
13: #include "metaphor.h"
14: #include "metautil.h"
15: #include "metaenum.h"
16: #pragma warning (disable: 4068)
17: // ----------------------------------------------------------
18: // Interface
19: // ----------------------------------------------------------
20:
21: // Variables
22: static HBRUSH FBrush;
23: static char szAppName[] = "Metaphor";
24: static HWND MainWindow;
25: static HINSTANCE hInstance;
26: static TDATA Dat;
27: static RECT OldRect;
28: static HMETAFILE GooberMeta;
```

```
29: static HDC GooberDC;
30: HMETAFILE hmf;
31: char TempName[256];
32:
33: // ----------------------------------------------------
34: // Initialization
35: // ----------------------------------------------------
36:
37: ////////////////////////////////////////////////////////
38: // Program entry point
39: ////////////////////////////////////////////////////////
40: #pragma argsused
41: int PASCAL WinMain(HINSTANCE hInst, HINSTANCE hPrevInstance,
42:                    LPSTR lpszCmdParam, int nCmdShow)
43: {
44:   MSG  Msg;
45:
46:   if (!hPrevInstance)
47:     if (!Register(hInst))
48:       return FALSE;
49:
50:   (MainWindow = Create(hInst, nCmdShow);
51:   if (MainWindow)
52:     return FALSE;
53:   while (GetMessage(&Msg, NULL, 0, 0))
54:   {
55:       TranslateMessage(&Msg);
56:       DispatchMessage(&Msg);
57:   }
58:
59:   return Msg.wParam;
60: }
61:
62: //////////////////////////////////////
63: // Register the window
64: //////////////////////////////////////
65: BOOL Register(HINSTANCE hInst)
66: {
67:   WNDCLASS WndClass;
68:
69:   WndClass.style         = CS_HREDRAW | CS_VREDRAW;
70:   WndClass.lpfnWndProc   = WndProc;
71:   WndClass.cbClsExtra    = 0;
72:   WndClass.cbWndExtra    = 0;
73:   WndClass.hInstance     = hInst;
74:   WndClass.hIcon         = 0;
75:   WndClass.hCursor       = LoadCursor(NULL, IDC_ARROW);
76:   WndClass.hbrBackground = GetStockBrush(WHITE_BRUSH);
77:   WndClass.lpszMenuName  = "MetaMenu";
78:   WndClass.lpszClassName = szAppName;
79:
```

18

continues

Listing 18.2. continued

```
80:    return RegisterClass (&WndClass);
81: }
82:
83: /////////////////////////////////////
84: // Create the window
85: /////////////////////////////////////
86: HWND Create(HINSTANCE hInst, int nCmdShow)
87: {
88:
89:    hInstance = hInst;
90:
91:    HWND hWindow = CreateWindow(szAppName, szAppName,
92:                    WS_OVERLAPPEDWINDOW,
93:                    CW_USEDEFAULT, CW_USEDEFAULT,
94:                    CW_USEDEFAULT, CW_USEDEFAULT,
95:                    NULL, NULL, hInst, NULL);
96:
97:    if (hWindow == NULL)
98:      return hWindow;
99:
100:   ShowWindow(hWindow, nCmdShow);
101:   UpdateWindow(hWindow);
102:
103:   return hWindow;
104: }
105:
106: // ----------------------------------------------------
107: // WndProc and Implementation
108: // ----------------------------------------------------
109:
110: /////////////////////////////////////
111: // The Window Procedure
112: /////////////////////////////////////
113: LRESULT CALLBACK _export WndProc(HWND hwnd, UINT Message,
114:                                  WPARAM wParam, LPARAM lParam)
115: {
116:   switch(Message)
117:   {
118:     HANDLE_MSG(hwnd, WM_CREATE, Meta_OnCreate);
119:     HANDLE_MSG(hwnd, WM_DESTROY, Meta_OnDestroy);
120:     HANDLE_MSG(hwnd, WM_COMMAND, Meta_OnCommand);
121:     HANDLE_MSG(hwnd, WM_LBUTTONDOWN, Meta_OnLButtonDown);
122:     HANDLE_MSG(hwnd, WM_LBUTTONUP, Meta_OnLButtonUp);
123:     HANDLE_MSG(hwnd, WM_MOUSEMOVE, Meta_OnMouseMove);
124:     HANDLE_MSG(hwnd, WM_PAINT, Meta_OnPaint);
125:
126:     default: return Meta_DefProc(hwnd, Message, wParam, lParam);
127:   }
128: }
```

```
129:
130: //////////////////////////////////
131: // Handle WM_CREATE
132: //////////////////////////////////
133: #pragma argsused
134: BOOL Meta_OnCreate(HWND hwnd, CREATESTRUCT FAR* lpCreateStruct)
135: {
136:   Dat.Color = RGB(0, 0, 0);
137:   FBrush = CreateSolidBrush(RGB(255, 255, 255));
138:   Dat.Thickness = 10;
139:   PostMessage(hwnd, WM_COMMAND, CM_STARTMETA, 0);
140:   _getdcwd(0, TempName, MAXSIZE);
141:   strcat(TempName, "\\goober.$$$");
142: hmf=NULL
143:
144:   return TRUE;
145: }
146:
147: //////////////////////////////////
148: // Handle WM_DESTROY
149: //////////////////////////////////
150: #pragma argsused
151: void Meta_OnDestroy(HWND hwnd)
152: {
153:   if (hmf)
154:     DeleteMetaFile(hmf);
155:   DeleteObject(FBrush);
156:   PostQuitMessage(0);
157: }
158:
159: //////////////////////////////////
160: // Handle WM_COMMAND
161: //////////////////////////////////
162: #pragma argsused
163: void Meta_OnCommand(HWND hwnd, int id, HWND hwndCtl,
                         UINT codeNotify)
164: {
165:   switch (id)
166:   {
167:     case CM_STARTMETA:
168:       GooberDC = CreateMetaFile(TempName);
169:       break;
170:
171:    case CM_ENDMETA:
172:       TurnOffSave(hwnd);
173:       if (hmf)
174:         DeleteMetaFile(hmf);
175:       hmf = CloseMetaFile(GooberDC);
176:       SaveFile(hwnd, TempName);
177:       break;
178:
```

continues

609

Listing 18.2. continued

```
179:      case CM_NEWMETA:
180:          CreateMeta(hwnd);
181:          break;
182:
183:      case CM_LOAD:
184:          TurnOffSave(hwnd);
185:          LoadFile(hwnd);
186:          break;
187:
188:      case CM_EXIT:
189:          DestroyWindow(hwnd);
190:          break;
191:
192:      case CM_RECTANGLE:
193:          Dat.Shape = RECTANGLE;
194:          break;
195:
196:      case CM_ERECTANGLE:
197:          Dat.Shape = ERECTANGLE;
198:          break;
199:
200:      case CM_ELLIPSE:
201:          Dat.Shape = ELLIPSE;
202:          break;
203:
204:      case CM_LINE:
205:          Dat.Shape = LINE;
206:          break;
207:
208:      case CM_RED:
209:          Dat.Color = RGB(255, 0, 0);
210:          break;
211:
212:      case CM_GREEN:
213:          Dat.Color = RGB(0, 255, 0);
214:          break;
215:
216:      case CM_BLUE:
217:          Dat.Color = RGB(0, 0, 255);
218:          break;
219:
220:      case CM_FRED:
221:          DeleteBrush(FBrush);
222:          FBrush = CreateSolidBrush(RGB(255, 0, 0));
223:          break;
224:
225:      case CM_FGREEN:
226:          DeleteBrush(FBrush);
227:          FBrush = CreateSolidBrush(RGB(0, 255, 0));
228:          break;
```

```
229:
230:      case CM_FBLUE:
231:        DeleteBrush(FBrush);
232:        FBrush = CreateSolidBrush(RGB(0, 0, 255));
233:        break;
234:
235:      case CM_ONE:
236:        Dat.Thickness = 1;
237:        break;
238:
239:      case CM_FIVE:
240:        Dat.Thickness = 5;
241:        break;
242:
243:      case CM_TEN:
244:        Dat.Thickness = 10;
245:        break;
246:
247:      case CM_TWENTY:
248:        Dat.Thickness = 20;
249:        break;
250:
251:      case CM_FORTY:
252:        Dat.Thickness = 40;
253:        break;
254:
255:      case CM_EIGHTY:
256:        Dat.Thickness = 80;
257:        break;
258:    }
259: }
260:
261: ///////////////////////////////////
262: // DRAWSHAPE
263: ///////////////////////////////////
264: #pragma argsused
265: void DrawShape(HWND hwnd, HDC PaintDC, RECT R)
266: {
267:   switch(Dat.Shape)
268:   {
269:
270:      case ELLIPSE:
271:        Ellipse(PaintDC, R.left, R.top, R.right, R.bottom);
272:        break;
273:
274:      case LINE:
275:        MoveTo(PaintDC, R.left, R.top);
276:        LineTo(PaintDC, R.right, R.bottom);
277:        break;
278:
```

continues

18

Listing 18.2. continued

```
279:     case ERECTANGLE:
280:     case RECTANGLE:
281:        Rectangle(PaintDC, R.left, R.top, R.right, R.bottom);
282:        break;
283:   }
284: }
285:
286: /////////////////////////////////////
287: // DrawFinalShape
288: /////////////////////////////////////
289: #pragma argsused
290: void DrawFinalShape(HWND hwnd, HDC PaintDC, RECT R)
291: {
292:   HBRUSH B, OldBrush, OldGBrush;
293:
294:   HPEN Pen = CreatePen(PS_INSIDEFRAME, Dat.Thickness, Dat.Color);
295:   HPEN OldPen = SelectPen(PaintDC, Pen);
296:   HPEN OldGPen = SelectPen(GooberDC, Pen);
297:
298:   switch(Dat.Shape)
299:   {
300:     case ELLIPSE:
301:        OldBrush = SelectBrush(PaintDC, FBrush);
302:        OldGBrush = SelectBrush(GooberDC, FBrush);
303:        Ellipse(PaintDC, R.left, R.top, R.right, R.bottom);
304:        Ellipse(GooberDC, R.left, R.top, R.right, R.bottom);
305:        SelectObject(PaintDC, OldBrush);
306:        SelectBrush(GooberDC, OldGBrush);
307:        break;
308:
309:     case LINE:
310:        MoveTo(PaintDC, R.left, R.top);
311:        LineTo(PaintDC, R.right, R.bottom);
312:        MoveTo(GooberDC, R.left, R.top);
313:        LineTo(GooberDC, R.right, R.bottom);
314:        break;
315:
316:     case RECTANGLE:
317:        OldBrush = SelectBrush(PaintDC, FBrush);
318:        OldGBrush = SelectBrush(GooberDC, FBrush);
319:        Rectangle(PaintDC, R.left, R.top, R.right, R.bottom);
320:        Rectangle(GooberDC, R.left, R.top, R.right, R.bottom);
321:        SelectObject(PaintDC, OldBrush);
322:        SelectBrush(GooberDC, OldGBrush);
323:        break;
324:
325:     case ERECTANGLE:
326:        B = GetStockBrush(NULL_BRUSH);
327:        OldBrush = SelectBrush(PaintDC, B);
```

```
328:        OldGBrush = SelectBrush(GooberDC, B);
329:        Rectangle(PaintDC, OldRect.left,
330:                OldRect.top, OldRect.right, OldRect.bottom);
331:        Rectangle(GooberDC, OldRect.left,
332:                OldRect.top, OldRect.right, OldRect.bottom);
333:        SelectObject(PaintDC, OldBrush);
334:        SelectBrush(GooberDC, OldGBrush);
335:        break;
336:    }
337:    SelectObject(PaintDC, OldPen);
338:    SelectObject(GooberDC, OldGPen);
339:    DeleteObject(Pen);
340: }
341:
342: //////////////////////////////////////////
343: // Handle WM_MOUSEMOVE
344: //////////////////////////////////////////
345: #pragma argsused
346: void Meta_OnMouseMove(HWND hwnd, int x, int y, UINT keyFlags)
347: {
348:    if (Dat.ButtonDown)
349:    {
350:      Dat.Drawing = TRUE;
351:
352:      HDC PaintDC = GetDC(hwnd);
353:
354:      SetROP2(PaintDC, R2_NOTXORPEN);
355:      if (OldRect.left != -32000)
356:        DrawShape(hwnd, PaintDC, OldRect);
357:      OldRect.left = Dat.DownX;
358:      OldRect.top = Dat.DownY;
359:      OldRect.right = x;
360:      OldRect.bottom = y;
361:      DrawShape(hwnd, PaintDC, OldRect);
362:      ReleaseDC(hwnd, PaintDC);
363:    }
364: }
365:
366: //////////////////////////////////////////
367: // WM_LBUTTONDOWN
368: //////////////////////////////////////////
369: #pragma argsused
370: void Meta_OnLButtonDown(HWND hwnd, BOOL fDoubleClick, int x,
371:                         int y, UINT keyFlags)
372: {
373:    Dat.ButtonDown = TRUE;
374:    Dat.Drawing = FALSE;
375:    OldRect.left = -32000;
376:    Dat.DownX = x;
```

18

continues

Listing 18.2. continued

```
377:    Dat.DownY = y;
378:    SetCapture(hwnd);
379: }
380:
381: ///////////////////////////////////////////////
382: // WM_LBUTTONUP
383: ///////////////////////////////////////////////
384: #pragma argsused
385: void Meta_OnLButtonUp(HWND hwnd, int x, int y, UINT keyFlags)
386: {
387:    if ((Dat.ButtonDown) && (Dat.Drawing))
388:    {
389:      Dat.Drawing = FALSE;
390:      HDC PaintDC = GetDC(hwnd);
391:      DrawFinalShape(hwnd, PaintDC, OldRect);
392:      ReleaseDC(hwnd, PaintDC);
393:      ReleaseCapture();
394:    }
395:    Dat.ButtonDown = FALSE;
396: }
397:
398: ///////////////////////////////////////////////
399: // WM_PAINT
400: ///////////////////////////////////////////////
401: void Meta_OnPaint(HWND hwnd)
402: {
403:    HDC PaintDC;
404:    PAINTSTRUCT PaintStruct;
405:    RECT R;
406:
407:    GetClientRect(hwnd, &R);
408:
409:    PaintDC = BeginPaint(hwnd, &PaintStruct);
410:
411:    if (IsAldusFile())
412:    {
413:      SetMapMode(PaintDC, MM_ANISOTROPIC);
414:      SetWindowExt(PaintDC, 1000, 1000);
415:      SetViewportExt(PaintDC, R.right, R.bottom);
416:      SetWindowOrg(PaintDC, R.right / 2, R.bottom / 2);
417:      PlayMetaFile(PaintDC, hmf);
418:    }
419:    else
420:      if(hmf) EnumTheMeta(hwnd, hmf);
421:
422:    EndPaint(hwnd, &PaintStruct);
423: }
```

Listing 18.3 shows the header file for Metaphor.

Type **Listing 18.3. META.H.**

```
 1: /////////////////////////////////
 2: // Module: META.H
 3: // Programmer: Charlie Calvert
 4: // Description: Part of Meta project
 5: /////////////////////////////////
 6:
 7: // Const
 8: #define CM_EXIT 101
 9: #define CM_LOAD 102
10: #define CM_NEWMETA 103
11: #define CM_STARTMETA 104
12: #define CM_ENDMETA 105
13:
14: #define CM_LINE 201
15: #define CM_ELLIPSE 202
16: #define CM_RECTANGLE 203
17: #define CM_ERECTANGLE 204
18:
19: #define CM_RED 301
20: #define CM_GREEN 302
21: #define CM_BLUE 303
22:
23: #define CM_FRED 401
24: #define CM_FGREEN 402
25: #define CM_FBLUE 403
26:
27: #define CM_ONE 501
28: #define CM_FIVE 502
29: #define CM_TEN 503
30: #define CM_TWENTY 504
31: #define CM_FORTY 505
32: #define CM_EIGHTY 506
33:
34: #define MAXSIZE 256
35:
36: // Type
37: enum TShape {ELLIPSE, LINE, RECTANGLE, ERECTANGLE};
38:
39: struct TDATA {
40:    int DownX, DownY;
41:    BOOL ButtonDown;
42:    BOOL Drawing;
43:    TShape Shape;
44:    int Thickness;
45:    COLORREF Color;
```

continues

Listing 18.3. continued

```
46: };
47:
48: // Declarations for class Meta
49: #define Meta_DefProc      DefWindowProc
50: BOOL Meta_OnCreate(HWND hwnd, CREATESTRUCT FAR* lpCreateStruct);
51: void Meta_OnDestroy(HWND hwnd);
52: void Meta_OnCommand(HWND hwnd, int id, HWND hwndCtl, UINT
codeNotify);
53: void Meta_OnLButtonDown(HWND hwnd, BOOL fDoubleClick, int x, int y,
54:                         UINT keyFlags);
55: void Meta_OnLButtonUp(HWND hwnd, int x, int y, UINT keyFlags);
56: void Meta_OnMouseMove(HWND hwnd, int x, int y, UINT keyFlags);
57: void Meta_OnPaint(HWND hwnd);
58:
59: // Funcs
60: LRESULT CALLBACK _export WndProc(HWND hwnd, UINT Message,
61:                                  WPARAM wParam, LPARAM lParam);
62: BOOL Register(HINSTANCE hInst);
63: HWND Create(HINSTANCE hInst, int nCmdShow);
```

Listing 18.4 shows the code for MetaUtil.

Type   Listing 18.4. METAUTIL.CPP.

```
1: ///////////////////////////////////////////////////////////
2: //   Program Name: METAUTIL.CPP
3: //   Programmer: Charlie Calvert
4: //   Description: Part of MetaFor Windows project
5: //   Date: 4/17/93
6: ///////////////////////////////////////////////////////////
7:
8: #define STRICT
9: #include <windows.h>
10: #include <windowsx.h>
11: #pragma hdrstop
12: #include <commdlg.h>
13: #include <string.h>
14: #include <direct.h>
15: #include <stdio.h>
16: #include <stdlib.h>
17: #include "metaphor.h"
18: #include "metautil.h"
19: #pragma warning (disable: 4068)
20: extern HMETAFILE hmf;
21: static METAHEADER mfHeader;
22: static BOOL bMetaInRam;
```

```
23: static BOOL IsAldus;
24:
25: //////////////////////////////////////////
26: // Create Meta
27: //////////////////////////////////////////
28: #pragma argsused
29: void CreateMeta(HWND hwnd)
30: {
31:    HDC MetaDC;
32:    HPEN OldPen;
33:    char FName[256];
34:
35:    _getdcwd(0, FName, MAXSIZE);
36:    strcat(FName, "\\quickmet.wmf");
37:    MetaDC = CreateMetaFile(FName);
38:    if (MetaDC != NULL)
39:    {
40:      HPEN Pen = CreatePen(PS_SOLID, 10, RGB(0, 255, 127));
41:      OldPen = SelectPen(MetaDC, Pen);
42:      Ellipse(MetaDC, 200, 200, 100, 100);
43:      SelectObject(MetaDC, OldPen);
44:      DeleteObject(Pen);
45:      Pen = CreatePen(PS_SOLID, 10, RGB(255, 0, 0));
46:      OldPen = SelectPen(MetaDC, Pen);
47:      Rectangle(MetaDC, 20, 20, 100, 100);
48:      SelectObject(MetaDC, OldPen);
49:      DeleteObject(Pen);
50:      hmf = CloseMetaFile(MetaDC);
51:    }
52: }
53:
54: //////////////////////////////////////////
55: // IsAldusFile
56: //////////////////////////////////////////
57: BOOL IsAldusFile(void)
58: {
59:    return IsAldus;
60: }
61:
62: //////////////////////////////////////////
63: // ReadPlaceableHeader
64: //////////////////////////////////////////
65: BOOL ReadPlaceableHeader(HWND hwnd, HFILE fh)
66: {
67:    char *ErrString = "Error reading placeable header";
68:    int wBytesRead;
69:    ALDUSMFHEADER AldusMFHeader;
70:
71:    wBytesRead = _lread(fh, (LPSTR)&AldusMFHeader,
                           sizeof(ALDUSMFHEADER));
```

18

continues

617

Listing 18.4. continued

```
 72:    if( wBytesRead == -1 ¦¦ wBytesRead < sizeof(ALDUSMFHEADER) )
 73:    {
 74:      MessageBox(hwnd, ErrString, NULL, MB_OK ¦ MB_ICONHAND);
 75:      return FALSE;
 76:    }
 77:    return TRUE;
 78: }
 79:
 80: /////////////////////////////////////////////
 81: // Read header of metafile
 82: /////////////////////////////////////////////
 83: BOOL ReadHeader(METAHEADER *mfHeader, HWND hwnd, HFILE fh)
 84: {
 85:    int wBytesRead;
 86:    char * ErrString = "Error reading metafile header";
 87:
 88:    _llseek(fh, sizeof(ALDUSMFHEADER), 0);
 89:    wBytesRead = _lread(fh, (LPSTR)mfHeader, sizeof(METAHEADER));
 90:
 91:    if( wBytesRead == -1 ¦¦ wBytesRead < sizeof(METAHEADER) )
 92:    {
 93:      MessageBox(hwnd, ErrString,  NULL, MB_OK ¦ MB_ICONHAND);
 94:      return(FALSE);
 95:    }
 96:
 97:    return TRUE;
 98: }
 99:
100: /////////////////////////////////////////////
101: // Allocate memory for meta bits
102: /////////////////////////////////////////////
103: HANDLE AllocMetaMemory(HWND hwnd, METAHEADER *mfHeader)
104: {
105:    char *ErrString1 = "Memory allocation error";
106:    HANDLE   hMem;
107:
108:    if (!(hMem = GlobalAlloc(GHND, (mfHeader->mtSize * 2L))))
109:    {
110:      MessageBox(hwnd, ErrString1, NULL, MB_OK ¦ MB_ICONHAND);
111:      return hMem = 0;
112:    }
113:    return hMem;
114: }
115:
116: BOOL ReadMetafileBits(HWND hwnd, HFILE fh, METAHEADER mfHeader,
117:                        LPSTR lpMem, HANDLE * hMem)
118: {
119:    int wBytesRead;
```

```
120:    char *ErrString = "Unable to read metafile bits";
121:
122:    _llseek(fh, sizeof(ALDUSMFHEADER), 0);
123:    wBytesRead = _lread(fh, lpMem, (WORD)(mfHeader.mtSize * 2));
124:
125:    if( wBytesRead == -1 )
126:    {
127:      MessageBox(hwnd, ErrString, NULL, MB_OK | MB_ICONHAND);
128:      GlobalUnlock(*hMem);
129:      GlobalFree(*hMem);
130:      return FALSE;
131:    }
132:    return TRUE;
133: }
134:
135: /////////////////////////////////////////////
136: // RenderMeta
137: /////////////////////////////////////////////
138: BOOL RenderPlaceableMeta(HWND hwnd, HFILE fh)
139: {
140:    LPSTR    lpMem;
141:    HANDLE   hMem;
142:
143:    if ((bMetaInRam) && (hmf))
144:      DeleteMetaFile(hmf);
145:    _llseek(fh, 0, 0);
146:
147:    if (!ReadPlaceableHeader(hwnd, fh)) return FALSE;
148:    if (!ReadHeader(&mfHeader, hwnd, fh)) return FALSE;
149:    if (!(hMem = AllocMetaMemory(hwnd, &mfHeader))) return FALSE;
150:    lpMem = (LPSTR)GlobalLock(hMem);
151:    if(!ReadMetafileBits(hwnd, fh, mfHeader, lpMem, &hMem))
152:      return FALSE;
153:    if (!(hmf = SetMetaFileBits(hMem))) return(FALSE);
154:    GlobalUnlock(hMem);
155:    return(TRUE);
156: }
157:
158: ///////////////////////////////////////////
159: // OpenMetaFile
160: ///////////////////////////////////////////
161: BOOL OpenMetaFile(HWND hwnd, char * lpFileName)
162: {
163:      HFILE fh;
164:      int wBytesRead;
165:      LONG dwIsAldus;
166:
167:      fh = _lopen(lpFileName, OF_READ);
168:
169:      if (fh != -1)
170:      {
```

18

continues

619

Listing 18.4. continued

```
171:        // See if it is a placeable wmf
172:        wBytesRead =
173:            _lread(fh,(LPSTR)&dwIsAldus, sizeof(dwIsAldus));
174:        if (wBytesRead == -1 ¦¦ wBytesRead < sizeof(dwIsAldus))
175:        {
176:          _lclose(fh);
177:          MessageBox(hwnd, "unable to read file", NULL,
178:                    MB_OK ¦ MB_ICONEXCLAMATION);
179:          return (FALSE);
180:        }
181:
182:        if (dwIsAldus != ALDUSKEY)
183:        {
184:          IsAldus = FALSE;
185:          hmf = GetMetaFile(lpFileName);
186:        }
187:        else
188:        {
189:          IsAldus = TRUE;
190:          RenderPlaceableMeta(hwnd, fh);
191:        }
192:        _lclose(fh);
193:      }
194:      return TRUE;
195: }
196:
197: //////////////////////////////////////
198: // GetFileName
199: //////////////////////////////////////
200: char * GetFileName(HWND hwnd, char * szFile, int StringSize)
201: {
202:    OPENFILENAME ofn;
203:    char szDirName[256];
204:    char szFileTitle[256];
205:    char szFilter[256];
206:
207:    memset(&ofn, 0, sizeof(OPENFILENAME));
208:    strcpy(szFilter, "Metafiles");
209:    strcpy(&szFilter[strlen(szFilter) + 1], "*.wmf");
210:
211:    ofn.lStructSize = sizeof(OPENFILENAME);
212:    ofn.hwndOwner = hwnd;
213:    ofn.lpstrFilter = szFilter;
214:    ofn.nFilterIndex = 1;
215:    ofn.lpstrFile= szFile;
216:    ofn.nMaxFile = StringSize;
217:    ofn.lpstrFileTitle = szFileTitle;
218:    ofn.nMaxFileTitle = sizeof(szFileTitle);
219:    ofn.lpstrInitialDir = szDirName;
220:    ofn.Flags = OFN_FILEMUSTEXIST;
```

```
221:
222:    GetOpenFileName(&ofn);
223:
224:    return szFile;
225: }
226:
227: ///////////////////////////////////////
228: // LoadFile
229: ///////////////////////////////////////
230: void LoadFile(HWND hwnd)
231: {
232:    char S[100];
233:    bMetaInRam = TRUE;
234:    memset(&S, 0, 100);
235:
236:    GetFileName(hwnd, S, 100);
237:
238:    OpenMetaFile(hwnd, S);
239:
240:    if (!hmf)
241:       MessageBox(hwnd, "No Meta", "sdf", MB_OK);
242:
243:    InvalidateRect(hwnd, NULL, TRUE);
244:
245: }
246:
247: ///////////////////////////////////////
248: // GetSaveName;
249: ///////////////////////////////////////
250: char *GetSaveName(HWND hwnd, char * SaveName)
251: {
252:    OPENFILENAME ofn;
253:    char szDirName[256];
254:    char szFile[256], szFileTitle[256];
255:    UINT  i;
256:    char  chReplace;
257:    char  szFilter[256];
258:
259:    _getdcwd(0, szDirName, 255);
260:
261:    strcpy(szFilter,
262:           "Metafiles(*.wmf)¦*.wmf¦Bitmap Files(*.bmp)¦*.bmp¦");
263:    chReplace = szFilter[strlen(szFilter) - 1];
264:    for (i = 0; szFilter[i] != '\0'; i++)
265:    {
266:       if (szFilter[i] == chReplace)
267:           szFilter[i] = '\0';
268:    }
269:
270:    /* Set all structure members to zero. */
```

continues

Listing 18.4. continued

```
271:
272:    memset(&ofn, 0, sizeof(OPENFILENAME));
273:
274:    /* Initialize the OPENFILENAME members. */
275:
276:    szFile[0] = '\0';
277:
278:    ofn.lStructSize = sizeof(OPENFILENAME);
279:    ofn.hwndOwner = hwnd;
280:    ofn.lpstrFilter = szFilter;
281:    ofn.lpstrFile= szFile;
282:    ofn.nMaxFile = sizeof(szFile);
283:    ofn.lpstrFileTitle = szFileTitle;
284:    ofn.nMaxFileTitle = sizeof(szFileTitle);
285:    ofn.lpstrInitialDir = szDirName;
286:
287:    ofn.Flags = OFN_OVERWRITEPROMPT;
288:
289:    if (GetSaveFileName(&ofn))
290:      strcpy(SaveName, ofn.lpstrFile);
291:    else
292:      strcpy(SaveName, "");
293:
294:    return SaveName;
295: }
296:
297: int FileExists(const char *path)
298: {
299:    FILE *f = fopen(path, "r");
300:    if (!f)
301:      return FALSE;
302:    else
303:    {
304:      fclose(f);
305:      return TRUE;
306:    }
307: }
308:
309: void SaveFile(HWND hwnd, char * OldName)
310: {
311:    char Name[256];
312:    int i;
313:
314:    GetSaveName(hwnd, Name);
315:
316:    if (strlen(Name) == 0) return;
317:
318:    if (FileExists(Name))
319:    {
```

```
320:    i = remove(Name);
321:    if (i != 0)
322:      MessageBox(hwnd, "Error deleting", "No", MB_OK);
323:    }
324:
325:    i = rename(OldName, Name);
326:    if (i != 0)
327:      MessageBox(hwnd, "Error renaming", "No", MB_OK);
328:
329:    OpenMetaFile(hwnd, Name);
330: }
331:
332: void TurnOffSave(HWND hwnd)
333: {
334:    HMENU hMenu = GetMenu(hwnd);
335:    EnableMenuItem(hMenu, CM_ENDMETA, MF_BYCOMMAND | MF_GRAYED);
336: }
```

Listing 18.5 shows the header file for MetaUtil.

Listing 18.5. METAUTIL.H.

```
 1: ///////////////////////////////////////
 2: // Module: METAUTIL.H
 3: // Programmer: Charlie Calvert
 4: // Description: Part of Meta project
 5: ///////////////////////////////////////
 6:
 7: #define   ALDUSKEY        0x9AC6CDD7L
 8:
 9: // types
10: typedef struct {
11:    DWORD    key;
12:    HANDLE   hmf;
13:    RECT     bbox;
14:    WORD     inch;
15:    DWORD    reserved;
16:    WORD     checksum;
17: } ALDUSMFHEADER;
18:
19: // Procs
20: void CreateMeta(HWND hwnd);
21: void LoadFile(HWND hwnd);
22: BOOL IsAldusFile(void);
23: void SaveFile(HWND hwnd, char * OldName);
24: void TurnOffSave(HWND hwnd);
```

Listing 18.6 shows the code for MetaEnum.

 Listing 18.6. METAENUM.CPP.

```
 1: ////////////////////////////////////////////////////////
 2: //   Program Name: METAENUM.CPP
 3: //   Programmer: Charlie Calvert
 4: //   Description: Part of Metaphor Windows project
 5: //   Date: 7/23/93
 6: ////////////////////////////////////////////////////////
 7:
 8: #define STRICT
 9: #include <windows.h>
10: #include <windowsx.h>
11: #pragma warning (disable: 4068)
12: int CALLBACK EnumMetaFileProc(HDC hdc, HANDLETABLE FAR* lpHTable,
13:     METARECORD FAR* lpMFR, int cObj, BYTE FAR* lpClientData);
14:
15: ////////////////////////////////////
16: // EnumTheMeta
17: ////////////////////////////////////
18: void EnumTheMeta(HWND hwnd, HMETAFILE AMeta)
19: {
20:    MFENUMPROC lpEnumMetaProc;
21:    HDC PaintDC;
22:    HINSTANCE hInst;
23:
24:    PaintDC = GetDC(hwnd);
25:    hInst = (HINSTANCE)GetClassWord(hwnd, GCW_HMODULE);
26:    lpEnumMetaProc = (MFENUMPROC) MakeProcInstance(
27:      (FARPROC) EnumMetaFileProc, hInst);
28:    EnumMetaFile(PaintDC, AMeta, lpEnumMetaProc, NULL);
29:    FreeProcInstance((FARPROC) lpEnumMetaProc);
30:
31:    ReleaseDC(hwnd, PaintDC);
32: }
33:
34: // -----------------------------------------------------
35: // Callbacks, etc
36: // -----------------------------------------------------
37:
38: ////////////////////////////////////
39: // EnumMetaFileProc
40: ////////////////////////////////////
41: #pragma argsused
42: int CALLBACK EnumMetaFileProc(HDC hdc, HANDLETABLE FAR* lpHTable,
43:     METARECORD FAR* lpMFR, int cObj, BYTE FAR* lpClientData)
```

```
44: {
45:     PlayMetaFileRecord(hdc, lpHTable, lpMFR, cObj);
46:     return 1;
47: }
```

Listing 18.7 shows the header file for MetaEnum.

Type

Listing 18.7. METAENUM.H.

```
1: /////////////////////////////////////////////////////////////
2: //   Program Name: METAENUM.H
3: //   Programmer: Charlie Calvert
4: //   Description: Part of Metaphor windows project
5: //   Date: 7/23/93
6: /////////////////////////////////////////////////////////////
7:
8: void EnumTheMeta(HWND hwnd, HMETAFILE AMeta);
```

Listing 18.8 shows the resource file for Metaphor.

Type

Listing 18.8. METAPHOR.RC.

```
1: /////////////////////////////////////
2: // File: METAPHOR.RC
3: // Description: Resource file for Metaphor project
4: /////////////////////////////////////
5: #include "metaphor.h"
6:
7: Head2 METAFILE "head2.wmf"
8:
9: MetaMenu MENU
10: BEGIN
11:   POPUP "&File"
12:   BEGIN
13:     MENUITEM "Load", CM_LOAD;
14:     MENUITEM SEPARATOR;
15:     MENUITEM "Save_Meta", CM_ENDMETA;
16:     MENUITEM SEPARATOR;
17:     MENUITEM "Quick_Meta", CM_NEWMETA;
18:     MENUITEM SEPARATOR;
19:     MENUITEM "Exit", CM_EXIT;
20:   END
21:
22:   POPUP "&Shape"
23:   BEGIN
24:     MENUITEM "Line", CM_LINE;
```

continues

18

625

Listing 18.8. continued

```
25:      MENUITEM "Ellipse", CM_ELLIPSE;
26:      MENUITEM "Rectangle", CM_RECTANGLE;
27:      MENUITEM "Empty Rectangle", CM_ERECTANGLE;
28:    END
29:
30:    POPUP "&Pen_Color"
31:    BEGIN
32:      MENUITEM "Red", CM_RED;
33:      MENUITEM "Green", CM_GREEN;
34:      MENUITEM "Blue", CM_BLUE;
35:    END
36:
37:    POPUP "&Fill_Color"
38:    BEGIN
39:      MENUITEM "Red", CM_FRED;
40:      MENUITEM "Green", CM_FGREEN;
41:      MENUITEM "Blue", CM_FBLUE;
42:    END
43:
44:    POPUP "Pen_&Size"
45:    BEGIN
46:      MENUITEM "1", CM_ONE;
47:      MENUITEM "5", CM_FIVE;
48:      MENUITEM "10", CM_TEN;
49:      MENUITEM "20", CM_TWENTY;
50:      MENUITEM "40", CM_FORTY;
51:      MENUITEM "80", CM_EIGHTY;
52:    END
53: END
```

Listing 18.9 shows the definition file for Metaphor.

 Listing 18.9. METAPHOR.DEF.

```
1: ; METAPHOR.DEF
2:
3: NAME          Metaphor
4: DESCRIPTION   'Metaphor Window'
5: EXETYPE       WINDOWS
6: STUB          'WINSTUB.EXE'
7: HEAPSIZE      4096
8: STACKSIZE     5120
9: CODE          PRELOAD MOVEABLE DISCARDABLE
10: DATA         PRELOAD MOVEABLE MULTIPLE
```

Listing 18.10 shows the Borland makefile for Metaphor.

Type **Listing 18.10. METAPHOR.MAK (Borland).**

```
 1: # METAPHOR.MAK
 2:
 3: # macros
 4: APPNAME = Metaphor
 5: OBJS = MetaUtil.obj MetaEnum.obj
 6: INCPATH = C:\BC\INCLUDE
 7: LIBPATH = C:\BC\LIB
 8: FLAGS = -H -ml -W -v -w4 -ml -I$(INCPATH) -L$(LIBPATH)
 9:
10: # link
11: $(APPNAME).exe: $(APPNAME).obj $(OBJS) $(APPNAME).def $(APPNAME).res
12:    bcc $(FLAGS) $(APPNAME).obj $(OBJS)
13:    brc $(APPNAME)
14:
15: # compile
16: .cpp.obj:
17:    bcc -c $(FLAGS) { $< }
18:
19: #resource
20: $(APPNAME).res: $(APPNAME).rc
21:    brc -r -i$(INCPATH) $(APPNAME).rc
```

18

Listing 18.11 shows the Microsoft makefile for Metaphor.

Type **Listing 18.11. METAPHOR.MAK (Microsoft).**

```
 1: #------------------
 2: # METAPHOR.MAK
 3: #------------------
 4:
 5: APPNAME = Metaphor
 6: OBJS = MetaUtil.obj MetaEnum.obj
 7:
 8: # linking
 9: $(APPNAME).exe : $(APPNAME).obj $(OBJS) $(APPNAME).def
    $(APPNAME).res
10:    link $(APPNAME) $(OBJS), /align:16, NUL,\
11:    /nod llibcew libw commdlg, $(APPNAME)
12:    rc $(APPNAME).res
13: # compile
14: .cpp.obj:
15:    cl -c AL -Gsw GA -Ow -W3 -AL -Zp { $< }
16:
17: # Compile
18: $(APPNAME).res: $(APPNAME).rc
19:    rc -r $(APPNAME).rc
```

Figure 18.3 shows the Metaphor program.

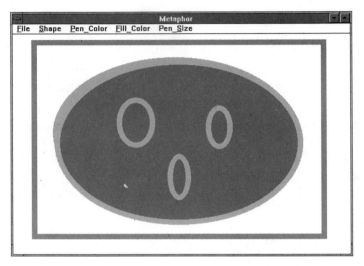

Figure 18.3. *The Metaphor program can be used to draw simple geometric shapes.*

The Metaphor program enables you to draw (with the mouse) lines, rectangles, and ellipses on its main window. By using the menu, you can change the color and thickness of the pen that outlines each shape, and also change the color of the solid fill pattern that forms the body of each shape.

The Metaphor program enables you to save the images you have created and reload them later. In order to simplify the design of the program, Metaphor only enables you to create one shape per session, and you must create the shape before loading any other files. You can't edit any of the designs you create, but the program could be expanded to include this feature.

Besides letting you draw metafiles, the Metaphor program supports loading and displaying these graphical images. The program is fully capable of reading and displaying the so-called "Aldus" metafiles that have a slightly different header than the one found in standard Windows metafiles. Metaphor examines any metafile you choose to read, and then automatically chooses the correct method for loading and displaying it.

The Shape of Things to Come

The rest of this chapter is divided into three sections:

1. An examination of *rubber banding*—the technique used for drawing shapes dynamically on the screen with the mouse

2. An examination of creating, reading, and saving metafiles

3. A brief introduction to the common dialogs—a theme that's carried to the next chapter

Rubber Banding

Before reading this section, fire up the Metaphor program and practice drawing ellipses and rectangles on-screen so you can see how the rubber band technique works. If for some reason you can't run the Metaphor program, open up Windows Paintbrush and draw some squares or circles with the appropriate tools from the Tools menu on the left edge of the program. Watch the way these programs create an elastic square or circle that you can drag around the desktop. Play with these shapes as you decide what dimensions and location you want for your geometric figure.

Such tools appear to be difficult for a programmer to create, but thanks to the Windows API, the code is relatively trivial. Following are the main steps involved, each of which will be explained in depth later in this section:

1. When the user clicks the left mouse button, Metaphor "memorizes" the x, y coordinates of the WM_LBUTTONDOWN event.

2. As the user drags the mouse across the screen, the left-button still down, Metaphor draws a square or circle each time it gets a WM_MOUSEMOVE message. Just before painting each new shape, the program blanks out the previous square or circle. The dimensions of the new shape are calculated by combining the coordinates of the original WM_LBUTTONDOWN message with the current coordinates passed in the WM_MOUSEMOVE message.

3. When the user generates a WM_LBUTTONUP message, Metaphor paints the final shape in the colors and pen size specified by the user.

Although this description obviously omits some important details, the outlines of the algorithm should take shape in your mind in the form of only a few, relatively simple, logical strokes. Things get a bit more complicated when the details are mulled over one by one, but the fundamental steps should be relatively clear.

Zooming in on the details now, here's a look at the response to a WM_LBUTTONDOWN message (lines 370-379):

```
void Meta_OnLButtonDown(HWND hwnd, BOOL fDoubleClick,
                        int x, int y, UINT keyFlags)
{
  Dat.ButtonDown = TRUE;
  Dat.Drawing = FALSE;
  OldRect.left = -32000;
  Dat.DownX = x;
  Dat.DownY = y;
  SetCapture(hwnd);
}
```

After initializing some variables, the final steps in Meta_OnLButtonDown involve "memorizing" the location of the event, and "capturing" the mouse. The call to SetCapture is necessary, because the user might drag the mouse off the window in the process of drawing a shape. If this happens, the user doesn't want the focus to drift off to some other window or program.

After the left mouse button is pressed, the program picks up all WM_MOUSEMOVE messages that come flying into Metaphor's kin (lines 346-364):

```
void Meta_OnMouseMove(HWND hwnd, int x,
                      int y, UINT keyFlags)
{
  if (Dat.ButtonDown)
  {
    Dat.Drawing = TRUE;

    HDC PaintDC = GetDC(hwnd);

    SetROP2(PaintDC, R2_NOTXORPEN);
    if (OldRect.left != -32000)
      DrawShape(hwnd, PaintDC, OldRect);
    OldRect.left = Dat.DownX;
    OldRect.top = Dat.DownY;
    OldRect.right = x;
    OldRect.bottom = y;
    DrawShape(hwnd, PaintDC, OldRect);
    ReleaseDC(hwnd, PaintDC);
  }
}
```

The first line of the function uses one of several possible techniques for checking to see if the left mouse button is down. If the button isn't down, the function ignores the message. If it is down, the function gets the device context, sets the drawing mode to R2_NOTXORPEN, memorizes the current dimensions of the figure, draws it, and releases the device context.

The SetROP2 function sets the current drawing mode in a manner similar to the way the last parameter in BitBlt sets the current painting mode. In this case, Metaphor uses the logical XOR and NOT operations to blit the elastic image to the screen. This logical operation is chosen because it paints the old shape directly on top of the original image, thereby effectively erasing each shape:

☐ If you XOR a square to the screen, the square will show up clearly.

☐ If you XOR that same image again in the same location, the image will disappear.

Such are the virtues of simple logical operations in graphics mode.

Note: Aficionados of graphics logic will note that the logical operation employed by Metaphor is a variation on the exclusive OR operation. This variation ensures that the fill in the center of the shape to be drawn won't blot out what's beneath it. The Microsoft documentation explains the difference like this:

```
R2_XOR:         final pixel = pen ^ screen pixel
R2_NOTXORPEN : final pixel = ~(pen ^ screen pixel)
```

Don't waste too much time worrying about logical operations and how they work. If they interest you, fine; if they don't, that's okay. The subject matter of this book is programming, not logic.

The *SetROP2* Function

Syntax

```
int SetROP2(HDC, int)

    HDC hdc;                Device context
    int fnDrawMode;         Drawing mode
```

SetROP2 determines the features of the current drawing mode. More specifically, it defines how the pen and the interior of an object are to be combined with the current contents of the screen.

The second parameter can contain a wide range of possible operations, all of which are listed in WINDOWS.H and in your online help files. A small sample includes the following options:

R2_BLACK	Draws shape in black pixels
R2_WHITE	Draws shape in white pixels
R2_NOP	Doesn't change the pixels
R2_NOT	Makes the current pixel the inverse of the screen color
R2_COPYPEN	Makes the pixel the color of the current pen

Example:

```
SetROP2(PaintDC, R2_NOT);
```

Notice that Meta_OnMouseMove calls DrawShape twice. The first time, it passes in the dimensions of the old figure that needs to be erased. That means it XORs the same image directly on top of the original image, thereby erasing it. Then, Meta_OnMouseMove records the location of the latest WM_MOUSEMOVE message and passes this new information to DrawShape, which paints the new image to the screen. This whole process is repeated over and over again (at incredible speeds) until the user lifts the left mouse button.

In the DrawImage function (line 265), Metaphor first checks to see which shape the user has selected and then proceeds to draw that shape to the screen using the default pen and fill color.

The final step in the whole operation occurs when the user lifts their finger off the mouse:

```
void Meta_OnLButtonUp(HWND hwnd, int x,
                      int y, UINT keyFlags)
{
  if ((Dat.ButtonDown) && (Dat.Drawing))
  {
    Dat.Drawing = FALSE;
    HDC PaintDC = GetDC(hwnd);
    DrawFinalShape(hwnd, PaintDC, OldRect);
    ReleaseDC(hwnd, PaintDC);
    ReleaseCapture();
  }
  Dat.ButtonDown = FALSE;
}
```

This code checks to see that the mouse is down and that the user is drawing a shape. If so, the following occurs:

☐ A flag is set stating that the user has decided to stop drawing.

- [ ] The final image is painted to the screen.

- [ ] The "captured" mouse is released.

The code that paints the final shape takes into account the colors and the pen thickness that the user selected with the menus. This excerpt from DrawFinalShape (line 290), shows what happens:

```
HPEN Pen = CreatePen(PS_INSIDEFRAME, Dat.Thickness, Dat.Color);
HPEN OldPen = SelectPen(PaintDC, Pen);

switch(Dat.Shape)
{
  case ELLIPSE:
    OldBrush = SelectBrush(PaintDC, FBrush);
    Ellipse(PaintDC, R.left, R.top, R.right, R.bottom);
    SelectObject(PaintDC, OldBrush);
    break;
        ... // code for drawing rectangles, lines, etc
```

Metaphor creates a pen in the user-selected color and thickness, and then copies the user-selected brush into the device context. The call to draw the shape follows, and the program carefully cleans up after itself. This code can be thought of in contrast to the code that's called to draw the "elastic shape." When drawing the "rubber band," Metaphor relies on the default brush and pen, but it employs the same switch statement and the same calls to Ellipse, Rectangle, and so forth.

Well, there you have it. That's how you draw shapes to the screen using the always popular rubber band technique. Overall, if you take one thing at a time, the process isn't complicated. Just so you can keep those steps clear in your mind, here they are again:

- [ ] Remember where the WM_LBUTTONDOWN took place.

- [ ] Draw the shape each time you get a WM_MOUSEMOVE message.

- [ ] Draw the final shape when you get a WM_LBUTTONUP message.

That's all there is to it.

What Are Metafiles?

When writing code for a book like this, I make design decisions based on the needs of students, rather than the needs of users. For instance, the Metaphor program contains a very short function which creates, designs, and writes a very simple metafile called QUICKMET.WMF to disk. This code serves no functional role in the program. It's just there for educational purposes.

Following is the code, which starts on line 30 of METAUTIL.CPP:

```cpp
void CreateMeta(HWND hwnd)
{
   HDC MetaDC;
   HPEN OldPen;
   char FName[256];

   _getdcwd(0, FName, MAXSIZE);
   strcat(FName, "\\quickmet.wmf");
   MetaDC = CreateMetaFile(FName);
   if (MetaDC != NULL)
   {
     HPEN Pen = CreatePen(PS_SOLID, 10, RGB(0, 255, 127));
     OldPen = SelectPen(MetaDC, Pen);
     Ellipse(MetaDC, 200, 200, 100, 100);
     SelectObject(MetaDC, OldPen);
     DeleteObject(Pen);
     Pen = CreatePen(PS_SOLID, 10, RGB(255, 0, 0));
     OldPen = SelectPen(MetaDC, Pen);
     Rectangle(MetaDC, 20, 20, 100, 100);
     SelectObject(MetaDC, OldPen);
     DeleteObject(Pen);
     hmf = CloseMetaFile(MetaDC);
   }
}
```

If you haven't done so already, run Metaphor, choose Quick_Meta from the menu, and load the QUICKMET.WMF file into the main window. The resulting image is shown in Figure 18.4.

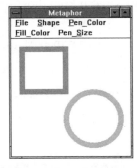

Figure 18.4. *The metafile produced by the* CreateMeta *function consists of two simple geometric shapes.*

Though it may look a bit intimidating at first, the previous code contains only one or two new ideas. The code starts by doing some hand waving to create a valid filename and then calls CreateMetaFile.

The *CreateMetaFile* Function

```
HDC CreateMetaFile(LPCSTR)
```

> LPCSTR lpszFile: String specifying the metafile's name

The CreateMetaFile function returns a valid device context for a metafile.

Example:

```
MyMetaDC = CreateMetaFile("c:\\Metafile.wmf");
```

After you've retrieved the DC for a metafile, all you need to do is copy shapes, pens, and brushes into it—just as you would with the device context for the screen. When you are done, call CloseMetafile, passing it the device context in its sole parameter. In return, it writes the file to disk and returns a handle to an in-memory copy of the file—which is of type HMETAFILE. An HMETAFILE is just like an HINSTANCE, HBITMAP, or HPEN. However, it's the handle to a metafile.

The final step is to display the metafile for the user with the easy-to-use PlayMetaFile function.

The *PlayMetaFile* Function

```
BOOL PlayMetaFile(hdc, hmf)
```

> HDC hdc;   The device context for the screen or printer
>
> HMETAFILE hmf;   The handle to a metafile

The PlayMetaFile function displays a metafile to the screen or the printer. Notice that the device context in its first parameter isn't the device context from the metafile; it's the DC of the device on which the file will be displayed.

Example:

```
PlayMetaFile(PaintDC, hmf);
```

In short, a metafile is nothing but a list of structures, each of which contains information about a basic GDI call, such as Rectangle, SelectObject, or Ellipse. The PlayMetaFile command simply iterates through this list, displaying each shape in turn and as defined.

Best of all, metafiles are extremely compact. A full 800x600 SuperVGA bitmap might use over 200,000 bytes when saved to disk as a BMP. An equivalent metafile might be as small as 200 or 300 bytes. Even a complex metafile, such as the one shown in Figure 18.5, is less than 15K bytes in size.

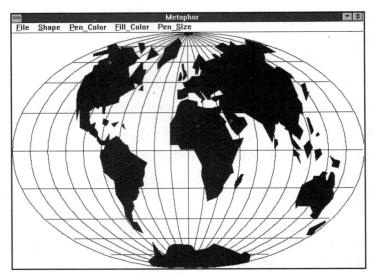

Figure 18.5. *An image that ships with CorelDRAW! can be transformed into a metafile 12,492 bytes in size.*

Because of the big savings in size, you should always see if it is possible to use a metafile instead of a bitmap. This is particularly true if you want to work with a bitmap larger than 64x64 pixels in size.

To review, here are the simplest possible set of steps involved in creating a metafile:

☐ Call CreateMetaFile and hang on to the device context it returns.

☐ Copy the pens, brushes, and figures you want to use into the device context.

☐ Call CloseMetaFile to write the image to disk and to retrieve a handle to the metafile.

☐ Show the metafile to the user by calling PlayMetaFile.

Creating Metafiles Interactively

It's easy to make the jump from CreateMeta to an interactive system that enables the user to design his or her own metafiles. In fact, this is the purpose of the code which lies at the heart of the metaphor program.

At startup, Metaphor calls CreateMetaFile in response to the user-defined CM_STARTMETA message:

```
case CM_STARTMETA:
  GooberDC = CreateMetaFile(TempName);
  break;
```

The device context retrieved from the call to `CreateMetaFile` is global to the program's main module; all the user-specified shapes and colors will be copied into it.

The actual figures to be placed in the file are defined by the user with the rubber band code. When the user-selected shape is drawn to the screen is in its final form, its type, color, and dimensions are also copied into the device context for the metafile. To see how this works, just take a moment to revisit the `DrawFinalShape` function (line 290, METAPHOR.CPP):

```
void DrawFinalShape(HWND hwnd, HDC PaintDC, RECT R)
{
  HBRUSH B, OldBrush, OldGBrush;

  HPEN Pen = CreatePen(PS_INSIDEFRAME, Dat.Thickness, Dat.Color);
  HPEN OldPen = SelectPen(PaintDC, Pen);
  HPEN OldGPen = SelectPen(GooberDC, Pen);

  switch(Dat.Shape)
  {
    case ELLIPSE:
      OldBrush = SelectBrush(PaintDC, FBrush);
      OldGBrush = SelectBrush(GooberDC, FBrush);
      Ellipse(PaintDC, R.left, R.top, R.right, R.bottom);
      Ellipse(GooberDC, R.left, R.top, R.right, R.bottom);
      SelectObject(PaintDC, OldBrush);
      SelectBrush(GooberDC, OldGBrush);
      break;
```

Here, Metaphor copies the geometric figure directly into both the screen's device context and the device context for the metafile. This same operation is repeated each time the user blocks out a new shape on-screen with the rubber band technique.

When the user is done, he or she can select Save from the File menu, and the device context can be passed to `CloseMetaFile`. This writes the final file to disk and returns an `HMETAFILE`, which can be displayed on-screen whenever a `WM_PAINT` message comes down the pike. (Metaphor is obviously not powerful enough to redraw the image during the time it's being created.)

The actual act of saving and loading a file is discussed in the section about common dialogs.

Turning a Metaphor into "Das Ding an Sich"

If you want to turn the metaphor program into a real paint program, that is, into the "thing itself," you obviously need to find some way to start iterating through the contents of an HMETAFILE. This functionality is not included in the Metaphor program, but the program does drop hints as to one possible course to pursue.

The technique that comes to the rescue is an old friend: the callback function. In this case, there happens to be a native Windows callback that iterates through the contents of a metafile. Appropriately enough, it's called EnumMetaFile.

Before I describe the details of the function, take a moment to consider how it works. As you recall, the EnumFontFamilies function sent copies of all the fonts on the system to a callback function. The callback function can pass descriptions of the fonts back to the main program. The same thing happens in this case. That is, when you pass EnumMetaFile a handle to a metafile, it will iterate through the records in the metafile, passing each in turn to your user-defined function—the address of which is passed in the third argument to EnumMetaFile. These records define the GDI function that will be called and the parameters to be passed to it.

The *EnumMetaFile* Function

```
BOOL EnumMetaFile(HDC, HLOCAL, MFENUMPROC, LPARAM)
```

HDC hdc;	Device context for the screen
HLOCAL hmf;	Handle of the metafile
MFENUMPROC mfenmprc;	The callback function
LPARAM lParam;	User-defined data to pass to the callback function

This function iterates through a series of structures containing information on all the calls used in the metafile. The key field in EnumMetaFile is the third, which contains the address of the callback function. The last parameter can be set to NULL, or it can contain any data the user wants to pass on to the EnumMetaFileProc.

Example:

```
EnumMetaFile(PaintDC, MyMetaFile, lpMyMetaProc, MyData);
```

Here's the actual callback, as defined in the Metaphor program:

```
int CALLBACK EnumMetaFileProc(HDC hdc,
                              HANDLETABLE FAR* lpHTable,
                              METARECORD FAR* lpMFR,
                              int cObj,
                              BYTE FAR* lpClientData)
{
    PlayMetaFileRecord(hdc, lpHTable, lpMFR, cObj);
    return 1;
}
```

As you can see, this particular callback does nothing with the records it receives except pass them to `PlayMetaFileRecord`, which displays them on-screen.

The parameters to the `EnumMetaFileProc` are listed in Table 18.2.

Table 18.2. `EnumMetaFileProc` **takes five parameters.**

`HDC hdc;`	Device context on which to paint
`HANDLETABLE FAR* lpht;`	Address of table the object handles
`METARECORD FAR* lpmr;`	Address of metafile record
`int cObj;`	Number of objects in handle table
`LPARAM lParam;`	Data defined by the user

The key parameter in Table 18.2 is the `METARECORD`, which is a pointer to a structure containing three fields:

```
struct {
  DWORD rdSize;
  WORD rdFunction;
  WORD rdParm[];
}
```

`rdSize` defines the size of the entire record, which can vary depending on the length of the last field. `rdFunction` specifies the GDI function—such as `Ellipse`, `Rectangle`, or `SelectObject`—packaged in the structure. The last argument lists the parameters passed to the function.

Consider the following call to `Rectangle`:

```
Rectangle(PaintDC, 0, 0, 96, 46);
```

The record designating this call would look like this:

```
rdSize: 7
rdFunction: 041B // Code for Rectangle function
rdParm 0046, 0096, 0000, 0000 // Parameters in reverse order
```

The codes designated in the second field are listed in the *Microsoft Windows 3.1 Programmers Reference, Vol 4: Resources.* For instance, `BitBlit` has a function number of 0x0922 or 0x0940. `TextOut` is associated with function number 0x0521.

Metaphor uses the `EnumMetaFileProc` solely to paint images to the screen quickly and efficiently. However, I've discussed the `METARECORDS`, because they reveal how metafiles are put together—and exactly how easy it is manipulating them.

Reading Metafiles from Disk

As mentioned, there are two different kinds of metafiles in use. One is the standard Windows metafile created by the Metaphor program. The other is the Aldus, or Placeable metafile, which is produced by programs commonly used throughout the industry.

When you are dealing with standard metafiles, all you need to do is call `GetMetaFile`, and it will suck the data up off the disk and pass it back in the form of an `HMETAFILE` handle. This is much simpler than the task you confront when you encounter a placeable metafile.

To identify an Aldus metafile, simply read the first `DWORD` size block from the file and compare it with the following constant: `0x9AC6CDD7L`. If you have a match, this is a placeable metafile. You should handle this file as follows:

☐ Strip off the 22-byte header which starts the file.

☐ Use the `SetMetaFileBits` function to transform what is left into a conventional metafile.

If you want to study this process in more depth, view the relevant code in the METAUTIL.CPP file, lines 66 - 243. In particular, you should note that the `OpenMetaFile` function determines whether or not the file is an Aldus metafile. If that is indeed the case, `RenderPlaceableMeta` is called. If the file isn't an Aldus metafile, the program relies on the `GetMetaFile` API function. The real grunt work of reading a placeable metafile is performed by `RenderPlaceableMeta`, which begins on line 138.

If you like, you can treat this whole process as a black box. In other words, the simplest way to proceed is to link the `MetaUtil` modules into your own programs. Then, call

LoadFile and be sure to pass in the HWND of the active window in your program. LoadFile pops up a common dialog enabling you to choose a file. When you do, it initializes a global variable called hmf, which is a handle to the metafile you selected.

Common Dialogs

Starting with Version 3.1, Windows includes a set of common dialogs meant to ease certain frequently performed tasks. For example, the Metaphor program uses the GetOpenFileName common dialog (Figure 18.6) and the GetSaveFileName common dialog (Figure 18.7) to aid in the loading and saving of files. The actual act of reading and writing files from disk still needs to be coded by the programmer. These dialogs are designed solely to handle the interface with the user.

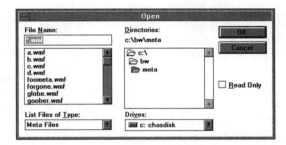

Figure 18.6. *The* GetOpenFileName *dialog enables you to choose files to be loaded into a program or window.*

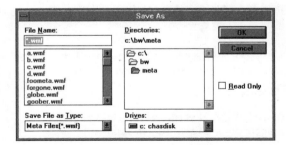

Figure 18.7. *The* GetSaveFileName *dialog is visually almost identical to the* GetOpenFileName *dialog.*

The difference between these two dialogs is not in the way they look, but in the way they behave. The GetSaveFileName dialog, for instance, has the capability of prompting the user before it overwrites a file.

Both of these functions involve working with a single large structure of type OPENFILENAME, which is described in the online help, or in COMMDLG.H. COMMDLG.H is to common dialogs as WINDOWS.H is to the rest of Windows. That is, it's the bible and main source of information. Here's a look at the OPENFILENAME structure, as it appears in COMMDLG.H, with a few sparse comments to define each field. For a more in-depth description, see the online documentation:

```
typedef struct tagOFN
{
    DWORD      lStructSize;          // Size of OPENFILENAME
    HWND       hwndOwner;            // Owner of dialog
    HINSTANCE  hInstance;            // Program that owns dialog
    LPCSTR     lpstrFilter;          // Types of files to view
    LPSTR      lpstrCustomFilter;    // Custom filters
    DWORD      nMaxCustFilter;       // Length of custom filter
    DWORD      nFilterIndex;         // Index for use with filters
    LPSTR      lpstrFile;            // Holds filename on success
    DWORD      nMaxFile;             // Size of lpstrFile
    LPSTR      lpstrFileTitle;       // Path & filename on success
    DWORD      nMaxFileTitle;        // Length of lpstrFileTitle
    LPCSTR     lpstrInitialDir;      // Initial file directory
    LPCSTR     lpstrTitle;           // String for caption bar
    DWORD      Flags;                // Initialization flags
    UINT       nFileOffset;          // Offset into lpstrFile
    UINT       nFileExtension;       // Offset into lpstrFile
    LPCSTR     lpstrDefExt;          // Default extension
    LPARAM     lCustData;            // Used with callbacks
    UINT       (CALLBACK *lpfnHook)(HWND, UINT, WPARAM, LPARAM);
    LPCSTR     lpTemplateName;       // Substitute resource for dlg
} OPENFILENAME;
typedef OPENFILENAME FAR* LPOPENFILENAME;
```

Whenever you are working with a common dialog, there are three steps you must follow:

1. Zero out the record associated with the common dialog and fill in its first field with the size of the structure itself:

   ```
   OPENFILENAME ofn;

   memset(&ofn, 0, sizeof(OPENFILENAME));
   ofn.lStructSize = sizeof(OPENFILENAME);
   ```

2. Fill in any of the other fields in the structure that are either required, or of special interest to your program. Of particular importance is the Flag field. This turns certain features of the dialog on and off, such as whether or not it will contain a help button, and whether or not it will prompt the user before overwriting an existing file.

3. Pass the structure to the API function that runs the dialog and handles input from the user. For instance, if you want to load a file from disk, make this call:

```
GetOpenFileName(&ofn);
```

In the lower-left corner of the common dialogs example is a drop-down combo box listing the types of files commonly used by a particular dialog. For instance, the GetSaveFileName dialog has both .WMF and .BMP files listed, as shown in Figure 18.8. As you can see, this list box includes both the file extension and a brief description.

Figure 18.8. *The combo box that displays the files that can be handled by a particular dialog.*

The text to be placed in the combo box is passed in with the lpstrFilter field of the OPENFILENAME struct. There are two ways to fill out this field. The first is relatively straightforward conceptually, but a bit clumsy to implement. The second is easy to implement, but a bit confusing at first glance.

The code for the first method works only if the lpstrFilter field has been filled with null characters. This is important, because the field contains pairs of null-terminated strings. The first contains the description of the file type and the second contains the extension itself. The end of the list should contain two contiguous NULL characters. Here's an example:

```
memset(&ofn, 0, sizeof(OPENFILENAME));
strcpy(szFilter, "Metafiles");
strcpy(&szFilter[strlen(szFilter) + 1], "*.wmf");
```

The second technique works with a string that contains placeholders designating where the NULL characters should be inserted. To make the following code work, the last character in this string should be an example of the placeholder. The for loop in the code replaces each of the placeholders with a NULL character.

```
strcpy(szFilter,
       "Metafiles(*.wmf)¦*.wmf¦Bitmap Files(*.bmp)¦*.bmp¦");
chReplace = szFilter[strlen(szFilter) - 1];
```

```
for (i = 0; szFilter[i] != '\0'; i++)
{
  if (szFilter[i] == chReplace)
  szFilter[i] = '\0';
}
```

If you want a more in-depth discussion of common dialogs, turn to the next chapter, which examines the ChooseFont common dialog. For now, you should be able to get your own programs up and running by using the GetFileName and GetSaveName functions (listed on lines 200 and 250 of METAUTIL.CPP).

Summary

A good deal of ground was covered in this chapter. The highlights include descriptions of how to

- ☐ Draw basic geometric shapes, such as ellipses and rectangles
- ☐ Keep a record of these shapes in a metafile
- ☐ Display a metafile (using two methods)
- ☐ Read placeable metafiles
- ☐ Work with the GetSaveFileName and GetOpenFileName common dialogs

Though not as important as bitmaps, metafiles can still play a prominent role in many applications because they are so small and fast. They also can be a convenient way of passing graphical or textual (don't forget that TextOut is a GDI function!) information between two applications or windows.

Q&A

1. Q: The makefile for this program looks different. What's up?

   A: The Metaphor program contains three separate .CPP files that need to be linked. Writing out explicit rules for compiling each of those files becomes a monotonous task that cries out for some form of automation. The solution provided by the creators of Make is to write something called an *implicit* rule, that says, in effect, "every time you need to perform a particular type of task, here's how to do it." For instance, the following code says: "Every time you see a file with an .OBJ extension, you can create it by running a .CPP file through the Borland command-line compiler."

```
.cpp.obj:
  bcc -c $(FLAGS) { $< }
```

Here's the same line applied to the Microsoft compiler:

```
.cpp.obj:
  cl -c -Gsw -Ow -W3 -AL -Zp { $< }
```

The `$<` syntax appended to the end of these statements is a built in macro that automatically supplies the name of the file in question, along with its extension.

2. Q: How do you gray the Save menu item in the File menu?

A: Sometimes, a programmer wants to prevent a user from selecting a particular menu item. To do this, simply call `EnableMenuItem` as follows:

```
HMENU hMenu = GetMenu(hwnd);
EnableMenuItem(hMenu, CM_ENDMETA, MF_BYCOMMAND | MF_GRAYED);
```

The `EnableMenuItem` function takes three parameters. The first is the handle to a menu; the second is the ID or position of the menu item in question. The third parameter is a set of flags specifying whether the second parameter is a position or command value, and whether or not you want the menu item grayed and disabled (`MF_GRAYED`), disabled but not grayed (`MF_DISABLED`), or enabled (`MF_ENABLE`).

3. Q: What are `NULL` brushes used for?

A: `NULL` brushes make a particular set of pixels invisible. For instance, if you paint the interior of a rectangle with a `NULL` brush, you'll be able to see through it to what lies beneath.

Workshop

The Workshop provides quiz questions to help you solidify your understanding of the material covered and exercises to provide you with experience in using what you've learned. Try to understand the quiz and exercise answers before continuing on to the next chapter. Answers are provided in Appendix A.

Quiz

1. What non-numerical field is common to every GDI function?

2. Name six GDI functions for creating geometric figures.

3. How do you change the color of the interior of an ellipse?

4. How do you change the color of the outline of a rectangle?

5. What's the difference between a placeable Windows metafile, and a standard Windows metafile?

6. Name two ways to display a metafile.

7. What is returned by CreateMetaFile and what do you do with it?

8. What is returned by CloseMetaFile and what can you do with it?

9. What is the second field in a METARECORD, how can you find the values listed in it, and how can you get hold of a METARECORD in the first place?

10. What is the first field in an OPENFILENAME struct, and what are you supposed to do with it?

Exercises

1. Write a program displaying a polygon with six sides.

2. (Optional) Create a metafile containing three ellipses and three rectangles. Modify the EnumMetaFileProc function so that every time it encounters one of the ellipses, it changes its color to green. (HINT: The function number for an ellipse is 0x0418. Its parameters are stored the same way as the parameters in the Rectangle function, as shown in the previous example.

3. (Optional) The function numbers for LineTo and MoveTo are 0x0213 and 0x0214. Create some metafiles with about 10 geometric figures in them, and then pop up a Message box which lists the order of the figures and their type. Obtain this information solely from an examination of the metafile itself. Sample output:

```
Figure 1: Rectangle
Figure 3: Ellipse
Figure 5: LineTo
...etc.
```

MDI: The Multiple Document Interface

In this chapter, you'll learn how to code applications that feature a multiple document interface (MDI). MDI programs enable you to have more than one document open inside an application at a time. Both the Borland and Microsoft IDEs are MDI applications, as well as the Program Manager and such well-known applications as Quattro Pro for Windows and Word for Windows.

Following is an overview of the main points covered in this chapter:

☐ An explanation of MDI and its purposes

☐ Registering and creating MDI Windows

☐ Working with MDI menus

☐ Using the WNDCLASS extra bytes to store data

☐ Using the WM_QUERYENDSESSION message

☐ Using MDI specific messages

☐ Sharing CPU time with other windows or applications

☐ The difference between MM_ANISOTROPIC and MM_ISOTROPIC

To demonstrate these ideas to you, I've included a stripped down MDI example called MDIPaint that displays four different types of child windows. This application has been divided into six different modules, one for the main program, one for a set of common routines, and one for each of the children. This approach enables a simple, clean design, with each module containing a relatively self-contained and easy to understand piece of the whole.

Overall, I find that the MDI interface presents a more complicated challenge than some of the other subjects approached in this book. However, it's not prohibitively difficult. You just need to take your time and take the trouble to think ahead.

What Is an MDI?

The first thing to understand about an MDI is that it is a standard. Way back in ancient computer history, when the earth's crust was still cooling, that is, in 1989, IBM wrote a specification for something called the multiple document interface .

This standard is explained in a book called *Systems Application Architecture Common User Access Advanced Interface Design Guide*, or more commonly, *SAA CUA Interface Design Guide*. This book was first published by IBM in June 1989. It was assigned

document number SY0328-300-R00-1089. The Windows MDI conforms to the standard laid out in this book. An example MDI application is shown in Figure 19.1.

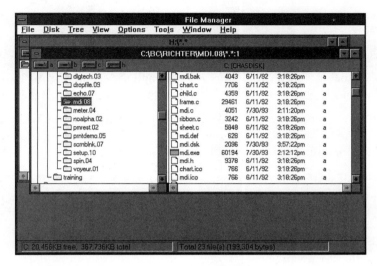

Figure 19.1. *The File Manager is an MDI application.*

This standard is not only a programmer's standard, but also a user's standard. MDI isn't just a technical specification for hackers, but an interface that users know, understand, and count on. More specifically, users count on the fact that each MDI program will behave in a similar fashion. In that way, users can catch on fairly quickly to the best methods for using the application. All Windows MDI applications automatically exhibit the following behavior:

☐ The application consists of a main window and a series of child windows. All the child windows stay within the parent's boundaries.

☐ The application, and each child window, can be maximized and minimized. Minimized child windows stay within the frame of the main window.

☐ A list of all the child windows is maintained in a pop-up menu usually named either File or Window. (The actual specification prefers the latter choice, but many programmers believe a list of files belongs in the File menu!)

☐ Alt-F4 closes an application, whereas Ctrl-F4 closes a child. Use Ctrl-F6 to switch between documents.

19

If you implement a Windows MDI application correctly, all these options are executed automatically. With some additional work, you can also teach your MDI app to

☐ Tile and cascade its child windows.

☐ Arrange the icons resting in the main window.

☐ Prompt the user before closing a child window. Even if the whole application is being shut down in one step (through the system menu or another mechanism), you should be able to prompt the user before closing a window.

The previous points specify the main features of any Windows MDI application. Of course, these ideas might be familiar to you from general experience, or from the use of the Borland or Microsoft IDEs.

From a technical point of view, you should remember these two key ideas:

1. Instead of using `CreateWindow`, send a `WM_MDICREATE` message when you want to create an MDI child window.

2. The "main window" really consists of two windows: the frame window and the client window.

`WM_MDICREATE` is discussed in-depth after the code is listed. However, it's important that you first come to terms with the frame and client windows.

Every MDI application creates a main window exactly the same way a normal main window is created. In addition, MDI applications should create a client window while responding to the `WM_CREATE` message. This child window uses the preregistered `MDICLIENT` class.

The client window is the key to all MDI applications. It manages all the chores (listed previously) while staying behind-the-scenes—hidden to the user and the programmer.

Note: On most machines, if you give the client and the frame windows different colors, you can actually see the client covering up the main window. The MDIPaint program creates a brush for its main window using the `COLOR_APPWORKSPACE` constant (line 87), which is the same constant used by the `MDICLIENT` class. If you use a stock `BLACK_BRUSH` or `WHITE_BRUSH` for the frame, you might see both windows for a moment when the application first appears on-screen:

```
wndclass.hbrBackground = GetStockBrush(BLACK_BRUSH)
```

The actual call to create a client window is fairly straightforward, except that you need to pass a CLIENTCREATESTRUCT in the last parameter of CreateWindow. The following excerpts from MDIPAINT.CPP show the code for creating a client window (starting at line 176).

```
175:    hMenuInit = LoadMenu(hInstance, "MdiMenuInit");
176:    hMenuMultiple = LoadMenu(hInstance, "MDIMultiple");
177:    SetMenu(hwnd, hMenuInit);
178:
179:    // Load accelerator table
180:    hWndClient = GetWindow (hwnd, GW CHILD);
181:    hAccel = LoadAccelerators (hInstance, "MdiAccel");
182:
183:    hMenuFileInit = GetSubMenu(hMenuInit, 0);
184:    hMenuFileInit = GetSubMenu(hMenuInit, 0);
185:
186:    clientcreate.hWindowMenu = hMenuFileInit;
187:    clientcreate.idFirstChild = IDM FIRSTCHILD;
188:
189:    hWndClient = CreateWindow ("MDICLIENT", NULL,
190:                        WS_CHILD ¦ WS_CLIPCHILDREN ¦ WS_VISIBLE,
191:                        0, 0, 0, 0, hwnd, HMENU(1), hInstance,
192:                        (LPSTR) &clientcreate);
```

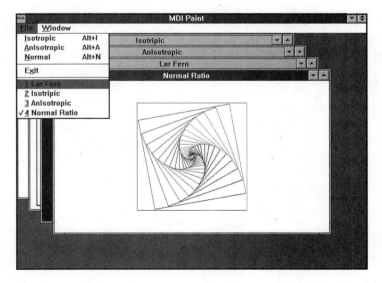

Figure 19.2. *The menu from the MDIPaint program can hold a numbered list of the current children.*

As you can see, a CLIENTCREATESTRUCT has two fields:

☐ The first field holds a menu. This is the menu that contains a list of the current child windows. (I discuss MDI menus later in this chapter, after the code.)

☐ The second field, called idFirstChild, holds the ID of the first MDI child window the application creates. To make this work, pass in an ID that is higher than any other ID used in your application. When you create MDI children, Windows automatically assigns them IDs based on idFirstChild. It uses these IDs to determine the number to be associated with each child window. These numbers are listed in the menu supplied by the first field of the CLIENTCREATESTRUCT (see Figure 19.2).

Note that the call to CreateWindow uses MDICLIENT in the szClass field. As mentioned, MDICLIENT is a preregistered class that responds to many of the key messages sent to an MDI application. In other words, that one field of CreateWindow looks small compared to the code in the rest of the program, but its significance is very large indeed!

Listing 19.1 shows the MDIPaint program, which draws geometric shapes and a simple fractal inside of four separate classes of an MDI window.

 Listing 19.1. MDIPAINT.CPP.

```
 1: ///////////////////////////////////////////////////////////
 2: // Program Name: MDIPAINT.CPP
 3: // Programmer: Charlie Calvert
 4: // Description: MDI example program
 5: // Note: Use Smart Callbacks or Explicit Exports
 6: // Date: 07/25/93
 7: ///////////////////////////////////////////////////////////
 8:
 9: #define STRICT
10: #include <windows.h>
11: #include <windowsx.h>
12: #include "mdipaint.h"
13: #pragma warning(disable : 4068)
14:
15: // global variables
16: static HWND hWndFrame, hWndClient;
17: static char szFrameClass[] = "MDI_Frame";
18: static char szIsotropic[] = "MDI_AnIsotropic";
19: static char szAnIsotropic[] = "MDI_Isotropic";
20: static char szNormal[] = "MDI_Normal";
21: static char szFern[] = "MDI_Fern";
22: static HINSTANCE hInstance;
23: HMENU   hMenuInit, hMenuMultiple;
```

```
24: HMENU  hMenuFileInit, hMenuFileMultiple;
25: HACCEL hAccel;
26:
27: //#define Frame_DefProc DefFrameProc
28: BOOL Frame_OnCreate(HWND hwnd, CREATESTRUCT FAR* lpCreateStruct);
29: void Frame_OnDestroy(HWND hwnd);
30: void Frame_OnClose(HWND hwnd);
31: void Frame_OnCommand(HWND hwnd, int id, HWND hwndCtl, UINT
32: codeNotify);
33: BOOL Frame_OnQueryEndSession(HWND hwnd);
34:
35: ////////////////////////////////
36: // DefProc for the Frame window.
37: ////////////////////////////////
38: LRESULT Frame_DefProc (HWND hwnd, UINT uMsg, WPARAM wParam,
39: LPARAM lParam)
40: {
41:    return(DefFrameProc(hwnd, hWndClient, uMsg, wParam, lParam));
42: }
43:
44: ////////////////////////////////
45: // Program entry point
46: ////////////////////////////////
47: #pragma argsused
48: int PASCAL WinMain (HINSTANCE hInst, HINSTANCE hPrevInstance,
49:                     LPSTR lpszCmdLine, int nCmdShow)
50: {
51:   MSG       msg;
52:
53:   if (!hPrevInstance)
54:     if (!Register(hInst))
55:       return FALSE;
56:
57:   if (!(hWndFrame = Create(hInst, nCmdShow)))
58:     return FALSE;
59:
60:   while (GetMessage (&msg, NULL, 0, 0))
61:   {
62:     if (!TranslateMDISysAccel (hWndClient, &msg) &&
63:         !TranslateAccelerator (hWndFrame, hAccel, &msg))
64:     {
65:       TranslateMessage (&msg);
66:       DispatchMessage (&msg);
67:     }
68:   }
69:   return msg.wParam;
70: }
71:
72: ////////////////////////////////
73: // Register classes with the OS
74: ////////////////////////////////
```

19

continues

Listing 19.1. continued

```
 75: BOOL Register(HINSTANCE hInst)
 76: {
 77:    WNDCLASS wndclass;
 78:
 79:    // Register the frame window class
 80:    wndclass.style          = CS_HREDRAW | CS_VREDRAW;
 81:    wndclass.lpfnWndProc    = FrameWndProc;
 82:    wndclass.cbClsExtra     = 0;
 83:    wndclass.cbWndExtra     = 0;
 84:    wndclass.hInstance      = hInst;
 85:    wndclass.hIcon          = LoadIcon (NULL, IDI_APPLICATION);
 86:    wndclass.hCursor        = LoadCursor (NULL, IDC_ARROW);
 87:    wndclass.hbrBackground =
 88:            CreateSolidBrush(GetSysColor(COLOR_APPWORKSPACE));
 89:    wndclass.lpszMenuName   = NULL;
 90:    wndclass.lpszClassName  = szFrameClass;
 91:
 92:    if(!RegisterClass (&wndclass))
 93:       return FALSE;
 94:
 95:    // Register the Isotropic window class
 96:    wndclass.lpfnWndProc    = IsotropicWndProc;
 97:    wndclass.hIcon          = LoadIcon (NULL, IDI_APPLICATION);
 98:    wndclass.hbrBackground  = GetStockBrush(WHITE_BRUSH);
 99:    wndclass.lpszMenuName   = NULL;
100:    wndclass.lpszClassName  = szIsotropic;
101:
102:    if(!RegisterClass (&wndclass))
103:       return FALSE;
104:
105:    // Register the AnIsotropic window class
106:    wndclass.lpfnWndProc    = AnIsotropicWndProc;
107:    wndclass.hIcon          = NULL;
108:    wndclass.lpszClassName  = szAnIsotropic;
109:
110:    if(!RegisterClass (&wndclass))
111:       return FALSE;
112:
113:    // Register the Normal window class
114:    wndclass.lpfnWndProc    = NormalWndProc;
115:    wndclass.lpszClassName  = szNormal;
116:
117:    if(!RegisterClass (&wndclass))
118:       return FALSE;
119:
120:    // Register the Normal window class
121:    wndclass.lpfnWndProc    = FernWndProc;
122:    wndclass.hbrBackground  = GetStockBrush(BLACK_BRUSH);
123:    wndclass.lpszClassName  = szFern;
124:
```

```
125:    return RegisterClass(&wndclass);
126: }
127:
128: ///////////////////////////////
129: // Create the main window
130: ///////////////////////////////
131: HWND Create(HINSTANCE hInst, int nCmdShow)
132: {
133:    hInstance = hInst;
134:
135:    HWND hwnd = CreateWindow (szFrameClass, "MDI Paint",
136:                              WS_OVERLAPPEDWINDOW | WS_CLIPCHILDREN,
137:                              CW_USEDEFAULT, CW_USEDEFAULT,
138:                              CW_USEDEFAULT, CW_USEDEFAULT,
139:                              NULL, hMenuInit, hInstance, NULL);
140:
141:    if (hwnd == NULL)
142:      return hwnd;
143:
144:    ShowWindow (hwnd, nCmdShow);
145:    UpdateWindow (hwnd);
146:
147:    return hwnd;
148: }
149:
150: LRESULT CALLBACK _export FrameWndProc (HWND hwnd, UINT message,
151: WPARAM wParam, LPARAM lParam)
152: {
153:    switch (message)
154:    {
155:        HANDLE_MSG(hwnd, WM_CREATE, Frame_OnCreate);
156:        HANDLE_MSG(hwnd, WM_DESTROY, Frame_OnDestroy);
157:        HANDLE_MSG(hwnd, WM_CLOSE, Frame_OnClose);
158:        HANDLE_MSG(hwnd, WM_COMMAND, Frame_OnCommand);
159:        HANDLE_MSG(hwnd, WM_QUERYENDSESSION,
160:                   Frame_OnQueryEndSession);
161:        default:
162:          return(DefFrameProc(hwnd, hWndClient, message, wParam,
                                  lParam));
163:
164:    }
165: }
166:
167: //////////////////////////////////////////
168: // WM_CREATE    Create the client window
169: //////////////////////////////////////////
170: #pragma argsused
171: BOOL Frame_OnCreate(HWND hwnd, CREATESTRUCT FAR* lpCreateStruct)
172: {
173:    CLIENTCREATESTRUCT clientcreate;
174:
```

continues

Listing 19.1. continued

```
175:    hMenuInit = LoadMenu(hInstance, "MdiMenuInit");
176:    hMenuMultiple = LoadMenu(hInstance, "MDIMultiple");
177:    SetMenu(hwnd, hMenuInit);
178:
179:    // Load accelerator table
180:    hWndClient = GetWindow (hwnd, GW_CHILD);
181:    hAccel = LoadAccelerators (hInstance, "MdiAccel");
182:
183:    hMenuFileInit = GetSubMenu(hMenuInit, 0);
184:    hMenuFileMultiple = GetSubMenu(hMenuMultiple, 0);
185:
186:    clientcreate.hWindowMenu  = hMenuFileInit;
187:    clientcreate.idFirstChild = IDM_FIRSTCHILD;
188:
189:    hWndClient = CreateWindow ("MDICLIENT", NULL,
190:                           WS_CHILD ¦ WS_CLIPCHILDREN ¦ WS_VISIBLE,
191:                           0, 0, 0, 0, hwnd, HMENU(1), hInstance,
192:                           (LPSTR) &clientcreate);
193:    if (hWndClient == NULL)
194:      return FALSE;
195:
196:    return TRUE;
197: }
198:
199: ////////////////////////////////////////////
200: // Handle WM_DESTROY
201: ////////////////////////////////////////////
202: #pragma argsused
203: void Frame_OnDestroy(HWND hwnd)
204: {
205:    DestroyMenu(hMenuMultiple);
206:    SetMenu(hwnd, NULL);
207:    DestroyMenu(hMenuInit);
208:    PostQuitMessage(0);
209: }
210:
211: ////////////////////////////////////////////
212: // Handle WM_CLOSE
213: ////////////////////////////////////////////
214: void Frame_OnClose(HWND hwnd)
215: {
216:    if (NULL != GetWindow (hWndClient, GW_CHILD))
217:      SendMessage (hwnd, WM_COMMAND, CM_CLOSEALL, 0L);
218:
219:    if (NULL != GetWindow (hWndClient, GW_CHILD))
220:      return;
221:
222:    DestroyWindow(hwnd);
223: }
```

SAMS
Sams
Learning
Center

SAMS
PUBLISHING

```
224:
225: ////////////////////////////////////////
226: // Create an MDI child, HANDLE WM_MDICREATE
227: ////////////////////////////////////////
228: HWND CreateMDIChild(LPCSTR szClass, LPCSTR szTitle)
229: {
230:   MDICREATESTRUCT    MCS;
231:
232:   MCS.szClass = szClass;
233:   MCS.szTitle = szTitle;
234:   MCS.hOwner  = hInstance;
235:   MCS.x       = CW_USEDEFAULT;
236:   MCS.y       = CW_USEDEFAULT;
237:   MCS.cx      = CW_USEDEFAULT;
238:   MCS.cy      = CW_USEDEFAULT;
239:   MCS.style   = 0;
240:   MCS.lParam  = NULL;
241:   return FORWARD_WM_MDICREATE(hWndClient, &MCS, SendMessage);
242: }
243:
244: ////////////////////////////////////////
245: // Handle WM_COMMAND
246: ////////////////////////////////////////
247: #pragma argsused
248: void Frame_OnCommand(HWND hwnd, int id, HWND hwndCtl, UINT
249: codeNotify)
250: {
251:   WNDENUMPROC           lpfnEnum;
252:   HWND                  hwndChild;
253:   MDICREATESTRUCT    MCS;
254:
255:   // Do default processing for any system commands (SC_*).
256:   if ((unsigned) id >= 0xF000u) goto DWP; // thanks to J. Richter
257:
258:   switch (id)
259:   {
260:     case CM_ANISOTROP:
261:       CreateMDIChild(szAnIsotropic, "AnIsotropic");
262:       break;
263:
264:     case CM_ISOTROP:
265:       CreateMDIChild(szIsotropic, "Isotripic");
266:       break;
267:
268:     case CM_NORMAL:
269:       CreateMDIChild(szNormal, "Normal Ratio");
270:       break;
271:
272:     case CM_FERN:
273:       CreateMDIChild(szFern, "Lar Fern");
274:       break;
```

continues

19

Listing 19.1. continued

```
275:
276:        case CM_CLOSE:              // Close the active window
277:          hwndChild = (HWND)LOWORD(SendMessage(hWndClient,
278:                                   WM_MDIGETACTIVE, 0, 0L));
279:          if (SendMessage(hwndChild, WM_QUERYENDSESSION, 0, 0L))
280:              SendMessage(hWndClient, WM_MDIDESTROY,
281:                          (WPARAM)hwndChild, 0L);
282:          break;
283:
284:        case CM_EXIT:               // Exit the program
285:          SendMessage (hwnd, WM_CLOSE, 0, 0L);
286:          break;
287:
288:        case CM_TILE:
289:          SendMessage (hWndClient, WM_MDITILE, 0, 0L);
290:          break;
291:
292:        case CM_CASCADE:
293:          SendMessage (hWndClient, WM_MDICASCADE, 0, 0L);
294:          break;
295:
296:        case CM_ARRANGE:
297:          SendMessage (hWndClient, WM_MDIICONARRANGE, 0, 0L);
298:          break;
299:
300:        case CM_CLOSEALL:           // Attempt to close all children
301:          lpfnEnum = (WNDENUMPROC)MakeProcInstance(
302:                             (FARPROC)EnumChildWnds, hInstance);
303:          EnumChildWindows (hWndClient, lpfnEnum, 0L);
304:          FreeProcInstance ((FARPROC)lpfnEnum);
305:          break;
306:
307:        default:                    // Pass to active child
308:          hwndChild = (HWND)LOWORD(SendMessage(hWndClient,
309:                        WM_MDIGETACTIVE, 0, 0L));
310:          if (IsWindow (hwndChild))
311:            SendMessage (hwndChild, WM_COMMAND, id, codeNotify);
312:          break;              // and then to DefFrameProc
313:    }
314:    DWP:
315:      FORWARD_WM_COMMAND(hwnd, id, hwndCtl,
316:                          codeNotify, Frame_DefProc);
317: }
318:
319: /////////////////////////////////////////////
320: // Handle WM_QUERYENDSESSION
321: /////////////////////////////////////////////
322: #pragma argsused
323: BOOL Frame_OnQueryEndSession(HWND hwnd)
```

```
324: {
325:   if (NULL != GetWindow (hWndClient, GW_CHILD))
326:     SendMessage (hwnd, WM_COMMAND, CM_CLOSEALL, 0L);
327:
328:   if (NULL != GetWindow (hWndClient, GW_CHILD))
329:     return FALSE;
330:   else
331:     return TRUE;
332: }
333:
334: // -------------------------------------
335: // Callbacks
336: // -------------------------------------
337:
338: /////////////////////////////////////////
339: // Callbacks
340: /////////////////////////////////////////
341: #pragma argsused
342: BOOL CALLBACK EnumChildWnds(HWND hwnd, LONG lParam)
343: {
344:   if (GetWindow(hwnd, GW_OWNER)) // Icon Title?
345:     return TRUE;
346:
347:   SendMessage (GetParent(hwnd), WM_MDIRESTORE, (WPARAM)hwnd, 0L);
348:   if (!SendMessage (hwnd, WM_QUERYENDSESSION, 0, 0L))
349:     return TRUE;
350:
351:   SendMessage (GetParent(hwnd), WM_MDIDESTROY, (WPARAM)hwnd, 0L);
352:     return TRUE;
353: }
```

19

Listing 19.2 shows the MDIPaint header file.

Listing 19.2. MDIPAINT.H.

```
1: /////////////////////////////////////////////////////////
2: // Program Name: MDIPAINT.H
3: // Programmer: Charlie Calvert
4: // Description: Multimedia MDI windows example program
5: // Date: 07/25/93
6: /////////////////////////////////////////////////////////
7:
8: #define CM_ISOTROP      100
9: #define CM_ANISOTROP    101
10: #define CM_NORMAL       112
11: #define CM_FERN         113
12: #define CM_CLOSE        114
13: #define CM_EXIT         115
14:
```

continues

Listing 19.2. continued

```
15: #define CM_TILE          130
16: #define CM_CASCADE       131
17: #define CM_ARRANGE       132
18: #define CM_CLOSEALL      133
19:
20: #define IDM_FIRSTCHILD   150
21:
22: // funcs
23: LRESULT CALLBACK _export AnIsotropicWndProc(HWND, UINT,
24:                                             WPARAM, LPARAM);
25: LRESULT CALLBACK _export IsotropicWndProc(HWND, UINT,
26:                                           WPARAM, LPARAM);
27: LRESULT CALLBACK _export NormalWndProc(HWND, UINT,
28:                                        WPARAM, LPARAM);
29: LRESULT CALLBACK _export FernWndProc(HWND, UINT, WPARAM, LPARAM);
30: LRESULT CALLBACK _export FrameWndProc(HWND, UINT,
31:                                       WPARAM, LPARAM);
32: BOOL CALLBACK _export EnumChildWnds(HWND, LONG);
33: BOOL Register(HINSTANCE hInst);
34: HWND Create(HINSTANCE hInst, int nCmdShow);
```

Listing 19.3 shows the code for AnIsotrop.

Type   **Listing 19.3. ANISOTROP.CPP.**

```
1:  //////////////////////////////////////////////////////
2:  // Program Name: ANISOTRP.CPP
3:  // Programmer: Charlie Calvert
4:  // Description: MDI example program
5:  // Date: 07/25/93
6:  //////////////////////////////////////////////////////
7:
8:  #define STRICT
9:  #include <windows.h>
10: #include <windowsx.h>
11: #pragma hdrstop
12: #include <stdlib.h>
13: #include "draw.h"
14: #pragma warning(disable : 4068)
15:
16: extern HMENU hMenuMultiple, hMenuInit;
17: extern HMENU hMenuFileMultiple, hMenuFileInit;
18: static HWND hwndClient, hwndFrame ;
19:
20: // AnIsotrop_Play Object
21: #define AnIsotrop_DefProc DefMDIChildProc
22: BOOL AnIsotrop_OnCreate(HWND hwnd,
23:                         CREATESTRUCT FAR* lpCreateStruct);
```

```
24: void AnIsotrop_MDIActivate(HWND hwnd, BOOL fActive,
25:                            HWND hwndActivate, HWND hwndDeactivate);
26: void AnIsotrop_OnPaint(HWND hwnd);
27:
28: ////////////////////////////////////
29: // The WndProc
30: ////////////////////////////////////
31: LRESULT CALLBACK AnIsotropicWndProc (HWND hwnd, UINT message,
32:                                      WPARAM wParam, LPARAM lParam)
33: {
34:   switch (message)
35:   {
36:     HANDLE_MSG(hwnd, WM_CREATE, AnIsotrop_OnCreate);
37:     HANDLE_MSG(hwnd, WM_MDIACTIVATE, AnIsotrop_MDIActivate);
38:     HANDLE_MSG(hwnd, WM_PAINT, AnIsotrop_OnPaint);
39:   default:
40:     return AnIsotrop_DefProc(hwnd, message, wParam, lParam) ;
41:   }
42: }
43:
44: ////////////////////////////////////
45: // Handle WM_CREATE
46: ////////////////////////////////////
47: #pragma argsused
48: BOOL AnIsotrop_OnCreate(HWND hwnd, CREATESTRUCT FAR* lpCreateStruct)
49: {
50:   hwndClient = GetParent (hwnd) ;
51:   hwndFrame  = GetParent (hwndClient) ;
52:   return TRUE;
53: }
54:
55: ////////////////////////////////////
56: // Handle WM_ACTIVATE
57: ////////////////////////////////////
58: #pragma argsused
59: void AnIsotrop_MDIActivate(HWND hwnd, BOOL fActive,
60:                            HWND hwndActivate,
61:                            HWND hwndDeactivate)
62: {
63:   if (fActive)
64:     SendMessage (hwndClient, WM_MDISETMENU, 0,
65:                  MAKELONG(hMenuMultiple, hMenuFileMultiple));
66:
67:   if (!fActive)
68:     SendMessage (hwndClient, WM_MDISETMENU, 0,
69:                  MAKELONG(hMenuInit, hMenuFileInit));
70:   DrawMenuBar (hwndFrame) ;
71: }
72:
73: ////////////////////////////////////
74: // Handle WM_PAINT
```

continues

Listing 19.3. continued

```
75: /////////////////////////////////////
76: void AnIsotrop_OnPaint(HWND hwnd)
77: {
78:   HDC PaintDC;
79:   PAINTSTRUCT PaintStruct;
80:   RECT R;
81:      '
82:   PaintDC = BeginPaint (hwnd, &PaintStruct);
83:
84:   SetMapMode(PaintDC, MM_ANISOTROPIC);
85:   GetClientRect(hwnd, &R);
86:   SetWindowExt(PaintDC, 210, 210);
87:   SetViewportExt(PaintDC, R.right, R.bottom);
88:   SetViewportOrg(PaintDC, R.right / 2, R.bottom / 2);
89:   DoDraw(PaintDC);
90:
91:   EndPaint (hwnd, &PaintStruct);
92: }
```

Listing 19.4 shows the code for Fern.

Type   **Listing 19.4. FERN.CPP.**

```
 1: ///////////////////////////////////////////////////////
 2: // Program Name: FERN.CPP
 3: // Programmer: Charlie Calvert
 4: // Description: MDI example program
 5: // Date: 07/25/93
 6: ///////////////////////////////////////////////////////
 7: #define STRICT
 8: #include <windows.h>
 9: #include <windowsx.h>
10: #include <stdlib.h>
11: #include "draw.h"
12: #pragma warning(disable : 4068)
13:
14: int FernTimer = 1;
15:
16: // constants
17: double a[4] = {0, 0.85,  0.2,  -0.15};
18: double b[4] = {0, 0.04, -0.26,  0.28};
19: double c[4] = {0, -0.04,  0.23,  0.26};
20: double d[4] = {0.16, 0.85,  0.22,  0.24};
21: double e[4] = {0,     0,     0,     0};
22: double f[4] = {0,    1.6,   1.6,   0.44};
23: double x = 0;
24: double y = 0;
25:
```

```
26: // variables
27: static double TempX, TempY;
28: static int MaxX, MaxY, k;
29: static long MaxIterations, Count;
30: static HWND hWndClient, hWndFrame;
31:
32: // externs
33: extern HMENU hMenuMultiple, hMenuInit;
34: extern HMENU hMenuFileMultiple, hMenuFileInit;
35: extern HACCEL hAccel;
36:
37: #define FernPlay_DefProc DefMDIChildProc
38: BOOL FernPlay_OnCreate(HWND hwnd,
39:                        CREATESTRUCT FAR* lpCreateStruct);
40: void FernPlay_OnClose(HWND hwnd);
41: void FernPlay_OnTimer(HWND hwnd, UINT id);
42: void FernPlay_MDIActivate(HWND hwnd, BOOL fActive,
43:                        HWND hwndActivate,
44:                        HWND hwndDeactivate);
45: BOOL FernPlay_OnQueryEndSession(HWND hwnd);
46: void FernPlay_OnPaint(HWND hwnd);
47: void FernPlay_OnSize(HWND hwnd, UINT state, int cx, int cy);
48:
49: /////////////////////////////////
50: // The Window Procedure
51: /////////////////////////////////
52: LRESULT CALLBACK FernWndProc(HWND hwnd, UINT message,
53:                        WPARAM wParam, LPARAM lParam)
54: {
55:   switch (message)
56:   {
57:     HANDLE_MSG(hwnd, WM_CREATE, FernPlay_OnCreate);
58:     HANDLE_MSG(hwnd, WM_CLOSE, FernPlay_OnClose);
59:     HANDLE_MSG(hwnd, WM_TIMER, FernPlay_OnTimer);
60:     HANDLE_MSG(hwnd, WM_MDIACTIVATE, FernPlay_MDIActivate);
61:     HANDLE_MSG(hwnd, WM_PAINT, FernPlay_OnPaint);
62:     HANDLE_MSG(hwnd, WM_QUERYENDSESSION,
63:                        FernPlay_OnQueryEndSession);
64:     HANDLE_MSG(hwnd, WM_SIZE, FernPlay_OnSize);
65:   default:
66:     return FernPlay_DefProc(hwnd, message, wParam, lParam);
67:   }
68: }
69:
70: /////////////////////////////////
71: // Handle WM_CREATE
72: /////////////////////////////////
73: #pragma argsused
74: BOOL FernPlay_OnCreate(HWND hwnd, CREATESTRUCT FAR* lpCreateStruct)
75: {
76:   hWndClient = GetParent (hwnd);
```

continues

Listing 19.4. continued

```
 77:    hWndFrame   = GetParent (hWndClient);
 78:    Count = 0;
 79:    SetTimer(hwnd, FernTimer, 0, NULL);
 80:    return TRUE;
 81: }
 82:
 83: ////////////////////////////////////
 84: // Handle WM_MDIACTIVATE
 85: ////////////////////////////////////
 86: #pragma argsused
 87: void FernPlay_MDIActivate(HWND hwnd, BOOL fActive, HWND
 88:                              hwndActivate, HWND hwndDeactivate)
 89: {
 90:    if (fActive)
 91:      SendMessage(hWndClient, WM_MDISETMENU, 0,
 92:                  MAKELONG(hMenuMultiple, hMenuFileMultiple));
 93:
 94:    if (!fActive)
 95:      SendMessage(hWndClient, WM_MDISETMENU, 0,
 96:                  MAKELONG(hMenuInit, hMenuFileInit));
 97:    DrawMenuBar (hWndFrame);
 98: }
 99:
100: ////////////////////////////////////
101: // Handle WM_CLOSE
102: ////////////////////////////////////
103: void FernPlay_OnClose(HWND hwnd)
104: {
105:    Count = MaxIterations;
106:    if (IDOK != MessageBox (hwnd, "OK to close window?",
107:                "Fern", MB_ICONQUESTION | MB_OKCANCEL))
108:      return;
109:    else
110:      FORWARD_WM_CLOSE(hwnd, FernPlay_DefProc);
111: }
112:
113: ////////////////////////////////////
114: // Handle WM_QUERYENDSESSION
115: ////////////////////////////////////
116: BOOL FernPlay_OnQueryEndSession(HWND hwnd)
117: {
118:    Count = MaxIterations;
119:    if (IDOK != MessageBox (hwnd, "OK to close window?",
120:                "Fern", MB_ICONQUESTION | MB_OKCANCEL))
121:      return FALSE;
122:    else
123:      return TRUE;
124: }
125:
```

```
126: ////////////////////////////////
127: // Handle WM_SIZE
128: ////////////////////////////////
129: #pragma argsused
130: void FernPlay_OnSize(HWND hwnd, UINT state, int cx, int cy)
131: {
132:   RECT R;
133:   GetClientRect(hwnd, &R);
134:   MaxX = R.right;
135:   MaxY = R.bottom;
136:   MaxIterations = long(MaxY) * 50;
137:   if (state == SIZE_MINIMIZED)
138:     MaxIterations = 175;
139:
140:   // MUST forward WM_SIZE messages
141:   FORWARD_WM_SIZE(hwnd, state, cx, cy, FernPlay_DefProc);
142: }
143:
144: ////////////////////////////////
145: // Handle WM_PAINT
146: ////////////////////////////////
147: void FernPlay_OnPaint(HWND hwnd)
148: {
149:   Count = 0;
150:   KillTimer(hwnd, FernTimer);
151:   SetTimer(hwnd, FernTimer, 0, NULL);
152:   FORWARD_WM_PAINT(hwnd, FernPlay_DefProc);
153: }
154:
155: ////////////////////////////////
156: // Paint the fern
157: ////////////////////////////////
158: void DoPaint(HWND hwnd)
159: {
160:   HDC PaintDC;
161:   k = rand() % 100;
162:   if ((k > 0 ) && (k <= 85))
163:     k = 1;
164:   if ((k > 85) && (k <= 92))
165:     k = 2;
166:   if (k > 92) k = 3;
167:   TempX = a[k] * x + b[k] * y + e[k];
168:   TempY = c[k] * x + d[k] * y + f[k];
169:   x = TempX;
170:   y = TempY;
171:   if ((Count >= MaxIterations) || (Count != 0))
172:   {
173:     PaintDC = GetDC(hwnd);
174:     SetPixel(PaintDC, (x * MaxY / 11 + MaxX / 2),
175:             (y * -MaxY / 11 + MaxY), RGB(0, 0XFF, 0));
176:     ReleaseDC(hwnd, PaintDC);
```

continues

Listing 19.4. continued

```
177:   }
178:   Count++;
179: }
180:
181: ////////////////////////////////
182: // Handle WM_TIMER
183: ////////////////////////////////
184: #pragma argsused
185: void FernPlay_OnTimer(HWND hwnd, UINT id)
186: {
187:   if (Count >= MaxIterations)
188:     KillTimer(hwnd, FernTimer);
189:
190:   for (int i = 0; i < 200; i++)
191:   {
192:     if (Count >= MaxIterations)
193:       return;
194:     DoPaint(hwnd);
195:   }
196: }
```

Listing 19.5 shows the code for Isotrop.

Listing 19.5. ISOTROP.CPP.

```
1: ///////////////////////////////////////////////////////
2: // Program Name: ISOTROP.CPP
3: // Programmer: Charlie Calvert
4: // Description: MDI example program
5: // Date: 07/25/93
6: ///////////////////////////////////////////////////////
7:
8: #define STRICT
9: #include <windows.h>
10: #include <windowsx.h>
11: #include "draw.h"
12: #pragma warning(disable : 4068)
13:
14: extern HMENU hMenuMultiple, hMenuInit;
15: extern HMENU hMenuFileMultiple, hMenuFileInit;
16: static HWND hwndClient, hwndFrame;
17:
18: #define Isotrop_DefProc DefMDIChildProc
19: BOOL Isotrop_OnCreate(HWND hwnd,
20:                       CREATESTRUCT FAR* lpCreateStruct);
21: void Isotrop_MDIActivate(HWND hwnd, BOOL fActive, HWND
22:                          hwndActivate, HWND hwndDeactivate);
23: void Isotrop_OnPaint(HWND hwnd);
24: BOOL Isotrop_OnQueryEndSession(HWND hwnd);
```

```
25:
26: ////////////////////////////////////
27: // The Windows Procedure
28: ////////////////////////////////////
29: LRESULT CALLBACK IsotropicWndProc(HWND hwnd, UINT message,
30:                                   WPARAM wParam, LPARAM lParam)
31: {
32:   switch (message)
33:   {
34:     HANDLE_MSG(hwnd, WM_CREATE, Isotrop_OnCreate);
35:     HANDLE_MSG(hwnd, WM_MDIACTIVATE, Isotrop_MDIActivate);
36:     HANDLE_MSG(hwnd, WM_PAINT, Isotrop_OnPaint);
37:     HANDLE_MSG(hwnd, WM_QUERYENDSESSION,
38:               Isotrop_OnQueryEndSession);
39:   default:
40:     return Isotrop_DefProc(hwnd, message, wParam, lParam);
41:   }
42: }
43:
44: ////////////////////////////////////
45: // HANDLE WM_QUERYENDSESSION
46: ////////////////////////////////////
47: BOOL Isotrop_OnQueryEndSession(HWND hwnd)
48: {
49:   if (IDOK != MessageBox (hwnd, "OK to close window?",
50:                   "Isotropic", MB_ICONQUESTION | MB_OKCANCEL))
51:     return FALSE;
52:   else
53:     return TRUE;
54: }
55:
56: ////////////////////////////////////
57: // HANDLE WM_CREATE
58: ////////////////////////////////////
59: #pragma argsused
60: BOOL Isotrop_OnCreate(HWND hwnd,
61:                       CREATESTRUCT FAR* lpCreateStruct)
62: {
63:   hwndClient = GetParent(hwnd);
64:   hwndFrame = GetParent(hwndClient);
65:   return TRUE;
66: }
67:
68: ////////////////////////////////////
69: // HANDLE WM_MDIACTIVATE
70: ////////////////////////////////////
71: #pragma argsused
72: void Isotrop_MDIActivate(HWND hwnd, BOOL fActive,
73:                          HWND hwndActivate, HWND hwndDeactivate)
74: {
75:   if (fActive)
76:     SendMessage(hwndClient, WM_MDISETMENU, 0,
```

continues

Listing 19.5. continued

```
 77:                     MAKELONG(hMenuMultiple, hMenuFileMultiple));
 78:   if (!fActive)
 79:     SendMessage(hwndClient, WM_MDISETMENU, 0,
 80:                     MAKELONG(hMenuInit, hMenuFileInit));
 81:   DrawMenuBar (hwndFrame);
 82: }
 83:
 84: /////////////////////////////////////
 85: // HANDLE WM_PAINT
 86: /////////////////////////////////////
 87: void Isotrop_OnPaint(HWND hwnd)
 88: {
 89:   HDC PaintDC;
 90:   PAINTSTRUCT PaintStruct;
 91:   RECT R;
 92:
 93:   PaintDC = BeginPaint (hwnd, &PaintStruct);
 94:
 95:   SetMapMode(PaintDC, MM_ISOTROPIC);
 96:   GetClientRect(hwnd, &R);
 97:   SetWindowExt(PaintDC, 210, 210);
 98:   SetViewportExt(PaintDC, R.right, R.bottom);
 99:   SetViewportOrg(PaintDC, R.right / 2, R.bottom / 2);
100:   DoDraw(PaintDC);
101:
102:   EndPaint (hwnd, &PaintStruct);
103: }
```

Listing 19.6 shows the code for Normal.

Type   **Listing 19.6. NORMAL.CPP.**

```
 1: /////////////////////////////////////////////////////////
 2: // Program Name: NORMAL.CPP
 3: // Programmer: Charlie Calvert
 4: // Description: MDI example program
 5: // Date: 07/25/93
 6: /////////////////////////////////////////////////////////
 7: #define STRICT
 8: #include <windows.h>
 9: #include <windowsx.h>
10: #include "draw.h"
11: #pragma warning(disable : 4068)
12:
13: extern HMENU hMenuMultiple, hMenuInit;
14: extern HMENU hMenuFileMultiple, hMenuFileInit;
15: static HWND hwndClient, hwndFrame;
16:
17: #define NormalPlay_DefProc DefMDIChildProc
```

```
18: BOOL NormalPlay_OnCreate(HWND hwnd,
19:                             CREATESTRUCT FAR* lpCreateStruct);
20: void NormalPlay_MDIActivate(HWND hwnd, BOOL fActive,
21:                             HWND hwndActivate,
22:                             HWND hwndDeactivate);
23: void NormalPlay_OnPaint(HWND hwnd);
24:
25: ////////////////////////////////////
26: // The Window Procedure
27: ////////////////////////////////////
28: LRESULT CALLBACK NormalWndProc(HWND hwnd, UINT message,
29:                                 WPARAM wParam, LPARAM lParam)
30: {
31:    switch (message)
32:    {
33:      HANDLE_MSG(hwnd, WM_CREATE, NormalPlay_OnCreate);
34:      HANDLE_MSG(hwnd, WM_MDIACTIVATE, NormalPlay_MDIActivate);
35:      HANDLE_MSG(hwnd, WM_PAINT, NormalPlay_OnPaint);
36:    default:
37:      return NormalPlay_DefProc(hwnd, message, wParam, lParam);
38:    }
39: }
40:
41: ////////////////////////////////////
42: // HANDLE WM_CREATE
43: ////////////////////////////////////
44: #pragma argsused
45: BOOL NormalPlay_OnCreate(HWND hwnd,
46:                             CREATESTRUCT FAR* lpCreateStruct)
47: {
48:    hwndClient = GetParent (hwnd);
49:    hwndFrame = GetParent (hwndClient);
50:    return TRUE;
51: }
52:
53: ////////////////////////////////////
54: // HANDLE WM_MDIACTIVATE
55: ////////////////////////////////////
56: #pragma argsused
57: void NormalPlay_MDIActivate(HWND hwnd, BOOL fActive,
58:                             HWND hwndActivate,
59:                             HWND hwndDeactivate)
60: {
61:    // Set the Normal menu if gaining focus
62:    if (fActive)
63:      SendMessage(hwndClient, WM_MDISETMENU, 0,
64:                  MAKELONG(hMenuMultiple, hMenuFileMultiple));
65:    if (!fActive)
66:      SendMessage(hwndClient, WM_MDISETMENU, 0,
67:                  MAKELONG(hMenuInit, hMenuFileInit));
68:    DrawMenuBar (hwndFrame);
69: }
```

continues

Listing 19.6. continued

```
70:
71: ////////////////////////////////////
72: // HANDLE WM_NORMAL
73: ////////////////////////////////////
74: void NormalPlay_OnPaint(HWND hwnd)
75: {
76:   HDC PaintDC;
77:   PAINTSTRUCT PaintStruct;
78:   RECT R;
79:
80:   PaintDC = BeginPaint (hwnd, &PaintStruct);
81:   GetClientRect(hwnd, &R);
82:   SetViewportOrg(PaintDC, R.right / 2, R.bottom / 2);
83:
84:   DoDraw(PaintDC);
85:   EndPaint (hwnd, &PaintStruct);
86: }
```

Listing 19.7 shows the code for Draw.

Type   **Listing 19.7. DRAW.CPP.**

```
1: ////////////////////////////////////////////////////////////
2: // Program Name: DRAW.CPP
3: // Programmer: Charlie Calvert
4: // Description: Multimedia MDI windows example program
5: // Date: 07/25/93
6: ////////////////////////////////////////////////////////////
7:
8: #define STRICT
9: #include <windows.h>
10: #include <windowsx.h>
11: #include <math.h>
12: #include "draw.h"
13:
14: #define PI 3.14159265358979323846
15:
16: ////////////////////////////////////
17: // Draw the shape
18: ////////////////////////////////////
19: void DrawSquare(HDC PaintDC, double Scale, int Theta)
20: {
21:   int x1,y1;
22:   int xt,yt;
23:   int i;
24:   HPEN Pens[5], OldPen;
25:   TCDS CDS;
26:
```

```
27:    Pens[1] = CreatePen(PS_SOLID, 1, RGB(255, 0, 0));
28:    Pens[2] = CreatePen(PS_SOLID, 1, RGB(0, 255, 0));
29:    Pens[3] = CreatePen(PS_SOLID, 1, RGB(0, 0, 255));
30:    Pens[4] = CreatePen(PS_SOLID, 1, RGB(255, 0, 255));
31:
32:    CDS[0].x = -100;
33:    CDS[0].y = -100;
34:    CDS[1].x = 100;
35:    CDS[1].y = -100;
36:    CDS[2].x = 100;
37:    CDS[2].y = 100;
38:    CDS[3].x = -100;
39:    CDS[3].y = 100;
40:    CDS[4].x = -100;
41:    CDS[4].y = -100;
42:
43:    for (i = 0; i < 5; i++)
44:    {
45:      x1 = CDS[i].x;
46:      y1 = CDS[i].y;
47:      xt = x1;
48:      yt = y1;
49:      xt = Scale * (x1 * cos(Theta * PI / 180) + y1 *
50:                   sin(Theta * PI/180));
51:      yt = Scale * (y1 * cos(Theta * PI / 180) - x1 *
52:                   sin(Theta * PI/180));
53:      if (i == 0)
54:        MoveTo(PaintDC, xt, yt);
55:      else
56:      {
57:        OldPen = SelectPen(PaintDC, Pens[i]);
58:        LineTo(PaintDC, xt, yt);
59:        SelectPen(PaintDC, OldPen);
60:      }
61:    }
62:    for (i = 1; i < 5; i++)
63:      DeleteObject(Pens[i]);
64: }
65:
66: ///////////////////////////////////
67: // Loop through the draw
68: ///////////////////////////////////
69: void DoDraw(HDC PaintDC)
70: {
71:    double Scale;
72:    int Theta;
73:    int Square;
74:
75:    Scale = 1.0;
76:    Theta = 0;
77:
78:    for (Square = 1; Square < 25; Square++)
```

19

```
79:    {
80:      DrawSquare(PaintDC, Scale, Theta);
81:      Theta = Theta + 10;
82:      Scale = Scale * 0.85;
83:    }
84: }
```

Listing 19.8 shows the header file for Draw.

Type **Listing 19.8. DRAW.H.**

```
 1: ///////////////////////////////////////
 2: // Program Name:l DRAW.H
 3: // Programmer: Charlie Calvert
 4: // Description: MDI windows example program
 5: // Date: 07/25/93
 6: ///////////////////////////////////////
 7:
 8: #define WM_FERNPAINT (WM_USER + 0)
 9: /* void Cls_OnFernPaint(HWND hwnd); */
10: #define HANDLE_WM_FERNPAINT(hwnd, wParam, lParam, fn) \
11:     ((fn)(hwnd), 0L)
12: #define FORWARD_WM_FERNPAINT(hwnd, fn) \
13:     (void)(fn)((hwnd), WM_FERNPAINT, 0, 0L)
14:
15: // type
16: typedef POINT TCDS[5];
17:
18: // func
19: void DoDraw(HDC PaintDC);
```

Listing 19.9 shows the resource file for MDIPaint.

Type **Listing 19.9. MDIPAINT.RC.**

```
 1: ///////////////////////////////////////////////////////
 2: // Program Name: MDIPAINT.RC
 3: // Programmer: Charlie Calvert
 4: // Description: MDI example program
 5: // Date: 07/25/93
 6: ///////////////////////////////////////////////////////
 7:
 8: #include <windows.h>
 9: #include "MDIPaint.h"
10:
11: MdiMenuInit MENU
12: BEGIN
13:   POPUP "&File"
```

```
14:    BEGIN
15:      MENUITEM "&Isotropic\tAlt+I", CM_ISOTROP
16:      MENUITEM "&AnIsotropic\tAlt+A", CM_ANISOTROP
17:      MENUITEM "&Normal\tAlt+N", CM_NORMAL
18:      MENUITEM "&Fern\tAlt+R", CM_FERN
19:      MENUITEM SEPARATOR
20:      MENUITEM "E&xit", CM_EXIT
21:    END
22: END
23:
24: MDIMultiple MENU
25: BEGIN
26:    POPUP "&File"
27:    BEGIN
28:      MENUITEM "&Isotropic\tAlt+I", CM_ISOTROP
29:      MENUITEM "&AnIsotropic\tAlt+A", CM_ANISOTROP
30:      MENUITEM "&Normal\tAlt+N", CM_NORMAL
31:      MENUITEM SEPARATOR
32:      MENUITEM "E&xit", CM_EXIT
33:    END
34:    POPUP "&Window"
35:    BEGIN
36:      MENUITEM "&Cascade\tShift+C", CM_CASCADE
37:      MENUITEM "&Tile\tShift+T", CM_TILE
38:      MENUITEM "Arrange &Icons", CM_ARRANGE
39:      MENUITEM "Close &All", CM_CLOSEALL
40:    END
41: END
42:
43: MdiAccel ACCELERATORS
44: BEGIN
45:    "C", CM_CASCADE, VIRTKEY, SHIFT
46:    "T", CM_TILE, VIRTKEY, SHIFT
47:    "I", CM_ISOTROP, VIRTKEY, ALT
48:    "A", CM_ANISOTROP, VIRTKEY, ALT
49:    "N", CM_NORMAL, VIRTKEY, ALT
50:    "R", CM_FERN, VIRTKEY, ALT
51: END
```

19

Listing 19.10 shows the definition file for MDIPaint.

Type **Listing 19.10. MDIPAINT.DEF.**

```
1: NAME           MDIPaint
2: DESCRIPTION    'MDIPaint program (c) Charlie Calvert'
3: EXETYPE        WINDOWS
4: STUB           'WINSTUB.EXE'
5: HEAPSIZE       1024
6: STACKSIZE      8192
```

continues

Listing 19.10. continued

```
7: CODE            PRELOAD MOVEABLE DISCARDABLE
8: DATA            PRELOAD MOVEABLE MULTIPLE
```

Listing 19.11 shows the Borland makefile for MDIPaint.

Listing 19.11. MDIPAINT.MAK (Borland).

```
1: # MDIPaint makefile
2: # Use /WE switch
3:
4: MAIN = MDIPaint
5: OBJS = $(MAIN).obj Isotrop.obj AnIsotrp.obj Normal.obj \
6:        Fern.obj Draw.obj
7: INCPATH = C:\BC\INCLUDE
8: LIBPATH = C:\BC\LIB
9: CFLAGS = -WE -ml -v -w4 -I$(INCPATH) -L$(LIBPATH)
10:
11: # Link
12: $(MAIN).exe: $(OBJS) $(MAIN).def $(MAIN).res
13:    bcc $(CFLAGS) $(OBJS)
14:    brc $(MAIN).res
15:
16: # Compile
17: .cpp.obj:
18:    bcc -c $(CFLAGS) { $< }
19:
20: # Resource
21: $(MAIN).res : $(MAIN).rc
22:    brc -r -i$(INCPATH) $(MAIN).rc
```

Listing 19.12 shows the Microsoft makefile for MDIPaint.

Listing 19.12. MDIPAINT.MAK (Microsoft).

```
1: # MDIPaint makefile
2: # Use /GA switch
3:
4: MAIN = MDIPaint
5: OBJS = $(MAIN).obj Isotrop.obj AnIsotrp.obj Normal.obj \
6:        Fern.obj Draw.obj
7:
8: # Link
9: $(MAIN).exe : $(OBJS) $(MAIN).def $(MAIN).res
10:    link/CO $(OBJS), /align:16, NUL, /nod llibcew libw, $(MAIN)
11:    rc $(MAIN).res
12:
```

```
13: # Compile
14: .cpp.obj:
15:   cl -c -AL -GA -Ow -W2 -Zp -Zi { $< }
16:
17: # Resource
18: $(MAIN).res : $(MAIN).rc
19:   rc -r $(MAIN).rc
```

 Figure 19.3 shows the output of this program.

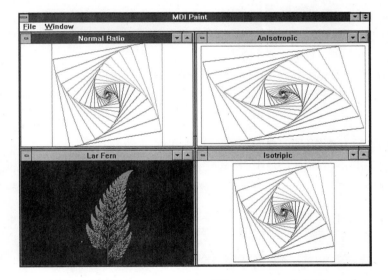

Figure 19.3. *The MDIPaint comes with different types of child windows.*

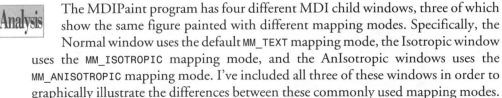 The MDIPaint program has four different MDI child windows, three of which show the same figure painted with different mapping modes. Specifically, the Normal window uses the default MM_TEXT mapping mode, the Isotropic window uses the MM_ISOTROPIC mapping mode, and the AnIsotropic windows uses the MM_ANISOTROPIC mapping mode. I've included all three of these windows in order to graphically illustrate the differences between these commonly used mapping modes. The fourth window shows an image of a fern, which is painted with standard fractal techniques.

MDIPaint has two different menus. The first appears at startup, and the second appears after the user opens a child window. If all the child windows are closed, the first menu reappears.

The difference between the two menus is twofold:

☐ The first menu has one popup, called File, which enables the user to open any·of the four child windows, or to exit the application.

☐ The second menu has two popups. The first, called File, enables the user to start the Normal, Isotropic, and AnIsotropic windows. The second, called Window, lets the user arrange the icons or tile, cascade, and close all the child windows.

MDIPaint enables only one copy of the Fern window on the desktop at a time. To enforce this rule, the program places the option to open the Fern window only in the File menu, which appears at startup, or when all other windows are closed. This means that you must display the Fern window first, or lose the option to open it.

Before the Fern window is closed (or when it's open and the entire application is being closed), it prompts the user. The Isotropic window prompts the user when the whole application is being closed (see Figure 19.4.) Normally, such a prompt asks the user whether he or she wants to save a file. In this particular case, however, the prompt is inserted merely to show you how to iterate through all the child windows, and how to respond to WM_QUERYENDSESSION messages.

Some children in the MDIPaint program set their WNDClass.hIcon field to NULL. As a result, the image seen in their main window gets duplicated in their icon when they are minimized.

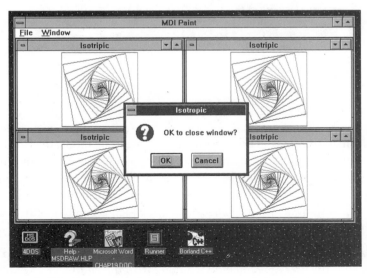

Figure 19.4. *The Isotrop window prompts the user before closing.*

Note: Once again, the makefile for this program uses an implicit rule to automatically compile all the CPP files into OBJ files. It's also very important that you use the /WE (Borland) or /GA (Microsoft) switches to the compiler to ensure that the window procedures for this application get properly exported. To do this in the Borland IDE, choose Options | Compiler | Entry/Exit Code—Windows explicit functions exported. In the MSVC IDE, choose Options | Project | Compiler | Windows Prolog/Epilog—Protected Mode Application Functions. The point of all this is to ensure that functions explicitly labeled _export do get exported. If you don't take these steps, the program might still run okay, but the debug version of Windows will complain of the omission.

Creating Child Windows

Each of the child windows can be started either through a menu or through an accelerator key (Alt-A for AnIsotropic, Alt-I for Isotropic, and so forth). In either case, a message is sent along with WM_COMMAND, and is responded to in the following manner (line 260, MDIPAINT.CPP):

```
case CM_ANISOTROP:
  CreateMDIChild(szAnIsotropic, "AnIsotropic");
  break;
```

CreateMDIChild is user-defined and hides a fair degree of complexity. The mechanism for creating MDI children involves using SendMessage to post a WM_MDICREATE message along with a structure called MDICREATESTRUCT, which holds most of the fields seen in a call to CreateWindow.

The *MDICREATESTRUCT* Stucture

Following is an MDICREATESTRUCT:

```
typedef struct tagMDICREATESTRUCT {
  LPCSTR    szClass;       // Class name
  LPCSTR    szTitle;       // A title for caption bar
  HINSTANCE hOwner;        // The Instance of the app
  int       x;             // X dimension of upper left corner
  int       y;             // Y dimension of upper left corner
  int       cx;            // X dimension of lower right corner
  int       cy;            // Y dimension of lower right corner
  DWORD     style;         // Is app minimized, maximized, etc
```

```
    LPARAM     lParam;      // User defined data, usually NULL
} MDICREATESTRUCT;
```

From an intellectual point of view, filling out the structure is no big challenge. However, the style field can host a combination of the following styles.

WS_MINIMIZE	Create window in a minimized state.
WS_MAXIMIZE	Create window in a maximized state.
WS_HSCROLL	Create window with a horizontal scroll bar.
WS_VSCROLL	Create window with a vertical scroll bar.

The following code shows how a typical call to create a window might look (note that the WPARAM field of SendMessage must be set to zero).

```
MDICREATESTRUCT MDICreate;

MDICreate.szClass = szMyMDIClass ;
MDICreate.szTitle = "MyMDIClass" ;
MDICreate.hOwner  = hInstance ;
MDICreate.x       = CW_USEDEFAULT ;
MDICreate.y       = CW_USEDEFAULT ;
MDICreate.cx      = CW_USEDEFAULT ;
MDICreate.cy      = CW_USEDEFAULT ;
MDICreate.style   = 0;
MDICreate.lParam  = NULL ;

hwndChild = SendMessage(hWndClient, WM_MDICREATE, 0,
                    (LPARAM)(LPMDICREATESTRUCT)&MDICreate);
```

The preceding syntax box tells you the basic facts about creating MDI children. However, the actual syntax you need to use can be simplified considerably with just a little work. MDIPaint, for instance, includes the following function, which can be used whenever you need to create a child window.

```
HWND CreateMDIChild(LPCSTR szClass, LPCSTR szTitle)
{
  MDICREATESTRUCT    MCS;

  MCS.szClass = szClass;
  MCS.szTitle = szTitle;
  MCS.hOwner  = hInstance;
  MCS.x       = CW_USEDEFAULT;
  MCS.y       = CW_USEDEFAULT;
  MCS.cx      = CW_USEDEFAULT;
  MCS.cy      = CW_USEDEFAULT;
  MCS.style   = 0;
  MCS.lParam  = NULL;
  return FORWARD_WM_MDICREATE(hWndClient, &MCS, SendMessage);
}
```

The `CreateMDIChild` call makes use of one of the WINDOWSX `FORWARD_WM_X` macros. This is a programmer's trick really, not part of the standard usage of WINDOWSX as defined by Microsoft in their documentation. I added it simply because it shows how to avoid getting hung up in a lot of unsightly typecasts, such as the one shown in the `SendMessage` statement from the last Syntax box.

If you use `CreateMDIChild`, creating an `MDIChild` involves simply passing in two string parameters:

```
CreateMDIChild(szFern, "Lar Fern");
```

in which the first parameter is the class name and the second is the title for the caption bar. You can copy `CreateMDIChild` into your own programs, but if you keep it in a separate module, you'll probably want to pass in the `HINSTANCE` as a third parameter.

Changing the Style of an MDI Child

In my experience, I've found that it's usually best to maintain the default behavior of MDI applications and their child windows. However, sometimes programmers want to vary the look and feel of a child window. If you decide this is necessary, you should pass the `MDIS_ALLCHILDSTYLES` in the `dwStyle` field of `CreateWindow` when you create the MDI client window:

```
hWndClient = CreateWindow ("MDICLIENT", NULL,
               WS_CHILD ¦ WS_CLIPCHILDREN ¦
               WS_VISIBLE ¦ MDIS_ALLCHILDSTYLES,
               0, 0, 0, 0, hwnd, HMENU(1), hInstance,
               (LPSTR) &clientcreate);
```

When you actually create the child windows, you should add some combination of the following styles to the style field of `MDICREATESTRUCT`:

```
WS_CHILD, WS_CLIPSIBLINGS, WS_CLIPCHILDREN,
WS_SYSMENU, WS_CAPTION, WS_THICKFRAME,
WS_MINIMIZEBOX, WS_MAXIMIZEBOX, WS_VISIBLE
```

If you add all these styles, you'll end up with a window that looks exactly like a standard MDI child. Remove the `WS_THICKFRAME`, `WS_MAXIMIZEBOX`, and `WS_MINIMIZEBOX`, and you'll get an MDI child like that shown in Figure 19.5.

19

Figure 19.5. *An MDI child window, with styles that have been changed to remove the frame and minimize and maximize box.*

Note: Remember that the moment you use the MDIS_ALLCHILDSTYLES flag, you must start specifying all or some portion of the styles (previously listed) every time you create an MDI child. One way to handle this is to create a single style containing all of the previously listed flags, similar to the way the WS_OVERLAPPEDWINDOW style is created in WINDOWS.H. Then, use logical bitwise operators to make any changes you deem necessary.

Special MDI Messages
That Must Be Forwarded

There are two sets of messages that you must pay special attention to when working with MDI applications. The first set involves messages that must be passed back to Windows from the window procedure of an MDI child:

WM_CHILDACTIVATE	Handles sizing, showing, and moving of children
WM_GETMINMAXINFO	Calculates the size of maximized window

WM_MENUCHAR	Passes keystrokes on to the main window
WM_MOVE	Needed for the scrollbars, if present
WM_SETFOCUS	Activates child windows when they get the focus
WM_SIZE	Essential when maximizing or restoring child windows
WM_SYSCOMMAND	Handles various default hot keys and commands

You've seen most of these messages before. In fact, the descriptions I've added for each message do little to explain the message itself. Rather, my notes are meant to point out why it is necessary to forward each of these messages on to Windows if you want your MDIChild to act as the user expects.

A key point to remember is that MDI child windows have a special default function called DefMDIChildProc, which they must use in lieu of DefWindowProc. To find which messages need to be passed on, look up DefMDIChildProc in the online help, and you'll find a copy of the list previously displayed.

Note: Remember that when you are using WINDOWSX, you have to explicitly pass messages to the DefMDIChildProc with one of the FORWARD_WM_X macros, such as the one used in the last section. So you understand how it works, following is an excerpt from FERN.CPP.

```
147: void FernPlay_OnSize(HWND hwnd, UINT state, int cx, int cy)
148: {
149:   RECT R;
150:   GetClientRect(hwnd, &R);
151:   MaxX = R.right;
152:   MaxY = R.bottom;
153:   MaxIterations = long(MaxY) * 50;
154:   if (state == SIZE_MINIMIZED)
155:     MaxIterations = 175;
156:
157:   // MUST forward WM_SIZE messages
158:   FORWARD_WM_SIZE(hwnd, state, cx, cy, FernPlay_DefProc);
159: }
```

The FernPlay_DefProc, referenced in the call to FORWARD_WM_SIZE, is declared like this:

```
#define FernPlay_DefProc DefMDIChildProc
```

All the other parameters sent to FORWARD_WM_SIZE are copied verbatim from the argument list to FernPlay_OnSize. This same pattern is followed in all the FORWARD_WM_X macros. As a result, the macros are virtually effortless to use.

Messages Specific to MDI Applications

Now that you know some basics about MDI child windows you're ready to turn your attention to the following messages. These messages define most of the behavior specific to MDI children. I've grouped these messages into four separate categories.

The first category includes the messages used to create and destroy MDI children:

```
WM_MDICREATE: Create an MDI window
WM_MDIDESTROY: Used to close an MDI child window
```

I've explained the WM_MDICREATE message in detail. WM_MDIDESTROY messages are easy to use because they require nothing more than the handle of the window to be closed in WPARAM.

The following messages can be used to find out which window has the focus. They can also be used to change the focus.

WM_MDIACTIVATE	Activates the window specified in WPARAM
WM_MDINEXT	Focuses the next window in the child list
WM_MDIGETACTIVE	Finds the active window

The WM_MDIACTIVATE message plays a dual role in Windows programming. The application first sends this message to the client window. At this point in its career, WM_MDIACTIVATE carries the handle of the window to be activated in WPARAM. After the client receives the message, it forwards it to both the child being activated and the one being deactivated.

Programmers rarely have to explicitly send WM_MDIACTIVATE messages, but they frequently must respond to these messages:

```
WM_MDIMAXIMIZE: Maximize a window
WM_MDIRESTORE: Restore a window
```

In the MDIPaint application, responding to these messages is important, because they tell the application when to change the menu.

The next message, WM_MDINEXT, is sent to the client window. This message activates the MDI child that is behind the currently active window. The window that was active is placed behind the other child windows. The list of child windows manipulated by this message is maintained by Windows and displayed in the program's menu.

The final message in this category, WM_MDIGETACTIVE, is an extremely useful message that every programmer absolutely requires sooner or later. When using this message,

set both WPARAM and LPARAM to 0, and expect the handle of the focused child in the low-order word of the return value. The high-order word is set to 1 if the window in question is maximized. You should send this message to the client window.

The following three messages need little explanation, though their importance is obvious:

WM_MDITILE	Tiles the children
WM_MDICASCADE	Cascades the children
WM_MDIICONARRANGE	Arranges iconic children

When you are tiling windows, you can arrange them horizontally or vertically, depending on the value of a flag passed in WPARAM. For instance, the MDITILE_HORIZONTAL flag creates the image shown in Figure 19.6, whereas the MDITILE_VERTICAL creates the image shown in Figure 19.7.

The final message specific to MDI children is WM_MDISETMENU. This is used in conjunction with WM_MDIACTIVATE messages, as shown in the next section.

WM_MDISETMENU: Changes the pop-up menu containing the list of children, the main MDI menu, or both the pop-up menu and the main menu.

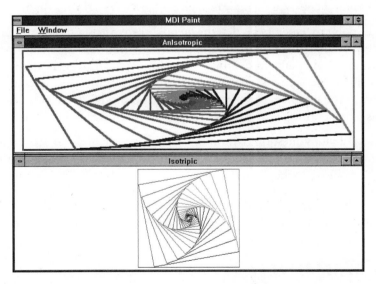

Figure 19.6. *Horizontal tiling with the* MDITILE_HORIZONTAL *flag.*

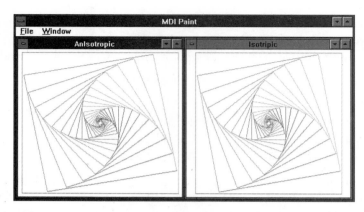

Figure 19.7. *Vertical tiling with the* MDITILE_VERTICAL *flag.*

Handling MDI Menus

The MDIPaint program only has two menus, but some MDI programs have five or ten different menus. An example of such a program is Borland's Resource Workshop.

The key point to remember is that the menu shown to a user should reflect the options available at the time. In normal applications, this isn't an issue, because these applications only perform one function. However, MDI applications can perform several different functions, depending on which MDI child the user has focused at any one time. For instance, users exploring the App Studio don't need the same set of menus when creating a string table as they do when creating an icon or bitmap.

The next obvious question is: how do you find out when a user activates a particular window? After reading the last section, astute readers should guess that the solution to this problem is the WM_MDIACTIVATE message, which gets sent down the pike whenever a window is about to get or lose the focus. As you recall, the WM_MDIACTIVATE message plays two roles in Windows programming. In its second incarnation, it gets sent to a child window whenever the window is about to get or lose the focus.

Syntax

The *WM_MDIACTIVATE* Message

When receiving WM_MDIACTIVATE:

WPARAM: If this is set to non-zero, the window is being activated.

LPARAM: The low word of LPARAM contains the handle of the child being activated; the high word contains the handle of the child being deactivated.

When sending WM_MDIACTIVATE:

WPARAM contains the handle of the window to activate.

LPARAM must be set to zero.

When this message is sent to a child window, WINDOWSX.H breaks it down so that WPARAM is contained in a Boolean variable called fActive, and the handles to the activated and deactivated windows are called hwndActivate and hwndDeactivate. Following is an example:

Example:

```
SendMessage(hwnd, WM_MDIACTIVATE, hMyMDIChild, 0);
```

The following code shows how the Fern window handles the WM_MDIACTIVATE message:

```
87: void FernPlay_MDIActivate(HWND hwnd, BOOL fActive,
88:              HWND hwndActivate, HWND hwndDeactivate)
89: {
90:   if (fActive)
91:     SendMessage(hWndClient, WM_MDISETMENU, 0,
92:               MAKELONG(hMenuMultiple, hMenuFileMultiple));
93:
94:   if (!fActive)
95:     SendMessage(hWndClient, WM_MDISETMENU, 0,
96:               MAKELONG(hMenuInit, hMenuFileInit));
97:   DrawMenuBar(hWndFrame);
98: }
```

As you can see, the center of attention is the fActive parameter. This parameter is set to true whenever a window is receiving the focus and to false whenever it's losing the focus. This enables the Fern menu to set its own menu whenever the window is coming into focus and to restore the main menu whenever it's losing the focus.

MDIPaint uses the WM_MDISETMENU message to manipulate its menus.

19

The *WM_MDISETMENU* Message

Syntax

When receiving WM_MDISETMENU:

WPARAM: Specifies whether to refresh the current menus or whether LPARAM specifies new menus. Refreshing the menus includes the act of updating the current list of children.

LPARAM: The low-order word specifies a new main menu (or a new menu for the frame window). The high-order word specifies a new menu to hold the list of child windows shown to the user.

Use WM_MDISETMENU to manipulate the menus of an MDI application and to specify which menu should hold the list of available child windows.

Example:

```
SendMessage(hWndClient, WM_MDISETMENU, 0,
            MAKELONG(hMyMenu, hMySubmenu));
```

MDIPaint uses this message to swap the main set of menus with the menus used whenever a child is open. It does this by keeping both sets of menus in memory as global variables, and then swapping them with WM_MDISETMENU whenever a WM_MDIACTIVATE message comes down the pike.

Instead of using SendMessage directly (which entails typecasting), you can use the WINDOWSX macros:

```
FORWARD_WM_MDISETMENU(hWndClient, 0, hMenuMultiple,
                      hMenuFileMultiple, SendMessage);
```

Every typecast a programmer makes is another platform-specific opportunity to make a careless error. As a result, the WINDOWSX macros are definitely worth careful consideration whenever you need to use SendMessage. Remember that these macros can help ensure that your code will run both on 16-bit and 32-bit platforms.

Note: MDIPaint sets new menus each time a child window is activated. It does this by sending the WM_SETMENU messages directly to the client window. This time-tested and commonly used technique has never caused me any trouble. However, Microsoft has recently released documents advocating that a programmer first post a message to the frame window, and then let the frame window notify the client that it's time to set new menus. I want to emphasize that you should *post* the message to the frame window. Don't use SendMessage.

Closing Up Shop

The next key point you need to know (about MDI applications) involves the proper way to go about closing them. This section makes the following points:

☐ When closing an MDI application, you can use the WM_QUERYENDSESSION and WM_CLOSE messages to ensure that the program gives the user a chance to save any work in progress.

- ☐ If a child window needs to prompt the user to save work, it responds to WM_CLOSE message whenever it's shut down by the user.

- ☐ Each child window can respond to WM_QUERYENDSESSION messages. These are sent out to each child by MDIPaint when the user wants to shut down the whole application.

- ☐ MDIPaint can iterate through all the child windows on its desktop, sending each a WM_QUERYENDSESSION message. To do this, it uses the EnumChildWindows callback function.

The next few paragraphs go through each of these points in detail, so you can get a balanced view of the issues involved in shutting down an MDI child or MDI application.

When it's time to shut down an application or window, you need to keep track of two different messages. The first message is WM_QUERYENDSESSION, and the second is WM_CLOSE. You need to respond to these messages so the user has a chance to save any work that might be in progress. (MDIPaint doesn't need to respond to these messages, because there isn't any work to save in any of its windows. However, I do so anyway, just so you can see how the process works.)

WM_QUERYENDSESSION messages are typically sent by the Program Manager or other Windows shell whenever it's time to shut down. If an application returns TRUE in response to this message, shut down proceeds; if it returns FALSE, the session continues.

It's traditional, or at least common, for an MDI application to send this WM_QUERYENDSESSION message to its children to see if they're ready to close. In other words, if the user wants to close the whole application, MDIPaint sends this message to each of its children. If they all return TRUE, the MDI application shuts down; otherwise the session continues.

By now, you should be able to take a good guess at how a window might respond to this message. For instance, here's how the Isotrop window reacts whenever it gets a WM_QUERYENDSESSION message:

```
BOOL Isotrop_OnQueryEndSession(HWND hwnd)
{
  if (IDOK != MessageBox (hwnd, "OK to close window?",
                "Isotropic", MB_ICONQUESTION | MB_OKCANCEL))
    return FALSE;
  else
    return TRUE;
}
```

If the user clicks the system icon of a child window, that window receives a WM_CLOSE message. Therefore, you should respond to WM_CLOSE messages in the same way you respond to WM_QUERYENDSESSION messages. For an example, take a look at the Fern_OnClose function (line 101 of FERN.CPP).

At first, you might be confused by the differences between the WM_CLOSE and WM_QUERYENDSESSION messages as they apply to MDI applications. To graphically illustrate the issues involved, I've supplied the Fern window with responses to both messages (whereas the Isotrope window responds only to WM_QUERYENDSESSION messages). Try closing both windows by clicking the child's system icon, by closing the MDIPaint application, and by shutting down Windows altogether. The different responses you see should help clarify exactly how the two messages work. Specifically

☐ The Fern window responds to all three methods of closing down a child window because it handles both WM_CLOSE and WM_QUERYENDSESSION.

☐ The Isotrop window closes without complaint if you shut it down with its system icon. However, it pops up a Message box if you close down the whole application, or if you shut down Windows. This occurs because it responds to WM_QUERYENDSESSION, not to WM_CLOSE.

When the user asks to close MDIPaint, the program can iterate through all the child windows on its desktop by calling EnumChildWindows. For instance, if the user clicks the system icon for the MDIPaint frame window, WM_CLOSE is called. WM_CLOSE then sends out a custom message called CM_CLOSEALL, which causes MDIPaint to respond like this:

```
300:    case CM_CLOSEALL:  // Children ready to close?
301:      lpfnEnum = (WNDENUMPROC)MakeProcInstance(
302:                        (FARPROC)EnumChildWnds, hInstance);
303:      EnumChildWindows (hWndClient, lpfnEnum, 0L);
304:      FreeProcInstance ((FARPROC)lpfnEnum);
305:      break;
```

These lines of code set up a classic windows callback of the type you have seen several times in this book. In particular, EnumChildWindows iterates through all the child windows belonging to any particular parent, such as a dialog, a main window, or an MDI client.

In MDIPaint, the callback that is set up to respond to the EnumChildWindows function looks like this:

```
BOOL CALLBACK EnumChildWnds(HWND hwnd, LONG lParam)
{
  if (GetWindow(hwnd, GW_OWNER)) // Icon Title?
    return TRUE;
```

```
SendMessage (GetParent(hwnd), WM_MDIRESTORE, (WPARAM)hwnd, 0L);
if (!SendMessage (hwnd, WM_QUERYENDSESSION, 0, 0L))
    return TRUE;

SendMessage (GetParent(hwnd), WM_MDIDESTROY, (WPARAM)hwnd, 0L);
    return TRUE;
}
```

This function gets called once for every child on the MDI desktop, and it receives the handle for that window in its first parameter.

The code first checks to see if the child window in question is the title for an icon. If so, it returns without doing anything. If the window is a real MDI child, the next step is to restore the window and send it a WM_QUERYENDSESSION message. If the child doesn't want to close, EnumChildWnds returns. If the window does want to close, EnumChildWnds shuts it down with a WM_MDIDESTROY message.

After the application has iterated through all the child windows, control returns to the original WM_CLOSE response function (line 212 of MDIPAINT.CPP). MDIPaint can then check to see if any child windows are still open. If so, the application knows that it shouldn't shut down; otherwise, it closes.

Obviously, there are a hundred variations that can be run on this theme, some of which are considerably more elegant than the relatively simplistic approach taken by MDIPaint. However, the code outlined in this section should be enough to show you how to go about shutting down an MDI application, and how to make sure the user doesn't lose any information in the process.

19

Extra Bytes and Sharing the CPU

Before moving on to a discussion of MM_ISOTROPIC and MM_ANISOTROPIC, I want to pause for a moment to make two quick, totally unrelated points:

- ☐ If you need to save window-specific information, do so by using the cbWndExtra field of the WNDCLASS structure.

- ☐ The Fern window is interesting because it shows one way of sharing CPU time with other windows and applications during the duration of a lengthy computation.

The first point mentioned is really very important. The issue is that you may have multiple copies of a particular type of window open on the MDI desktop, and each one of these windows might have a certain amount of specific data associated with it. For instance, if you have three edit windows open at one time in an MDI program, each of them might have a different block of text associated with it.

To handle a situation like this, you should use the cbWndExtra bytes, as illustrated in the child window's program you saw on Day 14. As you recall, the keys to this process are the SetWindowWord, SetWindowLong, GetWindowWord, and GetWindowLong functions.

The next point to consider involves the loop that draws the fractal fern in the Fern window. This code is a translation of a Pascal program written by Lar Mader, a technical support engineer and an ace Windows hacker who works at Borland.

Lar's original code used a function called PeekMessage to ensure that the program did not steal CPU time from other applications. The issue is that the Fern window can take a sizable period of time to complete its drawing. If it does so without ever yielding control back to Windows, the application could hog the available clock cycles—even if the user wants to do something else, such as switch applications or tile windows. Doing this is not only impolite and annoying, but it can be dangerous, because Windows users expect to be able to respond to a variety of different circumstances on relatively short notice.

As I implied, one solution to this problem is to call PeekMessage. Another solution, which is generally a bit easier to implement, involves sending WM_TIMER messages to a function. Each time the message comes zooming in, the function can perform a few iterations of its task and then yield control back to Windows. Because timers are fairly slow, the best course is to perform two or three hundred iterations of a loop and then pass control back to windows. Doing just one iteration at a time can make the process unbearably lengthy.

MDIPaint uses the WM_TIMER message to draw its fern. However, when applications have more sophisticated demands, they should use PeekMessage. Regardless, the key point is that no first-rate Windows application should ever steal the CPU for a lengthy period of time, except in the most dire circumstances. Certainly drawing a fern on the screen isn't a dire circumstance.

The Old Isotropic versus AnIsotropic Issue

The MDIPaint program gives me an opportunity to fulfill a promise I gave you on Day 18, "GDI and Metafiles." That chapter explained the MM_TEXT, MM_LOENGLISH, MM_HIENGLISH, MM_LOMETRIC, MM_HIMETRIC, and MM_TWIPS mapping modes. The two

modes left out were MM_ISOTROPIC and MM_ANISOTROPIC. MDIPaint illustrates these latter two mapping modes by drawing the same image, with the same dimensions, once in both of these mapping modes and once in the MM_TEXT mapping mode. (See Figure 19.8.)

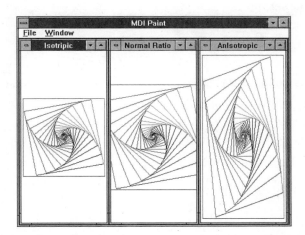

Figure 19.8. *MDIPaint shows the results of changing the mapping mode while drawing the same figure with the same dimensions.*

Both of these modes are used primarily when a programmer wants to draw as big an image as possible inside a window that's likely to be frequently resized. The classic examples of this type of application are the Clock program and Paintbrush program that come with Windows. When the Clock application is small, the clock face is small. If the user expands the application, the clock grows to fill the space available. Put as simply as possible, the following is the difference between MM_ISOTROPIC, MM_ANISOTROPIC, and standard mapping modes:

- [ ] Use MM_ISOTROPIC when you want your picture to maintain the ratio of its dimensions, just as the clock program does.

- [ ] Use MM_ANISOTROPIC when you want your drawing to stretch to fill up all available space, as seen in the Paintbrush program.

- [ ] Use any other mode when you want the drawing to maintain its same dimensions, regardless of how often the window is changed. This is the way the Program Manager works.

With the MDIPaint program, you should notice that the geometric shapes drawn in the AnIsotropic window distort themselves to fill the available space as completely as possible. (See Figure 19.9.) This functionality has a great deal in common with the `StretchBlt` function.

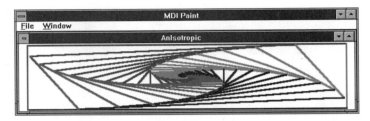

Figure 19.9. *No matter how you distort an* `MM_ANISOTROPIC` *window, the image inside attempts to stretch to fill the available space.*

The shapes inside the `MM_ISOTROPIC` window, on the other hand, always maintain the ratio of their original dimensions. The concepts involved have a lot in common with those you encounter when calculating the proper aspect ratio in a typical DOS graphics program. (See Figure 19.10.)

Finally, notice that the shape in the Normal window never changes, regardless of how you change the dimensions of the window in which it resides. The end result is that portions of the shape can be obscured when the window is shrunk.

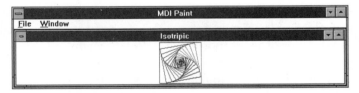

Figure 19.10. *The image inside an* `MM_ISOTROPIC` *window always maintains its original shape.*

The following code is used to set up the Isotrop window:

```
95  SetMapMode(PaintDC, MM_ISOTROPIC);
96  GetClientRect(hwnd, &R);
97  SetWindowExt(PaintDC, 210, 210);
98  SetViewportExt(PaintDC, R.right, R.bottom);
99  SetViewportOrg(PaintDC, R.right / 2, R.bottom / 2);
```

MDIPaint first sets the mapping mode; then, it sets the windows extent. Look at the DRAW.CPP module, and you'll see that the largest rectangle drawn in the Isotrop

window has a dimension of 200x200. Therefore, the Isotrop window sets itself up to always be just a little larger than 200x200 *logical* units in size.

The calls to SetWindowExt and SetViewportExt are mandatory when working with MM_ISOTROPIC windows. The purpose of these two calls is to give Windows enough information so it can figure out how to translate physical device coordinates into logical coordinates (and vice versa).

An Isotrop window with dimensions of 420x420 will have two physical pixels for every logical pixel specified by its user. The key is that the Isotrop window will always have 210x210 logical pixels, regardless of how the user reshapes it. Therefore, if the user sizes a window so its device (physical) coordinates are 420x420, Windows must paint two physical pixels for every one logical pixel—or the shape won't properly fill its bounding window.

The final step is to move the origin to the center of the screen by calling SetViewportOrg. This call isn't mandatory, but MDIPaint makes the call to simplify the drawing of the rotated squares that it displays.

The code for setting up the AnIsotropic window looks exactly like the code shown previously, except the mapping mode is set to MM_ANISOTROPIC instead of MM_ISOTROPIC. If you want to compare the samples, see line 77 in the ANISOTRP.CPP file.

Summary

In this chapter, you've learned about MDI windows, and about the MM_ISOTROPIC and MM_ANISOTROPIC mapping modes. Specifically, the main points covered in this chapter are as follows:

☐ MDI windows follow a standard called CUA, which was set up by IBM.

☐ You can create an MDI window by sending WM_MDICREATE messages.

☐ You need to respond to WM_MDIACTIVATE messages in order to set up an MDI child's menu.

☐ Use the extra bytes found in the WNDCLASS structure to store data specific to a window.

☐ Respond to WM_QUERYENDSESSION and WM_CLOSE messages to prompt a user before a child window closes.

☐ There are a number of messages that MDI applications must pass on to the DefMDIChildProc.

☐ Be sure to share CPU time with other windows or applications.

☐ Use MM_ANISOTROPIC and MM_ISOTROPIC when you want an image to automatically expand or shrink with the window it occupies.

All in all, the MDI specification is a fairly tricky bit of work, which almost all Windows programmer's have to master sooner or later. Although working with this kind of application isn't prohibitively difficult, you must pay attention while coding. The reward is an interface that's both powerful and easy to use.

Q&A

1. Q: I still don't understand the difference between a frame window and a client window. What's up?

   A: The frame window is the standard main window for an MDI application. It has a child called a client window. The MDIClient class is predefined by Windows and contains most of the functionality associated with MDI applications. It is literally painted over the top of the frame window, and it knows how to respond to most of the MDI specific messages. The user needs to set up a window procedure for frame windows, but not for client windows. Rather than calling DefWindowProc, MDI frame windows should call DefFrameProc. Be sure to pass WM_COMMAND messages to DefFrameProc!

2. Q: What's the difference between PeekMessage and GetMessage?

   A: The PeekMessage function keeps checking to see if any Windows messages are coming down the pike. If a message is in the queue, this function returns it; otherwise, the function returns and enables you to process information. The GetMessage function won't return unless it has a message to deliver. Because PeekMessage uses up clock cycles, you should use the function only when necessary; then, return to a standard Windows message loop as soon as possible.

Workshop

The Workshop provides quiz questions to help you solidify your understanding of the material covered and exercises to provide you with experience in using what you've learned. Try to understand the quiz and exercise answers before continuing on to the next chapter. Answers are provided in Appendix A.

Quiz

1. What class do you use when creating client windows?

2. What function is used to iterate through the child windows on an MDI desktop?

3. What message can you send to find out which MDI child has the focus?

4. What message is sent when a particular MDI child is getting or losing the focus?

5. What is the purpose of the LPARAM field accompanying a WM_MDISETMENU message?

6. How do you know the Clock program that comes with Windows uses the MM_ISOTROPIC style?

7. What structure do you have to fill out every time you create an MDI child?

8. What message does a Windows shell send out when the user wants to close the entire environment?

9. When iterating through the windows on the desktop, how can you tell if the window you have is a real window, or just the title of an icon?

10. If you have multiple copies of a specific class of an MDI child on the desktop, how can you store data associated with each instance of that class?

Exercises

1. Change calls to CreateWindow and MDICreateChild so that the MDIPaint program creates children that have no border and can't be minimized.

2. Add an option to the MDIPaint menu that will enable the user to tile windows either horizontally or vertically.

Multimedia

Today, you'll learn about dynamic link libraries and the multimedia extensions to Windows. The core of this chapter is a program called Harmony, which uses dynamic link libraries (DLLS) to demonstrate easy-to-use techniques for playing CD ROMs, MIDI files, and WAVE files. Along the way, you'll also learn about creating something called a *dialog window,* which is really just a standard dialog used as the main window for a program.

A list of specific topics to be covered today include

- [ ] The media control interface (MCI), which forms one of the key nexus in the multimedia extensions to Windows

- [ ] The `mciSendCommand` function, which plays a central role in the MCI

- [ ] The `ImpLib` utility and the `_export` keyword, which can be used to simplify the task of creating DLLs

- [ ] How to use `CreateDialog` in lieu of `CreateWindow`, when you want a dialog to form the center of attention in a Windows program

When you roll the phrase "dynamic link library" or "the multimedia extensions to Windows" around on your tongue, it's hard not to get the feeling that these must be terribly difficult subjects that will immerse programmers in a sea of technical details. It turns out, however, that both subjects are surprisingly easy to master. In fact, even the technique of using a dialog as a main window turns out to be so simple it needs no more than a few paragraphs of explanation.

So sit back and be prepared to have a little fun. All of the material in this chapter is relatively easy to master. This is payoff time. You've done the hard work, and now (in this chapter and the next) you can sit back and reap the harvest.

Groping for a Definition of Multimedia

Multimedia tools are so new that it would be helpful to spend a few moments clarifying exactly what this subject encompasses.

The first term to come to grips with is MPC, or Multimedia PC. This is a hardware standard meant to define the minimum configuration of any personal computer that can play multimedia programs. The key elements in the MPC standard are a 386 or better computer with a VGA video system, a mouse, a sound board, and a CD-ROM.

The program in this chapter was tested on two 486s, one equipped with Creative Labs' Sound Blaster Pro card and the other with an NEC CD-ROM drive. A sound card like the one I used is a requirement for playing MIDI and WAVE files with the code presented in this book. And of course, you won't be able to play compact disks unless you have CD-ROM drive or comparable hardware.

Note: If you don't have any of the previously listed tools, you won't be able to run any of the code in this chapter. It's important to understand that the widely distributed SPEAKER.DRV file won't be enough to enable you to run the included code. The reason for this is that the calls used in this chapter are too low level for the limited WAV file support available with SPEAKER.DRV.

Now that you've read about the hardware requirements, it's time to move on to a discussion of the various devices referenced in this chapter. It is probably safe to assume that everyone now knows what a CD-ROM is, but there may be some lingering confusion about WAV and MIDI files.

A WAV file is a Microsoft standard file format generally used for recording non-musical sounds, such as the human voice or a car horn. The key fact to know about a WAV file is that it can store about one second of sound in 11K of disk space, or one minute of sound in one meg of disk space. As a result, this medium tends to be extremely disk-intensive and is used mostly for adding short sound effects to a program or to the entire Windows environment.

The word MIDI stands for Musical Instrument Digital Interface. Put in the simplest possible terms, MIDI files can be thought of as containing a series of notes, such as C sharp or A flat. These notes are sent to a synthesizer with instructions to play the note using the sounds associated with a particular instrument such as a piano, horn, or guitar.

The synthesizer I used when writing the Harmony program came as a standard part of the Sound Blaster Pro card. Most sound cards and MIDI files can play between 6 and 16 notes at once, and can imitate between 3 and 9 instruments. MIDI files can store one minute of fairly high quality musical sound in about 5K of disk space. Because they take up about one-twentieth the space, MIDI files are much more useful than WAV files for many purposes.

Narrowing the Focus

Now that you know something about the media involved, it's time to focus on the programming techniques used to make computer-generated sounds. As it happens, Microsoft provides three separate interfaces that can enable you to access multimedia devices. Two of these are part of MCI; the third is a low-level API, which is very rigorous and demanding.

The low-level API is not appropriate for this book, and so that leaves only two remaining programming techniques. The first is a string-based interface meant primarily to provide support for very high-level languages, such as Visual Basic. Because this is a C programming book, it is possible to use the third technique—a powerful message-based interface.

The MCI command-message interface relies very heavily on a single routine called mciSendCommand, which takes four parameters. Though this might sound limiting at first, in practice it turns out to be a flexible system.

Syntax

The *mciSendCommand* Function

```
DWORD mciSendCommand(UINT, UINT, DWORD, DWORD);
```

UINT	wDeviceID	ID used to identify the current device
UINT	wMessage	Message specifying requested action
DWORD	dwParam1	Flags qualifying the wMessage field
DWORD	dwParam2	Pointer to structure containing additional data

mciSendCommand returns zero if the function was successful. Otherwise, it returns error information that can be passed to mciGetErrorString. The function itself sends a command to the MCI, which automatically carries out the requested action. See the following text for further details.

Example:

```
MCI_STATUS_PARMS Info;
DWORD ErrorNum, Flags;

memset(&Info, 0, sizeof(MCI_STATUS_PARMS));
Info.dwItem = MCI_STATUS_LENGTH;
Flags = MCI_STATUS_ITEM;
mciSendCommand(wDeviceID, MCI_STATUS, Flags, DWORD(&Info));
```

The first parameter passed to MciSendCommand is a handle or ID number used to identify the particular device in question. When Harmony first opens up a CD drive,

it passes 0 in this parameter, because it doesn't yet have an ID for the device. Thereafter, however, it passes in the ID that was returned by Windows.

Key to this interface is the second parameter, which is a message conveying a particular command. Following is a list of the twelve most common of these messages and their meanings:

MCI_GETDEVCAPS	Queries the devices capabilities
MCI_CLOSE	Closes a device
MCI_INFO	Queries type of hardware being used
MCI_OPEN	Opens a device
MCI_PLAY	Plays a song or piece on a device
MCI_RECORD	Records to a device
MCI_RESUME	Resumes playing or recording
MCI_SEEK	Moves media forward or backward
MCI_SET	Changes the settings on device
MCI_STATUS	Is device paused, playing, and so on
MCI_STOP	Stops playing or recording

Complementing these commands are a set of flags and records giving programmers the kind of fine tuned control they need to do the job right. For instance, the MCI_PLAY message has four important flags that can be OR'd together to form its third parameter:

MCI_NOTIFY	Posts MM_MCINOTIFY message on completion
MCI_WAIT	Completes operation before returning
MCI_FROM	Specifies starting position
MCI_TO	Specifies finishing position

The last two flags presented can be OR'd together like this:

```
MCI_FROM ¦ MCI_TO
```

This way, they inform MCI that a starting and finishing position will be specified in the last parameter.

The fourth parameter is a pointer to a structure that varies in composition, depending on which message is being sent. The structure accompanying MCI_PLAY looks like this:

```
typedef struct {
    DWORD dwCallback;
    DWORD dwFrom;
    DWORD dwTo;
} MCI_PLAY_PARMS;
```

Note: This naming convention is followed over and over again, so that MCI_STATUS works with MCI_STATUS_PARMS, and MCI_OPEN works with MCI_OPEN_PARMS.

All the multimedia structures or constants discussed in this paper are listed in the online help, and in MMSYSTEM.H. You should definitely take the time to become familiar with these files.

Sometimes it's necessary to fill out all three fields of this structure; at other times, some, or none of them can be filled out. For instance, if you set the MCI_NOTIFY flag in the second parameter of mciSendCommand, you'll probably want to set dwCallback equal to the HWND of the Window you want MCI to notify. Specifically, if you are inside a dialog when you start playing a WAV file, you should pass the dialog's HWND in dwCallback, so that the dialog would be informed with an MM_NOTIFY message when the WAV file stops playing.

Of course, if you set both the MCI_FROM and MCI_TO flags, you should fill out both the dwFrom and the dwTo fields of the MCI_PLAY_PARMS record (and so on).

The only major aspect of the mciSendCommand function that I've not discussed is its return value, which happens to be an error number kept in the low-order word of a LongInt. Microsoft comes through with a nice touch at this point, by adding the mciGetErrorString function, which provides you with a ready-made string that explains the error. mciGetErrorString will even send you back a pleasant little message that all has gone well, if that is the case.

The *mciGetErrorString* Function

```
UINT mciGetErrorString(DWORD, LPSTR, UINT)
```

DWORD	dwError:	Error code returned from mciSendCommand
LPSTR	lpstrBuffer:	Buffer to hold error message
UINT	wLength:	Length of the buffer in lpstrBuffer

mciGetErrorString returns TRUE if successful.

mciSendCommand returns a number listing the error that has occurred. The mciGetErrorString function returns a string, which describes an error, as shown in Figure 20.1.

Example:

```
char S[MsgLen];

if (!mciGetErrorString(RC, S, MsgLen))
    strcpy(S, "No message available");
```

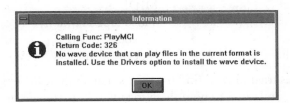

Figure 20.1. *The strings retrieved from* `mciGetErrorString` *are well-written and informative.*

Coming to Terms with MCI

If you have never dealt with code similar to the MCI interface, a few words of explanation are in order. MCI encapsulates the multimedia API inside a message-based system that isolates multimedia programmers from the details of the code base's actual implementation. In other words, when using this mid-level interface, there is no point at which you or I would actually call a true multimedia API function.

The reason for this is that hardware and operating systems change over time. As a result, APIs are forced to change with them. When APIs change, existing code bases are rendered obsolete, and last year's work has to be done all over again.

The MCI command-message interface protects the programmer from any fluctuations in the API. For all practical purposes, all you are doing is sending messages into a dark hole. What goes on inside of that hole is of little concern. (To get some ideas, run Harmony with the debug version of Windows!) Five years from now, CDs may have doubled their capacity and cut their access time down to a fifth of its current snail-like pace. But none of that is going to affect the code now. All we do is say that we want a particular track to be played. How it's played is of no concern to us.

Another crucial advantage of this style of programming is that it gives the user a common interface to a series of radically different pieces of hardware. For instance, the MCI command interface works with the following different types of devices, which are listed here opposite their MCI name:

animation	Animation device
cdaudio	CD Audio
dat	Digital audio tape device
digitalvideo	Digital video device
scanner	Image scanner
sequencer	MIDI
vcr	Video tape Harmony
videodisc	Videodisc device
waveaudio	A device that plays WAV files

What MCI has tried to do is find the things that all these devices have in common, and use those similarities to bind them together. In particular, it makes sense to ask all of these devices to play something, to stop playing, to pause, to seek to a particular location in their media, and so on. In other words, they all respond to the set of commands (previously listed) as the primary MCI messages.

Talk about device independence! The Windows multimedia extensions not only protect you from the details of how a particular device might work, they also frequently enable you to treat one device exactly the same way you treat another. For instance, Harmony uses the same code to play a WAV file as a MIDI file. The only difference is that in one case you tell MCI that you want to work with a "waveaudio" device, and the next time you say that you want to work with a "sequencer."

The Harmony Program

Listing 20.1 shows the code for the Harmony program.

Type   **Listing 20.1. HARMONY.CPP.**

```
 1: ///////////////////////////////////////
 2: //   Program Name: HARMONY.CPP
 3: //   Programmer: Charlie Calvert
 4: //   Description: Harmony windows program
 5: //   Date: 08/07/93
 6: ///////////////////////////////////////
 7:
 8: #define STRICT
 9: #include <windows.h>
10: #include <windowsx.h>
11: #include <mmsystem.h>
12: #include <stdio.h>
13: #include <string.h>
14: #include "harmony.h"
15: #include "playinfo.h"
```

```
16: #include "cdinfo.h"
17: #include "cdutil.h"
18: #include "wavemidi.h"
19: #pragma warning (disable: 4068)
20: // -------------------------------------
21: // Interface
22: // -------------------------------------
23:
24: static char szAppName[] = "Harmony";
25: static HWND MainWindow;
26: static HINSTANCE hInstance;
27:
28: BYTE State;
29: BYTE PlayType;
30: char DirStr[DIRSTRSIZE];
31: char DeviceString[DEVICESTRSIZE];
32: static char NoCDOnSystem;
33:
34: // ---------------------------------------------------------
35: // Initialization
36: // ---------------------------------------------------------
37:
38: ////////////////////////////////////////////////////////////
39: // Program entry point
40: ////////////////////////////////////////////////////////////
41: #pragma argsused
42: int PASCAL WinMain(HINSTANCE hInst, HINSTANCE hPrevInstance,
43:                    LPSTR lpszCmdParam, int nCmdShow)
44: {
45:   MSG  Msg;
46:
47:   if (!hPrevInstance)
48:     if (!Register(hInst))
49:       return FALSE;
50:
51:   (MainWindow = Create(hInst, nCmdShow);
52:   if (MainWindow)
53:     return FALSE;
54:   while (GetMessage(&Msg, NULL, 0, 0))
55:   {
56:     TranslateMessage(&Msg);
57:     DispatchMessage(&Msg);
58:   }
59:
60:   return Msg.wParam;
61: }
62:
63: ////////////////////////////////////////////////////////////
64: // Register the window
65: ////////////////////////////////////////////////////////////
```

continues

20

Listing 20.1. continued

```
 66: BOOL Register(HINSTANCE hInst)
 67: {
 68:   WNDCLASS WndClass;
 69:
 70:   WndClass.style        = CS_HREDRAW | CS_VREDRAW;
 71:   WndClass.lpfnWndProc  = WndProc;
 72:   WndClass.cbClsExtra   = 0;
 73:   WndClass.cbWndExtra   = DLGWINDOWEXTRA;
 74:   WndClass.hInstance    = hInst;
 75:   WndClass.hIcon        = LoadIcon(NULL, IDI_APPLICATION);
 76:   WndClass.hCursor      = LoadCursor(NULL, IDC_ARROW);
 77:   WndClass.hbrBackground = GetStockBrush(WHITE_BRUSH);
 78:   WndClass.lpszMenuName  = NULL;
 79:   WndClass.lpszClassName = szAppName;
 80:
 81:   return RegisterClass (&WndClass);
 82: }
 83:
 84: ////////////////////////////////////////////////////////////
 85: // Create the window
 86: ////////////////////////////////////////////////////////////
 87: HWND Create(HINSTANCE hInst, int nCmdShow)
 88: {
 89:
 90:   hInstance = hInst;
 91:
 92:   HWND hwnd = CreateDialog(hInst, szAppName, 0, NULL);
 93:
 94:   if (hwnd == NULL)
 95:     return hwnd;
 96:
 97:   if (NoCDOnSystem)
 98:     EnableWindow(GetDlgItem(hwnd, CM_COMPACT), FALSE);
 99:
100:   ShowWindow(hwnd, nCmdShow);
101:
102:   return hwnd;
103: }
104:
105: // ----------------------------------------------------------
106: // WndProc and Implementation
107: // ----------------------------------------------------------
108:
109: ////////////////////////////////////////////////////////////
110: // The Window Procedure
111: ////////////////////////////////////////////////////////////
112: LRESULT CALLBACK _export WndProc(HWND hwnd, UINT Message, WPARAM
113:                                        wParam, LPARAM lParam)
```

```
114: {
115:   switch(Message)
116:   {
117:     HANDLE_MSG(hwnd, WM_CREATE, Harmony_OnCreate);
118:     HANDLE_MSG(hwnd, WM_DESTROY, Harmony_OnDestroy);
119:     HANDLE_MSG(hwnd, WM_FILLLISTBOX, Harmony_OnFillListBox);
120:     HANDLE_MSG(hwnd, WM_COMMAND, Harmony_OnCommand);
121:     HANDLE_MSG(hwnd, MM_MCINOTIFY, Harmony_OnMCINotify);
122:     HANDLE_MSG(hwnd, WM_TIMER, Harmony_OnTimer);
123:     default: return Harmony_DefProc(hwnd, Message, wParam, lParam);
124:   }
125: }
126:
127: #pragma argsused
128: BOOL Harmony_OnCreate(HWND hwnd, CREATESTRUCT FAR* lpCreateStruct)
129: {
130:   PlayType = WAVE;
131:   State = CLOSED;
132:   strcpy(DeviceString, "waveaudio");
133:   GetWindowsDirectory(DirStr, 200);
134:   FORWARD_WM_FILLLISTBOX(hwnd, PostMessage);
135:   if (!DoesDeviceExistOnSystem("cdaudio"))
136:     NoCDOnSystem = TRUE;
137:   else
138:     NoCDOnSystem = FALSE;
139:   return TRUE;
140: }
141:
142: //////////////////////////////////////
143: // Handle WM_DESTROY
144: //////////////////////////////////////
145: #pragma argsused
146: void Harmony_OnDestroy(HWND hwnd)
147: {
148:   PostQuitMessage(0);
149: }
150:
151: //////////////////////////////////////
152: // Handle WM_COMMAND
153: //////////////////////////////////////
154: #pragma argsused
155: void Harmony_OnCommand(HWND hwnd, int id, HWND hwndCtl, UINT
                           codeNotify)
156: {
157:   char S[100];
158:
159:   switch (id)
160:   {
161:     case CM_MIDI:
162:       CheckForClose();
```

continues

Listing 20.1. continued

```
163:        strcpy(DeviceString, "sequencer");
164:        PlayType = MIDI;
165:        FORWARD_WM_FILLLISTBOX(hwnd, PostMessage);
166:        break;
167:
168:    case CM_WAVE:
169:        CheckForClose();
170:        strcpy(DeviceString, "waveaudio");
171:        PlayType = WAVE;
172:        FORWARD_WM_FILLLISTBOX(hwnd, PostMessage);
173:        break;
174:
175:    case CM_COMPACT:
176:        if (PlayType != COMPACT)
177:        {
178:          CheckForClose();
179:          PlayType = COMPACT;
180:          strcpy(DeviceString, "cdaudio");
181:          FORWARD_WM_FILLLISTBOX(hwnd, PostMessage);
182:        }
183:        break;
184:
185:    case CM_DIRECTORY:
186:        LoadFile(hwnd);
187:        FORWARD_WM_FILLLISTBOX(hwnd, PostMessage);
188:        break;
189:
190:    case IDOK:
191:        CheckForClose();
192:        FORWARD_WM_CLOSE(hwnd, Harmony_DefProc);
193:        break;
194:
195:    case CM_PAUSE:
196:    case CM_STOP:
197:        switch (PlayType)
198:        {
199:          case MIDI: HandleMIDIPAndS(hwnd, id); break;
200:          case WAVE: HandleWAVEPAndS(hwnd, id); break;
201:          case COMPACT: HandleCDPAndS(hwnd, id); break;
202:        }
203:        break;
204:
205:    case CM_WAVEPLAY:
206:        if (State == PLAYING)
207:          return;
208:
209:        if (PlayType == COMPACT)
210:        {
211:          PlayCD(hwnd);
```

```
212:        return;
213:      }
214:
215:      if (FileOpen(hwnd))
216:      {
217:        State = PLAYING;
218:        SetWindowText(GetDlgItem(hwnd, ID_MODE), "Playing");
219:        SetTimeFormatMs();
220:        DWORD Result = GetLen();
221:        sprintf(S, "%ld ms", Result);
222:        SetWindowText(GetDlgItem(hwnd, ID_LENGTH), S);
223:        SetWindowText(GetDlgItem(hwnd, ID_NUMTRACKS),
224:                      GetInfo(S));
225:        if (PlayMCI())
226:          SetTimer(hwnd, HARMONY_TIMER, 10, NULL);
227:        else
228:        {
229:          CloseMCI();
230:          State = CLOSED;
231:          SetWindowText(GetDlgItem(hwnd, ID_MODE), "CLOSED");
232:        }
233:      }
234:      break;
235:
236:    case ID_FILELIST:
237:      if (codeNotify == LBN_DBLCLK)
238:        MessageBox(hwnd, "They're talking to me!", NULL, MB_OK);
239:      break;
240:
241:    case CM_RECORD:
242:      if ((PlayType == MIDI) || (PlayType == COMPACT))
243:        return;
244:      if (OpenMCI(hwnd, "", DeviceString))
245:      {
246:        DoRecord(10000);
247:        State = RECORDING;
248:        SetTimer(hwnd, HARMONY_TIMER, 10, NULL);
249:      }
250:      break;
251:  }
252: }
253:
254: //////////////////////////////////////
255: // Handle WM_FILLLISTBOX
256: //////////////////////////////////////
257: #pragma argsused
258: void Harmony_OnFillListBox(HWND hwnd)
259: {
260:   if (PlayType == COMPACT)
261:   {
262:     FillCDTrackBox(hwnd);
```

continues

Listing 20.1. continued

```
263:    return;
264:  }
265:
266:  char S[200];
267:
268:  strcpy(S, DirStr);
269:  switch (PlayType)
270:  {
271:    case MIDI: strcat(S, "\\*.mid"); break;
272:    case WAVE: strcat(S, "\\*.wav"); break;
273:  }
274:
275:  if(!DlgDirList(hwnd, S, ID_FILELIST, 0, DDL_ARCHIVE))
276:    MessageBox(hwnd, "No way", NULL, MB_OK);
277:
278:  switch (PlayType)
279:  {
280:    case COMPACT:
281:      Button_SetCheck(GetDlgItem(hwnd, CM_COMPACT), TRUE); break;
282:    case MIDI:
283:      Button_SetCheck(GetDlgItem(hwnd, CM_MIDI), TRUE); break;
284:    case WAVE:
285:      Button_SetCheck(GetDlgItem(hwnd, CM_WAVE), TRUE); break;
286:  }
287:  SetWindowText(GetDlgItem(hwnd, ID_DIREDIT), DirStr);
288:
289:  ListBox_SetCurSel(GetDlgItem(hwnd, ID_FILELIST), 0);
290: }
291:
292: //////////////////////////////////////
293: // Handle MM_ONMCINOTIFY
294: //////////////////////////////////////
295: #pragma argsused
296: void Harmony_OnMCINotify(HWND hwnd, UINT status, int DeviceID)
297: {
298:   char S[100];
299:
300:   if (State == ERROR_OCCURED)
301:     return;
302:
303:   switch (status)
304:   {
305:     case MCI_NOTIFY_ABORTED:
306:       strcpy(S, "Aborted");
307:       break;
308:
309:     case MCI_NOTIFY_SUCCESSFUL:
310:       if (State == RECORDING)
311:         {
```

```
312:            SaveFile("Albert.wav");
313:            DlgDirList(hwnd, S, ID_FILELIST, 0, DDL_ARCHIVE);
314:          }
315:          State = CLOSED;
316:          if (PlayType == COMPACT)
317:            CloseCDMCI();
318:          else
319:            CloseMCI();
320:          strcpy(S, "Success");
321:          break;
322:
323:        case MCI_NOTIFY_SUPERSEDED:
324:          strcpy(S, "Superseded");
325:          break;
326:
327:        case MCI_NOTIFY_FAILURE:
328:          State = CLOSED;
329:          if (PlayType == COMPACT)
330:          CloseCDMCI();
331:          else
332:            CloseMCI();
333:          strcpy(S, "Failure");
334:          break;
335:      }
336:    SetWindowText(GetDlgItem(hwnd, ID_MODE), S);
337:    SetWindowText(GetDlgItem(hwnd, ID_LENGTH), "...");
338:    SetWindowText(GetDlgItem(hwnd, ID_POSITION), "...");
339:    SetWindowText(GetDlgItem(hwnd, ID_NUMTRACKS), "...");
340: //   MessageBox(hwnd, S, "MCI_NOTIFY", MB_OK);
341: }
342:
343: ///////////////////////////////////////////
344: // Handle WM_TIMER
345: ///////////////////////////////////////////
346: #pragma argsused
347: void Harmony_OnTimer(HWND hwnd, UINT id)
348: {
349:    char S[100];
350:
351:    switch (State)
352:    {
353:      case PAUSED:
354:        KillTimer(hwnd, HARMONY_TIMER);
355:        break;
356:
357:      case STOPPED:
358:        KillTimer(hwnd, HARMONY_TIMER);
359:        break;
360:
361:      case RECORDING:
362:      case PLAYING:
```

continues

20

711

Listing 20.1. continued

```
363:        if (PlayType == COMPACT)
364:        {
365:          HandleCDTimer(hwnd);
366:          return;
367:        }
368:
369:        DWORD Result = GetLocation();
370:        if (Result == -1)
371:        {
372:          KillTimer(hwnd, HARMONY_TIMER);
373:          State = ERROR_OCCURED;
374:          SetWindowText(GetDlgItem(hwnd, ID_MODE), "ERROR");
375:          return;
376:        }
377:        sprintf(S, "%ld ms", Result);
378:        SetWindowText(GetDlgItem(hwnd, ID_POSITION), S);
379:        break;
380:    }
381: }
```

Listing 20.2 shows the Harmony header file.

 Listing 20.2. HARMONY.H.

```
1: //////////////////////////////////////
2: //   Module Name: HARMONY.H
3: //   Programmer: Charlie Calvert
4: //   Description: Harmony windows program
5: //   Date: 08/07/93
6: //////////////////////////////////////
7:
8: // User defined messages
9: #define WM_FILLLISTBOX (WM_USER + 0)
10:
11: // Buttons the user can push
12: #define CM_WAVEPLAY 101
13: #define CM_PAUSE 102
14: #define CM_STOP 103
15: #define CM_DIRECTORY 104
16: #define CM_RECORD 105
17: #define CM_HELP      106
18:
19: // Listbox and Combo
20: #define ID_FILELIST 120
21: #define ID_PLAYLIST 121
22:
23: // Controls that report to user
```

```
24: #define ID_MODE 140
25: #define ID_NUMTRACKS 141
26: #define ID_POSITION 142
27: #define ID_LENGTH 143
28: #define ID_DIREDIT 145
29:
30: // The radio buttons for selecting mode
31: #define ID_GROUP 5000
32: #define CM_COMPACT 5001
33: #define CM_WAVE 5002
34: #define CM_MIDI 5003
35:
36: // States
37: #define PAUSED 1
38: #define PLAYING 2
39: #define STOPPED 3
40: #define CLOSED 4
41: #define OPENNED 6
42: #define RECORDING 7
43: #define ERROR_OCCURED 8
44:
45: // Devices
46: #define WAVE 1
47: #define COMPACT 2
48: #define MIDI 3
49:
50: // Misc
51: #define DIRSTRSIZE 200
52: #define DEVICESTRSIZE 50
53: #define HARMONY_TIMER 1
54:
55: // WindowsX extensions
56: #define HANDLE_MM_MCINOTIFY(hwnd, wParam, lParam, fn) \
57:     ((fn)((hwnd), (UINT)(wParam), (int)LOWORD(lParam)), 0L)
58: #define FORWARD_MM_MCINOTIFY(hwnd, status, DeviceID, fn) \
59:     (void)(fn)((hwnd), MM_MCINOTIFY, (WPARAM)(status), \
60:     MAKELPARAM((UINT)(DeviceID), 0))
61:
62: #define HANDLE_WM_FILLLISTBOX(hwnd, wParam, lParam, fn) \
63:     ((fn)(hwnd), 0L)
64: #define FORWARD_WM_FILLLISTBOX(hwnd, fn) \
65:     (void)(fn)((hwnd), WM_FILLLISTBOX, 0, 0L)
66:
67: // Declarations for class Harmony
68: #define Harmony_DefProc     DefWindowProc
69: BOOL Harmony_OnCreate(HWND hwnd,
70:                         CREATESTRUCT FAR* lpCreateStruct);
71: void Harmony_OnDestroy(HWND hwnd);
72: void Harmony_OnFillListBox(HWND hwnd);
73: void Harmony_OnCommand(HWND hwnd, int id, HWND hwndCtl,
                            UINT codeNotify);
```

continues

Listing 20.2. continued

```
74: void Harmony_OnMCINotify(HWND hwnd, UINT status, int DeviceID);
75: void Harmony_OnTimer(HWND hwnd, UINT id);
76:
77: // The sum of frustrations
78: LRESULT CALLBACK _export WndProc(HWND hwnd, UINT Message,
79:                                 WPARAM wParam, LPARAM lParam);
80: BOOL Register(HINSTANCE hInst);
81: HWND Create(HINSTANCE hInst, int nCmdShow);
```

Listing 20.3 shows the HARMONY definition file.

Listing 20.3. HARMONY.DEF.

```
 1: ; HARMONY.DEF
 2:
 3: NAME           Harmony
 4: DESCRIPTION    'Harmony Music (c) 1993 by Charlie Calvert'
 5: EXETYPE        WINDOWS
 6: STUB           'WINSTUB.EXE'
 7: CODE           PRELOAD MOVEABLE DISCARDABLE
 8: DATA           PRELOAD MOVEABLE MULTIPLE
 9:
10: HEAPSIZE       4096
11: STACKSIZE      5120
```

Listing 20.4 shows the CDUTIL source file.

Listing 20.4. CDUTIL.CPP.

```
 1: /////////////////////////////////////////
 2: //   Module Name: CDUTIL.CPP
 3: //   Programmer: Charlie Calvert
 4: //   Description: Harmony windows program
 5: //   Date: 08/07/93
 6: /////////////////////////////////////////
 7: #define STRICT
 8: #include <windows.h>
 9: #include <windowsx.h>
10: #include <mmsystem.h>
11: #include "harmony.h"
12: #include "cdinfo.h"
13: #include "stdio.h"
14: #include "playinfo.h"
15:
16: extern BYTE State;
17: extern BYTE PlayType;
```

```
18:
19: /////////////////////////////////////////
20: // HandleDCPAndS
21: /////////////////////////////////////////
22: void HandleCDPAndS(HWND hwnd, int id)
23: {
24:   switch(id)
25:   {
26:     case CM_PAUSE:
27:       State = PAUSED;
28:       SetWindowText(GetDlgItem(hwnd, ID_MODE), "Paused");
29:       PauseCDMCI();
30:       break;
31:
32:     case CM_STOP:
33:       State = STOPPED;
34:       SetWindowText(GetDlgItem(hwnd, ID_MODE), "Stopped");
35:       StopCDMCI();
36:       break;
37:   }
38: }
39:
40: /////////////////////////////////////////
41: // OpenCDFile
42: ///////////////////////////////////////////
43: BOOL OpenCDFile(HWND hwnd)
44: {
45:   if ((State == PAUSED) || (State == STOPPED) ||
         (State == OPENED))
46:     return TRUE;
47:
48:   if (OpenCD(hwnd))
49:   {
50:     State = OPENED;
51:     SetTMSFasFormat();
52:     return TRUE;
53:   }
54:   else
55:     return FALSE;
56: }
57:
58: /////////////////////////////////////////
59: // GetTrackString
60: /////////////////////////////////////////
61: LPSTR GetTrackString(LPSTR S, DWORD i, BOOL LongString)
62: {
63:   BYTE Min,Sec,Frame;
64:
65:   GetCDTrackLength(i, &Min, &Sec, &Frame);
66:   Min = Min;
67:   Sec = Sec;
```

continues

20

Listing 20.4. continued

```
68:    Frame = Frame;
69:    if (LongString)
70:      sprintf(S, "Track: %ld  >> Time: %d:%d", i, Min, Sec);
71:    else
72:      sprintf(S, "%d:%d", Min, Sec);
73:    return S;
74: }
75:
76: ///////////////////////////////////////////
77: // PlayCD
78: ///////////////////////////////////////////
79: void PlayCD(HWND hwnd)
80: {
81:    char S[100];
82:
83:    if (OpenCDFile(hwnd))
84:    {
85:      SetTimer(hwnd, HARMONY_TIMER, 10, NULL);
86:      // PlayMciCD(4, 5);
87:      DWORD Index =
88:        ListBox_GetCurSel(GetDlgItem(hwnd, ID_FILELIST));
89:      if (Index == LB_ERR)
90:      {
91:        MessageBox(hwnd, "You must select a file", NULL, MB_OK);
92:        return;
93:      }
94:      PlayCDOneTrack(Index + 1);
95:      State = PLAYING;
96:      SetWindowText(GetDlgItem(hwnd, ID_MODE), "Playing");
97:      GetTrackString(S, Index + 1, FALSE);
98:      SetWindowText(GetDlgItem(hwnd, ID_LENGTH), S);
99:    }
100: }
101:
102: ///////////////////////////////////////////
103: // HandleDCPTimer
104: ///////////////////////////////////////////
105: void HandleCDTimer(HWND hwnd)
106: {
107:    DWORD Track;
108:    DWORD Time;
109:    int TimeAry[2];
110:    char S[50];
111:
112:    Track = GetCurrentCDTrack();
113:    sprintf(S, "%ld", Track);
114:    SetWindowText(GetDlgItem(hwnd, ID_NUMTRACKS), S);
115:    SetTMSFasFormat();
116:    Time = GetCDLocation();
```

```
117:    sprintf(S, "%d:%d", MCI_TMSF_MINUTE(Time),
118:            MCI_TMSF_SECOND(Time));
119:    SetWindowText(GetDlgItem(hwnd, ID_POSITION), S);
120: }
121:
122: /////////////////////////////////////////
123: // FillCDTrackBox
124: /////////////////////////////////////////
125: void FillCDTrackBox(HWND hwnd)
126: {
127:    DWORD i;
128:    char S[100];
129:
130:    if (!OpenCDFile(hwnd))
131:      return;
132:
133:    ListBox_ResetContent(GetDlgItem(hwnd, ID_FILELIST));
134:    DWORD NumTracks = GetCDNumTracks();
135:    if (NumTracks == -1) return;
136:
137:    HCURSOR Cursor1 = LoadCursor(0, IDC_WAIT);
138:    SetCursor(Cursor1);
139:    HCURSOR OldCursor = (HCURSOR)SetClassWord(hwnd, GCW_HCURSOR,
140:                                   (WORD)Cursor1);
141:    SetCapture(GetDlgItem(hwnd, ID_LENGTH));
142:    for (i = 1; i <= NumTracks; i++)
143:    {
144:      GetTrackString(S, i, TRUE);
145:      ListBox_AddString(GetDlgItem(hwnd, ID_FILELIST), S);
146:    }
147:    ListBox_SetCurSel(GetDlgItem(hwnd, ID_FILELIST), 0);
148:    SetCursor(OldCursor);
149:    SetClassWord(hwnd, GCW_HCURSOR, (WORD)OldCursor);
150:    ReleaseCapture();
151: }
152:
153: /////////////////////////////////////////
154: // CloseCompact
155: /////////////////////////////////////////
156: void CloseCompact(void)
157: {
158:    if (State == CLOSED) return;
159:    if (State == PLAYING)
160:      StopCDMCI();
161:    CloseCDMCI();
162: }
163:
164: /////////////////////////////////////////
165: // CheckForClose
166: /////////////////////////////////////////
167: void CheckForClose(void)
```

continues

20

Listing 20.4. continued

```
168: {
169:   if (State != CLOSED)
170:     if (PlayType == COMPACT)
171:       CloseCompact();
172:     else
173:       CloseMCI();
174:
175:     State = CLOSED;
176: }
```

Listing 20.5 shows the code for CDUtil.

Listing 20.5. CDUTIL.H.

```
 1: ////////////////////////////////////////////
 2: //   Module Name: CDUTIL.H
 3: //   Programmer: Charlie Calvert
 4: //   Description: Harmony windows program
 5: //   Date: 08/07/93
 6: ////////////////////////////////////////////
 7:
 8: // Utility functions
 9: void HandleCDPAndS(HWND hwnd, int id);
10: void HandleCDTimer(HWND hwnd);
11: void FillCDTrackBox(HWND hwnd);
12: void CheckForClose(void);
```

Listing 20.6 shows the source file for WaveMidi.

Listing 20.6. WAVEMIDI.CPP.

```
 1: ////////////////////////////////////////////
 2: //   Program Name: WAVEMIDI.CPP
 3: //   Programmer: Charlie Calvert
 4: //   Description: Harmony windows program
 5: //   Date: 08/07/93
 6: ////////////////////////////////////////////
 7: #define STRICT
 8: #include <windows.h>
 9: #include <windowsx.h>
10: #include <commdlg.h>
11: #include <direct.h>
12: #include <mmsystem.h>
13: #include <string.h>
14: #include "harmony.h"
15: #include "cdinfo.h"
```

```
16: #include "stdio.h"
17: #include "playinfo.h"
18:
19: extern BYTE State;
20: extern BYTE PlayType;
21: extern char DirStr[DIRSTRSIZE];
22: extern char DeviceString[DEVICESTRSIZE];
23:
24: ///////////////////////////////////////
25: // GetFileName
26: ///////////////////////////////////////
27: BOOL FileOpen(HWND hwnd)
28: {
29:   char S[100];
30:   char S1[200];
31:
32:   if (State == PAUSED)
33:     return TRUE;
34:
35:   S[1] = '\0';
36:   int Index =
37:     ListBox_GetCurSel(GetDlgItem(hwnd, ID_FILELIST));
38:   if (Index == LB_ERR)
39:   {
40:     MessageBox(hwnd, "Select a valid file",
41:                 NULL, MB_OK | MB_ICONSTOP);
42:     return FALSE;
43:   }
44:   ListBox_GetText(GetDlgItem(hwnd, ID_FILELIST), Index, S);
45:   strcpy(S1, DirStr);
46:   strcat(S1, "\\");
47:   strcat(S1, S);
48:
49:   if (!OpenMCI(hwnd, S1, DeviceString))
50:     return FALSE;
51:   else
52:     return TRUE;
53: }
54:
55: ///////////////////////////////////////
56: // GetFileName
57: ///////////////////////////////////////
58: char * GetFileName(HWND hwnd, char * szFile, int StringSize)
59: {
60:   OPENFILENAME ofn;
61:   char szDirName[256];
62:   char szFileTitle[256];
63:   char szFilter[256];
64:   char chReplace;
65:
66:   memset(&ofn, 0, sizeof(OPENFILENAME));
```

continues

20

Listing 20.6. continued

```
67:
68:    strcpy(szFilter,
69:         "Wave Files(*.wav)¦*.wav¦MIDI Files(*.mid)¦*.mid¦");
70:    chReplace = szFilter[strlen(szFilter) - 1];
71:    for (int i = 0; szFilter[i] != '\0'; i++)
72:    {
73:        if (szFilter[i] == chReplace)
74:            szFilter[i] = '\0';
75:    }
76:
77:    ofn.lStructSize = sizeof(OPENFILENAME);
78:    ofn.hwndOwner = hwnd;
79:    ofn.lpstrFilter = szFilter;
80:    ofn.nFilterIndex = 1;
81:    ofn.lpstrFile= szFile;
82:    ofn.nMaxFile = StringSize;
83:    ofn.lpstrFileTitle = szFileTitle;
84:    ofn.nMaxFileTitle = sizeof(szFileTitle);
85:    ofn.lpstrInitialDir = szDirName;
86:    ofn.Flags = OFN_FILEMUSTEXIST;
87:
88:    GetOpenFileName(&ofn);
89:
90:    return szFile;
91: }
92:
93: /////////////////////////////////////
94: // LoadFile
95: /////////////////////////////////////
96: void LoadFile(HWND hwnd)
97: {
98:    char S[100];
99:
100:    memset(&S, 0, 100);
101:
102:    if (PlayType == WAVE)
103:      strcpy(S, "*.wav");
104:    else
105:      if (PlayType == MIDI)
106:        strcpy(S, "*.mid");
107:
108:    GetFileName(hwnd, S, 100);
109:    _getdcwd(0, DirStr, DIRSTRSIZE);
110: }
111:
112: /////////////////////////////////////
113: // HandleMIDIPAndS
114: /////////////////////////////////////
115: void HandleMIDIPAndS(HWND hwnd, int id)
```

```
116: {
117:    switch(id)
118:    {
119:      case CM_PAUSE:
120:        State = PAUSED;
121:        SetWindowText(GetDlgItem(hwnd, ID_MODE), "Paused");
122:        PauseMCI();
123:        break;
124:
125:      case CM_STOP:
126:        State = CLOSED;
127:        SetWindowText(GetDlgItem(hwnd, ID_MODE), "Stopped");
128:        StopMCI();
129:        CloseMCI();
130:        break;
131:    }
132: }
133:
134: ////////////////////////////////////////
135: // HandleWAVEPAndS
136: ////////////////////////////////////////
137: void HandleWAVEPAndS(HWND hwnd, int id)
138: {
139:    switch(id)
140:    {
141:      case CM_PAUSE:
142:        State = PAUSED;
143:        SetWindowText(GetDlgItem(hwnd, ID_MODE), "Paused");
144:        PauseMCI();
145:        break;
146:
147:      case CM_STOP:
148:        State = CLOSED;
149:        SetWindowText(GetDlgItem(hwnd, ID_MODE), "Stopped");
150:        StopMCI();
151:        CloseMCI();
152:        break;
153:    }
154: }
```

Listing 20.7 shows the header file for WaveMidi.

Type **Listing 20.7. WAVEMIDI.H.**

```
1: ////////////////////////////////////////
2: //   Module Name: WAVEMIDI.H
3: //   Programmer: Charlie Calvert
4: //   Description: Harmony windows program
5: //   Date: 08/07/93
```

continues

Listing 20.7. continued

```
 6: ////////////////////////////////////
 7:
 8: BOOL FileOpen(HWND hwnd);
 9: void PlayCD(HWND hwnd);
10: void HandleMIDIPAndS(HWND hwnd, int id);
11: void HandleWAVEPAndS(HWND hwnd, int id);
12: void LoadFile(HWND hwnd);
```

Listing 20.8 shows the resource file for the Harmony program.

 Listing 20.8. HARMONY.RC.

```
 1: ////////////////////////////////////
 2: //   Module Name: HARMONY.RC
 3: //   Programmer: Charlie Calvert
 4: //   Description: Harmony windows program
 5: //   Date: 08/07/93
 6: ////////////////////////////////////
 7: #include <windows.h>
 8: #include "harmony.h"
 9:
10: Harmony DIALOG 18, 23, 246, 208
11: STYLE DS_MODALFRAME ¦ WS_OVERLAPPED ¦ WS_CAPTION
          ¦ WS_SYSMENU ¦ WS_MINIMIZEBOX
12: CLASS "Harmony"
13: CAPTION "Harmony"
14: BEGIN
15:         CONTROL "", ID_GROUP, "BUTTON", BS_GROUPBOX ¦
16:           WS_CHILD ¦ WS_VISIBLE, 6, 5, 107, 93
17:         CONTROL "Mode", -1, "STATIC", SS_LEFT ¦ WS_CHILD ¦
18:           WS_VISIBLE, 17, 15, 39, 11
19:         CONTROL "...", ID_MODE, "STATIC", SS_LEFT ¦ WS_CHILD ¦
20:           WS_VISIBLE, 56, 15, 53, 11
21:         CONTROL "Track", -1, "STATIC", SS_LEFT ¦ WS_CHILD ¦
22:           WS_VISIBLE, 17, 37, 39, 11
23:         CONTROL "...", ID_NUMTRACKS, "STATIC", SS_LEFT ¦
24:           WS_CHILD ¦ WS_VISIBLE, 56, 37, 53, 11
25:         CONTROL "Position", -1, "STATIC", SS_LEFT ¦ WS_CHILD ¦
26:           WS_VISIBLE, 17, 59, 39, 11
27:         CONTROL "...", ID_POSITION, "STATIC", SS_LEFT ¦
28:           WS_CHILD ¦ WS_VISIBLE, 56, 59, 53, 11
29:         CONTROL "Length", -1, "STATIC", SS_LEFT ¦ WS_CHILD ¦
30:           WS_VISIBLE, 17, 81, 39, 11
31:         CONTROL "...", ID_LENGTH, "STATIC", SS_LEFT ¦
32:           WS_CHILD ¦ WS_VISIBLE, 56, 81, 53, 11
33:         CONTROL "", ID_FILELIST, "LISTBOX", LBS_NOTIFY ¦
34:           LBS_USETABSTOPS ¦ WS_CHILD ¦ WS_VISIBLE ¦
35:           WS_BORDER ¦ WS_VSCROLL, 132, 9, 107, 94
```

```
36:        CONTROL "", ID_PLAYLIST, "COMBOBOX", CBS_DROPDOWNLIST ¦
37:          WS_CHILD ¦ WS_VISIBLE ¦ WS_TABSTOP, 6, 115, 107, 33
38:        CONTROL "", ID_DIREDIT, "EDIT", ES_LEFT ¦ WS_CHILD ¦
39:          WS_VISIBLE ¦ WS_BORDER ¦ WS_TABSTOP, 132, 115, 107, 12
40:        CONTROL "", 102, "button", BS_GROUPBOX ¦ WS_CHILD ¦
41:          WS_VISIBLE, 7, 156, 71, 45
42:        CONTROL "Help", CM_HELP, "BUTTON", BS_PUSHBUTTON ¦
43:          WS_CHILD ¦ WS_VISIBLE ¦ WS_TABSTOP, 7, 135, 71, 17
44:        CONTROL "Compact Disk", CM_COMPACT, "BUTTON",
45:          BS_AUTORADIOBUTTON ¦ WS_CHILD ¦ WS_VISIBLE ¦
46:          WS_GROUP ¦ WS_TABSTOP, 13, 162, 58, 12
47:        CONTROL "WAVE", CM_WAVE, "BUTTON", BS_AUTORADIOBUTTON ¦
48:          WS_CHILD ¦ WS_VISIBLE ¦ WS_TABSTOP, 13, 174, 28, 12
49:        CONTROL "MIDI", CM_MIDI, "BUTTON", BS_AUTORADIOBUTTON ¦
50:          WS_CHILD ¦ WS_VISIBLE ¦ WS_TABSTOP, 13, 186, 28, 12
51:        CONTROL "Directory", CM_DIRECTORY, "BUTTON",
52:          BS_PUSHBUTTON ¦ WS_CHILD ¦ WS_VISIBLE ¦ WS_GROUP ¦
53:          WS_TABSTOP, 88, 135, 71, 17
54:        CONTROL "Play", CM_WAVEPLAY, "BUTTON", BS_PUSHBUTTON ¦
55:          WS_CHILD ¦ WS_VISIBLE ¦ WS_TABSTOP, 88, 160, 71, 17
56:        CONTROL "Close", IDOK, "BUTTON", BS_PUSHBUTTON ¦ WS_CHILD ¦
57:          WS_VISIBLE ¦ WS_TABSTOP, 88, 184, 71, 17
58:        CONTROL "Record", CM_RECORD, "BUTTON", BS_PUSHBUTTON ¦
59:          WS_CHILD ¦ WS_VISIBLE ¦ WS_TABSTOP, 169, 135, 71, 17
60:        CONTROL "Pause", CM_PAUSE, "BUTTON", BS_PUSHBUTTON ¦
61:          WS_CHILD ¦ WS_VISIBLE ¦ WS_TABSTOP, 169, 160, 71, 17
62:        CONTROL "Stop", CM_STOP, "BUTTON", BS_PUSHBUTTON ¦
63:          WS_CHILD ¦ WS_VISIBLE ¦ WS_TABSTOP, 169, 184, 71, 17
64:        CONTROL "Now Playing", -1, "STATIC", SS_LEFT ¦ WS_CHILD ¦
65:          WS_VISIBLE ¦ WS_GROUP, 6, 105, 57, 8
66:        CONTROL "Current Directory", -1, "STATIC", SS_LEFT ¦
67:          WS_CHILD ¦ WS_VISIBLE ¦ WS_GROUP, 132, 105, 99, 8
68: END
```

Listing 20.9 shows the PlayInfo source file.

Type   **Listing 20.9. PLAYINFO.CPP.**

```
 1: ////////////////////////////////////////
 2: // Program: PLAYINFO.CPP
 3: // Programmer: Charlie Calvert
 4: // Date: August 6, 1993
 5: // Description: DLL Module from Harmony program
 6: ////////////////////////////////////////
 7:
 8: #define STRICT
 9: #include <windows.h>
10: #include <windowsx.h>
11: #include <mmsystem.h>
```

continues

Listing 20.9. continued

```
12: #include <stdio.h>
13: #include <string.h>
14: #include "playinfo.h"
15: #pragma warning (disable : 4068)
16: #pragma argsused
17:
18: ////////////////////////////////////////
19: // LibMain
20: ////////////////////////////////////////
21: int CALLBACK LibMain(HINSTANCE hInstance, WORD wDataSeg,
22:                      WORD wHeapSize, LPSTR lpszCmdLine)
23: {
24:   if (wHeapSize > 0)
25:         UnlockData(0);
26:
27:   return 1;
28: }
29:
30: ////////////////////////////////////////
31: // WEP
32: ////////////////////////////////////////
33: #pragma argsused
34: int CALLBACK WEP (int nParameter)
35: {
36:   return 1;
37: }
38:
39: ////////////////////////////////////////
40: // GetDeviceID
41: ////////////////////////////////////////
42: WORD CALLBACK _export GetDeviceID(void)
43: {
44:   return wDeviceID;
45: }
46:
47: ////////////////////////////////////////
48: // GetErrorMessage
49: ////////////////////////////////////////
50: LPSTR GetErrorMessage(DWORD RC, LPSTR S)
51: {
52:   if (!mciGetErrorString(RC, S, MsgLen))
53:     strcpy(S, "No message available");
54:   return S;
55: }
56:
57: ////////////////////////////////////////
58: // ErrorMs
59: ////////////////////////////////////////
60: BOOL CALLBACK _export ErrorMsg(DWORD Error, LPSTR CallingFunc)
```

```
61: {
62:   char S[MsgLen + 50];
63:   char S1[MsgLen];
64:
65:   GetErrorMessage(Error, S1);
66:   sprintf(S, "Calling Func: %s\nReturn Code: %ld\n %s",
67:           CallingFunc, Error, S1);
68:   if (Error)
69:   {
70:     MessageBox(0, S, "Information", MB_OK | MB_ICONINFORMATION);
71:     return FALSE;
72:   }
73:   return TRUE;
74: }
75:
76: ////////////////////////////////////////////
77: // CloseMCI
78: ////////////////////////////////////////////
79: BOOL CALLBACK _export CloseMCI(void)
80: {
81:   DWORD ErrorNum;
82:
83:   ErrorNum = mciSendCommand(wDeviceID, MCI_CLOSE, 0, 0);
84:   if (ErrorNum)
85:   {
86:     ErrorMsg(ErrorNum, "CloseMCI");
87:     return FALSE;
88:   }
89:   wDeviceID = 0;
90:   return TRUE;
91: }
92:
93: ////////////////////////////////////////////
94: // GetInfo
95: ////////////////////////////////////////////
96: LPSTR CALLBACK _export GetInfo(LPSTR S)
97: {
98:   MCI_INFO_PARMS Info;
99:   DWORD Flags, ErrorNum;
100:
101:   Info.dwCallback = 0;
102:   Info.lpstrReturn = S;
103:   Info.dwRetSize = MsgLen;
104:   Flags = MCI_INFO_PRODUCT;
105:   ErrorNum =
106:     mciSendCommand(wDeviceID, MCI_INFO, Flags, DWORD(&Info));
107:   if (ErrorNum)
108:   {
109:     ErrorMsg(ErrorNum, "GetInfo");
110:     return NULL;
111:   }
```

continues

Listing 20.9. continued

```
112:    return S;
113: }
114:
115: ////////////////////////////////////////////
116: // GetLen
117: ////////////////////////////////////////////
118: DWORD CALLBACK _export GetLen(void)
119: {
120:   MCI_STATUS_PARMS Info;
121:   DWORD ErrorNum, Flags;
122:
123:   memset(&Info, 0, sizeof(MCI_STATUS_PARMS));
124:   Info.dwItem = MCI_STATUS_LENGTH;
125:   Flags = MCI_STATUS_ITEM;
126:   ErrorNum =
127:     mciSendCommand(wDeviceID, MCI_STATUS, Flags, DWORD(&Info));
128:   if (ErrorNum)
129:   {
130:     ErrorMsg(ErrorNum, "GetLen");
131:     return -1;
132:   }
133:   return Info.dwReturn;
134: }
135:
136: ////////////////////////////////////////////
137: // GetLocation
138: ////////////////////////////////////////////
139: DWORD CALLBACK _export GetLocation(void)
140: {
141:   MCI_STATUS_PARMS Info;
142:   DWORD Flags, ErrorNum;
143:
144:   Info.dwItem = MCI_STATUS_POSITION;
145:   Flags = MCI_STATUS_ITEM;
146:   ErrorNum = mciSendCommand(wDeviceID, MCI_STATUS,
147:                             Flags, DWORD(&Info));
148:   if (ErrorNum)
149:   {
150:     ErrorMsg(ErrorNum, "GetLocation");
151:     return -1;
152:   }
153:   return Info.dwReturn;
154: }
155:
156: ////////////////////////////////////////////
157: // GetMode
158: ////////////////////////////////////////////
159: DWORD CALLBACK _export GetMode(void)
160: {
```

```
161:    MCI_STATUS_PARMS Info;
162:    DWORD ErrorNum, Flags;
163:
164:    memset(&Info, 0, sizeof(MCI_STATUS_PARMS));
165:    Info.dwItem = MCI_STATUS_MODE;
166:    Flags = MCI_STATUS_ITEM;
167:    ErrorNum = mciSendCommand(wDeviceID, MCI_STATUS,
168:                                 Flags, DWORD(&Info));
169:    if (ErrorNum)
170:    {
171:      ErrorMsg(ErrorNum, "GetMode");
172:      return -1;
173:    }
174:    return Info.dwReturn;
175: }
176:
177: /////////////////////////////////////////////
178: // OpenMCI
179: /////////////////////////////////////////////
180: BOOL CALLBACK _export OpenMCI(HWND PWindow, LPSTR FileName,
181:                                 LPSTR DeviceType)
182: {
183:    MCI_OPEN_PARMS OpenParms;
184:    DWORD Style, ErrorNum;
185:
186:    PlayWindow = PWindow;
187:    OpenParms.lpstrDeviceType = DeviceType;
188:    OpenParms.lpstrElementName = FileName;
189:    Style = MCI_OPEN_TYPE ¦ MCI_OPEN_ELEMENT;
190:    ErrorNum = mciSendCommand(0, MCI_OPEN,
191:                                 Style, DWORD(&OpenParms));
192:    if ( ErrorNum)
193:    {
194:      ErrorMsg(ErrorNum, "OpenMCI");
195:      return FALSE;
196:    }
197:    wDeviceID = OpenParms.wDeviceID;
198:    return TRUE;
199: }
200:
201: /////////////////////////////////////////////
202: // PauseMCI
203: /////////////////////////////////////////////
204: BOOL CALLBACK _export PauseMCI(void)
205: {
206:    MCI_GENERIC_PARMS Info;
207:    DWORD ErrorNum;
208:    char S1[MsgLen];
209:
210:    memset(&Info, 0, sizeof(MCI_GENERIC_PARMS));
211:    ErrorNum = mciSendCommand(wDeviceID, MCI_PAUSE,
```

continues

Listing 20.9. continued

```
212:                                    0, DWORD(&Info));
213:    if (ErrorNum)
214:    {
215:       ErrorMsg(ErrorNum, "PauseMCI");
216:       return FALSE;
217:    }
218:    return TRUE;
219: }
220:
221: ////////////////////////////////////////////
222: // PlayMCI
223: ////////////////////////////////////////////
224: BOOL CALLBACK _export PlayMCI(void)
225: {
226:    DWORD ErrorNum;
227:    MCI_PLAY_PARMS Info;
228:
229:    Info.dwCallback = DWORD(PlayWindow);
230:    ErrorNum = mciSendCommand(wDeviceID, MCI_PLAY,
231:                              MCI_NOTIFY, DWORD(&Info));
232:    if (ErrorNum)
233:    {
234:       ErrorMsg(ErrorNum, "PlayMCI");
235:       return FALSE;
236:    }
237:    return TRUE;
238: }
239:
240: ////////////////////////////////////////////
241: // SetTimeFormatMS
242: ////////////////////////////////////////////
243: BOOL CALLBACK _export SetTimeFormatMs(void)
244: {
245:    MCI_SET_PARMS Info;
246:    DWORD ErrorNum, Flags;
247:
248:    Info.dwTimeFormat = MCI_FORMAT_MILLISECONDS;
249:    Flags = MCI_SET_TIME_FORMAT;
250:    ErrorNum = mciSendCommand(wDeviceID, MCI_SET,
251:                              Flags, DWORD(&Info));
252:    if (ErrorNum)
253:    {
254:       ErrorMsg(ErrorNum, "SetTimeFormatMS");
255:       return FALSE;
256:    }
257:    return TRUE;
258: }
259:
```

```
260: /////////////////////////////////////////
261: // StopMCI
262: /////////////////////////////////////////
263: BOOL CALLBACK _export StopMCI(void)
264: {
265:   DWORD ErrorNum;
266:   MCI_GENERIC_PARMS Info;
267:
268:   Info.dwCallback = 0;
269:   ErrorNum = mciSendCommand(wDeviceID, MCI_STOP,
270:                               MCI_NOTIFY, DWORD(&Info));
271:   if (ErrorNum)
272:   {
273:     ErrorMsg(ErrorNum, "StopMCI");
274:     return FALSE;
275:   }
276:   return TRUE;
277: }
278:
279:
280: /////////////////////////////////////////
281: // Can a device perform a function such
282: // as record, or pause, etc.
283: /////////////////////////////////////////
284: BOOL CALLBACK _export CanPerformFunction(DWORD Test)
285: {
286:   DWORD ErrorNum, Flags;
287:   MCI_GETDEVCAPS_PARMS Info;
288:
289:   memset(&Info, 0, sizeof(MCI_GENERIC_PARMS));
290:   Info.dwItem = Test;
291:   Flags = MCI_GETDEVCAPS_ITEM;
292:   ErrorNum = mciSendCommand(wDeviceID, MCI_GETDEVCAPS,
293:                               Flags, DWORD(&Info));
294:   if (ErrorNum)
295:   {
296:     ErrorMsg(ErrorNum, "CanPerformFunction");
297:     return FALSE;
298:   }
299:
300:   return Info.dwReturn > 0;
301: }
302:
303: /////////////////////////////////////////
304: // Can this system play "waveaudio", or
305: // "cdaudio" or "sequencer" etc.
306: /////////////////////////////////////////
307: BOOL CALLBACK _export DoesDeviceExistOnSystem(LPSTR DeviceType)
308: {
309:   DWORD ErrorNum, Flags;
310:   MCI_OPEN_PARMS Info;
311:
```

20

Listing 20.9. continued

```
312:    Info.lpstrDeviceType = DeviceType;
313:    Flags = MCI_OPEN_TYPE;
314:    ErrorNum = mciSendCommand(0, MCI_OPEN, Flags, DWORD(&Info));
315:
316:    if (ErrorNum)
317:      return FALSE;
318:    else
319:    {
320:      wDeviceID = Info.wDeviceID;
321:      CloseMCI();
322:      return TRUE;
323:    }
324: }
325:
326: ////////////////////////////////////////////
327: // DoRecord
328: ////////////////////////////////////////////
329: DWORD CALLBACK _export DoRecord(DWORD MMSecs)
330: {
331:   MCI_RECORD_PARMS Info;
332:   DWORD Result, Flags;
333:
334:   Info.dwCallback = (DWORD)PlayWindow;
335:   Info.dwTo = MMSecs;
336:   Flags = MCI_TO | MCI_NOTIFY;
337:   Result = mciSendCommand(wDeviceID, MCI_RECORD,
338:                           Flags, DWORD(&Info));
339:   if (Result)
340:   {
341:     ErrorMsg(Result, "DoRecord");
342:     return FALSE;
343:   }
344:   return TRUE;
345: }
346:
347: ////////////////////////////////////////////
348: // SaveFile
349: ////////////////////////////////////////////
350: BOOL CALLBACK _export SaveFile(char *FileName)
351: {
352:   MCI_SAVE_PARMS MCISave;
353:   DWORD Result, Flags;
354:   char S1[MsgLen];
355:
356:   MCISave.lpfilename = FileName;
357:   Flags = MCI_SAVE_FILE | MCI_WAIT;
358:   Result = mciSendCommand(wDeviceID, MCI_SAVE,
359:                           Flags, DWORD(&MCISave));
360:   if (Result)
```

```
361:    {
362:      ErrorMsg(Result, "SaveFile");
363:      return FALSE;
364:    }
365:    return TRUE;
366: }
```

Listing 20.10 shows the PlayInfo header file.

Type   **Listing 20.10. PLAYINFO.H.**

```
1: /////////////////////////////////////
2: // Program: PLAYINFO.H
3: // Programmer: Charlie Calvert
4: // Date: August 6, 1993
5: // Description: DLL Module from Harmony program
6: /////////////////////////////////////
7:
8: // This file shows how to use extern "C", which is needed to
9: // link a DLL into a Pascal or straight C programs.
10:
11: #define MsgLen 200
12:
13: static HWND PlayWindow;
14: static WORD wDeviceID;
15:
16: extern "C" {
17: BOOL CALLBACK _export CloseMCI(void);
18: BOOL CALLBACK _export ErrorMsg(DWORD Error, LPSTR CallingFunc);
19: WORD CALLBACK _export GetDeviceID(void);
20: LPSTR CALLBACK _export GetInfo(LPSTR S);
21: DWORD CALLBACK _export GetLen(void);
22: DWORD CALLBACK _export GetLocation(void);
23: DWORD CALLBACK _export GetMode(void);
24: BOOL CALLBACK _export OpenMCI(HWND PWindow,
25:                              LPSTR FileName, LPSTR DeviceType);
26: BOOL CALLBACK _export PauseMCI(void);
27: BOOL CALLBACK _export PlayMCI(void);
28: BOOL CALLBACK _export SetTimeFormatMs(void);
29: BOOL CALLBACK _export StopMCI(void);
30: BOOL CALLBACK _export DoesDeviceExistOnSystem(
                                 LPSTR DeviceType);
31: DWORD CALLBACK _export DoRecord(DWORD MMSecs);
32: BOOL CALLBACK _export SaveFile(char *FileName);
33: }
```

20

Listing 20.11 shows the PlayInfo definition file.

 Listing 20.11. PLAYINFO.DEF.

```
1: ; PLAYINFO.DEF
2:
3: LIBRARY        PlayInfo
4: DESCRIPTION    'PlayInfo (C) 1993 Charlie Calvert'
5: EXETYPE        WINDOWS
6: CODE           PRELOAD MOVEABLE DISCARDABLE
7: DATA           PRELOAD MOVEABLE SINGLE
8: HEAPSIZE  5200
```

Listing 20.12 shows the CDInfo source file.

 Listing 20.12. CDINFO.CPP.

```
1: /////////////////////////////////////////
2: // Program: CDINFO.CPP
3: // Programmer: Charlie Calvert
4: // Date: August 6, 1993
5: // Description: DLL Module from Harmony program
6: /////////////////////////////////////////
7:
8: #define STRICT
9: #include <windows.h>
10: #include <windowsx.h>
11: #include <mmsystem.h>
12: #include <stdio.h>
13: #include <string.h>
14: #pragma warning (disable : 4068)
15:
16: static HWND PlayWindow;
17: static WORD wDeviceID;
18: #define MsgLen 200
19:
20:
21: /////////////////////////////////////////
22: // LibMain
23: /////////////////////////////////////////
24: #pragma argsused
25: int CALLBACK LibMain(HINSTANCE hInstance, WORD wDataSeg,
26:                      WORD wHeapSize, LPSTR lpszCmdLine)
27: {
28:    if (wHeapSize > 0)
29:        UnlockData(0);
30:
31:    return 1;
```

```
32: }
33:
34: /////////////////////////////////////////
35: // Wep
36: /////////////////////////////////////////
37: #pragma argsused
38: int CALLBACK WEP (int nParameter)
39: {
40:   return 1;
41: }
42:
43: /////////////////////////////////////////
44: // GetErrorMessage
45: /////////////////////////////////////////
46: LPSTR GetErrorMessage(DWORD RC, LPSTR S)
47: {
48:   if (!mciGetErrorString(RC, S, MsgLen))
49:     strcpy(S, "No message available");
50:   return S;
51: }
52:
53: /////////////////////////////////////////
54: // ErrorMsg
55: /////////////////////////////////////////
56: BOOL CALLBACK _export ErrorMsg(DWORD Error,
57:                                 LPSTR CallingFunc)
58: {
59:   char S[MsgLen + 50];
60:   char S1[MsgLen];
61:
62:   GetErrorMessage(Error, S1);
63:   sprintf(S, "Calling Func: %s\nReturn Code: %ld\n %s",
64:           CallingFunc, Error, S1);
65:   if (Error)
66:   {
67:     MessageBox(0, S, "Information",
68:               MB_OK | MB_ICONINFORMATION);
69:     return FALSE;
70:   }
71:   return TRUE;
72: }
73:
74: /////////////////////////////////////////
75: // OpenCD
76: /////////////////////////////////////////
77: BOOL CALLBACK _export OpenCD(HWND PWindow)
78: {
79:   MCI_OPEN_PARMS Info;
80:   DWORD Result, Flags;
81:
82:   memset(&Info, 0, sizeof(MCI_OPEN_PARMS));
```

continues

Listing 20.12. continued

```
 83:    Info.dwCallback = DWORD(PWindow);
 84:    Info.lpstrDeviceType =
 85:                    MAKEINTRESOURCE(MCI_DEVTYPE_CD_AUDIO);
 86:    Flags = MCI_OPEN_TYPE | MCI_OPEN_TYPE_ID;
 87:    Result = mciSendCommand(0, MCI_OPEN, Flags, DWORD(&Info));
 88:
 89:    wDeviceID = Info.wDeviceID;
 90:
 91:    if (Result)
 92:    {
 93:      ErrorMsg(Result, "OpenCD");
 94:      return FALSE;
 95:    }
 96:    return TRUE;
 97: }
 98:
 99: ////////////////////////////////////////////
100: // CloseCDMCI
101: ////////////////////////////////////////////
102: BOOL CALLBACK _export CloseCDMCI(void)
103: {
104:    DWORD ErrorNum;
105:    MCI_GENERIC_PARMS Info;
106:
107:    memset(&Info, 0, sizeof(MCI_GENERIC_PARMS));
108:    ErrorNum = mciSendCommand(wDeviceID, MCI_CLOSE,
109:                        MCI_NOTIFY, DWORD(&Info));
110:    if (ErrorNum)
111:    {
112:      ErrorMsg(ErrorNum, "CloseCDMCI");
113:      return FALSE;
114:    }
115:    return TRUE;
116: }
117:
118: ////////////////////////////////////////////
119: // StopCDMCI
120: ////////////////////////////////////////////
121: BOOL CALLBACK _export StopCDMCI(void)
122: {
123:    DWORD ErrorNum;
124:    MCI_GENERIC_PARMS Info;
125:
126:    Info.dwCallback = 0;
127:    ErrorNum = mciSendCommand(wDeviceID, MCI_STOP,
128:                        MCI_NOTIFY, DWORD(&Info));
129:    if (ErrorNum)
130:    {
131:      ErrorMsg(ErrorNum, "StopCDMCI");
```

```
132:      return FALSE;
133:    }
134:    return TRUE;
135: }
136:
137: ///////////////////////////////////////
138: // PauseCDMCI
139: ///////////////////////////////////////
140: BOOL CALLBACK _export PauseCDMCI(void)
141: {
142:    MCI_GENERIC_PARMS Info;
143:    DWORD ErrorNum;
144:    char S1[MsgLen];
145:
146:    memset(&Info, 0, sizeof(MCI_GENERIC_PARMS));
147:    ErrorNum = mciSendCommand(wDeviceID, MCI_PAUSE,
148:                              0, DWORD(&Info));
149:    if (ErrorNum)
150:    {
151:      ErrorMsg(ErrorNum, "PauseCDMCI");
152:      return FALSE;
153:    }
154:    return TRUE;
155: }
156:
157: ///////////////////////////////////////
158: // SetTMSFasFormat
159: ///////////////////////////////////////
160: void CALLBACK _export SetTMSFasFormat(void)
161: {
162:    MCI_SET_PARMS Info;
163:    DWORD Result;
164:
165:    Info.dwCallback = 0;
166:    Info.dwTimeFormat = MCI_FORMAT_TMSF;
167:    Info.dwAudio = 0;
168:
169:    Result = mciSendCommand(wDeviceID, MCI_SET,
170:                            MCI_SET_TIME_FORMAT, DWORD(&Info));
171:
172:    if (Result)
173:      ErrorMsg(Result, "SetTMSFasFormat");
174: }
175:
176: ///////////////////////////////////////
177: // PlayCDOneTrack
178: ///////////////////////////////////////
179: void CALLBACK _export PlayCDOneTrack(BYTE StartTrack)
180: {
181:    MCI_PLAY_PARMS Info;
182:    DWORD Flags, Result;
```

continues

Listing 20.12. continued

```
183:
184:    memset(&Info, 0, sizeof(MCI_PLAY_PARMS));
185:    Info.dwFrom = MCI_MAKE_TMSF(StartTrack,0,0,0);
186:
187:    Flags = MCI_FROM | MCI_NOTIFY;
188:    Result = mciSendCommand(wDeviceID, MCI_PLAY,
189:                            Flags, DWORD(&Info));
190:
191:    if (Result)
192:      ErrorMsg(Result, "PlayCDOneTrack");
193: }
194:
195: //////////////////////////////////////////
196: // PlayMCICD
197: //////////////////////////////////////////
198: void CALLBACK _export PlayMciCD(BYTE StartTrack, BYTE EndTrack)
199: {
200:    MCI_PLAY_PARMS Info;
201:    DWORD Flags, Result;
202:    char S1[MsgLen];
203:
204:    memset(&Info, 0, sizeof(MCI_PLAY_PARMS));
205:    Info.dwFrom = MCI_MAKE_TMSF(StartTrack,0,0,0);
206:    Info.dwTo   = MCI_MAKE_TMSF(EndTrack,  0,0,0);
207:
208:    Flags = MCI_FROM | MCI_TO | MCI_NOTIFY;
209:    Result = mciSendCommand(wDeviceID, MCI_PLAY,
210:                            Flags, DWORD(&Info));
211:
212:    if (Result) ErrorMsg(Result, "PlayCDMCI");
213: }
214:
215: //////////////////////////////////////////
216: // GetCDNumTracks
217: //////////////////////////////////////////
218: DWORD CALLBACK _export GetCDNumTracks(void)
219: {
220:    MCI_STATUS_PARMS Info;
221:    DWORD Result;
222:
223:
224:    Info.dwCallback = 0;
225:    Info.dwReturn   = 0;
226:    Info.dwItem     = MCI_STATUS_NUMBER_OF_TRACKS;
227:    Info.dwTrack    = 0;
228:    Result = mciSendCommand(wDeviceID, MCI_STATUS,
229:                       MCI_STATUS_ITEM, DWORD(&Info));
230:    if (Result)
231:    {
232:      ErrorMsg(Result, "GetCDNumTracks");
```

```
233:     return -1;
234:   }
235:
236:   return Info.dwReturn;
237: }
238:
239: ///////////////////////////////////////////
240: // GetCDTrackLength
241: ///////////////////////////////////////////
242: void CALLBACK _export GetCDTrackLength(DWORD TrackNum,
243:                        BYTE *Min, BYTE *Sec, BYTE *Frame)
244: {
245:   MCI_STATUS_PARMS Info;
246:   DWORD Result, MSF;
247:   char MessageText[MsgLen];
248:
249:   memset(&Info, 0, sizeof(MCI_STATUS_PARMS));
250:   Info.dwTrack    = TrackNum;
251:   Info.dwItem     = MCI_STATUS_LENGTH;
252:
253:   Result = mciSendCommand(wDeviceID, MCI_STATUS,
254:                        MCI_STATUS_ITEM | MCI_TRACK,
255:                        DWORD(&Info));
256:
257:   if (Result)
258:   {
259:     ErrorMsg(Result, "GetCDTrackLength");
260:     return;
261:   }
262:
263:   MSF =Info.dwReturn;
264:
265:   *Min = MCI_MSF_MINUTE(MSF);
266:   *Sec = MCI_MSF_SECOND(MSF);
267:   *Frame = MCI_MSF_FRAME(MSF);
268: }
269:
270: ///////////////////////////////////////////
271: // GetLengthofEachTrack
272: ///////////////////////////////////////////
273: void CALLBACK _export GetLengthOfEachTrack(DWORD TrackNum,
                                           BYTE *Min, BYTE *Sec,
274:                                           BYTE *Frame)
275: {
276:   MCI_STATUS_PARMS Info;
277:   DWORD Result, Flags, MSF;
278:
279:   memset(&Info, 0, sizeof(MCI_STATUS_PARMS));
280:   Info.dwTrack = TrackNum;
281:   Info.dwItem = MCI_STATUS_LENGTH;
282:   Flags = MCI_STATUS_ITEM | MCI_TRACK;
283:   Result = mciSendCommand(wDeviceID, MCI_STATUS,
```

Listing 20.12. continued

```
284:                                  Flags, DWORD(&Info));
285:
286:    if (Result)
287:    {
288:      ErrorMsg(Result, "GetLengthOfEachTrack");
289:      return;
290:    }
291:
292:    MSF = Info.dwReturn;
293:    *Min = MCI_MSF_MINUTE(MSF);
294:    *Sec = MCI_MSF_SECOND(MSF);
295:    *Frame = MCI_MSF_FRAME(MSF);
296: }
297:
298: /////////////////////////////////////////
299: // GetCurrentCDTrack
300: /////////////////////////////////////////
301: DWORD CALLBACK _export GetCurrentCDTrack(void)
302: {
303:    MCI_STATUS_PARMS Info;
304:    DWORD Result;
305:
306:    memset(&Info, 0, sizeof(MCI_STATUS_PARMS));
307:    Info.dwItem     = MCI_STATUS_CURRENT_TRACK;
308:
309:    Result = mciSendCommand(wDeviceID, MCI_STATUS,
310:                         MCI_STATUS_ITEM, DWORD(&Info));
311:
312:    if (Result)
313:    {
314:      ErrorMsg(Result, "GetCurrentCDTrack");
315:      return FALSE;
316:    }
317:    return Info.dwReturn;
318: }
319:
320: /////////////////////////////////////////
321: // HasDiskInserted
322: /////////////////////////////////////////
323: BOOL CALLBACK _export HasDiskInserted(void)
324: {
325:    MCI_STATUS_PARMS Info;
326:    DWORD Flags, Result;
327:
328:    memset(&Info, 0, sizeof(MCI_STATUS_PARMS));
329:    Info.dwItem = MCI_STATUS_MEDIA_PRESENT;
330:
331:    Flags = MCI_STATUS_ITEM;
```

```
332:    Result=mciSendCommand(wDeviceID, MCI_STATUS,
333:                          Flags, DWORD(&Info));
334:
335:    if (Result)
336:    {
337:      ErrorMsg(Result, "HasDiskInserted");
338:      return FALSE;
339:    }
340:
341:    return Info.dwReturn > 0;
342: }
343:
344: /////////////////////////////////////////
345: // EjectCD
346: /////////////////////////////////////////
347: void CALLBACK _export EjectCD(void)
348: {
349:    MCI_SET_PARMS Info;
350:    DWORD Flags, Result;
351:
352:    memset(&Info, 0, sizeof(MCI_SET_PARMS));
353:    Flags = MCI_SET_DOOR_OPEN;
354:    Result = mciSendCommand( wDeviceID, MCI_SET,
355:                          Flags, DWORD(&Info));
356:    if (Result)
357:      ErrorMsg(Result, "EjectCD");
358: }
359:
360: /////////////////////////////////////////
361: // GetCDLocation
362: /////////////////////////////////////////
363: DWORD CALLBACK _export GetCDLocation(void)
364: {
365:    MCI_STATUS_PARMS Info;
366:    DWORD Flags, ErrorNum;
367:
368:    Info.dwItem = MCI_STATUS_POSITION;
369:    Flags = MCI_STATUS_ITEM;
370:    ErrorNum = mciSendCommand(wDeviceID, MCI_STATUS,
371:                          Flags, DWORD(&Info));
372:    if (ErrorNum)
373:    {
374:      ErrorMsg(ErrorNum, "GetLocation");
375:      return -1;
376:    }
377:    return Info.dwReturn;
378: }
```

20

Listing 20.13 shows the CDInfo header file.

    Listing 20.13. CDINFO.H.

```
 1: ////////////////////////////////////////
 2: // Program: CDINFO.H
 3: // Programmer: Charlie Calvert
 4: // Date: August 6, 1993
 5: // Description: DLL Module from Harmony program
 6: ////////////////////////////////////////
 7: BOOL CALLBACK _export OpenCD(HWND PWindow);
 8: BOOL CALLBACK _export CloseCDMCI(void);
 9: BOOL CALLBACK _export PauseCDMCI(void);
10: void CALLBACK _export PlayMciCD(BYTE StartTrack,
11:                                BYTE EndTrack);
12: void CALLBACK _export PlayCDOneTrack(BYTE StartTrack);
13: void CALLBACK _export SetTMSFasFormat(void);
14: DWORD CALLBACK _export GetCDNumTracks(void);
15: void CALLBACK _export GetCDTrackLength(DWORD TrackNum,
16:                      BYTE *Min, BYTE *Sec, BYTE *Frame);
17: DWORD CALLBACK _export GetCurrentCDTrack(void);
18: BOOL CALLBACK _export HasDiskInserted(void);
19: void CALLBACK _export EjectCD(void);
20: BOOL CALLBACK _export StopCDMCI(void);
21: DWORD CALLBACK _export GetCDLocation(void);
```

Listing 20.14 shows the CDInfo definition file.

    Listing 20.14. CDINFO.DEF.

```
1: LIBRARY CDInfo
2:
3: DESCRIPTION 'CDInfo (C) 1993 Charlie Calvert'
4: EXETYPE WINDOWS
5: CODE PRELOAD MOVEABLE DISCARDABLE
6: DATA PRELOAD MOVEABLE SINGLE
7: HEAPSIZE 5120
```

Listing 20.15 shows the Borland makefile for the Harmony program.

Listing 20.15. HARMONY.MAK (Borland).

```
1: # HARMONY.MAK
2:
3: APPNAME = Harmony
4: PATHS = -IC:\BC\INCLUDE -LC:\BC\LIB
5: FLAGS = -H -ml -R -2 -W -v -w4 -vi -wpro -weas -wpre
```

```
 6: DLLFLAGS = -ml -R -WDE -2 -v  -wpro -weas -wpre
 7: LIBS = PlayInfo.lib CDInfo.lib
 8: OBJS = Harmony.obj WaveMidi.obj CDUtil.obj
 9:
10: # goal
11: ALL: PlayInfo.dll CDInfo.dll $(APPNAME).exe
12:
13: # link EXES
14: $(APPNAME).exe: $(OBJS) $(APPNAME).def $(LIBS) $(APPNAME).res
15:   bcc $(FLAGS) $(PATHS) $(OBJS) $(LIBS)
16:   rc $(APPNAME).res
17:
18: # link DLLS
19: playinfo.dll: playinfo.obj playinfo.def
20:   bcc $(DLLFLAGS) $(PATHS) playinfo.obj
21:
22: cdinfo.dll: cdinfo.obj cdinfo.def
23:   bcc $(DLLFLAGS) $(PATHS) cdinfo.obj
24:
25: # compile
26: $(APPNAME).obj: $(APPNAME).cpp
27:   bcc -c $(FLAGS) $(PATHS) $(APPNAME).cpp
28:
29: # compile
30: CDUtils.obj: CDUtils.cpp
31:   bcc -c $(FLAGS) $(PATHS) CDUtils.cpp
32:
33: # compile
34: WaveMidi.obj: WaveMidi.cpp
35:   bcc -c $(FLAGS) $(PATHS) WaveMidi.cpp
36:
37: # compile
38: .cpp.obj:
39:   bcc -c $(DLLFLAGS) $(PATHS) { $< }
40:
41: # resource
42: .rc.res:
43:   brc -r $(PATHS) { $< }
44:
45: # libraries
46: .dll.lib:
47:   implib $&.lib $&.dll
```

Listing 20.16 shows the Microsoft makefile for Harmony.

Type   ## Listing 20.16. HARMONY.MAK (Microsoft).

```
1: # HARMONY.MAK
2:
3: APPNAME = Harmony
```

20

Listing 20.16. continued

```
 4: DLLCOMPFLAGS = -c -ALw -Gsw -Ow -W2 -Zp
 5: DLLLINKFLAGS = /align:16, NUL, /nod ldllcew libw mmsystem
 6: COMPFLAGS = -c -Gsw -Ow -W3 -AL -Zp
 7: LINKFLAGS = /align:16, NUL, /nod llibcew libw
 8: OBJS = Harmony.obj WaveMidi.obj CDUtil.obj
 9: LIBS = PlayInfo.lib CDInfo.lib
10:
11: # goal
12: ALL: $(APPNAME).exe PlayInfo.dll CDInfo.dll
13:
14: # link EXES
15: $(APPNAME).exe: $(OBJS) $(APPNAME).def $(APPNAME).res $(LIBS)
16:    link $(OBJS), $(LINKFLAGS) $(LIBS) CommDlg, $(APPNAME)
17:    rc $(APPNAME).res
18:
19: # link DLLS
20: playinfo.dll: playinfo.obj playinfo.def
21:    link playinfo, playinfo.dll $(DLLLINKFLAGS), playinfo
22:
23: cdinfo.dll: cdinfo.obj cdinfo.def
24:    link cdinfo, cdinfo.dll $(DLLLINKFLAGS), cdinfo
25:
26: # compile
27: $(APPNAME).obj: $(APPNAME).cpp
28:    cl $(COMPFLAGS) $(APPNAME).cpp
29:
30: # compile
31: CDUtils.obj: CDUtils.cpp
32:    cl $(COMPFLAGS) CDUtils.cpp
33:
34: # compile
35: WaveMidi.obj: WaveMidi.cpp
36:    cl $(COMPFLAGS) WaveMidi.cpp
37:
38: # compile
39: .cpp.obj:
40:    cl $(DLLCOMPFLAGS) $(PATHS) { $< }
41:
42: # resource
43: harmony.res: harmony.rc
44:    rc -r harmony.rc
45:
46: # libraries
47: playinfo.lib: playinfo.dll
48:    implib playinfo.lib playinfo.dll
49:
50: cdinfo.lib: cdinfo.dll
51:    implib cdinfo.lib cdinfo.dll
```

Figure 20.2 shows the Harmony program.

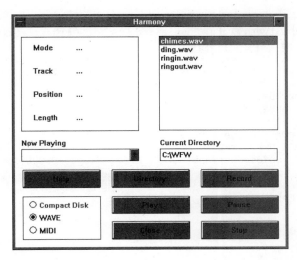

Figure 20.2. *The Harmony program enables the user to play MIDI files, WAVE files, and CDs.*

The Harmony program is divided into two major sections: a main file and a set of DLLs. Specifically, there are two DLLs, one containing the MCI code for playing WAV and MIDI files (PLAYINFO.DLL), and one containing the MCI code for playing CDs (CDINFO.DLL).

The section that explains DLLs lies near the end of this chapter. At this point I can only say that DLLs are a lot like EXE Files except that they use a function called `LibMain` in lieu of the `WinMain` Function. In addition, Functions in DLLs that are called from the main progtam are declared using the `CALLBACK` and `export` keywords:

```
BOOL CALLBACK _export CloseMCI(void);
```

Remember that Harmony uses the same code to play, close, stop, pause, and get the length (in milliseconds) of both MIDI and WAVE files.

The other half of the program, the part that is not a DLL, is written in standard Windows code. It pops up a main window cum dialog, which enables the user to play files (see Figure 20.2). Code used for playing MIDI, WAVE, and CD files is kept in the HARMONY.CPP module; code specific to CD files is kept in CDUTIL.CPP, and code specific to WAVE or MIDI files is kept in WAVEMIDI.CPP.

20

On Startup

The first MCI specific code used in Harmony checks to see if the current system supports CD files. If it doesn't, the radio button, which switches the program into CD mode, is disabled with a call to EnableWindow. The code that checks for CD capabilities is located in PLAYINFO.CPP:

```
BOOL CALLBACK _export DoesDeviceExistOnSystem(LPSTR DeviceType)
{
  DWORD ErrorNum, Flags;
  MCI_OPEN_PARMS Info;

  Info.lpstrDeviceType = DeviceType;
  Flags = MCI_OPEN_TYPE;
  ErrorNum = mciSendCommand(0, MCI_OPEN, Flags, DWORD(&Info));

  if (ErrorNum)
    return FALSE;
  else
  {
    wDeviceID = Info.wDeviceID;
    CloseMCI();
    return TRUE;
  }
}
```

As you can see, this code first checks to see if it can open a CD driver. If that code fails, the function returns false. Otherwise, it calls CloseMCI so the device is not left open while the program runs. Notice that the DLL carefully saves the device ID in a global variable before calling CloseMCI. If it did not do this, Windows would complain, and the call would fail.

The end result of these activities is that the user is informed immediately if CD capabilities are available. This same technique could be used to query Windows about WAVE or MIDI files, or any other device.

Note: It's possible to test specifically to see if the Windows MIDI mapper is installed. This call might be worth making because the MIDI drivers for Windows often cause trouble. If you have trouble getting the MIDI services to work, you might try tweaking the Drivers and MIDI Mapper tools in the Control Panel (Figure 20.3). In addition, it sometimes helps to literally rearrange the order in which the MIDI drivers are listed in the

> "drivers" and "mci" section of the SYSTEM.INI FILE. Furthermore, you can use the Media Player utility that comes with Windows to test whether your code, or the system, is causing trouble.

Figure 20.3 shows the driver and MIDI Mapper tools in the Control Panel.

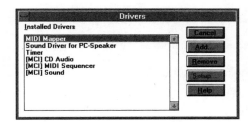

Figure 20.3. *Using the drivers utility from the Control Panel to initialize multimedia capabilities.*

General MCI Strategies

The Harmony program checks to see if the user's attempts to open a device and/or file are successful. If either or both of these steps fail, the program exits as gracefully as possible. Because of the mciGetErrorString function, it is easy for you to post an appropriate error message for the user.

After opening up the file, it's a good idea to report on its length and format before playing it. While the user is listening to the file, Harmony reports on the file's progress, which is particularly important when playing CD or MIDI files (that can last for several minutes or longer).

When the file stops playing, or when the user aborts the play, the program closes the device before exiting. At all times, Harmony checks the results of particular calls so that it responds appropriately if an error occurs. This process needs to be taken considerably further in programs that are aimed at the general public, rather than a group of programmers.

20

Details

At this point, all that remains to be covered are a few details that might cause confusion to the reader. In particular, you should notice the function called `SetTimeFormatMS`:

```
BOOL CALLBACK _export SetTimeFormatMs(void)
{
  MCI_SET_PARMS Info;
  DWORD ErrorNum, Flags;

  Info.dwTimeFormat = MCI_FORMAT_MILLISECONDS;
  Flags = MCI_SET_TIME_FORMAT;
  ErrorNum = mciSendCommand(wDeviceID, MCI_SET,
                            Flags, DWORD(&Info));
  if (ErrorNum)
  {
    ErrorMsg(ErrorNum, "SetTimeFormatMS");
    return FALSE;
  }
  return TRUE;
}
```

This code uses the `MCI_SET_PARMS` struct:

```
typedef struct  {
    DWORD dwCallback;
    DWORD dwTimeFormat;
    DWORD dwAudio;
} MCI_SET_PARMS;
```

The key member of this structure is `dwTimeFormat`, which is used to select a particular time format. The Harmony program uses milliseconds to measure the length of WAVE and MIDI files, and seconds and minutes for CD files.

Notice that `SetTimeFormatMS` receives `MCI_SET_TIME_FORMAT` in the flag parameter. Other messages I could have passed in its stead include `MCI_SET_DOOR_CLOSED` and `MCI_SET_DOOR_OPEN`. This latter flag can be used to eject a CD from a CD player, as shown in CDINFO.CPP.

It might not seem intuitively obvious to search out the `MCI_SET` message as the place to issue the command to eject a cassette. This highlights one possible criticism of the MCI command interface, namely that it lacks some of the intuitive feel of an API, which might feature a command such as EjectCD.

One final point involves the posting of `MM_NOTIFY` messages to the dialog objects in the main program. These messages are routed to standard Windows message handler functions, such as this one quoted in part from HARMONY.CPP:

```
void Harmony_OnMCINotify(HWND hwnd, UINT status, int DeviceID)
{
  char S[100];

  if (State == ERROR_OCCURED)
    return;

  switch (status)
  {
    case MCI_NOTIFY_ABORTED:
      strcpy(S, "Aborted");
      break;

    ... // addition code

    case MCI_NOTIFY_SUPERSEDED:
      strcpy(S, "Superseded");
      break;

  }
  SetWindowText(GetDlgItem(hwnd, ID_MODE), S);
}
```

To fully understand the Harmony_OnMCINotify method, you have to understand that Harmony receives a message whenever anything important happens to the file being played. For instance, if the file ends, or if the user presses the Pause button, an MM_NOTIFY message is posted.

Note: To fill in the gaps between MM_NOTIFY messages, Harmony uses a timer to check on the status of the device being played. For instance, if a MIDI file is being played, the timer enables you to check up on its progress at set intervals. In this particular program, the intervals are 10 milliseconds in duration.

When the file currently being played finishes, or when the user asks to abort the play, the proper response is to close the device. Of course, this is not what you want to do if the user has simply paused the file. To distinguish between these two events, the harmony program maintains a variable called State, which can be set to one of the following values:

```
// States
#define PAUSED 1
#define PLAYING 2
#define STOPPED 3
#define CLOSED 4
```

```
#define OPENED 6
#define RECORDING 7
#define ERROR_OCCURED 8
```

By setting the `State` variable, the program can always know what is taking place, and it can respond appropriately. If you want, you can handle this same task with the `MCI_STATUS` message.

Introducing DLLs

DLLs are very similar in concept to DOS libraries, or even to a standard .OBJ file. The purpose of a DLL is to give programmers a place to store routines that can be called by one or more programs. Unlike .OBJ files or .LIB files, the routines stored in a DLL are linked at runtime. During compilation and linking, a program is merely informed of the presence of a DLL that contains the routines the program needs. After the program is loaded, these routines are linked in dynamically.

All DLLs sport a function called `LibMain`, which has a rough correspondence with `WinMain`, and a function called `WEP`, which has at least a remote relationship to a `Cls_OnDestroy` function.

Syntax

The *LibMain* Function

```
int FAR PASCAL LibMain (HINSTANCE, WORD, WORD, LPSTR);
```

HINSTANCE hInstance	Contains instance handle of the DLL
WORD wDataSeg	The data segment (DS) for the DLL
WORD cbHeapSize	The size of the local heap
LPSTR lpCmdLine	The command line passed to the DLL

`LibMain` is called automatically when a DLL is loaded into memory. You must supply this routine. If it doesn't exist, your file will not compile.

Example:

```
int CALLBACK LibMain(HINSTANCE hInstance, WORD wDataSeg,
                     WORD wHeapSize, LPSTR lpszCmdLine)
{
  if (wHeapSize > 0)
      UnlockData(0);

  return 1;
}
```

Just before a DLL is unloaded from memory, Windows calls the `WEP` routine. As a result, this is a good place to deallocate any memory allocated for the DLL. Borland

automatically supplies a WEP for all DLLs, but users of the Microsoft compiler should be sure to explicitly include one.

Exporting a Function from a DLL

It is now standard practice for programmers to declare the routines that they want to export from a DLL in the following manner:

```
DWORD CALLBACK _export GetLocation(void)
```

The key elements of this declaration are the use of the words CALLBACK and _export. As you already know, CALLBACK tells the compiler that the function is declared FAR, and that it uses the Pascal calling convention. The _export keyword is also familiar to you, because you've used it with window procedures and callbacks.

Once you have declared a DLL function in this manner, you need to perform two additional steps in order to call it from your program. The first step is to include a header file in your project containing the declarations of the files you want to link into your program. The second step is to run a utility called ImpLib on the DLL containing the functions you want to call.

ImpLib is run from the DOS prompt. It expects two parameters. The first is the name of the library you want to create, and the second is the name of the DLL in question:

```
ImpLib MyFuncs.lib MyFuncs.dll
```

The end result is a file called MYFUNCS.LIB, which you can link into your program just as you would any other library. The difference here, however, is that this library file does not contain the actual code for the functions you want to use. Instead, it simply refers your program to the DLL, which will be linked in at runtime.

Another Borland file, called IMPLIPW, runs from inside of Windows. It is shown in Figure 20.4.

> **Note:** It's important to understand that you need to compile a DLL with different settings than you use for the normal portions of your program. If you are using the Borland or Microsoft IDEs, you can simply use the supplied menus to automatically obtain these settings, as described in your documentation. If you are using a makefile, you should use the settings shown in HARMONY.MAK.

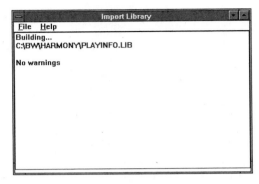

Figure 20.4. *The IMPLIBW.EXE program is easier to use than IMPLIB.EXE, and you can use it from inside Windows.*

DLLs and Memory

If you compare the DEF file for the CDInfo DLL with the other DEF files used in this book you will see that it:

- [ ] Uses the LIBRARY statement instead of the NAME statement

- [ ] Declares its DATA as single rather than multiple

- [ ] Does not have a STUB statement

- [ ] Doesn't have a STACKSIZE statement

For ready comparison, here is the CDINFO.DEF file:

```
LIBRARY CDInfo

DESCRIPTION 'CDInfo (C) 1993 Charlie Calvert'
EXETYPE WINDOWS
CODE   PRELOAD MOVEABLE DISCARDABLE
DATA   PRELOAD MOVEABLE SINGLE
HEAPSIZE 5120
```

The key points here are that the DATA segment for a DLL is single (at least under DOS Windows), because only one copy of a DLL is loaded into memory at a time. Secondly, the DLL has no stack. This means that it uses the stack of the program that calls it! This is a factor you must consider when you call a DLL. Note also that you sometimes can devise methods of increasing the data space available to your program by moving variables out of your local DGROUP and into a DLL.

The final point to make in this quick overview of DLLs is that it is possible to load a DLL into memory dynamically at runtime by calling LoadLibrary. Conversely, you can unload the library by calling FreeLibrary. If you are using this technique, you shouldn't link an ImpLib created LIB file into your program. Instead, you should count on GetProcAddress to create a pointer to the function. When using this technique, you sometimes need to know the index of a function. You'll find out how to obtain that index in the next section.

The difference between using ImpLib and LoadLibrary is that the first technique loads the DLL into memory when your program is loaded, and unloads it when your program ends. If you use LoadLibrary and FreeLibrary, you can load and unload the DLL dynamically.

Pulling Back the Veil from DLLs

Not only will DLLs enable you to store reusable code outside of your main executable, they also reveal the technique used for storing all the Windows API routines. Functions, such as CreateWindow or BitBlt, are actually stored in DLLs called by names like USER.EXE, GDI.EXE, and KRNL386.EXE. This means you have been using DLLs since (literally) Day 1. The only difference is that now you are writing some of your own.

DLLs are great, but sometimes they can appear as black boxes that stubbornly refuse to reveal their secrets. One way to find out about the contents of a DLL is to run a Borland program called ImpDef that ships with the Borland compiler. This will tell you what functions are in a DLL, and what index is associated with each function. The syntax to ImpDef is just like the syntax for ImpLib, except you specify a text file to hold the output in the second parameter.

```
impdef MyDLL.txt MyDLL.dll
```

The following command line will echo the output to the console, as shown in Figure 20.5.

```
impdef con MyDLL.dll
```

Note: When exporting functions from a DLL, you have to decide whether or not to use name mangling. Figure 20.5 shows one function that uses name mangling, whereas the others are exported as they would be from a standard C or Pascal compiler. The name mangling, which

> C++ compilers use by default, will make it very difficult for you to link your DLL into a Pascal or straight C program. The header file for CDINFO.CPP leaves name mangling turned on; PLAYINFO.H shows how to turn it off by using extern "C." One way to find out whether a DLL or other binary file uses name mangling is with TDump or ExeHdr.

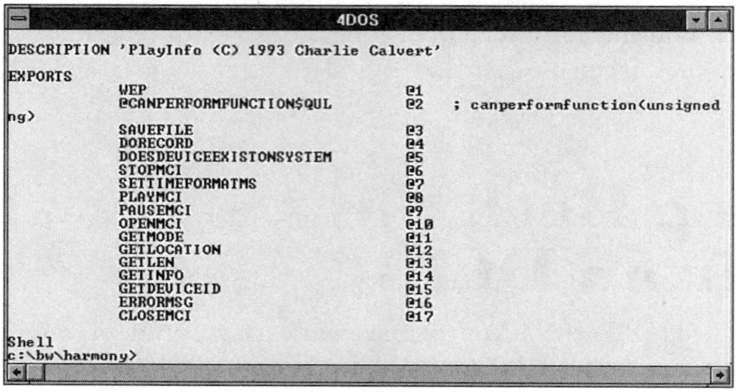

Figure 20.5. *The results of running ImpDef on PLAYINFO.DLL. In this example,* CanPerformFunction *has name mangling, whereas the others use* extern C.

An excellent way to find out what is happening inside a DLL is to use the Microsoft ExeHdr utility or the TDump utility from Borland. If you run TDump on a DLL or executable, you can learn all about its structure, as well as which functions it exports or imports.

Sooner or later, all good Windows programmers spend an afternoon or evening running ExeHdr or TDump on KRNL386.EXE, GDI.EXE, and USER.EXE. The output you see will be voluminous, but it will serve to lift back the veil on the inner workings of Windows. An added bonus is that this technique reveals the existence of numerous undocumented functions, as shown in this excerpt from KRNL386.EXE:

```
Name: GETPROCADDRESS          Entry:    50
Name: _HWRITE                 Entry:   350
Name: __A000H                 Entry:   174
Name: LSTRLEN                 Entry:    90
Name: DIRECTRESALLOC          Entry:   168
Name: GETSYSTEMDIRECTORY      Entry:   135
Name: BUNNY_351               Entry:   351
Name: GETTEMPFILENAME         Entry:    97
Name: GETWINFLAGS             Entry:   132
Name: __B000H                 Entry:   181
```

That's all I'm going to say about DLLs in this book. The central point to remember is that if you stick with ImpLib, CALLBACK, and _export, DLLs can be very flexible and extremely easy to use.

Dialog Windows

The other technique you need to master before you can understand the Harmony program is the use of a dialog as the main window. This is a suprisingly simple little trick that has three key steps.

The first step is that you need to use CreateDialog, instead of CreateWindow, when launching the program's main window:

```
HWND hwnd = CreateDialog(hInst, szAppName, 0, NULL);
```

You've seen this routine before; the only difference is that this time you don't pass in the handle to a parent, because this dialog does not have a parent.

The second step involves setting the window extra bytes to a constant called DLGWINDOWEXTRA:

```
WndClass.cbWndExtra    = DLGWINDOWEXTRA;
```

This constant, when declared in WINDOWS.H, looks like this:

```
/* cbWndExtra needed by dialog manager for dialog classes */
#define DLGWINDOWEXTRA  30
```

The third and final step necessary to create a dialog is to use the CLASS statement in the dialog definition:

```
Harmony DIALOG 18, 23; 246, 208
STYLE DS_MODALFRAME ¦ WS_OVERLAPPED ¦ WS_CAPTION ¦ WS_SYSMENU
CLASS "Harmony"
CAPTION "Harmony"
BEGIN
        CONTROL "", ID_GROUP, "BUTTON", BS_GROUPBOX ¦
          WS_CHILD ¦ WS_VISIBLE, 6, 5, 107, 93

... // additional code
```

Note that the CLASS name Harmony matches up with the contents of the szAppName parameter passed to CreateDialog. If this string matching is not successful, your program may still run, but messages will not be properly passed on to your window procedure.

That's all there is to it. Dialog windows are really much easier to use than ordinary windows. As an extra bonus, you get to use the Resource Workshop or the App Studio to create all the controls in your windows. All of these controls will be initialized for you automatically at start up. This means you can create the visual side of your program in only a few minutes.

The rest of the harmony program looks just like any ordinary Windows program. That is, there is a window procedure that receives all the same messages, and respond in the same way as any standard main window. The only major difference is the `Cls_OnCreate` function, which isn't supplied with a valid `HWND`. To make up for this, however, the Create function automatically creates all the child windows on your main window.

Summary

This chapter introduced DLLs and the multimedia extensions to Windows. In particular, you learned

☐ How to use `mciSendCommand` to control multimedia functions

☐ How to get error strings with `mciGetErrorString`

☐ How to find out about available multimedia capabilities on a system

☐ How to create a DLL and how to export functions from it

☐ How to use a dialog as the main window of your program

If you want to learn more about multimedia, the best thing you can do is study the included example and the MMSYSTEM.H interface unit, which ships with your compiler. Microsoft also ships additional documentation with the SDK, and separately in the form of two books: *The Microsoft Windows Multimedia Programmer's Reference* and *Microsoft Windows Multimedia Programmer's Workbook*. Both volumes are published by the Microsoft Press.

Q&A

1. Q: Are there any additional ways of finding out about the capabilities of the system on which a multimedia program is running?

   A: Yes, you can use the `MCI_GETDEVCAPS` message. When sending this message, fill in the `MCI_GETDEVCAPS_PARMS.dwItem` with constants that ask whether a particular device can Play, Pause, Record, and so forth. One way to use this message is to query to see if a particular device is available (as shown in the DoesDeviceExistOnSystem function). If the device is available, send an MCI_GETDEVCAPS message.

2. Q: Besides using ImpLib, is there another method for exporting functions from a DLL?

A: Yes. You can also list functions declared FAR and PASCAL in the EXPORTS section of a DEF file:

```
EXPORTS    MyFunc1
           MyFunc2
```

This technique used to be fairly popular. However, it's not as easy to use as ImpLib because you have to explicitly import all the functions in the DEF file of your program:

```
IMPORTS
        MyDLL.MyFunc1
        MyDLL.MyFunc2
```

Workshop

The Workshop provides quiz questions to help you solidify your understanding of the material covered and exercises to provide you with experience in using what you've learned. Try to understand the quiz and exercise answers before continuing on to the next chapter. Answers are provided in Appendix A.

Quiz

1. What does MCI stand for?

2. In terms of disk space, what is the difference between MIDI files and WAVE files?

3. What do you do with the device ID field when you are first opening a multimedia device?

4. What value does mciSendCommand return?

5. What does the MCI_NOTIFY flag do?

6. What two words are included in the declaration of functions exported from a DLL?

7. How can you inform the linker that certain functions used in your program reside inside a DLL?

8. Harmony uses the PLAYINFO.H and CDINFO.H file for learning about the declarations of routines in CDINFO.DLL and PLAYINFO.DLL. How does your program know about the declarations of the routines in GDI.EXE and USER.EXE?

9. What is the purpose of the CLASS statement in HARMONY.RC?

10. If you use TDump or ExeHdr on both HARMONY.EXE and PLAYINFO.DLL, you'll find that they have very similar structures and are both examples of something called the new executable format. Given this similarity, it follows that there should be an equivalent to WinMain inside a DLL. What is it?

Exercises

1. Use the empty ComboBox in the left-center of the Harmony main window to display a list of files queued up to play. The user should be able to double-click files in the program's list box, and then have them transferred to the ComboBox. When the user clicks the play button, the files should be selected one at a time for the ComboBox.

2. The Harmony program only enables the user to record a message in a .WAV file that lasts for a preset period of time. Using Windows controls, such as radio buttons, edits, and scrollbars, create a dialog that will enable the user to designate how long he or she wants a recording to last. You could also extend the functionality of the record button by letting the user gracefully terminate a recording any time.

Snako for Windows

M T W R F S

Today, you'll see the final version of the Snako program. The main purpose of this chapter is to allow you to have some fun with the skills you have learned, and to discuss some of the principles behind creating and designing Windows programs.

A few new ideas do come up in this chapter. In particular, you will find a discussion of

- [ ] Memory issues: the DGROUP and its data, stack, and local heap
- [ ] Using pointers to move data out of the local heap
- [ ] Simple file I/O
- [ ] Centering dialogs

Though pointers are an extremely important aspect of Windows programming, none of these subjects will tax your intellect to any great degree. They basically involve concepts which should already be very familiar to you from your experience in the DOS world.

Besides memory allocation, the main theme of this chapter is that it is important to get back to our roots as avid hackers. Presumably most programmers enter the profession because they love to code. Certainly, most of us got interested in this field simply because it is fascinating and entertaining. I believe that losing this initial sense of playfulness is the death knell that destroys many good programmers. I feel all programmers need to take some time out to have some fun with the tools of their trade. If that's not happening, no amount of money can compensate for our efforts, and any accolades we might receive will taste like bitter ash.

Snako

The Snako program that comes with this book consists of eight screens arranged on two different levels. An ever-lengthening snake winds its way through these screens, eating all the red dots on one screen in order to open a door that leads to the next screen (Figure 21.1). At any time, the snake is free to go back and visit any previously visited screen on the current level.

The danger in the game springs from running into the sides of the screen, the "grass" through which the snake's path winds its way, or any part of the snake's tail. Once you are past the first screen, you can take as many cracks as you want at completing any one screen. Victory comes when the snake makes it all the way to the eighth screen and eats all the red dots there.

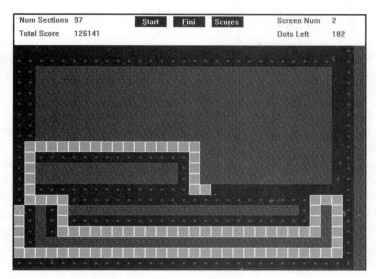

Figure 21.1. *The Snako program and its snake.*

The nature of the game is such that the first few screens are only moderately challenging. It's only after the snake gets some fifty sections or more in length that the action begins to heat up. If you design sufficiently complex screens, the last levels can get to be extremely intense, so you need to combine physical coordination, logic, forethought, and a nimble mind in order to find your way to victory.

Though the Snako program is presented as a complete and original entertainment, this is a programming book and so I assume you'll want to modify the code to suit your needs. For instance, it would be interesting if the user could adjust the snake's speed and its growth rate. Other interesting improvements might be enabling the snake to climb through more than two levels, and letting the user save a game in progress to disk.

At any rate, you should feel free to modify the game in any way you like, though the version that ships with this book, and any future versions of the game that I may design, are mine to do with as I like. As with all the code in this book, however, you should feel free to distribute copies of this game to anyone who wants it, as long as you don't actually charge a fee for the transaction. This is a learning tool, not an exercise in entrepreneurship. Education is primary: it is the foundation on which all social ventures rest.

21

The Code

The primary reason this chapter introduces so few new topics is simply that Snako is a relatively lengthy program. As such, it presents its own challenges and reveals much about the design issues faced by real-world Windows programmers.

The code that drives the program is presented in the following listings, but much of the challenge in the game comes from the appearance of individual screens. In other words, you could design screens that make it a cakewalk to move all the way to the end of the game, and in fact I kept a set of those screens available for when I was debugging. On the other hand, creating overly complex screens can make it all but impossible to get off the first level. The figures in this chapter show suggested designs for the eight screens used in the program. These are just suggestions, and I more or less assume that anyone interested in this game will want to create screens of their own (or modify the ones shown here).

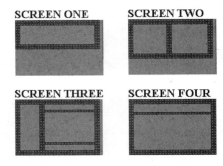

Figure 21.2. *Suggested screens 1-4 for level 1.*

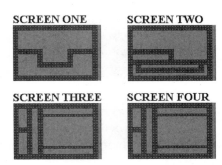

Figure 21.3. *Suggested screens 1-4 for level 2.*

Listing 21.1 shows the logic for the Snako program.

Type **Listing 21.1. The Snako program is an arcade type game for windows.**

```
 1: /////////////////////////////////////////////////////
 2: //   Program Name: SNAKO.CPP
 3: //   Programmer: Charlie Calvert
 4: //   Description: A Windows game
 5: //   Date: 08/05/93
 6: /////////////////////////////////////////////////////
 7:
 8: #define STRICT
 9: #include <windows.h>
10: #include <windowsx.h>
11: #pragma hdrstop
12: #include <string.h>
13: #include <stdlib.h>
14: #include "snako.h"
15: #include "score.h"
16: #include "grunt.h"
17: #include "snakutil.h"
18: #pragma warning (disable : 4068)
19: #pragma warning (disable : 4100)
20:
21: static char szAppName[] = "Snako";
22: static char szScoreClass[] = "ScoreKeeper";
23: HWND hWindow;
24:
25: // Varialbles
26: HINSTANCE hInstance;
27: HWND hScoreWindow;
28: TSNAKEMAP SMap;
29: PGAMEINFO G, SaveGame;
30: //----------------------------------------------------------
31: // Setup
32: //----------------------------------------------------------
33:
34: #pragma argsused
35: int PASCAL WinMain(HINSTANCE hInst, HINSTANCE hPrevInstance,
36:                    LPSTR  lpszCmdParam, int nCmdShow)
37: {
38:   MSG  Msg;
39:
40:   if (!hPrevInstance)
41:     if (!Register(hInst))
42:       return FALSE;
43:
44:   if (!(hWindow = Create(hInst, nCmdShow)))
45:     return FALSE;
```

21

continues

Listing 21.1. continued

```
46:
47:    while (GetMessage(&Msg, NULL, 0, 0))
48:    {
49:      TranslateMessage(&Msg);
50:      DispatchMessage(&Msg);
51:    }
52:    return Msg.wParam;
53: }
54:
55: ///////////////////////////////////////////
56: // Save hInstance, Create window,
57: //   Show window maximized
58: ///////////////////////////////////////////
59: HWND Create(HINSTANCE hInst, int nCmdShow)
60: {
61:    hInstance = hInst;
62:
63:    HWND hWindow = CreateWindow(szAppName,
64:                   "A Snake and its Tail",
65:                   WS_POPUP, CW_USEDEFAULT, CW_USEDEFAULT,
66:                   CW_USEDEFAULT, CW_USEDEFAULT,
67:                   NULL, NULL, hInst, NULL);
68:
69:    if (hWindow == NULL)
70:      return hWindow;
71:
72:    nCmdShow = SW_SHOWMAXIMIZED;
73:
74:    ShowWindow(hWindow, nCmdShow);
75:    UpdateWindow(hWindow);
76:
77:    return hWindow;
78: }
79:
80: ///////////////////////////////////////////
81: // Register window
82: ///////////////////////////////////////////
83: BOOL Register(HINSTANCE hInst)
84: {
85:    WNDCLASS WndClass;
86:
87:    WndClass.style          = CS_HREDRAW | CS_VREDRAW;
88:    WndClass.lpfnWndProc    = WndProc;
89:    WndClass.cbClsExtra     = 0;
90:    WndClass.cbWndExtra     = 0;
91:    WndClass.hInstance      = hInst;
92:    WndClass.hIcon          = LoadIcon(NULL, IDI_APPLICATION);
93:    WndClass.hCursor        = LoadCursor(NULL, IDC_ARROW);
94:    WndClass.hbrBackground  = GetStockBrush(BLACK_BRUSH);
95:    WndClass.lpszMenuName   = NULL;
```

```
 96:    WndClass.lpszClassName  = szAppName;
 97:
 98:    if (!RegisterClass (&WndClass))
 99:      return FALSE;
100:
101:    WndClass.lpfnWndProc    = ScoreWndProc;
102:    WndClass.hIcon          = NULL;
103:    WndClass.hbrBackground  = NULL;
104:    WndClass.lpszClassName  = szScoreClass;
105:
106:    return RegisterClass (&WndClass);
107: }
108:
109: // ------------------------------------------------
110: // The Implementation
111: // ------------------------------------------------
112:
113: // ------------------------------------------------
114: // WndProc
115: // ------------------------------------------------
116: LRESULT CALLBACK __export WndProc(HWND hwnd, UINT Message,
117:                                   WPARAM wParam, LPARAM lParam)
118: {
119:    switch(Message)
120:    {
121:      HANDLE_MSG(hwnd, WM_CREATE, Snake_OnCreate);
122:      HANDLE_MSG(hwnd, WM_DESTROY, Snake_OnDestroy);
123:      HANDLE_MSG(hwnd, WM_CHAR, Snake_OnChar);
124:      HANDLE_MSG(hwnd, WM_KEYDOWN, Snake_OnKey);
125:      HANDLE_MSG(hwnd, WM_PAINT, Snake_OnPaint);
126:      HANDLE_MSG(hwnd, WM_TIMER, Snake_OnTimer);
127:      HANDLE_MSG(hwnd, WM_START, Snake_OnStart);
128:      HANDLE_MSG(hwnd, WM_SIZE, Snake_OnSize);
129:      default: return Snake_DefProc(hwnd, Message, wParam, lParam);
130:    }
131: }
132:
133: /////////////////////////////////////////////
134: // Handle WM_CREATE
135: /////////////////////////////////////////////
136: #pragma argsused
137: BOOL Snake_OnCreate(HWND hwnd, CREATESTRUCT FAR* lpCreateStruct)
138: {
139:    if((G = (PGAMEINFO)malloc(sizeof(TGAMEINFO))) == NULL)
140:    {
141:      MessageBox(hwnd, "Memory is hosed!", "Closing Snako", MB_OK);
142:      return FALSE;
143:    }
144:
145:    InitializeSections();
```

continues

Listing 21.1. continued

```
146:
147:    G->Dat.Speed = 250;
148:    int XScreen = GetSystemMetrics(SM_CXSCREEN);
149:
150:    if (XScreen == 1024)
151:    {
152:      G->Dat.GrassX = G->Dat.SizeX = 32;
153:      G->Dat.GrassY = G->Dat.SizeY = 32;
154:    }
155:
156:    if (XScreen == 800)
157:    {
158:      G->Dat.GrassX = G->Dat.SizeX = 25;
159:      G->Dat.GrassY = G->Dat.SizeY = 25;
160:    }
161:
162:    if (XScreen == 640)
163:    {
164:      G->Dat.GrassX = G->Dat.SizeX = 20;
165:              G->Dat.GrassY = G->Dat.SizeY = 20;
166:    }
167:
168:    G->Dat.MaxScore = 3 * G->Dat.GrassX;
169:    G->Dat.MenuSpace = 3;
170:    G->Dat.TotalClicks = 0;
171:
172:    SMap.Grass = LoadBitmap(hInstance, "Grass");
173:    SMap.Road = LoadBitmap(hInstance, "Road");
174:    SMap.Road2 = LoadBitmap(hInstance, "Road2");
175:    if ((!SMap.Grass) ¦¦ (!SMap.Road) ¦¦ (!SMap.Road2))
176:    {
177:      MessageBox(hwnd, "No Grass! No Road! No Road2!", "Fatal Error",
178:                  MB_OK ¦ MB_ICONSTOP);
179:      return FALSE;
180:    }
181:
182:    SMap.Head = LoadBitmap(hInstance, "Head");
183:    if (!SMap.Head)
184:    {
185:      MessageBox(hwnd, "No head", "Fatal Error", MB_OK);
186:      return FALSE;
187:    }
188:
189:    SMap.Body = LoadBitmap(hInstance, "Body");
190:    if (!SMap.Body)
191:    {
192:      MessageBox(hwnd, "No body", "Fatal Error", MB_OK);
193:      return FALSE;
194:    }
195:
```

```
196:    hScoreWindow = CreateWindow(szScoreClass, "Score",
197:                      WS_CHILD | WS_VISIBLE | WS_CLIPSIBLINGS,
198:                      10, 10, 100, 100, hwnd,
199:                      HMENU(50), hInstance, NULL);
200:
201:    if(!hScoreWindow)
202:            return FALSE;
203:
204:    G->ScoreRep.Level = 1;
205:    ReadArray(hwnd);
206:    SaveGame = NULL;
207:
208:    return TRUE;
209: }
210:
211: ///////////////////////////////////////////
212: // Handle WM_DESTROY
213: ///////////////////////////////////////////
214: #pragma argsused
215: void Snake_OnDestroy(HWND hwnd)
216: {
217:    if (SMap.Head) DeleteObject(SMap.Head);
218:    if (SMap.Body) DeleteObject(SMap.Body);
219:    if (SMap.Grass) DeleteObject(SMap.Grass);
220:    if (SMap.Road) DeleteObject(SMap.Road);
221:    if (SMap.Road2) DeleteObject(SMap.Road2);
222:    free(G);
223:    if (SaveGame)
224:      free(SaveGame);
225:    PostQuitMessage(0);
226: }
227:
228: ///////////////////////////////////////////
229: // Handle WM_CHAR -- Stub code to implement
230: // a pause feature by pressing the p key
231: ///////////////////////////////////////////
232: #pragma argsused
233: void Snake_OnChar(HWND hwnd, UINT ch, int cRepeat)
234: {
235:    switch (ch)
236:    {
237:      case 'p':
238:        KillTimer(hwnd, SNAKETIMER);
239:        break;
240:      case 's':
241:        SendMessage(hwnd, WM_START, 0, 0L);
242:        break;
243:      case 'r':
244:        SendMessage(hScoreWindow, WM_COMMAND, ID_SCORE, 0);
245:        break;
```

continues

Listing 21.1. continued

```
246:    case 'f':
247:        SendMessage(hScoreWindow, WM_COMMAND, ID_FINI, 0);
248:        break;
249:    }
250: }
251:
252: //////////////////////////////////////
253: // Handle WM_KEYDOWN
254: //////////////////////////////////////
255: #pragma argsused
256: void Snake_OnKey(HWND hwnd, UINT vk, BOOL fDown,
                       int cRepeat, UINT flags)
257: {
258:    switch(vk)
259:    {
260:      case VK_DOWN:
261:        SetNewDir(DOWN);
262:        MoveBitMap(hwnd);
263:        break;
264:      case VK_UP:
265:        SetNewDir(UP);
266:        MoveBitMap(hwnd);
267:        break;
268:      case VK_LEFT:
269:        SetNewDir(LEFT);
270:        MoveBitMap(hwnd);
271:        break;
272:      case VK_RIGHT:
273:        SetNewDir(RIGHT);
274:        MoveBitMap(hwnd);
275:        break;
276:    }
277:
278:    // In case you hit no accidentally
279:    if (G->Dat.NewScreenStarted == 2)
280:    {
281:      G->Dat.NewScreenStarted = FALSE;
282:      SetTimer(hwnd, SNAKETIMER, G->Dat.Speed, NULL);
283:      InvalidateRect(hwnd, NULL, TRUE);
284:    }
285: }
286:
287: //////////////////////////////////////
288: // -- Snake_OnPaint --
289: // Repaint the playing board
290: //////////////////////////////////////
291: void Snake_OnPaint(HWND hwnd)
292: {
293:    PAINTSTRUCT PaintStruct;
294:
```

```
295:    HDC PaintDC = BeginPaint(hwnd, &PaintStruct);
296:    PaintPlayingField(PaintDC);
297:    EndPaint(hwnd, &PaintStruct);
298:
299:    G->SectInfo[0].DirChange = FALSE;
300:    InvalidateRect(hScoreWindow, NULL, FALSE);
301: }
302:
303: ///////////////////////////////////////
304: // Set the position of the score window
305: ///////////////////////////////////////
306: void Snake_OnSize(HWND hwnd, UINT state, int cx, int cy)
307: {
308:    MoveWindow(hScoreWindow, 0, 0, cx, G->Dat.MaxScore - 1, FALSE);
309:    FORWARD_WM_SIZE(hwnd, state, cx, cy, Snake_DefProc);
310: }
311:
312:
313: ///////////////////////////////////////
314: // Handle the user defined WM_START message
315: // when the start button is pressed
316: ///////////////////////////////////////
317: void Snake_OnStart(HWND hwnd)
318: {
319:    HDC PaintDC;
320:
321:    SetFocus(hwnd);
322:    InitializeSections();
323:    ReadArray(hwnd);
324:    PaintDC = GetDC(hwnd);
325:    PaintPlayingField(PaintDC);
326:    ReleaseDC(hwnd, PaintDC);
327:    SetUpWindow(hwnd);
328:    InvalidateRect(hScoreWindow, NULL, TRUE);
329: }
330:
331: ///////////////////////////////////////
332: // -- Snake_OnTimer --
333: // Gets called when the timer runs out.
334: // Call MoveBitMap to move the snake.
335: // If the Timer has been called 15 times in
336: // a row, then add a new section to the Snake
337: ///////////////////////////////////////
338: #pragma argsused
339: void Snake_OnTimer(HWND hwnd, UINT id)
340: {
341:    MoveBitMap(hwnd);
342:    G->Dat.TotalClicks++;
343:    //  QuickScan(); // debug routine found in SnakUtil
```

continues

Listing 21.1. continued

```
344:     SendMessage(hScoreWindow, WM_SETNUMSEGS, 0,
                     (LPARAM)&G->ScoreRep);
345:
346:     if (G->ScoreRep.NumPrizes > 60000) G->ScoreRep.NumPrizes = 0;
347:
348:     #ifdef _DEBUG
349:       if (G->ScoreRep.NumPrizes <= 20)
350:         if(G->Map[BRIDGEX1][G->Dat.MaxCols - 1] != ROADMAP)
351:           MakeGateWay(hwnd);
352:     #else
353:       if (G->ScoreRep.NumPrizes <= 0)
354:         if((G->Map[BRIDGEX1][G->Dat.MaxCols - 1] != ROADMAP) ¦¦
355:            (G->ScoreRep.ScreenNum == 4))
356:           MakeGateWay(hwnd);
357:     #endif
358:
359:     if ((G->Dat.TotalClicks % 15) == 0)
360:       AddSection();
361:
362:     G->ScoreRep.NumSects = G->Dat.Sections;
363:
364:     if (G->Dat.NewScreenStarted == 2)
365:     {
366:       G->Dat.NewScreenStarted = FALSE;
367:       SetTimer(hwnd, SNAKETIMER, G->Dat.Speed, NULL);
368:       InvalidateRect(hwnd, NULL, TRUE);
369:     }
370: }
```

Listing 21.2 shows the Snako header file.

Type **Listing 21.2. SNAKO.H.**

```
 1: /////////////////////////////////////////
 2: //  Program Name: SNAKO.H
 3: //  Programmer: Charlie Calvert
 4: //  Description: A windows game
 5: //  Date: 08/05/93
 6: /////////////////////////////////////////
 7:
 8: #if !defined _SNAKE_H
 9: #define _SNAKE_H
10:
11: // const
12: #define SNAKETIMER 1
13: #define GRASSMAP 1
14: #define PRIZEMAP 2
```

```
15: #define ROADMAP 3
16:
17: #define MAXY 21        // Max rows for maze on one level
18: #define MAXX 32 * 4    // Max cols for maze on one level
19: #define JUMPSPACE 32   // Width of one screen in bitmaps
20: #define XWIDTH 25      // Bitmap width in pixels
21: #define YHEIGHT 25     // Bitmap height in pixels
22: #define MAXSECTS 512   // Max length of snake: very flexible
23:
24: #define BRIDGEX1 0     // Row for bridge to next screen
25: #define BRIDGEX2 1     // Row for bridge to next screen
26:
27: #define LEFT 0
28: #define RIGHT 1
29: #define UP 2
30: #define DOWN 3
31:
32: // Type
33: struct TSCOREREP{
34:   int NumSects;
35:   WORD NumPrizes;
36:   LONG TotalScore;
37:   WORD ScreenNum;
38:   WORD Level;
39: };
40:
41: // Types
42: typedef struct  {
43:     HDC CompDC;
44:     HDC TCompDC;
45:     HBITMAP CompBmp;
46:     HBITMAP OldBmp;
47:     HBITMAP OldTBmp;
48: } TSAVEBITMAP;
49: typedef TSAVEBITMAP TSAVEBITMAPARY[6];
50:
51: typedef struct
52: {
53:   int MaxScore;
54:   int MaxCols;
55:   int MinCols;
56:   int GrassX;
57:   int GrassY;
58:   int XPos;
59:   int MenuSpace;
60:   int SizeX;
61:   int SizeY;
62:   long TotalClicks;
63:   BOOL NewScreenStarted;
64:   int Speed;
65:   int NumTurns, Sections;
```

continues

Listing 21.2. continued

```
 66: } TDATA;
 67:
 68: typedef struct TSNAKEMAP {
 69:   HBITMAP Head, Body, Grass, Road, Road2;
 70: }SNAKEMAP;
 71:
 72: typedef struct TSECTINFO {
 73:   BOOL DirChange;
 74:   int Dir;
 75:   int Col, Row;
 76:   int OldCol, OldRow;
 77: } SECTINFO;
 78:
 79: typedef struct {
 80:   TSCOREREP ScoreRep;
 81:   char Map[MAXY][MAXX];
 82:   TDATA Dat;
 83:   TSECTINFO SectInfo[MAXSECTS];
 84: } TGAMEINFO;
 85: typedef TGAMEINFO *PGAMEINFO;
 86:
 87: #endif
 88:
 89: // Macros
 90: #define HANDLE_WM_START(hwnd, wParam, lParam, fn) \
 91:     ((fn)(hwnd), 0L)
 92: #define FORWARD_WM_START(hwnd, fn) \
 93:     (void)(fn)((hwnd), WM_START, 0, 0L)
 94:
 95: // Class Snake
 96: #define Snake_DefProc      DefWindowProc
 97: BOOL Snake_OnCreate(HWND hWindow,
 98:                     CREATESTRUCT FAR* lpCreateStruct);
 99: void Snake_OnDestroy(HWND hWindow);
100: void Snake_OnChar(HWND hWindow, UINT ch, int cRepeat);
101: void Snake_OnKey(HWND hWindow, UINT vk, BOOL fDown,
102:                  int cRepeat, UINT flags);
103: void Snake_OnPaint(HWND hWindow);
104: void Snake_OnSize(HWND hwnd, UINT state, int cx, int cy);
105: void Snake_OnStart(HWND hwnd);
106: void Snake_OnTimer(HWND hWindow, UINT id);
107:
108: // Procs
109: HWND Create(HINSTANCE hInst, int nCmdShow);
110: BOOL Register(HINSTANCE hInst);
111: BOOL SetUpWindow(HWND hWindow);
112: void PaintPlayingField(HDC PaintDC);
113: LRESULT CALLBACK __export WndProc(HWND, UINT, WPARAM, LPARAM);
114: void InitializeSections(HWND hwnd);
115: int ReadArray(HWND hwnd);
```

Listing 21.3 shows the Grunt source file.

Listing 21.3. GRUNT.CPP.

```
1:  ///////////////////////////////////////////////////////
2:  // Module: GRUNT.CPP
3:  // Project: Snake
4:  // Programmer: Charlie Calvert
5:  // Date: May 29, 1993
6:  // Description: Do the real work of moving the snake.
7:  ///////////////////////////////////////////////////////
8:
9:  #define STRICT
10: #include <windows.h>
11: #include <windowsx.h>
12: #pragma hdrstop
13: #include <stdlib.h>
14: #include <string.h>
15: #include "grunt.h"
16: #include "snako.h"
17: #include "score.h"
18: #include "snakutil.h"
19: #include "snakopnt.h"
20: #pragma warning (disable : 4100)
21:
22: extern TSNAKEMAP SMap;
23: extern HWND hScoreWindow;
24: extern PGAMEINFO G;
25:
26: int FindSafe(HWND hwnd)
27: {
28:   int Result;
29:
30:   KillTimer(hwnd, SNAKETIMER);
31:   if ((G->ScoreRep.Level != 1) || (G->ScoreRep.ScreenNum != 1))
32:   {
33:     Result = MessageBox(hwnd,
34:       "Yes to try this level again, no to start over.",
35:       "Snako by Charlie Calvert!", MB_YESNO | MB_ICONSTOP);
36:   }
37:   else
38:   {
39:     Result = MessageBox(hwnd, "Dead Snake!",
40:             "Snako by Charlie Calvert!", MB_OK | MB_ICONSTOP);
41:   }
42:   if ((Result == IDOK) || (Result == IDNO))
43:   SendMessage(hScoreWindow, WM_SCORE, 0,
44:               (LPARAM)G->ScoreRep.TotalScore);
```

continues

Listing 21.3. continued

```
45:   if (Result != IDYES)
46:   {
47:     DoSnakePainting(hwnd);
48:     memset(&G->SectInfo, '\0', sizeof(G->SectInfo));
49:     memset(&G->ScoreRep, '\0', sizeof(TSCOREREP));
50:     G->ScoreRep.Level = 1;
51:   }
52:   else
53:     G->Dat.NewScreenStarted = 2;
54:   return FALSE;
55: }
56:
57: ////////////////////////////////////////
58: // Will the snake hit its own body if it
59: // goes in the direction user asked for?
60: ////////////////////////////////////////
61: BOOL DidSnakeHitSnake(HWND hwnd)
62: {
63:   int C = G->SectInfo[0].Col;
64:   int R = G->SectInfo[0].Row;
65:
66:   for (int i = 1; i <= G->Dat.Sections; i++)
67:     if ((C == G->SectInfo[i].Col) && (R == G->SectInfo[i].Row))
68:     {
69:       FindSafe(hwnd);
70:       return TRUE;
71:     }
72:
73:   return FALSE;
74: }
75:
76: ////////////////////////////////////////
77: // This only gets called for the head.
78: // It tests if head is going to hit the
79: // body of the snake or if it hits the grass.
80: // In either case it returns FALSE, else TRUE
81: ////////////////////////////////////////
82: BOOL FindNextSpace(HWND hwnd)
83: {
84:   int Test;
85:
86:   switch(G->SectInfo[0].Dir)
87:   {
88:     case UP:
89:       if (G->SectInfo[0].Row <= 0)
90:         return FindSafe(hwnd);
91:       Test = G->Map[G->SectInfo[0].Row - 1][G->SectInfo[0].Col];
92:       if ((Test == GRASSMAP) || (G->SectInfo[0].Row <= 0))
93:         return FindSafe(hwnd);
94:       G->SectInfo[0].Row -= 1;
```

```
95:        break;
96:
97:     case DOWN:
98:       Test = G->Map[G->SectInfo[0].Row + 1][G->SectInfo[0].Col];
99:       if ((Test == GRASSMAP) || (G->SectInfo[0].Row >= MAXY - 1))
100:         return FindSafe(hwnd);
101:       G->SectInfo[0].Row += 1;
102:       break;
103:
104:     case LEFT:
105:       Test = G->Map[G->SectInfo[0].Row][G->SectInfo[0].Col - 1];
106:       if ((Test == GRASSMAP) || (G->SectInfo[0].Col < 1))
107:         return FindSafe(hwnd);
108:       G->SectInfo[0].Col -= 1;
109:       break;
110:
111:     case RIGHT:
112:       Test = G->Map[G->SectInfo[0].Row][G->SectInfo[0].Col + 1];
113:       if ((Test == GRASSMAP) || (G->SectInfo[0].Col > MAXX))
114:         return FindSafe(hwnd);
115:       G->SectInfo[0].Col += 1;
116:       break;
117:   }
118:
119:   if (Test == PRIZEMAP)
120:   {
121:     G->ScoreRep.TotalScore += (LONG)100;
122:     G->ScoreRep.NumPrizes--;
123:   }
124:
125:   G->Map[G->SectInfo[0].Row][G->SectInfo[0].Col] = ROADMAP;
126:
127:   if(DidSnakeHitSnake(hwnd))
128:     return FALSE;
129:   else
130:     return TRUE;
131: }
132:
133: ///////////////////////////////////////////
134: // This moves each section of the
135: // snake on one place. It never
136: // gets called for the head.
137: ///////////////////////////////////////////
138: void SetNextSection(int i)
139: {
140:   switch(G->SectInfo[i].Dir)
141:   {
142:     case UP: G->SectInfo[i].Row -= 1; break;
143:     case DOWN: G->SectInfo[i].Row += 1; break;
144:     case LEFT: G->SectInfo[i].Col -= 1; break;
```

continues

21

Listing 21.3. continued

```
145:        case RIGHT: G->SectInfo[i].Col += 1; break;
146:    }
147: }
148:
149: //////////////////////////////////////////
150: // When ever the snake moves back and forth
151: // across a screen, we need to know which
152: // number screen he is on so we can tell the user.
153: //////////////////////////////////////////
154: void SetScreenNum(void)
155: {
156:   switch (G->Dat.MaxCols)
157:   {
158:     case JUMPSPACE: G->ScoreRep.ScreenNum = 1; break;
159:     case JUMPSPACE * 2: G->ScoreRep.ScreenNum = 2; break;
160:     case JUMPSPACE * 3: G->ScoreRep.ScreenNum = 3; break;
161:     case JUMPSPACE * 4: G->ScoreRep.ScreenNum = 4; break;
162:   }
163: }
164:
165: //////////////////////////////////////////
166: // Move things left one screen or
167: // right one screen if we hit end of screen
168: //////////////////////////////////////////
169: void CheckForEndScreen(HWND hwnd, int i)
170: {
171:   if ((i == 0) && (G->SectInfo[i].Col >= G->Dat.MaxCols))
172:   {
173:     if (G->Dat.XPos != (MAXX - JUMPSPACE))
174:     {
175:       G->Dat.XPos += JUMPSPACE;
176:       G->Dat.MaxCols += JUMPSPACE;
177:       G->Dat.MinCols += JUMPSPACE;
178:       G->ScoreRep.NumPrizes = 10000;
179:       InvalidateRect(hwnd, NULL, TRUE);
180:       SetScreenNum();
181:       G->Dat.NewScreenStarted = TRUE;
182:     }
183:   }
184:
185:   if ((i == 0) && (G->SectInfo[i].Col < G->Dat.MinCols))
186:   {
187:     if (G->Dat.XPos != 0)
188:     {
189:       G->Dat.XPos -= JUMPSPACE;
190:       G->Dat.MaxCols -= JUMPSPACE;
191:       G->Dat.MinCols -= JUMPSPACE;
192:       G->ScoreRep.NumPrizes = 10000;
193:       InvalidateRect(hwnd, NULL, TRUE);
```

```
194:        SetScreenNum( );
195:      }
196:    }
197: }
198:
199: /////////////////////////////////////////////
200: // Move the whole snake forward. The calls to
201: // FindNextSpace move the head and test to see
202: // if move is legal. Once we know the move is legal,
203: // then move everything else by calling SetNextSection.
204: // CheckForEndScreen moves to next screen or back.
205: /////////////////////////////////////////////
206: void SetColRow(HWND hwnd)
207: {
208:   int i;
209:   BOOL Result;
210:
211:   for (i = 0; i <= G->Dat.Sections; i++)
212:   {
213:     G->SectInfo[i].OldCol = G->SectInfo[i].Col;
214:     G->SectInfo[i].OldRow = G->SectInfo[i].Row;
215:
216:     if (i == 0)
217:     {
218:       Result = FindNextSpace(hwnd);
219:       if(G->Dat.NewScreenStarted == 2)
220:         return;
221:     }
222:     else
223:       SetNextSection(i);
224:
225:     if (Result)
226:       CheckForEndScreen(hwnd, i);
227:   }
228:
229:   if (Result)
230:     for (i = G->Dat.Sections; i > 0; i--)
231:     {
232:       if (G->SectInfo[i - 1].DirChange)
233:       {
234:         G->SectInfo[i].DirChange = TRUE;
235:         G->SectInfo[i].Dir = G->SectInfo[i - 1].Dir;
236:         G->SectInfo[i - 1].DirChange = FALSE;
237:       }
238:     }
239: }
240:
241: /////////////////////////////////////////////
242: // Set New Direction when we turn
243: /////////////////////////////////////////////
```

continues

Listing 21.3. continued

```
244: void SetNewDir(int NewDir)
245: {
246:   G->SectInfo[0].Dir = NewDir;
247:   G->SectInfo[0].DirChange = TRUE;
248: }
249:
250: //////////////////////////////////////////
251: // Make the snake a little longer
252: //////////////////////////////////////////
253: void AddSection(void)
254: {
255:   G->Dat.Sections++;
256:
257:   G->SectInfo[G->Dat.Sections].Dir =
258:     G->SectInfo[G->Dat.Sections - 1].Dir;
259:   G->SectInfo[G->Dat.Sections].DirChange = FALSE;
260:
261:   switch (G->SectInfo[G->Dat.Sections].Dir)
262:   {
263:     case LEFT:
264:     {
265:       G->SectInfo[G->Dat.Sections].Col =
266:         G->SectInfo[G->Dat.Sections - 1].Col + 1;
267:       G->SectInfo[G->Dat.Sections].Row =
268:         G->SectInfo[G->Dat.Sections - 1].Row;
269:       break;
270:     }
271:     case RIGHT:
272:     {
273:       G->SectInfo[G->Dat.Sections].Col =
274:         G->SectInfo[G->Dat.Sections - 1].Col - 1;
275:       G->SectInfo[G->Dat.Sections].Row =
276:         G->SectInfo[G->Dat.Sections - 1].Row;
277:       break;
278:     }
279:
280:     case UP:
281:     {
282:       G->SectInfo[G->Dat.Sections].Col =
283:         G->SectInfo[G->Dat.Sections - 1].Col;
284:       G->SectInfo[G->Dat.Sections].Row =
285:         G->SectInfo[G->Dat.Sections - 1].Row + 1;
286:       break;
287:     }
288:
289:     case DOWN:
290:     {
291:       G->SectInfo[G->Dat.Sections].Col =
292:         G->SectInfo[G->Dat.Sections - 1].Col;
```

```
293:            G->SectInfo[G->Dat.Sections].Row =
294:              G->SectInfo[G->Dat.Sections - 1].Row - 1;
295:            break;
296:        }
297:    } // end switch
298:
299:    G->SectInfo[G->Dat.Sections].OldCol =
300:      G->SectInfo[G->Dat.Sections - 1].Col;
301:    G->SectInfo[G->Dat.Sections].OldRow =
302:      G->SectInfo[G->Dat.Sections - 1].Row;
303: }
304:
305:
306: //////////////////////////////////////////////////
307: // Game is over
308: //////////////////////////////////////////////////
309: void YouWin(HWND hwnd)
310: {
311:    KillTimer(hwnd, SNAKETIMER);
312:    MessageBox(hwnd, "You Win!", "Victory!",
313:               MB_ICONEXCLAMATION | MB_OK);
314:    SendMessage(hScoreWindow, WM_SCORE, 0,
315:               (LPARAM)G->ScoreRep.TotalScore);
316: }
317:
318: //////////////////////////////////////////////////
319: // Make a bridge to the next screen,
320: // start the next level or proclaim victory.
321: //////////////////////////////////////////////////
322: void MakeGateWay(HWND hwnd)
323: {
324:    if (G->ScoreRep.ScreenNum == 4)
325:    {
326:      if (G->ScoreRep.Level == 2)
327:      {
328:        YouWin(hwnd);
329:        return;
330:      }
331:      G->ScoreRep.Level++;
332:      StartNewScreen(hwnd);
333:      KillTimer(hwnd, SNAKETIMER);
334:      MessageBox(hwnd, "Get Ready for a new Level", "Snako",
335:               MB_OK | MB_ICONEXCLAMATION);
336:      if (!SetTimer(hwnd, SNAKETIMER, G->Dat.Speed, NULL))
337:        MessageBox(hwnd,"No Timers Available","Snako",MB_OK);
338:
339:      SaveGameToMemory(hwnd);
340:      return;
341:    }
342:    MakeAndPaintBridge(hwnd);
```

continues

Listing 21.3. continued

```
343: }
344:
345: ////////////////////////////////////////
346: // Command Central for the whole of Grunt
347: ////////////////////////////////////////
348: void MoveBitMap(HWND hwnd)
349: {
350:   SetColRow(hwnd);
351:   if (G->Dat.NewScreenStarted == 2)
352:   {
353:     ReadGameFromMemory();
354:     G->Dat.NewScreenStarted = 2;
355:   }
356:   DoSnakePainting(hwnd);
357:   G->ScoreRep.TotalScore += 1;
358:   G->SectInfo[0].DirChange = FALSE;
359:   if (G->Dat.NewScreenStarted == 1)
360:   {
361:     G->Dat.NewScreenStarted = FALSE;
362:     SaveGameToMemory(hwnd);
363:   }
364: }
```

Listing 21.4 shows the Grunt header file.

Type   **Listing 21.4. GRUNT.H.**

```
 1: ////////////////////////////////////
 2: // Module: GRUNT.H
 3: // Project: Snake
 4: // Programmer: Charlie Calvert
 5: ////////////////////////////////////
 6:
 7: #include "snako.h"
 8:
 9: // Procs
10: void AddSection(void);
11: void MoveBitMap(HWND hwnd);
12: void SetNewDir(int NewDir);
13: void MakeGateWay(HWND hwnd);
```

Listing 21.5 shows the SnakoPnt source file.

Type **Listing 21.5. SNAKOPNT.CPP.**

```cpp
1: //////////////////////////////////////////////
2: //    Program Name: SNAKOPNT.CPP
3: //    Programmer: Charlie Calvert
4: //    Description: Draw playing field and the snake
5: //    Date: 08/05/93
6: //////////////////////////////////////////////
7:
8: #define STRICT
9: #include <windows.h>
10: #include <windowsx.h>
11: #include "snako.h"
12: #include "snakutil.h"
13:
14: extern PGAMEINFO G;
15: extern TSNAKEMAP SMap;
16: enum Bmps {EHead, EBody, EGrass, ERoad, ERoad2};
17:
18: // ----------------------------------------
19: //    The Paint Section
20: // ----------------------------------------
21:
22: //////////////////////////////////////////
23: // The Drawing of the snake
24: //////////////////////////////////////////
25: int PaintTheSnake(HDC PaintDC, HDC HeadDC, HDC BodyDC)
26: {
27:   BitBlt(PaintDC,
28:         (G->SectInfo[0].Col - G->Dat.XPos) * G->Dat.SizeX,
29:         (G->SectInfo[0].Row + G->Dat.MenuSpace) * G->Dat.SizeY,
30:          G->Dat.SizeX, G->Dat.SizeY, HeadDC, 0, 0, SRCCOPY);
31:
32:   for (int i = 1; i <= G->Dat.Sections; i++)
33:     BitBlt(PaintDC,
34:         (G->SectInfo[i].Col - G->Dat.XPos) * G->Dat.SizeX,
35:         (G->SectInfo[i].Row + G->Dat.MenuSpace) * G->Dat.SizeY,
36:          G->Dat.SizeX, G->Dat.SizeY, BodyDC, 0, 0, SRCCOPY);
37:   return --i;
38: }
39:
40: //////////////////////////////////////////
41: // After snake has been somewhere, get rid of prize
42: // bitmap and just put in regular road.
43: //////////////////////////////////////////
44: void FillInWhereSnakeHasBeen(HDC PaintDC, int i)
45: {
46:   TSAVEBITMAPARY SaveBmp;
47:   HDC RoadDC;
```

21

continues

Listing 21.5. continued

```
48:
49:    RoadDC = GetScaledDC(PaintDC, SaveBmp, SMap.Road, ERoad);
50:
51:    BitBlt(PaintDC,
52:      (G->SectInfo[i].OldCol - G->Dat.XPos) * G->Dat.SizeX,
53:      (G->SectInfo[i].OldRow + G->Dat.MenuSpace) * G->Dat.SizeY,
54:       G->Dat.SizeX, G->Dat.SizeY, RoadDC, 0, 0, SRCCOPY);
55:
56:    DisposeScaledDC(SaveBmp, ERoad);
57: }
58:
59: /////////////////////////////////////////////
60: // Command central for painting the snake
61: // GetScaledDC in SnakUtils
62: /////////////////////////////////////////////
63: void DoSnakePainting(HWND hwnd)
64: {
65:    TSAVEBITMAPARY SB;
66:    HDC DC = GetDC(hwnd);
67:
68:    HDC HeadDC = GetScaledDC(DC, SB, SMap.Head, EHead);
69:    HDC BodyDC = GetScaledDC(DC, SB, SMap.Body, EBody);
70:
71:    int i = PaintTheSnake(DC, HeadDC, BodyDC);
72:
73:    DisposeScaledDC(SB, EHead);
74:    DisposeScaledDC(SB, EBody);
75:
76:    if ((G->SectInfo[i].OldRow > -1) &&
77:        (G->SectInfo[i].OldCol > -1))
78:      FillInWhereSnakeHasBeen(DC, i);
79:
80:    ReleaseDC(hwnd, DC);
81: }
82:
83: /////////////////////////////////////////////
84: // Used with PaintBitmaps below
85: /////////////////////////////////////////////
86: void BlitIt(HDC PaintDC, HDC BmpDC, int i, int j)
87: {
88:    BitBlt(PaintDC, (j - G->Dat.XPos) * G->Dat.GrassX,
89:        (i * G->Dat.GrassY) + (G->Dat.GrassY * G->Dat.MenuSpace),
90:         G->Dat.GrassX, G->Dat.GrassY, BmpDC, 0, 0, SRCCOPY);
91: }
92:
93: /////////////////////////////////////////////
94: // This is used to paint the background
95: // not to paint the snake.
96: /////////////////////////////////////////////
```

```
 97: void PaintBitmaps(HDC PaintDC, HDC GrassDC,
 98:                   HDC RoadDC, HDC Road2DC)
 99: {
100:   G->ScoreRep.NumPrizes = 0;
101:   for (int i = 0; i < MAXY; i++)
102:     for (int j = G->Dat.MinCols; j < G->Dat.MaxCols; j++)
103:     {
104:       switch (G->Map[i][j])
105:       {
106:         case ROADMAP:
107:           BlitIt(PaintDC, RoadDC, i, j);
108:           break;
109:
110:         case GRASSMAP:
111:           BlitIt(PaintDC, GrassDC, i, j);
112:           break;
113:
114:         case PRIZEMAP:
115:           BlitIt(PaintDC, Road2DC, i, j);
116:           G->ScoreRep.NumPrizes++;
117:           break;
118:       }
119:     }
120: }
121:
122: /////////////////////////////
123: // Paint The Field of Play
124: /////////////////////////////
125: void PaintPlayingField(HDC PaintDC)
126: {
127:   TSAVEBITMAPARY SB;
128:
129:   HDC GrassDC = GetScaledDC(PaintDC, SB, SMap.Grass, EGrass);
130:   HDC RoadDC = GetScaledDC(PaintDC, SB, SMap.Road, ERoad);
131:   HDC Road2DC = GetScaledDC(PaintDC, SB, SMap.Road2, ERoad2);
132:
133:   PaintBitmaps(PaintDC, GrassDC, RoadDC, Road2DC);
134:
135:   DisposeScaledDC(SB, EGrass);
136:   DisposeScaledDC(SB, ERoad);
137:   DisposeScaledDC(SB, ERoad2);
138: }
139:
140: /////////////////////////////////////////////
141: // Draw the actual bridge to next screen
142: /////////////////////////////////////////////
143: void MakeAndPaintBridge(HWND hwnd)
144: {
145:   TSAVEBITMAPARY SB;
146:
147:   G->Map[BRIDGEX1][G->Dat.MaxCols - 1] = ROADMAP;
```

continues

Listing 21.5. continued

```
148:    G->Map[BRIDGEX2][G->Dat.MaxCols - 1] = ROADMAP;
149:
150:    HDC PaintDC = GetDC(hwnd);
151:    HDC RoadDC = GetScaledDC(PaintDC, SB, SMap.Road, ERoad);
152:
153:    BitBlt(PaintDC, (JUMPSPACE - 1) * G->Dat.GrassX,
154:          (BRIDGEX1 * G->Dat.GrassY) +
155:          (G->Dat.GrassY * G->Dat.MenuSpace),
156:           G->Dat.GrassX, G->Dat.GrassY, RoadDC, 0, 0, SRCCOPY);
157:    BitBlt(PaintDC, (JUMPSPACE - 1) * G->Dat.GrassX,
158:          (BRIDGEX2 * G->Dat.GrassY) +
159:          (G->Dat.GrassY * G->Dat.MenuSpace),
160:           G->Dat.GrassX, G->Dat.GrassY, RoadDC, 0, 0, SRCCOPY);
161:
162:    DisposeScaledDC(SB, ERoad);
163:    ReleaseDC(hwnd, PaintDC);
164: }
```

Listing 21.6 shows the SnakoPnt header file.

Listing 21.6. SNAKOPNT.H.

```
 1: //////////////////////////////////////////////
 2: // Program Name: SNAKOPNT.H
 3: // Programmer: Charlie Calvert
 4: // Description: Draw playing field and the snake
 5: // Date: 08/05/93
 6: //////////////////////////////////////////////
 7:
 8: void MakeAndPaintBridge(HWND hwnd);
 9: void DoSnakePainting(HWND hwnd);
10: void PaintPlayingField(HDC PaintDC);
11: void PaintNewSection(HWND hwnd);
```

Listing 21.7 shows the SnakUtil source file.

Listing 21.7. SNAKUTIL.CPP.

```
 1: //////////////////////////////////////////////
 2: // Program Name: SNAKUTIL.CPP
 3: // Programmer: Charlie Calvert
 4: // Description: Miscellaneous routines
 5: // Date: 08/05/93
 6: //////////////////////////////////////////////
```

```
 7:
 8: #define STRICT
 9: #include <windows.h>
10: #include <windowsx.h>
11: #include <stdlib.h>
12: #include <string.h>
13: #include <stdio.h>
14: #include "snako.h"
15:
16: extern PGAMEINFO SaveGame;
17: extern PGAMEINFO G;
18:
19: ////////////////////////////////
20: //  Save Game from Memory
21: ////////////////////////////////
22: BOOL ReadGameFromMemory(void)
23: {
24:   memcpy(G, SaveGame, sizeof(TGAMEINFO));
25:   return TRUE;
26: }
27:
28: ////////////////////////////////
29: //  Save Game to Memory
30: ////////////////////////////////
31: BOOL SaveGameToMemory(HWND hwnd)
32: {
33:   if (!SaveGame)
34:   {
35:     free(SaveGame);
36:     SaveGame = NULL;
37:   }
38:
39:   if((SaveGame = (PGAMEINFO)malloc(sizeof(TGAMEINFO))) == NULL)
40:     MessageBox(hwnd,"Memory is hosed!","Closing Snako",MB_OK);
41:     return FALSE;
42:   }
43:   memcpy(SaveGame, G, sizeof(TGAMEINFO));
44:   return TRUE;
45: }
46:
47:
48: /////////////////////////////////////////
49 // Stretch the bitmaps to fit users
50: // screen resolution
51: /////////////////////////////////////////
52: HDC GetScaledDC(HDC PaintDC, TSAVEBITMAPARY SB,
53:                 HBITMAP Bmp, int Num)
```

continues

Listing 21.7. continued

```
54: {
55:    SB[Num].CompDC = CreateCompatibleDC(PaintDC);
56:    SB[Num].TCompDC = CreateCompatibleDC(PaintDC);
57:    SB[Num].CompBmp = CreateCompatibleBitmap(PaintDC,
58:                          G->Dat.GrassX, G->Dat.GrassY);
59:    SB[Num].OldBmp = SelectBitmap(SB[Num].CompDC, Bmp);
60:    SB[Num].OldTBmp = SelectBitmap(SB[Num].TCompDC,
61:                          SB[Num].CompBmp);
62:
63:    StretchBlt(SB[Num].TCompDC,
64:                 0, 0, G->Dat.GrassX, G->Dat.GrassY,
65:                   SB[Num].CompDC, 0, 0, XWIDTH, YHEIGHT, SRCCOPY);
66:
67:    return SB[Num].TCompDC;
68: }
69:
70: ///////////////////////////////////////
71: // Dispose resources created in GetScaledDC
72: ///////////////////////////////////////
73: BOOL DisposeScaledDC(TSAVEBITMAPARY SB, int Num)
74: {
75:    SelectBitmap(SB[Num].CompDC, SB[Num].OldBmp);
76:    SelectBitmap(SB[Num].TCompDC, SB[Num].OldTBmp);
77:    DeleteBitmap(SB[Num].CompBmp);
78:    DeleteDC(SB[Num].CompDC);
79:    DeleteDC(SB[Num].TCompDC);
80:    return TRUE;
81: }
82:
83: ///////////////////////////////////////
84: // Called whenever a new game is started
85: ///////////////////////////////////////
86: void InitializeSections(void)
87: {
88:    int i, StartCol, StartRow;
89:
90:    StartCol = -1;
91:    StartRow = 0;
92:    G->Dat.XPos = 0;
93:    G->Dat.Sections = 1;
94:    G->Dat.MaxCols = 32;
95:    G->Dat.MinCols = 0;
96:    G->Dat.NewScreenStarted = FALSE;
97:
98:    G->ScoreRep.ScreenNum = 1;
99:    G->ScoreRep.TotalScore = 0;
100:   G->ScoreRep.NumPrizes = 0;
101:   G->ScoreRep.Level = 1;
102:
103:   for (i = 0; i < 2; i++)
```

```
104:     {
105:       G->SectInfo[i].Dir = RIGHT;
106:       G->SectInfo[i].DirChange = FALSE;
107:       G->SectInfo[i].Col = StartCol - i;
108:       G->SectInfo[i].Row = StartRow;
109:       G->SectInfo[i].OldCol = G->SectInfo[i].Col;
110:       G->SectInfo[i].OldRow = G->SectInfo[i].Row;
111:     }
112: }
113:
114: ///////////////////////////////////////
115: // So you made it level two...
116: ///////////////////////////////////////
117: void InitializeNewLevel(void)
118: {
119:     int i, StartCol, StartRow;
120:
121:     StartCol = -1;
122:     StartRow = 0;
123:     G->Dat.XPos = 0;
124:     G->Dat.MaxCols = 32;
125:     G->Dat.MinCols = 0;
126:     G->ScoreRep.ScreenNum = 1;
127:
128:     // line 'em up off screen one behind next
129:     for (i = 0; i <= G->Dat.Sections; i++)
130:     {
131:       G->SectInfo[i].Dir = RIGHT;
132:       G->SectInfo[i].DirChange = FALSE;
133:       G->SectInfo[i].Col = StartCol - i;
134:       G->SectInfo[i].Row = StartRow;
135:       G->SectInfo[i].OldCol = G->SectInfo[i].Col;
136:       G->SectInfo[i].OldRow = G->SectInfo[i].Row;
137:     }
138: }
139:
140: ///////////////////////////////////////
141: // Crossing the border...
142: ///////////////////////////////////////
143: void StartNewScreen(HWND hwnd)
144: {
145:     InitializeNewLevel();
146:     ReadArray(hwnd);
147:     InvalidateRect(hwnd, NULL, FALSE);
148: }
149:
150: ///////////////////////////////////////
151: // Read screen arrays into memory
152: // Change case statement to add levels
153: ///////////////////////////////////////
```

continues

Listing 21.7. continued

```
154: int ReadArray(HWND hwnd)
155: {
156:   FILE * fp;
157:   char FileName[50];
158:
159:   switch (G->ScoreRep.Level)
160:   {
161:     case 1: strcpy(FileName, "Screen.Dta"); break;
162:     case 2: strcpy(FileName, "Screen1.Dta"); break;
163:   }
164:
165:   if ((fp = fopen(FileName, "r")) == NULL)
166:   {
167:     MessageBox(hwnd, "No Stream", "NULL", MB_OK);
168:     return FALSE;
169:   }
170:
171:   if((fread(G->Map, sizeof(G->Map), 1, fp)) == 0)
172:   {
173:     MessageBox(hwnd, "No map", "Grunt", MB_OK);
174:     return FALSE;
175:   }
176:
177:   fclose(fp);
178:
179:   return TRUE;
180: }
181:
182: /////////////////////////////////////
183: // If you ever get caught on a level
184: // and can't get out even though
185: // you've eaten all dots, call this
186: // from third line of Snako_OnTimer
187: /////////////////////////////////////
188: void QuickScan(void)
189: {
190:   G->ScoreRep.NumPrizes = 0;
191:   int TotalX = G->Dat.MinCols + JUMPSPACE;
192:
193:   for (int i = 0; i < MAXY; i++)
194:     for (int j = G->Dat.MinCols; j < TotalX; j++)
195:       if(G->Map[i][j] == PRIZEMAP)
196:         G->ScoreRep.NumPrizes++;
197: }
198:
199: /////////////////////////////////////
200: // Perform setup => initialize Timer
201: /////////////////////////////////////
202: BOOL SetUpWindow(HWND hwnd)
```

```
203: {
204:   if (!SetTimer(hwnd, SNAKETIMER, 175, NULL))
205:   {
206:     MessageBox(hwnd, "No Timers Available", "Snako", MB_OK);
207:      return FALSE;
208:   }
209:      return TRUE;
210: }
```

Listing 21.8 shows the SnakUtil header file.

 Listing 21.8. SNAKUTIL.H.

```
1: /////////////////////////////////////////////
2: // Program Name: SNAKUTIL.H
3: // Programmer: Charlie Calvert
4: // Description: Miscellaneous routines
5: // Date: 08/05/93
6: /////////////////////////////////////////////
7:
8: #include "snako.h"
9:
10: BOOL ReadGameFromMemory(void);
11: BOOL SaveGameToMemory(HWND hwnd);
12: BOOL DisposeScaledDC(TSAVEBITMAPARY SB, int Num);
13: void StartNewScreen(HWND hwnd);
14: int ReadArray(HWND hwnd);
15: void InitializeSections(void);
16: void QuickScan(void);
17: BOOL SetUpWindow(HWND hwnd);
18: HDC GetScaledDC(HDC PaintDC, TSAVEBITMAPARY SB,
19:                 HBITMAP Bmp, int Num);
```

Listing 21.9 shows the Score source file.

 Listing 21.9. SCORE.CPP.

```
1: /////////////////////////////////////////////
2: // Program Name: SCORE.CPP
3: // Programmer: Charlie Calvert
4: // Description: Score window and SaveScore dialog
5: // Date: 08/05/93
6: /////////////////////////////////////////////
```

continues

Listing 21.9. continued

```
 7:
 8: #define STRICT
 9: #include <windows.h>
10: #include <windowsx.h>
11: #pragma hdrstop
12: #include <stdLib.h>
13: #include <stdio.h>
14: #include <string.h>
15: #include "snako.h"
16: #include "score.h"
17: #pragma warning(disable: 4068)
18: #pragma warning(disable: 4100)
19: #define TOTALSCORES 16
20:
21: struct TSCORESTRUCT {
22:   char Name[SCORESIZE];
23:   LONG Total;
24: } SCORESTRUCT;
25:
26: // Variables
27: LONG NewScore;
28: HBRUSH Pattern;
29: TSCORESTRUCT Scores[TOTALSCORES];
30: HWND hStaticWind, hStaticScore;
31: HWND hStatScreen, hDotsLeftWin;
32: HBITMAP Patternmap;
33: BOOL ScoreRecorded = FALSE;
34: extern BOOL ChangeScore = FALSE;
35: FILE * fp;
36:
37: //////////////////////////////////////
38: // ScoreDlgProc
39: //////////////////////////////////////
40: void DoScoreDlg(HWND hwnd)
41: {
42:   HINSTANCE hInstance;
43:   FARPROC ScoreBox;
44:
45:   hInstance = (HINSTANCE)GetWindowWord(hwnd, GWW_HINSTANCE);
46:   ScoreBox = MakeProcInstance((FARPROC)ScoreDlgProc, hInstance);
47:   DialogBox(hInstance, "Scores", hwnd, (DLGPROC)ScoreBox);
48:   FreeProcInstance(ScoreBox);
49:   ChangeScore = FALSE;
50: }
51:
52:
53: //////////////////////////////////////
54: // The window procedure
55: //////////////////////////////////////
```

```
56: LRESULT CALLBACK __export ScoreWndProc(HWND hwnd, UINT Message,
57:                                  WPARAM wParam, LPARAM lParam)
58: {
59:   TSCOREREP * ScoreRep;
60:   char S[10];
61:
62:   switch(Message)
63:   {
64:     case WM_SETNUMSEGS:
65:       ScoreRep = (TSCOREREP *)lParam;
66:       SetWindowText(hStaticWind,itoa(ScoreRep->NumSects,S,10));
67:       SetWindowText(hDotsLeftWin,ltoa(ScoreRep->NumPrizes,S,10));
68:      SetWindowText(hStaticScore,ltoa(ScoreRep->TotalScore,S,10));
69:       SetWindowText(hStatScreen,itoa(ScoreRep->ScreenNum,S,10));
70:       return 0;
71:
72:     case WM_SCORE:
73:       ChangeScore = TRUE;
74:       NewScore = lParam;
75:       DoScoreDlg(hwnd);
76:       return 0;
77:
78:     HANDLE_MSG(hwnd, WM_CREATE, Score_OnCreate);
79:     HANDLE_MSG(hwnd, WM_DESTROY, Score_OnDestroy);
80:     HANDLE_MSG(hwnd, WM_COMMAND, Score_OnCommand);
81:     HANDLE_MSG(hwnd, WM_CTLCOLOR, Score_OnCtlColor);
82:     default: return Score_DefProc(hwnd, Message, wParam, lParam);
83:   }
84: }
85:
86: /////////////////////////////////////////
87: // Handle WM_CREATE
88: /////////////////////////////////////////
89: #pragma argsused
90: BOOL Score_OnCreate(HWND hwnd, CREATESTRUCT FAR* lpCreateStruct)
91: {
92:   int YTopRow = 5;    // Place where top row of statics appear
93:   int YSecRow = 30;   // Second row of statics start here
94:   int SHeight = 17;   // Height of statics
95:   int BHeight = 22;   // Height of Buttons
96:
97:   HINSTANCE hInstance =
98:           (HINSTANCE)GetWindowWord(hwnd, GWW_HINSTANCE);
99:
100:   Patternmap = LoadBitmap(hInstance, "Pattern");
101:   if (!Patternmap)
102:   {
103:     MessageBox(hwnd, "No Pattern", "Fatal Error", MB_OK);
104:     return FALSE;
105:   }
```

continues

Listing 21.9. continued

```
106:
107:     Pattern = CreatePatternBrush(Patternmap);
108:     SetClassWord(hwnd, GCW_HBRBACKGROUND, (WORD)Pattern);
109:
110:     CreateWindow("static", "Num Sections",
111:                     WS_CHILD | WS_VISIBLE | SS_LEFT,
112:                     10, YTopRow, 95, SHeight, hwnd, NULL,
113:                     hInstance, NULL);
114:
115:     hStaticWind = CreateWindow("static", "0",
116:                     WS_CHILD | WS_VISIBLE | SS_LEFT,
117:                     110, YTopRow, 50, SHeight, hwnd, NULL,
118:                     hInstance, NULL);
119:
120:     CreateWindow("static", "Total Score ",
121:                     WS_CHILD | WS_VISIBLE | SS_LEFT,
122:                     10, YSecRow, 95, SHeight, hwnd, NULL,
123:                     hInstance, NULL);
124:
125:     hStaticScore = CreateWindow("static", "0",
126:                     WS_CHILD | WS_VISIBLE | SS_LEFT,
127:                     110, YSecRow, 50, SHeight, hwnd, NULL,
128:                     hInstance, NULL);
129:
130:     // Right Screen
131:
132:     int XVal = GetSystemMetrics(SM_CXFULLSCREEN) - 160;
133:
134:     CreateWindow("static", "Screen Num",
135:                     WS_CHILD | WS_VISIBLE | SS_LEFT,
136:                     XVal, YTopRow, 95, SHeight, hwnd, NULL,
137:                     hInstance, NULL);
138:
139:     hStatScreen  = CreateWindow("static", "0",
140:                     WS_CHILD | WS_VISIBLE | SS_LEFT,
141:                     XVal + 100, YTopRow, 50, SHeight, hwnd, NULL,
142:                     hInstance, NULL);
143:
144:     CreateWindow("static", "Dots Left",
145:                     WS_CHILD | WS_VISIBLE | SS_LEFT,
146:                     XVal, YSecRow, 95, SHeight, hwnd, NULL,
147:                     hInstance, NULL);
148:
149:     hDotsLeftWin = CreateWindow("static", "0",
150:                     WS_CHILD | WS_VISIBLE | SS_LEFT,
151:                     XVal + 100, YSecRow, 50, SHeight, hwnd, NULL,
152:                     hInstance, NULL);
153:
154:     int Width = GetSystemMetrics(SM_CXSCREEN) / 2;
155:
```

```
156:    CreateWindow("button", "&Start",
157:                  WS_CHILD | WS_VISIBLE | BS_PUSHBUTTON,
158:                  Width - 100, YTopRow, 60, BHeight, hwnd,
159:                  HMENU(ID_START), hInstance, NULL);
160:
161:    CreateWindow("button", "&Fini",
162:                  WS_CHILD | WS_VISIBLE | BS_PUSHBUTTON,
163:                  Width - 30, YTopRow, 60, BHeight, hwnd,
164:                  HMENU(ID_FINI), hInstance, NULL);
165:
166:    CreateWindow("button", "Sco&res",
167:                  WS_CHILD | WS_VISIBLE | BS_PUSHBUTTON,
168:                  Width + 40, YTopRow, 60, BHeight, hwnd,
169:                  HMENU(ID_SCORE), hInstance, NULL);
170:
171:    return TRUE;
172: }
173:
174: /////////////////////////////////////
175: // Handle WM_DESTROY
176: /////////////////////////////////////
177: #pragma argsused
178: void Score_OnDestroy(HWND hwnd)
179: {
180:    SetClassWord(hwnd, GCW_HBRBACKGROUND, NULL);
181:    DeleteBrush(Pattern);
182:    DeleteBitmap(Patternmap);
183:    PostQuitMessage(0);
184: }
185:
186: /////////////////////////////////////
187: // Handle WM_COMMAND
188: /////////////////////////////////////
189: #pragma argsused
190: void Score_OnCommand(HWND hwnd, int id,
191:                      HWND hwndCtl, UINT codeNotify)
192: {
193:    switch(id)
194:    {
195:     case ID_START:
196:       SendMessage(GetParent(hwnd), WM_START, 0, 0L);
197:       break;
198:
199:     case ID_FINI:
200:       SendMessage(GetParent(hwnd), WM_CLOSE, 0, 0L);
201:       break;
202:
203:     case ID_SCORE:
204:       DoScoreDlg(hwnd);
205:       break;
```

continues

Listing 21.9. continued

```
206:    }
207: }
208:
209: /////////////////////////////////////
210: // Color of controls for ScoreWindow
211: /////////////////////////////////////
212: HBRUSH Score_OnCtlColor(HWND hwnd, HDC hdc,
213:                             HWND hwndChild, int type)
214: {
215:    switch(type)
216:    {
217:      case CTLCOLOR_STATIC:
218:      case CTLCOLOR_BTN:
219:      case CTLCOLOR_EDIT:
220:        SetTextColor(hdc, RGB(0, 127, 0));
221:         SetBkMode(hdc, TRANSPARENT);
222:        return GetStockBrush(BLACK_BRUSH);
223:    }
224:    return FORWARD_WM_CTLCOLOR(hwnd, hdc, hwndChild,
225:                                type, Score_DefProc);
226: }
227:
228: /////////////////////////////////////
229: // ScoreDlgProc
230: /////////////////////////////////////
231: int OpenScores(FILE * fp)
232: {
233:    if ((fp = fopen("Scores.Dta", "r+")) == NULL)
234:    {
235:      fp = fopen("Scores.Dta", "w+");
236:      memset(Scores, '\0', sizeof(Scores));
237:    }
238:    else
239:      fread(&Scores, sizeof(Scores), 1, fp);
240:
241:    fclose(fp);
242:    return 1;
243: }
244:
245: /////////////////////////////////////
246: // File io
247: /////////////////////////////////////
248: BOOL CloseScores(HWND hwnd, FILE * fp)
249: {
250:    int Result;
251:
252:    if ((fp = fopen("Scores.Dta", "w+")) == NULL)
253:    {
254:      MessageBox(hwnd, "Error", "er", MB_OK);
```

```
255:     return 0;
256:   }
257:
258:   Result = fwrite(&Scores, sizeof(Scores), 1, fp);
259:   if (!Result)
260:   {
261:     MessageBox(hwnd, "Error", "er", MB_OK);
262:     return 0;
263:   }
264:
265:   fclose(fp);
266:   return 1;
267: }
268:
269: /////////////////////////////////////////
270: // FillListBox
271: /////////////////////////////////////////
272: void FillListBox(HWND hDlg)
273: {
274:   char S[150];
275:
276:   for (int i = 1; i < TOTALSCORES; i++)
277:   {
278:     if (strlen(Scores[i].Name) == 0)
279:       strcpy(Scores[i].Name, "Sammy");
280:     sprintf(S, "%2i) %-20s %10ld", i,
281:             Scores[i].Name, Scores[i].Total);
282:     SendDlgItemMessage(hDlg, ID_SCOREBOX,
283:                        LB_ADDSTRING, 0, (LPARAM)S);
284:       }
285: }
286:
287: /////////////////////////////////////////
288: // Swap routine
289: /////////////////////////////////////////
290: void Swap(int i, int j)
291: {
292:   TSCORESTRUCT temp;
293:   temp = Scores[i];
294:   Scores[i] = Scores[j];
295:   Scores[j] = temp;
296: }
297:
298: /////////////////////////////////////////
299: // SortScores
300: /////////////////////////////////////////
301: void SortScores(void)
302: {
303:   for (int i = TOTALSCORES; i >= 1; i--)
304:     for (int j = 2; j <= i; j++)
```

continues

21

Listing 21.9. continued

```
305:         if (Scores[j - 1].Total < Scores[j].Total)
306:            Swap(j-1, j);
307: }
308:
309: ///////////////////////////////////////////
310: // RecordScore
311: ///////////////////////////////////////////
312: void RecordScore(HWND hDlg)
313: {
314:   SendDlgItemMessage(hDlg, ID_SCORENAME, WM_GETTEXT, SCORESIZE,
315:                         (LPARAM)Scores[TOTALSCORES - 1].Name);
316:   Scores[TOTALSCORES-1].Total = NewScore;
317:   SortScores();
318:     SendDlgItemMessage(hDlg, ID_SCOREBOX, LB_RESETCONTENT,0,0);
319:   FillListBox(hDlg);
320: }
321:
322: ///////////////////////////////////////////
323: // Automatically center a dialog
324: ///////////////////////////////////////////
325: void CenterDialog(HWND hDlg)
326: {
327:   RECT R;
328:   int i = GetSystemMetrics(SM_CXSCREEN);
329:   int j = GetSystemMetrics(SM_CYSCREEN);
330:   int Height = GetSystemMetrics(SM_CYCAPTION);
331:   Height += (GetSystemMetrics(SM_CYDLGFRAME) * 2);
332:   int Width = GetSystemMetrics(SM_CXDLGFRAME) * 2;
333:   GetClientRect(hDlg, &R);
334:   MoveWindow(hDlg, (i / 2)-(R.right / 2),  (j / 2)-R.bottom / 2,
335:             R.right + Width, R.bottom + Height, FALSE);
336: }
337:
338: ///////////////////////////////////////////
339: // The Score Dialog Proc so user can
340: // see lists of scores and add his own
341: ///////////////////////////////////////////
342: #pragma argsused
343: BOOL CALLBACK ScoreDlgProc(HWND hDlg, WORD Message,
344:                             WPARAM wParam, LPARAM lParam)
345: {
346:   switch(Message)
347:   {
348:     case WM_INITDIALOG:
349:       SetWindowFont(GetDlgItem(hDlg, ID_SCOREBOX),
350:                     GetStockObject(SYSTEM_FIXED_FONT), FALSE);
351:       Edit_LimitText(GetDlgItem(hDlg, ID_SCORENAME), 20);
352:       OpenScores(fp);
353:       FillListBox(hDlg);
```

```
354:        if (ChangeScore)
355:          PostMessage(hDlg, WM_FOCUS, 0, 0);
356:        else
357:          {
358:             MoveWindow(GetDlgItem(hDlg, ID_SCOREBOX),
359:                        10, 6, 365, 225, FALSE);
360:             MoveWindow(GetDlgItem(hDlg, IDOK),
361:                        8, 240, 370, 25, FALSE);
362:             ShowWindow(GetDlgItem(hDlg, ID_SCORENAME), SW_HIDE);
363:             ShowWindow(GetDlgItem(hDlg, ID_SCORESTAT), SW_HIDE);
364:             ShowWindow(GetDlgItem(hDlg, ID_NEWNAME), SW_HIDE);
365:          }
366:        CenterDialog(hDlg);
367:        return TRUE;
368:
369:      case WM_FOCUS:
370:        SetFocus(GetDlgItem(hDlg, ID_SCORENAME));
371:        break;
372:
373:      case WM_COMMAND:
374:        switch(wParam)
375:          {
376:            case IDOK:
377:            case IDCANCEL:
378:              if (!ScoreRecorded)
379:                RecordScore(hDlg);
380:              if (ChangeScore)
381:                CloseScores(hDlg, fp);
382:              ScoreRecorded = FALSE;
383:              EndDialog(hDlg, TRUE);
384:              return TRUE;
385:
386:            case ID_NEWNAME:
387:              RecordScore(hDlg);
388:              ScoreRecorded = TRUE;
389:              return TRUE;
390:          }
391:     }
392:   return FALSE;
393: }
```

21

Listing 21.10 shows the Score header file.

 Listing 21.10. SCORE.H.

```
 1: ////////////////////////////////////////////////
 2: // SCORE.H
 3: // Used in SNAKE.CPP
 4: // Programmer: Charlie Calvert
 5: ////////////////////////////////////////////////
 6:
 7: #if !defined _SCORE_H
 8: #define _SCORE_H
 9:
10: // Const
11: #define SCORESIZE 75
12: #define WM_SETNUMSEGS (WM_USER + 0)
13: #define WM_START (WM_USER + 1)
14: #define WM_FINI (WM_USER + 2)
15: #define WM_SCORE (WM_USER + 3)
16: #define WM_FOCUS (WM_USER + 4)
17: #define ID_START 190
18: #define ID_FINI 191
19: #define ID_SCORE 192
20:
21: #define ID_SCOREBOX 175
22: #define ID_SCORENAME 176
23: #define ID_SCORESTAT 177
24: #define ID_NEWNAME 178
25:
26: // Class Score
27: #define Score_DefProc     DefWindowProc
28: BOOL Score_OnCreate(HWND hwnd, CREATESTRUCT FAR* lpCreateStruct);
29: void Score_OnDestroy(HWND hwnd);
30: void Score_OnCommand(HWND hwnd, int id,
31:                      HWND hwndCtl, UINT codeNotify);
32: HBRUSH Score_OnCtlColor(HWND hwnd, HDC hdc,
33:                         HWND hwndChild, int type);
34:
35: #endif
36:
37: // Procs
38: LRESULT CALLBACK __export ScoreWndProc(HWND, UINT,
39:                                        WPARAM, LPARAM);
40: BOOL CALLBACK ScoreDlgProc(HWND hDlg, WORD Message,
41:                            WPARAM wParam, LPARAM lParam);
```

Listing 21.11 shows the Snako resource file.

 Listing 21.11. SNAKO.RC.

```
 1: /////////////////////////////////////////////
 2: //   Program Name: SNAKO.RC
 3: //   Programmer: Charlie Calvert
 4: //   Description: A windows game
 5: //   Date: 08/05/93
 6: /////////////////////////////////////////////
 7:
 8: #include <windows.h>
 9: #include "score.h"
10:
11: Body    BITMAP "body.bmp"
12: Head    BITMAP "head.bmp"
13: Pattern BITMAP "pattern.bmp"
14: Grass   BITMAP "grass.bmp"
15: Road    BITMAP "road.bmp"
16: Road2   BITMAP "road2.bmp"
17:
18: #define NORMALSTY WS_CHILD ¦ WS_VISIBLE ¦ WS_TABSTOP
19: #define LISTBOXSTY LBS_NOTIFY ¦ WS_CHILD ¦ WS_VISIBLE ¦ \
20:                    WS_BORDER ¦ WS_VSCROLL
21:
22: Scores DIALOG 18, 18, 193, 136
23: STYLE DS_MODALFRAME ¦ WS_POPUP ¦ WS_VISIBLE ¦
         WS_CAPTION ¦ WS_SYSMENU
24: CAPTION "Score Dialog"
25: BEGIN
26:         PUSHBUTTON "Close", IDOK, 8, 121, 176, 10, NORMALSTY
27:         LISTBOX ID_SCOREBOX, 10, 6, 172, 91, LISTBOXSTY
28:         LTEXT "Enter Name", ID_SCORESTAT, 13, 104, 41, 8
29:         EDITTEXT ID_SCORENAME, 56, 102, 124, 12
30: END
```

BODY.BMP (25X25)   *HEAD.BMP (25X25)*   *PATTERN.BMP (8X8)*

GRASS.BMP (25X25)   ROAD.BMP (25X25)   ROAD2.BMP (25X25)

Listing 21.12 shows the Snako definition file.

Type   **Listing 21.12. SNAKO.DEF.**

```
 1: ;SNAKO.DEF
 2:
 3: NAME                SNAKO
 4: DESCRIPTION         'Snako (c) 1993 Charlie Calvert'
 5: EXETYPE             Windows
 6: STUB                'WINSTUB.EXE'
 7: CODE                PRELOAD MOVEABLE DISCARDABLE
 8: DATA                PRELOAD MOVEABLE MULTIPLE
 9: HEAPSIZE            20000
10: STACKSIZE           5120
```

Listing 21.13 shows the Borland makefile for Snako.

Type   **Listing 21.13. SNAKO.MAK (Borland).**

```
 1: # SNAKO.MAK
 2:
 3: APPNAME = Snako
 4: INCPATH = C:\BC\INCLUDE
 5: LIBPATH = C:\BC\LIB
 6: OBJS = SNAKO.OBJ SCORE.OBJ GRUNT.OBJ SNAKUTIL.OBJ SNAKOPNT.OBJ
 7: CFLAGS = -ml -WE -v -w4 -I$(INCPATH) -L$(LIBPATH)
 8:
 9: # linking
10: $(APPNAME).exe: $(OBJS) $(APPNAME).def $(APPNAME).res
11:   bcc $(CFLAGS) $(OBJS)
12:   brc $(APPNAME).res
13:
14: # compiling
15: .cpp.obj:
16:   bcc -c $(CFLAGS) { $<        }
```

```
17:
18: # resource
19: $(APPNAME).res: $(APPNAME).rc
20:    brc -r -I$(INCPATH) $(APPNAME).rc
```

Listing 21.14 shows the Microsoft makefile for Snako.

 Listing 21.14. SNAKO.MAK (Microsoft).

```
 1: # Snako makefile
 2:
 3: MAIN = Snako
 4: OBJS = SNAKO.OBJ SCORE.OBJ GRUNT.OBJ SNAKUTIL.OBJ SNAKOPNT.OBJ
 5:
 6: # Link
 7: $(MAIN).exe : $(OBJS) $(MAIN).def $(MAIN).res
 8:    link /CO$(OBJS), /align:16, NUL, /nod llibcew libw oldnames,
    $(MAIN)
 9:    rc $(MAIN).res
10:
11: # Compile
12: .cpp.obj:
13:    cl -c -AL -GA -Ow -W4 -Zp -Zi { $< }
14:
15: # Resource
16: $(MAIN).res : $(MAIN).rc
17:    rc -r $(MAIN).rc
```

 Figure 21.4 shows an error box appearing in the Snako program.

 To make things comprehensible and maintainable, I have divided the code into five modules:

☐ SNAKO.CPP: This is where you find the hard-core Windows material. There's a WndProc, a WinMain, and various message response functions.

☐ SNAKOPNT.CPP: This is the code that paints the snake to the screen. It gets called in response to WM_PAINT and WM_TIMER messages.

☐ GRUNT.CPP: This is the logic that makes the snake move around the screen.

☐ SNAKUTIL.CPP: This is a place to store generic routines used by one or more of the previous modules.

☐ SCORE.CPP: A return to Windows basics, this module controls the child window in which the program's score is displayed, as well as the dialog that enables the user to record his or her forays onto the playing field.

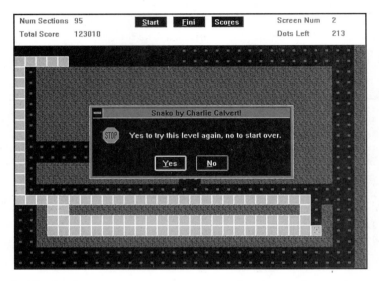

Figure 21.4. *The Snake program as it appears just after the user has made an error.*

This outline should serve as your guide to finding your way around the Snako program. The key point to grasp is that each major function of the program takes place in its own module. Once you grasp the basic categories involved, you should know where to look for a particular routine.

Note that the Snako program is designed to be compiled in the Large memory model. In general, this is probably the best model for all Windows programs, but it is especially useful in this particular case because of the way the program uses pointers.

Remember that the Mapper program, presented on Day 16, is used to design the screens for the Snako program. At some point, you should probably take the time to reread what is said there, because it reveals much about the basic structure behind Snako.

Strategic Overview

In its simplest possible form, here's the logic that drives the program:

1. The entire state of the game is stored in a single variable called G, which is of type PGAMEINFO. PGAMEINFO is a pointer to a structure defined in SNAKO.H.

2. The game is driven by a single timer. Snake_OnTimer calls MoveBitMap, which is found in the GRUNT.CPP module.

3. MoveBitMap first calls SetColRow. This function is the guiding hand in the Grunt module. It calculates where the snake will go next and updates the program's data accordingly. If the snake is going to die, this is where the error is detected.

4. MoveBitMap then calls DoSnakePainting, which is located in SNAKOPNT.CPP. This is where all the painting takes place. Notice that the snake is painted separately from the background. If the snake and the background were painted in the same procedure, the whole background would have to be drawn whenever the snake moves. Such a solution proves to be too expensive in terms of clock cycles.

5. Whenever the user moves on to a new screen, the current state of the game is saved into a pointer of type PGAMEINFO. If the user makes a mistake, the game can be restored from the information kept in this pointer. The logic that decides when to store and restore the game is in GRUNT.CPP. The actual copying of the pointer is performed in SNAKUTIL.CPP.

6. Every time the user earns the right to move on to a new screen, the MakeGateWay function, found in GRUNT.CPP, gets called. This function detects a change in level and whether or not the user has won the game.

As I stated earlier, this chapter is included in this book so that you can have a little fun both playing and hacking the Snako game. As a result, I'm not going to spend a lot of time discussing technical issues. But I am going to take a few minutes to describe pointers, file I/O, and a method for centering a dialog. The first two of these subjects are relatively easy to master, but they are essential cornerstones in the construction of most Windows programs.

21

Using Pointers

The Snako program allocates memory for two pointers. To understand why this is necessary, you have to understand something about the way a typical 16-bit Windows program treats memory.

Most Windows programs are forced to keep their data, stack, and local heap in a single 64K segment called the DGROUP. This means that there is usually very little room for a program's data. To make up for this lack of available real estate, most Windows programs end up allocating memory from the global heap.

Because the snake in the Snako program could become very large, there is a potential need for a good deal of memory. Furthermore, when the user starts a new screen, all the program's data is copied into a variable where it can be retrieved if the user needs to take a second crack at a particular screen. In other words, the Snako program needs to keep track of two fairly large chunks of memory. Because of the way Windows programs are structured, there is little room for the program's data. As a result, there is a need to create one or more additional segments in memory with an allocation from the system.

It's time now to become a little more specific, and to mention some of the key data structures in the Snako program. In order to keep things simple, Snako initializes a single struct that holds the current state of the game. This structure is called G; its memory is allocated during the call to Snako_OnCreate and deallocated during the call to Snako_OnDestroy.

Struct G is of type PGAMEINFO and holds the current state and shape of the snake, the current appearance of the screen, the score, and the screen and level numbers. More specifically, it encapsulates three additional structs and an array, all of which are defined in SNAKO.H:

```
typedef struct {
  TSCOREREP ScoreRep;
  char Map[MAXY][MAXX];
  TDATA Dat;
  TSECTINFO SectInfo[MAXSECTS];
} TGAMEINFO;
```

If you want to understand Snako, you have to become familiar with TGAMEINFO. Remember, it contains all the variables that define the current state of the game. Following is a brief overview of the structure:

☐ TSCOREREP is a structure that keeps track of the current level, screen, score, and the number of sections in the snake's body. Most of this information is displayed to the user in the SCORE.CPP module.

☐ Map holds the two-dimensional array that defines the current appearance of the game board. Each item in the array is set to either one, two, or three (GRASSMAP, PRIZEMAP, or ROADMAP), depending on whether it designates the grass bitmap, prize bitmap, or road bitmap.

☐ TDATA contains information about the current screen dimensions, as well as a number of other miscellaneous variables that need a home.

☐ TSECTINFO is used in an array in which each member defines the current state of a particular section of the Snake.

Here's how Snako allocates the memory for G:

```
if((G = (PGAMEINFO)malloc(sizeof(TGAMEINFO))) == NULL)
{
    MessageBox(hwnd, "No Memory!", "Closing Snako", MB_OK);
    return FALSE;
}
```

As you can see, nothing unusual is going on here. This is just a simple call to malloc, exactly as it would be performed in DOS. The end result is an allocation of memory designated explicitly for Snako's data. In other words, it moves the program's data out of the cramped DGROUP and into the wide open spaces of the heap!

The *malloc* Function

Syntax

```
void *malloc(size_t size);
```

This function returns a block of memory from the heap. It takes one parameter that designates the desired size of the memory allocation. Programmers typically use the sizeof keyword in this parameter in order to let the compiler calculate the size of a variable. Most of the time it's necessary to typecast the result of malloc to the type of the variable for which you are allocating memory. In DOS, programmers always need to be aware that a call to malloc might fail due to a lack of memory. This is much less likely on most Windows machines, but it is still an issue that you can't afford to overlook.

21

Example:

```
#define MAXSTRLEN 100
char * MyString;

if((MyString = (char *)malloc(MAXSTRLEN)) == NULL)
{
    MessageBox(hwnd, "No Memory!", "Error", MB_OK);
    return FALSE;
}
```

When it comes time to destroy the memory allocated by malloc, you need to do nothing more than make a simple call to free:

```
free(G);
```

I have chosen to concentrate on malloc, because it should be familiar to the widest possible audience. However, you can use either the new and delete operators, or the native Windows functions called GlobalAlloc and GlobalFree. However, it's often both simpler and wiser to call either new or malloc rather than calling GlobalAlloc directly (see the Note following the Syntax section).

Syntax

The *GlobalAlloc* Function

```
HGLOBAL GlobalAlloc(UINT fuAlloc, DWORDcbAlloc)
```

UINT fuAlloc;   A flag designating the traits of the memory to be allocated. Use this field to state whether you want the memory to be moveable, fixed, discardable, and so forth.

DWORD cbAlloc;   Parameter to specify how much memory you want to allocate

Every time you call GlobalAlloc, you should also make a call to GlobalLock before you attempt to use the memory. To deallocate the memory, call GlobalUnlock and GlobalFree.

Example:

```
HGLOBAL hglb;
char FAR* MyString;

hglb = GlobalAlloc(GPTR, 1024);
MyString = (char *)GlobalLock(hglb);
strcpy(MyString, "Fine Tuna");
MessageBox(hwnd, MyString, "Info", MB_OK);
GlobalUnlock(hglb);
GlobalFree(hglb);
```

Note: Smaller allocations of memory are often handled by a compiler's suballocator. Suballocators exist because no 16-bit protected mode program can ask the system for more than 8,192 memory allocations. In other words, on any one system, only 8,192 pointers can be requested from the operating environment at any one time. This means that if your program makes 8,000 allocations in a linked list, all other programs on the system only have 192 allocations available to them.

As a result, many compilers automatically allocate blocks of memory and then parcel chunks out to programs with a suballocator when needed. That is, the compiler allocates a chunk of some 4,000 bytes and then parcels this memory out to you in bits and pieces when you need it. As a result, only the initial 4,000-byte hit takes up one of the 8K of available handles. Each suballocation comes to you free, at least in terms of the 8,192 available handles.

This whole process takes place transparently, without the programmer ever having to worry about how it works. Requests for relatively large blocks of memory, however, are passed directly to Windows with a call to GlobalAlloc. The results of this call are passed back to your program. The presence of these suballocator schemes is one of the major reasons for using malloc or new rather than calling GlobalAlloc directly. See your compiler documentation for details. Really. Go look at the docs!

Here's the portion of the SNAKUTIL.CPP file in which a backup copy of the game's data is copied to a second pointer of type PGAMEINFO:

```
31: BOOL SaveGameToMemory(HWND hwnd)
32: {
33:   if (!SaveGame)
34:   {
35:     free(SaveGame);
36:     SaveGame = NULL;
37:   }
38:
39:   if((SaveGame =
          (PGAMEINFO)malloc(sizeof(TGAMEINFO))) == 40 NULL)
40:   {
41:     MessageBox(hwnd, "No Memory!", "Closing Snako", MB_OK);
42:     return FALSE;
43:   }
44:   memcpy(SaveGame, G, sizeof(TGAMEINFO));
45:   return TRUE;
46: }
```

21

Once again, this code should look very familiar to anyone who has used pointers in DOS, UNIX, or elsewhere.

The basic plan is simply to allocate some memory, and then use memcpy to move the program's data from one place on the heap to another. When it's time to get it back, the process is carried out in reverse. Notice that Snako is careful to check to see whether it needs to dispose of the SaveGame pointer before allocating new memory and copying the program's data into it. The program can always tell whether memory has been allocated for SaveGame by checking if the pointer has been set to NULL. To make this system work, you must specifically assign NULL to a pointer at startup time.

When the game is done, both G and SaveGame are deallocated, if necessary, in response to a WM_DESTROY message. You have to be absolutely certain that you always destroy every pointer you allocate, because allocations can remain intact even after your program has ended. This can muddy the waters so badly that the entire Windows system can come crashing down around the user's ears.

Note: In protected mode, programmers no longer have to worry about the famous 640K limitation that has hampered DOS programs for years. Windows programs that run in enhanced mode can have access to 10M, 20M, even 30M of memory, depending on the resources available in the current system. As a result, you can allocate many different 64K chunks of memory with malloc or new. Furthermore, you can allocate much larger chunks of memory with calls to GlobalAlloc. For instance, a 286 can allocate up to just under 1M at a time, and a 386 can allocate some 16M at a time. However, you should know that 16-bit systems need to page through large blocks of memory 64K at a time, with the good graces of a function called ahIncr—found in the Windows Kernal, index number 114.

After reading this last section, it should be clear that memory is a radically different beast in Windows than in DOS. The presence of functions like malloc, or operators like new, can serve to make the strange familiar; but you should always be aware that there are many new ideas to master. However, if all you need to do is create additional data space for your program, your DOS- or UNIX-based knowledge of pointers will stand you in good stead.

To sum up:

☐ Always remember and never forget that your stack, data, and local heap have to share one 64K data segment! This means many Windows programs have to use pointers to store their data!

☐ As a rule, it's better to use `malloc` or the `new` operator rather than `GlobalAlloc`, because they are familiar and take advantage of the suballocator.

☐ Use `GlobalAlloc` to grab chunks of memory up to 16M in size!

A Little File I/O

The main theme of the last section was that you can handle pointers in Windows much the way they are handled in DOS or UNIX. The same is true of file I/O.

For instance, here is a function from SCORE.CPP that opens up the file containing a list of people's names and their scores. The information retrieved from disk in the `OpenScores` function is displayed in a dialog, as shown in Figure 21.5.

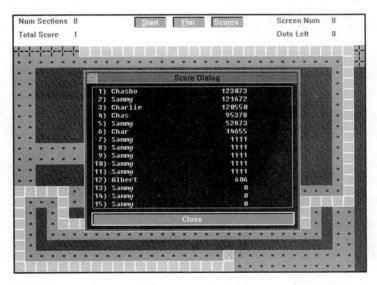

Figure 21.5. *The* `OpenScores` *dialog.*

```
231: int OpenScores(FILE * fp)
232: {
233:   if ((fp = fopen("Scores.Dta", "r+")) == NULL)
234:   {
235:     fp = fopen("Scores.Dta", "w+");
236:     memset(Scores, '\0', sizeof(Scores));
237:   }
238:   else
239:     fread(&Scores, sizeof(Scores), 1, fp);
240:
241:   fclose(fp);
242:   return 1;
243: }
```

This is the same type of code you might see in a primer for the C language. The calls to fopen, fread, and fclose are all totally standard, though there is a dearth of error checking.

The point here is simply that you should perform file I/O in DOS-based Windows applications exactly as you do in UNIX or DOS. The only possible exception is when you need to copy a file from one location to another. In that case, you might want to call on the handy LZCopyFile API function.

The *LZCopy* Function

```
LONG LZCopy(hfSource, hfDest)
```

HFILE hfSource;	Handle obtained from LzOpenFile, lopen, OpenFile, or any other "C" routine that opens a file in binary mode.
HFILE hfDest;	Handle to a destination file obtained from the previously listed sources.

If the file in question were compressed with the COMPRESS.EXE program, which comes with Borland's and Microsoft's compilers, this function would decompress and copy the file. Otherwise it would simply copy the file.

Example:

```
#include <lzexpand.h>
  ...

  char szSrc[] = {"c:\\goober.txt"};
  char szDst[] = {"c:\\goober.foo"};
  OFSTRUCT ofStrSrc;
  OFSTRUCT ofStrDest;
  HFILE Source, Dest;
```

```
Source = OpenFile(szSrc, &ofStrSrc, OF_READ);
Dest = OpenFile(szDst, &ofStrDest, OF_CREATE);
LZCopy(Source, Dest);
_lclose(Source);
_lclose(Dest);
```

That's all I'm going to say about file I/O. The reason this subject is so easy to explain is simply that it's one part of the Windows 3.1 environment that is inherited almost entirely intact from the DOS world. Except for this one long familiar facet of the DOS world, Windows tends to take over nearly every aspect of system operation.

Dynamic Dialogs and Centering a Dialog

The Score dialog, shown in Figures 21.5 and 21.6, is interesting because it can be seen in one of two different states. In one case, all that appears at the bottom of the dialog is a single close button, whereas at other times, there are a close button, an edit control, and a static control.

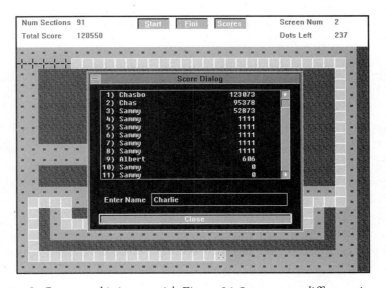

Figure 21.6. *Compare this image with Figure 21.5 to see two different views of the Score dialog.*

Rather than design two separate dialogs, Snako opts to change the appearance of the ScoreDlg at runtime. It does so with the following code, drawn from lines 358 through 363 of SCORE.CPP.

```
MoveWindow(GetDlgItem(hDlg, ID_SCOREBOX), 10,6,365,225, FALSE);
MoveWindow(GetDlgItem(hDlg, IDOK), 8, 240, 370, 25, FALSE);
ShowWindow(GetDlgItem(hDlg, ID_SCORENAME), SW_HIDE);
ShowWindow(GetDlgItem(hDlg, ID_SCORESTAT), SW_HIDE);
```

This code first decreases the size of the list box, which holds the scores for the program. Then, it adjusts the size of the Close button and hides both the static text and the edit control normally found at the bottom of the dialog. Notice that the HWND of the controls is obtained through calls to GetDlgItem, and that any window can be hidden by calling ShowWindow with the SW_HIDE identifier.

In addition to the hand waving that changes the appearance of the score dialog, SCORE.CPP also contains a useful little function that ensures that the dialog always appears in the middle of the screen (see Figure 21.6). This function, called CenterDialog, can be used with any standard dialog that is declared with the WS_CAPTION and DS_MODALFRAME styles:

```
325: void CenterDialog(HWND hDlg)
326: {
327:   RECT R;
328:   int i = GetSystemMetrics(SM_CXSCREEN);
329:   int j = GetSystemMetrics(SM_CYSCREEN);
330:   int Height = GetSystemMetrics(SM_CYCAPTION);
331:   Height += (GetSystemMetrics(SM_CYDLGFRAME) * 2);
332:   int Width = GetSystemMetrics(SM_CXDLGFRAME) * 2;
333:   GetClientRect(hDlg, &R);
334:   MoveWindow(hDlg, (i / 2)-(R.right / 2),
335:             (j / 2)-R.bottom / 2,
336:             R.right + Width, R.bottom + Height, FALSE);
337: }
```

This function uses GetSystemMetrics to query Windows for the resolution of the current screen and GetClientRect to obtain the size of the dialog. It then uses this information to calculate where the dialog should be placed to find the center of the screen. The additional code takes into account the thickness of the dialog's frame and caption. Notice that the frame's width and height have to be factored in twice, because they are found on both the top and bottom, as well as the left and right, of every dialog.

Closing Thoughts: Is Snako Really a Windows Program?

In terms of design, Snako breaks every stricture laid down in the rule book. If you are curious, I enjoyed breaking all those carefully thought-out rules, and I definitely got a kick out of Snako's iconoclastic spirit.

Intellectual experimentation has always lain at the heart of the computer world. I believe individual programmers, and not bureaucratic committees, should decide how applications are constructed. If we cease to honor creativity, we might as well roll over and die, because someone else will take over the future of computers.

On the other hand, I want to make it clear that the classic Windows interface, used in 90 percent of the programs in this book, is anything but trivial. Most of the time, it's best to write programs that everyone can readily understand. The best way to do that is to give your application an interface that's already familiar — thanks to the good graces of thousands of other well-crafted programs. The heritage of interface design, represented by the classic Windows program, is the fruit of many years of experience. Use it and enjoy it.

In particular, see if you can obtain a copy of *Systems Application Architecture Common User Access Advanced Interface Design Guide (SAA CUA Interface Design Guide)*, published by IBM.

This is the book that lays down all the key rules and illustrates them with numerous drawings and diagrams. If you want to create a program that conforms to industry standards, and that many users will feel at home with right away, this should be one of your bibles.

My main point, however, is that if you have an idea for a totally different type of program, you should try to bring it to fruition. Windows shouldn't be allowed to become a strait jacket, and all these silly committees can outlaw everything but our imagination!

Whatever happens, remember the following key rules:

☐ Good programmers write reams of code. Most of the programs in this book are meant to be starting points and clues for dedicated, hard-working hackers. Don't be content with these starting points. Push the code to the limit and go on to develop your own ideas.

☐ Windows can be difficult at times, but it's also extremely seductive. If you're not having fun and are not fascinated by what you are doing, it will become more and more difficult to write good code. Willpower and ambition are two important ingredients in the mix required for a good programmer, but they don't tell the whole story. You need more than discipline; you need passion, carefully leavened with a lively sense of humor. The passion helps you write the best possible code; the humor helps you preserve your sanity.

Summary

This chapter contained an overview of the Snako program, some general discussion of Windows coding techniques, and a coverage of the following issues:

☐ Using `malloc`, `new`, and `GlobalAlloc` to obtain memory from the heap

☐ Simple file I/O in Windows

☐ Centering dialogs

Q&A

1. Q: I'm having trouble working inside the limitations of the 64K DGROUP. What else can I do to save data space?

   A: If possible, you should save all your program's strings into a string resource, or a user-defined resource. Techniques for doing this were explored in Days 6 and 7. If you need to move things onto the heap, remember that arrays are the data structures that tend to take up the most space. If you can move an array onto the heap, you'll probably gain back a sizable chunk of your data segment. Remember also that you can change the structure of your heap by working with the HEAPSIZE and STACKSIZE variables in a projects DEF file.

2. Q: What is the difference between the local heap and the global heap?

   A: The local heap resides inside the 64K of the DGROUP, along with a program's stack and its data. The global heap is really just another name for any free-floating, unassigned memory available on a system. It is limited in size only by the amount of RAM and virtual RAM available on a particular machine. Windows has two sets of memory allocation routines, one for the local heap and one for the global heap. For instance, the local counterpart of GlobalAlloc is called LocalAlloc, which has an accompanying LocalFree function. In general, LocalAlloc is somewhat faster than GlobalAlloc and should be used for small, short-term memory needs.

3. Q: Is there a relationship between a local heap and the resources that get expended when a program calls the GDI?

A: Good question. The reason you have to be so careful to free the resources obtained from GDI calls is that they are all stored on the GDI.EXE local heap. When you make calls to RegisterClass or CreateWindow, the information you supply is stored in the USER.EXE local heap. Because these areas are never larger than 64K in size, you have to be very careful to free the memory back up again; if not, the GDI heap will be expended. If you want to see the contents of your own, or any other local heap, you can do so by using the ToolHelp DLL and the LocalInfo, LocalFirst and LocalNext functions.

Workshop

The Workshop provides quiz questions to help you solidify your understanding of the material covered and exercises to provide you with experience in using what you've learned. Try to understand the quiz and exercise answers before continuing on to the next chapter. Answers are provided in Appendix A.

Quiz

1. What book defines the elements of the Windows interface and who publishes it?

2. The acronym CUA stands for what three words?

3. What does the malloc function return?

4. What three functions are normally called whenever you call GlobalAlloc?

5. What three types of memory appear in the DGROUP?

6. How many times can a single program call GlobalAlloc?

7. What is a suballocator, and why would you ever want to use one?

8. How can you hide a window so that the user does not know it is in memory?

21

9. What single native Windows function can be used to copy a file from one subdirectory to another?

10. Name at least one function used to change the location of a dialog.

Exercises

1. Change Snako so that it is possible to go through 4 different levels and a total of 16 screens.

2. Work out a way to enable users to save the state of a Snako game to disk and then reload it later.

3. Change the Snako program so it will not save the state of the game to memory if a user is entering a screen for the second time. In other words, save the state of the game only the first time the user enters a new screen.

4. Enable the user to select the speed at which the snake moves, and the speed at which it grows.

Having finished Week 3, you have reason to feel proud. By this time, you've covered most of the major topics involved in Windows programming. You should feel as though the most significant projects you might want to undertake should now be within your grasp. All you need to do is apply the knowledge you have obtained, and any reasonable Windows programming goal should now yield to your efforts.

The final version of the SysInfo program (see Listing R3.1) makes extensive use of dialogs to offer an in-depth look at the current state of a 16-bit Windows machine. This new version gives a more in-depth, interrelated look at the classes, modules, and tasks available on your system. It also adds the capability to list all the objects on the GDI local heap, thereby giving you a specific look at how system resources are handled.

Type Listing R3.1. **Final version of the SysInfo program.**

```
 1: //////////////////////////////////////////////////
 2: //   Program Name: SYSINFO.CPP
 3: //   Programmer: Charlie Calvert
 4: //   Description: What I did on my system's vacation
 5: //   Date: 08/09/93
 6: //////////////////////////////////////////////////
 7:
 8: #define STRICT
 9: #include <windows.h>
10: #include <windowsx.h>
11: #include <toolhelp.h>
12: #include <stdio.h>
13: #include <string.h>
14: #include "SysInfo.h"
15:
16: #pragma warning (disable: 4068)
17: #pragma warning (disable: 4100)
18:
19: // ----------------------------------------
20: // Interface
21: // ----------------------------------------
22:
23: static char szAppName[] = "SysInfo";
24: static HWND MainWindow;
25: static HINSTANCE hInstance;
26: HBRUSH BlueBrush;
27:
28: // ----------------------------------------
29: // Initialization
30: // ----------------------------------------
31:
32: //////////////////////////////////////////////
33: // Program entry point
34: //////////////////////////////////////////////
35: #pragma argsused
36: int PASCAL WinMain(HINSTANCE hInst, HINSTANCE hPrevInstance,
37:                    LPSTR  lpszCmdParam, int nCmdShow)
38: {
39:   MSG  Msg;
```

```
40:
41:    if (!hPrevInstance)
42:      if (!Register(hInst))
43:        return FALSE;
44:
45:    (MainWindow = Create(hInst, nCmdShow);
46:    if (MainWindow)
47:      return FALSE;
48:    while (GetMessage(&Msg, NULL, 0, 0))
49:    {
50:        TranslateMessage(&Msg);
51:        DispatchMessage(&Msg);
52:    }
53:
54:    return Msg.wParam;
55: }
56:
57: //////////////////////////////////////////
58: // Register the window
59: //////////////////////////////////////////
60: BOOL Register(HINSTANCE hInst)
61: {
62:    WNDCLASS WndClass;
63:
64:    WndClass.style          = CS_HREDRAW | CS_VREDRAW;
65:    WndClass.lpfnWndProc    = WndProc;
66:    WndClass.cbClsExtra     = 0;
67:    WndClass.cbWndExtra     = 0;
68:    WndClass.hInstance      = hInst;
69:    WndClass.hIcon          = LoadIcon(NULL, IDI_APPLICATION);
70:    WndClass.hCursor        = LoadCursor(NULL, IDC_ARROW);
71:    WndClass.hbrBackground  = GetStockBrush(LTGRAY_BRUSH);
72:    WndClass.lpszMenuName   = "MENU_1";
73:    WndClass.lpszClassName  = szAppName;
74:
75:    return RegisterClass (&WndClass);
76: }
77:
78: //////////////////////////////////////////
79: // Create the window
80: //////////////////////////////////////////
81: #pragma argsused
```

continues

817

Listing R3.1. continued

```
 82: HWND Create(HINSTANCE hInst, int nCmdShow)
 83: {
 84:   hInstance = hInst;
 85:
 86:   HWND hWindow = CreateWindow(szAppName, szAppName,
 87:                     WS_OVERLAPPEDWINDOW,
 88:                     CW_USEDEFAULT, CW_USEDEFAULT,
 89:                     CW_USEDEFAULT, CW_USEDEFAULT,
 90:                     NULL, NULL, hInstance, NULL);
 91:
 92:   if (hWindow == NULL)
 93:     return hWindow;
 94:
 95:   ShowWindow(hWindow, nCmdShow);
 96:   UpdateWindow(hWindow);
 97:
 98:   return hWindow;
 99: }
100:
101: // -------------------------------------
102: // WndProc and Implementation
103: // -------------------------------------
104:
105: ////////////////////////////////////////
106: // The Window Procedure
107: ////////////////////////////////////////
108: LRESULT CALLBACK _export WndProc(HWND hWindow, UINT Message,
109:                                  WPARAM wParam, LPARAM lParam)
110: {
111:   switch(Message)
112:   {
113:     HANDLE_MSG(hWindow, WM_CREATE, SysInfo_OnCreate);
114:     HANDLE_MSG(hWindow, WM_DESTROY, SysInfo_OnDestroy);
115:     HANDLE_MSG(hWindow, WM_COMMAND, SysInfo_OnCommand);
116:     HANDLE_MSG(hWindow, WM_PAINT, SysInfo_OnPaint);
117:     default: return SysInfo_DefProc(hWindow, Message,
118:                                     wParam, lParam);
118:   }
119: }
120:
```

```
121: /////////////////////////////////////
122: // Handle WM_CREATE
123: /////////////////////////////////////
124: #pragma argsused
125: BOOL SysInfo_OnCreate(HWND hwnd, CREATESTRUCT FAR*
                            lpCreateStruct)
126: {
127:   BlueBrush = CreateSolidBrush(RGB(0, 0, 255));
128:   return TRUE;
129: }
130:
131: /////////////////////////////////////
132: // Handle WM_DESTROY
133: /////////////////////////////////////
134: #pragma argsused
135: void SysInfo_OnDestroy(HWND hwnd)
136: {
137:   DeleteBrush(BlueBrush);
138:   PostQuitMessage(0);
139: }
140:
141: #pragma argsused
142: void SysInfo_OnCommand(HWND hwnd, int id,
143:                        HWND hwndCtl, UINT codeNotify)
144: {
145:   switch(id)
146:   {
147:     case CM_ABOUT:
148:     {
149:       FARPROC AboutBox =
              MakeProcInstance((FARPROC)AboutDlgProc, hInstance);
150:       DialogBox(hInstance, "About", hwnd, (DLGPROC)AboutBox);
151:       FreeProcInstance(AboutBox);
152:       break;
153:     }
154:
155:     case CM_CLASS:
156:     {
157:       FARPROC ClassBox =
              MakeProcInstance((FARPROC)ClassDlgProc, hInstance);
158:       DialogBox(hInstance, "ClassList", hwnd,
                    (DLGPROC)ClassBox);
```

continues

Listing R3.1. continued

```
159:        FreeProcInstance(ClassBox);
160:        break;
161:    }
162:
163:    case CM_GDIWALK:
164:    {
165:      FARPROC LocalWalk =
            MakeProcInstance((FARPROC)LocalDlgProc, hInstance);
166:      DialogBox(hInstance, "LocalWalk", hwnd,
                  (DLGPROC)LocalWalk);
167:      FreeProcInstance(LocalWalk);
168:      break;
169:    }
170:
171:    case CM_MODULE:
172:    {
173:      FARPROC ModuleBox =
            MakeProcInstance((FARPROC)ModuleDlgProc, hInstance);
174:      DialogBox(hInstance, "ModuleList", hwnd,
                  (DLGPROC)ModuleBox);
175:      FreeProcInstance(ModuleBox);
176:      break;
177:    }
178:
179:    case CM_TASK:
180:    {
181:      FARPROC TaskBox = MakeProcInstance((FARPROC)TaskDlgProc,
182:                                           hInstance);
183:      DialogBox(hInstance, "TaskList", hwnd,
                  (DLGPROC)TaskBox);
184:      FreeProcInstance(TaskBox);
185:      break;
186:    }
187:  }
188: }
189:
190: void SystemOutLine(HDC PaintDC, int Y)
191: {
192:   int len;
193:   int YInc = 25;
```

```
194:    char S[100];
195:    DWORD dwFlags;
196:
197:    dwFlags = GetWinFlags();
198:
199:    len = sprintf(S, "This is an %s system.",
200:       (dwFlags & WF_CPU286) ? "80286" :
201:       (dwFlags & WF_CPU386) ? "80386" :
202:       (dwFlags & WF_CPU486) ? "80486" : "unknown");
203:    TextOut(PaintDC, 10, Y + YInc, S, len);
204:
205:    len = sprintf(S, "A coprocessor is %s ",
206:       (dwFlags & WF_80x87) ? "present" : "not present");
207:    TextOut(PaintDC, 10, Y + 2 * YInc, S, len);
208:
209:    len = sprintf(S, "Mode: %s",
210:       (dwFlags & WF_ENHANCED) ? "Enhanced" : "Standard");
211:    TextOut(PaintDC, 10, Y + 3 * YInc, S, len);
212:
213:    len = sprintf(S, "Paging is %s",
214:        (dwFlags & WF_PAGING) ? "available" : "unavailable");
215:    TextOut(PaintDC, 10, Y +  4 * YInc, S, len);
216: }
217:
218: ///////////////////////////////////////
219: // Handle WM_PAINT
220: ///////////////////////////////////////
221: void SysInfo_OnPaint(HWND hwnd)
222: {
223:    HDC PaintDC;
224:    PAINTSTRUCT PaintStruct;
225:    SYSHEAPINFO Info;
226:    char S[100];
227:
228:    Info.dwSize = sizeof(SYSHEAPINFO);
229:    SystemHeapInfo(&Info);
230:    DWORD FreeSpace = GetFreeSpace(0) / 1024;
231:
232:    PaintDC = BeginPaint(hwnd, &PaintStruct);
233:    SetBkMode(PaintDC, TRANSPARENT);
234:    sprintf(S, "Percent free in the USER heap: %d",
235:             Info.wUserFreePercent);
```

continues

Listing R3.1. continued

```
236:    TextOut(PaintDC, 10, 10, S, strlen(S));
237:    sprintf(S, "Percent free in the GDI heap: %d",
238:            Info.wGDIFreePercent);
239:    TextOut(PaintDC, 10, 35, S, strlen(S));
240:    sprintf(S, "Kilobytes free on Global heap: %ld", FreeSpace);
241:    TextOut(PaintDC, 10, 60, S, strlen(S));
242:
243:    SystemOutLine(PaintDC, 60);
244:
245:    EndPaint(hwnd, &PaintStruct);
246: }
247:
248: // ----------------------------------------------
249: // SysInfo Dialog
250: // ----------------------------------------------
251:
252: /////////////////////////////////////////////////
253: // The SysInfo Dialog Procedure
254: /////////////////////////////////////////////////
255: #pragma argsused
256: BOOL CALLBACK AboutDlgProc(HWND hDlg, WORD Message,
257:                            WPARAM wParam, LPARAM lParam)
258: {
259:    switch(Message)
260:    {
261:      case WM_INITDIALOG:
262:        return TRUE;
263:
264:      case WM_COMMAND:
265:        if (wParam == IDOK || wParam == IDCANCEL)
266:        {
267:          EndDialog(hDlg, TRUE);
268:          return TRUE;
269:        }
270:        break;
271:    }
272:    return FALSE;
273: }
```

Listing R3.2 shows the header file for SysInfo.

 Listing R3.2. SYSINFO.H.

```
 1: ////////////////////////////////////////////////
 2: //   Program Name: SYSINFO.H
 3: //   Programmer: Charlie Calvert
 4: //   Description: What I did on my system's vacation version 2
 5: //   Date: 08/09/93
 6: ////////////////////////////////////////////////
 7:
 8: #define CM_GDIWALK 105
 9: #define CM_ABOUT 101
10: #define CM_CLASS 102
11: #define CM_TASK 103
12: #define CM_MODULE 104
13:
14: #define ID_MODULELISTBOX 120
15: #define ID_MODULEEDIT 121
16:
17: #define ID_TASKLISTBOX 160
18: #define ID_TASKEDIT 161
19: #define ID_TASKCLASSLIST 162
20:
21: #define ID_CLASSLISTBOX 110
22: #define ID_CLASSSTYLE 111
23: #define ID_CLASSWINSTYLE 112
24:
25: #define ID_LOCALLIST 140
26:
27: typedef struct {
28:   UINT Style;
29:   LPSTR StyleStr;
30: }TCLASSSTYLE;
31:
32: // Declarations for class SysInfo
33: #define SysInfo_DefProc     DefWindowProc
34: BOOL SysInfo_OnCreate(HWND hwnd,
35:                      CREATESTRUCT FAR* lpCreateStruct);
36: void SysInfo_OnDestroy(HWND hwnd);
37: void SysInfo_OnCommand(HWND hwnd, int id,
```

continues

Listing R3.2. continued

```
38:                              HWND hwndCtl, UINT codeNotify);
39: void SysInfo_OnPaint(HWND hwnd);
40:
41: // Funcs
42: BOOL Register(HINSTANCE hInst);
43: HWND Create(HINSTANCE hInst, int nCmdShow);
44: LRESULT CALLBACK _export WndProc(HWND hWindow, UINT Message,
45:                                  WPARAM wParam, LPARAM
                                     lParam);
46: BOOL CALLBACK AboutDlgProc(HWND hDlg, WORD Message,
47:                            WPARAM wParam, LPARAM lParam);
48: BOOL CALLBACK ClassDlgProc(HWND hDlg, WORD Message,
49:                            WPARAM wParam, LPARAM lParam);
50: BOOL CALLBACK ModuleDlgProc(HWND hDlg, WORD Message,
51:                             WPARAM wParam, LPARAM lParam);
52: BOOL CALLBACK TaskDlgProc(HWND hDlg, WORD Message,
53:                           WPARAM wParam, LPARAM lParam);
54: BOOL CALLBACK LocalDlgProc(HWND hDlg, WORD Message,
55:                            WPARAM wParam, LPARAM lParam);
56: BOOL HandleSysColor(WPARAM wParam, LPARAM lParam);
```

Listing R3.3 shows the source file for SysClass.

 Listing R3.3. SYSCLASS.CPP.

```
1: /////////////////////////////////////////////
2: //   Module Name: SYSCLASS.CPP
3: //   Programmer: Charlie Calvert
4: //   Description: Part of SysInfo Application
5: //   Date: 08/09/93
6: /////////////////////////////////////////////
7:
8: #define STRICT
9: #include <windows.h>
10: #include <windowsx.h>
11: #include <toolhelp.h>
12: #include <stdio.h>
13: #include <string.h>
14: #include "sysinfo.h"
```

```
15: #pragma warning (disable: 4068)
16:
17: static int TotalStyles = 13;
18:
19: TCLASSSTYLE ClassStyle[] =
20: {
21:   CS_VREDRAW, "CS_VREDRAW",
22:   CS_HREDRAW, "CS_HREDRAW",
23:   CS_OWNDC, "CS_OWNDC",
24:   CS_CLASSDC, "CS_CLASSDC",
25:   CS_PARENTDC, "CS_PARENTDC",
26:   CS_SAVEBITS, "CS_SAVEBITS",
27:   CS_DBLCLKS, "CS_DBLCLKS",
28:   CS_BYTEALIGNCLIENT, "CS_BYTEALIGNCLIENT",
29:   CS_BYTEALIGNWINDOW, "CS_BYTEALIGNWINDOW",
30:   CS_NOCLOSE, "CS_NOCLOSE",
31:   CS_KEYCVTWINDOW, "CS_KEYCVTWINDOW",
32:   CS_NOKEYCVT, "CS_NOKEYCVT",
33:   CS_GLOBALCLASS, "CS_GLOBALCLASS",
34: };
35:
36: ////////////////////////////////////////
37: // SetClassContents
38: ////////////////////////////////////////
39: BOOL SetClassContents(void)
40: {
41:   CLASSENTRY Class;
42:   BOOL Result;
43:
44:   ListBox_ResetContent(hListBox);
45:   Class.dwSize = sizeof(CLASSENTRY);
46:   Result = ClassFirst(&Class);
47:   while (Result)
48:   {
49:     ListBox_AddString(hListBox, Class.szClassName);
50:     Result = ClassNext(&Class);
51:   }
52:   return TRUE;
53: }
54:
55:
56:
```

continues

Listing R3.3. continued

```
57:
58: ////////////////////////////////////////
59: // GetClass Instance
60: ////////////////////////////////////////
61: HINSTANCE GetClassInstance(LPSTR S)
62: {
63:   CLASSENTRY Class;
64:   BOOL Result = TRUE;
65:
66:   Class.dwSize = sizeof(CLASSENTRY);
67:   Result = ClassFirst(&Class);
68:   while (Result)
69:   {
70:     if (!strcmp(S, Class.szClassName))
71:       return Class.hInst;
72:     Result = ClassNext(&Class);
73:   }
74:   return NULL;
75: }
76:
77: ////////////////////////////////////////
78: // SetClassStyles
79: ////////////////////////////////////////
80: void SetClassStyles(HWND hDlg, UINT style)
81: {
82:   HWND hLBWnd = GetDlgItem(hDlg, ID_CLASSSTYLE);
83:   ListBox_ResetContent(hLBWnd);
84:
85:   for (int i = 0; i < TotalStyles; i++)
86:     if((style & ClassStyle[i].Style) == ClassStyle[i].Style)
87:       ListBox_AddString(hLBWnd, ClassStyle[i].StyleStr);
88: }
89:
90: ////////////////////////////////////////
91: // SpecifyAppsUsingClass
92: ////////////////////////////////////////
93: BOOL SpecifyAppsUsingClass(HWND hDlg, HINSTANCE hTempInst)
94: {
95:   TASKENTRY Task;
96:   BOOL Result = TRUE;
```

```
 97:
 98:    HWND hLBWnd = GetDlgItem(hDlg, ID_CLASSWINSTYLE);
 99:    ListBox_ResetContent(hLBWnd);
100:    Task.dwSize = sizeof(TASKENTRY);
101:    Result = TaskFirst(&Task);
102:    while (Result)
103:    {
104:      if (hTempInst == Task.hModule)
105:        ListBox_AddString(hLBWnd, Task.szModule);
106:      Result = TaskNext(&Task);
107:    }
108:    return TRUE;
109: }
110:
111: /////////////////////////////////////////
112: // FillClassBox
113: /////////////////////////////////////////
114: BOOL FillClassBox(HWND hDlg, LPSTR S)
115: {
116:    WNDCLASS WndClass;
117:    HINSTANCE hTempInst;
118:    hTempInst = GetClassInstance(S);
119:    GetClassInfo(hTempInst, S, &WndClass);
120:    SetClassStyles(hDlg,  WndClass.style);
121:    SpecifyAppsUsingClass(hDlg, hTempInst);
122:    return TRUE;
123: }
124:
125: /////////////////////////////////////////
126: // The SysInfo Class Dialog Procedure
127: /////////////////////////////////////////
128: #pragma argsused
129: BOOL CALLBACK ClassDlgProc(HWND hDlg, WORD Message,
130:                               WPARAM wParam, LPARAM lParam)
131: {
132:    int Index;
133:    char S[100];
134:
135:
136:    switch(Message)
137:    {
138:      case WM_INITDIALOG:
```

continues

Listing R3.3. continued

```
139:        {
140:          SetClassContents(hDlg);
141:          ListBox_SetCurSel(GetDlgItem(hDlg, ID_CLASSLISTBOX), 0);
142:          HWND hLBWnd = GetDlgItem(hDlg, ID_CLASSWINSTYLE);
143:          SetWindowFont(hLBWnd, GetStockFont(ANSI_FIXED_FONT), 0);
144:          hLBWnd = GetDlgItem(hDlg, ID_CLASSSTYLE);
145:          SetWindowFont(hLBWnd, GetStockFont(ANSI_FIXED_FONT), 0);
146:          return TRUE;
147:        }
148:
149:      case WM_CTLCOLOR:
150:          return HandleSysColor(wParam, lParam);
151:
152:      case WM_COMMAND:
153:        switch (wParam)
154:        {
155:          case IDOK:
156:          case IDCANCEL:
157:            EndDialog(hDlg, TRUE);
158:            return TRUE;
159:
160:          case
161:            ID_CLASSLISTBOX:
162:            {
163:              if (HIWORD(lParam) == LBN_SELCHANGE)
164:              {
165:                HWND hListBox = (HWND)LOWORD(lParam);
166:                Index = ListBox_GetCurSel(hListBox);
167:
168:                strcpy(S, "Trouble");
169:                if (Index != LB_ERR)
170:                {
171:                  ListBox_GetText(hListBox, Index, S);
172:                  FillClassBox(hDlg, S);
173:                }
174:              }
175:              return TRUE;
176:            }
177:        }
178:
```

```
179:      break;
180:    }
181:   return FALSE;
182: }
```

Listing R3.4 shows the SysMod source file.

Type **Listing R3.4. SYSMOD.CPP.**

```
1: //////////////////////////////////////////////
2: //   Module Name: SYSMOD.CPP
3: //   Programmer: Charlie Calvert
4: //   Description: Part of SysInfo Application
5: //   Date: 08/09/93
6: //////////////////////////////////////////////
7:
8: #define STRICT
9: #include <windows.h>
10: #include <windowsx.h>
11: #include <toolhelp.h>
12: #include <stdio.h>
13: #include <string.h>
14: #include "sysinfo.h"
15: #pragma warning (disable: 4068)
16:
17: extern HBRUSH BlueBrush;
18:
19: ///////////////////////////////////////
20: // SetModuleContents
21: ///////////////////////////////////////
22: #pragma argsused
23: BOOL SetModuleContents(void)
24: {
25:   MODULEENTRY Module;
26:   BOOL Result;
27:
28:   ListBox_ResetContent(hListBox);
29:   Module.dwSize = sizeof(MODULEENTRY);
30:   ModuleFirst(&Module);
31:   while (Result)
```

continues

Listing R3.4. continued

```
32:   {
33:     ListBox_AddString(hListBox, Module.szModule);
34:     Result = ModuleNext(&Module);
35:   }
36:   return TRUE;
37: }
38:
39: /////////////////////////////////////////
40: // FillModuleBox
41: /////////////////////////////////////////
42: FillModuleBox(HWND hDlg, LPSTR S)
43: {
44:   MODULEENTRY Module;
45:   BOOL Result = TRUE;
46:
47:   HWND hEdWnd = GetDlgItem(hDlg, ID_MODULEEDIT);
48:   SetWindowFont(hEdWnd, GetStockObject(ANSI_FIXED_FONT), 0);
49:   Module.dwSize = sizeof(MODULEENTRY);
50:   ModuleFirst(&Module);
51:   if (!strcmp(Module.szModule, S))
52:     SetWindowText(hEdWnd, Module.szExePath);
53:
54:   while (Result)
55:   {
56:     Result = ModuleNext(&Module);
57:     if (!strcmp(Module.szModule, S))
58:       SetWindowText(hEdWnd, Module.szExePath);
59:   }
60:   return TRUE;
61: }
62:
63: /////////////////////////////////////////
64: // HandleSysColor
65: /////////////////////////////////////////
66: BOOL HandleSysColor(WPARAM wParam, LPARAM lParam)
67: {
68:   if (GetDlgCtrlID((HWND)LOWORD(lParam)) == -1)
69:   {
70:     SetTextColor((HDC)wParam, RGB(0, 0, 255));
71:     SetBkMode((HDC)wParam, TRANSPARENT);
```

```
 72:     return (BOOL) GetStockBrush(GRAY_BRUSH);
 73:   }
 74:
 75:   switch(HIWORD(lParam))
 76:   {
 77:     case CTLCOLOR_STATIC:
 78:     case CTLCOLOR_LISTBOX:
 79:       SetTextColor((HDC)wParam, RGB(255, 255, 0));
 80:       SetBkMode((HDC)wParam, TRANSPARENT);
 81:       return (BOOL) BlueBrush;
 82:
 83:     case CTLCOLOR_DLG:
 84:       return (BOOL) GetStockBrush(GRAY_BRUSH);
 85:   }
 86:   return FALSE;
 87: }
 88: ////////////////////////////////////////
 89: // The SysInfo Module Dialog Procedure
 90: ////////////////////////////////////////
 91: #pragma argsused
 92: BOOL CALLBACK ModuleDlgProc(HWND hDlg, WORD Message,
 93:                             WPARAM wParam, LPARAM lParam)
 94: {
 95:   int Index;
 96:   char S[100];
 97:
 98:   switch(Message)
 99:   {
100:     case WM_INITDIALOG:
101:       SetModuleContents(hDlg);
102:       return TRUE;
103:
104:     case WM_CTLCOLOR:
105:       return HandleSysColor(wParam, lParam);
106:
107:     case WM_COMMAND:
108:       switch (wParam)
109:       {
110:         case IDOK:
111:         case IDCANCEL:
112:           EndDialog(hDlg, TRUE);
113:           return TRUE;
```

continues

Listing R3.4. continued

```
114:
115:          case ID_MODULELISTBOX:
116:            if (HIWORD(lParam) == LBN_SELCHANGE)
117:            {
118:              HWND hListBox = (HWND)LOWORD(lParam);
119:              Index = ListBox_GetCurSel(hListBox);
120:
121:              strcpy(S, "Trouble");
122:              if (Index != LB_ERR)
123:              {
124:                ListBox_GetText(hListBox, Index, S);
125:                FillModuleBox(hDlg, S);
126:              }
127:            }
128:          return TRUE;
129:        }
130:      }
131:      return FALSE;
132: }
```

Listing 3.5 shows the source file for SysTask.

Type Listing R3.5. **SYSTASK.CPP.**

```
 1: /////////////////////////////////////////
 2: //   Module Name: SYSTASK.CPP
 3: //   Programmer: Charlie Calvert
 4: //   Description: Part of SysInfo Application
 5: //   Date: 08/09/93
 6: /////////////////////////////////////////
 7:
 8: #define STRICT
 9: #include <windows.h>
10: #include <windowsx.h>
11: #include <toolhelp.h>
12: #include <stdio.h>
13: #include <string.h>
14: #include "sysinfo.h"
15: #pragma warning (disable: 4068)
```

```
16: #pragma warning (disable: 4100)
17:
18: static HWND hTaskWnd, hLBWnd, hEdWnd;
19:
20: ////////////////////////////////////
21: // SetTaskContents
22: ////////////////////////////////////
23: BOOL SetTaskContents(void)
24: {
25:   TASKENTRY Task;
26:   BOOL Result;
27:
28:   ListBox_ResetContent(hListBox);
29:   Task.dwSize = sizeof(TASKENTRY);
30:   Result = TaskFirst(&Task);
31:   while(Result)
32:   {
33:     ListBox_AddString(hListBox, Task.szModule);
34:     Result = TaskNext(&Task);
35:   }
36:   return TRUE;
37: }
38: ////////////////////////////////////
39: // GetModule
40: ////////////////////////////////////
41: HMODULE GetModule(LPSTR S)
42: {
43:   MODULEENTRY Module;
44:   BOOL Result = TRUE;
45:
46:   Module.dwSize = sizeof(MODULEENTRY);
47:   ModuleFirst(&Module);
48:   if (!strcmp(Module.szModule, S))
49:   {
50:     SetWindowText(hEdWnd, Module.szExePath);
51:     return Module.hModule;
52:   }
53:
54:   while (Result)
55:   {
56:     Result = ModuleNext(&Module);
57:     if (!strcmp(Module.szModule, S))
```

continues

Listing R3.5. continued

```
58:     {
59:         SetWindowText(hEdWnd, Module.szExePath);
60:         return Module.hModule;
61:     }
62:   }
63:   return NULL;
64: }
65:
66: /////////////////////////////////////
67: // ShowWindowClasses
68: /////////////////////////////////////
69: BOOL ShowWindowClasses(HMODULE hModule)
70: {
71:   CLASSENTRY Class;
72:   BOOL Result = TRUE;
73:
74:   ListBox_ResetContent(hLBWnd);
75:
76:   Class.dwSize = sizeof(CLASSENTRY);
77:   Result = ClassFirst(&Class);
78:   if (hModule == Class.hInst)
79:     ListBox_AddString(hLBWnd, Class.szClassName);
80:
81:   while (Result)
82:   {
83:     Result = ClassNext(&Class);
84:     if (hModule == Class.hInst)
85:       ListBox_AddString(hLBWnd, Class.szClassName);
86:   }
87:   return NULL;
88: }
89:
90: /////////////////////////////////////
91: // The FillTaskBox
92: /////////////////////////////////////
93: #pragma argsused
94: BOOL FillTaskBox(HWND hDlg, LPSTR S)
95: {
96:   HMODULE hModule = GetModule(S);
97:   ShowWindowClasses(hModule);
```

```
 98:    return TRUE;
 99: }
100:
101: ////////////////////////////////////////
102: // The SysInfo Task Dialog Procedure
103: ////////////////////////////////////////
104: #pragma argsused
105: BOOL CALLBACK TaskDlgProc(HWND hDlg, WORD Message,
106:                                  WPARAM wParam, LPARAM lParam)
107: {
108:   char S[100];
109:   int Index;
110:
111:   switch(Message)
112:   {
113:     case WM_INITDIALOG:
114:       hTaskWnd = GetDlgItem(hDlg, ID_TASKLISTBOX);
115:       hLBWnd = GetDlgItem(hDlg, ID_TASKCLASSLIST);
116:       hEdWnd = GetDlgItem(hDlg, ID_TASKEDIT);
117:       SetWindowFont(hTaskWnd,
118:                       GetStockObject(ANSI_FIXED_FONT), 0);
119:       SetWindowFont(hLBWnd,
                        GetStockObject(ANSI_FIXED_FONT), 0);
119:       SetWindowFont(hEdWnd,
                        GetStockObject(ANSI_FIXED_FONT), 0);
120:       SetTaskContents();
121:       ListBox_SetCurSel(GetDlgItem(hDlg, ID_TASKLISTBOX), 0);
122:       return TRUE;
123:
124:     case WM_CTLCOLOR:
125:       return HandleSysColor(wParam, lParam);
126:
127:     case WM_COMMAND:
128:       switch (wParam)
129:       {
130:         case IDOK:
131:         case IDCANCEL:
132:           EndDialog(hDlg, TRUE);
133:           return TRUE;
134:
135:         case
136:           ID_TASKLISTBOX:
```

continues

Listing R3.5. continued

```
137:                if (HIWORD(lParam) == LBN_SELCHANGE)
138:                {
139:                  HWND hListBox = (HWND)LOWORD(lParam);
140:                  Index = ListBox_GetCurSel(hListBox);
141:
142:                  strcpy(S, "Trouble");
143:                  if (Index != LB_ERR)
144:                  {
145:                    ListBox_GetText(hListBox, Index, S);
146:                    FillTaskBox(hDlg, S);
147:                  }
148:                }
149:                return TRUE;
150:        }
151:    }
152:    return FALSE;
153: }
```

Listing 3.6 shows the source file for SysWalk.

Type

Listing R3.6. SYSWALK.CPP

```
1: ///////////////////////////////////////////////
2: //   Program Name: SYSWALK.CPP
3: //   Programmer: Charlie Calvert
4: //   Description: What I did on my system's vacation
5: //   Date: 08/09/93
6: ///////////////////////////////////////////////
7:
8: #define STRICT
9: #include <windows.h>
10: #include <windowsx.h>
11: #include <toolhelp.h>
12: #include <stdio.h>
13: #include <string.h>
14: #include "SysInfo.h"
15:
16: char *GDITypes[] = {"Normal",
17:     "Pen", "Brush", "Font",
```

```
18:     "Palette", "Bitmap", "RGN",
19:     "DC", "Disabled_DC",
20:     "MetaDC", "Metafile", "Free"};
21:
22: char *WFlags[] = {"-", "Fixed",
23:                     "Free", "-",
24:                     "Moveable"};
25:
26: void FillLocalDlg(HWND hDlg)
27: {
28:    SYSHEAPINFO Info;
29:    LOCALENTRY LocalEntry;
30:    int Result = TRUE;
31:    char S[150];
32:    char *T = "Type: ";
33:    char *R = "Size: ";
34:    char *F = "Flags: ";
35:
36:    HWND hLocalList = GetDlgItem(hDlg, ID_LOCALLIST);
37:    SetWindowFont(hLocalList,
                     GetStockObject(ANSI_FIXED_FONT), 0);
38:    Info.dwSize = sizeof(SYSHEAPINFO);
39:    if (!SystemHeapInfo(&Info)) return;
40:    LocalEntry.dwSize = sizeof(LocalEntry);
41:    Result = LocalFirst(&LocalEntry, Info.hGDISegment);
42:    while (Result)
43:    {
44:      if (LocalEntry.wType < 12)
45:        sprintf(S, "%5s%-8s  %s%-6u %s%s", T,
46:                GDITypes[LocalEntry.wType],
47:                R, LocalEntry.wSize, F,
48:                WFlags[LocalEntry.wFlags]);
49:      else
50:        sprintf(S, "%5s%-8s  %s%-6u %s%s", T,
51:                GDITypes[11],
52:                R, LocalEntry.wSize, F,
53:                WFlags[LocalEntry.wFlags]);
54:      ListBox_AddString(hLocalList, S);
55:      Result = LocalNext(&LocalEntry);
56:    }
57: }
```

continues

Listing R3.6. continued

```
58: ////////////////////////////////////////////////
59: // The SysInfo Dialog Procedure
60: ////////////////////////////////////////////////
61: #pragma argsused
62: BOOL CALLBACK LocalDlgProc(HWND hDlg, WORD Message,
63:                            WPARAM wParam, LPARAM lParam)
64: {
65:   switch(Message)
66:   {
67:     case WM_INITDIALOG:
68:       FillLocalDlg(hDlg);
69:       return TRUE;
70:
71:     case WM_CTLCOLOR:
72:       return HandleSysColor(wParam, lParam);
73:
74:     case WM_COMMAND:
75:       switch(wParam)
76:       {
77:         case IDOK:
78:         case IDCANCEL:
79:           EndDialog(hDlg, TRUE);
80:           return TRUE;
81:       }
82:       break;
83:   }
84:   return FALSE;
85: }
```

Listing R3.7 shows the recource file for SysInfo.

 Listing R3.7. SYSINFO.RC.

```
1: ////////////////////////////////////////////////
2: //   Module Name: SYSINFO.RC
3: //   Programmer: Charlie Calvert
4: //   Description: Resource File
5: //   Date: 08/09/93
6: ////////////////////////////////////////////////
7:
```

```
8: #include <windows.h>
9: #include "SysInfo.h"
10:
11: MENU_1 MENU
12: BEGIN
13:     POPUP "Local Walks"
14:     BEGIN
15:         MENUITEM "GDI Walk", CM_GDIWALK
16:         MENUITEM "E&xit", 3003
17:     END
18:     MENUITEM "Classes", CM_CLASS
19:     MENUITEM "Tasks", CM_TASK
20:     MENUITEM "Modules", CM_MODULE
21:     MENUITEM "About", CM_ABOUT
22: END
23:
24: About DIALOG 18, 24, 141, 58
25: STYLE DS_MODALFRAME ¦ WS_POPUP ¦ WS_CAPTION ¦ WS_SYSMENU
26: CAPTION "About Dialog"
27: BEGIN
28:     CTEXT "What I Did on My System's Vacation",
29:      -1, 1, 9, 140, 8, WS_CHILD ¦ WS_VISIBLE ¦ WS_GROUP
30:     CTEXT "Copyright (c) 1993 Charlie Calvert",
31:      -1, 1, 23, 140, 10, WS_CHILD ¦ WS_VISIBLE ¦ WS_GROUP
32:     PUSHBUTTON "Ok", IDOK,
33:      5, 39, 132, 12, WS_CHILD ¦ WS_VISIBLE ¦ WS_TABSTOP
34: END
35:
36:
37: ClassList DIALOG 18, 16, 212, 181
38: STYLE DS_MODALFRAME ¦ WS_POPUP ¦ WS_CAPTION ¦ WS_SYSMENU
39: CAPTION "Classes"
40: BEGIN
41:     CONTROL "", ID_CLASSLISTBOX, "LISTBOX",
42:      LBS_STANDARD ¦ WS_CHILD ¦ WS_VISIBLE ¦ WS_TABSTOP,
43:      11, 9, 189, 90
44:     PUSHBUTTON "Ok", IDOK, 5, 162, 201, 14,
45:      WS_CHILD ¦ WS_VISIBLE ¦ WS_TABSTOP
46:     LISTBOX ID_CLASSSTYLE, 11, 114, 70, 41
47:     LISTBOX ID_CLASSWINSTYLE, 130, 114, 70, 41
48:     LTEXT "Styles", -1, 14, 104, 27, 8
49:     LTEXT "Modules", -1, 131, 104, 32, 8
```

continues

Listing R3.7. continued

```
50: END
51:
52: TaskList DIALOG 18, 18, 214, 149
53: STYLE DS_MODALFRAME ¦ WS_POPUP ¦ WS_CAPTION ¦ WS_SYSMENU
54: CAPTION "Tasks"
55: BEGIN
56:     CONTROL "", ID_TASKLISTBOX, "LISTBOX",
57:      LBS_STANDARD ¦ WS_CHILD ¦ WS_VISIBLE ¦ WS_TABSTOP,
58:      7, 15, 90, 90
59:     PUSHBUTTON "Ok", IDOK, 6, 130, 202, 14,
60:     WS_CHILD ¦ WS_VISIBLE ¦ WS_TABSTOP
61:     LTEXT "", ID_TASKEDIT, 7, 114, 200, 8
62:     LISTBOX ID_TASKCLASSLIST, 117, 15, 90, 90,
63:      LBS_NOTIFY ¦ WS_CHILD ¦ WS_VISIBLE ¦ WS_BORDER ¦
          WS_VSCROLL
64:     LTEXT "Tasks", -1, 7, 4, 62, 8,
65:      WS_CHILD ¦ WS_VISIBLE ¦ WS_GROUP
66:     LTEXT "Classes in Task", -1, 117, 4, 80, 8,
67:      WS_CHILD ¦ WS_VISIBLE ¦ WS_GROUP
68: END
69:
70: ModuleList DIALOG 18, 18, 180, 159
71: STYLE DS_MODALFRAME ¦ WS_POPUP ¦ WS_CAPTION ¦ WS_SYSMENU
72: CAPTION "Modules"
73: BEGIN
74:     CONTROL "", ID_MODULELISTBOX, "LISTBOX",
75:      LBS_STANDARD ¦ WS_TABSTOP ¦ WS_CHILD ¦ WS_VISIBLE,
76:      23, 11, 133, 107
77:     PUSHBUTTON "Ok", IDOK, 10, 140, 160, 14,
78:      WS_CHILD ¦ WS_VISIBLE ¦ WS_TABSTOP
79:     LTEXT "", ID_MODULEEDIT, 23, 123, 134, 10,
80:      SS_LEFT ¦ WS_CHILD ¦ WS_VISIBLE ¦ WS_BORDER ¦ WS_GROUP
81: END
82:
83: LocalWalk DIALOG 31, 16, 248, 214
84: STYLE DS_MODALFRAME ¦ WS_POPUP ¦ WS_CAPTION ¦ WS_SYSMENU
85: CAPTION "Local Walk"
86: BEGIN
87:     CONTROL "", ID_LOCALLIST, "LISTBOX",
88:      LBS_NOTIFY ¦ WS_CHILD ¦ WS_VISIBLE ¦ WS_BORDER ¦
```

```
89:        WS_VSCROLL ¦ WS_TABSTOP, 18, 12, 213, 171
90:        PUSHBUTTON "Close", IDOK, 10, 194, 231, 14
91: END
```

Listing R3.8 shows the definition file for SysInfo.

Type   Listing R3.8. **SYSINFO.DEF.**

```
 1: ; SYSINFO.DEF
 2:
 3: NAME            SysInfo
 4: DESCRIPTION     'SysInfo Vacation (c) 1993
                      by Charles Spence Calvert'
 5: EXETYPE         WINDOWS
 6: STUB            'WINSTUB.EXE'
 7: CODE            PRELOAD MOVEABLE DISCARDABLE
 8: DATA            PRELOAD MOVEABLE MULTIPLE
 9:
10: HEAPSIZE        4096
11: STACKSIZE       5120
```

Listing R3.9 shows the Borland makefile for SysInfo.

Type   Listing R3.9. **SYSINFO.MAK (Borland).**

```
 1: # SYSINFO.MAK
 2:
 3: # macros
 4: APPNAME = SysInfo
 5: INCPATH = C:\BC\INCLUDE
 6: LIBPATH = C:\BC\LIB
 7: OBJS = $(APPNAME).obj SysMod.obj SysClass.obj SysTask.obj
    SysWalk.obj
 8: FLAGS = -ml -W -v -w4 -I$(INCPATH) -L$(LIBPATH)
 9:
10: # link
11: $(APPNAME).exe: $(OBJS) $(APPNAME).def $(APPNAME).res
12:   bcc $(FLAGS) $(OBJS)
13:   brc $(APPNAME).res
```

continues

841

Listing R3.9. continued

```
14:
15: # compile
16: .cpp.obj:
17:    bcc -c $(FLAGS) { $< }
18:
19: $(APPNAME).res: $(APPNAME).rc
20:    brc -r -I$(INCPATH) $(APPNAME).rc
```

Listing R3.10 shows the Microsoft makefile for SysInfo.

Listing R3.10. SYSINFO.MAK (Microsoft).

```
 1: # SYSINFO.MAK for Microsoft
 2:
 3: APPNAME = SysInfo
 4: LIBS = llibcew libw toolhelp
 5: OBJS = $(APPNAME).obj SysMod.obj SysClass.obj SysTask.obj
    SysWalk.obj
 6:
 7: # linking
 8: $(APPNAME).exe : $(OBJS) $(APPNAME).def $(APPNAME).res
 9:    link $(OBJS), /align:16, NUL, /nod $(LIBS), $(APPNAME)
10:    rc $(APPNAME).res
11:
12: # compile
13: .cpp.obj:
14:    cl -AL -c -GA -Ow -W4 -Zp  { $< }
15:
16: # Compile
17: $(APPNAME).res: $(APPNAME).rc
18:    rc -r $(APPNAME).rc
```

The big changes apparent in Week 3's version of the SysInfo program are evident from the presence of several new dialog boxes and the menu item that enables you to walk the GDI heap.

Stripped down to its essentials, C++ psuedocode for the function that walks the local heap looks like this:

```
void FillLocalDlg(HWND hDlg)
{
  SYSHEAPINFO Info;
  LOCALENTRY LocalEntry;
  int Result = TRUE;
  char S[150];

  ... // Code to set the font
  Info.dwSize = sizeof(SYSHEAPINFO);
  if (!SystemHeapInfo(&Info)) return;
  LocalEntry.dwSize = sizeof(LocalEntry);
  LocalFirst(&LocalEntry, Info.hGDISegment);
  while (Result)
  {
    ... // Code to make the string "S"
    ListBox_AddString(hLocalList, S);
    Result = LocalNext(&LocalEntry);
  }
}
```

The core of this function is represented by the calls to SystemHeapInfo, LocalFirst, and LocalNext.

You've seen the SystemHeapInfo function in earlier versions of this program; it was used to retrieve the current free space in the GDI and User heaps. This time, SysInfo enlists the function to retrieve a handle to the GDI heap. This handle is one of the pieces of information required by LocalFirst function.

By now, the act of calling LocalFirst and LocalNext should be familiar, because this same pattern was followed when calling similar TOOLHELP functions, such as ClassFirst and ClassNext. The difference, here, of course, is that LocalFirst and LocalNext retrieve information about the actual objects stored on the GDI or User heap. This enables you to see the device contexts, brushes, pens, and so forth, that your program allocates. If you want, you can extend this program to compare the state of the GDI heap before and after you run a program or perform a particular function. (See Figure R3.1.) The information you obtain can help you be sure that your program properly cleans up after itself, and help you see exactly what memory your program is allocating (in terms of GDI resources).

The actual act of retrieving and displaying information, obtained from TOOLHELP, has been explained either in the earlier weeks in review or in the chapters on advanced dialog issues. However, it still might be helpful for me to point out the exact purpose of each dialog, as seen from the user's perspective.

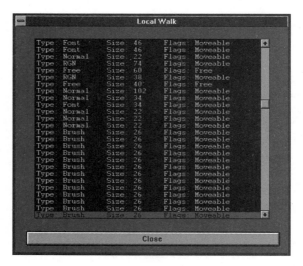

Figure R3.1. *The GDI Walk dialog displays information about the GDI heap.*

The GDI Walk dialog, shown in Figure R3.1, is used to display all the objects on the GDI local heap. In the left-hand column is the type of object itself, which might be a system resource, such as a brush, pen, or device context. Of course, it could also be nothing more than a free space on the heap, made available when some other resource was destroyed. The next column of information informs the user about the size of the object in question. The final column states whether the memory is fixed, moveable, or free. As you can see, most objects on the heap are moveable, which means Windows can change the address to which their selector points. This latter technique enables the system to use virtual memory, or to employ other tricks that maximize the power and functionality of the current system.

The Classes dialog box, shown in Figure R3.2, displays all the classes currently in memory. The two list boxes, shown at the bottom of the dialog, display information about the styles defined for the current class, as well as the module with which the class is associated.

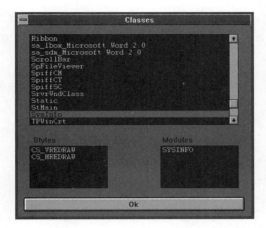

Figure R3.2. *The Classes dialog displays information about the classes currently in use on the user's system.*

The Tasks dialog box, shown in Figure R3.3, presents the user with a list of the currently available tasks. It also shows the classes used in that task, as well as the path to the actual executable in question.

Figure R3.3. *The Tasks dialog displays information about the Tasks currently running on the user's system.*

The Modules dialog (see Figure R3.4) shows the modules that have been loaded into memory, as well as the path to the module. This information can be particularly useful, because it enables you to see which copy of a DLL, font, or what-have-you, is actually being used.

Figure R3.4. *The Modules dialog displays information about the modules currently in memory on the user's system.*

The Modules dialog also shows the remarkable number of tools that must be loaded into memory before Windows is ready to run. I think it helps to remember that a DLL is really just a special form of the standard Windows new executable format. Furthermore, the FON files and DRV files are just DLLs with special extensions. As a result, all the various DLLs, FON files, DRV files, and so forth, that are loaded into memory, are really separate executables; they need to be running before Windows can operate properly.

The Modules dialog is a reminder that Windows is a vast, complex, and intricately interrelated operating environment. If you have mastered the material in this book, you now should feel confident of your ability to tackle almost any standard Windows programming task—no matter how large or complex. If this is the case, you have reason to feel proud. This is no average accomplishment, and it means you have acquired a very valuable and sophisticated skill. Congratulations!

Answers

Day 1 Quiz

1. Use the WinExec function to launch a Windows or DOS application.

2. Windows is a multitasking environment with built-in mouse support that runs in graphics mode, whereas DOS was designed to run only one application at a time and by default runs in text mode. Programmers must design their own mouse interface if they want to use a mouse in a DOS program.

3. A GUI is a Graphical User Interface. Traditionally, these interfaces feature mouse support and familiar graphical features such as windows, scrollbars, buttons, and dialogs. Most GUIs are designed to present a relatively uniform interface to the user, regardless of which application is being run at the time.

4. No. Windows (that runs on top of DOS) is really only a very elaborate extension to DOS. It does take over many of the duties associated with an operating system, but will farm other tasks, such as file IO, out to DOS. It also lacks some of the more elaborate features, such as preemptive multitasking, that are often associated with true operating systems.

5. A PIF is a place for storing information that Windows can use when it runs a DOS session. For instance, users can utilize PIF files to specify whether a DOS session should be full screen or windowed, or to specify the amount of memory Windows should allocate for a DOS session.

6. The Borland Debugger is called Turbo Debugger for Windows, and the Microsoft Debugger is called Codeview. A very popular third-party tool is called Bounds Checker for Windows.

7. No. Windows uses the HINSTANCE assigned to a program to distinguish that program from other executables currently running on the system.

8. From the programmer's point of view, the program entry point is the WinMain function. However, you should be aware that there is some startup code that executes before WinMain is called.

9. hPrevInstance is set to NULL if there is no previous instance of a program available. This provides the clue you need in order to check to see whether a previous instance is running.

10. If more than one instance of a program is running, the hPrevInstance is set to the hInstance of the last copy of the program to be loaded into memory.

Day 2 Quiz

1. The WinStub is the DOS program that is executed if a Windows program is run from the DOS command line. It usually puts up a message that says something like, "This program requires Microsoft Windows."

2. The Module Definition file contains information about the size of the stack and heap, as well as the name of the WinStub, the module name, and a short description of the file.

3. `WinMain` and `WndProc`.

4. Code to register the `mainWindow`, code to create the main window, and code to define the main message loop.

5. `WM_DESTROY`.

Day 3 Quiz

1. `WNDCLASS` is a structure used to define the major features of a window class such as its name, its icon and its cursor.

2. Use the Register function to define the fields of the `WNDCLASS` structure and to register this structure with windows by calling `RegisterClass`.

3. Use the create function to realize and make visible a program's main windows. These functions are performed with calls to `CreateWindow`, `ShowWindow`, and `UpDateWindow`.

4. `ShowWindow` sets a windows visibility state. It is usually used to make a window either visible or hidden. The `UpDateWindow` function sends a `WM_PAINT` message to a window, thereby causing its interior to be redrawn.

5. `WndProc` enables you to define the behavior associated with a particular window. Specifically, it gives the programmer a chance to say how a window will handle any of the messages sent to it.

6. The message loop acts as a guardian at the gate of the window procedure. It can be used to filter, coordinate, or modify messages before they are sent to the window procedure.

7. `DefWindowProc` is used to pass a message on to Windows proper. In some cases, a programmer might want to swallow a message without sending it on. To do this, it is only necessary to exit the window procedure without ever passing the message to `DefWindowProc`.

The following answers apply to 16-bit Windows:

8. `WORD unsigned short.`

9. `LONG signed long.`

10. `LPSTR char _far*.` (That is, it's a pointer to null-terminated string.)

Day 4 Quiz

1. `HANDLE_MSG` lets programmers avoid creating `case` statements such as this:

   ```
   case WM_CREATE:
     return HANDLE_WM_CREATE(hwnd, wParam,
                               lParam, MyCls_OnCreate);
   ```

   and to replace them with easy to read code that looks like this:

   ```
   HANDLE_MSG(hwnd, WM_CREATE, MyCls_OnCreate);
   ```

2. The second macro is called `FORWARD_WM_xxx`, and it can be used to pass a message back to the default window procedure.

3. `TextOut` and `DrawText`.

4. `GetDC`. When you are done, don't forget to call `ReleaseDC`. It is not appropriate to call `GetDC` when responding to `WM_PAINT` messages.

5. Most information is kept in the `WPARAM` and `LPARAM` parameters, though the message itself is the `UINT` parameter, which is the second parameter.

6. The printer.

7. It either gets ignored altogether or passed on to the default window procedure.

8. Look it up in WINDOWS.H. For instance:

   ```
   #define WM_CREATE            0x0001
   ```

9. Windows programs usually start with at least two files, one with a .CPP or .C extension, and one with a .DEF extension. Many projects also include a makefile and a resource file. One good way to start a new project is to copy a generic set of these files into a new subdirectory.

10. Traditional DOS programs run in text mode, one task at a time, and with no mouse support. Windows programs come with built-in mouse support, run in graphics mode, and can be multitasked. Another important difference is that Windows programs are event-oriented by default.

Day 5 Quiz

1. `WM_LBUTTONDBLCLK` and `WM_LBUTTONDOWN`

2. The `VK` constants specify virtual keys, such as `VK_DOWN` or `VK_UP`. For a complete list, see WINDOWS.H.

3. `CS_DBLCLK` is a class style. Use it with windows that you want to respond to double-clicks on the mouse.

4. Black.

5. The following code checks to see if the `MK_CONTROL` flag is set:

```
if ((keyFlags & MK_CONTROL) == MK_CONTROL)
   DoSomething
```

6. The system key is also called the ALT key.

7. Use a `FORWARD_WM_xxx` macro.

8. To the system icon in the upper-left hand corner of the window.

9. `KeyMouse_OnKey`, because nearly all key presses get passed on to it. Some of these messages are then translated and passed on to `Cls_OnChar` function.

10. Failure to call `ReleaseDC` results in the slow depletion of system resources. The end result is a complete failure of the system.

Day 6 Quiz

1. For Microsoft products, type

```
rc -r emerson.rc
```

For Borland, type

```
brc -r emerson.rc
```

2. For Microsoft products, type

   `rc emerson.res.`

   For Borland, type

   `brc emerson.res`

3. `CM_ABOUT` is the identifier associated with a menu item. When the user selects this item from a menu, the numeric value associated with `CM_ABOUT` is sent to the program's window procedure via a `WM_COMMAND` message.

4. A pop-up menu has a small window associated with it that drops down when the user selects that portion of the menu. A menu item is merely one of the words listed in a pop-up menu, or a single word listed along the menu bar at the top of the program.

5. `HINSTANCE`. A `HINSTANCE` is the unique handle that identifies an application.

6. `WPARAM`. This gets translated into the parameter `id` that is passed to the `Cls_OnCommand` function.

7. `FindResource` searches through a file for a particular resource, such as an icon or user-defined text, while `LoadResource` actually moves the item into memory.

8. `GlobalUnlock` decrements an internal counter associated with a chunk of memory. If the counter reaches zero, that memory can be moved or discarded—if the memory is declared to be `MOVEABLE` or `DISCARDABLE`. `FreeResource` does more than this; it actually deallocates the memory associated with a resource.

9. A *new executable* is the format used by EXE's and DLLs under Windows and OS2. It is different from the format used by DOS executables.

10. Yes.

Day 7 Quiz

1. `DialogBox.`

2. None. The About dialog is a modal dialog, and so nearly all messages associated with a program are sent to it while it is on-screen. There are a few minor exceptions to this rule, but the main point is simply that a modal dialog takes over an application while it is on-screen, effectively rendering the application itself inert until the dialog box is closed.

3. `WM_COMMAND`.

4. `FreeProcInstance` is used to free up a function that has been bound to a data segment with a call to `MakeProcInstance`.

5. Use `DeleteObject` to free the memory associated with a bitmap. Even better, if you have included WINDOWSX, use the `DeleteBitmap` macro, which includes type checking.

6. Use `LoadString` to retrieve text from a string resource.

7. `WM_VSCROLL` messages are sent whenever the user clicks a scrollbar. It carries information about the direction or manner in which the user wants to scroll, as well as the current position of the scrollbox.

8. The `TEXTMETRIC` structure contains detailed information about a font. It is defined in WINDOWS.H and in Borland's and Microsoft's online help.

9. The OK button in a dialog generates an `IDOK` message, which is sent to the dialog procedure associated with a dialog.

10. `MakeProcInstance` binds a function to a chunk of prolog code. This prolog code gives a function access to a programs data segment (`mov ax, ds`), thereby ensuring that a function will have access to a program's variables and data.

Day 8 Quiz

1. First register its class (if necessary) and then call `CreateWindow`.

2. The first time it is called for the main window of the application, and the second time for the child window.

3. `GameWndProc`.

4. Because this is not necessary for child windows. `PostQuitMessage` tells Windows that an application wants to close, and most of the time users don't want the entire application to close just because they've closed a child window. (In this program, the two occur at more or less the same time, but that is just coincidence. There is no reason why the first window can't be closed while the application is still running.)

5. `SetTimer` is the API function to use when you want to create a timer. Be sure to check the result, because the timer is not always available.

6. Because it resides in the WM_DESTROY function for the child window, and Windows always calls this function automatically before the app is closed.

7. SRCINVERT.

8. Call GetSystemMetrics to find out about many important facts regarding the hardware and software settings on the current system.

9. Answers will vary, but here is one possible selection:

   Width of a window frame
   Height of a window frame
   Width of a cursor
   Height of a cursor
   Width of an icon
   Height of an icon
   Width of the screen
   Height of the screen
   Whether or not a mouse is present
   Whether or not the current version of Windows is a debugging version

10. I threw Game_OnChar into the program to enable the user to pause the snake at a particular point on its path. You would need to call SetTimer to get things moving again.

Day 9 Quiz

1. CreateFont and CreateFontIndirect.

2. GetStockObject or, if you are using WINDOWSX, GetStockFont.

3. TrueType fonts were developed by Microsoft for Windows 3.1. Their main virtue is that they are a high quality, highly portable set of fonts that can be used for free by all Windows owners.

4. A stock font is just like any other font on the system, except it has been predefined. In other words, a stock font might be an ordinary Courier font that could be created with a call to CreateFontIndirect. However, the tedious part of the job has already been done for you, so all you need to do is call GetStockObject or GetStockFont.

5. `GetTextFace` retrieves the name of the currently selected font.

6. To find the size of the current font, call `GetTextMetrics` to retrieve a `TEXTMETRIC` structure. The `TEXTMETRIC` structure has the information you need.

7. Answer varies depending on your system.

8. Answer varies depending on your system.

9. Copy the font into a device context via a call to `SelectObject`, or, if you are using WINDOWSX, a call to `SelectFont`.

10. The type of the font. For instance, the font could be TrueType, Vector, or Fixed_Pitch.

Day 10 Quiz

1. To create a control, call `CreateWindow`.

2. Because it has been preregistered by Windows.

3. The eighth parameter to `CreateWindow` is called `hwndParent`, and it should hold the `HWND` of the owner of a control.

4. `ID`. To get the `HWND` of a control from its `ID`, call `GetDlgItem`.

5. By typecasting the `hmenu` field while calling `CreateWindow`.

6. You should OR the various styles of a control together.

7. `SetWindowText` and `GetWindowText`. Also the WINDOWSX macros `Edit_GetText`, `Edit_SetText`, `Static_GetText`, and `Static_SetText`.

8. List boxes and check boxes can be used to *control* the flow of a program (the same way the knob on a stereo can be used to *control* the volume of a piece of music).

9. An `EM_SETSEL` message is associated with edit controls. You know this because it begins with the letters `EM`. It enables you to select a particular range of letters in an edit control.

10. Call `SendMessage` with a `BM_GETCHECK` message, or call the WINDOWSX macro, `Button_GetCheck`.

Day 11 Quiz

1. Call `SetFocus` and pass it the handle to the control.

2. `SendMessage` will send a message directly to the appropriate window procedure, while `PostMessage` will place the message in the application message queue. As a result, `PostMessage` tends to be slower than `SendMessage`.

3. `ButtonMessage`.

4. The best way is to look up the information in an online help file. Another good method is to look up the information in a reference book. The important thing is to find a simple way of obtaining this information. You should make the process as close to effortless as possible, because you will frequently need to look up this type of information.

5. A callback is a function that is called directly by Windows, rather than by some other routine in your application. Typically, you pass the address of a callback to Windows and use the `MakeProcInstance` function to ensure that the function will have access to your program's data. Once you have this process down cold, you can sometimes "cheat" by using the "smart callbacks" option instead of `MakeProcInstance`.

6. `MakeProcInstance` links in some prolog code that gives the function access to your programs variables and other data.

7. `FreeProcInstance`.

8. Pound (#) define an identifier and use `WM_USER` as the starting offset:

   ```
   #define MyMessage (WM_USER + 0)
   ```

9. `WM_USER`.

10. Nothing. The `BM_GETCHECK` message is a button message, and the main window will simply ignore it.

Day 12 Quiz

1. `ExitWindows`, the first parameter of which can contain either `EW_REBOOTSYSTEM` or `EW_REBOOTWINDOWS`.

2. `IsDialogMessage` enforces normal tabbing among controls when you place them inside a window. This function automatically handles special key combinations such as Tab or Shift-Tab.

3. Both group boxes and radio buttons are part of the button class.

4. The macros are listed in WINDOWSX.H. Other places to look include the WINDOWSX.TXT file that ships with Microsoft's compiler, or the WIN31.DOC file that ships with Borland's compiler.

5. The `BM_SETCHECK` is sent every time you call the WINDOWSX `Button_SetCheck` macro.

6. Give it the `BS_AUTORADIOBUTTON` style.

7. Group Boxes have no built-in functionality. Their primary purpose is merely visual. They give the user a clue as to how to think about certain controls, and about how the tabbing system for the controls works.

8. Give the first item in any group of controls the `WS_GROUP` style. The end of one group of controls is marked by the beginning of the next group.

9. The `WS_TABSTOP` style designates that the user can tab to a particular control, but it does not state that the user will always automatically tab to that control if it is next to the child window list. The `WS_GROUP` style marks the beginning of a group of controls. Sometimes a group of controls, such as a set of radio buttons, will handle tabs in a special way, even though the `WS_TABSTOP` style is set for every member of the group. For instance, if you tab to a group of radio buttons, only the currently selected button will receive the focus, even though all of the buttons in the group have the `WS_TABSTOP` style. This is very convenient for the user, but a bit confusing to the programmer who is trying to understand how the `WS_GROUP` and `WS_TABSTOP` styles actually work.

10. Check to see if the return value from `WinExec` is less than 32. If it is, you should pop up a message box that displays one of the predefined errors shown below:

    0 Out of memory, executable corrupt, or relocation error.
    2 File not found.
    3 Path not found.
    5 Attempt to dynamically link to task, or sharing error.
    6 Library required separate data segments for each task.
    8 Insufficient memory to start the application.
    10 Windows version incorrect.
    11 Executable file invalid.
    12 Application designed for a different operating system.
    13 Application designed for MS-DOS 4.0.

14 Type of executable file unknown.

15 Can't load real-mode apps from old Windows versions.

16 Attempt to load a second instance of an executable file containing multiple data segments that were not marked read-only.

19 Attempt to load a compressed executable file.

20 DLL required to run this file is invalid.

21 This app requires 32-bit extensions.

Day 13 Quiz

1. BS_PUSHBUTTON and BS_RADIOBUTTON.

2. ListBox_Dir.

3. Here's a relatively complete list:

```
ListBox_Enable(hwnd, fEnable)
ListBox_GetCount(hwnd)
ListBox_ResetContent(hwnd)
ListBox_AddString(hwnd, lpsz)
ListBox_InsertString(hwnd, lpsz, index)
ListBox_AddItemData(hwnd, data)
ListBox_InsertItemData(hwnd, lpsz, index)
ListBox_DeleteString(hwnd, index)
ListBox_GetTextLen(hwnd, index)
ListBox_GetText(hwnd, index, lpszBuffer)
ListBox_GetItemData(hwnd, index)
ListBox_SetItemData(hwnd, index, data)
ListBox_FindString(hwnd, indexStart, lpszFind)
ListBox_FindItemData(hwnd, indexStart, data)
ListBox_SetSel(hwnd, fSelect, index)
ListBox_SelItemRange(hwnd, fSelect, first, last)
ListBox_GetCurSel(hwnd)
ListBox_SetCurSel(hwnd, index)
ListBox_SelectString(hwnd, indexStart, lpszFind)
ListBox_SelectItemData(hwnd, indexStart, data)
ListBox_GetSel(hwnd, index)
ListBox_GetSelCount(hwnd)
ListBox_GetTopIndex(hwnd)
ListBox_GetSelItems(hwnd, cItems, lpIndices)
```

```
ListBox_SetTopIndex(hwnd, indexTop)
ListBox_SetColumnWidth(hwnd, cxColumn)
ListBox_GetHorizontalExtent(hwnd)
ListBox_SetHorizontalExtent(hwnd, cxExtent)
ListBox_SetTabStops(hwnd, cTabs, lpTabs)
ListBox_GetItemRect(hwnd, index, lprc)
ListBox_SetCaretIndex(hwnd, index)
ListBox_GetCaretIndex(hwnd)
ListBox_SetAnchorIndex(hwnd, index)
ListBox_GetAnchorIndex(hwnd)
ListBox_Dir(hwnd, attrs, lpszFileSpec)
ListBox_AddFile(hwnd, lpszFilename)
ListBox_SetItemHeight(hwnd, index, cy) 3.1 only
ListBox_GetItemHeight(hwnd, index) 3.1 only
```

4. You'll need to typecast the LPARAM argument to get ahold of the MINMAXINFO structure if you are not using WINDOWSX.

5. The WM_GETMINMAXINFO message ensures that the user cannot change the shape of window beyond certain limits defined by the programmer. CreateWindow starts a window out at a certain size, but will not prevent the user from resizing a framed window.

6. Use SetWindowLong (in combination with MakeProcInstance) whenever you want to subclass a control.

7. Edit_SetSel is the macro you want to use. It relies on the EM_SETSEL message.

8. Use the TrackPopupMenu function.

9. Use GetProfileString to retrieve information from the WIN.INI file, and use GetPrivateProfileString to retrieve information from any other .INI file.

10. InvalidateRect generates WM_PAINT messages. The second parameter is the size of the rectangle that you want to update. If this is set to NULL, the whole window is updated. Compare to UpDateWindow.

Day 14 Quiz

1. The big difference is that a child window will always stay within the confines of its parent's client rectangle, whereas a pop-up window is free to rove anywhere on-screen.

2. `GetClientRect` gets the dimensions of a window with the upper-left hand coordinate, expressed as 0, 0. `GetWindowRect` retrieves the dimensions of a window with the upper-left hand corner expressed in terms of that corner's location relative to the entire screen.

3. The `WS_OVERLAPPEDWINDOW` style is used to define a standard window with a frame, caption bar, system menu, and minimize and maximize box. It literally consists of the following styles OR'd together into one style:

```
WS_OVERLAPPEDWINDOW = WS_OVERLAPPED | WS_CAPTION |
                      WS_SYSMENU | WS_THICKFRAME |
                      WS_MINIMIZEBOX | WS_MAXIMIZEBOX;
```

4. Either `MoveWindow` or `SetWindowPos`.

5. Use `GetSystemMetrics` to retrieve information about the width of a window's frame. Pass in `SM_CXFRAME` and `SM_CYFRAME`.

6. Call `EnableWindow`, passing in the `HWND` of the window you want to disable in the first parameter. The second parameter is set to `FALSE` to disable the window, and `TRUE` to enable the window.

7. Balance all calls to `CreateSolidBrush` with calls to `DeleteObject`.

8. `GetClassWord` retrieves information about an entire class of windows, and `GetWindowWord` retrieves information about a specific instance of a window.

9. When you are calling `GetClassWord`, this identifier can be used to retrieve the handle of the background brush. It is actually an offset into a structure.

10. In most cases, this is up to the programmer. Use the extra bytes you associate with a window to store information specific to the window, such as variables owned by that window.

Day 15 Quiz

1. Mapping modes define the relationship between device units and logical units, as well as the orientation of the x and y axes.

2. A pixel is the smallest single point of light that can be manipulated on the screen at one time by the programmer. There is a one-to-one correspondence between pixels and device units.

3. It is smaller. A logical unit in the MM_LOMETRIC is equal to .1 mm, which is considerably smaller than a pixel on virtually all VGA systems. To see this relationship, open up the size dialog in the WinSize program and compare the coordinates of the window in the MM_TEXT mode to those in the MM_LOMETRIC mode.

4. The viewport origin is the origin, or (0, 0) point, of the device coordinate system as opposed to the logical coordinate system.

5. Device coordinates are based on the physical pixels seen on-screen, or the physical dots drawn on a printer. Logical coordinates ignore these device-dependent factors and attempt to base GDI coordinates on logical units such as inches or millimeters.

6. SetViewportOrg sets the origin for the device coordinate system, and SetWindowOrg sets the origin for the logical coordinate system.

7. Modeless dialogs give the user access to the rest of the program to which they belong. While modal dialogs are on-screen, they are the sole focus of user input for the program to which they belong.

8. You can create a modeless dialog by calling CreateDialog.

9. You can create a modal dialog by calling DialogBox.

10. (Answers may vary.) Dialog procedures receive WM_INITDIALOG messages rather than WM_CREATE messages. You should pass messages intended for default processing to DefDlgProc rather than DefWndProc. You might also be interested to know that dialogs have a standard window procedure (that looks just like any other window procedure) that actually calls your dialog procedure. When you return TRUE or FALSE from a dialog procedure, the result is handled by the dialog's window procedure.

Day 16 Quiz

1. You can use `SendDlgItemMessage` to handle communications between a dialog and its controls. `SendMessage`, on the other hand, can be used whenever you need to send messages between any two points in a program or on the desktop.

2. Use `GetDlgItem` to retrieve the handle of a control if all you know is its ID.

3. Use `DPtoLP` to convert device coordinates into logical coordinates.

4. Use `GetParent` to find the `HWND` of a window's parent.

5. Yes, a modal dialog can communicate freely with its parent with the `SendMessage` function. Communications in the other direction are more difficult, although by no means impossible. For instance, you could use a timer to send messages at specified intervals between a parent and a modal dialog.

6. Set breakpoints on the portion of the dialog procedure you want to examine. (I should perhaps qualify this point by saying that at the deepest level, that is, at the machine level, a Windows program running on an Intel processor is still very much a linear program. However, this is not at all the way things appear to a C++ programmer who writes standard Windows code. For all practical purposes, C++ Windows code is nonlinear, however, the processor still executes machine instructions in a linear fashion.)

7. The mapper program subclasses a static control in order to display a bitmap inside the control's boundaries.

8. There are a number of possible answers, but one important explanation is that it enables you to circumvent the unusual coordinate system in dialogs. That is, you can design the dialog and locate the static control using the Resource Workshop or the AppStudio, and then simply paint the bitmap at the (0, 0) coordinates of the static control. This saves you the trouble of making a calculation at runtime that must be based on the size of the current font.

9. `StretchBlt` will, if necessary, compress or stretch a bitmap when it copies it from a source to a destination. `BitBlt`, on the other hand, simply copies a bitmap from one device context to the next.

10. The program calls StretchBlt so the original bitmaps can be stretched into a new shape. This means they must be copied from one bitmap to another. The call to CreateCompatibleBitmap creates the new bitmaps into which the old bitmaps will be copied.

Day 17 Quiz

1. Hotkeys designated in menus are separated from the rest of the menu text with tab character. Specifically, they use the '\t' syntax: "&Round Cursor\tAlt+F1."

2. To place an underline beneath a letter in a menu, use the ampersand symbol &. The end result is that the user can select that item by pressing Alt and the specified key. If you are inside a POPUP menu, pressing the Alt key is optional, that is, you can select the option by pressing the letter alone.

3. Add a call to TranslateAccelarators to your message loop whenever you use accelerators.

4. See if the itemState field of DRAWITEMSTRUCT has the ODS_SELECTED flag set.

5. Answers will vary, but here's a complete list from WINDOWS.H that includes the associated constants:

```
#define MF_BYCOMMAND          0x0000
#define MF_BYPOSITION         0x0400
#define MF_SEPARATOR          0x0800
#define MF_ENABLED            0x0000
#define MF_GRAYED             0x0001
#define MF_DISABLED           0x0002
#define MF_UNCHECKED          0x0000
#define MF_CHECKED            0x0008
#define MF_USECHECKBITMAPS    0x0200
#define MF_STRING             0x0000
#define MF_BITMAP             0x0004
#define MF_OWNERDRAW          0x0100
#define MF_POPUP              0x0010
#define MF_MENUBARBREAK       0x0020
#define MF_MENUBREAK          0x0040
```

```
#define MF_UNHILITE        0x0000
#define MF_HILITE          0x0080
#define MF_SYSMENU         0x2000
#define MF_HELP            0x4000
#define MF_MOUSESELECT     0x8000
```

6. The MF_BYPOSITION flag designates the position of the menu item in question in terms of the other menu items in the menu. For instance, it might be the fifth menu item, or the sixth menu item. MF_BYCOMMAND identifies a menu item with its ID.

7. BY_POSITION is a zero-based offset.

8. The SS_ICON style can be used to designate that a particular static control has an icon associated with it.

9. A call to SetCapture must be matched with a call to ReleaseCapture.

10. Use the GetObject function to obtain the dimensions of bitmap at runtime.

Day 18 Quiz

1. The HDC field is part of every GDI funciton.

2. chord, ellipse, polygon, rectangle, pie, and roundrect are all GDI functions that draw geometric shapes.

3. To change the color that fills an ellipse, select a new brush into the current device context.

4. To change the color of the boundary of a rectangle, select a new pen into the current device context.

5. A placeable, or Aldus, metafile has a 22-byte header.

6. To display a metafile, use PlayMetaFile, or use the EnumMetaFile and EnumMetaFileProc callback along with the PlayMetaFileRecord function.

7. CreateMetaFile returns a device context. You can copy pens, brushes, and other GDI elements into this device context.

8. If you pass the HDC obtained from CreateMetaFile to CloseMetaFile, it will return an HMETAFILE object. An HMETAFILE can be shown to the screen simply by passing it to PlayMetaFile.

9. The second field in a METARECORD is a function number. Each GDI function has a function number associated with it. For instance, Polygon is assigned function number 0x0324. You can find this information in the *Microsoft Windows 3.1 Programmer's Reference Volume 4: Resources*, which is available from the Microsoft Press.

10. The first field of OPENFILENAME is called lStructSize. You should set this field equal to the size of the OPENFILENAME struct before passing the struct to GetOpenFileName:

```
OpenFileName.lStructSize = sizeof(OPENFILENAME);
```

Day 19 Quiz

1. When creating client windows, assign the szClass field to MDICLIENT.

2. Use EnumChildWnds and the EnumChildWindows function to iterate through all the windows on the desktop.

3. The WM_MDIGETACTIVE function finds the active window.

4. The client window sends a WM_MDIACTIVATE message to each child window about to gain or lose the focus.

5. The lParam field accompanying the WM_MDISETMENU message contains a new menu or pop-up menu.

6. The easiest way to tell is to make it very wide and very shallow. In other words, make the clock about one-half inch high and four or five inches wide. The actual image of the clock stays symetrical, even though its frame has been distorted.

7. You need to fill out an MDICREATESTRUCT before creating an MDI child.

8. A WM_QUERYENDSESSION message is sent out whenever a properly constructed Windows shell is about to close down.

9. Call GetWindow and pass it the HWND of your window and the GW_OWNER constant. If it returns TRUE, you're dealing with the child of an icon:

```
if (GetWindow(hwnd, GW_OWNER)) // Icon Title?
    return TRUE;
```

10. Use the cbWndExtra bytes to store information specific to each window.

Day 20 Quiz

1. MCI stands for the Media Control Interface.

2. WAVE files can hold one second in 11K, or one minute in 1 meg. MIDI files can hold one minute in about 5K of disk space.

3. When you first open a multimedia device, you should pass zero in this field. After opening a multimedia device, you should save the device ID so that you can use it in future calls relating to the device.

4. `mciSendCommand` returns zero if the call is a success. Otherwise, it returns an error code. You can pass the error codes to `mciGetErrorString` if you want to retrieve an error string to show your users.

5. If you pass in an `HWND` along with the `MCI_NOTIFY` flag, it will send `MM_MCINOTIFY` messages to the designated window. The `WPARAM` associated with the `MM_MCINOTIFY` message reveals information about the state of the current multimedia device. For instance, `WPARAM` can be set to `MCI_NOTIFY_ABORTED`, or `MCI_NOTIFY_SUCCESSFUL`.

6. All the functions in the book that are exported from a DLL use the keywords `_export` and `CALLBACK`. `_export` ensures that the function is properly exported from the DLL, that is, that it is placed in an export table. It also creates prolog code that will properly set up the data segment after the function is linked. `CALLBACK` is shorthand for ensuring that a function is declared `FAR PASCAL`.

7. To inform your program about the routines in a DLL, use `IMPLIB` to create a .LIB file that can be linked into your program.

8. The declarations for the standard Windows API routines are placed in WINDOWS.H.

9. When you are creating a dialog window to act as the main window of an application, you need to give it a unique class name so that Windows can send messages to the right location.

10. Inside a DLL, the function called `LibMain` plays a role very similar to the one usually played by `WinMain` in a standard Windows executable.

Day 21 Quiz

1. The elements of the Windows interface are described in the *SAA CUA Advanced Interface Design Guide*, published by IBM.

2. CUA stands for Common User Interface.

3. On success, the malloc function returns a pointer of type void; on failure, it returns NULL.

4. Calls to GlobalAlloc are usually accompanied by calls to GlobalLock, GlobalUnlock, and GlobalFree.

5. The program's data, stack, and local heap are all normally kept in the DGROUP.

6. GlobalAlloc only can be called 8,192 times on a protected-mode 16-bit system such as the one used by the version of Windows that runs on top of DOS.

7. Suballocators use GlobalAlloc to grab chunks of memory from the operating environment. They then parcel this memory out to a program in bits and pieces whenever the program allocates memory through calls to malloc or new. This system helps a program or suite of programs circumvent the 8K limit on the number of global memory objects that can be allocated during the course of a single 16-bit Windows session.

8. To make a window invisible, pass SW_HIDE to ShowWindow.

9. Use LZCopy to copy a file from one directory to another.

10. Use either MoveWindow or SetWindowPos to move a window from one location to another.

Index

C

E

F

G

M

N

O

T

Order Your Program Disk Today!

You can save yourself hours of tedious, error-prone typing by ordering the companion disk to *Teach Yourself Windows Programming in 21 Days*. This disk contains the source code for all the programs in the book. Each disk is only $15.00 (U.S. currency only). Foreign orders must enclose an extra $5.00 to cover additional postage and handling.

Fill in the following information and mail the form (or a copy) with your check or postal money order to

Charlie Calvert
P.O. Box 66115
ScottsValley, CA 95067

Please **print** the following information:

Number of disks: _____ @ $15.00 (U.S. Dollars) = _____
Name: _____
Address: _____
City: _____ State: _____
ZIP: _____

Disk format (check one):

5.25-inch _____   3.5-inch _____

On foreign orders, use a separate page (if needed) to give your exact mailing address in the format required by your postal service.

Make checks and postal money orders payable to **Charlie Calvert**. Sorry, we cannot accept credit cards or checks drawn on a non-U.S. bank.

(This offer is made by the author, not by Sams Publishing.)

Add to Your Sams Library Today with the Best Books for Programming, Operating Systems, and New Technologies

The easiest way to order is to pick up the phone and call

1-800-428-5331

between 9:00 a.m. and 5:00 p.m. EST.

For faster service please have your credit card available.

ISBN	Quantity	Description of Item	Unit Cost	Total Cost
0-672-30168-7		Advanced C (Book/Disk)	$39.95	
0-672-30158-X		Advanced C++ (Book/Disk)	$39.95	
0-672-30287-X		Tom Swan's Code Secrets (Book/Disk)	$39.95	
0-672-30309-4		Programming Sound for DOS and Windows (Book/Disk)	$39.95	
0-672-30292-6		Programming Windows Games with Borland C++ (Book/Disk)	$34.95	
0-672-30299-3		Uncharted Windows Programming (Book/Disk)	$34.95	
0-672-30274-8		Mastering Borland C++ (Book/Disk)	$39.95	
0-672-30236-5		Windows Programmer's Guide to DLLs & Memory Management (Book/Disk)	$34.95	
0-672-30030-3		Windows Programmer's Guide to Serial Communications (Book/Disk)	$39.95	
0-672-30177-6		Windows Programmer's Guide to Borland C++ Tools (Book/Disk)	$39.95	
0-672-30097-4		Windows Programmer's Guide to Resources (Book/Disk)	$34.95	
0-672-30067-2		Windows Programmer's Guide to Microsoft Foundation Class Library (Book/Disk)	$34.95	
0-672-30106-7		Windows Programmer's Guide to ObjectWindows Library (Book/Disk)	$34.95	
0-672-30249-7		Multimedia Madness (Book/Disk-CD ROM)	$44.95	
		Shipping and Handling: See information below.		
		TOTAL		

❏ 3 ½" Disk

❏ 5 ¼" Disk

Shipping and Handling: $4.00 for the first book, and $1.75 for each additional book. Floppy disk: add $1.75 for shipping and handling. If you need to have it NOW, we can ship product to you in 24 hours for an additional charge of approximately $18.00, and you will receive your item overnight or in two days. Overseas shipping and handling adds $2.00 per book and $8.00 for up to three disks. Prices subject to change. Call for availability and pricing information on latest editions.

201 West 103rd Street, Indianapolis, Indiana 46290

1-800-428-5331 — Orders   1-800-835-3202 — FAX   1-800-858-7674 — Customer Service

Book ISBN 0-672-30344-2